The New Pragmatist Sociology

LIBRARY OF
CONGRESS
SURPLUS
DUPLICATE

The New Pragmatist Sociology

INQUIRY, AGENCY, AND DEMOCRACY

Edited by Neil Gross, Isaac Ariail Reed,
and Christopher Winship

COLUMBIA UNIVERSITY PRESS

NEW YORK

Columbia University Press
Publishers Since 1893
New York   Chichester, West Sussex
cup.columbia.edu

Copyright © 2022 Columbia University Press
All rights reserved
Library of Congress Cataloging-in-Publication Data
Names: Gross, Neil, 1971- editor. | Reed, Isaac (Isaac Ariail), editor.|
Winship, Christopher, editor.
Title: The new pragmatist sociology: inquiry, agency, and democracy/edited by
Isaac Ariail Reed, Neil Gross and Christopher Winship.
Description: New York: Columbia University Press, [2022] | Includes
bibliographical references and index.
Identifiers: LCCN 2021045756 (print) | LCCN 2021045757 (ebook) |
ISBN 9780231203784 (hardback) | ISBN 9780231203791 (trade paperback) |
ISBN 9780231555234 (ebook)
Subjects: LCSH: Sociology—Philosophy. | Sociology—Methodology. | Pragmatism.
Classification: LCC HM585 .I54 2022 (print) | LCC HM585 (ebook) | DDC
301.01—dc23/eng/20211207
LC record available at https://lccn.loc.gov/2021045756
LC ebook record available at https://lccn.loc.gov/2021045757

Columbia University Press books are printed on permanent
and durable acid-free paper.
Printed in the United States of America

CONTENTS

INTRODUCTION

The New Pragmatist Sociology

Introduction

1. Pragmatist Sociology

HISTORIES AND POSSIBILITIES

ISAAC ARIAIL REED, NEIL GROSS, AND CHRISTOPHER WINSHIP

In the third decade of the twenty-first century, the sociologist who has not heard of pragmatism has not been paying attention. Scores of articles are published each year in leading sociology journals that draw either directly from the writings of Charles S. Peirce (1839–1914), William James (1842–1910), and John Dewey (1859–1952)—the main architects of pragmatism as a distinctive approach to philosophy—or from the thought of later thinkers, whether philosophers or social scientists, who pushed pragmatism in new directions. In some cases, these articles by sociologists are works of pure theory, but most are empirical studies that utilize pragmatism for diverse purposes, whether to develop more productive models of the social action under investigation, to elaborate new methodologies, or to provide intellectual warrant for undertaking the inquiry in the first place. On the book side of things, we are equally awash in monographs by sociologists who see themselves as having been shaped by pragmatism and whose contributions turn on pragmatist conceptions of the self, agency, rationality, habit, and creativity. Contemporary sociologists can be found busily synthesizing pragmatism with other approaches: field theory, analytical sociology, dual-process theory, feminist theory, or critical race theory. And the classical sociologist most closely studied by the current generation of graduate students—W. E. B. Du Bois—was both a contributor to pragmatist theories of action and education and an engaged and careful critic of pragmatist philosophy.

For sociologists not steeped in pragmatist thought—surely still the majority—all this must make for a perplexing situation. If all you know of pragmatism is the work of George Herbert Mead that you read in graduate school (Mead having been a close colleague of Dewey) or the symbolic interactionism of Herbert Blumer (who had been a student of Mead), or if you have only encountered pragmatist philosophy as the backdrop for Erving Goffman's writings, the sheer volume and range of pragmatist-inspired work being produced today is bound to seem puzzling. Perhaps pragmatism can help us understand the self, the uninitiated sociologist might say. But can it really explain such core sociological phenomena as social structures or meso- or macro-orders? Can it account for power? Can it contribute meaningfully to the development of middle-range theory? Doesn't pragmatism sit uncomfortably with rigorous methodology?

For committed pragmatists, the situation is odd for a different reason. Mention of Mead and Du Bois serves as a reminder that—in the United States, anyway—pragmatism and sociology have long been intertwined. But it was back in the late 1980s and early 1990s that sociologists, along with scholars across the social sciences and humanities, first began to speak of a revival of interest in pragmatism after a long mid-twentieth century period when other intellectual perspectives seemed more compelling. Who could have predicted that only now, more than twenty-five years later, pragmatism would come to count so many sociological admirers? Although no pragmatist sociologist would want to look a gift horse in the mouth, questions naturally arise about the reason for pragmatism's current popularity, the fidelity and intellectual coherence of contemporary appropriations, and which intellectual problems in the discipline pragmatism is best suited to shed light on.

With this volume, we offer something to newcomers and old hands alike. With chapters by established as well as emerging scholars of pragmatism and the social sciences, the volume simultaneously (re)introduces pragmatism to the sociological community—pragmatism as it stands as a living, evolving tradition of thought—and considers how some of its lesser-known features might inform investigations being carried out on the cutting edge of research.

An important feature of classical pragmatism, as we describe here, is attention to the social and historical context out of which thought develops. C. Wright Mills, a champion of pragmatism, wrote his PhD dissertation on its social origins, highlighting the affinities between pragmatism and the sociology of knowledge.[1] Given this history, it would be rather unpragmatist of us to argue that the tradition's return to the forefront in the contemporary social sciences is entirely a function of "intrinsic" merit. Surely there are other factors involved: a paucity of new, competing theoretical approaches emanating from Europe; the centrality of empirical, policy-oriented sociology in many leading U.S. graduate departments (also narrowing the field of competitors); the growth of a strong progressive movement in the political field, its academic supporters in sociology eager to connect to an intellectual approach that gave succor to progressives of an earlier era; and the concerted efforts of a network of pragmatist sociologists to push their—our— agenda forward.

But it would be equally alien to the premises of pragmatism if we failed to note some of the fundamental intellectual problems of sociology that pragmatism can solve. Pragmatism's service in this regard also helps account for its popularity and provides inner motivation for both writing and reading this book. Here are six distinct questions that pragmatism—and the essays on pragmatism in this volume—address.

(1) How should we think about human rationality, strategic action, and problem solving in relation to constraint once it has become clear that the explanatory limits of rational choice theory and other utilitarian approaches to social action have been reached?

(2) How should we think about the relations between thought, talk, and action, outside of the dichotomies between mind and body that sociologists have repeatedly criticized but that seem nonetheless to reappear in our theoretical languages and terms of art?

(3) How should we conceive of truth in social scientific accounts—and with it such criteria of epistemic goodness as accuracy, reliability, richness, and explanatory productivity—in ways that are neither problematically realist nor relativist?

(4) How should we understand the relationship between facts and values and use this understanding to navigate the politics of sociological knowledge, that is, the way in which sociology seeks to be an evidence-based endeavor yet also recognizes that it cannot avoid normative claims?

(5) How should sociologists understand the distinction between lay versus expert knowledge?

(6) How can sociology in the twenty-first century develop a rigorous theoretical pluralism, recognizing that no one theoretical approach—including, most certainly, pragmatism itself—could ever hope to provide all the guidance that social scientists need as they attempt to grasp intellectually the dappled and ever-changing social universe?

If these different but overlapping questions had to be summed up, we might say that pragmatism offers a particularly perspicacious way to address the widely felt yet not well-articulated *symmetry problem* that attends all of the social sciences and humanities but tends to vex sociology in particular.[2] The symmetry problem refers to how sociology, at a bedrock level, involves people studying other people. As such, any theory is potentially equally applicable to both those doing the studying and those who are the object of study. As we address in this introduction, we believe that the language of pragmatism—and especially its attention to action, careful theoretical elaboration of terms such as *conduct* or *project*, and long-standing insistence on bridging specific scholarship with public communication and democratic imperatives—is especially well suited for dealing with the issue. The symmetry problem is also evident in the way in which the chapters in this volume migrate back and forth between using pragmatism to talk about how sociologists and other social investigators do their work and make their claims and using it to talk about the actions taken and institutions made and unmade by the people sociologists study. This can be, initially at least, a bit disconcerting or disorienting. But it should be seen as a feature, rather than a bug, of pragmatist thinking.

For these reasons and others, pragmatism is an approach whose time has come, and our hope is that this volume will shore up pragmatist sociology's intellectual foundations and move the enterprise forward.

CLASSICAL PRAGMATISM

Those unfamiliar with the thought of Peirce, James, and Dewey can consult myriad secondary sources, each offering a somewhat different account of the intellectual content of pragmatism and its place in the history of thought and the history of the United States. For the purposes of this volume, what we wish to stress is that classical pragmatism, originally developed in discussion circles in Cambridge, Massachusetts in the 1870s, was a philosophical position before it became a social-scientific one.

At its base stands Peirce's "pragmatic maxim," which first saw the light of day in an article published in 1878: "Consider what effects, which might conceivably have practical bearings, we conceive the object of our conception to have. Then, our conception of these effects is the whole of our conception of the object."[3] The meaning of every idea, in other words—no matter how abstract or scientific—is to be found exclusively in its consequences for experience. Although the significance of this move might not be immediately apparent, it was profound. The pragmatic maxim is in line with the notion that the human capacity for thought and reason is not a God-given faculty, as many philosophers had believed, but a product of evolution selected to facilitate human adaptation. We think *so that* we may act. The maxim allowed Peirce—a brilliant but eccentric polymath who could not hold down an academic post—to dispense with all sorts of metaphysical debates in philosophy that had no practical consequence while also providing the basis for a novel definition of belief: to believe an idea means to consistently act on it, to have a rule or habit of acting in a particular way. This definition, in turn, allowed Peirce to formulate a powerful response to the skepticism of René Descartes, whose rationalism had become the cornerstone of Western philosophy.

Descartes questioned the validity of every belief that could not be held indubitably, making it the primary job of philosophy to provide a foundation of certainty for our beliefs. But if, as Peirce maintained, a belief is a rule or habit of action, then in actuality we must believe a great many things we are not certain about because human life is characterized by far more regular action than inaction and certainty is rare. The doubts raised by philosophers were often "paper doubts," Peirce argued, irrelevant to real human experience. That is not to say that doubt does not matter: just the opposite. We frequently experience real doubts not when we lack complete certainty but when we simply do not know how to act, an experience character-ized by frustration and irritation. It is these doubts that lead us to engage in inquiry so that we can "attain belief," Peirce proposed. From these claims he went on to formulate a distinctive theory of truth—not as an ideational copy of reality but as those ideas that an unfettered community of human inquirers would eventually find the most suitable for bringing about particular consequences (in a scientific experiment, for example). All in all, Peirce's pragmatism—or as he preferred, "prag-maticism"—started with human beings purposively trying to solve problems in the world (no Kantian apriorist, Peirce was nevertheless influenced by the German philosopher's notion of "pragmatisch," denoting an experimentalist mindset) and worked out the range of philosophical implications. Indeed, if there is one concept that recurs in nearly all pragmatist writing, classical or contemporary, it is that of the problem that demands to be solved.

James, essayist rather than systematic philosopher, professed allegiance to Peirce's pragmatic maxim. But, working from a position at Harvard at the inter-section of philosophy and psychology (which was only beginning to emerge, in the late nineteenth century, as a distinct, experimental science), he was led in dif-ferent directions. In his 1890 book, *The Principles of Psychology*, James reviewed what psychological research then existed, offering a synthetic account of human thought and consciousness consistent with certain features of Peircean pragma-tism and inconsistent with others.[4] Central for James was experience: humans out and about, interacting with one another and with things, experiencing an endless stream of sensations and feels. It is the job of the brain to find some order and con-tinuity in this chaos, James asserted, nominating as key order-making devices a per-sonal sense of self (which he saw as emergent from experience and as an anchor for memory), the ability to formulate and use general concepts, and the apparatus of selective attention.

The Principles of Psychology also argued for the importance of habit in human life, though in a different way than Peirce had done. Most complex tasks, phys-ical and mental, require significant brain power when we first attempt them. It would be impossible for humans to do all the things asked of them if they could not become habituated to these tasks, gaining the ability to execute them in subsequent iterations without much conscious thought so that they can attend to other matters. Certain habits, moreover, can be passed down through the generations, so that, for James, much of civilization, culture, and tradition—and thus, also, ingrained hier-archy and domination—should be regarded as habit, "the enormous fly-wheel of society," in his memorable phrase. Though vigorously defending the possibility of free will against various forms of determinism, with these arguments James pre-sented a vision of cognition and behavior less voluntaristic and purposeful than that of some of his peers, including Peirce. For James, persons are carried along by facets of the psyche over which they do not always have conscious control.

Later in his career, as he became a celebrated intellectual figure on both sides of the Atlantic, James coupled his ideas about the stream of experience with an open-minded metaphysics, suggesting that the world is many-sided and that the search for truth must include acceptance of radical pluralism. More interested than Peirce in moral and spiritual matters, James let his pluralism lead him toward an individualistic and even relativistic theory of truth that many found intriguing and others irresponsible. As Horace Thayer put it in his classic interpretation of the pragmatist tradition, *Meaning and Action,* since for James people are "differently situated, with differences of needs, wants, and satisfactions, the 'value'—the meaning and truth—of ideas is subject to the same range of local and relative differences."[5] With respect to morality and spirituality, James argued, "the true is the name of whatever proves itself to be good in the way of belief."[6]

Dewey, a generation younger than Peirce or James, was not around for the initial conversations in Cambridge out of which pragmatism arose. He began his career as a Hegelian. With time, however, he came to find less value in German idealism and more in the pragmatic method and in James's approach to philosophical psychology. A turning point came with the publication of his paper "The Reflex Arc Concept in Psychology" in 1896. Whereas most writers on the reflex arc regarded stimuli experienced by the human organism and responses to those stimuli to be "distinct psychical existences," Dewey showed that they are really phases in a continuous, coordinated process by which the organism prepares itself to receive and process stimuli and to act on them in the service of some end in the world.[7] Thus was born Dewey's "instrumentalism," under the banner of which he insisted that many of the dualisms philosophers had long regarded as unbridgeable, such as mind and body, needed to be discarded in light of the recognition that thinking is always in service of acting. Peirce had used such a recognition to rethink core questions in the philosophy of his day, and Dewey did the same as the twentieth century unfolded, bringing to the effort a more progressive spirit than did Peirce. Peirce developed a distinctive approach to formal logic, whereas Dewey offered a broader logical theory centered on the operations necessary to produce the human organism's meaningful adjustment to the world.

As Thayer also notes, the key notions in Dewey's theory were *value,* or what is striven for; *situation,* or the circumstances humans find themselves in, the elements and contours of which may be either familiar or novel and perplexing; and *inquiry,* the experimental investigation of different possibilities for action. As with his work on the reflex arc, Dewey saw these elements as interrelated. Inquiry makes no sense except in relation to value and situational adjustment—and this means, among other things, that both science and philosophy must be undertaken in relation to human values and needs. Concerning philosophy, Dewey worked, over the course of a long career, to develop not just an approach to logic but also an original social and political philosophy—stressing the need for collective, democratic experimentation to better adjust to the social realities of the time, especially laissez-faire capitalism and the brutal inequalities it produced—a philosophy of education centered on fostering an experimentalist mindset, and a philosophy of art focused on the transformative potential of aesthetic experience. While arguing that an increasingly professionalized academic philosophy was too far removed from pressing social concerns, Dewey contextualized many of his own claims by offering a history of philosophy that stressed its social and historical roots.

PRAGMATISM AND THE SOCIAL SCIENCES

Pragmatism's history as a way of thinking and practicing *social* science is deeply intertwined with the social reform movement in Chicago, often identified with Jane Addams, and with the academic ethos of the University of Chicago, often identified with Dewey and Mead. In its early forms, it provided a conceptual framework for University of Chicago sociologists who sought to make the city a living laboratory for sociological research. While in Chicago, Dewey engaged in extensive dialogue with Addams concerning the meaning and purpose of a democratic society; both authors worked through a fundamental premise of pragmatist thinking, namely, that thoroughgoing inquiry into the workings of social institutions is vital to democratic experimentation. Meanwhile, Mead, whose pragmatism is well known by sociologists, built out the inherent sociality of the self implicit in the work of James into an elaborate and influential social theory. When Chicago sociologists attended to actors' "definitions of the situation" or to the dynamics of urban ecology, it was pragmatism that provided the frame of reference for these arguments about and interpretations of social life.

As various scholars of W. E. B. Du Bois from Aldon Morris and Ross Posnock to, in this volume, Karida Brown and Luna Vincent have shown, the preeminent early scholar of race in America was another thinker who brought pragmatism and sociology together.[8] Du Bois had studied with James at Harvard, moving James's concerns with the self forward in a different way than Mead had: toward an account of racialized selves and double consciousness. He was also drawn to pragmatism's empiricism—its orientation toward science and facts (which pragmatists refused to see as entirely separate from values)—and became, at least partly under the influence of pragmatism, a pioneer of empirical sociology, intended to inform the project of racial reconstruction. What Morris tracks as Du Bois's rejection of "armchair" social philosophy in favor of the empirical social science he built at the Atlanta University school of sociology resonates with Dewey's turn away from speculative Hegelian philosophy. Finally, as Posnock argues—citing Du Bois's own statements— Jamesian pragmatism in particular, with its emphasis on pluralism and moral strenuousness, left him feeling excited to be an intellectual who turned as the circumstances called for it, traversing disciplinary boundaries, methodologies, genres of writing, and even political positions when faced with different sets of problems and evolving sociopolitical circumstances.[9] Such a turning would eventually lead Du Bois toward a radicalism at odds with what some have seen as Dewey's meliorism.

The early story of pragmatism and social science is not limited to sociology, however. Just as early American sociologists turned to pragmatism for guidance, so did influential figures in political science, economics, and anthropology. In political science, Charles Merriam and Harold Lasswell drew on Dewey to articulate non-technocratic visions of political inquiry designed to enhance the intelligence of the public. In economics, pragmatism was central to the institutionalist approach developed by John R. Commons, Thorstein Veblen, and others, which sought to understand the workings of the economy by examining the history, logic, and psychology of the institutions that structure and support it, a project understood to be simultaneously scientific and reconstructive in intent. In anthropology, some of the influence went the other way, as Dewey's views of culture were arguably shaped by his engagement with the thought of thinkers like Franz Boas, but Ruth Benedict was a close reader of Dewey.

In the middle of the twentieth century, however, a difference emerged between the influence of pragmatism on sociology and its influence in other social science disciplines. In other fields, pragmatism's stature radically declined; it was replaced by behavioralism in psychology, neoclassicism in economics, and structuralism in anthropology. This was in part the result of a double movement, as these fields became increasingly disengaged from their philosophical roots and pragmatism became far less important in academic philosophy. But in sociology, though it was never dominant, pragmatism remained an important part of the ambient background for sociological thinking.

One important renewal occurred in the 1960s and 1970s, as Herbert Blumer made an impassioned case for what he termed "symbolic interactionism" as an alternative to the structural functionalism of Talcott Parsons and the rise of methodological positivism centered on the quantitative analysis of data from large-scale social surveys. Blumer embraced pragmatist principles when he argued that "in order to act the individual has to identify what he [sic] wants, establish an objective or goal, map out a prospective line of behavior, note and interpret the actions of others, size up his [sic] situation."[10]

Then, in the 1980s and early 1990s, pragmatism became central to a crisis in the humanities, specifically philosophy and literary theory. A set of humanist intellectuals—Richard Rorty, Hilary Putnam, Richard Bernstein, Stanley Fish, and W. J. T. Mitchell and, in Germany, Jürgen Habermas—brought pragmatism back to the attention of certain key intellectual communities. Although their interpretations of original pragmatist authors were far from orthodox, the controversy and debate surrounding their work (Rorty's in particular) had the ironic effect of creating a large audience for efforts that were under way simultaneously to bring classical pragmatism into fuller textual and contextual view. It was during this time that the collected papers of Peirce began to appear in print in a more comprehensive format than previously, the historian Robert Westbrook's magisterial biography of Dewey was released, there was an explosion of exegetical scholarship in journals such as *The Transactions of the Charles S. Peirce Society,* and the literary scholar Louis Menand brought classical pragmatism to popular attention with his book *The Metaphysical Club.*[11] Soon it became routine for academic conferences to be held—and to issue edited volumes such as Morris Dickstein's *The Revival of Pragmatism*—proclaiming that pragmatism, once at the center of American thought, was back.[12]

All this attention to pragmatism in the humanities led a number of established social scientists—sociologists especially—to look again, this time much more closely, at pragmatic philosophical ideas and social-theoretical assumptions to which they had been exposed earlier in their careers. Could those ideas, seen in a new way, help them solve pressing theoretical and empirical puzzles? For sociologists, pragmatism offered the possibility of addressing three concerns that were widely felt but often experienced as distinct: (a) that sociologists were students of *action*, which could and should be distinguished from *behavior*; (b) that sociologists were, via this focus on action, engaged in earnest scientific inquiry, even though that inquiry was, as a form of conduct, different from the inquiry of a biologist or physicist; and (c) that the persistence of this form of inquiry was related to its participation in societies in which democratic ideals were, in part, institutionalized and pursued. Pragmatism, in other words, could imagine sociology as a *human science*, with equal emphasis on both words in the phrase.

Especially influential for social theory during this period was the reinterpretation of pragmatism offered by the German sociologist Hans Joas. Responding in part to the uses of pragmatism made by Habermas in *Knowledge and Human Interests* and *The Theory of Communicative Action*, Joas began his voyage into pragmatism with a book on G. H. Mead.[13] From there he launched a full-scale effort to understand pragmatism's place in the history of social theory and—importantly for the American social sciences—to articulate how pragmatism's understanding of social change and its approach to social action differed radically from both modernization theory and structural Marxism.

In his 1996 book *The Creativity of Action*, Joas demonstrated that despite the sometimes individualistic bent of William James's thought and the fact that the original pragmatists were philosophers, not sociologists, pragmatism was deeply concerned with the explanation of social action and thus belonged squarely within the animating concerns of any social science.[14] At pragmatism's core, Joas argued, is a theory of social action emphasizing the creative and intrinsically social problem-solving potential of the human species—a theory that is not subsidiary to pragmatism's signature anti-Cartesian epistemology but key to it.

Although Joas's reading of pragmatism was not the only vehicle by which late twentieth-century sociologists renewed their interest in the tradition, it provided an intellectual gathering point for scholars who were moved by pragmatism and unconvinced that previous attempts at incorporating it into sociology exhausted its potential. In this phase of the pragmatist renaissance in sociology, pragmatism was drawn upon primarily to serve a few key ends: to stake out positions on projectivity and future orientation, the self, rationality, habit, science and truth, democratic citizenship, and culture and agency, often in conjunction with cognate approaches in the broader family of practice theory.[15] In all of this, the pragmatist approach to social action—and its variable interpretation—provided the unified background against which different arguments could be made. And it is worth noting that in terms of longer-arc shifts in commitments, this renaissance participated in, and was buoyed by, the efflorescence of cultural sociology, which sought new ways to think of culture that departed both from the approach of Talcott Parsons and from that of his critics from the generation of 1968.[16]

Parallel moves toward a rediscovery of pragmatism were evident elsewhere in the social sciences, too, although the disciplinary impact of such moves was more limited.[17] At the current juncture, it is in American sociology—not surprisingly, given the narrative here—that things have now progressed the furthest, as research and writing in a pragmatist vein has moved well beyond the initial phase of rediscovery. Turning to empirical matters, sociologists have begun to make a case that pragmatist ideas can yield better explanations of such important phenomena for sociology as racial and ethnic inequality, the emergence of social and political movements, dynamics within organizational fields, and social network formation.[18] And they have been not only synthesizing pragmatism and other approaches but also asking after the limits of such syntheses, such that pragmatism does not just become another word for laissez-faire pluralism. Key articles and books on pragmatism from the early 2000s have now become part of the accepted background of arguments in the field that new graduate students are expected to learn.

THE CURRENT SITUATION

In the opening pages of Jane Austen's *Pride and Prejudice*, Mrs. Bennet complains to her husband that he enjoys vexing her. "You have no compassion on my poor nerves," she declares. And so comes the reply: "I have a high respect for your nerves. They are my old friends. I have heard you mention them with consideration these twenty years at least." Pragmatism and sociology are surely old friends, but at the present moment they are also nervous ones. Pragmatism sits—especially vis-à-vis sociology, but also in some broader sense in relationship to the behemoth of American social science—as a querying and querulous companion philosophy, repeatedly getting on the nerves of supposedly more straightforward approaches to social science as the accumulation of facts and theories about behavior. Pragmatism asks irritating questions about whether or not values and facts can be separated. Pragmatism demands that our core theories of social structure and political power be articulated in relationship to ambitious normative goals for human individuals and groups: community, democracy, transparent communication, and fulfilling aesthetic experience.

Finally, pragmatism proposes to span a notoriously difficult chasm in the human sciences. Specifically, pragmatists pursue a naturalistic understanding of the human being as a creature of sinews and nerves negotiating its varying environments and beset with problems that must be overcome. Yet pragmatists also pursue a deeply historicized and context-sensitive account of human subjectivity and purposiveness, a moral philosophy or axiology, and a critique of taken-for-granted understandings of value and valuation produced by industrial and postindustrial capitalism. Pragmatism, in other words, sits at the difficult, even openly conflictual, meeting point of historicism and philosophical anthropology.

How, then, should pragmatism and social science—sociology specifically—be practiced together moving forward? Which version or aspect of pragmatism should sociologists most heartily embrace? To what extent are syntheses with other theories and approaches logically possible and fruitful? Conversely, when it comes to social science, what are pragmatism's limits? This volume takes up these issues directly and seeks to jumpstart a new phase in sociological practice, one in which principled but nondogmatic, multidimensional, and forthrightly uncertain inquiry into social processes and the workings of institutions comes to be undertaken with the aim of advancing collective problem-solving and social intelligence.

Our authors give different answers to the questions posed in this introduction. This is itself an old pragmatist habit. Peirce and James seldom agreed with each other, and more recent pragmatist philosophers such as Rorty and Putnam rarely did either. So it is with the contributors to our volume, each of whom develops their own line of thought.

MAPPING PRAGMATIST SOCIOLOGY TODAY: INQUIRY, AGENCY, AND DEMOCRACY

Consider the metaphor of the map. What are maps for, and how do humans use them? Readers may be familiar with the parable from Jorge Luis Borges in which a guild of cartographers "struck a Map of the Empire whose size was that of the Empire, and which coincided point for point with it." The power of the parable lies in its demonstration that exhaustive description is not only impossible but useless. Maps are useful as much for what they leave out as for what they keep in.

This insight applies to both the use of sociological theory to develop explanations and the metatheoretical effort, undertaken in this introductory essay and in this volume as a whole, to map the new pragmatist sociology. The quality of a map depends on its relationship to what we want to do in the world; different maps help us do different things—"there is a nondenumerable infinity of possible maps we could draw for our planet; the ones we draw, and the boundaries they introduce, depend on our evolving purposes."[19] A map we draw specifically for a guest trying to find our house will be of little use for most city dwellers trying to find their way between two other points in the city. Thus pragmatism, as well as particular pragmatist thinkers, do not seek to have the final word on which maps social scientists should draw; but they do demand that in evaluating maps, sociologists consider them in the context of their purposes both explicit and implicit. What follows, then, are a series of deliberations on the use of pragmatism in sociology. As the philosopher Elizabeth Anderson put it, "deliberation is a kind of thought experiment, in which we rehearse proposed solutions to problems in imagination, trying to foresee the consequences of implementing them, including our favorable or unfavorable reactions to them. We then put the policies we decide upon to an actual test by acting in accordance with them and evaluating the results."[20] What Anderson says about policy, we would like to apply to sociological thought.

Our own map for understanding the new pragmatist sociology, with its deep attention to problem solving and careful philosophy of thought-in-action, finds its focus via three central themes: inquiry, agency, and democracy.

Inquiry

As mentioned earlier, pragmatist social science tacks back and forth between two reference points:

(a) The actions and relations of the human beings who happen to be engaged in scholarship and science, and whose *research practices* and *modes of inference* come in for examination and scrutiny in pragmatist philosophy or metatheory of science. Here the terms of art are *controlled conduct*, deliberation within a *community of inquiry*, or *habits of thought*.

(b) The actions and relations of the human beings and their social formations that are the central points of empirical inquiry for modern social science, especially contemporary sociology. Here the terms of art are *ends-in-view, habit, publicity,* and *communication*.

This oscillation—between scrutinizing scholarly inquiry as action and theorizing action in general—was a central tendency of the classical pragmatists and recurs in our volume's chapters.

To be clear, pragmatists do not collapse scientific research into action in general. The point is to provide a ground from which to judge different practices of language and experience and thereby better understand certain formats of social-scientific inquiry from other formats of social practice. To do this, it is useful to recognize scientific reasoning as itself a form of symbolic action. In his reconstruction of classical pragmatism, Charles Morris put the matter in the following way: "What is most novel in pragmatic methodology is the attempt to deal with the traditional problems of the theory of knowledge within the context of a theory of inquiry. And since inquiry involves the use of symbols, the study of inquiry must make use of semiotic. Hence pragmatic methodology . . . is a semiotically oriented methodology. Knowing is a form of sign behavior, and open to objective inquiry."[21]

Inquiry, then, is one of the key points whereby pragmatism moves, as Richard Bernstein once argued, "beyond objectivism and relativism." But how? Several of our authors develop arguments about this "how," including arguments directed specifically at certain subfields of sociology (e.g., the sociology of science, comparative-historical sociology).

Of particular interest in this regard is the way in which pragmatism has developed an account of inquiry that emphasizes not only empirical evidence but also the social context of scientific inference that makes the pursuit of truth possible—and, in particular, sees that context in pragmatist terms as creating problems, inducing doubts, and relying on (or disrupting) habits. Simultaneously, pragmatist thought explores the possibility that moral inquiry might share with scientific inquiry many of the features that pragmatism ascribes to the latter. In pragmatism, then, two possibilities that are often held far apart in academic discourse come together: (a) the possibility that scientific inference—including natural-scientific inference—can be adequately described in terms that are also used to philosophize action, such that both the specialness of scientific inquiry and its all-too-human aspects can be grasped, and (b) the possibility that a *theory of value* and ethics can be developed "in terms of the general pragmatic view of meaning . . . which maintains that evaluations (as inquiries into what objects or actions are to be valued) are amenable to the same general pattern of inquiry that occurs in science."[22]

And so, in this volume, we *re*focus this classical pragmatist conversation about knowledge (as Du Bois did in the "classical" era of social theory) on the *social* sciences in particular, and especially sociological inquiry.[23] Almost all of the chapters herein have something to say about inquiry—though for some it is a primary focus, whereas for others inquiry is connected to the other major themes of pragmatist social science, agency, and democracy.

Agency

In American sociology today, pragmatism is perhaps best known for its theorization of *action* and in particular for the way its account of social action promises to transcend the opposition between an instrumental and a voluntarist or value- and norm-driven understanding of action. This opposition, originally designed by Talcott Parsons as part of his interpretation of Karl Marx, Max Weber, Émile Durkheim, and Vilfredo Pareto, has often been used as a starting point for teaching social theory to undergraduate and graduate students. In contrast, pragmatism, with its emphasis on ends-in-view and the consistent intertwining of means and ends in writing about action, and with its careful renderings of *people with projects* as the starting point for theorizing even macro phenomena such as power and states, promises a different starting point for theorizing institutions, culture, and political economy.[24] Related to this, pragmatism is also deeply concerned with the social conditions that destroy or open the possibility for "new action" and the creativity of individuals and groups—and so, it is drawn to the recurrent concern, in social theory, with "agency."[25]

From a pragmatist perspective, *agency* refers to the way in which human action in the world can have purpose, be the result of reflection, and thus exemplify what Peirce called "controlled conduct." Although some earlier pragmatists wrote about human agency using the term *behavior* (and, indeed, Peirce's pragmatism was once understood as a "behavioral semiotic," a term that rings oddly to contemporary ears), the concern was the same: to articulate an approach to philosophy and the human sciences that centered on the human person. By so doing, pragmatists sought to address both the core questions found in the tradition of Western philosophy that they knew (e.g., questions centered by Plato, Kant, and Hegel) and yet also do this in a way that connected philosophy to empirical inquiry and actual human experience.

Pragmatist thought about action, then, develops in counterpoint to two well-known positions on action. On the one hand, the pragmatist project is anti-Cartesian, in the sense of opposing Descartes's intuitive and thought-centered approach to knowledge, and seeking instead to connect questions about thought to questions about action. On the other hand, the pragmatist project is anti-Skinnerian, in the sense of opposing the reduction of human science to a science only of observable behavior, stimulus-response, and so on. Perhaps one way to put this is that for the pragmatist approach to action, Descartes renders *ego* far too close to an ideal subject (or God), whereas Skinner renders the human individual far too close to a pigeon. Instead, pragmatism takes as its home space the human (all-too-human) world of habit, problems to be overcome, and communication. Underneath many of the papers in this volume lies the fundamental reorientation of social science research via its focus on action rather than behavior (with the latter understood not as it was classically but as forming the basis for behaviorism). And out of this reorientation comes a series of studies of human agency—and, especially, agency as *problem-solving*.

Democracy

It is perhaps common knowledge in academic circles that John Dewey and other pragmatist philosophers routinely reject the fact/value distinction, imagine a deep link between democratic norms and the nature of inquiry, and therefore advocate some sort of public-facing encounter between social-scientific "experts" and the societies in which they work. The very possibility of a public sociology has become a vibrant topic of debate in the last twenty years of American sociology. Moreover, since Dewey's death in 1952, political theory has developed an entire genre of writing dedicated to the development and clarification of Dewey's work on democracy, publics, and communication.

This volume also takes up the democratic strand in pragmatist thinking, but it does so in a way that is grounded in empirical social science rather than political theory. Specifically, several chapters take up pragmatist concerns with community relations (including communities of inquiry), publicity and public deliberation, and the pursuit of a more just and democratic polity. They do so, however, by starting with the working problems of empirical social science. Out of these emerge novel investigations into the complex ways in which normativity (or *values*) does, can, and should or should not inflect inquiry and the presentation of research findings.

In this regard, it can be said that Dewey was prescient when he wrote that "the problem of restoring integration and cooperation between man's beliefs about the world and his beliefs about the values and purposes that should direct his conduct is the deepest problem of modern life."[26] For in an age of merchants of doubt, attacks on scientific expertise, and the remaking of academic institutions on a for-profit model, it is no small matter to take up the fraught relationship between scientific truth and the pursuit of human emancipation, as several of our authors do with aplomb.

THE VOLUME

The chapters in this volume cohere around the themes of inquiry, agency, and democracy, and many of them also discuss at length the pragmatist thematic — touched on repeatedly here, and unavoidably present in almost any discussion of pragmatism — of problem-solving, resulting in a set of four points of focus to unify what follows. The matrix in table 1.1 provides a rough guide to which papers take up which of the four points of focus. As can be seen, many (though not all!) of the papers focus on problem-solving. Mische and Winship touch on all four, and many involve at least three, and all but two focus on at least two. What this demonstrates,

TABLE 1.1
Theme Matrix

	Problem-Solving	Inquiry	Agency	Democracy
Martin	X	X		
Huebner		X		
Flores and Gross	X	X		
Silver	X	X		
Whitford		X	X	X
Tavory and Timmermans	X	X	X	
Elfakhani	X	X	X	
Small et al.	X		X	
Aviles	X	X		
Silbey	X		X	
Winship	X	X	X	X
Reed and Lichterman		X	X	X
Brown and White	X		X	X
Cefai	X	X	X	X
Mische	X	X	X	X

as claimed previously, is that pragmatism involves a set of interconnected themes that are difficult to separate out and often provide mutual intellectual support to one another.

John Martin's goal in "What Sociologists Should Get Out of Pragmatism" (chapter 2) is "to use pragmatist ideas to think about how sociology can improve its practice." As such, it provides an excellent entrée to the volume. Martin begins with a discussion of how pragmatism is a response to and rejection of rationalism. Following this he considers the difficult pragmatist proposition that what is true is what is expedient, revealing the subtlety implied by this phrase. Next, he looks at the pragmatist conception of inference that is understood as the ability to generalize from and beyond the specific. Turning to the question of the usefulness of science for solving problems, Martin argues that pragmatism must grapple with the problem of *what is a problem* and *for whom is a problem a problem*. Here Du Bois is the clear model for inquiry; he was driven by problems as well as the question of "problem for whom?" (as anyone who has opened the *Souls of Black Folk* has been compelled to consider). Du Bois's work, then, provides a workable, cartographical model for sociology as an observational science. Finally, Martin discusses the importance for pragmatists of the integration of lay and expert critiques so that science is truly useful.

In "Self-Reflection and Social Responsibility in Research: Lessons from Early Pragmatist Historical Investigations" (chapter 3), Daniel Huebner renovates and revises our understanding of both pragmatist approaches to history and the history of pragmatism. Drawing on the work of several noncanonical, less-attended-to, and marginalized figures in the first wave of pragmatism, Huebner reconstructs the importance—for early pragmatists and social scientists today—of the dynamic relationship to the past implied by a philosophy that understands historical research itself as "action in the present," which "interprets a past to a future." Huebner thereby develops a subtle understanding of the relationship between evidence-driven inference in archival research and the kinds of projectivity theorized by Mische and Elfakhani in their chapters.

Huebner develops this pragmatist understanding of historical investigation via a meditation on "inference" (where he engages Peirce and Tavory and Timmermans on abduction), "interpretation" (where he engages Josiah Royce's study of Christianity—a key reference point for Hans Joas in his writings on pragmatism), and, finally, "Values and the Selection of Facts," which engages W. E. B. Du Bois, Alain Locke, Charlotte Perkins Gilman, and Lucy Maynard Salmon. Here Huebner looks closely at the making of Du Bois's *Black Reconstruction in America* to develop an account of how "the documentation and preservation of materials from people in socially marginalized positions is an essential aspect of social progress because of the ways in which they can serve to recover a more inclusive history."

This, then, leads Huebner to a highly original historical reinterpretation of pragmatist semiotics, in which he combines the careful consideration of how "signs of the past" work in investigation with the ethics of "historical self-reflection" and "social responsibility." Can responsibility to the past in historical research also be responsibility to "conscious social progress"? Huebner argues that this can and should be so. His reconstruction of pragmatist historical consciousness, then, segues into the final chapter in the volume, which uses the pragmatist concept of conduct to address debates in comparative-historical sociology.

In "Problem Situation Misassessment and the Financial Crisis" (chapter 4), Luis Flores and Neil Gross focus on the general problem of inquiry and the misassessment of situations, in their case the financial crisis. They begin their chapter by reviewing the pragmatist model of action and the central role accorded to habit. In the pragmatist tradition, habits are understood as routines, as the way individuals typically do and think about things. Change occurs when individuals believe that their normal habits will not work in the situation they are in; or, in the language of pragmatism, when they find themselves in a problematic situation. But this returns us to the core question: when is a problem a problem? When do individuals correctly assess whether or not there is a problem and correctly understand the nature of the situation? Flores and Gross explore this idea in the work of Dewey, Thomas and Znaniecki, symbolic interaction generally, Goffman, Schutz, and, finally, Berger and Luckmann. Building on this earlier work, they offer their own theory of "problem-situation misassessment."

In their argument, three aspects of problem-situation misassessment are key: first, that assessment is aesthetic in nature; second, that an important benchmark of assessment is determining whether "actors grasp circumstances in roughly the same way that an ideal community of social scientists would"; and third, that a range of social factors can be identified as linked to a higher probability of correct assessment.

Flores and Gross conclude by applying their theory to the 2007–8 financial crisis. They examine how both home purchasers and regulators misassessed the situation, failing to understand, respectively, the implications of the structure of the housing market and the rapidly changing mortgage market. Home purchasers had come to believe that housing prices would go up indefinitely and that, as such, a home was not just a place where one lived but also a smart investment. Similarly, regulators failed to understand how the mortgage market was changing—specifically, that the way in which mortgages were being sold in bundles created greater risk.

Daniel Silver's chapter, "Pragmatism, Aesthetics, and Sociology"(chapter 5), makes a compelling and provocative case that sociologists should be concerned with aesthetics. He starts by pointing out how aesthetics was of fundamental importance to Dewey, something that sociologists have largely ignored. "Attention to creative problem solving and flexible, intelligent action—the common refrain of contemporary pragmatist sociology—is pointless unless we have some sense of what solving a problem is for," Silver writes. For Dewey, the answer was clear: it is for the completed, satisfying, consummatory experience that he designated "aesthetic." Silver's argument is that from a Deweyan perspective, sociological research is a kind of art, providing perspective on the individual's experience and, in this way, "being subject to criticism and experimentation."

Silver then examines and critiques the work of two sociologists, Cesar Graña and John Levi Martin, for whom Dewey's aesthetics have been important. Key in Silver's argument is the notion of judgment, or, to use the word in the chapter by Flores and Gross, "assessment." For Silver, both the execution and the suspension of judgment are critical. Silver contrasts Dewey's thinking with Bourdieu's field theory and its extensions. Finally, he discusses in specific details the Chicago School's maps of social process as art.

In "Disambiguating Dewey; Or Why Pragmatist Action Theory Neither Needs nor Asks Paradigmatic Privilege" (chapter 6) Josh Whitford begins by describing three versions of Dewey. The first is the Dewey of *Human Nature and Conduct*, in which he argues that understanding habit is foundational to an adequate social psychology. The second is the author of *The Public and Its Problems*, with its focus on the processes whereby publics come to understand themselves and the need for them to do so. This version of Dewey is explicitly antagonistic to a model of government by experts. Finally, there is the Dewey of *The Quest for Certainty* and *Logic: The Theory of Inquiry*. It is in these works that Dewey critiques how knowledge is structured and understood in society; here Whitford adeptly leads the reader through deep epistemological thickets. Specifically, he explicates Dewey's opposition to the idea that there can be a purely objective understanding in the sense that people can stand wholly outside of the phenomena that they are studying—what Dewey calls the spectator theory of knowledge.

Whitford ends by recommending that we understand all three iterations of Dewey's philosophy as aimed at creating a pragmatist theory of knowledge. In summary, he concludes that Dewey provides a guide to good research practice, a means to sidestep some unproductive disciplinary quandaries, *and* a source of theories akin in some sense to Hogben's "recipes for correct conduct" that can and should be deployed in inquiries far and wide to see what "consequences . . . arise if and when they are operationally instituted."

"Problem Solving in Action: A Peircean Account," by Iddo Tavory and Stefan Timmermans (chapter 7), like so many other papers in this volume, begins with the crucial importance of problem-solving to the pragmatist theory of action. Developing this insight, they ask, how does pragmatist theory help us parse out how people both define and solve problems? Tavory and Timmermans expand Peirce's theory of semiotics to approach not just how an individual understands the meaning of a situation but also how meaning is negotiated intersubjectively. Their chapter makes the particular contribution of developing Peirce's complex, multipart terminology for signs in a way that is directly applicable to ethnographic interpretation.

These authors use a toy example to develop their argument. Briefly, a couple is living together; the man has left a towel on the floor; the woman asks if it is his towel; and an argument about the towel escalates into a spat about the patterning of their relationship. In Tavory and Timmermans's analysis of this situation, the towel begins as a specific and indexical sign but quickly changes across the three dimensions to become both a type and a symbol (and, as a category of the interpretant, a "rheme").

In their analysis of this interaction, Tavory and Timmermans introduce the notions of upshifting and downshifting of semiotic categories. They show that making signification specific and indexical takes as much interactional work as does rendering signs general and symbolic. This rigorous Peircean approach to ethnography is notable for its careful use of Peircean categories that have usually been the province of exegetical work on Peirce in philosophy and religious studies.

In his paper, "Projective and Responsive Creativity Among On-Demand Workers" (chapter 8), Mazen Elfakhani is concerned with people's projections about the future. Specifically, he examines how Uber drivers use the flexibility of the job to creatively design lives that "work." Linking this problem to a notion of positive freedom, he wants to understand how individuals use their agency to create future lives even when there are no immediate problems.

Elfakhani proposes three types of creative action: slack, responsive, and projective. Slack creativity occurs when problem-solving is sufficiently challenging that an individual engages in tunnel vision. Responsive creativity is the type of problem-solving that pragmatists have typically been concerned with. An individual is engaged in habitual action until she encounters a situation in which her standard understandings and practices no longer work. Creative inquiry and action follow in a responsive attempt to develop new habits that will work.

Elfakhani's main interest, however, is projective creativity, situations in which an individual's life and habits are unproblematic but in which they are looking forward to solving potential problems in the future. One set of drivers Elfakhani studied are involved in financial projects—Uber as a way to balance debt and income, or to save money in order to start a business or buy a boat. A second set are drivers who have family aspirations—to be able to provide gifts for their children from whom they are separated by divorce, to better coordinate work plans with a spouse, or simply to start a family. The third set are drivers who use Uber as a means of regulating their smoking and drinking.

This empirical study of projective creativity connects to Peircian semiotics (see also Tavory and Timmermans in this volume), because for Elfakhani, Peirce's concept of *interpretant*, when combined with the distinction between responsive and projective creativity, provides a new account of that recurrent pragmatist phrase: "problem-solving."

Chapter 9, by Mario Small et al., "Words vs. Actions in the Network Behavior of Low-Income African Americans," seeks to understand how action works in the concrete. Specifically, the authors are interested in an apparent contradiction between the distrust that people living in poverty express and their action in relying on others. Their research involves an ethnographic study of three neighborhoods in New York, Chicago, and Houston and interviews with 133 mothers. The authors provide rich evidence of the same women expressing broad distrust but wide dependence on others.

How should we resolve these seemingly contradicting findings? Are they even contradictory? On the face of it, as the authors point out, these women's distrust is toward people in general, whereas their reliance is on specific individuals. Digging deeper, Small et al. argue that people rely on individuals with whom they connect through various *institutions*—family, coworkers, church members, social clubs, their children's schools. The importance of these institutionally embedded ties, to quote Small, is that "they constitute sets of institutional rules, norms, and practices that to a lesser or greater extent affect how their members or participants interact, form personal connections, think of one another, build trust, develop obligations, and share information and other resources."[27]

Small et. al.'s contribution brings together a recurrent pragmatist concern—the way in which both speech and action can be considered "conduct" (speech act theory, etc.)—with a sociological institutionalism. In this regard, their meso-level analysis stands in contrast to more interactionally focused sociologies of action, representing a kind of meeting point between pragmatist-inspired sociologies of action and the study of organizations and institutions that has always been at the center of mainstream sociology.

Natalie Aviles, in "Scientific Innovation as Environed Social Learning" (chapter 10), leans on pragmatism to develop an account of innovation in the life sciences that attends to both the social worlds scientists inhabit and the scale-variant ontological domains they must navigate and manipulate in order to solve scientific problems. Aviles begins by briefly retracing the intellectual history of sociological work on scientific innovation, from studies of scientific institutions pioneered by Robert K. Merton to work by Pierre Bourdieu and his colleagues on the scientific field to studies of scientific knowledge-making undertaken by Bruno Latour, Michel Callon, and those who have embraced their actor-network theory (ANT). While Aviles finds all of these approaches insightful, she notes that the normatively or strategically oriented actors who populated Merton's and Bourdieu's models never got their hands dirty in the laboratory; these theorists, and their contemporary followers, offer no meaningful account of how the social is implicated in scientific practice. ANT, for its part, in trying to theorize the interaction between human and nonhuman "actants," "propose[s] a syndochic ontology of the world," imagining all actants to exist on the same plane, such that relationships between them can be traced. But this, Aviles argues, fails to attend to a key feature of science: that scientists must grapple theoretically, methodologically, and practically with the challenge of tracing causal processes across diverse ontological levels that resist exactly the kind of flattening that ANT presupposes.

Aviles argues that pragmatism, with its forthright acknowledgment of ontological pluralism, provides the theoretical and philosophical basis for a more robust conception of scientific discovery and innovation. She finds particular value in the approach of philosopher of science Joseph Rouse, who draws on neopragmatist Robert Brandom to develop an account of "the joint articulation of conceptual, technical, and organizational commitments in science over time as a process of niche construction;" and of "social worlds" scholars such as Susan Leigh Star, Adele Clarke, and Joan Fujimura—influenced by symbolic interactionism—who analyze the "complex and multi-scalar material, technological, and discursive environments characterizing different social worlds involved in scientific innovation." To these, Aviles adds that the writings of Peirce and Mead can be further mined for an understanding of how scientists innovate by iteratively learning how to meliorate or solve problems in the complex, heterogenous socio-material environments that are their laboratories. Aviles offers an illustrative example of this dynamic from her research on how scientists at a National Cancer Institute laboratory were able to develop a vaccine for the human papillomavirus.

In "Why Do Biologists and Chemists Do Safety Differently? The Reproduction of Cultural Variation Through Pragmatic Regulation" (chapter 11), Susan Silbey examines the distinctive ways in which a research university's chemistry and biology departments respond to the United States government's demands that they satisfy various environmental and safety regulations. Silbey asks, given the autonomy that professors generally enjoy, why is it that neither department resisted this imposition? For faculty members, the proposed changes would have inhibited and disrupted their research agendas, wasted time, and made some avenues of exploration more difficult to pursue. Silbey documents in considerable detail how the two departments have distinctly different cultures and practices. Chemistry labs were independent from each other and generally did not share resources. Biology labs were linked and shared equipment. Silbey tells about how those seeking compliance were able to seduce (her word) each department into conforming by allowing the specifics of implementation to vary to fit the culture and history of the respective departments. The result was that each department met the new regulations in totally different ways, but in each case, compliance was achieved pragmatically based on the discipline's history and the department's culture and how it organized research. Sibley concludes that it was precisely the flexibility in the process that resulted in a high degree of compliance. A strict and narrow application of the regulations would not have worked.

Sibley's chapter connects pragmatism, the sociology of science, and the sociology of organizations. In this regard it serves—as did the chapters by Small et. al. and Winship—to suggest that robust organizational analysis in sociology benefits tremendously from engagement with pragmatist ideas.

In "Accidental Discovery and the Pragmatist Theory of Action: The Emergence of a Boston Police and Black Ministers Partnership" (chapter 12), Christopher Winship mobilizes his study of a Boston community-police partnership in the 1990s and early 2000s to illuminate a series of theoretical issues within pragmatism: how action can lead to retrospective sensemaking, how problems can be solved via accidental discovery (a different form of creativity than usually assumed), how events can create solutions to problems, and how shared participation in events and actions can result in the emergence of new intersubjective understandings.

By using the pragmatist-influenced organizational theorist Karl Weick's theory of sensemaking, Winship tells the history of how a community-police partnership in Boston that focused on violence prevention came about. Winship divides the story into five periods. First was a period of established senses and habits. Police and Black ministers in Boston at best lived separate lives and at worst had a highly antagonistic relationship. This was followed by a collapse of sense. For the police, there was a court case, a formal commission, and a series of newspaper articles all revealing police ineptness and misconduct. For the ministers, an attempted gang slaying in a church during a funeral for a gang member burst their ability to carry on with their congregations as they normally would.

Subsequently, there was a period of what Winship calls "liminality," characterized by general confusion and ambiguity for both groups. It is important to note that both groups during this time experienced various crises that *the other group* was able to help resolve, which pushed toward sensemaking and, eventually, the emergence of shared goals. When a Black drug dealer murdered an assistant district attorney, sensemaking and mutual public recognition emerged in response: both the ministers and the police recognized this to be a serious crime deserving thorough investigation, and both also recognized that the police should refrain from indiscriminate and arbitrary harassment of young Black men in the process. Finally, there was the shared sense (continuing today) consisting of a common understanding of how both groups can work together in partnership, with a shared, though arguably thin, understanding of youth violence and an agreement on methods and goals: a formal institutionalized partnership.

Beginning from a pragmatist-inspired theory of "the social world as chains of meaningful actions" (chapter 13), Isaac Ariail Reed and Paul Lichterman investigate the specific methodological problems of historical sociology from a pragmatist perspective. Noting that historical sociology has always grappled with the tension-filled interaction between two fields (history and sociology) with different epistemic norms, they posit their own understanding of historical sociology as a counterpoint to a well-known development in the field: the approach to explanation grounded in fuzzy set qualitative comparative analysis. They analyze this approach, which developed as a reconstruction of the Millian method of similarity and difference used by the classics in the field, as "causal combinatorics." If causal combinatorics was taken as the foundational understanding of the community of inquiry in historical sociology, then what Peirce called the economy of effort in science would dictate that historical sociologists turn toward medium-N and large-N studies. And yet, this is far from the case within the comparative-historical subfield or community of inquiry, wherein "comparative-historical dissertations in sociology continue to involve the careful study of between two and five cases." Why?

Reed and Lichterman argue that comparative-historical sociology has an implicit mode of inquiry that is pragmatist in its understanding of inference in pursuit of interpretive explanations. They seek to make explicit and refine this logic of inquiry. In so doing, they develop an extended account of how comparison works via the theoretical work of casing and "comparison via theoretical translation." They then address how comparisons and the use of counterfactuals are judged to have contributed to an efficacious interpretive explanation, positing a process of *metacommunicative dialogue* as the essence of concept critique and progress in knowledge in historical sociology.

This leads Reed and Lichterman to meditate on the anatomy and purpose of comparison and, in particular, how the specific *contrast class* for a historical explanation is developed (a contrast class is a series of counterfactuals in contrast to which the process under study occurred). How are contrast classes developed in historical sociology? To answer this question, they consider the methodological implications of Du Bois's *Black Reconstruction in America*. They posit that Du Bois's masterwork considers the sociopolitical trajectory of reconstruction in America via a carefully drawn contrast to (a) a theoretical translation of Marxist concepts of modernity centered on Europe and applied to the United States and (b) a *historically grounded normative counterfactual* of a historical process that could and should have taken place—and toward which incipient efforts were made—namely, a "union of democratic forces" that would have drawn together the "champions of universal suffrage and the rights of the freedmen, together with the leaders of labor, the small landholders of the West, and logically, the poor whites of the South."[28] It is via this artfully constructed contrast space that Du Bois's explanation of what actually happened emerges.

Reed and Lichterman's chapter, then, connects the overarching concern with inquiry that animates many of the chapters in this volume to the pragmatist theory of action on the one hand and to the pragmatist concern with democracy on the other. In particular, they posit a novel way in which certain incipient or emergent democratic possibilities, when detected in the historical evidence, can enter into inquiry fairly—not as "politicized interpretation" of what happened but, rather, as part of the contrast space against which the social processes and conduct under study are explained interpretively. And so, a "pragmatist historical sociology" provides a different way to think through the pursuit of truth in historical sociology.

Karida Brown and Luna Vincent's "American Pragmatism and the Dilemma of the Negro" (chapter 14) focuses on the intellectual and activist biography of W. E. B. Du Bois to both examine his engagement with pragmatism and insist that a key implication of Du Bois's work is that *pragmatism is not enough*.

Brown and Vincent carefully consider Du Bois's time as a student of William James at Harvard and, furthermore, the influence of pragmatism on Du Bois's foundational (or "architectural") efforts to invent, define, and develop the nascent human science of sociology. In his construction of the discipline, Du Bois rejected the abstract concerns with philosophy and metaphysics that he encountered during his postdoctoral studies in Germany; he conceptualized instead a discipline that was systematic and pragmatically connected to the identification and amelioration of social problems. Du Bois's early framework for understanding the rapid changes transforming American society was thus, in some sense, pragmatist.

However, Brown and Vincent also detail Du Bois's lifelong engagement with and theorization of subaltern experience, the *global* color line. His was a global sociology of racialized modernity. This, they argue, also separates Du Bois from pragmatism in a way that is worthy of extended meditation. In the end, the authors conclude that "pragmatism does not go far for theorizing the subaltern condition without employing other analytical frameworks that have been used to understand modernity from the margins, such as Black feminism, the Black radical tradition, racial capitalism, Du Boisian sociology, and decolonial theory." There is a place for pragmatism in the larger human project of abolition and liberty, they argue, but it is not as large as some pragmatists (including the editors of this volume) might think it is.

In "The Public Arena: A Pragmatist Concept of the Public Sphere" (chapter 15), Daniel Cefai has three goals: to distinguish a public arena—in Dewey's sense of the term—from a market, a social field, or an agora; to explain the different processes through which public arenas emerge and their ecological background; and to describe what public arenas do and why they are important for democracy.

Cefai starts by analyzing how it is that a public arena forms. As do other authors in this volume, he begins with a discussion and definition of a "problematic situation." (It is worth noting that this question—what makes a problem a problem?—appears across many contributions to this volume and appears to constitute one of the ways in which this generation of pragmatist authors have criticized previous pragmatist sociology.) In the case where "troubles" are not simply those of an individual, people come to understand from one another the nature of an issue and whether it should be understood as a problem. Consistent with Dewey's model, this making of a public experience goes with an inquiry, both empirical and moral, attributing causes, identifying victims, ascribing responsibility, and potentially deciding on a solution. For Cefai it is crucial to understand that this process involves more than the "social construction" of a problem—rather, there is, in the making of public problems, an *ecology of public experience* that is simultaneously affective, evaluative, perceptive, moral, and political in nature.

Having described how a public arena emerges, Cefai then contrasts public arenas with markets, fields in Bourdieu's sense, and agora, and he argues that it is in fact public arenas that are foundational for democracy. How can they be nurtured? Here Cefai turns to Cooley's words, insisting on the necessity of a "public mind" that grows up and is educated to support democratic life.[29] Such a mind grows when myriad civic institutions are interlinked: public schools and colleges, community centers, and municipal bureaus to scientific labs, libraries, and various media.

In "Finding the Future in Pragmatist Thought: Imagination, Teleologies, and Public Deliberation" (chapter 16), Ann Mische develops a pragmatist theory of future thinking. She starts by demonstrating that Dewey was not as strictly presentist as many people assume. She then extends Dewey's thinking by turning to the work of Alfred Schutz and Paul Ricoeur. She uses this effort to examine the role of future thinking in democratic politics and public debate, with a particular focus on what she calls "soft teleology."

Mische begins by asking why, in the study of social change, it is so difficult to theorize the role of the future. She points out that although the future does not yet exist, it plays a critical role in human action "through our expectations and aspirations, institutional scaffoldings, routinized temporal schemas, and heuristics for practical decision-making." Futures are also essential for publics, in the Deweyean sense, as people debate the appropriate directions for social change. Mische suggests that pragmatism gives us not only the (well-known) concept of "ends-in-view" but also a deeper set of conceptual tools for understanding the "cultural scaffoldings" and "rehearsals in imagination" by which individuals and groups think. She argues that by considering different possible futures, we analyze and deliberate about the consequences of actions. Choices are made not because they are optimal but because they provide courses of action. The result is a significant theoretical reinterpretation, by Mische, of the pragmatist account of action in sociology.

CONCLUSION

Although sociology has a long history of drawing on pragmatism for inspiration, we see the essays in our volume as signaling a new phase in the relationship between the two intellectual projects. This phase is characterized by increasing reflexivity and awareness by sociologists of the great many theoretical possibilities that pragmatism opens up—above and beyond those associated with symbolic interactionism—and at the same time by a movement away from theoretical reconstruction of pragmatism's precepts and toward the use of pragmatist language to produce fuller engagement with and orientation toward empirical studies of the social world. Pragmatism, then, is not merely a theory of action or a philosophy of science but, rather, an essential part of the development of sociology.

We are hopeful that in the years to come, an even wider array of sociologists will develop and reinterpret pragmatism for the coming generations. Given pragmatism's internal diversity, its emphasis on creativity, and its skepticism toward teleology, we cannot pretend to know what the cumulative impact of such work may be or the directions it will take. We hold out hope, however—and we speak now not just for ourselves, the editors, but also for all the authors in our volume—that any pragmatist-influenced social science to come will be, as we have emphasized already, a fundamentally human science, a democratic science, a pluralistic science, a science focused simultaneously, as it should be, on explanation and achieving social good.

NOTES

1. C. Wright Mills, *Sociology and Pragmatism: The Higher Learning in America* (New York: Oxford University Press, 1964).

2. Charles Taylor, "Interpretation and the Sciences of Man," *Review of Metaphysics* 25, no. 1 (1971): 3–51; and Isaac Ariail Reed, *Interpretation and Social Knowledge: On the Use of Theory in the Human Sciences* (Chicago: University of Chicago Press, 2011).

3. Charles S. Peirce, "How to Make Our Ideas Clear," *Popular Science Monthly* 12 (1878): 286–302.

4. William James, *The Principles of Psychology*, 2 vols. (New York: Henry Holt, 1890).

5. Horace Standish Thayer, *Meaning and Action: A Critical History of Pragmatism* (Indianapolis: Hackett, 1981), 140.

6. William James, *Pragmatism, a New Name for Some Old Ways of Thinking: Popular Lectures on Philosophy* (New York: Longmans, Green, 1907), 76.

7. John Dewey, "The Reflex Arc Concept in Psychology," *Psychological Review* 3, no. 4 (1896): 357–70.

8. Aldon D. Morris, *The Scholar Denied: W. E. B. Du Bois and the Birth of Modern Sociology* (Berkeley: University of California Press, 2015); Ross Posnock, "Going Astray, Going Forward: Du Boisian Pragmatism and Its Lineage, in *The Revival of Pragmatism: New Essays on Social Thought, Law, and Culture*, ed. Morris Dickstein (Durham, NC: Duke University Press, 1998), 176–89.

9. Posnock, "Going Astray," 176–89.

10. Herbert Blumer, *Symbolic Interactionism: Perspective and Method* (Berkeley: University of California Press, 1986), 64.

11. Robert B. Westbrook, *John Dewey and American Democracy* (Ithaca, NY: Cornell University Press, 1991); and Louis Menand, *The Metaphysical Club* (New York: Farrar, Straus and Giroux, 2001).

12. Morris Dickstein, *The Revival of Pragmatism: New Essays on Social Thought, Law, and Culture* (Durham, NC: Duke University Press, 1998).

13. Hans Joas, *G. H. Mead: A Contemporary Re-Examination of His Thought* (Cambridge: Polity, 1985).

14. Hans Joas, *The Creativity of Action* (Chicago: University of Chicago Press, 1996).

15. Mustafa Emirbayer and Ann Mische, "What Is Agency?," *American Journal of Sociology* 103, no. 4 (1998): 962–1,023; Norbert Wiley, *The Semiotic Self* (Chicago: University of Chicago Press, 1994); Josh Whitford, "Pragmatism and the Untenable Dualism of Means and Ends: Why Rational Choice Theory Does Not Deserve Paradigmatic Privilege," *Theory and Society* 31, no. 3 (2002): 325–63; Charles Camic, "The Matter of Habit," *American Journal of Sociology* 91, no. 5 (1986): 1,039–87; Steven Shapin, *A Social History of Truth: Civility and Science in 17th Century England* (Chicago: University of Chicago Press, 1994); Robert N. Bellah, *The Good Society* (New York: Knopf, 1991); and Ann Swidler, *Talk of Love: How Culture Matters* (Chicago: University of Chicago Press, 2001).

16. Talcott Parsons, *The Structure of Social Action: A Study in Social Theory with Special Reference to a Group of Recent European Writers*, (New York: Free Press, 1949).

17. In political science, pragmatism resurfaced in political theory when, for example, Matthew Festenstein examined the implications of Dewey's thought—as well as Rorty's—for contemporary debates about liberalism and democracy and Archon Fung incorporated Deweyan ideas about participatory democracy into his normatively oriented inquiries

about the workings of public institutions. Perhaps most relevant for the chapters in this volume, Elizabeth Anderson comingled pragmatism, feminist epistemology, and social-scientific research on race to develop new understandings of justice and injustice. See Festenstein, *Pragmatism and Political Theory: From Dewey to Rorty* (Chicago: University of Chicago Press, 1997); Fung, *Empowered Participation: Reinventing Urban Democracy* (Princeton, NJ: Princeton University Press, 2002); and Anderson, *The Imperative of Integration* (Princeton, NJ: Princeton University Press, 2010).

Pragmatism's return in anthropology arose in efforts to advance semiotic anthropology "post-Geertz," as Alfred Gell's *Art and Agency* and Roy Rappaport's *Ritual and Religion in the Making of Humanity* began from Peircian premises and developed their research via the use of Peircean vocabulary. More broadly, pragmatism provided a philosophical ground from which to consider the purpose of ethnographic inquiry after the displacement of scientism, to explore the social and cultural worlds where scientific truth is produced (the intersection of anthropology and science and technology studies), and to gain a deeper understanding of the "practice turn" taken by anthropologists in the 1980s and 1990s. See Gell, *Art and Agency: An Anthropological Theory* (London: Clarendon, 1998); and Rappaport, *Ritual and Religion in the Making of Humanity* (Cambridge: Cambridge University Press, 1999).

Mainstream economics has remained resistant to pragmatist forms of inquiry. But where cracks appeared in the edifice of the neoclassical approach, pragmatism was often involved. Geoffrey Hodgson mounted a large-scale effort to resuscitate institutional economics, drawing heavily on Veblen and pragmatist understandings of habit (e.g., *Economics in the Shadows of Darwin and Marx: Essays on Institutional and Evolutionary Themes* [London: Edward Elgar, 2006]). And behavioral economics made significant strides shaped by psychological studies of the limits of human rationality, but that often resulted in depictions of economic actors as information-limited cognitive misers and heuristically guided problem solvers that were not far from the account offered by Dewey, even if they continued to assume—as Dewey had not—that instrumental rationality was the baseline against which bias and deviation should be measured. In psychology, dual-process models took over. It was routinely acknowledged that the idea of an alternation between system 1 and system 2 cognition, triggered, respectively, by routine situations and novel, problematic situations, was first developed in the writings of James.

18. Mustafa Emirbayer and Matthew Desmond, *The Racial Order* (Chicago: University of Chicago Press, 2015); Robert S. Jansen, *Revolutionizing Repertoires: The Rise of Populist Mobilization in Peru* (Chicago: University of Chicago Press, 2017); Neil Fligstein and Doug McAdam, *A Theory of Fields* (New York: Oxford University Press, 2012); and Jorge Fontdevila, M. Pilar Opazo, and Harrison C. White, "Order at the Edge of Chaos: Meanings from Netdom Switchings Across Functional Systems," *Sociological Theory* 29, no. 3 (2011): 178–98.

19. Philip Kitcher, "Does 'Race' Have a Future?," *Philosophy and Public Affairs* 35, no. 4 (2007): 293–317.

20. Elizabeth Anderson, "The Epistemology of Democracy," *Episteme: A Journal of Social Epistemology* 3, no. 1 (2006): 8–22.

21. Charles Morris, *The Pragmatic Movement in American Philosophy* (New York: G. Braziller, 1970) 75.

22. Morris, *The Pragmatic Movement*, 83.

23. Many of the most-read texts of pragmatism on scientific inference (e.g., Peirce's papers and Richard Rorty's *Philosophy and the Mirror of Nature* [Princeton, NJ: Princeton University Press, 1979]) start from certain paradigmatic natural sciences and their philosophies, and only sometimes—we would say, not nearly often enough—move from there to social science.

24. Isaac Ariail Reed, *Power in Modernity: Agency Relations and the Creative Destruction of the King's Two Bodies* (Chicago: University of Chicago Press, 2020).

25. Harrison C. White, *Identity and Control*, 2nd ed. (Princeton, NJ: Princeton University Press, 2008).

26. John Dewey, "The Quest for Certainty: A Study of the Relation of Knowledge and Action," in *John Dewey: The Latter Works, 1925-1933*, volume 4 (1929), ed. Jo Ann Boydston (Carbondale, IL: Southern Illinois University Press), 204.

27. Mario Luis Small, *Unanticipated Gains: Origins of Network Inequality in Everyday Life* (New York: Oxford University Press, 2009).

28. W. E. B. Du Bois, *Black Reconstruction in America: Toward a History of the Part Which Black Folk Played in the Attempt to Reconstruct Democracy in America, 1860–1880* (1935; London: Routledge, 2014).

29. Charles H. Cooley, *Social Organization: A Study of the Larger Mind* (New York: Scribner's Sons, 1909).

PART I. Inquiry

2. What Sociologists Should Get Out of Pragmatism

JOHN LEVI MARTIN

INTRODUCTION

It is common to hear contemporary sociologists express their appreciation for the fact that the days of obeisance to windbag system-builders is over, and that we, having passed the immature stage of such implausible grandiosity, all agree that theory is simply what "works" for us.[1*] This is often taken to be a pragmatic orientation, whether or not there is any interest in pragmatism as an actually existing historical-intellectual phenomenon. My argument is that our current disciplinary approach is not at all pragmatic, and, instead, is a worrisome development. While joining others in celebrating our exodus from systems-building, I find no reason to be sanguine about our current understanding of theory "working" for us. It is because the faux pragmatism of our current directionless roll downhill threatens the core of the sociological project—one which turns on the interplay of action and pattern—that I argue that we must give a serious consideration to pragmatism as a coherent theory of science.

I will begin by indicating what I think sociologists can get out of pragmatism. This then raises the question of what we must see as the core of pragmatism (as in, if you deny this, it is a perverse mockery to call yourself a pragmatist). This core is the opposition to rationalism, or, equivalently, it is the coherent and nontranscendental employment of the principle of the primacy of practical reason at all decision points in theorizing. I will then review what this primacy means for the closely related conceptions of truth and inference.

Next, I consider the issue of the application of these core principles to the social sciences. I will argue—and here I think this is an easy and conventional argument to make—that despite the logic of the pragmatist position seeming to naturally apply itself to the social world, there are many problems in deriving clear principles for the development of a social science in an imperfect world. There are some coherent principles that might be derived—some worked out by Habermas—but they seem implausible in practice. However, pragmatism does not require that we demonstrate how our knowledge can be *right*, but merely how it can be *better*. This, I believe, is tractable, even without solving all the problems before us. Indeed, I suggest that the work of W. E. B. Du Bois has much to offer as an exemplar. Finally, I argue that these problems are, to some degree (as Critical Theorists argued before, if with unnecessary pessimism), inherent in many non-social sciences as well. Thus sociology can—perhaps—bring something to pragmatism.

WHAT IS PRAGMATISM?

What Do We Need from Pragmatism?

When we examine how contemporary sociologists draw on pragmatism, we see three main clusters. First, there are a number of scholars who build on the *substantive* interests that were key to many of the pragmatists, most notably, collective problem-solving and democratic deliberation. (A key example here is the work of Lichterman and Eliasoph.[2]) Second, we have those who take *terminology* and *analytic* structures from leading pragmatists and attempt to repurpose it. (A key example here would be Timmermans and Tavory's use of Peircean terminology.[3]) Third, we have those who want to use pragmatists' account of science to more accurately describe what sociology *is*. (A key example here would the work of Whitford.[4]) Here I want to do something different: to use pragmatist ideas to think about how sociology can improve its practice.

Although any pragmatist will initially rankle at this division, we must recognize that a *descriptively* valid account of science may lack any sort of *prescriptive* validity for those who are attempting to improve, as opposed to describe, their practice. For example, it may be true that social scientists overfit data by running too many models. If we were attempting to write a training manual for students, one that would, we believe, lead them to good as opposed to bad practice, we do not simply want to note that sociologists overfit but use our better understanding of scientific practice to get them to *stop* overfitting.

Here I want to suggest how sociologists can turn to one version of American pragmatism to improve our practice. The relation of American pragmatism to the sociological work of the early Chicago school is, of course, well known. However, it is my belief (to be explicated later) that this approach has a built-in limitation. I propose that the closest exemplar that we have for a contemporary, pragmatist-influenced, sociological science is the work of Du Bois, which comes from the underappreciated Jamesian version of pragmatism. This may be a surprising choice, as his engagement with sociological research was relatively short-lived, and he gave little attention to explicating his philosophy of science. However, the context—that he left sociology before the limitations of data mongering had become clear, and that (as I discuss in this chapter) he closely identified with what he considered a truth-deprived population—led him to develop a vision that has much to offer for current work, and to couple it with some of the grandest and most florid inspirational language, without which we are likely to prefer to stick with current practice.

Contra Rationalism

I begin by discussing what we must consider to be the core of pragmatism. This is necessary if we are not to throw up an ersatz version of pragmatism, one that simply codifies what we already do. We can expect that, like the churchgoers pleased that their parson has chosen to expound on the scripture "be thou not righteous overmuch," sociologists will always prefer to hear from "theorists" whose theory is simply a generalization of existing practice.

If pragmatism is not simply "what I want to do," then what are its core characteristics? Here there is the awkward complication that one of the founders, perhaps *the* founder, of pragmatism, C. S. Peirce, differed greatly from the other important founders (whom I consider to be William James, John Dewey, and G. H. Mead) in a number of respects. However, it is also the case that Peirce's own views changed over the course of his anti-career, and that his earlier conceptions are obviously in line with the core notions of pragmatism. (His later conceptions, to my mind, are also related, though not obviously.) Thus we can delimit the core contributions of pragmatism and use this to determine what the practical goals of pragmatism as a movement were.

Pragmatism was proposed as a solution to what was understood by its adherents as a *problem*. If there was no problem, there would have been no solution. And this problem stemmed from the inherent paradoxes of rationalism.[5] Now, it might seem as though we have made no progress by defining pragmatism as opposition to rationalism, given that *rationalism* is also a term whose referent may be obscure, as it has been used to denote any number of somewhat different notions. But the heart of nineteenth-century rationalism was the claim that human reason is *more than a mental process*; it gets to something inherent in the nature of the world, something greater than humans. Human thought is a reflection—perhaps distorted, weak, or partial—of the inherent truth of Reason.[6]

In a very small nutshell, rationalism refuses to recognize that anything fundamentally foreign to mind can be known, or *should* be known; it starts by hypothesizing the real (the "real" being a coherent mental extrapolation from the actuality of experience data) and then determines how we can come to know the real as it truly is. In other words, the attempt is to rederive the conditions of possible experience of actuality from this reality, but this turns out to involve hypostatizing mind.

(For example, because our minds are oriented to a notion of space, and space is an incredibly useful axiom for manipulating cognitions, we declare that space "is real" and that this explains the experiences with which we began.) Much of what the pragmatists wrote was a careful and eloquent description of the paradoxes that come from this approach.

In contrast to the rationalists, the pragmatists began by taking Kant's principle of the primacy of practical reason with deadly seriousness, but they refused to accept Kant's transcendental solution—one that says that for purposes of practice, we must treat certain things "as if they were true." This solution, although logically invincible, took the teeth out of the principle: effective control was quickly returned to theoretical reason. But still, it was to honor Kant's bravery in making this first step that Peirce and/or James chose the term *pragmatism*. In this view, the organism is not created to serve the spirit; the spirit was created to serve the organism. For this reason, the pragmatists started with the experience of the organism, and considered the question to be how this organism moved further toward intelligence, toward adequacy, toward anything that deserved the name of truth.

It all comes down to the Humpty-Dumptyish question of who is to be inside of whom. Rationalists of all stripes see *Homo sapiens* as perhaps a uniquely favored species because it understands that it dwells within the overarching sphere of truth and reason. Pragmatists see truth and reason as something humans do. This does not mean that truth is not defensible (in Dewey's terms, that it has "warranted assertibility")—indeed, truth might be said to be *uniquely* defensible (as we may consider it the class of all cognitions worthy of defense by any open-minded, honest, and informed inquirer). Nor does the pragmatist conception require that no other intelligent species be able to have a reason completely homologous to ours. But still, our reason is *ours*, in the same way that our sense of beauty is *our* beauty; our sense of ethics *our* ethics. This vision is not as tidy as the rationalist competitor. There, the knowledge that is worth defending is true knowledge, and though sometimes we are wrong about what we think is true, it really always was (or wasn't) true—even before human minds came on the scene. The pragmatist must reject this as unsound reasoning while avoiding collapsing truth and error. Almost all of the core planks of pragmatism were developed to support this task, to accept the primacy of practical reason without renouncing a means of cognitive orientation to *better*.

Chapter and Verse

There is no way to reject the primacy of the practical and have anything to do with pragmatism.[7*] But although pragmatism handily disposes of all the paradoxes associated with rationalism, it brings problems of its own. It is all very well to say, as did James, that "in every genuine metaphysical debate some practical issue, however conjectural and remote, is involved,"[8*] but it is difficult to know what a "practical issue" is and whether a "conjectural" practical issue may be a contradiction in terms. The greatest pitfall for sociological pragmatism is our tendency (well pointed to by Marx) to take abstractions and think that they are concrete—to think that we root things in practice when, in fact, we root them only in our own ideas. For this reason, I think it will be important to take seriously the work of the first generation of pragmatists, who gave these difficult issues sustained attention. Their efforts would have been foolish were the solutions to these problems obvious, and who would want to follow a theoretical tradition established by fools?

WHAT DOES PRAGMATISM SAY ABOUT SCIENCE?

The Project of Truth

I noted earlier that the key to pragmatism was its commitment to the primacy of practical reason and its rejection of rationalism. This does not mean that the pragmatists downgraded the importance of theory when it came to science. However, it did mean that they had work to do if they were to be able to distinguish science from technology, truth from efficacy. And in fact, much of the work of the first generation of pragmatists was to accomplish precisely this and thereby to develop a coherent theory of science—and, accordingly, a set of principles for the conduct of scientific inquiry. But it is easy for those who have not actually read the work by James, Peirce, or Dewey to confuse having *pragmatist* principles with having *no* principles. For this reason, it is necessary for us to approach the confusing issue of the role of truth in pragmatist philosophy.

James, Peirce, and Dewey struggled with formulating their ideas of truth, and all changed over time. My treatment, therefore, is necessarily only a thumbnail, although it is not, I believe, a biased selection. The key point is that while the pragmatists never meant anyone to think that "truth is just what works," it is also the case that they certainly did mean that truth, as a quality of cognitions or statements, was a quality of an endeavor oriented around engagement with the world, and it had to be judged—ultimately—in those terms. I want to focus here on James's approach, as I will argue that it offers us a good starting point for a reconstruction of sociology.

James is often misunderstood here, in two ways. First, he is often unfairly thought of as the "dumb pragmatist," someone not in the same league as Peirce or Dewey.[9*] It is indeed true that James's way of working was to orient to great masses of empirical material and to bring insight to them, as opposed to systematizing vocabulary. But a difficult relationship with vocabulary marked all the pragmatists: Dewey, too, found words often unreliable auxiliaries in his assault on previous philosophy, and Mead, though a stunning lecturer (and a fine popular writer), was nearly incapable of writing academic philosophy so that it could be read. Peirce's own struggle with vocabulary was lost relatively early in his career, but his capacity to construct two neologisms for every term that failed him has perhaps distracted readers from this fact. Thus all the pragmatists must be read somewhat like a three-dimensional "magic eye" picture—one must have a focal point somewhat beyond the page if the whole is to snap into coherence. James had, however, in addition to the problems of an inadequate inherited vocabulary, the tendency to make impressive and unqualified statements. That is not at all surprising, given that his work on pragmatism is disproportionately from popular lectures (whereas, in contrast, most of Peirce's is in the form of notes to himself, thus reaching an audience less in need of inspiration or simplicity of exposition).

Second, James is misremembered as giving the definition of truth that collapsed it with expediency (something that he did at times explicitly state, though this is merely half the story) and, most vulgar to the sociological ear, equated it with the "cash value" of statements.[10]* More important was James's clarification that truth was a species of good[11]—that is, it is something that is good in the Greek sense, that meaning "good for a human being who is him- or herself rightly oriented." In any case, James later made clear his "regret" at the "unguarded language" of his earlier presentations.[12]

Yet James also hit on something that we need to take seriously: the commonsense knowledge that contradicts the results of experimental science certainly is not scientific knowledge, but it is hardly obvious that it is less true for that.[13] Rather than glibly solve our problems by declaring that what we *mean* by true is what we, as academics, decide to *treat* as true, the pragmatists all considered closely the continuity between scientific truth and everyday knowledge.

The Growth of Truth

As James brilliantly says, "our knowledge grows *in spots*," and "the knowledge never grows all over."[14] Most of the time, truth lives "on a credit system," in that our ideas " 'pass,' so long as nothing challenges them, just as bank-notes pass so long as nobody refuses them."[15] This is a key to the notion of the "cash value" of truth—and it is a metaphor that Peirce used as well.[16] The point of the metaphor is not the glorification of immanence and narrow-minded hucksterism but that talk, like printing paper, is cheap, and we need to see if our promissory notes have real value, value in the worlds of intervention and experience. The pivot of the pragmatist approach to truth, formulated by Peirce (1877), is that we can treat as axiomatic that which we cannot doubt, but where we actually *do* doubt, there we may begin inquiry.[17] The *root* notion of truth—the adequate coordination between our practical activity and the world[18]—is one that shades gradually into science as, in an effort to increase the robustness of our knowledge, we consciously begin using specific techniques, especially experimental ones. But the results are true for the same reason that commonsense thoughts may be true—they are expedient. However, as James said, by "expediency" we do not mean what we want to do right *now*—we only grace our thoughts with the appellation "true" when they prove to work time and time again, especially when we are able to draw other conclusions from them. Then the "spots" get bigger, and some link to one another.

There is thus a continuity between our everyday knowledge and our scientific knowledge. No one begins with radical "Cartesian doubt"—that is a pretense. Rather, we assume what we have never had cause to doubt and concentrate our inquiry on the parts we *do* doubt. Even the most sophisticated scientific inquiry involves commonsense assumptions (for example, that our capacity to read a dial does not alter with the velocity of a reference frame) . . . until we find that we do have reason to doubt an assumption. The only true forks in the road of inquiry are those that matter, sooner or later, for our practical engagement with the world, for our experience, but this includes the rarified experience of scientific inquiry itself. Finally, we have, as Dewey emphasized, the capacity for intelligence—for critical reflection and reorganization of our own thoughts in the light of their relation to experience.

There is one final aspect of the pragmatist conception of truth that is worthy of emphasis: that it refers always to a community and not to an individual. Something that is efficacious for *you* to believe but not for anyone else is not what we mean by "true." It is really only this seemingly small plank that separates the pragmatist approach from that of Nietzsche, who was perhaps the first to grapple seriously with the radical implications of the notion that reason was nothing but a means used by (evolved, not created) biological organisms in their attempt to deal with their worlds.

It might seem obvious to sociologists that truth should refer to a community—yet our own working conception seems to be quite different from that of the pragmatists. For we do not carry out research to clarify issues about which we are unsure, and where knowledge is important to us. This is easily seen by the serious amount of sociological work that is carried out in the answering of questions that raise no doubt whatsoever. Consider the extremely popular research into cultural influence, in which we attempt to estimate the value of a parameter tapping, say, the increase in the probability that one person likes a cultural product, given that her friends say they like it. We go to a great deal of trouble to see whether we can disprove the hypothesis that this parameter is exactly zero. Questions like this, whose answers are so obvious that they are hardly worth asking (do we really doubt that interpersonal influence *ever* occurs?), let alone answering, compose far more of sociological practice than directed—and much more difficult, often necessarily unelegant—research into the questions that we find truly puzzling.[19]* The reason that we need to take seriously the pragmatist conception of truth, then, is that it might lead us to change our evaluation of the comparative worth of different forms of research. In particular, grappling with the various pragmatist conceptions of scientific truth leads us to revise our understanding of the importance of *inference*.

The Project of Inference

The notion of inference is, I believe, central to pragmatist conceptions of science, and pragmatism offers a different way of thinking about this issue than our current notions (including specifically statistical understandings, both frequentist and Bayesian). Peirce gave the most thought to this issue;[20]* although his particular approach and vocabulary do not represent all pragmatists here, the basic orientation does. Inference is the capacity to extend knowledge developed in some situation to other situations. This sort of extension is at the very heart of the notions of truth and reality proposed by James and Dewey. To Dewey, although all experiences were equally "real," we could still prefer some theorizations of our experience as more robust: for example, we find that the "snake" that we saw, now that we come closer and look more carefully, is a stick.[21] The belief that it is a snake was fine in the moment, but breaks down when we want to build on this (for example, if we were inclined to try to eat some snake meat).[22]* James's point about our "efficacy" being our *long*-term, enlightened efficacy, gets to the same thing: the reason truth refers to "all people over all time" is that this is the widest range of inference, and the truer something is, the less likely it is to disappoint when we shift venues.

In a nutshell, the thing about "true" knowledge is not that it makes you richer or happier (though it might), but that it supports inference. The reason we have neural systems is so that we can process the pattern of environmental regularity and change. Were we sessile animals that strained their medium for nutrients, we would not waste the protein to make nerves, as we would have few decisions to make. We have a cognitive apparatus to help us with the world we find ourselves in, one that displays a level of order between total randomness and total homogeneity. That is, there are complex alternations of sameness and change, producing patterns that can, to a greater or lesser extent, be grasped by organisms. Knowledge is a way of navigating these conditions, and intelligence is (in part) an understanding of the scope conditions of our knowledge. Science, finally, is a determined and focused effort to use responsible inquiry to settle questions about which we have doubt, as well as the development of the technologies that are required for such inquiry.

But the sociological understanding of inference is heavily stamped by its historical derivation from issues of *sampling* and not of science. We (to use quantitative examples for reasons of simplicity) ask questions like, "*Given that my model is correct*, how likely is a population parameter to be close to this sample estimate?" We have very good answers to this sort of question. But that is not a very good question to ask in the first place. Bayesian approaches are somewhat closer to what we want: they allow us to also ask questions like, "*Given that one of the following models is correct*, which one has the weight of the evidence?" (It is also possible to construct such criteria for model selection from information-theoretic bases and to have meaningful estimates when the correct model is not in the set investigated, but still. . . .) The Bayesian approach is most consistently interpretable, however, when its probabilities are understood as subjective states of certainty of an individual investigator—a radical difference from the pragmatist focus on a *community*'s distribution of belief. More important, both the information-theoretical and the Bayesian approach are dealing with the make-believe world in which something at least *like* one of these models *is* correct. But these models are only rough approximations of whatever the hell is going on in the world. The inference we care about is at the level not of *models* but of *social interaction*.

Thus we do not want the answers to the questions that are easiest to ask, such as (a) "Would this parameter in this (untrue) model, estimated using data from the complete population, be zero?"; (b) "Is this (untrue) model the single most likely model of all the ones I thought of?"; or (c) "Given the differential weight of the different models I've considered (all of which are wrong), what is the distribution of my confidence in the belief that the true parameter is any particular value?" We may want to ask these questions, but only as a means to an end, to allow us to answer questions like, "Can folks whose parents are poor get a fair shake?", "Do we expect further political polarization?", or "How has the occupational structure facing newer cohorts changed?" These sorts of questions are ones that we (that is, all competent and involved investigators) make not on the basis of any one analysis, but only via the surveying of the results of many different types of analyses, designed to tease apart competing explanations and clarify obscurities where we still have doubts. At least, that is what we would do if there was a true social science. Can there be?

IS THERE A POSSIBILITY OF SOCIAL SCIENCE?

The Purifying of Science and the Problems with Reformism

In one light, the possibility of a coherent, pragmatist social science is utterly obvious. If we start with perhaps the most fundamental aspects of human life — our social interdependence — we realize that different forms of social organization make it easier or harder for us to succeed in our goals, collective and individual. This relation should be amenable to empirical inquiry and, hence, social science. And it was in fact precisely the desire to orient to these sorts of collective problems in a way that was more rigorous and informed that gave birth to empirical social science.[23]

Yet sociology as a science largely marks its birth from the point at which it rejected and delegitimated such concerns as do-goodism. Sociology's turn away from such a pragmatist conception of its mission may have come from reasons associated with the professionalization project[24] — and not from epistemic unease. But the dismissal of do-goodism as paternalistic (actually, given the gendering, one might say maternalistic, were it not for the obsession of critics with the spinsterism of social reformers[25*]) can be given strong justification. The project of "fixing society" makes a great deal of sense so long as either everyone agrees about the nature of the problems that face them, or that even if there is disagreement, only some people's way of thinking matters. Given that the first is implausible, the enthusiasm for a coherently grounded pragmatist social science of reform was tempered as soon as the right of some to define the problems was questioned (and this was quite soon indeed).

The difficulty with rooting social science in practical efficacy, then, is that the identification of problems is the greatest problem of all. There are, of course, attempted responses and various attempted solutions to this meta-problem, but no one can make it go away. Who gets to assume that they know how the lower classes ought to live? Should they have neater houses and cleaner faces, drink and swear less, or just get higher wages?[26]* If we accept that we cannot solve the meta-problem, there are, so far as I can see, only three logical ways of attempting to derive a pragmatist social science. The first is for social sciences to define the problems that they solve as the internally generated problems of a scientific community. The second is what we can call "pragmatism in detail." Just as the physical sciences do not need to solve all our problems at once, but prove that they can be useful for many people's particular problems, so, too, the social sciences need only to produce knowledge that can be of use to some given their projects. The third is to propose that the sciences are not oriented to solving problems but, rather, providing a more general infrastructure that can be used for the solution of problems. I want to consider each of these in turn.

Smaller Communities

Science is what a community does as it goes about solving its intellectual problems. That certainly sounds congenial to the current sociological imagination. For isn't that what disciplines do? Aren't they social orders that have their own senses of what is a problem? Indeed, this rendition of a quasi-pragmatist theory of science fits our most common understanding of social sciences as "fields" that have their own autonomous logic, setting their goals as to what is to be accomplished, establishing their own criteria of what constitutes success, and allocating rewards accordingly. It seems that we already have the pragmatist vision of a social science at hand.

But there are two problems with this interpretation of how we should bring pragmatism to bear on sociology, which I have called the "descriptive" approach. The first is that we have all been forced to recognize that research programs can take on what we can (borrowing from Lakatos) call a "degenerate" character[27]—one that, like a degenerate solution to a system of equations (all variables set to zero, for example), seems to satisfy our criteria but is definitely not compatible with the substantive questions that gave rise to our model. Whatever the vision of "science as a field" may be, it seems to also include not simply pseudo-sciences but anti-sciences. The falsest and most twisted authoritarian ideology also can be defined as a social order setting its own problems requiring cognitive solutions. And the lies produced therein may be very "useful" in helping the liars achieve their various goals. Clearly, something else is going to be needed if we are to derive principles for *scientific* inquiry.

That something else is, at least as a first approximation, technological realization and material practice and, most important, the connection of these external considerations to the internal processes of the field. When Rousseau forecast that a corrupt society would develop "useless or pernicious arts" and "silly sciences," it was based on the assumption of "the extreme inequality of conditions and fortunes" that made such activities the self-constructed province of a few.[28] The sort of involution that is often assumed to be necessary for a progressive field would allow for such silliness to survive. It is heteronomy, not autonomy, that is key for science—as Bacon said, we compel nature by obeying it—and this is true for most other fields as well. Put simply, if sociology is not to orient to technological projects of making artifacts in the world, it cannot be trusted to turn inward like an ouroboros. Recall the key metaphor of the "cash value" for truth—there is no pragmatist science that allows us simply to write checks to ourselves, ones that no one else ever has to cash.[29]*

Pragmatism in Detail

The second approach would be to propose that while the social sciences must solve real-world problems, they do not need to solve the problems of the *whole* world. Rather, they can solve the specific problems of different persons or sets of persons. There are two ways in which this can be interpreted, a narrower and a broader conception. The narrower is that the social sciences should find regularities that allow people to do things they want to do—no matter what these are. I cannot see how one can deny that this is indeed implied as a possibility by the notion of a pragmatist social science. If theories of fluid mechanics are right, because airplanes stay up, so theories of decision-making are right, if some people can convince others to buy worthless junk. True social theories lead to effective social engineering. If we find this vision of sociology as marketing an unappealing one, it should not be because we react in prurient horror to its being "sullied" by its connection with the economic world. Detached knowledge is rarely good knowledge, and it is better for a science to be sullied than silly.

The real problem with this vision is that although true theories may lead to effective engineering, effective engineering does not require true theories in any but the most degenerate sense: that of performative self-actualization. For example, Hannah Arendt argued that totalitarian governments held to a strange idea of truth that involved them merely hastening the destiny of history—but at the same time, they could apply overwhelming power to create what they predicted ("you are members of a dying class").[30] More innocuously, we are aware that a theory can make itself true, in the sense of Merton's "self-fulfilling prophecy,"[31] when it is used by actors to solve coordination problems, for example, by channeling their expectations of what others will treat as the case. Simply declaring the pattern can be enough to start the pattern—one need not enforce it.[32] Thus we cannot rely upon sheer efficacy as a proof of truth in the social sciences.

All this means is that while we must accept that some social-scientific knowledge should lead to the solution of at least some people's problems, the greater reactivity of our subjects to our own notions makes it a bit difficult to work out the principles of the relations among efficacy, prediction, and truth. Still, can we build on this to lead to a general vision of sociology as a problem-solving science, but one that lets different communities define their problems themselves? This is the somewhat broader interpretation of pragmatism in detail: we are oriented less to technical problems and more to the larger problems of *some* groups. It is the notion underlying participatory action research, in which the investigator teams with a community to study the problems they want solved.[33] Although I believe that this is coherent and has a number of serious advantages, it does not get beyond the understanding of social science as a fragmented set of techniques that allow some people to do what they want, whether for good or evil. It is not that I personally find this a disappointing resolution; rather, I believe that it is an unstable one.

And this is because the problems that groups confront are not always inert, technical ones. The reason "we" haven't been "able" to solve the problem of poverty is that many of us don't want to.[34] The problem with our social problems is that most of them are solutions to *other people's problems* (such as, how can I get as much money as I possibly can? How can I ensure that my children are secure in their social position?). Even more, looking closely at the nature of our problems can lead to somewhat frightening reorientations. The social "problems" associated with African Americans occupy a great deal of American journal space; sociological researchers quite rightly resist any attempt to answer such problems with a one-word solution. Still, should such a first approximation be searched for, it seems that one cannot deny that the chief problem that Blacks have had, historically, is simple: Whites. Thinking in these terms—and then considering what a "solution" to this problem means—is not exactly what the reformers had in mind.

Seen in this light, orienting the social science of a divided society—and all societies *are* divided—around so-called problems is a recipe not for science but for civil war. We cannot assume that there is a single "we" for whom problems should be fixed, nor can we identify a privileged vantage point of those who "know best" and hence can determine how all should live. We cannot even find a safe choice of an all-purpose underdog whose position can be used as the identification of the "right" formulation of problems (in the way that the proletariat seemed to Marxists to be a universal class). Within any group there always are divisions, and if they aren't there to begin with, having experts promising to intervene is likely to open some up. There is, it seems, little chance of defining a stable epistemology for social science on the basis of "problem solving."

Things, then, do not look good for the project of a pragmatist social science. The "this-sidedness" of our knowledge cannot simply be determined by practice, because people's behavior is changed by their beliefs. We cannot simply let each group solve its own problems, because very often their problem is (at least in their minds) the behavior or sometimes very existence of another group.

I can see two responses. The first is to accept that, in a literal way, there is no "truth" to be had—yet—in a fundamentally divided society.[35] But this gives us little orientation toward what we should do *now*. Indeed, it might be thought to justify an attitude of resignation: if we cannot demonstrate the possibility of truth, let's just do what we want to do anyway. Such a response, however, goes against the core ethos of pragmatism. Science is something that does not start with absolute grounds or with absolute truth, but with what we already have—our everyday knowledge. Our everyday knowledge has some value, and the job of science is to increase the quality of that knowledge. That can be possible—indeed, it appears to me that it *must* be possible—even if we cannot determine how, even in principle, we could conclude our investigation with *perfect* thought.[36]*

And thus the other response is to attempt to chart the ways in which social science can improve on existing knowledge without being in a position to resolve conflicts over interest and goals. Although this falls short of what the pragmatists might have hoped for, I propose that we can best achieve these goals by moving toward something akin to a half-way covenant, a value-free pragmatism.[37]* It thus takes the form of that provision of general infrastructure that I listed as a third response to the incapacity of social science to solve all social problems. I go on to sketch how I understand such an infrastructural project.

A PRAGMATIC VERSION OF PRAGMATISM

The Value of Value-Freedom

There is, to my mind, no doubt that any attempt to strictly bracket valuation from other statements of experience flies in the face of the writings of Dewey, James, and Peirce. However, that does not mean that such thinkers would have supported the intermixing of *individual* valuations in science. Indeed, their core commitment to democracy and collectivity was fundamentally at odds with the sorts of defenses of mixing our own valuations with our axioms that come easiest to reformist sciences (for example, "most people don't really know what they want, anyway"; "you can't bracket your values, so why try?"; or "at least I'm honest about my biases").

We often turn to Max Weber to justify this sort of necessary use of values. Although Weber's use of this idea, and that of value-freedom, is a bit tricky,[38] he basically drew on the classic Ciceronian distinction between *invention* and *justification* and proposed that values (intellectual interests) were *necessarily* involved in the formation of the research question, but, having delivered the psychological interest to the investigator, were now required to depart the scene and allow the science to take over. Thus every scientist must contain within herself the polarities that Weber worked out in his theory of politics—first, a value-driven politician, setting the agenda, and then a will-less administrative official, mechanically implementing the directives.

In this vision, a left-wing researcher might well ask the interesting question, "why are conservatives so rigid, authoritarian, and irrational?" and a right-wing researcher the interesting question, "why are liberals so wimpy, cowardly, and irrational?" *Given* the acceptance of the formation of the concepts and/or types implied by the intellectual interest, both should agree on the results of the other. But we probably also recognize that each will insist that the other's work is meaningless because of the poor choice of orienting concepts and their operationalization. Something is wrong, then, with allowing individuals to use their values to create idiosyncratic and tendentious concepts—no matter how "honest" they are about it. Valuation, in the eyes of the pragmatists, is a job not for a knight-errant, but for an intelligent community.

Of course, if we had that intelligent community, everything would be a lot easier. We do not, not because of a lack of intelligence, but because of a lack of *communitas*—even when there are common interests, the "general will" is not something that can be correctly formulated in a society with nontrivial amounts of exploitation—or even transfers of resources carried out grudgingly. In the absence of such community, "values" are likely to be rhetorical sublimations of interests, and hence social science must aim to be "value-free,"—in the sense of removing the role of assumptions about preferability—to the fullest extent possible (and I am convinced that this extent is greater than "nothing"). For one thing, the public is unlikely to support the establishment of a secular church of self-proclaimed experts, because they would suspect that the sociologists are simply not to be trusted. For another, I agree with the hypothetical public here. Social scientists, who may be entrusted to do rigorous work, and to honestly report all their results, still have no particular claim to altruism. We do not teach graduate students how to repackage refined self-interest as noble service to transcendent ideals, but then again, neither do we need to.[39]

Some might argue that it is misplaced to put the institutional survival of the social sciences above their "rightness." Perhaps it would imperil our support, but it is (according to this way of thinking) both morally and intellectual sound that our science should incorporate our values, public be dammed. If that means the end of university-situated social science, perhaps this is preferable. But then again, there are plenty of ways of empirically informing social action outside of social science. Social science is that particular version which thrives in an academic environment, and if it can have worth, we should seek to bring out its strengths, as opposed to collapsing it with other existing forms of inquiry.

This notion of separating valuation from science may seem to be completely antithetical to the writings of the pragmatists, especially those of Dewey. I am not so sure. Dewey certainly argued that the reality of experience—a core principle of his whole approach—implied not only that the qualities of objects were as real as anything else about them but that values existed.[40] There were "ends" in nature as well as in our subjectivities. Yet Dewey's conception was one that stressed these values as aspects of *experience*; the reason that they partake of objectivity is that they are aspects of objects.

Very different are the abstract values that we claim justify our fall from impartiality. These values are little more than hypostasized regimes of justification that we have learned to employ in place of a more honest admission of sides. No one doubts that people are valuable or that they value one another. This does not mean that a scientist weighs in on whose ox gets gored. Thus I think there is less incompatibility of *this* version of value-freedom— namely, the commitment to making knowledge that is not *sided* knowledge—with the core tenets of pragmatism than it might first appear.

An Observational Science

Still, to reject a clear place for values seems to undermine any capacity to closely orient sociology around problems, because to identify situations as problematic is (or so we think) in effect to orient to values, whether explicitly or not. (While I am not so sure that this is so, if only because the notion of "values" may be less useful than Dewey believed, I will accept the implication as valid for current purposes.) But we saw that a science that solves no problems is no science. Is there a way of resolving this seeming antinomy?

I believe that the best way to approach sociology is to consider it not a science of practical intervention, but an observational science, like astronomy. The development of astronomy was pursued for both speculative and practical reasons: astronomy was necessary for calendar systems (quite important for all humans but probably especially agriculturalists) as well as for navigation. Thus although astronomy was driven in part by practical problems, these were not "astronomical" problems. Astronomy could produce stable information on regularities of the universe that were then accessible to people pursuing their own projects.

So, too, sociology can be a science that assembles the regularities that persons might refer to when they have practical problems. These practical problems might indeed be ones related to registers of action like the economic, but they also might be political projects. They would not, however, need to be "global" political solutions (the sort pursued by a society without major fault lines). What sociology can do for people, then, is to improve upon their knowledge of social regularities. As far as I can see, the most promising approach is a cartographic one.[41]* A map is an instrument, a tool that can be used to solve many problems, but it is not itself the solution to any particular one.[42] So, too, we should seek to organize information in ways that can be used for many purposes.

In this approach, we recognize, with the pragmatists, that we start out in everyday life with some workable knowledge of social life—disconnected circles of knowledge, to follow James's vision. Science, if it is doing its job right, increases the width of these circles and attempts to connect them. The cartographic vision is one that is the logical endpoint of the scientific project à la James: the progressive reduction of *terra incognita*. There is, however, a weakness with this appealing approach, and it is that in between "where we are now" and a perfect mapping, we are likely to have an uneven allocation of attention: our explorers—moved by their personal interests, professional sponsors, and political projects—go in some directions and not others. Our maps are likely to have intrinsic biases as a result. Such biases are unlikely to be totally correctable, but that does not mean that they cannot be reduced through dialogue and critique. However, I believe that the implication of these biases is more worrisome than might first appear.

Terra Cognita and Incognita

The problem of biased maps may be greater than simply having given attention to some areas and not others. The usefulness of the cartographic metaphor encounters a limitation if—as I believe—the very objects that we map are constellations of relations connecting persons scattered far across social space. Omitting attention to some means not simply an unevenness in overall attention but a bias in the construction of all of our objects.[43]

One possible response would be to try to codify principles of symmetric investigation. This would seem to follow from one version of the identification of this problem, that of Martin Nicolaus, who famously charged that American sociologists turn their eyes downward "and their palms upward."[44] However, as Nicolaus would have known, it matters not only where we turn our eyes but whether our subjects are inclined to, or compelled to, appear before us when we do so. Our need to have respectful and honest relations with our subjects—a need that I consider an epistemic one, not "merely" an ethical one[45]—means that we cannot have a vision of our science that is premised on the coerced disclosure of data. And it is hard to remove biases that are implicit in the uneven attention to different terrae incognitae when our subjects (or some of them) can veil their actions.

There is indeed something coherent and defensible about Kant's maxim of *publicity* (openness) that he worked out for international relations: namely, that all parties should conduct themselves according to maxims that they would be willing to have made public.[46] However—as Weber insisted—if only some play by these rules, the results can be worse than if none does.[47] And, given that we must also act in accordance with a maxim of *privacy*—that the social sciences cannot align themselves with forces that invade privacy if they are to expect the continued toleration of the public—it seems that we have only one possible solution.

That solution is to organize debate in two ways. The first is to encourage lay critique of sociological claims. This is not to offer subjects a veto over findings; rather, the circle of the community of investigators that pragmatists always understood as vital for the project of inquiry should be as wide as possible. The second is that debate should be conducted in such a way as to give participants an incentive to choose publicity over privacy. Fieldworkers often note that potential subjects can be recruited because they are concerned that their side of the story will otherwise not be told, to their discredit in the eyes of those attempting to come to general conclusions. The assumption here is that opinion, once swayed in one direction, will stay there unless countermanding evidence comes from another source. How do we make this initial allocation of the weight of the evidence? To do this, I believe that we must change our understanding of the relation between inquiry and our acceptance of claims about the world.

In sociology, our reliance on classical statistics has led us to adopt what I suggest we call a "criminal" standard of proof—that the null hypothesis is accepted until it is proven guilty. We can contrast this to the logic of civil trials, in which whichever side the burden of proof falls on is the one we provisionally accept.[48] The criminal standard is, I think, a reasonable one when we have persons all proposing their own somewhat idiosyncratic theories. As Peirce emphasized in his work on the computation of probabilities, we cannot coherently imagine that the equiprobable distribution across cases is 50/50 when dealing with the alternative theories A and *not-A*, if there are twenty-five other competing theories. The criminal standard prevents us from according too much credibility to a claim simply because it has been raised.

But in other cases, in which we have, on the basis of previous research, narrowed down the set of possibilities to a well-defined (and relatively small) set, moving to a civil understanding might help push us to a format in which, without violation of the right to privacy, the system of social science is such as to facilitate the extension of invitations by potential subjects that allow us to explore terra incognita, as opposed to giving an additional incentive for secretiveness.

I believe that we have some reasonable models for such a pragmatist-inspired sociology; significantly, they come before the recognition of the limitations of vast data collation projects. I believe that the single best inspiration that we might select is W. E. B. Du Bois, and I would like to briefly suggest what we can take as orienting principles from his work.

Du Bois as Exemplar

There is, as many note, often something a bit incongruous in writing programmatic claims for pragmatic inquiry—if one really is so oriented to practice, why talk about it, why not just do it? While writing about doing is hardly a strong logical contradiction (there can be reasons why, for example, we sometimes need abstract defenses of the concrete), it is largely true in terms of overall *habitus* or *mien*—those who are good exemplars of a pragmatist approach may leave behind frustratingly little in the way of epistemic guidelines for others, and this characterizes Du Bois. However, in targeted methodological pieces (most important, "Sociology Hesitant"),[49] in scattered statements about his research, and by the contours of the research he did carry out, Du Bois outlined enough of his approach that, also drawing on work by others,[50] we can use him as an existence proof for a particular—and, I believe, particularly pragmatist—vision of sociological research.

First, I would like to emphasize that Du Bois (influenced by James, not Dewey or Peirce[51*]), never adopted a *descriptive* understanding of the search for truth but always considered truth (often capitalized, as if it were a Platonic Idea) not merely a goal to strive for, but an inspiration. Perhaps because he saw the situation of the enslaved as, among other things, to involve a deprivation of truth,[52] Du Bois, unlike many twentieth-century thinkers, always took for granted that we had too little truth, not too much.

Second, he believed that sociology was an *aspiration* to science. Lacking a complacency that characterized better-situated academics, he saw science as a grand, inspiring, unified, and intrinsically worthy endeavor. It held out a promise that

social researchers could pursue, without guarantee of success. But he also emphasized that "whether or not this study may eventually lead to a systematic body of
knowledge deserving the name of science, it cannot in any case fail to give the
world a mass of truth worth the knowing."[53] This notion of a "mass of truth" well
expresses much of the zeal found among workers in the fledgling social sciences in
the late nineteenth century. After the turn of the century, there was increasing recognition that the quest for masses of precise data had yielded very little. (An example would be Weber's own early work for the *Verein für Sozialpolitik*.) Sociology
increasingly focused on attempting to answer theoretically guided research questions as opposed to pursuing precision for its own sake. As these new standards in
sociology developed, however, Du Bois exited the field, locking in this earlier faith
in objectivity and precision.

And (third) Du Bois had taken a fundamentally *cartographic* understanding of
science that was shared by other late-nineteenth-century social researchers, stemming from Charles Booth's famous studies of London. We see this done in a traditional fashion most impressively in *The Philadelphia Negro*.[54] But I believe that
Du Bois's cartographic conception goes somewhat beyond the use of these familiar
techniques and is related to his recognition of the wrinkle for a pragmatist philosophy of social science: that often our problems are, if not simply other people, then,
still, other people's solutions.

To Du Bois, the great question that he was implicitly asked was, "How does it
feel to be a problem?"[55] His orientation to the enormous falsity—untruth—of what
might seem as "pragmatism in detail" answers to questions like "how do we reduce
Negro crime?" (given that the *we* was, literally, rich whites posing the question) prevented him from prematurely finding facile satisfaction in the notion that a pragmatist sociology could simply "solve social problems" (this is the fourth point).

And this understanding that narrow questions contained falsehoods seems to be
connected to Du Bois's cartographic sensibility, which was deeper than the mere
reliance on maps and graphs.[56]* Regarding science, Du Bois wrote, "Its results lie
open for the use of all men—merchants, physicians, men of letters, and philanthropists, but the aim of science itself is simple truth."[57] Of course, we must bear in
mind Du Bois's skill as a rhetorician, and his capacity to unswervingly stick to a tone
of compromise and moderation when it served him. However, I am convinced that,
even when (according to some) he had made the transition from science to propaganda, he retained this vision of the openness and sharedness of truth. Further, I
also hold that he was sincere in his conviction that truth could be attained only by
open and public interchange and the piling up of facts against facts, and that this
was necessary for social progress. Thus in his (relatively late) work *Black Reconstruction*, Du Bois sympathetically saw some of the reasons for the tragedy of the South
being its stubborn refusal to allow open debate.[58]

However, his conviction as to the importance of inclusion in science goes beyond
this practical issue of maximizing the effectiveness of decisions. In a fundamental
way, Du Bois's conception of sociology was one that required the compilation of

lives and experiences. "Sociology," he famously said, "is the science that seeks to measure the limits of chance in human action, or if you will excuse the paradox, it is the science of free will."[59] In contrast to the French social scientists, for whom individual deviation from the "law" was intrinsically *non*-social, Du Bois saw both of these moments—the general pattern and the actions taken by human beings—as part of the domain of sociology.[60]

To Du Bois, lives are neither mere random dispersion from social laws nor a refuge of individuality; rather, they are forms of patterned experience. These patterns reflect not only the actions of those living the life, but the actions of others—and what appear as general conditions are themselves the results of actions that are no less willful than our responses to these conditions. To understand a life, it must be placed in context (thus he interlaces the facts of his own autobiography with world-historical political-economic changes!), but the question of the force of that context is not one that can be answered via assumption. It is for the reason that an investigation of law does not imply the abrogation of ethical responsibility. I noted earlier that Du Bois emphasized the weakness of social formations caused by suppressed opinion; in a different place, considering this issue, Du Bois proposed that aristocracies collapse because they disconnect themselves from the common people. "In the last analysis only the sufferer knows his sufferings and . . . no state can be strong which excludes from its expressed wisdom the knowledge possessed by mothers, wives, and daughters."[61] I think that this general principle—that pragmatism must understand not merely activity but suffering[62]—is one that fits James's vision of experience rather well. But I believe that for Du Bois, unlike James, this orientation to the concrete experience of suffering is joined to a conception of sociology being a science that is always oriented to internal differentiation and not merely aggregate pattern.

For this reason, I think that this conception is different from that of Karl Mannheim, for whom a mature sociology had to examine its object from the many points of view deriving from social variations.[63] Instead, for Du Bois, the variation itself, and its relation to both will and suffering, is to be the object of sociology. The interplay of general statistics and close understanding of lives—the sort of work recently done by Matthew Desmond[64]—can allow a science that is rigorously objective, yet one that need not even raise questions of relativism that once seemed inherently destabilizing to a nomothetic understanding of science.

At the time that Du Bois was writing, this program was, for technical reasons, impossible—and this mismatch between the most promising theoretical conceptions and the possibilities of actual research was characteristic of the period. Thus in France, Gabriel de Tarde's brilliant outline of an interactional sociology was steamrolled by the Durkheimian vision, which conveniently hypostatized the sorts of tabular statistics produced by the governments of the day. But Tarde's conception of influence (and his yearning for the sorts of data now garnered by Amazon) fits the practice and challenges of contemporary researchers using digital exhaust data far better than does the Durkheimian.[65] So, too, Du Bois's idea of social science, impractical as it was a century ago, may be a perfect place to begin a sociology that uses a cartographic conception to compile and organize data on lives, turning it into visual representations that, in his words, "lie open for the use of all."

Thus, following Du Bois, it seems that pragmatism can offer principles that would make for a more robust, and more scientific, sociology. I want to close by suggesting that some of the principles that a pragmatist-inspired sociology would develop may turn out to be relevant to the other sciences—perhaps especially the technological ones.

WHAT SOCIOLOGISTS CAN BRING INTO PRAGMATISM

The Critical Theory

My appeal to the notions of the unbounded increase of openness (or "publicity") probably reminds us of the approach of Jürgen Habermas. Pragmatists in sociology may now tend to dismiss his efforts, in part because they were often based on a provisional reception of the core insights of pragmatism, coming from a thoroughly Charles W. Morris-ed version of Mead.[66] However, I cannot think of anyone who has gone further in the solution of this problem, insoluble though it may be. I therefore think that some aspects of Habermas's system[67] must be grappled with, although this is not the place to do so.

Instead, I wish to draw on his earlier work, as he was making the transition from Critical Theory to his quasi-pragmatism via the interest in publicity. Habermas, considering the differences between the human and natural sciences, which once corresponded to examinations of *praxis* as opposed to *technē*, accepted the gist of Arendt's argument that our capacity to impose reason *successfully* on nature does not mean the *truth* of our cognition.[68] Thus, Habermas argued, it is not simply that the social sciences have the problem of self-fulfilling prophecy but that "we are no longer able to distinguish between practical and technical power."

The natural sciences, as Ian Hacking has emphasized, are all about artifacts—our capacity to make certain phenomena, and to make the referents of our theories real thereby. That is a sign of their truth, not their falsity. (Hacking on electrons: "if you can spray them, they are real."[69]). But if there are options regarding which phenomenon we should concentrate on attempting to make—and given that it took the combined efforts of dozens of countries, and thousands of researchers, to the approximate cost of over \$13 billion[70] to make the Higgs boson appear, one foresees that there are trade-offs—then we cannot always divorce the political/technical questions from the scientific. I share most readers' convictions that most imaginable worlds are not to be had for either love or money: Habermas's point is not that we can either vote on or buy the constants of the universe but that what we *do* do (at least, what we *try* to do) is endogenous to the same complex systematic mess of social relations that we familiarly appeal to when attempting to understand our political and economic relations. This might seem obvious to sociologists who are familiar with social studies of science, but not all of the implications are equally obvious.

The Integration of Lay and Expert Critiques

The one implication that follows automatically is that without pressure for lay critique, the sciences, too, fall short of the truth they could have. (Again, these points have been made many times before, but I believe that they can be made here in a brief and noncontroversial form, especially given that here they are derived from a value-free orientation, and by someone who has no particular animus against scientists of any stripe, whether they vivisect cats, make nuclear weapons, or merely tire us with implausible reductionism.) A good example can be found by drawing on arguments long made by sociologists of deviance.

There is a fair amount of current work on genetic determinants of behavior, some of which—perhaps especially that using well-crafted twin subsamples— should be judged to be of reasonably high scientific caliber. It is often used to determine the proportion of variance in some trait or activity that is explainable by genetic heritage (say, a whopping 16 percent of the variance in some crime statistic is explained by genotype—equivalent to the Blau/Duncan estimate of father-son occupational persistence). But they rarely, for one, consider that monozygotic twins share not only a *genotype*, but also a *phenotype*—they *look* very similar, and may be treated similarly by others. The distortion thus goes beyond the mere issue of selective focus, whereby we walk away remembering that, say, "crime is genetic," even though, given the 84 percent of unexplained variance, the opposite conclusion might be more reasonable. For by setting up our research without, say, speaking to our subjects in the "crime = 1" cell, we might not learn that, of the five people arrested at the same time, four were released on their own recognizance. This information might lead us to extend inferences in new directions. (Perhaps the phenotype that leads to conviction is not related to behavior at all, but to physiognomy—those with innocent-looking faces are not prosecuted.)

This example, of course, involves human subjects, though analogous problems have arisen in animal behavior, in which the capacity to make animals do this or that (or, more commonly, *fail* at this or that) allowed for the creation of knowledge which lacked the degree of inferential strength—the capacity to be transported across venue—that we rightly demand of truth (being restricted to laboratory conditions). For example, rats placed in tubes in which they lack an overview of the terrain and cannot use smell seem a lot less intelligent than rats out of the apparatus. But the logic goes all the way down, as they say: given alternative ways of theorizing reality, ways that all successfully solve practical problems, but *different* problems, the allocation of attention may shift the allocation of reality. For example, until the quantum revolution, the two great theories of light were the particle theory and the wave theory. If one is making reflecting telescopes, the particle theory of light is all one needs, but if one is making refracting telescopes, one will encounter anomalies that call out for a wave theory of light.[71]*

The pragmatist conception of truth, then, reminds us that what communities hold to be true is a function not only of the way of the world, but of what they are trying to do. The fullest participation of all may (or may not) be important in its own terms, as an ethical imperative, but it also seems to increase the robustness of our knowledge, if it helps us explore recesses of that patterning of potential experience that we call the universe, recesses that would otherwise be left alone.

The notion that we should crown our thoughts with the blue ribbon of "true" before all sincere, competent, and interested inquirers had come to agreement was, to Peirce, an absurdity. This, of course, does not mean that one has to wait for the insincere, the incompetent, or the uninterested to have their say. But, given the many ways in which we mischaracterize and misjudge, we might do well to set a high bar for our determinations that others are indeed undeserving of inclusion, if we are not to unwittingly increase the fragility of our findings.

CONCLUSION

As Nietzsche saw, a comet was coming to wipe out the Western philosophy based on rationalism in various guises. Rationalism allows us to approve of those thoughts (thoughts by human neural systems, that is) that would correspond to the thoughts that an omniscient being—but one who still happens to think a lot like a human— would have. A truly disenchanted philosophy is one in which this very idea makes no sense whatsoever, no more than the idea of a *truly* delicious cannoli, the kind that God would like. Whatever truth is, it is something inside human life, not outside it.

If we accept this disenchanted view, there are, so far as I can see, two consistent and coherent responses. The first is a radically individual one; Nietzsche gives us the bookish version—the creed of Bartol's assassins ("nothing is true— everything is permitted") a more practical spin. The other coherent response is that of pragmatism—to acknowledge the humanness of truth but in such a way that renounces neither science nor human decency, and, in fact, finds compelling (and, in a way, value-free!) reasons why the two support each other. It gives us the only avenue of which I am aware by which we can reform our practice in such a way that it is defensible as an endeavor worthy of lay support, and that is because it is the only way I can see to found a stable epistemology for social inquiry. Perhaps now, after a century of stalling, we will do so.

NOTES

1. The first version of the title of this paper was "*Which* Sociologists Should Get Out of Pragmatism." I have pragmatically changed it. I am grateful to all the participants of the

2015 miniconference at Chicago and the 2017 meeting at Radcliffe, the editors of this volume, and especially Clem Aeppli, B. Robert Owens, and Josh Whitford for comments and dialogue that greatly increased the cogency of this chapter.

2. For example, Paul Lichterman and Nina Eliasoph, "Civic Action," *American Journal of Sociology* 120 (2014): 798–863.

3. Stefan Timmermans and Iddo Tavory, "Theory Construction in Qualitative Research: From Grounded Theory to Abductive Analysis," *Sociological Theory* 30 (2012): 167–86.

4. Josh Whitford, "Pragmatism and the Untenable Dualism of Means and Ends: Why Rational Choice Theory Does Not Deserve Paradigmatic Privilege," *Theory and Society* 31 (2002): 325–63. Also see his chapter in this volume.

5. For explicit introductions of pragmatism as the opposite of rationalism, see William James, *Pragmatism, a New Name for Some Old Ways of Thinking: Popular Lectures on Philosophy* (1907; New York: Longmans, Green, 1946), 66, 257; and *Essays in Radical Empiricism* (1912; New York: Longmans, Green, 1943), 41, 96.

6. Also see Charles S. Peirce, "Treatise on Metaphysics," in *Writings of Charles S. Peirce, Volume 1*, ed. Nathan Houser et al. (1861; Bloomington: Indiana University Press, 1982), 57–84; 65.

7. In his later life, Peirce seems to have rejected this as he became more and more concerned with what strikes most of us as speculative metaphysics. But his conception of what a person *is*—indeed, what matter itself is—was such as to make any application of this principle of the primacy of the practical very abstruse.

8. James, *Pragmatism*, 100. Note that he did not say that metaphysical debates were irrelevant because they did not matter!

9. James was a kindly soul, always willing to support others and boost them at his own expense, and not all of his friends repaid him as they should, affecting his historical reputation.

10. James, *Pragmatism*, 222, 53. Susan Haack, "The Pragmatist Theory of Truth," *British Journal of Philosophical Science* 27 (1976): 231–49 has built upon this in a useful article, though I believe that she is wrong to read "agreement with reality" to be the same thing as a correspondence theory of truth. Further, it is important to distinguish between the times that a theorist (especially James) is giving a *predicate* of truth from the times that our theorist is giving a *definition*. For James's unqualified dismissal of the notion of correspondence, see William James, *The Meaning of Truth: A Sequel to "Pragmatism"* (1909; New York: Longmans, Green, 1946), 396f.

11. James, *Pragmatism*, 75.

12. James, *Meaning of Truth*, 306.

13. James, *Pragmatism*, 188.

14. James, *Pragmatism*, 167.

15. James, *Pragmatism*, 207.

16. Charles S. Peirce, "On the Logic of Science [Harvard Lectures of 1865]," in *Writings of Charles S. Peirce, Volume 1*, ed. Nathan Houser et al. (1865; Bloomington: Indiana University Press, 1982), 162–302; 248.

17. Charles S. Peirce, "The Fixation of Belief," *Popular Science Monthly*, 12 (1877): 1–15. Also see John Dewey, *Theory of Valuation* (Chicago: University of Chicago Press, 1939), 54.

18. See, importantly, Michael Strand and Omar Lizardo, "Beyond World Images: Belief as Embodied Action in the World," *Sociological Theory* 33 (2015): 44–70.

19. Let me briefly expand on this point. As Peirce would have pointed out, it is rare that a hypothesis that some *x* causes *y* comes into a mind in a world in which *x* can *never*, ever cause *y*. The question of whether we can find evidence of *x* causing *y*—that is, enough to reject the null hypothesis of no effect in the population from which we sample—then often really boils down into how large a sample we have gone about constructing. And that often boils down to how determined we are, and/or how much money we have. There are many problems with an attempt to remake sociology in the mold of experimental causality, some particularly important for those who want to focus on numerical estimates of causal effects, but one grave problem for those attached to classical statistics is that it easily degenerates into a system that is equivalent to bidding on the laws of reality.

20. I discuss some aspects of this in John Levi Martin, "Peirce and Spencer-Brown on Probability, Chance and Lawfulness," *Cybernetics and Human Knowing* 22 (2015): 9–33.

21. See especially these works by John Dewey: "The Postulate of Immediate Empiricism," *Journal of Philosophy, Psychology and Scientific Methods* 2 (1905): 393–99; "Brief Studies in Realism. I," *Journal of Philosophy, Psychology and Scientific Methods* 8 (1911): 393–400; and Dewey, *Experience and Nature* (New York: Norton, 1929).

22. This all may seem obvious, but it actually contradicts not only realist approaches to the relation between cognition and truth but the phenomenology associated with Husserl, who founds all knowledge on an originary seeing without acknowledging a capacity for ever *un*-seeing the most fundamental essences. See Edmund Husserl, *Ideas for a Pure Phenomenology and Phenomenological Philosophy I*, trans. Daniel O. Dahlstrom (1913; Indianapolis: Hackett, 2014), 36.

23. See, for example, Anthony Oberschall, *Establishment of Empirical Sociology* (New York: Harper & Row, 1972).

24. See Mary Jo Deegan, *Jane Addams and the Men of the Chicago School, 1892–1918* (New Brunswick, NJ: Transaction, 1988).

25. Indeed, such a focus led to innuendos about Marianne Weber that provoked Max to offer at least one challenge to the field of honor.

26. It is important to note that the engaged social scientists in the early twentieth century were themselves often the source of this critique, and some (most notably, Jane Addams and W. E. B. Du Bois), recognizing the problem of defending the Archimedean point from which problems were defined, moved to more radical politics, as opposed to more politically insulated research.

27. Imre Lakatos, "Falsification and the Methodology of Scientific Research Programmes," in *Criticism and the Growth of Knowledge*, ed. Imre Lakatos and Alan Musgrave (Cambridge: Cambridge University Press, 1970), 118.

28. Jean-Jacques Rousseau, *Discourse on Inequality*, trans. Franklin Philip (1755; New York: Oxford, 1994), 81.

29. To stick with the economic metaphor, I would like to propose what I will call "Wanna Say's" law for such involuted sciences. Say's law in economics is that supply creates its own demand. Wanna Say's law is that intellectual supply creates its own "demand"—we come up with reasons why we *should* say just what we *wanna* say.

30. Hannah Arendt, *The Origins of Totalitarianism* (New York: Harcourt, Brace, 1951), 339.

31. Robert K. Merton, "The Self-Fulfilling Prophecy," *Antioch Review* 8 (1948): 193–210.

32. See, e.g., Donald MacKenzie and Yuval Millo, "Constructing a Market, Performing Theory: The Historical Sociology of a Financial Derivatives Exchange," *American Journal of Sociology* 109 (2003): 107–45.

33. See William Foote Whyte, *Participatory Action Research* (Newbury Park, CA: SAGE, 1991).

34. See Adam Przeworksi, "Could We Feed Everyone? The Irrationality of Capitalism and the Infeasibility of Socialism," *Politics and Society* 19 (1991): 1–38.

35. This is the argument I made in the conclusion of my *The Explanation of Social Action* (New York: Oxford University Press, 2011).

36. To steal vocabulary from Erik Olin Wright ("Compass Points. Towards a Socialist Alternative," *New Left Review* 41 [2006]: 93–124), we can say that we can move forward without a map, so long as we have a compass.

37. I do have some thoughts on how to more closely connect social science research to a democratic community's attempt to repair itself; it is just that these thoughts are no better than anyone else's.

38. See John Levi Martin and Alessandra Lembo, "On the Other Side of Values," *American Journal of Sociology* 126 (2020): 52–98.

39. Karl Marx and Frederick Engels, *The German Ideology*, in *Collected Works*, vol. 5 (1845–46; New York: International Publishers, 1976).

40. Dewey, *Experience and Nature*, 2, 112, 394, 396; also see John Dewey, "The Objects of Valuation," *Journal of Philosophy, Psychology and Scientific Methods* 15 (1918): 253–58; Dewey, "Values, Liking, and Thought," *Journal of Philosophy, Psychology and Scientific Methods* 20 (1923): 617–62; and Dewey, *Human Nature and Conduct: An Introduction to Social Psychology* 1922; (New York: Modern Library, 1930), 326f.

41. Here, see Christopher Muller and Christopher Winship's chapter in this volume, as well as Monica Lee and John Levi Martin, "Coding, Counting, and Cultural Cartography," *American Journal of Cultural Sociology* 3 (2015): 1–33. My reasons to be doubtful as to the promise of a resolutely causal approach are given in Martin, *Explanation of Social Action*.

42. See Edwin Hutchins, *Cognition in the Wild* (Cambridge: MIT Press, 1995).

43. Matthew Desmond, "Relational Ethnography," *Theory and Society* 43 (2014): 547–79.

44. Martin Nicolaus, "Remarks at ASA Convention," *American Sociologist* 4, no. 2 (May 1969): 154–56.

45. John Levi Martin, *Thinking Through Methods: A Social Science Primer* (Chicago: University of Chicago Press, 2017).

46. Immanuel Kant, "Perpetual Peace: A Philosophical Sketch," in *Political Writings*, trans. H. B. Nisbet, (1796; Cambridge: Cambridge University Press, 1970), 93–130.

47. Max Weber, "Politics as a Vocation," in *From Max Weber: Essays in Sociology*, trans. H. H. Gerth and C. Wright Mills(1918; New York: Oxford University Press, 1946), 120.

48. See Charles S. Peirce, "The Logic Notebook," in *Writings of Charles S. Peirce, Volume 1*, ed. Nathan Houser et al. (1865–66; Bloomington: Indiana University Press, 1982), 337–350; 339. Also see Lecture III in *The Lowell Lectures*, in *Writings of Charles S. Peirce, Volume 1*, ed. Nathan Houser et al. (1866; Bloomington: Indiana University Press, 1982), 357–504.

49. W. E. B. Du Bois, "Sociology Hesitant," in *The Problem of the Color Line*, ed. Nahum Dimitri Chandler (1905; New York: Fordham University Press, 2015), 272–84.

50. See the chapter by Karida Brown in this volume.

51. In Du Bois's very early student days, he has rapturous notes on a geometric interpretation of the relation among Truth, Goodness, and Beauty that could have been inspired by Peirce but more likely by Peirce's own inspiration, Schelling. See W. E. B. Du Bois, *The Autobiography of WEB Du Bois* (1968; New York: Oxford University Press, 2007), 107.

52. See, e.g., W. E. B Du Bois, *Black Reconstruction in America: An Essay Toward a History of the Part Which Black Folk Played in the Attempt to Reconstruct Democracy in America, 1860–1880* (1935; New York: Oxford University Press, 2014), 44.

53. W. E. B. Du Bois, "The Study of the Negro Problems," in *The Problem of the Color Line*, ed. Nahum Dimitri Chandler (1898; New York: Fordham University Press, 2015), 77.

54. W. E. B. Du Bois, *The Philadelphia Negro: A Social Study* (1899; New York: Oxford University Press, 2014).

55. W. E. B. Du Bois, "Strivings of the Negro People," in *The Problem of the Color Line*, ed. Nahum Dimitri Chandler (1897; New York: Fordham University Press, 2015), 67.

56. It also seems to be related to his attempt to always begin a report with historical context.

57. Du Bois, "Study of the Negro Problems," 89.

58. Du Bois, *Black Reconstruction*, 134, 576f, also 44.

59. W. E. B. Du Bois, "The Atlanta Conferences," in *On Sociology and the Black Community*, ed. Dan S. Green and Edwin D. Driver (1904; Chicago: University of Chicago Press 1978), 53; also see *Autobiography*, 208.

60. Du Bois, "Sociology Hesitant."

61. W. E. B. Du Bois, *Darkwater: Voices from Within the Veil* (Washington, DC: Austin Jenkins, 1920), 143.

62. Also see Cornel West, *The American Evasion of Philosophy: A Genealogy of Pragmatism* (Madison: University of Wisconsin Press, 1989).

63. Karl Mannheim, *Ideology and Utopia*, trans. Louis Wirth and Edward Shils (1929; New York: Harcourt Brace Jovanovich, 1936).

64. Matthew Desmond, *Evicted: Poverty and Profit in the American City* (New York: Crown, 2016).

65. Monica Lee and John Levi Martin, "Surfeit and Surface," *Big Data and Society* 2 (2015), https://doi.org/10.1177/2053951715604334.

66. See Daniel R. Huebner, "The Construction of *Mind, Self, and Society*: The Social Process Behind G. H. Mead's Social Psychology," *Journal of the History of the Behavioral Sciences* 48 (2012): 134–53.

67. See especially Jürgen Habermas, *The Theory of Communicative Action. Volume 1: Reason and the Rationalization of Society*, trans. Thomas McCarthy (1981; Boston: Beacon, 1984) and *The Theory of Communicative Action. Volume 2: Lifeworld and System: A Critique of Functionalist Reason*, trans. Thomas McCarthy (1981; Boston: Beacon, 1987).

68. Jürgen Habermas, *Theory and Practice*, trans. John Viertel (1963; London: Beacon, 1973), 20, 46, 255; Hannah Arendt, *The Human Condition* (Chicago: University of Chicago Press, 1958).

69. Ian Hacking, *Representing and Intervening: Introductory Topics in the Philosophy of Natural Science* (Cambridge: Cambridge University Press, 1983).

70. Alex Knapp, "How Much Does It Cost to Find a Higgs Boson?" *Forbes* July 5, 2012.

71. Because different frequencies of light refract differently, it is impossible to crisply focus such a telescope on more than one color at a time.

3. Self-Reflection and Social Responsibility in Research

LESSONS FROM EARLY PRAGMATIST HISTORICAL INVESTIGATIONS

DANIEL R. HUEBNER

How can an approach centered on the practical future consequences of social action in the present tell us anything about the past, and why should we care what historical figures had to say about even older events? In seeking to answer these questions, this chapter charts an unusual course that challenges us to expand our view of pragmatism and reflect on our own contemporary enterprise of social science. I argue that it is precisely in early pragmatists' neglected historical investigations that they develop the tools to turn pragmatism from a general philosophy into a social science epistemology and methodological guide by having to articulate clear understandings of interpretation and inference, the nature of evidence, the role of value commitments, and, perhaps especially, the necessity of retrospection in self-reflective action and social reconstruction.

In the course of the chapter, different strands of pragmatist analysis in history are reconstructed and pulled together in an effort to reveal the guidelines they offer in our enterprise of adapting pragmatist philosophy to the problems of contemporary social science. To preview the argument, I will propose that in reflections on history, classical pragmatists conceptualized research in the human sciences as action in the present and argued that it necessarily involves ongoing dynamic relationships to the past. This approach helps us to reflect on the situatedness of our own claims and to recognize the ethical questions we face regarding the anticipated future consequences of our work. In the course of investigation, according to classical pragmatists, we construct sign relationships in which we treat items in our own present as evidence of past action (even if that past action is only moments before).

We, in effect, interpret a past to a future in a present. Thus, the practical processes of searching for evidence and of interpreting that evidence are implicated in constructing the limits of who we see ourselves as historically—how inclusive we are in responding to some and not other possible evidence and how we pursue continuities and explanations that appeal to the terms of some communities and not others. Because evidence and facts are located in practical acts of selection and representation, they can be subjected to critical reflection as ethical, political, value-laden problems. Our evidence and interpretive processes, likewise, are always historical, in that they are determined by a host of already given factors and in that we treat evidence as historically given in the moment in which it is subjected to analysis.

Classical pragmatists considered the nature of material evidence, as well as their relationship to symbolic or linguistic claims and embodied memories, and sought to show that our evidence is already constitutive of the fabric of human relations. We social scientists (historical or not) participate in processes of social consciousness formation and memorializing that tie us to others and extend the practical actions already integral to society. Value commitments are inherent in this embodied social action and are thus constitutive for the enterprise of research. Far from being something we can and should try to opt out of, we are urged to become self-reflective, explicit, and critical in our commitment to values so as to harness them to yield better results. Finally, pragmatist investigations in history show us that efforts at democratic social inclusiveness are always also retrospective and reconstructive endeavors that involve reappraising the past from the new perspectives we gain in the emerging present. We participate in the composition of that present through the ways in which we interpret the past as relevant to the future, so we are impelled to reflect on how what we do makes a difference. This practice in self-reflection, the pragmatists' argued, makes us better able to take the role of disparate others and think critically over time, and thus offers the promise of knowledge that is more universal in both its epistemology and its ethics. Although the classical pragmatists were criticized for their supposed neglect of history, this chapter attempts to show that they did much of their most rigorous thinking about how to account for human action when they were confronted with historical problems.

A couple of points of orientation are relevant at the outset. This chapter focuses on the broad tradition of classical pragmatists, their interlocutors, and those they influenced, but it does not treat these theorists and ideas merely as amusing bedtime reading. Instead, I introduce their work in the service of reconstructing how knowing about their work can help us do ours better. Although the chapter will introduce literature in historiography and the philosophy of history, I will not be particularly concerned to recreate the nuances and quagmires of debates in these fields, or in whether the classical pragmatists sound dated in the language of contemporary historiography, but rather in how pragmatists responded to the critical challenges of investigating the past and how their ideas may serve as useful conceptual tools. And these tools will not be directed only to the subfield of historical sociology that studies "the past"; rather, they are directed to all of us who represent human acts, who treat our data as given facts, who rely on symbolic or written documents and memories, and who participate in the ongoing processes of exclusion and inclusion in our own scholarly efforts.

Additionally, this approach is not limited to the canonical American pragmatists Charles Peirce, William James, and John Dewey but is, instead, especially emphatic in the work of a number of social theorists who have been marginalized from the disciplinary canon. In this sense, the chapter is in part an attempt to rearticulate an often unrecognized aspect of the pragmatist tradition and to reinterpret that tradition pragmatically as a historically dynamic and self-reflective movement. We should not suppose that we know dogmatically what pragmatism is; instead, pragmatic social theory should lead us to conclude that the question of who is a pragmatist is to be answered from within the ongoing social process and should be continually reevaluated in light of the kinds of problems contemporary actors face. We should conceptualize pragmatism in the same manner that we, drawing from pragmatism, conceptualize our various objects of study. The chapter seeks to show that as we undertake this reevaluation, the understanding of social processes is enriched. We find striking formulations and uniquely valuable insights into the nature of social processes from some of those scholars who have been marginalized historically, and we gain a better grounding of our principles when we consider pragmatism inclusively rather than dogmatically.

The chapter is organized as follows. The first section outlines the historical approach to social action in canonical pragmatists, their relationship to the "new history" of American social and intellectual historians, and the importance of considering pragmatism as an inclusive and dynamic approach. I show that although history was thought of as a challenge for classical pragmatists, they addressed this supposed problem by elaborating a novel understanding of human action that helps us understand our own work as investigators in pragmatic terms. The second section considers the methodology of conducting historical social research pragmatically, focusing especially on the nature of inference and interpretation, value commitments, and the presentation of facts. The third section takes on the topic of the historical evidence for inquiry into human social action, including the given nature of evidence, the ways in which something comes to be treated as evidence, and the constitutive role of symbolic materials and memory in studying human action. The chapter concludes by considering how inquiry that takes the early pragmatist approach to history seriously can ground the importance of inclusive, epistemologically richer, self-reflective, and socially responsible research as we come to conceptualize the practices of research as social action processes that unfold over time.

I. PRAGMATIST PHILOSOPHIES AND SOCIAL HISTORIES

For several of the major critics of pragmatism in the early twentieth century, including Émile Durkheim, the supposed inability to explain knowledge of past events was a fundamental problem for the philosophy.[1] However, these critics missed the pragmatists' serious work to theorize the nature of historical processes and to ground their own philosophy in the emergent features of social history (at least in part because they focused on a partial, selective reading of early pragmatism). John Dewey's exchanges with philosopher and historian of ideas Arthur O. Lovejoy are particularly acute in their formulations of pragmatist understandings of history and their contrast from dominant "realist" histories.[2] For Dewey, knowledge of the past is logically "knowledge of past-as-connected-with-present-or-future" or, corrected for the actual temporal course of inquiry, "the present and the future as implicating a certain past." Verification of claims about the past must be in the present or the future, because there is no way for thought about the past to be verified if its meaning does not have a future reference, and to say this is to say that it is implicated in future-oriented human action in the present. Dewey wrote repeatedly on historical issues, going so far as to criticize all "non-historical" political theories because they invalidly abstract action away from "time, place, and concrete conditions." Dewey's monumental *Logic: The Theory of Inquiry* builds on the historical reasoning developed in his exchanges with Lovejoy. Subsequent pragmatist philosophers drew on Dewey's articulations in their own work on the philosophy of history and the history of philosophy, noting that the investigation of history is vital for critical social reflection and emancipation.[3]

The exemplars of the so-called new American social history—Frederick Jackson Turner, James Harvey Robinson, Carl Becker, Charles and Mary Ritter Beard, Lucy Maynard Salmon—were either explicitly in dialogue with the pragmatist philosophers or exemplified much the same attitude toward historical investigation.[4] In one of the earliest pieces to express a presentist, social, anti-formalist sensibility toward historical investigation, Turner wrote that "history is the self-consciousness of this [societal] organism" ever growing and that "each age writes the history of the past anew with reference to the conditions uppermost in its own time."[5] All of these authors insisted that history must attend to social development, broadly defined, as its subject matter and draw from the social sciences for its analysis; that the nature and topics of historical investigation change with changes in pressing practical social concerns; and that history as a self-reflective enterprise is done in the service of intelligent social reconstruction.[6] Still, these intellectual historians who drew on the emerging social sciences have not figured prominently in social-scientific considerations of pragmatist philosophy.

To take seriously this focus on self-reflexivity and social reconstruction should mean an approach to our own intellectual and social history that is ongoing, seeking to progress through engagement with those voices that can enrich the dialogue. This task should be undertaken because, as I hope to show, the work of pragmatists excluded from the canon profoundly improves pragmatic social science, especially as it is recognized as a historically dynamic enterprise. The excluded and marginalized tell us about history not just as their marginalization serves as an object lesson in historical processes but, more important, as they are found to be creative thinkers situated in and practically responding to the capacities and resources of social processes in ways that the canonical authors have not.[7] Patricia Hill Collins, in new work seeking to create a historically informed dialogue between pragmatism and intersectionality in the social sciences, argues that we can both use the historical simultaneity of scholars as a critical tool (that Jane Addams or Alain Locke wrote at the same time about the same topics as John Dewey) and self-consciously evaluate the contested, historical construction of such mutually exclusive lineages of scholars in this way.[8] This effort is an invitation to pursue inclusive dialogue that draws from the experiences of a broader tradition for both epistemological and ethical progress. The approach likewise allows us to maintain the pragmatist democratic critique of forms of domination and authoritarianism (including intellectual domination) by "self-inclusion," treating our own claims as contextually shaped and committed to values and avoiding the "moral smugness" of historical accounts that covertly identify success with righteousness.[9]

Taken seriously, a pragmatic view of history as "that which works best" actually cautions us against making snap judgments or acquiescing to the idea that "what is, is right."[10] Because a pragmatic stance invites us to consider the plurality and contextuality of what it means for something to work or to be useful, a thoroughgoing pragmatism would also need to consider how what appears in one instance to be failure may come to have made vital contributions as new consequences emerge in time and across situations. Thus, because pragmatism is consequentialist, it implies that we must remain open to the ways in which new developments change our understanding of the past. This is what Richard Bernstein has elsewhere called the process of "argumentative retellings" of pragmatist tradition, a process that is inherent in the reconstruction of traditions and, thus, constitutive of tradition itself.[11]

For the purposes of this chapter, I outline how ideas from Jane Addams, W. E. B. Du Bois, Charlotte Perkins Gilman, Alain Locke, Josiah Royce, Lucy Maynard Salmon, and Ella Flagg Young, alongside American intellectual "new" historians, as well as canonical pragmatists Peirce, James, Dewey, and Mead, help to develop the epistemology and methods of a more democratically inclusive social science that reflects conscientiously on the lessons of history. Each of these individuals has been associated with pragmatism in reconstructive scholarship in the history of philosophy, the social sciences, and progressive education.[12] This is not intended as a closed list but, rather, an invitation to rummage through our intellectual history for more forgotten treasures and varieties. The retrospective reconstruction of our own disciplinary history is always an ongoing project, and this chapter is certainly not intended as the final word. Each of the following sections will show how these authors provide a more thoroughgoing pragmatist elaboration of the temporal and historically conscious processes of research in the social sciences and, by doing so, come to a more satisfying self-reflective position with regard to the critical advocacy of social justice and democracy, scientific research, and the integrative study of human society.

II. CONDUCTING HISTORICAL INQUIRY AS SOCIAL SCIENCE

Pragmatist scholars beginning with Peirce have considered the methodology or practical epistemology of historical inquiry; that is, how we conceive of the study of historical human actions and what our principles lead us to propose with regard to the nature of interpretation, value commitments, and the materials from which narratives may be constructed. Of course, historical social research is a human endeavor, and its methodologies are enacted as processes of action. In this generic sense, it is no different from other human actions, and we can bring to the analysis of social research the same social, practical, and processual theory that pragmatists elaborate to study action in all its diversity. Hans Joas has been explicit in arguing that a fully elaborated pragmatist theory of action is preferable to other available social-scientific accounts precisely because its conceptual apparatus can claim to account for action in all of its myriad forms without residual categories.[13] It must follow from this that pragmatist theory is also a tool for analysis of social science as action. The lessons that early pragmatists derived from the study of history are eminently applicable to contemporary social-scientific investigation, which involves the same problems of inference through an iterative process of guessing and exploring consequences, of interpretation in which the investigator is situated in a temporal process of relating a past to a future, and of selection of facts in relation to the investigator's values. Authors outside the canon of classical pragmatism are especially important in showing not only how value judgments are necessary to the research process but also how conceptualization of and reflection on values provides a ground for a dynamic, critical advocacy of democratic pluralism and historical preservation of human records. We can, thus, trace a strand of pragmatist theorizing on history that can help to inform the development of pragmatic social science.

A. *Inference*

Peirce wrote a treatise in 1901 entitled "On the Logic of Drawing History from Ancient Documents Especially from Testimonies," which treats the problem of researching human history as a way to develop and illustrate his logic of science.[14] For Peirce, the process of knowledge in any discipline begins with the "discovery that there has been an erroneous expectation of which we had before hardly been conscious."[15] The notion of erroneous expectation should be treated broadly because, for example, we can be surprised just as easily by unexpected regularities as by anomalies. Peirce's approach to the logic of the scientific process is often called "abductive analysis." Abduction is a form of reflective or disciplined guessing that proposes a hypothesis that renders the observed facts possible and entertains it "on probation" while testing out probable experiential consequences of adopting it.[16] History, like any other field of knowledge that seeks to be scientific, has a processual logic with definable inferential steps over time and a recursion to previous steps if the process fails to proceed smoothly. This method acknowledges, on the one hand, that although the possible explanations for facts are in a certain sense innumerable, there is reason to believe that the human mind may guess productively at them in a finite course of investigation (indeed, that the historical advances of science demonstrate as much).[17] On the other hand, the method acknowledges that we rarely find a hypothesis that proves entirely satisfactory to all the facts, and so an intrinsic part of scientific method is skillfully reflecting on the best ways to seek hypotheses and to anticipate their breakdown.[18]

In the most detailed recent application of Peirce's logic of inference to social science methodology, Tavory and Timmermans note that abductive analysis aims at producing new theory through speculative hunches based on evidence that is found to be surprising or unexpected. Those hunches are then scrutinized, altered, and refined iteratively by carefully evaluating variation in the assembled data, assessing possible cases that do not fit the hypotheses, comparing hypotheses with others in terms of plausibility, and interpreting the relevance of the hypotheses to a community of inquiry.[19] They stress Peirce's social approach to the scientific process, including both how the hypotheses an investigator develops are responsive to investigators' social contexts and how research is validated and scrutinized in the ongoing collective endeavor of scientific inquiry. Drawing from sociologist Robert MacIver's pragmatist-informed *Social Causation*, historian Morton White also developed the logic of this position, arguing that of all existing logical approaches to studying human history, only abduction acknowledges the fundamental pluralism built into research because of the way that investigators' values and interests are intrinsic to it while they also retain an understanding of the determinate relationship between facts and their explanation.[20] There can be legitimate and even fundamental differences in what one takes to be the cause of a phenomenon, but such explanations are always continually tested against the traces of the historical reality described.

Dewey and others echoed Peirce's "experimental" or "explorative" approach, noting that although the meanings of history are hypothetical, this does not make them "subjective." They are submitted to the test of reference to future situations; all our meanings are of this "tentative" kind: "indications of relevance" or "estimates of value" that have an "empirical status" in the sense of both really orienting us in the present and continually having to prove themselves true in the future.[21]

B. Interpretation

Among early pragmatist-influenced authors, the historical account that drew most explicitly and substantively from Peirce's logic is Josiah Royce's study of Christianity, which Joas argues holds key insights.[22] For Royce, history consists of a sequence of interpretations of signs. For example, an Egyptologist who translates an ancient inscription involves the translator as interpreter, the text to be interpreted, and the implied reader of the translation and hence the language and context for the act of interpretation.[23] In his view, the past is a "realm of events whose historical sense, whose records, whose lessons, we may now interpret, in so far as our memory and the documents furnish us the evidences for such interpretation," and the "future" is the "realm of events which we view as more or less under the control of the present will of voluntary agents, so that it is worthwhile to give to ourselves, or to our fellows, counsel regarding this future."[24] This process of the present interpreting the meaning of our past experiences to the future is, for Royce, a continuous and ultimately infinite one as each act of interpretation becomes itself an event of the past to be interpreted.[25]

There are further implications to this realization for Royce. To be an interpreter of history is to adopt a definite position in a "community of interpretation." It requires a "self-surrender" and a double conformity to ideas that are not one's own, to both the past minds to be interpreted and the minds to whom the interpretation is addressed—a responsibility to understand both "languages," so to speak.[26] Interpretation is a profoundly ethical and social act both because of this double responsibility and because it gives a determinate order to the relationships between the elements: the interpreter interprets one meaning, language, or speaker to another (and not vice versa).[27] Interpretation is a creative act in that it involves the discovery or invention of a third element that mediates between the two ideas compared; a creation that "shows us ourselves, as we are," that "enriches our world of self-consciousness," that "broadens our outlook and gives our mental realm definiteness and self-control," that "teaches one of our ideas what another of our ideas means," or that "connects" the fragments of experience by showing "how to live as if life had some coherent aim."[28] Interpretation is enriched and continually renewed by the "inexhaustible resources of our social relations" and is undertaken in the expectation of endless further "mutual interpretations" made in the community that will serve to verify or modify one's interpretation by the community's own further experiences.[29] To report that you have discovered a fact is not, in Royce's view, to report the workings of an individual's psychology or a self-contained object of the world but, rather, to "interpret" in the sense of appealing to a community within which that fact may be recognized.[30] Indeed, Royce is often credited with coining the pragmatist notion of the "scientific community," building on and elaborating Peirce's ideas in this regard.[31] Royce's identification of interpretation with temporality suggests that not only historians but all human inquiries are constituted by this temporal progress of interpreting the past to the future in a situated present.

To this view, Dewey adds that the things that form a part of our present experiences can be said to "represent" or "stand for" some event in the past only as they take on an "anticipatory reference" to some practical consequences in the future.[32] That is, when we ask about an object or assert that it has such a meaning, the object acquires or serves a representative function that it does not inherently possess. Treating an object as a sign or representation is an inference that does not become "knowledge" in a complete sense until the indication is borne out in something immediately experienced.[33] As both professional researchers and everyday actors, we go looking, by means of "tentative inference," for evidence that would satisfactorily demonstrate whether or not some event happened.[34] For Dewey, this approach should lead us to a "pluralistic realism" in our treatment of knowledge: that "the things which are taken as meaning or intending other things are indefinitely diversified, and so are the things meant."[35]

William James, in his own excursion into historical reasoning, provided an analysis of a prosaic example.[36] Whether a statement ("Caesar really existed") refers to an event in the past may be known by the ways in which the practical effects of the statement run together with the practical effects of the event in the past. If Caesar wrote a manuscript of which the investigator can see a reprint and say "the Caesar I mean is the author of *that*," then there is a ground for establishing a "determinate cognitive relation" between the statement and the past event it supposedly grasps. That is, James advocated looking for "finite intermediaries" (chains of facts with practical effects, such as the writing and reprinting of Caesar's manuscript) that serve as signs in a universe of discourse by the effects they have on the functional working of statements, like "Caesar really existed."

Stefan Niklas offers, as contemporary examples of this process, the use of a fingerprint or DNA sample in forensics; and, drawing from pragmatist logician C. I. Lewis, he identifies these as "material extensions" that become identified with the past as "concrete parts of the whole" or "effects of the past event which endure after it has ceased to exist."[37] They are not transcendentally or completely established as true—this is not ultimately a "correspondence theory" between claim and reality—but they provide a practical medium in which agreement on truth, falsehood, or irrelevance can be assessed and reassessed in light of subsequent practical effects. Bernstein traces this grounding of claims about truth and objectivity in "justificatory inferential social practices" as one of the central common themes throughout the modern pragmatist tradition.[38] This historical reasoning is, for James, no different in principle from the process of making and evaluating truthful claims about a contemporaneous fact outside one's immediate environment (such as whether there are tigers in India), because both involve this process of indicating signs that, if pursued, bear out practical consequences that unfold in time (e.g., traveling to India and searching for tigers).[39]

C. Values and the Selection of Facts

In this pragmatic view, to talk of the "facts" of history is to take some occurrence "out of a swirling dumb anonymity and give it *public* rank and status," to "confer upon it a *rightful* claim, the *authority*, to determine belief and decide the conclusion to be reached."[40] Dewey's language is explicitly ethical and political: a fact is something acknowledged and committed to publicly (with all the Deweyan connotations of that word), and this act of selecting facts as worthy of consideration must be undertaken responsibly precisely because it confers authority and asserts the consequences that follow from it. But on the converse, whether one notes an occurrence and what one notes about it depend on one's antecedent "constellation of habits, including attitudes of belief," which are "determined under and by social conditions including language" and the "means and material of communication."[41] It is not that the researcher arbitrarily chooses among facts but that what constitutes a fact is inextricable from the practical orientation of sociohistorically situated investigators, undertaken as a process of reasoning tentatively to an end.[42] Whereas in one sense it is correct to say that pragmatists reject a substantive fact value (or cognitive-normative) distinction, a more fully elaborated view shows how both facts and values emerge and function in relation to embodied and situated action.

Alain Locke, an often-neglected pragmatist philosopher, thoroughly examined the nature of professing and adhering to values, and his approach overcomes the caricatured (but often implicitly held) pragmatist understanding of values.[43] For Locke, values must be conceptualized not merely (as they are typically treated in the logical positivist tradition and elsewhere) as formal value judgments but, rather, as bodily/emotionally mediated forms of experiencing.[44] To treat only propositional judgments is to limit what can be said about values to logical-experimental form rather than to acknowledge the active, embodied, nonrational experience of selectively preferring, of being guided by affinities. This more fundamental notion of values is important for recovering and being self-reflective about their fundamentally "normative" and sociopolitical nature. We should acknowledge that "we must live in terms of our own particular institutions and mores, assert and cherish our own specific values, and we could not, even if it were desirable, uproot our own traditions and loyalties."[45] But we should also acknowledge that our mode of living gives us no justification for treating the particular structure of the values by which we live as the "perfect set of architectural specifications" for democracy or some other ideal society, because such an assumption entails huge consequences in social practice and is ultimately associated with bigotry and authoritarianism.[46]

As contemporary intersectional feminist scholars have argued, the pluralism of values should not lead pragmatism into a directionlessness or pretended noncommitment to all values, especially in light of the pragmatic political projects of socially marginalized groups.[47] Instead, Locke sought a way of grounding the commitment to democratic social values pragmatically and hence in terms of their continual reconstruction and experiment. In his historical social research, Locke showed how, without this reflective awareness of the "moral associations and relationships" of our view on historical facts, we end up treating the fact of practical political domination as an indication of innate (often racialized) superiority or inferiority.[48] This challenges the idea that there can be a fundamental separation between our seemingly universal values and the particular practices of domination that they seem to critique. For example, Locke notes that nineteenth-century European missionaries, although they typically conceived of themselves as having altruistic, universal religious values, were also implicated in the race practices of economic and political imperialism.[49]

In a major contribution to historiography that helps flesh out the practical consequences of value commitments, Du Bois showed how dominant—and, indeed, virtually unquestioned—were blatantly racist and demonstrably false views in the professional historical literature about the American Civil War and Reconstruction period.[50] One aspect of this problem is the popular view that history should be written for "our pleasure and amusement, for inflating our national ego, and giving us a false but pleasurable sense of accomplishment," or, more tersely, "lies agreed upon"—Pierre Bourdieu likewise scorned this as the reason history (but not sociology) books could be produced so as to be given as "Christmas presents."[51] This propagandism is a commitment to the idea that the wrongs of history should be forgotten, distorted, or skimmed over so that history can serve as a kind of edifying moral example of "perfect humans and noble nations."[52]

Indeed, a supposed commitment to the value of "impartiality" or "objectivity" (to use Weber's much-debated term) can participate in this propagandism when history is written in such a way that no one seems to have done any wrong: history depicted by "sweeping mechanistic interpretation" as if it were the clash of "winds and waters" or the working out of "cosmic social and economic law."[53] Even supposedly radical historians (Du Bois singles out Charles and Mary Beard) succumb to such a pseudo-depoliticizing approach. This propaganda may even be, in a limited sense, "useful," but Du Bois emphasizes that propaganda cannot continue to hold a "permanent benefit" as a guide to humanity. Although he does not fully elaborate this point, Du Bois points to a consequentialist and ethical criterion for what leads historical study to be more "scientific." We are implicitly asked to consider what kinds of accounts stand the test of time, where the "test of time" is continual beneficial guidance in new situations. And Du Bois suggests, in *Black Reconstruction*, that such guidance comes only from emphasizing rather than eliding the reality of the wrongs committed in history.[54]

In Du Bois's study, it is clear that such an approach is most obvious when the supposed usefulness of history fails and thereby shows itself to be propaganda. The propagandistic history of Reconstruction was, Du Bois pointed out, part of the "foundation of our present lawlessness and loss of democratic ideals" in the Jim Crow South; and its caricature of race relations was part of leading "the world to embrace and worship the color bar as social salvation" in eugenics and segregation.[55] To get history wrong may placate our sense of righteousness or complacency, but it has devastating consequences for the future. Scientific history, to Du Bois, is simultaneously humane history in that it records as accurately and faithfully as possible the "real plot," which is human action with all its mistakes, guilt, courage, sacrifice, hurt, and struggle.[56] The people in history books are not archetypal villains, idiots, or saints but "just men; men who crave ease and power, men who know want and hunger, men who have crawled."[57]

For Du Bois, the right and wrong of history is a judgment about the real human and social costs of past events.[58] E. H. Carr, drawing from Weber, noted further that it is important to pass judgment on social events, institutions, and policies (not individuals) in the past precisely because such an act prevents facile attempts to explain away the moral responsibility of the past merely as the properties of individuals (e.g., blaming Hitler as a way of ignoring questions about the society that produced and supported him or pointing to the "good slave-owner" to justify the institution of slavery).[59]

Such a human, scientific approach to history as Du Bois proposes requires a reading of the total and authoritative records, an endeavor that is inseparable from a value-laden assessment of the real "witness" of history (that is, who the event is "about").[60] The records of the past are doubly important to marginalized people, because they serve to document the hardships and inequalities those people face and demonstrate the integral roles they nevertheless play in social institutions, while also illuminating the demonstrable social causes that have led to the destruction of progress.[61] The lack of documentation becomes a self-perpetuating problem that the historical researcher—and, indeed, all researchers—must recognize: documents are not preserved because they are presumed to be the records of poor and ignorant people, which means that the most unfair caricatures are carefully preserved while the documents of "serious speeches, successful administration and upright character" are ignored and forgotten.[62] In post–Civil War Reconstruction, the chief witness was, Du Bois proposed, the formerly enslaved people, whose testimonies had been "almost barred from court" and whose records had been systematically disregarded, discredited, and purposefully destroyed, because historians sought to find support for their racial beliefs already presupposed rather than to investigate what really happened.[63]

The bulk of Du Bois's seven-hundred-page *Black Reconstruction* consists of quotations from little-used sources seeking to preserve and demonstrate what may be called the "embarrassment of facts" on Reconstruction. The facts are not just necessary in a literal sense (that without them a determinate history cannot be written) but also in a moral sense, that they serve as the arbiter of truth, which is the only sure basis on which to build "Right in the future."[64] Indeed, Du Bois is joined in this sentiment by Locke, Charlotte Perkins Gilman, Lucy Maynard Salmon, and many others who argued that the documentation and preservation of materials from people in socially marginalized positions is an essential aspect of social progress because of the ways in which they can serve to recover a more inclusive history.[65]

If people are alike in enacting value commitments, but if those values are nonconvergent, then there is only one practical way, according to Locke, to develop a healthy democratic pluralism and better social self-knowledge.[66] Comparative-historical exposure to, and critical evaluation of, other cultures and their value systems as they change in response to social conditions "free[s] our minds" from provincial limitations and dogmatisms of our value-commitments. This brings a surprising and rather unique answer to the question of value commitments: whereas a Weberian may advocate self-reflection on values in order to strive to overcome them in the service of "value-neutrality," a pragmatist may argue that we are more self-consciously and critically able to understand and commit to our own values by seriously studying the values of others in comparative-historical investigations. At the same time, this enterprise trains us in better democratic practice by having to develop approaches to the conceptualization of differences without inequalities, equivalences without identities, cooperation without conformity.[67]

Locke developed an explicit and thorough justification of a democratic pluralism of value commitments on this critical, interrogative basis and sought to show that in tracing the ways in which values change in modified social conditions, we find a starting place for a "moral responsibility of society" to exercise social control and deliberately cultivate progressive changes.[68] So, the pragmatist confronted with the problem of value commitments in all forms of social research may answer: it is through self-reflective investigation of historical human action that we come to learn what our values are and how to best hold them in relation to others. Indeed, Locke explicitly argued that the critical, comparative-historical study of values not only reveals "an entirely different type of fact"—the history of cultural contacts, dynamics, changes, and composites—but also creates a "radical reversal of values through which discoveries and inventions become more important than disasters and battles, peoples and varieties of living more interesting than heroes and dynastic successions, and cultural contacts and interchanges more significant than treaties and annexations."[69] The real study of values in history actually *changes* our values, leading us to seek out and see precisely the kinds of social contacts that are unfamiliar and not yet documented.[70]

For further discussion of the pragmatic selection of cases in comparative-historical analysis and the self-reflective scientific dialogue possible on that basis, see Reed and Lichterman's contribution in this volume.

III. EVIDENCES OF HISTORY

An essential part of examining the research act is considering the materials with which interpretation is performed. As already noted, early pragmatist authors argued that the interpretation of signs is constitutive of the conduct of inquiry, and in this section the emphasis is placed on how what count as signs is defined by their practical effects on that inquiry. Pragmatist authors reflecting on the problems of historiography provide a subtle, yet practical, guide to understanding the materials from which social investigations can be constructed, beginning with the conceptualization of the "given" nature of the past, its selection or isolation within human social processes, and the ways in which physical traces become signs of past human endeavors. Again, Peirce and Dewey provide substantive contributions, but a fully elaborated understanding of the breadth of human documents, the role of documents in mediating human action, and the fundamentally social and material nature of memory require acknowledgment of the contributions of historians and social scientists who are traditionally excluded from the classical pragmatist canon.

A. *The Given Past*

The materials from which to build an account of social action must exist in the investigator's present—that is, in the time that the investigator is researching and building an interpretation. As Dewey forcefully argued, there can be no sense in which a past could be meaningfully verified if this were not the case.[71] Many events—perhaps the vast majority—that happened in the past are meaningless as the object of historical knowledge because they have left no "consequences" that are now definitely observable in the investigator's present. On the one hand, this means that the investigator must and does rely on a taken-for-granted "givenness" of the past within which problems of interpretation develop.[72] The investigator must "work with" the past in a profound sense: not only the immediate object investigated but also the ideas, assumptions, methods, techniques—the "entire stock of intellectual resources"—is a heritage of the past, an "embodied history" in the present.[73] The given past thus exercises formidable control over the enterprise, because the investigator has no way of proceeding without practically accepting what is prior as authoritative.[74] But on the other hand, the given past never forms a "self-complete" object; seeking to treat it as such arbitrarily "mutilates" the complete object of knowledge, which is necessarily relational in that it involves the ongoing practical-social concerns of the investigator.[75]

As discussed earlier, something becomes a "sign" of the past as it is located in the ongoing social action of the investigator, not because of a special substance or essence of the material itself. Indeed, a number of pragmatists pointed out that even when new materials are lacking, the historical record still *requires* restatement and reinterpretation, because the course of subsequent human events changes the meaning of past events—as when the audiences for some historical narrative change, the social division of research is restructured, social changes bring new problems to the fore or suggest connections between previously unconnected events.[76] This means that the given facts of the past are not merely found but, rather, made in the course of inquiry, in the sense that they are practically "analyzed out" or separated from the total value-filled social experience of the investigator so as to be the basis of purposive experimentation.[77] What constitutes the material for such an investigation, thus, is subject to the problems raised by the investigator, is continually subject to revision and reevaluation, and can be made the subject of critical self-reflection on the part of the investigator on this basis.

B. *Human Materials*

In practical terms, myriad phenomena can potentially be treated as the materials from which to construct social accounts. Salmon's posthumous *Historical Materials* pointed not only to political documents but also to institutions and customs, archaeological remains and inscriptions, place and biological names, literature, art, everyday objects—all the things that may comment on people and customs, including not only social relationships but also the record of humanity's relationship to the natural environment.[78] She noted especially that one of the often unrecognized practical functions of contemporary social institutions is to gather up and preserve the cumulative records of the past. This stress on the breadth and ubiquity of records was, for Salmon, connected with a democratization of historical investigation: it can be found in your own "backyard" (both literally and figurative) and all of humanity, not just rulers and geniuses, serves as the object of investigation.

Where Salmon stressed the manifold possibilities of historical evidence and the ways in which practical, everyday affairs determine what is treated as historical material, Peirce stressed the commonality that unites all of these disparate things as enduring material references to human action. Peirce wrote, in an incisive and critical letter to sociologist Franklin Giddings (who wanted to write a comprehensive "history of civilization"), that "all history must be founded upon *monuments*," meaning physical traces in the present of past human action. Peirce cautioned that "'materials' mined from 'documents'" were insufficient as a conception of the totality of the materials on which social investigation is to be undertaken.[79] Indeed, Peirce proposed that written documents should be conceptualized as a particular subset or species of the broader genus of "monuments" (a subset with the additional feature of testimonies or assertions inscribed on them), and he noted that the study of monuments by archaeologists often demonstrated the fallacies of drawing conclusions from the content of documents alone.[80]

To this discussion Addams added somewhat speculatively that what is considered evidence of human action in the past may itself be the product of a historically variable sense of humanism.[81] That is, the development of a more universalizing humanitarian orientation in recent history—which Addams noted has developed through new forms of connection to socially distant others in modern society—is perhaps what allows us to relate to the remains of previous human civilizations as records of a common, familiar human life to which we may compare our own, rather than as merely physical objects.[82] This approach suggests that a conscientious reflection on how and why we treat certain phenomena as data of social life is linked to the modes and extent of our ability to take the role of socially distant others.

C. Written Documents

Written documents, of course, remain the dominant category of such historical materials. For our purposes, the challenges of interpreting written documents considered by classical pragmatists can point beyond strictly paper documents and offer suggestions for the interpretation of symbolic forms more generally. The most adequate logical approach to interpreting historical documents, according to Peirce, is "experiment," in the sense of rigorous and iterative hypothesis testing; and the hypotheses an investigator develops should seek to explain all the facts related to the "testimonies" or claims represented in documents.[83] That is, one should not seek to debunk documents (as the overly "incredulous" critical historians of his day seemed inclined to do), and if a testimony is determined to be untrue, this does not dissolve one's responsibility for explaining how the document and its content came to be such as it is (which would otherwise amount to *explaining away* one's data).[84]

Peirce thought testimonies should be treated as true until refuted, in accord with the "deep and primary instinct" in humans to believe testimony, "without which human society could not exist."[85] He thought abduction was the only method that allowed historical materials the rational possibility to educate us or enlarge our knowledge rather than merely to demonstrate the assumptions already brought to the subject matter. Peirce shares with Addams, Charles H. Cooley, Du Bois, Mead, and others a view of documents as an avenue for social contact with distant others, which accounts for their special value and necessity to the development of social consciousness over extended time and place.[86]

Although not explicit in Peirce's discussion, written documents do not just passively record events of which they are not a part. Salmon noted how newspapers have been integral to the making—not just the documenting—of modern society, in that they are inseparable from the shaping of events and confer authority on the events that make up their contents.[87] Gilman and Cooley went further, noting that written documents give humans an extended capacity for receiving and retaining impressions that shape their conduct, allow the engineering of wider plans of action, and provide for the social use and distribution of memory by more people over longer periods.[88] In this sense, documents are a kind of master tool—an "extraphysical paper brain" or "social brain" that allows people to remember, teach, order, inform, and stimulate action more effectively, enlarging our universe of feeling and experience and mediating or coordinating the vast and disparate social body.[89] For Gilman, different forms of document are connected with different social purposes, our changing and unequal social conditions influence our readings of these documents, and the social processes of production of documents shape their functions.[90]

These capacities make documents an important subject of ethics and explain the often pathological concern in society over the control and access to documents. Thus, understanding documents as intrinsic to, rather than just accompanying, social actions is important for understanding how documents become traces of human action and how those documents can be implicated in our own acts of accounting for the past—a topic reemphasized in recent formulations of "institutional ethnography."[91] And, as Cooley stressed, social scientists not only depend on the reading and writing of human documents but also *produce* human documents, the composition and interpretation of which they should reflect on sociologically.[92]

D. Memories

Early pragmatist authors proposed that memories, along with documents, are a necessary aspect of the conduct of history (as they are of everyday conduct); that memories are not in essential opposition to the accuracy found in documents; that memories are inherently part of a social-communicative process; and that they have future-oriented effects that should not be ignored in inquiry. Memory is no less constitutive of the bonds in the scientific community of inquiry than in any other community, and memory is no less inherent in the conduct of social research than in everyday life, so acknowledgment of its features provides another avenue to reflect critically on research practice.

In perhaps his most famous work, "new historian" Carl Becker built on the work of James to propose that memory is a way of deliberately enlarging, enriching, diversifying, and reinforcing the "specious present" (the durational or tense present in which we act and which experientially extends beyond the instant into the past and future).[93] Although centering the analysis of memory would seem to challenge a focus on the material remains of human action and raise further questions about accuracy, Becker understood documents as "artificial extensions of memory" that orient one in a broader world of endeavor or prepare one for what is to come by recalling certain past events that help to anticipate the future.[94] Indeed, this intelligent extension of memory is what Becker saw as the "natural function" of history as a field of study. The extent and direction of historical "researches" in our own everyday lives are set by definite practical goals, which typically make it very clear which documents to consult and which facts to seek out. That is, the everyday person is a good historian "precisely because he [sic] is not disinterested: he will solve his problems, if he does solve them, by virtue of his intelligence and not by virtue of his indifference."[95] In this way, the criterion of memory is not whether the whole is accurate—although accuracy and exactness are subject to continual confirmation in one's practical affairs with others (try misremembering whether you paid your utility bill)—but, rather, that it functions within one's socially contextual actions and goals.

But memory is social in senses other than those stressed by Becker. Royce's historical study of Christianity highlighted how collective memory is key to understanding the unification of a community: people who do not share the same course of personal experience nevertheless may be united in finding the same events of the past as a part of their memory.[96] One of the fundamental ways in which people form a community in a practical sense (while not dismissing real social divisions) is the constitution of a common remembered past connected with anticipated or hoped-for common future events. This is true of all "communities of interpretation," including the scientific community. This approach prefigures the claim by Robert Bellah and others, which has become integral to the field of collective memory studies, that genuine community is a community of memory and that, therefore, the practical social processes whereby collective memories are formed and transmitted should be studied as essential features of society.[97] Mead went even further, according to Max Pensky, by proposing that we are in continually revised dialogue with the voices from the past to whom we recognize an obligation to include in our collective memory, and this "eminently democratic practice" of dialogue generates appeals to a moral community unbounded in time whereby victims of historical injustice may expand our social consciousness and reconstruct our sense of community—an argument, as we've seen, that Du Bois also made.[98]

The best extended study of the social nature and functions of memory in the early pragmatist tradition is Addams's *The Long Road of Woman's Memory*.[99] "Memory," in this work, refers not to individual psychological processes but to self-narratives given by women in the course of conversations. Addams demonstrated the interpretive and selective value that such memories had for a generation of immigrant women in America's industrializing cities. They provided an altered, reflective perspective on the often brutal hardships and inequalities women faced, "transmuting" and isolating them from the practical immediacies of the moment through storytelling and advice, but without detaching the events reflected on from a moral register of responsibility or from the emotions that allow these events to be embodied as personal experiences.[100] Memories not only interpret and ameliorate the individual's experiences; they also become the basis for challenges to social conventions and the formation of new social norms when conceptualized as communicative or dialogic rather than individual. Although such memories are about past experience, they are articulated in present conversations and have practical consequences in the future. By sharing mutual reminiscences of diverse experiences, people who have no other basis for like-mindedness can "accumulate into a social protest," a process demonstrated in the building of collective memories of grievances and unfulfilled promises in the modern labor and women's movements, among others.[101] Throughout this work, Addams suggests that the sharing of memories has an especially valuable and critical social function among those marginalized from effective public social action by age, gender, disability, nationality, or other basis of social exclusion.

Addams's work also illustrates a self-reflective listening approach that seeks to learn about others by hearing them tell about themselves and to build a sense of taking the role of the other over the course of a dialogue. The long quotations and paraphrases from these women that Addams includes in the work allow readers to participate in this exercise vicariously and to hear in their own words the articulate voices of everyday people striving to understand their perplexing, often devastating experiences. Again, far from being a recondite issue of historiography, a pragmatist orientation to memory returns us to reflections on the role of the investigator as a participant in and extender of ongoing social action from within.

IV. LESSONS OF HISTORICAL SOCIAL SCIENCE

The investigation of the past is a key process of human self-reflexivity, especially as such a process is conceived not in terms of individual humans thinking and studying in isolation but as the process of the social group continually coming to know itself. Such an acknowledgment can provide an orientation to social research that grounds better inquiry in more democratically inclusive and self-reflective social practices and that provides a firm social grounding for treating the past as a domain of ethical concern and responsibility on the part of scholars. Getting history "right," although never a finished endeavor, is in this view a process of serving a more inclusive social order; that is, more universalizable claims are developed by more practically inclusive social referents.

Such a position is supported in this concluding section by intellectual historians and philosophers in dialogue with the canonical pragmatists who provide additional orientation to the values and functions of pluralism in historical investigation and the essential place of pedagogy in such an enterprise. Ultimately, the chapter seeks to make the case not only for a more inclusive reading of early pragmatism but, more importantly, for the imperative ethical and epistemological rationales for historical self-reflection in social research more generally, a case made strongly by early pragmatists but neglected in their subsequent influence in social science.

A. *Historical Self-Reflection*

Pragmatist philosophers of history note that the writing of historical accounts is an event in history, just as are the events studied, and therefore may be studied as a subject of historical inquiry.[102] And the production of narratives about events is itself a particularly significant historical event, in that it is self-reflective: through this work we can become aware, to a certain extent, of the course of human events, appraise them, and anticipate new directions and impulses for the future.[103] Indeed, by studying how humans study history, we learn something about our human experience of self-reflection on the present and the making of sign relationships to the past and future.[104] As the student and critic of pragmatism Randolph Bourne noted, it is the past that we "really make" or "author" by carefully constructing and "lovingly beautifying" it with our thoughts, interests, delights, and hopes—because the present is always still in the making, because we are not really self-aware about the making of the present (what we leave behind as monuments of ourselves and which of our customs will become the roots of institutions), and because the fuller meaning of the present comes as it is reflected on in the past.[105] To locate a historical actor's views in their sociohistorical context is, from this point of view, not to diminish them but to increase their significance by connecting them with settings within which they have pertinence and meaning.[106]

Of course, when every point of view is understood historically, we ourselves cannot claim to stand outside of history, and we run up against problems of historicism.[107] Pragmatist historical investigators have sought to address this problem by grounding the study of history in the social self of pragmatic philosophy, which both provides for the mind as emerging from the "pragmatic context of the conflict of social forces" while also acknowledging its situated capacity for creative "self-transcendence" or "imaginative understanding" of others that appear at first to be alien and unintelligible.[108] Historical social research is not just an end; it is also a means: the process of coming to understand another viewpoint may be productively approached historically by reconstructing and following the problems that faced historical actors, along with the intellectual and material resources that the actors had available and the ideas and recalcitrant assumptions with which they set about their tasks and which simultaneously limited their possibilities.[109]

This is, implicitly, what we do as researchers regardless of whether we think of it as historical reconstruction or just accounting for another's actions—as, for example, Alfred Schutz's reconstruction of Weber's interpretive sociology sought in part to show.[110] Such work to understand is simultaneously a work of self-reflection that expands our understanding of our own position by training us to more competently and critically debate with ourselves from various viewpoints and to see the relationship between intellectual positions and their contexts.[111] In their chapter in this volume, Reed and Lichterman identify such deliberative self-reflection on the normative orientations inherent in the research process as "metacommunicative dialogue."

B. Social Responsibility

A number of early pragmatist authors have turned their attention toward the ethics of research in a way that can help to inform us. In Becker's view, the apparatus of scholarship is so many investigative and rhetorical devices for extending the "social memory" and deriving satisfactory "meaning" from the succession of events under the conditions imposed by the sheer weight of public opinion and conviction.[112] Thus, if we are aware of the value-laden nature of explaining historical social actions, it is the obligation of us as researchers to hold ourselves responsible for the employment of those value judgments.[113] And although we should expect interpretations to abound, each interpretation should be tested to see what light it gives to events and where it fails to illuminate.[114]

An essential part of this social responsibility is its pedagogy. Ella Flagg Young, colleague and student of Dewey and Mead, superintendent of Chicago Public Schools, and the first woman president of the National Education Association, argued that history should not be made educative by blotting out the wrongs done—like Du Bois, she criticized Civil War historiography for taking this approach.[115] She noted that students may feel an easy self-aggrandizement through "spontaneous identification of self with a masterful past," but this does not advance public virtues of morality and citizenship.[116] In order for history to enlarge public opinion and present the best educative example—in order for it truly to be useful—learners must be in a position to bring to bear their originality and independence of thought, to treat history as investigation into how society grows, and to forecast the future by means of the past.[117] This sympathetic contact with others, facilitated by orienting oneself to the situated problems facing sociohistorical actors, is stressed not only by Young but also by Addams, Cooley, Du Bois, Mead, and Salmon.[118]

Such an approach, according to Locke, teaches critical thinking; that is, it seeks to educate the student in improved "*way*[s] of thinking," not just an increased "*scope* of thinking"—tracing head-on the development of conflict and difference, grappling realistically with value judgments, and "bravely" taking normative stands by showing how values emerge in relation to historical and cultural contexts.[119] This simultaneously "integrated" and "particular" study of historically contextualized actions and values would ground a pragmatic criterion of "relativistic normativism" by which diversity and inclusiveness may be advocated, in place of the "doctrinaire normativism of agreement."[120] This approach, then, refers not only to the teaching of history as a special subject but to the teaching of any topic historically, and the approach these pragmatist authors underscore is that a historical orientation is especially educative to the extent that it captures the social interest of the student and encourages exploration and knowledge of sociocultural diversity.

The notion of a responsibility to the past, and hence to a conscious social progress, follows as a consequence from virtually all versions of pragmatism and indeed may be considered one of the features that constitutes a pragmatist family resemblance. As shown in this chapter, such a conclusion is explicitly drawn not only by the canonical pragmatists but also by other pragmatist philosophers of history, by American intellectual and cultural historians in dialogue with pragmatism, and, perhaps most emphatically, by pragmatist social theorists who have typically been excluded from the canon of American philosophy. In the hands of the pragmatists, responsibility is emphatically social: dependent on the dynamic community of inquiry and constrained by the inclusive and ongoing public deliberation not just of specialists in history but of all who make history.

Our social awareness is an ongoing process in which the shortcomings and forewarnings that emerge in the course of social action provide the means to subject our own study to deliberative critique in an effort to influence subsequent research practices. It is perhaps not incidental that it is in reflecting on history that we see the responsibility of research most poignantly, as the writing of history prompts reflection on wrongs, errors, and our relationship to what has come before. This pragmatic approach urges us as social researchers, not just those who explicitly pursue historiography, to reflect on how our obligations to an inclusive sense of past human action relate to the future consequences we anticipate of our research.

NOTES

1. Bertrand Russell, *Philosophical Essays. Russell on Metaphysics* (London: Longmans, Green, 1910); Josiah Royce, *The Problem of Christianity, Vo. 2: The Real World and the Christian Ideas* (New York: Macmillan, 1913); George Santayana, *Winds of Doctrine: Studies in Contemporary Opinion* (New York: Charles Scribner's Sons, 1913), 124–31; G. E. Moore, *Philosophical Studies* (New York: Harcourt, Brace, 1922); Émile Durkheim, *Pragmatism and Sociology*, trans. J. C. Whitehouse, ed. John B. Allcock (1913–14; Cambridge: Cambridge University Press, 1983).

2. John Dewey, "Realism Without Monism or Dualism—I: Knowledge Involving the Past," *Journal of Philosophy* 19, no. 12 (1922a): 309–17; Dewey, "Realism Without Monism or Dualism—II," *Journal of Philosophy* 19, no. 13 (1922b): 351–61; Dewey, "Some Comments

on Philosophical Discussion," *Journal of Philosophy* 21, no. 8 (1924): 197–209; A. O. Lovejoy, "Pragmatism Versus the Pragmatist," in *Essays in Critical Realism: A Co-Operative Study of the Problem of Knowledge*, ed. Durant Drake, A. O. Lovejoy, James B. Pratt, Arthur K. Rogers, George Santayana, Roy Wood Sellars, and C. A. Strong (New York: Macmillan, 1920), 35–81; Lovejoy, "Time, Meaning and Transcendence—I: The Alleged Futurity of Yesterday," *Journal of Philosophy* 19, no. 19 (1922a): 505–15; Lovejoy, "Time, Meaning and Transcendence—II: Professor Dewey's Tertium Quid," *Journal of Philosophy* 19, no. 20 (1922b): 533–41; Lovejoy, "Pastness and Transcendence," *Journal of Philosophy* 21, no. 22 (1924): 601–11; and Stefan Niklas, "The Anticipated Past of Historical Inquiry: A. O. Lovejoy, C. I. Lewis and E. Wind on Accounting for Knowledge of the Past Within a Pragmatist Theory," *European Journal of Pragmatism and American Philosophy* 8, no. 2 (2016): 1–21.

3. John Dewey, *The Public and Its Problems* (New York: Henry Holt, 1927), 193; Dewey, *Logic: The Theory of Inquiry* (New York: Henry Holt, 1938). Pragmatist philosophers who have written about historical matters in dialogue with Dewey include, among others, Richard Bernstein, Horace L. Friess, Sidney Hook, Hans Joas, Horace M. Kallen, Colin Koopman, Sterling P. Lamprecht, Joseph Margolis, Cheryl Misak, Addison W. Moore, John Herman Randall, Jr., Richard Rorty, and Cornel West.

4. Cushing Strout, *The Pragmatic Revolt in American History: Carl Becker and Charles Beard* (New Haven, CT: Yale University Press, 1958); Morton White, *Pragmatism and the American Mind* (New York: Oxford University Press, 1973); John Pettegrew, "Introduction," in *A Pragmatist's Progress? Richard Rorty and American Intellectual History*, ed. John Pettegrew (Lanham: Rowman & Littlefield, 2000), 1–17; and James T. Kloppenberg, "Pragmatism and the Practice of History: From Turner and Du Bois to Today," *Metaphilosophy* 35, nos. 1–2 (2004): 202–25. Although Salmon is often overlooked as one of the "new historians," her body of work puts her in line with these authors. British historian E. H. Carr, although not often linked with the pragmatists, articulated a pragmatic approach to history more emphatically and lucidly than many self-proclaimed acolytes, and for this reason he is also included in this chapter.

5. Frederick Jackson Turner, "The Significance of History," *Wisconsin Journal of Education* 21 (1891): 230–34, 253–56.

6. Frederick Jackson Turner, "Social Forces in American History," *American Historical Review* 16 (1911): 217–33; James Harvey Robinson, *The New History: Essays Illustrating the Modern Historical Outlook* (New York: Macmillan, 1912); and Carl Becker, "Some Aspects of the Influence of Social Problems and Ideas Upon the Study and Writing of History," *Papers and Proceedings of the American Sociological Society* 7 (1913): 73–112.

7. Charlene Haddock Seigfried, *Pragmatism and Feminism: Reweaving the Social Fabric* (Chicago: University of Chicago Press, 1996), 102–3.

8. Patricia Hill Collins, "Piecing Together a Genealogical Puzzle: Intersectionality and American Pragmatism," *European Journal of Pragmatism and American Philosophy* 3, no. 2 (2011): 88–112; Collins, "Social Inequality, Power, and Politics: Intersectionality and American Pragmatism in Dialogue," *Journal of Speculative Philosophy* 26, no. 2 (2012): 442–57; and Collins, "Intersectionality, Experience, and Community," in

Intersectionality as Critical Social Theory (Durham, NC: Duke University Press, 2019), 157–88.

9. Alain Locke, *The Philosophy of Alain Locke: Harlem Renaissance and Beyond*, ed. Leonard Harris (Philadelphia: Temple University Press, 1989), 142; Edward Hallett Carr, *What Is History? The George Macaulay Trevelyan Lectures Delivered at the University of Cambridge January–March 1961* (New York: Vintage, 1961), 53–54; Strout, *Pragmatic Revolt*, 36.

10. Carr, *What Is History?*, 171–72. In this regard, Adam Greteman, drawing on work by Cleo Cherryholmes and Eve K. Sedgwick, notes that pragmatism's consequentialism seeks results that are "fulfilling"—a pursuit determined inclusively, not because of some detached aesthetic value in "diversity" but because of the realization that a built-in openness to otherness is the only sure basis on which to decide about things that will have future consequences. In the same work, Greteman sketches a unique, historically grounded warrant for pragmatism. He proposes that pragmatism becomes more important as an analytical approach precisely to the extent that the object of analysis becomes more institutionalized. That is, when the probability of the object having an effect increases (or the extent of its effect increases), so, too, does the relevance of a theory that defines an object in terms of its practical consequences. Adam J. Greteman, "On Reading Practices: Where Pragmatism and Queer Meet," in *Sexualities and Genders in Education: Towards Queer Thriving* (New York: Palgrave Macmillan, 2018), 37–56.

11. Richard Bernstein, "The Resurgence of Pragmatism," *Social Research* 59, no. 4 (1992): 813–40. See also Bernstein, "Pragmatism, Pluralism and the Healing of Wounds," *Proceedings and Addresses of the American Philosophical Association* 63, no. 3 (1989): 5–18.

12. Collins, "Piecing Together"; Collins, "Social Inequality"; Mary Jo Deegan, *Jane Addams and the Men of the Chicago School, 1892–1918* (New Brunswick, NJ: Transaction, 1988); Leonard Harris, "Rendering the Text," in *The Philosophy of Alain Locke: Harlem Renaissance and Beyond*, by Alain Locke (Philadelphia: Temple University Press, 1989), 3–30; Leonard Harris, ed., *The Critical Pragmatism of Alain Locke: A Reader on Value Theory, Aesthetics, Community, Culture, Race, and Education* (Lanham, MD: Rowman & Littlefield, 1999); Patricia Lengermann and Jill Niebrugge-Brantley, *The Women Founders: Sociology and Social Theory* (New York: McGraw-Hill, 1998); José Medina, "Pragmatism and Ethnicity: Critique, Reconstruction, and the New Hispanic," *Metaphilosophy* 25, nos. 1–2 (2004): 115–46; Kelly A. Parker and Piotr Krzysztof Skowronski, "Contemporary Readings of Josiah Royce," in *Josiah Royce for the Twenty-First Century: Historical, Ethical, and Religious Interpretations*, ed. K. A. Parker and P. K. Skowronski (Lanham, MD: Lexington, 2012), 1–8; Alan R. Sadovnik and Susan F. Semel, eds., *Founding Mothers and Others: Women Educational Leaders During the Progressive Era* (New York: Palgrave, 2002); Seigfried, *Pragmatism and Feminism*; Charlene Haddock Seigfried, ed., *Feminist Interpretations of John Dewey* (University Park: Pennsylvania State University Press, 2002); Paul C. Taylor, "What's the Use of Calling Du Bois a Pragmatist?" *Metaphilosophy* 35, nos. 1–2 (2004): 99–114; and Cornel West, *The American Evasion of Philosophy* (Madison: University of Wisconsin Press, 1989).

13. Hans Joas, *The Creativity of Action*, trans. Jeremy Gaines and Paul Keast (Chicago: University of Chicago Press, 1996).

14. Charles S. Peirce, *Historical Perspectives on Peirce's Logic of Science: A History of Science*, ed. Carolyn Eisele (New York: Mouton, 1985); and Tullio Viola, *Peirce and the Uses of History: The Legacy of a Realist* (Berlin: DeGruyter, 2020).

15. Peirce, *Historical Perspectives*, 724.

16. Peirce, *Historical Perspectives*, 732–33, 753.

17. Peirce, *Historical Perspectives*, 753.

18. Peirce, *Historical Perspectives*, 756–57.

19. Iddo Tavory and Stefan Timmermans, *Abductive Analysis: Theorizing Qualitative Research* (Chicago: University of Chicago Press, 2014).

20. Morton White, *Foundations of Historical Knowledge* (New York: Harper & Row, 1965), 115; and Robert MacIver, *Social Causation* (Boston: Ginn, 1942); see also Carr, *What Is History?*

21. Sterling P. Lamprecht, "Historiography of Philosophy," *Journal of Philosophy* 36, no. 17 (1939): 449–60; and Sterling P. Lamprecht, José Ferrater-Mora, and Maurice Mandelbaum, "Comments on the Symposium 'What Is Philosophy of History?'" *Journal of Philosophy* 49, no. 10 (1952): 350–62.

22. Hans Joas, "Pragmatism and Historicism: Mead's Philosophy of Temporality and the Logic of Historiography," in *The Timeliness of George Herbert Mead*, ed. Hans Joas and Daniel R. Huebner (Chicago: University of Chicago Press, 2016), 67–70. Josiah Royce was sometimes grouped with the classical pragmatists and sometimes with their critics, and he counted Mead and Locke among his students. He wrote an early social history of California that was an important inspiration for his philosophical writings. Royce's *The Problem of Christianity* also contains key points of his absolute idealism, which he sometimes called "absolute pragmatism" but in which he parted ways with the other pragmatists in formulating a definite metaphysics. Parker and Skowronski, "Introduction"; Earl Pomeroy, "Josiah Royce, Historian in Quest of Community," *Pacific Historical Review* 40, no. 1 (1971): 1–20; Robert Hine, "The American West as Metaphysics: A Perspective on Josiah Royce," *Pacific Historical Review* 58, no. 3 (1989): 267–21.

23. Royce, *Problem of Christianity*, 140–41.

24. Royce, *Problem of Christianity*, 145–46.

25. Royce, *Problem of Christianity*, 147–49, 284.

26. Royce, *Problem of Christianity*, 214–17.

27. Royce, *Problem of Christianity*, 140–41, 214–15.

28. Royce, *Problem of Christianity*, 187.

29. Royce, *Problem of Christianity*, 151, 227.

30. Royce, *Problem of Christianity*, 247.

31. Royce, *Problem of Christianity*, 227–32, 249–52; Struan Jacobs, "Models of Scientific Community: Charles Sanders Peirce to Thomas Kuhn," *Interdisciplinary Science Reviews* 31, no. 2 (2006): 163–73.

32. Dewey, "Realism Without . . . II," 352.

33. Dewey, "Realism Without . . . II," 353.

34. Dewey, "Realism Without . . . I," 309; see also Carl Becker, "Everyman His Own His-torian," *American Historical Review* 37, no. 2 (1932): 221–36; and John Herman Randall, Jr., "On Understanding the History of Philosophy." *Journal of Philosophy* 36, no. 17 (1939): 467.

35. Dewey, "Realism Without . . . II," 356; see also Sterling P. Lamprecht, "A Note on Pro-fessor Dewey's Theory of Knowledge," *Journal of Philosophy* 20, no. 18 (1923): 488–94.

36. William James, "The Existence of Julius Caesar," in *The Meaning of Truth: A Sequel to "Pragmatism"* (New York: Longmans, Green, 1909), 221–25. Although James is some-times seen as an ahistorical scholar, several of his essays evince historically informed engagement with social problems and epistemology, and recent research has uncovered the surprising extent of James's reading in the history of thought. Pettegrew, "Introduc-tion," 4–5; John Kaag, *American Philosophy: A Love Story* (New York: Farrar, Strauss and Giroux, 2016), 207–8.

37. Niklas, "The Anticipated Past," 9–10.

38. Richard Bernstein, "Pragmatism, Objectivity, and Truth," *Philosophical Topics* 36, no. 1 (2008): 37–55.

39. James, *Meaning of Truth*, 43–50.

40. John Dewey, *Unmodern Philosophy and Modern Philosophy*, ed. Phillip Deen (Car-bondale: Southern Illinois University Press, 2012), 137–38, emphasis in original; see also Carr, *What Is History?*, chap. 1.

41. Dewey, *Unmodern Philosophy*, 138.

42. Randall, "On Understanding," 469–70; see also Carr, *What Is History?*, 173–75 passim.

43. George Hutchinson, *The Harlem Renaissance in Black and White* (Cambridge, MA: Harvard University Press, 1995); Mark Helbling, "African Art and the Harlem Renais-sance: Alain Locke, Melville Herskovits, Robert Fry, and Albert C. Barnes," in *The Critical Pragmatism of Alain Locke: A Reader on Value Theory, Aesthetics, Community, Culture, Race, and Education*, ed. Leonard Harris (Lanham, MD: Rowman & Little-field, 1999), 53–84.

44. Locke, *Philosophy of Alain Locke*, 37.

45. Locke, *Philosophy of Alain Locke*, 59.

46. Locke, *Philosophy of Alain Locke*, 59–60.

47. See, for example, Seigfried, *Pragmatism and Feminism*, 10; Collins, "Piecing Together"; and Collins, "Social Inequality."

48. Alain Locke, *Race Contacts and Interracial Relations: Lectures on the Theory and Prac-tice of Race*, ed. Jeffrey C. Stewart (1916; Washington, DC: Howard University Press, 1992), 23–27.

49. Locke, *Race Contacts*, 26–27.

50. W. E. B. Du Bois, "The Propaganda of History," in *Black Reconstruction in America: An Essay Toward a History of the Part Which Black Folk Played in the Attempt to Reconstruct Democracy in America, 1860–1880* (New York: Harcourt, Brace, 1935), 711–29.

51. Du Bois, *Black Reconstruction*, 714–15; Pierre Bourdieu and Roger Chartier, *The Sociol-ogist and the Historian*, trans. David Fernbach (Cambridge, UK: Polity, 2015), 47.

52. Du Bois, *Black Reconstruction*, 722.

53. Du Bois, *Black Reconstruction*, 714–15.

54. Du Bois, *Black Reconstruction*, 714.

55. Du Bois, *Black Reconstruction*, 723.

56. Du Bois, *Black Reconstruction*, 714.

57. Du Bois, *Black Reconstruction*, vii, 727–28; see also W. E. B. Du Bois, "Sociology Unbound (ca. 1905)," *boundary 2* 27, no. 3 (2000): 37–44.

58. Du Bois, *Black Reconstruction*, 715.

59. Carr, *What Is History?*, 100–101.

60. Du Bois, *Black Reconstruction*, 722. A related part of this reconstructive task, for Du Bois, is a kind of critical sociology of historiography, the work to ground the writing of historical social research in the contextual social experiences of the historian. Du Bois showed how the particular socially situated beliefs of Southern students and historians dominated the historiography of the leading post–Civil War Northern universities; that they had "plain reasons" rooted in their early experiences of domination and inequality for their demonstrably false histories and inability to "conceive Negroes as men"; that the inequality of opportunities for white and nonwhite students to study and publish further segregated this group of historians; and that therefore—in almost Gramscian language—the supposedly universal, objective histories they wrote exhibited the "general agreement and determination of the dominant classes," a "convenient fairy tale that the masters of men wish." Du Bois *Black Reconstruction*, 717–20, 724–26; W. E. B. Du Bois, "Postscript," in *The Black Flame: A Trilogy: Book One, The Ordeal of Mansart* (New York: Mainstream, 1957), 315–16.

61. Du Bois, *Black Reconstruction*, 727.

62. Du Bois, *Black Reconstruction*, 721; Du Bois, "Postscript."

63. Du Bois, *Black Reconstruction*, 721–25.

64. Du Bois, *Black Reconstruction*, 725.

65. Locke, *Philosophy of Alain Locke*; Charlotte Perkins Gilman, *The Man-Made World: Or, Our Androcentric Culture* (New York: Charlton, 1911); Lucy Maynard Salmon, *Historical Material* (New York: Oxford University Press, 1933); Salmon, *Why Is History Rewritten?* (New York: Oxford University Press, 1929); and Salmon, *The Newspaper and the Historian* (New York: Oxford University Press, 1923b).

66. Locke, *Race Contacts*, 53–54.

67. Locke, *Race Contacts*, 49, 57, 60.

68. Locke, *Race Contacts*, 53–54; Locke, *Philosophy of Alain Locke*, 60; see also Carr, *What Is History?*, 101–9. This "engaged fallibilistic pluralism" that places new responsibilities on each of us is what Bernstein says represents "the best in our pragmatic tradition." Throughout his work, Bernstein contrasts this pragmatic ethos with other supposed versions of pluralism, which do not fully acknowledge the fundamentally ethical, dialogic, and self-transformative nature of a commitment to pluralism. Bernstein, "Pragmatism, Pluralism," 15–17.

69. Alain Locke and Bernhard J. Stern, eds., *When Peoples Meet: A Study in Race and Culture Contacts* (New York: Progressive Education Association, 1942), 30.

70. Locke and Stern, *When Peoples Meet*, 6, 30.

71. Dewey, "Realism Without . . . I"; see also Niklas, "Anticipated Past"; and Lamprecht, "A Note on . . ."

72. George Herbert Mead, *The Philosophy of the Present*, ed. A. E. Murphy (Chicago: Open Court, 1932), 3–5.

73. John Herman Randall, Jr., *How Philosophy Uses Its Past* (New York: Columbia University Press, 1963), 77.

74. Lamprecht, "Historiography of Philosophy," 450.

75. Dewey, "Realism Without . . . I," 313–15.

76. Salmon, *Why Is History Rewritten?*; Mead, *Philosophy of the Present*; Sterling P. Lamprecht, "Philosophy of History," *Journal of Philosophy* 33, no. 8 (1936): 197–204.

77. Locke, *Philosophy of Alain Locke*, 126.

78. Salmon, *Historical Material*.

79. Peirce, *Historical Perspectives*, 996–97.

80. Peirce, *Historical Perspectives*, 705, 760–61.

81. Jane Addams, *The Long Road of Women's Memory* (New York: Macmillan, 1917), 166.

82. Jane Addams, *Democracy and Social Ethics* (New York: Macmillan, 1902); Addams, *The Newer Ideals of Peace* (New York: Macmillan, 1906).

83. Peirce, *Historical Perspectives*, 760, 255.

84. Peirce, *Historical Perspectives*, 164, 167, 217, 1003.

85. Peirce, *Historical Perspectives*, 760–61.

86. Addams, *Long Road*; Charles H. Cooley, *Human Nature and the Social Order*, rev. ed. (New York: Charles Scribner's Sons, 1922); W. E. B. Du Bois, "The Criteria of Negro Art," *Crisis* 32, no. 6 (1926): 290–97; and George Herbert Mead, *Mind, Self, and Society: The Definitive Edition*, ed. D. R. Huebner and H. Joas, originally edited by C. W. Morris (Chicago: University of Chicago Press, 2015).

87. Lucy Maynard Salmon, "Newspaper and Research," *American Journal of Sociology* 32, no. 2 (1926): 217–26.

88. Charlotte Perkins Gilman, "Effect of Literature Upon the Mind," in *Our Brains and What Ails Them*, chap. 5, serialized in *The Forerunner* 3, no. 5 (1912): 133–39; Charles H. Cooley, *Sociological Theory and Social Research*, ed. Robert Cooley Angell (New York: Henry Holt, 1930).

89. Gilman, "Effect of Literature Upon the Mind," 135–37.

90. Gilman, "Effect of Literature Upon the Mind," 135–36, 138; see also Lucy Maynard Salmon, *The Newspaper and Authority* (New York: Oxford University Press, 1923a).

91. Dorothy E. Smith and Susan Marie Turner, *Incorporating Texts Into Institutional Ethnographies* (Toronto: University of Toronto Press, 2014).

92. Cooley, *Sociological Theory*; Daniel R. Huebner, "Cooley's Social Theory of Reading and Writing," in *Updating Charles Cooley: Contemporary Perspectives on a Sociological Classic*, ed. Natalia Ruiz-Junco and Baptiste Brossard (Abingdon, UK: Routledge, 2018), 83–110.

93. Carl Becker, "Everyman His Own Historian." James makes a distinction between "memory proper" and what he called "primary memory," which is part of the "specious present." Primary memory is, for James, not really memory but the lingering impressions of

immediate past events as they continue to be a part of one's awareness (akin to retinal afterimages), which are not really "brought back" or "recalled" because they have not yet been lost; and, of course, most of what passes through our present stream of consciousness does not survive into true memory proper. For James, memory proper has a semiotic and affective character, because it involves not just the revival of an image in the mind but also a *reference* to the past that is constructed through its systematic or networked association with names, dates, and other events (its "setting"), and a *feeling* of belief that comes from relation to one's present sensations or emotional activities. Memory can thus be understood as an active, selective process of associating, representing, and appropriating past events to the tasks of a person's future-oriented action. William James, "Memory," in *The Principles of Psychology*, vol. I (New York: Henry Holt, 1890), 643–89.

94. Becker, "Everyman His Own Historian," 224–26.

95. Becker, "Everyman His Own Historian," 228.

96. Royce, *Problem of Christianity*, chap. 9.

97. Robert N. Bellah, Richard Madsen, William Sullivan, Ann Swidler, and Steven M. Tipton, *Habits of the Heart: Commitment and Individualism in American Life* (New York: Harper & Row, 1985), 153.

98. Mead, *Philosophy of the Present*; Max Pensky, "Pragmatism and Solidarity with the Past," in *Pragmatism, Nation, and Race: Community in the Age of Empire*, ed. Chad Kautzer and Eduardo Mendieta (Bloomington: Indiana University Press, 2009), 73–88. Peirce makes the case that we have a responsibility to adapt ourselves to the past precisely because of its "brute actuality," the enduring effects of which place constraints on our inferences, so that we are impelled by a social impulse to seek understanding and continuity with the past. Viola, *Peirce and the Uses of History*, 157–58.

99. Addams, *Long Road*.

100. Addams, *Long Road*, 21–22, 30, 101.

101. Addams, *Long Road*, 53, 99ff.

102. Dewey, *Unmodern Philosophy*, 144; Lamprecht "Historiography of Philosophy"; Lamprecht, "Philosophy of History"; and Carr, *What Is History?*, 25–26.

103. Lamprecht, "Philosophy of History," 197.

104. Lamprecht, "Historiography of Philosophy," 449.

105. Randolph Bourne, "Seeing, We See Not," in *Youth and Life* (Boston: Houghton Mifflin, 1913), 217–18.

106. Lamprecht "Historiography of Philosophy," 458.

107. Strout, *Pragmatic Revolt*, 2; Joas, "Pragmatism and Historicism."

108. Strout, *Pragmatic Revolt*, 42–43, 47; see also Addams, *Democracy and Social Ethics*; Addams, *Newer Ideals*; Addams, *Long Road*; Du Bois, "Criteria of Negro Art"; Mead, *Mind, Self, and Society*; and Daniel R. Huebner, "History and Social Progress: Reflections on Mead's Approach to History," *European Journal of Pragmatism and American Philosophy* 8, no. 2 (2016): 120–42.

109. Randall, *How Philosophy*, 90.

110. Alfred Schutz, *The Phenomenology of the Social World*, trans. George Walsh and Frederick Lehnert (Evanston, IL: Northwestern University Press, 1967).

111. Lamprecht, "Historiography of Philosophy," 459–60; Becker, "Everyman His Own Historian," 230; and Carr, *What Is History?*, 53–54, 163.

112. Becker, "Everyman His Own Historian."

113. White, *Foundations of Historical Knowledge*, 271ff.

114. Lamprecht et al., "Comments on the Symposium," 351; Carr, *What Is History?*, 163.

115. Ella Flagg Young, *Isolation in the School* (PhD dissertation, Chicago: University of Chicago Press, 1900).

116. Young, *Isolation in the School*, 52.

117. Ella Flagg Young, *Some Types of Modern Educational Theory* (Chicago: University of Chicago Press, 1902), 48; see also Lucy Maynard Salmon, "The Teaching of History in Academies and Colleges," in *Women and the Higher Education*, ed. Anna C. Brackett (New York: Harper & Brothers, 1893), 145–46.

118. Addams, *Democracy and Social Ethics*; Cooley, *Human Nature*; Du Bois, "Criteria of Negro Art"; Mead, *Mind, Self, and Society*; Salmon, "Teaching of History," 150–51; and Carr, *What Is History?*, 26–27.

119. Locke, *Philosophy of Alain Locke*, 268–71.

120. Locke, *Philosophy of Alain Locke*, 272.

4. Problem Situation Misassessment and the Financial Crisis

LUIS FLORES

NEIL GROSS

As developed in the writings of Hans Joas, the pragmatist model of action looks like this. An actor finds herself in a situation endowed with certain habits—some primarily cognitive, others affective, still others to do with language use, bodily movement, material technique, etc.—that derive from individual or social experience or the evolutionary experience of the human species.[1] If, as is frequently the case, the situation as a set of environing cues and practical challenges strikes the actor as familiar, as containing patterns, features, and logics she has encountered before and dealt with successfully, then some of those habits will be activated alongside other capacities, like intentionality and projectivity. Using the habits as a resource, the actor gains the ability to move through the situation with a degree of automaticity and ease. When, by contrast, the situation feels novel and unfamiliar, the actor will find herself in a state of tension. The perception that a situation is problematic—in the specifically pragmatist sense of the actor lacking habits needed to cope with circumstances at hand—can prompt anxiety or despair. But it can also become the occasion for productive inquiry and experimentation, as the actor, alone or working jointly with others, tries out new (if still habit-informed) strategies of action, looking for ones that render the situation navigable. Joas has shown that for the classical pragmatists, social action and interaction involve a constant cycling through of more or less unproblematic and problematic moments of this sort, and hence an alternation between habit and creativity, with new habits emerging out of adaptive innovations.

This is an exciting model. Joas and others have demonstrated its coherence and phenomenological plausibility and have made a case that it can be productively synthesized with competing sociological theories of action, such as norm-based ones or approaches stressing the roots of action in identity, in ways that help these approaches overcome critical lacunae. The empirical value of the model has become apparent as well, as scholars have used it to shed light on a range of phenomena, from entrepreneurial innovation to stability and dynamism in racial fields to the advent of game-changing political repertoires.[2]

But there is an aspect that has not been fleshed out—an aspect that, were it developed, could further extend pragmatism's explanatory reach. Central to the pragmatist action model is an assessment by an actor, or group of actors, as to whether or not a situation encountered is problematic—an assessment of situational familiarity and manipulability, and thus as to the applicability of more habitual or creative response. What, however, is involved in judgments of this sort, and what happens when actors get it wrong, perceiving unfamiliarity in a situation that should have called for the rollout of established habits or familiarity in the face of unrecognized novelty? We refer to this as problem situation misassessment, an important but neglected facet of generic situational misassessment (encompassing every failure to properly grasp a situation's parameters.)

In this chapter we develop a theory of problem situation misassessment, as an amendment to pragmatist action theory. Problem situation misassessment is pervasive in social life, and the factors and circumstances occasioning it, and the social processes surrounding it contribute causally to many outcomes and events of interest to sociology, not least because misassessment often leads to improper calibrations of certainty and risk. Our chapter is primarily theoretical, proceeding from a discussion of how perceptions of problematicity are treated by Joas to a consideration of other relevant pragmatist work, and from there to a statement of our key claims. But to illustrate the empirical utility of the theory, we turn in the last section to the case of the 2007–8 financial crisis, when problem situation misassessment was evident in the behavior of certain classes of homeowners and the failure of regulators to properly identify and act to counter emergent risks in an era of mortgage securitization.

A note about terminology before we proceed. Problem situation misassessment, as we understand it, can be prereflexive or reflexive. That is, actors can err with regard to the novelty of situations when they are in the midst of the flow of action and automaticity is high or when action has slowed and they have time to contemplate. We are aware that the terms *assessment* and *misassessment* (along with related terms like *judgment*) have reflexive connotations. Lacking better options, we use misassessment to refer to mistakes made in both prereflexive and reflexive moments while attempting to illuminate the different processes involved in each.

ROUTINE AND PROBLEMATICITY IN JOASIAN PRAGMATISM

American pragmatism is a multifaceted body of philosophical thought. The genius of Joas's contribution, made across a series of essays and books but set out most fully in *The Creativity of Action*, was to demonstrate that despite pragmatism's scope and internal diversity, a common core to the tradition does exist and can be found precisely in the pragmatist action model.[3] On Joas's account, pragmatism's signature theory of truth, as reflecting not a view-from-nowhere correspondence between ideas and properties of the world but an honorific bestowed on ideas when they do the work of helping us to better adjust, is seen as stemming from its theory of action, which is held as primary. Ideas for the pragmatists are habits of action, and as their evolutionary function is to facilitate adjustment to situations, the correct standard for judging ideas must involve reference to that facilitation. Philosophical commentators on pragmatism before Joas also attended to the connections between its evolutionary psychology and critique of Cartesian rationalism. But Joas shifted the discussion by showing that action is at the core of pragmatic naturalism. Although this made clear why so many early sociologists perceived an affinity between pragmatism and sociology, the point had not been brought out well before and opened the door for new and important pragmatist interventions into long-standing theoretical debates.

Joas's writings on pragmatism span widely. Yet it is difficult to find a sustained discussion by him of how individual or collective actors come to judge the situations they are facing as familiar or problematic, and of what it would mean for them to err in this regard.

There are two places in *The Creativity of Action* where Joas comes close to such a treatment. The first occurs as Joas explains why, for the pragmatists, action should not be seen as teleological—as unfolding in a predetermined fashion from goals, values, and other commitments held prior to situational entry. Dewey, in his work on ethics, aesthetics, and valuation, argued that although occasionally humans have a clear sense, at the outset of situations, about what aims and goals they hope to attain, more commonly aims are inchoate and evolve in the course of action, functioning as what he called "ends-in-view." Sociologists are familiar with this claim from pragmatism because it represents a powerful critique of strands of rational choice theory: if ends are vague and ambiguous and evolve from action, then action is not best characterized in most circumstances as an efficient selection of means to a stable end.[4]

But Joas's argument runs deeper: another reason action is not teleological is that much of the selection among means happens prereflexively, as the perceptual system of the human organism interfaces with its environment. For the pragmatists, actors experience situations via the frames of reference, capabilities, and limitations of their prior experience. *Inter alia*, these enable actors to ascertain what *type* of situation they are facing, in so doing priming them to mobilize or consider pertinent classes of response while leaving wholly unsuitable actions by the wayside. This is what Joas means when he writes that "our perception of situations already incorporates a judgment on the appropriateness of certain kinds of action. This explains why situations are not neutral fields of activity for intentions which were conceived outside of that situation, but appear to call forth, to provoke certain actions already in our perception."[5] When habits are triggered, they, alongside these preconscious perceptual judgments, may substitute for a reflexive consideration of means. But

preconscious judgments play a role in narrowing choice sets even in circumstances
in which actors end up consciously weighing means to an end. No action model
that is inattentive to such judgments will suffice, Joas insists, highlighting problems
not just with rational choice theory but also with normatively oriented theoretical
frameworks that begin with sets of means that are constituted analytically rather
than empirically through the action process.

The perceptual judgments Joas seems to have in mind are similar to judgments
of situational type and relevance as analyzed by sociologists in the tradition of
Alfred Schutz, about whom more will be said later. The judgments preselect certain means, bypassing what Anthony Giddens called "discursive consciousness," by
sensitizing the actor to the fact that the situation is of this sort rather than that: one
calling for an investment decision to be made, for example, rather than good parenting.[6] It is to Joas's credit that he emphasizes the essential role played by these
judgments in the pragmatist action model, pointing toward a continual (if pha-
sic) preconscious monitoring of the action environment—a monitoring emphasized not just in pragmatism but in several different approaches to practice theory
(including Giddens's own). In the work of practice theorists, monitoring and the
environment-perception interchange are sometimes discussed under the heading of
"affordances." Presumably, quasi-automatic judgments, assessments, or affordances
are also at play in alerting the actor to the familiarity or novelty of a situation. But
Joas says little about this aspect of perceptual judgment, beyond suggesting that it is
linked to attention and affectivity in that an unfamiliar situation resists our efforts to
move through it, demands cognitive energy, and frustrates.

The other place in *The Creativity of Action* where Joas approaches a theory of
the assessment of routine or problematicity is in the concluding chapter, where he
attempts to show the salience of an account of creative action for macro sociology.
Much of his effort involves reinterpreting lines of thought in collective action theory through a pragmatist lens. Eventually this issues in a novel account of functional differentiation processes, an account that acknowledges societal-level drivers,
such as population density and growing social complexity, but also examines how
these and other factors and events are experienced by particular, historically situated groups of actors as problems or crises in need of solution, generating collective
projects that push differentiation down specific paths.

Joas sees his claims to this effect as consistent with Shmuel Eisenstadt's writings
on "multiple modernities" and of a piece not just with pragmatist action theory
but also with Mead and Dewey's understanding of the challenges and opportunities presented by the early twentieth century.[7] During this period a series of profound crises—World War I, the Great Depression (which Mead died in the midst
of), and the rise of fascism—shattered complacent ideals of social progress and stim-
ulated mass collective experimentation in the institutional and cultural arenas (a
claim Joas further develops in the essays collected for his book *War and Modernity*).[8] Although the discussion in the chapter is geared toward a higher level of
social complexity than the earlier treatment of perceptual judgment, in identifying,

as Joas does, certain classes of macro-events and experiences as likely to generate experimentation, he can be seen as making a parallel theoretical move by suggesting that a now collective sense of routines being broken may be necessary to bring about the major social developments of interest to macro sociology. Wars, economic crises, the sudden emergence of authoritarian regimes—when these occur, life does not go on as normal, catalyzing collective action. Yet even in these contexts, there is little warrant for the assumption that a sense of problematicity must appear spontaneously and in all sectors of society at once. Joas leaves it to others—perhaps to analysts of social problems, social movement scholars, or students of collective trauma or "eventful" social history—to work out a theory of collective situational assessment and misassessment.

Other Relevant Pragmatist Work

If Joas does not theorize as much as he could how actors come to perceive the situations they are in as routine or problematic, is that because the issue had already been addressed at length by other, prior pragmatists? Alas, it had not—though the scattered things that pragmatist writers, and those in allied intellectual traditions like phenomenology, had to say on the subject represent insights worth building on.

One line of thinking that deserves attention, even if it has not been the subject of much sociological elaboration, is Dewey's philosophy of education. In a chapter of his 1910 book, *How We Think*, Dewey addressed judgment, giving the term a more formal-logical gloss than Joas. For Dewey, judgment relates to inference: "The aim of inference is to terminate itself in an adequate judgment of a situation, and the course of inference goes on through a series of partial and tentative judgments."[9] But what is involved in coming to a sound judgment on some question, how are sound judgments socially distributed, and what may be done in the educational sphere to enhance judgmental capacity? Dewey understood sound judgment as mastery of relevance: "To be a good judge is to have a sense of the relative indicative or signifying values of the various features of the perplexing situation; to know what to let go of as of no account; what to eliminate as irrelevant; what to retain as conducive to outcome; what to emphasize as a clue to the difficulty."[10] Good judgment in this sense requires experience in delimited domains of activity. More generally, however, Dewey viewed certain habits of mind as conducive to sound judgment and others as inhibitory. Required is "alertness, flexibility, curiosity," whereas "dogmatism, rigidity, prejudice, caprice arising from routine, passion, and flippancy are fatal."[11]

Part of the reason, Dewey suggested—and here lies the connection to our project—is that humans in the grip of dogma, incuriousness, and related complexes may fail to recognize problematic situations as problematic, demanding inquiry and judgment as opposed to utilization of convention. "Our progress in genuine knowledge," Dewey insists, "always consists *in part in the discovery of something not understood in what had previously been taken for granted as plain, obvious, matter-of-course.*"[12] As for which groups in society are likely to evince alertness and curiosity, refusing to take things for granted, Dewey saw these as distinguishing characteristics of the scientific profession and of the artist. In passages in the book, and in *Human Nature and Conduct*, he argued that the young are also natural repositories of mental suppleness, whereas fully acculturated adults, set in their ways, display the opposite tendency.[13] The latter often fail to notice perplexity in what should be perplexing situations. That is why Dewey rejected traditional approaches to pedagogy that emphasize rote learning of established knowledge. Such approaches endeavor to get the young thinking like the old, when the need of a rapidly changing modern society is for adaptability.

Similar concerns arise in W. I. Thomas and Florian Znaniecki's *The Polish Peasant in Europe and America*, an early sociological contribution inspired by pragmatism and one of the first to put "the situation" at the analytic center.[14] Despite their debt to pragmatism, Thomas and Znaniecki resist the concept of habituation, which they see as applicable to the biological sphere but not the social, given that in the latter—in their view—the meaning of situations for actors is never automatic but depends on the work that actors put in to develop a "life-organization" that effectively combines their "temperamental attitudes" with the meaning structures of their culture: "the individual does not find passively ready situations exactly similar to past situations; he must consciously define every situation as similar to certain past situations, if he wants to apply to it the same solution applied in those situations."

But what determines whether an actor will define a given situation as familiar or novel? The objective content of the situation matters, Thomas and Znaniecki claim, but so does the actor's character, as this is shaped by her social and cultural surround. It is in this context that the authors develop their threefold distinctions among the "Philistine," the "Bohemian," and "the creative man"—distinctions that inform their empirical analysis of immigrant adaptation. The first character type, nurtured by traditional communities, sees few situations as genuinely new: "every class of situation is defined in the same way once and forever." This leads the Philistine to error, as in the "case with any conservative and intellectually limited member of a stable community, whatever may be his social class, when he finds himself transferred into another community or when his own group undergoes some rapid and sudden change." Failing to recognize novelty, he applies established routines—for example, the mores and customs of the Polish peasantry to life in turn-of-the-twentieth-century Chicago—and is flummoxed when they do not work out as expected. The Bohemian is far more adaptable, prone to adopt new interpretive schemes on a whim and therefore better able to recognize novelty. Yet she also may see novelty when none is present and is so transient in her commitments that novelty properly grasped today need not mean novelty properly grasped tomorrow. Only the third type, the creative man, "searches for new situations in order to widen the control of his environment, to adapt to his purposes a continually increasing sphere of social reality." These are tantalizing suggestions about the individual and social correlates of perceiving novelty or familiarity in situations, but they fall short of an elaborated theory.

Does symbolic interactionism perhaps have more to say on this front? Yes and no. By virtue of its greater orientation to Mead than Dewey, interactionism is concerned with assessments by actors not simply of their ends but of the meaning of situations. Key here are the intentions and identities of interaction partners. A situation means what it does, *is* the situation it is, in large part because of the intentions and identities of those with whom one is interacting, as these are inferred by the actor decoding behavioral signs and cues emitted by other actors, particularly linguistic signs—inferences that become the basis for action that is then reciprocally interpreted and acted on in a process by which meanings evolve.

But according to interactionists, we must not assume that interpreting signs of intentionality or identity is an easy thing, even when interaction partners have clear and consistent intentions (which often they do not.) On the one hand, in some forms of interaction (such as "strategic interaction," as discussed by Erving Goffman, or nonopen "awareness contexts," as discussed by Barney Glaser and Anselm Strauss), actors may disguise their intentions, tricking the other for strategic gain or in order to uphold some value (e.g., a doctor concealing from a patient that he is dying, or a con man seeking to gain the trust of a mark.)[15] On the other hand, in contemporary societies a great many instances of interaction occur when actors do not share a lifeworld. Social and cultural heterogeneity throw together actors with divergent experiences and backgrounds, making it challenging even for the most sophisticated and forthright to correctly assess what the other is up to and devise an appropriate response. Intersubjective failure is therefore to be expected. In Blumerian terms—terms that extend Thomas and Znaniecki—this is to say that often actors do not share the same definition of the situation.

Interactionist analysis gains much of its empirical traction by examining the work that people do, and the techniques and conventions and institutions they rely on, to coordinate their actions against the backdrop of these frequent misunderstandings or partial understandings. And though Blumer emphasized the agentic, creative side of action more than the habitual—owing to his commitment to Mead's metaphysics of creativity and desire to elaborate a theoretical program that could serve as a counterweight to the ostensible determinism of structural-functionalism—it was here, in his scheme, that something like an alternation between habit and creativity became evident. When it is obvious that actors' definitions of the situation do line up—that is, when intersubjectivity is plainly assured—situations have no real problematic component. Interpretation of meaning becomes straightforward and ritualistic, and then action can unfold in an almost automatic fashion. Problematicity happens when things are not so clear, and in these circumstances interpretation and the action it funds take on a provisional, experimental quality akin to Deweyan inquiry, as actors engage in a behavioral back and forth to feel each other out. It was C. Wright Mills, not Herbert Blumer, who stated this mostly explicitly in "Situated Actions and Vocabularies of Motive," when he wrote that "men live in immediate acts of experience and their attentions are directed outside themselves until acts are in some way frustrated. It is then that awareness of self and of motive occur."[16] So interactionism does address, in its own way, perceptions of situational familiarity or problematicity. And the premises of the approach would lead the analyst to expect many circumstances in which one actor in a situation perceives it as unproblematic and thinks she has a clear grasp on the others' intentions when actually there is disjuncture.

Goffman explored these ideas under the specific theoretical banner of frames. Inspired by William James's work on attention, Schutz's on "multiple realities," and the writings of anthropologist Gregory Bateson, Goffman argued that interaction always involves application of interpretive frameworks for situational understanding that help actors answer the question, "'What is it that's going on here?'[17] Such frameworks are "principles of organization which govern [social] events."[18] Although frameworks may "vary in degree of organization," all those that coalesce in a society and acquire basic coherence "allow [their] user[s] to locate, perceive, identify, and label a seemingly infinite number of concrete occurrences defined in its terms."[19]

Yet according to Goffman, framing presents actors with "ordinary troubles."[20] First, situations can be ambiguous, so that it is not clear to actors which frame they should be using. Second, ambiguity aside, actors can make mistakes in situational framing. This may become apparent to them and their interaction partners as the action process unfolds, occasioning confusion, embarrassment, and sometimes conflict. Goffman saw the study of ambiguity and error in framing, and their consequences for interaction, as important components of his program for frame analysis. Most of the ambiguity and error he considered revolved around uncertainty or misunderstanding of what the other is up to.

Interactionist ideas figure in the theoretical approach we develop. But we would not want to reduce assessments of familiarity or problematicity to shared definitions of the situation, as definitions are but one aspect of the social and natural worlds.

The final body of pragmatist-related thought that bears on problem situation assessment and misassessment is phenomenological sociology. Phenomenological sociology and pragmatism do not share a philosophical provenance, the former tracing its roots to the foundationalist intellectual project of Edmund Husserl. Nevertheless, the two sociologies have much in common, including a focus on practice, an antipathy toward objectivism, and a shared interest in habit. For Schutz—as the discussion of Joas on preconscious judgments suggests—the most important typifications are situational (though Schutz recognizes other typifications). Actors figure out what to do, which actions are relevant, by assessing the kind of situation they are in. In this Schutz agreed with Thomas and Znaniecki. But Schutz insisted, first, that actors make these assessments with the help of culturally shared schemes that classify situations, imbue them with meaning, and direct attention—stocks of knowledge that were not as central to the authors of *The Polish Peasant*. Second, Schutz insisted that definitions of the situation depend not simply on characterological differences among actors but on potentially idiosyncratic life projects that they happen to be pursuing, such that—in the classic example Schutz gave—chopping a log presents itself as a very different kind of situation for someone trying to warm his house for the winter than for someone trying to exercise.[21] Situational typifications, for Schutz, also include formal and practical knowledge of interaction with material objects.

Peter Berger and Thomas Luckmann were interested in life projects as well and in the critique of objectivist social science implied by the concept. But the main typificatory schemes that concerned them, in *The Social Construction of Reality*, related to types of actors experienced as others in situations and to types of actions: "The reality of everyday life contains typificatory schemes in terms of which others are apprehended and 'dealt with' in face-to-face encounters. Thus I apprehend the other as 'a man,' 'a European,' 'a buyer,' 'a jovial type,' and so on. All these typifications ongoingly affect my interaction with him as, say, I decide to show him a good time on the town before trying to sell him my product."[22]

Whichever the relative emphasis—whether on types of situations for Schutz or types of others and actions for Berger and Luckmann (which provided, for the later authors, a connection to role theory)—typification was understood as bound up with habit, in that there is a prereflexive automaticity and learned component to it. Actors acquire typifications from experience and culture and apply them without much conscious thought to understand, order, and orient themselves to the world around them. As with pragmatist habits, only when typifications fail do actors encounter a distinctly problematic situation that demands their attention and may lead them to apply different typifications than they did initially, or, potentially, to revise their typificatory schemes. Berger and Luckmann built a theory of institutionalization around the idea of habitualized typification.

Like the interactionists, phenomenological sociologists thought that actors often get it wrong: they apply an unsuitable typification given the circumstances. This could involve resort to an element of typological knowledge that inappropriately codes a novel situation as routine, or simply resort to the wrong typification. Where Berger and Luckmann viewed this mostly as a question of the degree to which actors become involved in interactions removed from their everyday experiences and competencies, Schutz gave it a more perspicacious framing. In an article first published in 1944 that built on the ideas of another pragmatist sociologist, Robert S. Lynd—and that also resonates with work in the tradition of critical theory, including Pierre Bourdieu's idea of "doxa"—Schutz put situational typification under the banner of "thinking-as-usual," and discussed the conditions under which such thinking comes about.

Thinking-as-usual may be maintained as long as some basic assumptions hold true, namely: (1) that life and especially social life will continue to be the same as it has been so far, that the same problems requiring the same solutions will recur and that, therefore, our former experiences will suffice for mastering future situations; (2) that we may rely on the knowledge handed down to us by parents, teachers, governments, traditions, habits, etc., even if we do not understand its origin and its real meaning; (3) that in the ordinary course of affairs it is sufficient to know something *about* the general type or style of events we may encounter in our life-world in order to manage or control them; and (4) that neither the systems of recipes as schemes of interpretation and expression nor the underlying basic assumptions just mentioned are our private affair, but that they are likewise accepted and applied by our fellow-men. If only one of these assumptions ceases to stand the test, thinking-as-usual becomes unworkable.[23]

This is closer to a general theory of problem situation misassessment. But we think there is value in a synthetic statement that pulls together the strands we have been discussing.

A THEORY OF PROBLEM SITUATION MISASSESSMENT

Our theory of problem situation misassessment grows out of the complexified view of the pragmatist actor immanent in Joas. With him, we see actors as engaged in pre-conscious assessments of their social and material environments, with these occurring through the deployment of classification schemes for situations that mediate the initiation, continuation, or cessation of habitual or creative action. The following points deserve fuller elaboration than space allows but have the benefit of distilling ideas previously reviewed.

1. *Situational classificatory schemes are a vital, if understudied, component of culture.* In the course of acquiring experience with the social and natural worlds—including through processes of socialization and communication—individual actors pick up classificatory schemes, frames, and stocks of knowledge that they use to code and understand the circumstances before them as comprising situations of such and such a kind. These schemes are bits of culture, anchored to broader meaning structures, that circulate in social networks and may become embedded in, and partially definitive of, groups, institutions, and organizations. Situational classifications, organized along the lines of fuzzy hierarchies and family resemblances, have social histories of emergence, diffusion, institutionalization, contestation and refiguring, and, ultimately, dissolution.

And yet, for all the use that has been made of Goffman's frame concept, sociologists have paid relatively little attention to situational classificatory schemes per se, except for the occasional ethnographer, historical sociologist, or organizational scholar who has sought to answer the question, for particular sets of actors, of what kinds of situations they understood themselves to be facing in light of restricted sets of situations they understood it *possible* for them to be facing. What we are flagging, by contrast—in line with Goffman—are entire vocabularies and grammars of situations that are part and parcel of social and cultural variability.

2. *Situational assessment is a phase of the action process.* Actors continually assess the action environment—with varying levels of intensity—with situational

classificatory schemes in mind, looking to ascertain what kind of situation they are in. This occurs whether they have entered a new situation or are trying to determine if the parameters of an ongoing situation have changed. Assessment is not an intellectual exercise but a phase of the action process. It helps to provide an actor's sense of "truth," in the pragmatist sense of denoting a practical interpretation of reality. Efforts at situational classification—typically, though by no means always, preconscious—are structured by life projects, organizational tasks, and trajectories through social space. As subjective contexts for action, these delimit the range of possible situations that actors expect to find themselves in, favor one situational classification over another where there is ambiguity, and set the temporal boundaries of situations by casting momentary encounters and action sequences as part of longer, meaningful chains. When an actor pragmatically classifies a situation as of type X versus Y, it both preselects certain means for action and sets up behavioral expectations for the situation's unfolding.

3. *Situational assessment is first and foremost aesthetic in nature, and success at it can mean one of three things.* We see situational classification as primarily an aesthetic enterprise: it involves interpolating visual, auditory, and bodily clues, along with cultural knowledge, to identify a gestalt pattern. Many mammals engage in tacit situational classification. Humans do so through the mediation of language and other symbolic systems and in the face of greater cultural and situational complexity. But it still remains on the order of "feeling out." Although this is a basic human competence we see as honed during childhood role-play, consistent with Mead's theory of self-development, we assume that actors vary in their capacity to engage in it successfully—across the board, in given situational domains, or in specific instances.

There are at least three meanings of success. One is classifying circumstances in much the same way that other members of one's group or community would—essential for intersubjectivity. This is success vis-à-vis the generalized other, and it is the kind of success Goffman generally had in mind when discussing errors in situational understanding. A second meaning of success is more practical. Does the actors' classification of the situation lead her to act in such a way that she is able to accomplish what she wants to in the moment? These first two meanings of success are interrelated. Practical success often requires interacting fruitfully with others through the same interpretive frame, whereas the situational classificatory schemes of groups may evolve over time in recognition of practical and material constraints. Yet the two meanings are not the same. One may classify a situation in the same way as one's peers and yet not achieve practical success, as in the use of widely accepted religious ritual to fight disease. Conversely, practical success may be had while departing from the interpretive frames of one's peers; entrepreneurs who successfully bring a product to market at a time when no one thought it possible stand as an example.

A third meaning of success—the one that serves as a benchmark for our theory of problem situation misassessment—is different: do actors grasp circumstances in roughly the same way that an ideal community of social scientists would? Whereas the first meaning of success depends on adequate socialization and the second on practical competency, the third is a function of how much "social intelligence," in Dewey's sense of the term, comes to be injected into the classificatory schemes, stocks of knowledge, and procedures of inquiry of the actor's group. Social intelligence is a somewhat vague concept in Dewey but refers in the end to the wisdom in social matters that can be gained through the application of a mindset that is simultaneously experimental and democratically oriented.

Our third meaning of success pairs this idea with Peirce's notion of truth as that which would be discovered by an ideal community of inquirers. We assume that if an ideal community of social-scientific inquirers turned its attention to a given situation, eventually the community would reach consensus on the situation's qualities. Success in situational assessment by real-world social actors, in the third sense we are developing, is a matter of the degree of convergence on the main points with that idealized consensus account. Given that the idealized end of inquiry can never be reached, real-world social analysts of assessment and misassessment can only seek to establish those points provisionally in light of the best social-scientific evidence that exists at the time their inquiries are being carried out. Although Dewey was no fan of Karl Marx, there is a parallel between our use of Dewey and Peirce here (based on our reading of Dewey's scattered comments on social science) and most strains of critical theory: both pragmatism and critical theory assume there is a "real" layer of social structures, relations, and forces that, in principle, social scientists should be able to uncover (although pragmatic realism is distinctive); and both assume that social actors often misrecognize what is happening in front of them.[24]

Given our third meaning of success, situational misassessment is bound to be commonplace, particularly in the premodern period before the development of the social sciences. But correct assessment is not unheard of. Historically, many groups, cultures, and institutions have displayed social intelligence without any input from the formal social sciences, whereas today, social intelligence is increasingly part of public culture, threats to democracy and scientific literacy notwithstanding. In theory, grasping a social situation as the community of social inquirers would should yield maximal control over it, including an enhanced ability to predict outcomes, though practical success *in situ* is not necessarily evidence of correct assessment in our third sense. And in fact, as we will argue in our empirical discussion, *sometimes repeated practical success in situational assessment is precisely what blinds actors to larger realities.*

Finally, although linking situational assessment to social intelligence may make the former sound like a fully reflexive enterprise and therefore not particularly aesthetic, what we are drawing attention to, ultimately, is how perspicacious and socially wise a group's culture is when it comes to situational classification and understanding. The application of culturally established classifications to situations at hand remains a more or less automatic process in most instances no matter how socially intelligent or myopic those classifications are.

4. *Habit is rooted in situational assessment.* Actors' habits are directly tied to their deployment of situational classificatory schemes. On the one hand, relevant habits can be activated only when the actor perceives that a particular kind of situation is being faced. On the other hand, consistent with work on affordances, we might say that every habit indexes a scheme for classifying situations, and that the practical availability of habits renders situations graspable by actors in particular kinds of ways.

5. *The assessment of problematicity is a key aspect of situational assessment.* Actors will assess a situation as problematic—as one for which their stocks of habit are ill-suited, prompting inquiry and experimentation—when, as a result of the environmental monitoring process we have been describing, the situation seems to contain features sufficiently unfamiliar that either the actors do not know how to classify it or it gets classified as a circumstance with which they have little personal experience (perhaps only abstract cultural knowledge), and hence few appropriate habits. It also may be the case that actors initially perceive a situation as familiar and unproblematic, only to find that over the course of the situation's development, the habits they mobilize yield strange and unexpected results; the situation resists their habit deployment. This, too, can lead to the puzzlement and "irritation of doubt" first incorporated into pragmatism by Peirce.

Expanding on Joas's social-theoretical interpretation of pragmatist epistemology, we would stress that this form of problematicity is not a function of habits failing to work in some mind-independent sense; rather, it is a function of an expectations/action/environmental manipulability gap. Here, as well, there is an aesthetic aspect. Dewey's theory of aesthetics examined the "fullness" or "roundness" of aesthetic experience, and it seems to us that the irritation of doubt often takes the form of engagements in a situation that, despite initial expectations, end up proving jarring or lacking in fullness because of unfamiliarity and that call out for aesthetic restoration and reintegration.

6. *Awareness of problematicity can become reflexive and collective.* The assessments we have been concerned with so far take place prereflexively for individuals. But awareness of problematicity can bring a situation to reflexive consciousness, and when this occurs, actors often engage others. Confused as to what is going on, they may turn to friends, family members, coworkers, coreligionists, intellectuals (as specialized problem situation diagnosticians), and so on, asking for help in coming to an adequate understanding. This can happen for select individuals or for many at once, in the case of confusing macro situations that present themselves to a group or whole society. Situational classificatory schemes are at play in interpersonal problem situation assessment, but so, too, are interactional, organizational, and institutional dynamics that have no individual-level counterpart.

7. *Problem situation misassessment defined.* We are now in a position to define problem situation misassessment. Whereas generic situational misassessment means any failure to properly grasp what is happening in one's environment, problem situation misassessment means specifically feeling a situation to be problematic—novel

and not routine, and habit inappropriate—when the community of social inquirers would not judge it to be so; or vice versa—unproblematic where the community of social inquirers would see a genuine break from routine. Whether actions under-taken as the result of an assessment of problematicity bring about consequences that actors desire, over the short or long term, may count as evidence that such a community of inquirers would draw on in forming judgments, as it would seem to suggest more accurate assessment. But the information would not be disposi-tive, as—under the right circumstances—actors can misassess problematicity, be unaware of having done so, and stumble nevertheless into what they would regard as favorable outcomes.

8. *Misassessment is correlated with social processes and conditions.* Generic situa-tional assessment turns on individual capacity, information, situational parameters, and social position. Problem situation assessment, too, is a contingent achievement. At higher levels of environmental complexity, many things must line up for actors to correctly and intuitively gauge whether the circumstances they are facing are sufficiently similar to those they have faced in the past that they can productively mobilize their habits, or whether creativity and inquiry are the more appropriate response. We can identify several factors that should affect the likelihood of prob-lem situation misassessment by individuals and therefore the extent of misassess-ment in a group or population. This is not intended as an exhaustive list.

(8a) *Unevenness in the pace of social change.* Social change in a given period that is either much faster or slower than normal should lead to more problem situation misassessment. Groups, organizations, and individuals can and do adapt to change, and an important part of adaptation is coming to recognize and develop suitable habits for new situations. Where the pace of change is usually rapid (for example, in countries on steep developmental trajectories), actors may become acclimated to dynamism and a near-constant revision of situational schemes and habit sets. Where the pace of change is always slow, procedures may be put in place to facili-tate gradual adaptation (in the justice system of the medieval church, for example). But where change occurs at an unexpected clip, established mechanisms for adap-tation can be expected to fail, with the result that people will either not come to rec-ognize novel situations for what they are or else not recognize genuine situational continuities.

(8b) *The nature of situations.* Situations vary in their interpretability. Just as inter-actional misassessment can result from confusion over an actor's intentions, prob-lem situation misassessment can come from a disorienting atmosphere around a situation, hard-to-interpret cultural and material objects, or fundamental ambigu-ity in the situation itself. Situations bring together individual and collective actors with not only varying degrees of social intelligence and nimbleness of assessment but often also diverging interests, aims, ambitions, rules and procedures, status and resource endowments, subjectivities, and more, each with its own history of social construction. Some situations will be constituted by these assemblages of social relations such that their main lines are more or less clear and understandable to the parties concerned, whereas other situations will be murky, multivalent, and evanescent. Winship has written in this regard about "extra-rational" behavior—behavior to which standard forms of rationality do not apply because it is a response to inchoate situations.[25] In a different vein, Ivan Ermakoff urges expansion of rational choice theory's scope from "small-world" problems with well-defined parameters to "situations of disruption and crisis," in which nobody can be sure what is transpiring.[26]

Although we see situational ambiguity as commonplace, action in some domains of activity seems to be more intrinsically ambiguous than in others; think of the difference between espionage and venture capitalism, on the one side, and small-business accounting on the other.[27] Ambiguity in a domain also may ebb and flow over time. We would expect actors located in domains high in ambiguity, and those who otherwise confront ambiguous situations on a regular basis, to routinely misassess problematicity.

(8c) *Experience*. We would expect a U-shaped curve in the relationship between an actor's level of experience in a given activity domain and the extent of problem situation misassessment. Low levels of experience generally result in a great deal of misassessment because actors are not yet fully conversant with relevant classificatory schemes, lack practical competency in domain-specific monitoring, and are not vested with germane habits. This changes as experience grows. But at the high end of the experience distribution, one often finds actors so sure of their own competency that they fail to attend to subtle but important environmental modifications.

(8d) *Network size and diversity*. All else being equal, we expect people with larger, more diverse social networks to be better positioned to recognize novel situations as would an idealized community of social inquirers. From such networks, people gain meaningful exposure to a wider variety of situational classificatory schemes, as well as a wider variety of habits. Their broader horizons include an understanding, informed by the experiences of others in different circumstances, of the many types of situations a person may encounter, which reduces the error rate in situational classification and action. We should also expect more churn in classification schemes in such networks: more new schemes coming on line quickly in response to social change. Additionally, discussion of situational confusion in larger networks should be more error correcting. Conversely, we would expect people to do a better job at classifying situations as would their immediate peers—with the associated benefits and drawbacks—the smaller and more tight-knit their networks. More generally, the social positions actors are in relative to others in a network may, for a variety of reasons, increase or decrease the likelihood that they will correctly grasp familiarity or novelty, irrespective of their personal traits or dispositions.

(8e) *Dogma as a feature of belief*. Although early sociologists saw dogma and traditionalism to decline with modernity, it now seems clear that dogmatic religious or ideological belief can be found in societies throughout history. Where dogmatism prevails—where, for any number of reasons, groups and individuals come to believe their worldview expresses singular spiritual, moral, or political truth—we should find elevated rates of problem situation misassessment, as people endeavor to squeeze the messiness and vicissitudes of social life into simplified frameworks and categories for understanding and staunchly resist meaningful updating. With Dewey, we see strongly developed artistic and scientific sectors as potential counterweights to dogmatic belief—and therefore buffers against problem situation misassessment, though under certain conditions art and science can become fountainheads for dogma. (Dewey saw laissez-faire economics as an example of the capture of science by dogma.)

(8f) *Institutions of socialization*. Analytically but not empirically distinct from dogmatism in belief systems is the nature of institutions that function to socialize the young. It seems to us, as it seemed to Dewey, that such institutions can prepare people more or less well to adapt to changing social circumstances. For example, schools that emphasize creativity and inquiry prepare people to recognize novel situations but perhaps less well to recognize the familiar. Rigid, backward-looking socializing institutions do just the opposite. Similarly, socializing institutions whose epistemic cultures have been influenced by the social sciences may help people recognize the true social parameters of the situations before them. Where different groups in society are exposed to institutions that vary in this regard—with the young from one social class attending one kind of school, for instance, and those from another class attending another kind—we may find differential rates of problem situation misassessment.

(8g) *Organizational environments*. In modern societies, a great deal of social action takes place in the context of formal organizations. Whether people are acting in their corporate capacity as employees or representatives of an organization, or as organizational clients (for example, students in a higher education setting or patients in a hospital), the organizational infrastructures and logics that surround them shape their interactions with others and the material world. Socialization and situational constitution aside, where these infrastructures and logics are out of step with social conditions—where they are inflexible and slow to change, for example, because of intransigence from elements of the organization with interests in preserving the status quo—or, alternatively, where the organization is characterized by thoroughgoing "dissonance" and "heterarchy" and is in *greater* flux than its environment, we should expect organizationally embedded actors to exhibit above-average rates of problem situation misassessment.[28] Such actors will be working with maladaptive templates and frameworks for situational understanding and action.

(8h) Finally, and in a somewhat different register, *exploitation*. Although we do not see problem situation misassessment as inherently good or bad, one of its most significant consequences is that it alters the risk profile of action. At the level of individual cognition, humans are not very good at assessing risk or uncertainty. But they are particularly bad at it when they cannot correctly determine the familiarity or novelty of the situations to which they are exposed. Among other things, habit is a way of controlling risk and reducing uncertainty. To enact a well-established routine is to repeat behavior that, in the past, has seemed successful at taming environmental challenge and keeping the hazards of life at arm's distance. Social habits allow actors to benefit from distributed cognition and collective learning around risk.

To be sure, even in rationalized domains, like those of the formal organization, there is an element of irrationality and magical thinking to habits: some of the habits people enact believing them to reduce risk are unrelated to actual risk reduction, on the order of "myth and ceremonies." But from a pragmatist/social-evolutionary point of view, institutionalized habits and practices—those that have survived over time—should be presumed to play a role in risk minimization. (Think of the evolutionary origin of food taboos, or the habits children are taught of distrusting strangers.)

When actors misassess problem situations, they fail to avail themselves of relevant action strategies for minimizing risk and controlling uncertainty, and they also close themselves off, via immersion in inapplicable situational frames, to new, risk-relevant information that may become apparent as the situation unfolds. Because this is so, however, often problem situation misassessment is not innocent: the result not of a natural mistake but of interested strategies of distortion. Precisely because it involves an alteration of risk and/or uncertainty, and because some social actors will be better positioned than others to correctly grasp changing environmental conditions, problem situation misassessment is rife with possibilities for exploitation. This occurs as better-positioned actors work to shore up situation-related information asymmetries and invest (economically and politically) in ways that bet against the situational assessments of others. To return to our discussion of correlates, when opportunities arise for one group of actors to exploit another in this fashion, we should see promotion of problem situation misassessment at the micro, meso, and macro levels—and more misassessment taking place unless the would-be exploited group finds ways to resist. Here (again) pragmatism and critical theory find common ground.

In short, in place of a simple pragmatist action model that sees actors acting in either a more habitual or more creative fashion depending on how much novelty is present in the situations they confront, we emphasize that the key is how much novelty they *feel or perceive* themselves to be facing, with the gap between perceptions and reality (as it appears to the analyst) socially patterned. Because problem situation misassessment—which leads to deployment of inapplicable habits or a failure to engage in productive inquiry—can have profound consequences for social relations and outcomes at various scales, a pragmatist sociology that is attentive to the extent and sources of misassessment has broad explanatory potential.

Problem Situation Misassessment, Behavioral Economics, and Hysteresis

Before we move on to empirical illustration, it is important to distinguish our approach from analogous theories in behavioral economics and field theory. These approaches capture certain aspects of misassessment but leave much of the phenomenon unexplored.

Behavioral economics is concerned with systemic irrationality in human judgment and decision-making. The biases of interest to behavioral economists are errors in decision-making situations that can be induced by a host of factors, including heuristics for automatic reasoning, situational cues or priming, and imperfect or incomplete information. Daniel Kahneman's behavioral theory of action, a synthesis of nearly four decades of research with collaborator Amos Tversky, rests on a dual model of cognition, with automatic and intuitive thinking said to constitute one cognitive system and effortful, calculative, and deliberative thought another.[29] This cognitive system is biased toward overconfidence, susceptible to priming by irrelevant details, reliant on norms, and "gullible and biased to believe."[30]

In contrast to the involuntary nature of system 1, the deliberative "remembering selves" of system 2 requires sustained attention and effort. Kahneman is clear that the clean distinction between systems is meant for ease of explication. In fact, the systems are interdependent and interactive. System 1, as the source of "impressions, intuitions, intentions, and feelings," supplies suggestions for system 2, whereas system 2 can "endorse" these in a process by which "impressions and intuitions turn into beliefs, and impulses turn into voluntary action."[31] This back and forth can be a major source of error for system 2, as deliberation takes as inputs heuristics and other forms of fast reasoning that may lead to misinterpretations, such as the "anchoring effect," in which estimation of a value is affected by exposure to an anchor value.[32]

Reminiscent of the pragmatist theory of action, Kahneman interprets the relatively infrequent activation of system 2 in terms of problematicity: "system 2 is activated when an event is detected that violates the model of the world that system 1 maintains."[33] The inverse problem, too, a failure to recognize a novel situation as problematic, is also considered. Kahneman explains that "impressions of familiarity" serve the function of achieving "cognitive ease" by system 1, which is biased toward belief and effortless evaluation.[34]

Kahneman's theorization has been justly celebrated and speaks to some of the psychological and social-psychological roots of problem situation misassessment. But misassessment is also socially and culturally underpinned in ways that behavioral economists ignore. The schemes for understanding situations we have been emphasizing make no appearance in conventional behavioral economic models, except as heuristics denuded of cultural content. Rather than fragmentary cognitive tools, we conceive of such schemes as meaningful, articulated with one another; embedded in future-oriented projects, notions of identity, and organizational architectures; and most important for our purposes, connected to prescriptions for lines of activity. Because behavioral economics is inattentive to situational schemes thus conceived, foregrounding individual cognition and decision-making, it cannot tap into most of the sources of problem situation misassessment identified earlier. Beyond that, behavioral economics takes formal rationality as its benchmark, where we have understood problem situation misassessment in relation to social intelligence. By eschewing the framework of rationality and bias, our conception of misassessment stays grounded in the experiential specificity and environmental context of the actor and problem situation being studied.

Bourdieusian and other field theory traditions have also developed accounts of mismatch between action and situation. Perhaps the most complementary field approach is Michael Strand and Omar Lizardo's elaboration of Bourdieu's "hysteresis effect," denoting "agent-environment mismatches."[35] Taking as their target representational notions of belief, which posit that ideas mediate between actor and environment, Strand and Lizardo propose a "dispositional" or "practical" notion of belief that they claim comes prior. Their notion of practical belief is not "content-bearing," and it is embodied.[36] They suggest that representational belief is called on by actors only when dispositional practical belief runs into trouble, "after repeated failure at matching practical belief to institutional patterns."[37] Mismatch in this model results from two asynchronous temporalities, one of environmental change and the other of adaptation in practical beliefs.[38] Strand and Lizardo argue that the condition of hysteresis, the effect of the lag between "a conditioning period in which practical belief is acquired and a deployment period in which practical belief becomes the engaged basis of action," is vital to a field conception of action, alongside the conceptual triad of habitus, field, and capital.[39]

Many theorists—including Bourdieu himself—have commented on the similarities between pragmatism and the Bourdieusian theory of action. But there are benefits to conceiving of the relevant dynamics through the lens of problem situation misassessment. First, and most obviously, hysteresis helps us understand circumstances only when actors apply the wrong habits. But, as we have been arguing, a no less important form of maladjustment in action occurs when actors perceive that a situation is novel and calls for creativity when in fact it is routine and familiar. Here it is not that actors apply the wrong habits; rather, they fail to engage habituality when they should. In agreement with Emirbayer and Desmond, who have argued that pragmatism is stronger than Bourdieusian theory when it comes to the projectivity side of action, the notion of problem situation misassessment, flagging as it does routine circumstances that are perceived as nonroutine, helps to explain why there is more agency and dynamism in social life than a strict Bourdieusian model would recognize.[40] Second, the pragmatist understanding of habit is relevant to both fielded and unfielded circumstances while also attending to crucial meso-level sources of habit that Bourdieusians have often overlooked. Problem situation misassessment carries these benefits into the analysis of situational mismatch, allowing us to consider diverse causes for what students of hysteresis rightly diagnose as—in a broad sense—failures of synchronicity. Third, Lizardo and Strand go too far in downplaying representational aspects of action. The schemes for understanding situations that we have highlighted as factoring into environmental assessment have a representational element and are in some cases linked to bodies of propositional belief. We see no reason to deny the existence of such schemes or conceive of them as secondary to action and think that our aesthetic approach bridges some of the distance between representationalism and dispositionalism.

PROBLEM SITUATION MISASSESSMENT AND
THE 2007–8 FINANCIAL CRISIS

Looking across the landscape of contemporary sociology, we see many empirical puzzles that our theory of problem situation misassessment could help to address. But to illustrate its explanatory potential, we focus on a large-scale, highly consequential phenomenon of particular concern to economic sociologists: the 2007–8 financial crisis. We contend that problem situation misassessment offers a way to makes sense of two enduring puzzles from the crisis: household decisions to continue borrowing and take on ever-riskier mortgages during an unprecedented housing price bubble (the topic to which we devote most of our attention, as it has been little addressed by sociologists), and government regulators' unresponsiveness to the high levels of financial risk produced around the circulation of mortgage-backed securities and collateralized debt obligations increasingly composed of subprime loans. While home buyers acted creatively, thinking there was a change to housing market fundamentals, regulators acted habitually as they downplayed the risks posed by the circulation of new financial instruments. These dimensions of the crisis can be understood as instances of misassessment when it comes to market situations.

The crisis of 2007–8, which precipitated the Great Recession, was both an asset and banking crisis. After a decade-long climb, in 2006, home prices in the United States stalled in many metropolitan areas and then began to fall. This sudden and largely unexpected halt in price increases, followed by a rapid decline, would ripple across the housing market and spill over to numerous financial institutions and millions of American households. The domestic and global consequences were overwhelming. An estimated nine million Americans lost their homes in foreclosure proceedings, with foreclosures affecting subprime and creditworthy "prime" or "Alt A" borrowers alike. More than eight million jobs were lost between July 2007 and October 2009 alone. Depreciation in home values, the evaporation of savings and equity, and the rise in unemployment caused declines in consumption that spread the effects of the crisis from the realm of finance to markets for commodities.

We argue that as homeowners embraced new mortgage instruments to solve practical problems, they erred in seeing a more fundamental transformation of housing values. They acted creatively when postwar habits of home buying would have been more situationally appropriate.

In the three decades preceding the financial crisis, the mortgage lending system had transformed dramatically. From the late 1990s, a growing share of U.S. mortgage lending had centered on so-called nonconventional mortgages, with features like adjustable interest rates, teaser introductory rates, and low down payments. Nonconventional mortgages passed on the risks of interest rate changes to borrowers rather than falling on lenders locked into charging a set rate, as was the case with "fixed-rate" loans. Popular in a time of low interest rates, nonconventional products also gave homeowners the option to renegotiate the terms of their mortgage if rates rose. Homeowners were confident that with steadily rising home prices, they would enjoy sufficient equity to refinance if it became necessary to do so.

A slight uptick in interest rates in 2006, along with the bursting of the real estate bubble, unraveled the precarious financial infrastructure that had buttressed a major expansion of homeownership—by six full percentage points—in the decade after 1994. Many new homeowners during this time were "subprime" borrowers, a term for loans made to those who lacked the standard markers of creditworthiness. After 2006, these homeowners were saddled with payments they could no longer afford, carrying the full cost of rising rates while seeing their home equity evaporate and the once-sure safety valve of refinancing options close. Between 2006 and 2007, foreclosure filings rose more than 80 percent, and subprime borrowers were among the first to default. The decline in housing prices that set off the first shock wave of foreclosures was followed by unemployment from a construction industry in standstill, resulting in even more foreclosures, and quickly unsettling an entire financial sector.

Irrational Exuberance?

Although it is broadly recognized that there would have been no financial crisis without the mass speculative activity of households—without large numbers of Americans taking out mortgages and home equity loans they could not afford—most social-scientific analyses have focused largely on macroeconomic and regulatory causes. Underspecified is an explanation of why Americans were receptive to the use of mortgage instruments that opened them up, both individually and collectively, to such risk and why they were willing to buy even when prices were high. We think a major part of the answer is that many American households misassessed their market situation: they perceived that in purchasing a property in the context of the "new economy," they were facing wholly different circumstances than had buyers in the past, necessitating the use of novel financial strategies, including speculation and substantial risk, when in fact important continuities remained that called for the use of collectively established habits and practices. Our argument intersects in some ways, but ultimately diverges from, one of the most influential explanations for homeowner behavior leading up to the crash. We briefly elaborate behavioral economist Robert Shiller's interpretation of homeowner behavior as a case of "irrational exuberance" fueled by the spread of distortionary news stories that proclaimed a change in the fundamentals of home prices.

Over the course of multiple books and articles, Shiller has proposed a central role in speculative manias for "oversimplified and easily transmitted variants of economic narratives"—stories about price changes that circulate and are amplified by news media.[41] Whereas much of his research draws on surveys to examine responses to financial news by stockbrokers, he has extended this model to interpret speculative behavior among homeowners. Shiller contends that home prices began to diverge from the standard metrics of real land values, rents, and labor and construction costs around 1994.[42] What changed, he contends, was the way in which homeowners thought about the financial affordances of housing. Just a few decades ago, Shiller explains, "there would be no more reason to think that one can make money by buying houses and holding them for resale than that one can make money by buying tables and chairs and holding them for resale."[43] This conception of housing as a passive investment changed as homeowners (and prospective homeowners) began to think about their homes as rapidly appreciating investments. The culprits for this transformation, Shiller argues, were stories. The availability of home price numbers increased the likelihood of news coverage of price changes, unleashing "attention cascades" that reverberated through the population, fueling speculative booms.[44] Substantively, a particular kind of story was behind the housing boom—what Shiller calls "new era stories." These are stories that frame rising prices as a sign that "[the] world is entering into a new era of capitalism . . . [warning] people that they have to join the capitalist world and buy their homestead now, before it is priced out of reach by hordes of wealthy investors."[45]

Shiller's attention to the role of stories in shaping economic trends, what he terms "narrative economics," centers on the exogenous effect of stories on market choices.[46] Adapting a contagion model from epidemiology, Shiller argues that media stories spread like a virus through a population that is susceptible to the behavioral biases of heuristics, myopic loss aversion, emotional contagion, and sensation seeking.[47] Without proper inoculation, exposure to new era stories leads to "contagion [occurring] from person to person through talk, whether in person, or through telephone or social media."[48] As new economy stories about home price changes spread, they generate a feedback effect, leading to speculative behavior that further drives prices up, resulting in more news coverage. For Shiller, the effects of narratives on market action are episodic. Like the spread of a virus, narratives affect "a rising number of infected people who spread the narrative for a while, followed by a period of forgetting."[49] Shiller lists a number of factors that affect the "contagion rate" of narratives, including the arrival of the internet, rise of business-dedicated news, and expansion of defined-contribution retirement plans that focus attention on market movements.[50]

Shiller's media-focused account of the sources of homeowner overconfidence illuminates some of the psychological contributors to market situation misassessment. We agree with Shiller's assertion of a shift in the way that homeowners thought about homes as appreciating assets. However, we find important limitations to Shiller's approach. In line with behavioral economics, Shiller highlights only one metric for assessment success: a baseline of rational action. This has two major consequences for the model he elaborates. The first is its inability to account for narrativity as constitutive of identity, future projects, and ultimately a feature of all social action—whether irrational or not. The reduction of narratives to bite-sized viral strains that infect a population provides little space to consider the coconstitution of narratives and lines of action—reflecting the pragmatist concern with practice as the basis of belief.

Second, Shiller's singular concern with divergences from rational action overlooks the practical, albeit short-term, solutions that speculation on home prices provided for homeowners. In reference to long-term home prices, it was "irrational" to buy homes, invest in costly renovations, and take on risky equity loans. But in the context of stalling wages, consumer desire, and rising inequality, the treatment of homes as investments provided solutions to short-term problems among homeowners. Finally, as a solution to practical problems, the conception of homes as appreciating assets began before the spread of new economy stories that Shiller highlights in the mid-1990s.

Market Situation Misassessment

With Shiller, we argue that in the decades before the collapse of the housing market, a cultural shift occurred whereby homes came to be seen not only as stable repositories of value but rapidly appreciating assets. This made purchasing a home, along with refinancing and assuming equity loans, seem to buyers like an unprecedented situation, one to which old rules did not apply.

Postwar policy interventions in mortgage markets, as well as the spread of suburban development and advertising, generated and distributed a particular set of schemas and orientations toward homeownership, along with associated financial habits. Remaining steady at around 40 percent for the first decades of the twentieth century, the American homeownership rate rose significantly between 1940 and 1960, from 44 to 62 percent.[51] New Deal institutions and regulations underwrote this expansion by encouraging lending. The culmination of federal mortgage insurance programs was the promotion of what became the standard thirty-year mortgage. In contrast to the "balloon mortgages" popular before the 1930s—nonamortized three- to five-year loans with high interest rates and low loan-to-value ratios—the standard mortgage, reaching fruition in the 1940s and 1950s, was amortized, had fixed interest rates, spanned for thirty years, and reached a 95 percent loan-to-value ratio.[52]

These loans proved immensely popular. Aided by federal credit programs and the circulation of media representations, homeownership became part of the repertoire of citizenship and family life across the nation, extending in influence even to those excluded from first-hand experience in mortgage markets. Home buyers in the postwar years associated *stability*, rather than rising wealth, with their purchase. Brian McCabe reports that in polls and studies done at the time, Americans said they did not think of buying principally as a vehicle for investment—and consistent with nearly a century of aggregate price trends, they did not expect their house values to appreciate all that much.[53] In suburban developments like Levittown, McCabe writes, "the promise of owning a single-family home was driven by media representations of suburban life, the social status of homeownership, and the desire for spacious yards and living space."[54] This is not to say, however, that homeowners before the 1980s were inattentive to the value of their homes. But their concerns were over depreciation rather than appreciation of home values.

Evidence for this claim can be found in the well-recorded history of white neighborhood opposition to racial integration. In contests over housing desegregation, white homeowners appealed to the protection of property values from depreciation — this value consciousness was fixated on loss rather than racial integration's effects in hindering property appreciation.[55] Even for the smaller but increasing number of Black families who secured suburban homeownership between 1940 and 1960, homeownership implied a source of security not tied to expectations of rising wealth. As historian Andrew Wiese explains, Black suburban homeowners "viewed home ownership as the basis of economic security through thrift and domestic production . . . [relishing] gardens and fruit trees, and many [insisting] on keeping livestock."[56] This older conception of homeownership not only circulated as narratives of middle-class consumer desire but carried with it a repertoire of practices, spanning from neighborhood resistance to public housing to home renovations aimed at upkeep, not appreciation.

The terms of the standard mortgage contract, with its emphasis on long duration, safeguards against volatility, and low risk, shaped postwar financial habits and norms around borrowing and buying. Although other options were available, most mortgages issued in the postwar years were fixed rate, reflecting borrower preferences; use of home equity credit was unheard of before 1980 and remained unpopular and utilized by only 17 percent of homeowners as late as 1996; and, most reflective of financial habits, the ratio of monthly housing costs to household income for mortgage holders rarely exceeded 30 percent. The latter was crystalized as a popular heuristic for home buying: never spend more than a third of your income on housing.

New mortgage and financial instruments that allowed homeowners to enact expectations of rising home prices began to emerge as solutions to distributional tensions in the late 1960s.[57] Greta Krippner argued that deregulation of interest rates in the 1980s, which had previously kept a lid on speculative lending by depository institutions, was a response to political activism among would-be homeowners who could not access mortgage credit during a mortgage credit crunch in the late 1970s.[58] These same deregulations also promoted liberalization of the postwar standard mortgage contract by encouraging adjustable-rate loans, higher debt-to-loan ratios, and options for second and third mortgages.

A crucial development that propelled asset conceptions of homes was the introduction of home equity loans — a kind of second mortgage. If, before the 1980s, homeowners could expect to make money on their homes only through resale, like chairs and tables, home equity loans provided them the ability to extract (or borrow on) the equity built into homes. Second mortgages were highly stigmatized before the late 1970s and seen as relics of speculative land booms in the 1920s. When used by prospective homeowners, they were meant to compliment a first mortgage in funding the initial purchase of a home, not to extract equity.

This began to change in the late 1970s as neighborhood associations promoted home equity as a solution to the problem of "cash-poor but house-rich" seniors in the context of rising inflation.[59] Between 1970 and 1981, home prices increased at an annual rate of 10.7 percent, versus an 8.1 percent increase in the consumer price index. Homeowners and regulators in the 1970s and 1980s reacted to the inflation in home values with revised expectations of continued growth. "A man's home may be his castle but, in the past five years, it also has become his very own bank," explained one 1981 *New York Times* article; homeownership came to provide "both an investment return exceeding inflation and a way for strapped consumers to borrow billions."[60] Homeowner support for new home equity extraction instruments made actionable conceptions of homes as a rapidly appreciating asset that owners could routinely tap into.

Increasingly, borrowers embraced new nonstandard mortgage products. Home equity extractions accounted for four-fifths of the rise in mortgage debt between 1990 and 2006.[61] In 1994, the market for refinancing led the expansion of subprime borrowing—meaning that not only were new home buyers assuming higher risks, but existing owners embraced new risks by refinancing homes under volatile terms.[62] But why, especially as prices climbed in the 1990s and early 2000s, such that taking out a nonstandard mortgage entailed exposure to major financial risk? The answer is that these risky mortgage instruments provided solutions for practical problems faced by homeowners, fueling a divergence from considerations about the fundamentals of home prices. People now thought of their houses more as assets, as vehicles for financial gain and for navigating new social and economic realities. Different groups of borrowers embraced riskier orientations to home borrowing as solutions to distinct problems.

One set of problems that an asset-based approach to homeownership addressed was the maintenance of social status amid rising inequality and wage stagnation. Neil Fligstein and Adam Goldstein demonstrate that "financial culture among households"—especially the use of home equity lines of credit—was in fact most concentrated among the income quintile just below the wealthiest.[63] In line with economist Robert Frank's notion that increasing inequality leads to conspicuous consumption through "expenditure cascades," Fligstein and Goldstein suggest that a desire to "keep up with the Joneses"—to emulate the consumption practices of those in the social stratum just above, who were pulling away—explains this concentration.[64] This theory also helps to make sense of why groups of borrowers previously excluded from mortgage markets took on subprime loans. Home Mortgage Disclosure Act data suggests that in the years of the bubble, Black and Latino mortgage applicants were twice as likely to be issued subprime loans compared with white applicants with the same credit profiles. Under pressure to sustain the supply of mortgage-backed securities, financial institutions expanded the market for subprime loans after 2004. Yet, consistent with Fligstein and Goldstein's description of equity extractions, the households of color most likely to be offered and take these subprime loans were not the poorest but the middle classes, who could have qualified for standard terms.[65]

Related to the cultural and status projects that drove homeowners to invest in the appreciation of values was the proliferation of house "flipping"—the practice of buying homes, renovating them, and quickly selling them for a higher price. Informed by a slew of home renovation shows, homeowners similarly rethought home improvement as not just about upkeep (redoing electrical work or a roof) but about value-boosting cosmetic renovations, such as high-end kitchens. As Shiller put it, even those not engaged in short-term flipping "imagined that they were engaged in 'long-term flipping' simply by purchasing a primary residence as a long-term investment."[66]

If, for many households, assuming higher risks was tied to projects of social status, markers of upward mobility, and assimilation, for others, investing in rising home values also provided ways to contend with material hardship. Atif Mian and Amir Sufi, in *House of Debt*, advance a theory of "levered losses" to suggest that the crisis was precipitated by a decline in consumer demand concentrated among highly indebted households who pulled back on their consumption of durable and semidurable goods as home values fell.[67] Finding a concentration in borrowing among low-credit households, they suggest that indebtedness was driven by the need to secure basic needs: "Home owners didn't just extract home equity—they spent it."[68] One study using Panel Study of Income Dynamics data found that in the years when subprime refinancing took off (between 1991 and 1994), households experiencing an unemployment shock and with limited liquidity were 25 percent more likely to refinance their mortgages.[69]

As one 1995 article noted of the change, "Just a generation or two ago . . . homeowners who needed a new washer and dryer would save until they had enough money to pay cash. . . . While lenders used to insist that home equity loans be used only to increase the value of the home itself, they now encouraged borrowers to use loans for everything from debt consolidation to college tuition."[70] Data on the uses of extracted equity between 1990 and 2006 suggest that homeowners made use of new equity instruments to address practical problems: one-third of equity extractions were used to repay nonmortgage debt, one-fourth to fund personal consumption expenditures (including education and medical costs), and one-third went toward home improvements, which, during this decade, became oriented toward value-boosting renovations.[71] News stories of price increases certainly affected expectations of rising home prices, but more important was the emergence of financial instruments that allowed homeowners to practice, and become invested in, beliefs of rising home values.

Our approach allows us to interpret homeowner willingness to embrace risky mortgages in the lead-up to the crisis as a disjuncture between practical assessment—of the practical ends enabled by new financial technologies—and the dismissal of assessments based on a longer-term, more perspicacious view of home prices that pointed to an inevitable collapse in prices. The pursuit of practical ends within the asset-based view of homeownership had clear implications for the willingness of borrowers to enter into nonstandard mortgage contracts. It seemed to many Americans in the heady days of the housing boom that they were living in entirely new economic times, which called for experimentation with all sorts of new financial arrangements and practices. Taking on considerable risk was worth it so as not to be left behind.

But in one fundamental respect not noticed by borrowers, the mortgage system had not changed: homes had not, in fact, been transformed into assets with the capacity to appreciate indefinitely. Even while packaged into homogenous and abstract mortgage-backed securities, enabled by an institutional and technological transformation of mortgage markets, the fundamentals of homes (as particular, material, and geographic goods) and mortgages (as resting on the creditworthiness and stable incomes of borrowers) remained the same. In effect, homeowners as well as investors misinterpreted the new institutional setup around mortgages as a transformation of the asset status of the homes—from singular, material, and a long-term and slow investment to aggregated, immaterial, and reliably liquid assets.

Providing a good example of how problem situation misassessment can be linked to exploitation, real estate agents and lenders pushed the same view of things, promising a market run that would go on forever, downplaying the risks of nonstandard mortgages, encouraging borrowers to pull equity from their properties, and, in many cases, disguising actual loan terms—a job made easier by the fact that financial literacy was lowest in segments of the population where some of the riskiest loans were concentrated[72] If borrowers had seen the market situational continuities underlying all the change—not just the fact that all bubbles burst but that (a) the key determinant of their own market situation, for those outside the most privileged classes, remained their job-related income; and (b) houses are unlike other kinds of assets with which one may speculate, because of how disruptive to one's life their loss is—they might have availed themselves of habits forged under the previous homeownership regime. They could have waited to buy until prices moderated and their credit and income permitted them to take out standard, fixed-rate loans, or opted to look in other markets.

By 2004, the average ratio of housing payment to income had come to exceed the historical norm, rising to an impossible-to-sustain 45 percent nationwide, with even higher ratios in expensive markets. Ultimately, this was a collective, not an individual, failure. The more prudent set of financial habits was waiting in the nation's repertoire, ready to be transmitted to the next generation of buyers. But there were no institutions in place to do the transmitting and money to be made in fostering risk.

Beyond the role of exploitation in encouraging problem situation misassessment, here we also see the effects of rapid social change (deregulation of mortgage markets had been ongoing for some time, but the price bubble and intense marketing of nonstandard loans developed quickly); ambiguity due to inherent situational complexity (wage stagnation and nonstandard loan terms were difficult to grasp); experience (some subprime buyers, as we have noted, lacked intergenerational experience with mortgage lending); and lack of network diversity (subprime loans were concentrated in neighborhoods with high levels of racial segregation, which speaks to both targeting and network composition).[73] Carmen Reinhart and Ken-neth Rogoff have argued that a general feature of financial crises is that investors persuade themselves, or are persuaded by others, that "this time is different"—that a bubble will never burst.[74] By highlighting effects of the sort we have been describ-ing, problem situation misassessment permits a more precise sociological character-ization of this phenomenon.

The Regulatory Side

Yet problem situation misassessment was at play in the financial crisis in its other form as well—in misperceptions of a novel situation as familiar. This was the case on the regulatory side of the equation, where regulators overlooked and downplayed the novel threat posed by an overheated housing market that propped up mort-gage-backed securities. In a recent paper, Fligstein, Jonah Brundage, and Michael Schultz point to regulators, professionalized with a macroeconomic "frame" of interpretation, who were susceptible to "positive asymmetry, or a tendency to see the best cases clearly and the worst cases only vaguely."[75] Analyzing transcripts from the Open Market Committee of the Federal Reserve, the central financial regulator and source of monetary policy, the authors find fateful justifications for the unprec-edented rise in home values. "It seems to me as if there are a lot of plausible stories one can tell about fundamentals that would explain or rationalize housing prices," reassured Richmond Reserve Bank President Jeffrey Lacker in a 2005 FOMC meet-ing on the housing market.[76] Fligstein et al. deploy tools from cognitive sociology to argue that training in macroeconomic theory and a frame of analysis that con-ceived of finance as a secondary system, with relative autonomy from the business cycle measured best through inflation, unemployment, interest rates, and growth, kept regulators from recognizing not just that the housing market was overvalued but that a correction would result in mass defaults, given the complex linkages of the system. While home buyers failed to perceive that their basic market situation had not changed completely, regulators failed to recognize how much the financial infrastructure around mortgages *had* changed, requiring new techniques of moni-toring and intervention.

Our view that problem situation misassessment often results in the downplaying of risk is particularly salient in the regulatory case, which Fligstein, Brundage, and Schultz interpret as a function of formal organization: "the structure and culture of most organizations lead actors to either downplay negative information or rein-terpret it in a positive light," they explain.[77] The growth of what the authors char-acterize as the "neo classical synthesis of macroeconomics" as the primary (and, we may say, dogmatic) frame for interpreting market trends emerged in a period when the institutional identity of the Federal Reserve, as shielded from politics, became the object of a legitimacy crisis. As Krippner argues, distributional ten-sions over the allocation of capital since the 1970s pushed the Federal Reserve to move from the practice of directly targeting interest rates (and thus the supply of credit) to "following rather than leading the market."[78] So much was this concern with appearing to overstep regulatory discretion ingrained by the time of the financial crisis that even as seven of fifteen members of the FOMC were swayed by evidence of a housing bubble, all eighteen decided that the appropriate response in June 2005 was to "wait and see."[79] At the same time, regulators ran up against the complexity and ambiguity of the financial system and did not yet have the social technology in place to fully understand the risk posed by mortgage-backed securities.

CONCLUSION

In this chapter we laid out a theory of problem situation misassessment, focused not principally on misperceptions of the intentions of interaction partners but on the adequacy of actors' judgments as to the familiarity or novelty of a situation. Synthesizing the insights of a variety of pragmatist and pragmatist-related scholars, we described what problem situation misassessment entails for individual as well as collective actors and identified factors associated with misassessment at multiple levels of analysis.

If we are correct that problem situation misassessment is related to but distinct from established sociological concepts and processes such as definitions of the situation or frames or hysteresis, then our discussion should be seen as opening new areas of investigation for pragmatist sociology. It now becomes possible to consider how actors' situational responses are a function not only of the availability of habit and the potential for creativity but also of the conditions under which they come to detect or misdetect social familiarity or its absence. Our empirical illustration was the 2007–8 financial crisis, but it seems to us that problem situation misassessment is also evident in such phenomena as police violence, the rise of (and reaction to) authoritarian populism, ethno-racial conflict, labor market mismatch, the population ecology of organizations, the slowness of adaptation to climate change, the global response to the COVID-19 pandemic, and much more. Systematic empirical research will be necessary to bear out this supposition.

Application of the misassessment approach across a range of cases could also provide a test of some of the more general propositions contained in our theory, as well as an opportunity for further theoretical development and refinement. Present in germinal form in the earliest versions of pragmatist action theory, and beginning to take root in the work of Hans Joas, problem situation misassessment is an idea whose time has come.

NOTES

1. Hans Joas, *Pragmatism and Social Theory* (Chicago: University of Chicago Press, 1993); Joas, *The Creativity of Action* (Chicago: University of Chicago Press, 1996).

2. Tiantian Yang and Howard E. Aldrich, "Who's the Boss? Explaining Gender Inequality in Entrepreneurial Teams," *American Sociological Review* 79, no. 2 (2014): 303–27; Robert Jansen, *Revolutionizing Repertoires: The Rise of Populist Mobilization in Peru* (Chicago: University of Chicago Press, 2017); and Mustafa Emirbayer and Matthew Desmond, *The Racial Order* (Chicago: University of Chicago Press, 2015).

3. Joas, *The Creativity of Action*.

4. Josh Whitford, "Pragmatism and the Untenable Dualism of Means and Ends: Why Rational Choice Theory Does Not Deserve Paradigmatic Privilege," *Theory and Society* 31, no. 3 (2002): 325–63.

5. Joas, *The Creativity of Action*, 160.

6. Anthony Giddens, *The Constitution of Society: Introduction of the Theory of Structuration* (Berkeley: University of California Press, 1984).

7. Shmuel Eisenstadt, *Comparative Civilizations and Multiple Modernities*, 2 vols. (Leiden: Brill, 2003), 1.

8. Hans Joas, *War and Modernity* (Oxford: Blackwell, 2003).

9. John Dewey, *How We Think* (Boston: D. C. Heath, 1910).

10. Dewey, *How We Think*, 104.

11. Dewey, *How We Think*, 105–6.

12. Dewey, *How We Think*, 120; emphasis in original.

13. John Dewey, *Human Nature and Conduct* (New York: Holt, 1922).

14. William Isaac Thomas and Florian Znaniecki, *The Polish Peasant in Europe and America*, vol. 3 (Boston: Badger, 1919), 26–30.

15. Erving Goffman, *Strategic Interaction* (New York: Ballantine, 1972); Barney G. Glaser and Anselm L. Strauss, "Awareness Contexts and Social Interaction," *American Sociological Review* 29, no. 5 (1965): 669–79.

16. C. Wright Mills, "Situated Actions and Vocabularies of Motive," *American Sociological Review* 5, no. 6 (1940): 904–13.

17. Erving Goffman, *Frame Analysis: An Essay on the Organization of Experience* (Cambridge, MA: Harvard University Press, 1974), 8.

18. Goffman, *Frame Analysis*, 10.

19. Goffman, *Frame Analysis*, 21.

20. Goffman, *Frame Analysis*, 301–44.

21. Alfred Schutz and Thomas Luckmann, *The Structures of the Life-World*, vol. 1, Studies in Phenomenology and Existential Philosophy, trans. Richard M. Zaner and H. Tristram Engelhardt, Jr. (Evanston, IL: Northwestern University Press, 1973), 116.

22. Peter Berger and Thomas Luckmann, *The Social Construction of Reality* (Garden City, NY: Doubleday, 1966), 29.

23. Alfred Schutz, *Collected Papers II: Studies in Social Theory* (The Hague: Martinus Nijhoff, 1964), 96.

24. On pragmatic realism, see Hilary Putnam, *Realism with a Human Face* (Cambridge, MA: Harvard University Press, 1992).

25. Christopher Winship, "Inchoate Situations in Extra-Rational Behavior," in *Rationality in the Social Sciences*, ed. Helmut Staubmann and Victor Lidz (New York: Springer, 2017), 223–43.

26. Ivan Ermakoff, "On the Frontiers of Rational Choice," in *Social Theory Now*, ed. Claudio Benzecry, Monika Krause, and Isaac Reed (Chicago: University of Chicago Press, 2017), 179.

27. Richard Whitley, *The Intellectual and Social Organization of the Sciences* (London: Oxford University Press, 1984).

28. David Stark, *The Sense of Dissonance: Accounts of Worth in Economic Life* (Princeton, NJ: Princeton University Press, 2009).

29. Daniel Kahneman, *Thinking, Fast and Slow* (New York: Farrar, Straus and Giroux, 2011).

30. Kahneman, *Thinking, Fast and Slow*, 81.

31. Kahneman, *Thinking, Fast and Slow*, 24.

32. Kahneman, *Thinking, Fast and Slow*, 120.

33. Kahneman, *Thinking, Fast and Slow*, 24.

34. Kahneman, *Thinking, Fast and Slow*, 60–61.

35. Michael Strand and Omar Lizardo, "The Hysteresis Effect: Theorizing Mismatch in Action," *Journal for the Theory of Social Behavior* 47, no. 2 (2017): 1.

36. Strand and Lizardo, "The Hysteresis Effect," 4.

37. Strand and Lizardo, "The Hysteresis Effect," 7.

38. Strand and Lizardo, "The Hysteresis Effect," 6.

39. Strand and Lizardo, "The Hysteresis Effect," 23.

40. Emirbayer and Desmond, *The Racial Order*.

41. Robert Shiller, *Narrative Economics: How Stories Go Viral and Drive Major Economic Events* (Princeton, NJ: Princeton University Press, 2020), 26.

42. Robert Shiller, "Understanding Recent Trends in Housing Prices and Homeownership," in *Housing, Housing Finance, and Monetary Policy: A Symposium Sponsored by the Federal Reserve Bank of Kansas City, Jackson Hole, Wyoming, August 20–September 1, 2007* (Kansas City, MO: Federal Reserve Bank of Kansas City, 2007), 90–93.

43. Shiller, "Understanding Recent Trends," 97.

44. Robert Shiller, *Irrational Exuberance* (Princeton, NJ: Princeton University Press, 2016), 108–9.

45. Shiller, "Understanding Recent Trends," 95.

46. Shiller, *Narrative Economics*.

47. Shiller, "Understanding Recent Trends," 94.

48. Shiller, *Narrative Economics*, 21.

49. Shiller, *Narrative Economics*, 21.

50. Shiller, *Irrational Exuberance*, 39–100; Shiller, *Narrative Economics*, 18–30.

51. Daniel K. Fetter, "The Twentieth-Century Increase in U.S. Homeownership: Facts and Hypotheses," in *Housing and Mortgage Markets in Historical Perspective*, ed. Eugene N. White, Kenneth Snowden, and Price Fishback (Chicago: University of Chicago Press, 2014), 329–50.

52. Jonathan Levy, *Freaks of Fortune: The Emerging World of Capitalism and Risk in America* (Cambridge, MA: Harvard University Press, 2012); Richard K. Green and Susan M. Watcher, "The American Mortgage in Historical and International Context," *Journal of Economic Perspectives* 19, no. 4 (2005): 93–114.

53. Brian J. McCabe, *No Place Like Home: Wealth Community, and the Politics of Homeownership* (Oxford: Oxford University Press, 2016).

54. McCabe, *No Place Like Home*, 62.

55. Lizabeth Cohen, *A Consumers' Republic: The Politics of Mass Consumption in Postwar America* (New York: Vintage, 2003), 194; Thomas J. Sugrue, *The Origins of Urban Crisis: Race and Inequality in Postwar Detroit* (Princeton, NJ: Princeton University Press, 1996), 231.

56. Andrew Wiese, *Places of Their Own: African American Suburbanization in the Twentieth Century* (Chicago: University of Chicago Press, 2004), 145–47.

57. Wolfgang Streeck, *Buying Time: The Delayed Crisis of Democratic Capitalism* (New York: Verso, 2014).

58. Greta Krippner, *Capitalizing on Crisis: The Political Origins of the Rise of Finance* (Cambridge, MA: Harvard University Press, 2011).

59. Ken Scholen and Yung-Ping Chen, *Unlocking Home Equity for the Elderly* (Cambridge, MA: Ballinger, 1980).

60. Diana Shaman, "Equity Conversion Plans Grow," *New York Times*, October 18, 1981.

61. Alan Greenspan and James Kennedy, "Sources and Uses of Equity Extracted from Homes," *Oxford Review of Economic Policy* 24, no. 1 (2008): 122

62. John C. Weicher, *The Home Equity Lending Industry: Refinancing Mortgages for Borrowers with Impaired Credit* (Indianapolis: Hudson Institute, 1997).

63. Neil Fligstein and Adam Goldstein, "The Emergence of a Financial Culture in American Households, 1989–2007," *Socio-Economic Review* 13, no. 3 (2015): 575–601.

64. Robert Frank, "Does Inequality Matter? How 'Expenditure Cascades' Are Squeezing the American Middle Class," *Slate*, December 5, 2011; Fligstein and Goldstein, "Emergence of a Financial Culture."

65. Jacob W. Faber, "Racial Dynamics of Subprime Mortgage Lending at the Peak," *Housing Policy Debate* 23, no. 2 (2013): 328–49.

66. Shiller, *Narrative Economics*, 224.

67. Atif R. Mian and Amir Sufi, *House of Debt: How They (and You) Caused the Great Recession and How We Can Prevent It from Happening Again* (Chicago: University of Chicago Press, 2014).

68. Mian and Sufi, *House of Debt*, 88.

69. Erik Hurst and Frank Stafford, "Home Is Where the Equity Is: Mortgage Refinancing and Household Consumption," *Journal of Money, Credit and Banking* 36, no. 6 (2004): 985–1014.

70. "Home Equity Loans," *New York Times*, October 15, 1995.

71. Greenspan and Kennedy, "Sources and Uses of Equity."

72. Kristopher Gerardi, Lorenz Goette, and Stephan Meier, "Numerical Ability Predicts Mortgage Default," *Proceedings of the National Academy of Sciences* 110, no. 28 (2013): 11267–271.

73. Derek Hyra, Gregory Squires, Robert Renner, and David Kirk, "Metropolitan Segregation and the Subprime Lending Crisis," *Housing Policy Debate* 23, no. 1 (2012): 177–98.

74. Carmen Reinhart and Kenneth Rogoff, *This Time Is Different: Eight Centuries of Financial Folly* (Princeton, NJ: Princeton University Press, 2009).

75. Neil Fligstein, Jonah Brundage, and Michael Schultz, "Seeing Like the Fed: Culture, Cognition, and Framing in the Failure to Anticipate the Financial Crisis of 2008," *American Sociological Review* 82, no. 5 (2017): 886.

76. Quoted in Fligstein et al, "Seeing Like the Fed," 899.

77. Fligstein et al., "Seeing Like the Fed," 899.

78. Greta Krippner, "The Making of U.S. Monetary Policy: Central Bank Transparency and the Neoliberal Dilemma," *Theory and Society* 36, no. 6 (2007): 504.

79. Fligstein et al., "Seeing Like the Fed," 898.

5. Pragmatism, Aesthetics, and Sociology

DANIEL SILVER

John Dewey believed that the "theory of aesthetics put forward by a philosopher . . . is a test of the capacity of the system he puts forth to grasp the nature of experience itself. There is no test that so surely reveals the one-sidedness of a philosophy as its treatment of art and aesthetic perception" (Dewey 2005, 274). Given that Dewey's own philosophy is a concerted effort to grasp the nature of experience itself, his theory of art and aesthetics must be considered a crucial test of his philosophy as a whole. Indeed, he held that art is "the greatest intellectual achievement in the history of mankind," the practice in which "hard and fast dualisms" are dissolved, and even "the culmination of nature" (Alexander 1987, 1).

These are, on their face, strange claims that defy straightforward interpretation. Yet interpret them we must if we want to learn how Dewey's philosophy could enrich sociology. However, the recent revival of pragmatism within American sociology has largely ignored Dewey's aesthetic theory. For example, while Hans Joas's *The Creativity of Action* (1996) explicitly notes the importance of *Art as Experience*, highly cited American sociological appropriations (e.g., Gross 2009; and Whitford 2002) do not mention *Art as Experience* or the discussion of aesthetics in *Experience and Nature*. Nor do other recent contributions, including those by highly sensitive readers of Dewey (e.g., Emirbayer and Schneiderhan 2013; Emirbayer and Maynard 2011). Even within the sociology of culture, Dewey's aesthetic theory is sidelined: in its nearly five hundred pages, *The Routledge International Handbook of the Sociology of Art and Culture* includes one sentence about Dewey; among the seven hundred pages of the *Handbook of Cultural Sociology* (2010) is one sentence about Dewey's aesthetics.

Habit, inference, situation, problem, solution, communication, creativity, intelligence, democracy, deliberation—these are the central terms of Deweyan philosophy that American sociologists have tended to elaborate. Yet for Dewey himself, these are intelligible only as moments in a process through which experience—social experience included—grows from discord and division toward moments of consummation. Attention to creative problem-solving and flexible, intelligent action—the common refrain of contemporary pragmatist sociology—is pointless unless we have some sense of what solving a problem is for. For Dewey, the answer was clear: it is for the completed, satisfying, consummatory experience he designated as "aesthetic." The aim of this chapter is to take Dewey at his word and ask what it would mean to place a pragmatist notion of art and aesthetics at the very center of a sociological formulation of his ideas.

What this would mean is far from obvious, however, and the main goal of the chapter is modest: to make a seemingly outlandish proposition at least plausible. My central argument is that according to Dewey's theory of art, sociological research is itself a kind of art. It involves the production of objects that are capable of not only faithfully retrieving the organization of our subjects' varied experiences but also being subject to criticism and experimentation that may extend and deepen that experience, both ours and theirs. It is (or should be) a platform for developing a social experience into *a* social *experience*.

I will proceed in three steps. First, I briefly elaborate two sociological efforts to take seriously Dewey's aesthetics, one by Cesar Graña and the other by John Levi Martin, highlighting the fact that appreciating the significance of Dewey's aesthetics means going beyond its narrow application to the sociology of culture. Second, I develop an original interpretation of the sociological significance of Dewey's aesthetics through a critical engagement with Martin's "social aesthetics." I contrast Dewey's conception of aesthetic experience with Martin's variant, which derives from field theory, highlighting three crucial differences in how they conceptualize aesthetics (and thus experience): the centrality of judgment, the significance of sociality, and the relation between aesthetics and art. All these differences arise from a fundamental disagreement about the developmental character of experience—in Dewey's terms, the trajectory from experience to *an* experience to artistic expression and aesthetic critique of experience, and around again. Third and finally, I articulate what sociological investigation in a Deweyan mode is like through an interpretation of the Chicago School's maps. I show how such diagrams can provide means for researchers to participate in an ongoing critical heightening of (in this case) urban experience.

I. DEWEY'S AESTHETICS IN SOCIOLOGICAL PERSPECTIVE: BEYOND THE SOCIOLOGY OF CULTURE

Although in general American sociology has largely ignored Dewey's aesthetics, there are some notable exceptions against which a contemporary interpretation can find its footing. Graña's 1962 "John Dewey's Social Art and the Sociology of Art" came in the early days of the sociology of culture as a separate subfield in American sociology. It offers a telling example of challenges in appropriating Dewey's thought in the field's formative period.

Graña found much to admire in Dewey's *Art as Experience*. For him, it confronts us with the challenge of why the notably "instrumentalist" pragmatist philosopher of the "common man" would spend so much time with the seemingly rarefied practice of art. To Graña, the book articulated Dewey's ideas about the creative interaction of the "live creature" with the world, highlighting that this interaction is full of stress and strain and that it is the work of art to move it toward moments of satisfaction, not only in museums and concert halls but in efforts to round out and fulfill the potential in, for instance, baseball or cutlery. Crucially, it held that for human beings, the "world" in question is primarily the social world, so that art is a "manifestation of [the] collective spirit."

Despite Graña's appreciation of Dewey's philosophical accomplishment, the major thrust of his article cautions sociologists against taking up Dewey's aesthetics. "It is one thing to speak of Dewey as the philosopher of the workaday world — or perhaps as the American aesthetician of democratic productivity and its inner life — and another to evaluate his work as a method for the analysis of art" (Graña 1962, 407). Graña criticizes Dewey for falling into a Romantic-Hegelian conception of culture, whereby great artists or works embody the collective spirit. Additionally, Graña admonishes Dewey for his "psychological populism." Graña does not quite accuse Dewey of advocating "kitsch sentimentalism," but he does indicate that valorizing "normal processes of living" offers no defense against the specter of "calendar scenes as aesthetic models" (1962, 411). And without such a defense, the "autonomy of art" against its surrounding social currents is at risk, which autonomy is, for Graña, one of its most critical social functions.

Graña's criticisms align with early interpreters of Dewey's aesthetics. When not utterly baffled, readers often saw *Art as Experience* as a relapse into Hegelism (Alexander 1987). Decades of careful hermeneutic scholarship have largely dispelled this view, especially through the work of Richard Shusterman, Richard Bernstein, and Thomas Alexander, among others. Perhaps the most sweeping result of this work involves the proposition that Dewey's philosophy of art and aesthetics is not actually about art and aesthetics, at least in the narrow sense of paintings on walls and professional critical discourse. *Art as Experience* is, rather, a realization of Dewey's entire philosophy of experience. From this vantage point, Graña makes a category error in taking the sociological significance of Dewey's aesthetics to consist in providing a sociological "method for the analysis of art." If it is to have the sort of sociological import commensurate with the generality Dewey ascribed to it, it must be as part of a general experientialist sociology, not a special sociology of culture or art.[1]

This broader aspiration is a characteristic achievement of Martin's "general cultural sociology." Aesthetic judgment is the keynote in this effort, which starts from the irreducibly qualitative character of experience. We do not first perceive the world as a blank neutral field, then make a judgment about it, and then act on it. "[J]udgment is not an analytically separable moment intervening between perception and action" (Martin 2011, 203). The world—including other people—appears to us as a field of motivating qualities: scary, intriguing, tacky. These judgments are already "in" the perception, which itself already indicates a line of action: run away from, talk with, look down on, smile at. Such "aesthetic" qualities thus lay out "vectors" that orient social actors in various ways to and from one another. These vectors can be mapped through a "cultural cartography," which codifies social life as an interconnected "field" of judgments-qualities. At the same time, shared response to a quality is itself characteristic of a common experience that lies at the basis of social groupings and, thus, social order.

Dewey is a central figure in this ambitious program. For Martin, Dewey is a moment in an intellectual narrative charting the promise and pitfalls of taking the aesthetic character of perception seriously, running from Kant's *Critique of Judgment* to the Gestalt theorists, Russian activity theorists, Deweyean pragmatism, and Bourdieusian field theory. In this narrative, Dewey illustrates how to transcend the Gestalt theorists' assumption that the perception of quality is passive and speaks for itself. This assumption is inadequate, since our perceptions of what a quality asks us to do can change and differ depending on our experiences. Dewey, by contrast, saw the perception of quality as an active process that "retain[ed] the phenomenological givenness of qualities" (Martin 2011, 195). In particular, Martin highlights how Dewey linked perception to a process of inquiry, in which mind and world coevolve as we seek to probe and revise experience in the light of new information.

But Dewey also comes up short for Martin, which in turn motivates Martin's turn to field theory. Field theory explicitly comprehends and thematizes the "many-sidedness" of a quality: that what is ugly for me can be pretty for you, and these divergent aesthetic responses in turn index our divergent social positions and corresponding relations, as well as corresponding dispositions to respond to one another in different ways. For Martin, Dewey lacks a coherent way to deal with this many-sidedness, which, by contrast, is the central motif of field theory.

II. SOME IMPLICATIONS OF THE DEVELOPMENTAL CHARACTER OF AESTHETIC EXPERIENCE

For Martin the path from Dewey to field theory leads from aesthetics in the narrow sense to an appreciation of the more general role of aesthetic judgment in the constitution of social order as such. This section argues that something important is lost on the way and that this becomes evident when contrasting key features of Dewey's aesthetics to Martin's field-theoretical version of social aesthetics.[2] The central difference lies in the basic conception of the qualitative character of experience— that is, its aesthetic dimension: for Dewey there is an inherently developmental character to the aesthetic perception of qualities, whereby the perception of quality may continuously build up from the inarticulate impression of a set of potentialities through interaction, interpretation, tension, and struggle to a felt perception of articulated wholeness. This developmental, growing character of experience is largely absent in field theory, which maps the perception of qualities to positions, relations, and dispositions.[3] I pursue this distinction across three areas: the centrality of judgment, the nature of sociality, and the relation between art and aesthetics.

The centrality of judgment. I start with a simple textual point: judgment is central to Martin's field-theoretic account of the social aesthetics of perception, but it is peripheral to Dewey's. The focus on judgment traces back to Kant's *Critique of Judgment,* in which Kant took the judgment "this is beautiful" as an entry point into a notoriously complex tangle of issues. Kant noticed that this sort of judgment cannot be understood as the application of a rule to a case, since there is no universally shared standard of taste. And yet he also was struck by the fact that we grant a general significance to aesthetic judgments in a way that we do not for sensuous judgments like "chocolate tastes good." We are put off when people do not agree with our aesthetic judgments but do not blame somebody for disliking chocolate, even if we might find it a bit unusual.

In a subtle interpretation of the basis of some of Bourdieu's insights, Martin rejects Kant's ensuing arguments that aesthetic judgment depends on postulated membership in a universal "community of sensibility." "We reverse Kant's 'we see that it is beautiful' to form the sociological 'who sees this as beautiful, let him join with me'" (Martin 2011, 203). Crucially for sociology, aesthetic judgment involves a prior openness and orientation to those who do, and opposition to those who do not, respond to the world as I do. Aesthetic perception is social perception is social aesthetics. This becomes explicit in "2nd order judgments," where we judge judgments, such as "that is just what somebody who likes garden gnomes would say"; "that is just what somebody who thinks garden gnomes are kitsch would say"; "that is just what somebody who looks down on people who like garden gnomes would say." Such valenced judgments issue in vectors that orient actors to and away from one another (Martin and Merriman 2015, 140–41). Thus the perception of qualities (e.g., in the garden gnome) reveals a set of social relations that are not neutral but directed (i.e., aesthetically charged), which in turn reveal the basic contours of social space. Accordingly, while rejecting Kant's particular theory of judgment, Martin retains his "judgmentalist" orientation, which discovers the order that is already contained in actors' mundane perceptual judgments of qualities—in social aesthetics.

Dewey, by contrast, makes judgment one part—albeit an important one—of his broader theory of "qualitative thought." This peripheral character of judgment is part and parcel with his deep-rooted skepticism toward Kantian aesthetics, including its very starting point from judgments of beauty (Shusterman 2000, chap. 1; Fesmire 1999, 534). For Dewey, by contrast, judging is relevant to experience in the ways it contributes to—or stymies—a build-up toward its climax in an experience of the pervasive qualities that permeate a situation (Frega 2010). Perception for Dewey does not begin in so articulate a form as "that is what a garden gnome lover would say." Experience begins with an "Oh!", a "first total unanalyzed qualitative impression" (Dewey 2005, 311). "Oh!" can embody a qualitative impression that there is something amiss in this person's lawn or this other person's reaction to the lawn, though exactly what and how is open. There is some feel to the room, the street, the meeting, in the light of which it fits together somehow (ominous, festive, sorrowful . . .), and we feel the situation moving forward in some direction where there is a fitting next step, even if we often don't take it. As the action unfolds, and we probe the situation, our perception of its quality can become more sensitive; lines of possible action move from the background to the foreground.

This processual character of aesthetic experience is central to Dewey's notion of judgment. Judgment then "supervenes" (Dewey 2005; 311) as a (social) activity building on this impression, helping to articulate its potential through processes of discrimination and unification—judgment as a living process of judging (Frega 2010a, 595–96). If this process is successful (and often it is not), this is in the service of heightened perception.[4] Participants perceive the gnome more richly, in all of its possibilities, as they work through the diverse potentials for animosity and alignment that it holds (not only intellectually but practically by, for example, probing how family members react to different statements or looks with respect to the gnome at a gathering, standing closer or farther from it and listening to songs or watching movies that expand on the significance of garden gnomes). As the experience builds, the garden gnome and all of our relations to one another embodied in it become powerfully evident, permeating the experience entirely. The mood deepens. We experience with a particularly radiant intensity the alliances and opposition it organizes. This "marks a change by which . . . events . . . connected by relations of push and pull . . . realize characters, meanings, and relations not hitherto possessed by them" (Dewey 1925, 459).

This is what Dewey might call *an* experience of a garden gnome, in which the valenced perception of the initial "oh" is developed into meaningful experience that we not only respond to but learn from. It is present as an organized set of social relations in which we ourselves are participants, for better or ill. "Oh" has grown to "good," a rounded-out articulation of the situation as suffused with (tension-riddled) meaning. But it is neither the "oh" nor the "good" but the movement from one to the other that characterizes the full aesthetic experience. Otherwise judging would be an empty exercise in classification and positioning.

Dewey contrasts this sort of open, developmental process of critical elaboration through discrimination and synthesis to a more common notion of judgment as a "verdict," which instead seeks to lay down the final word. Such verdicts tend to interrupt the build-up of a situation to its climax by predetermining its direction (Anderson 2014). Instead, for Dewey, judgments are by their nature provisional. Childress (2017), in a rare move within Bourdieusian-inspired sociology of culture, empirically demonstrates this provisional and developmental character of judgment in his analysis of book club meetings. He shows that participants tended to revise their judgment through interactions, and that the book club itself is consti-tuted as a venue that permits such developmental build-up toward a shared percep-tion of the book. The valences in the situation point us not only toward one another but toward their own growing self-revelation as such.

The nature of sociality. These different conceptions of judgment's centrality lead to alternative ideas about the nature of sociality. In Martin's field-theoretic concep-tion, social order is a field of mutual judgments, which orient us to and away from one another. The model for this notion of sociality is "Judgment 2.0"—not the kind of top-down order produced by authorities and influential institutions determining evaluative standards (as in, say, college ranking regimes) but a more emergent pro-cess of the form that occurs in online venues (Martin and Merriman 2015). In such settings, we do not just find product and restaurant reviews and learn about what "people like you" might like. We also rate the raters and in so doing position our-selves and them as a certain type of person with certain types of tastes. Such sites have the added advantage for the sociologist of providing massive amounts of fine-grained data recording how peoples' tastes—their judgments and their judgments of judgments—clump into distinct groupings. They allow us to map an emergent order revealed in actors' own perceptions and experiences.

As Martin and Merriman (2015) acknowledge, the theoretically relevant question is not how prevalent or important this sort of activity is but, rather, how well it works as a theoretical model for the organization of social life. The pragmatist answers this question by putting it to the pragmatic test: what would the world be like if it were organized on the principles of "Judgment 2.0?" I think that for Dewey it would be a nightmare, but an instructive one that reveals both the limits of a "judgment-cen-tric" conception of social life.

To see why it would be a nightmare, imagine a world in which Amazon or Yelp ratings were not restricted to online shopping but informed all our interactions. This in fact is the theme of an episode of the science fiction series *Black Mirror*. In "Nosedive," people routinely use their smart phones to scan one another on beginning and ending any personal interaction. After the interaction, they rate one another on a five-point scale; before the interaction they learn the other's rating. The ratings of higher-rated raters count for more; a good rating from a low-rated person can have negative value. Let us call this "Judgment 3.0: things get real."

The pathos of the episode comes from the fact that this is not a very far-fetched scenario. It builds as we follow the main character, Lacie Pound, descending into madness as she obsessively tries to increase her rating by conforming to the sorts of judgments she expects others to judge her by and judging others by those same standards. Strong order definitely emerges, and without any central coordination: there are neighborhoods and jobs reserved only for "4.5s"; low-rated people are passed over for organ transplants and shunned by their higher-rated siblings. Judg-ment 3.0 produces spontaneous order, but it is a crushing order, in which any form of fulfilling social experience is replaced by performances designed to elicit approv-ing judgments, and judgments of judgments. Effort to escape this order proves futile; it is immediately assimilated into a set of judgments about what a person who seeks to escape judgment would do. There is No Exit. As Lacie spirals toward a zero rating, the only relief she finds is in a prison cell, where she can speak freely to others whose ratings have also reached bottom. They revel in the freedom to insult one another.

"Nosedive" invites questions about what is missing in a world where social relations are defined on the model of Judgment 2.0. Dewey helps to articulate what is going wrong and to elaborate a different notion of the role of aesthetics in social life. Consider three issues: (1) the ability to suspend judgment, (2) communication as mutual exposure and vulnerability, and (3) the immanence of ideal possibilities.

First, "Nosedive" highlights how impoverished social life would be without the capacity to suspend judgment.[5] Experience begins without well-formed judgment and builds as judgments become more articulated into and formative of interaction. But they can also become self-validating loops in which every action confirms and hardens them. Now judgment becomes debilitating, and the growth of social life can continue only by opening oneself to perceiving others in a new way. This requires, for Dewey, a kind of releasement, or a "passive intentionality," in which one lets go of the perceptual habits that have hitherto patterned one's interactions (Joas 2000, 112). The capacity to periodically act beyond and without judgment prevents social life from hardening into camps that are incapable of communicating with one another.

The sociological and democratic significance of this capacity is evident in Winship's chapter in this volume. He shows how a group of Boston ministers were able to open up new possibilities for communication with community members and police through setting aside their judgments and simply wandering through their neighborhoods, remaining open to whatever came their way: "purposeless engagement." In this way—by temporarily suspending judgment but continuing to act—they allowed a situation that had hardened into clearly delineated camps to loosen up and admit new possibilities. "As I heard in interviews with different ministers, they did not know what they were trying to accomplish with their walks. All they knew was that they were called by God to be present." Faith in the possibility of renewed experience enabled a broken situation to begin to knit itself together and to continue to build toward a mutual perception of what the situation could become.

Second is the difference between communication and interaction. From a Deweyan point of view, "Nosedive" embodies a world with the latter but without the former. Communication involves an essential moment of vulnerability and exposure, approach and retreat, discomfort and revelation, which grows through mutual participation toward a (possible) consummation.[6] "For Dewey, conversation or dialogue is the place where we are confronted with the values of others, and, when we truly open ourselves up, where we consider our own values anew. . . . [P]rovided that it grants us this experience, conversation produces a value commitment to the consummation of intercommunication itself" (Joas 2000, 118). On the model of a field-theoretic social aesthetics of judgments, we may gravitate toward those who share our tastes (and experiences) and away from those who do not, and delight in the easy comfort of experiencing ourselves as fitted to one another (whether as allies or opponents). Dewey's philosophy, despite its undercurrents of melioristic optimism, is harder: if the aesthetic character of experience must grow to culmination, it grows only when there is a problem, and without facing the discomfort of encountering others who do not see what I see as beautiful, there can be no (social) problem meriting a satisfying resolution worthy of the name "consummation." We may thus reverse again the Kantian dictum from the field-theoretic "who sees this as beautiful, let him join with me" to the pragmatist-Deweyean injunction: "who does *not* see this as beautiful, let me reach out to them."

Third, the example highlights another implication of the developmental character of Dewey's aesthetics: its inherent ideality. Most experience does not develop into *an* experience. Yet once we experience our world as one that *might* become like the one in "Nosedive," our present experience is transformed. This is why Dewey tends to speak in terms of possibility when he describes aesthetic experience in its fullness.[7] On this basis Dewey's aesthetics acquires its oft-neglected critical potential (but see Shusterman 2015, 446). For Dewey, this shows up most clearly in his critique of the contemporary split between menial work and fulfilling leisure, where the former is deemed mere means to the latter and the latter is deemed the more fulfilling the less it is mixed with the former. Standard "museum theories of art" are the result, where the aesthetic is contained, classified, decontextualized, and reduced to whatever institutional professionals say it is (Shusterman 2000, chap. 2).[8] Dewey's philosophy, by contrast, treats this situation not as a taken-for-granted reality but as a problem to be confronted.

Similarly, we might suggest that ideality in Dewey's philosophy points toward a constructive critical-moral potential for social theory in a highly polarized society in which every judgment reconfirms one's position as the sort of person who eats these vegetables, drives this car, drinks this sort of caffeinated beverage, enjoys this music, votes for this party, and so on. A theory of judgment might properly describe this situation, but it does not provide a way to articulate the (social) aesthetic problem it embodies—namely, the problem of producing a shared experience with those whose experiences are not shared with us yet with whom we must live. And just as "the museum theory of art" is an expression of a society fractured by a debilitating split between work and leisure, so, too, might a field theory of aesthetics be an expression of a society fractured by a debilitating clustering of tastes into circumscribed areas. Deweyan aesthetics is a crucial impetus toward a social theory that is open to imagining alternatives.

Art and aesthetics. How can experience be grown and widened where it is stunted and narrow? This is the work of art, and granting a core place to art in his aesthetics is another crucial difference between Dewey's aesthetics and Martin's field-theoretic version. Martin's aesthetics in fact dismisses art, even for Dewey. For instance, after reiterating that Dewey's insight into the "inherently qualitative" character of first-person experience led him to "highlight the importance of aesthetics," Martin immediately writes that "this sense of aesthetics has nothing to do with . . . art" (Martin 2011, 196). This is a evidently an odd claim about the author of *Art as Experience*, for whom art was the fulfillment of experience as such! And so Martin grudgingly acknowledges in a footnote that Dewey "argued against a complete separation of art and aesthetic" by highlighting how the artist creates objects that are designed to "effect a certain qualitative experience in the perceiver" and therefore must anticipate the audience, even when alone. This is true enough, but Dewey did much more than "not separate" art and aesthetics: he sought to thoroughly fuse them, so much so that he lamented the necessity of using the two words separately, experimenting with alternatives such as his awkward "consummation."

The difference reveals another crucial divergence between Deweyean pragmatism and (aesthetic) field theory. From Dewey's point of view, an aesthetics without art is hardly worth the name; such an aesthetics merely confirms and retrieves experience as we happen to find it currently funded. Yet building up a fund requires sustained investment. And for Dewey it is through art that we gain *greater control* over the qualities of our experiences and (experimentally) learn how to *share them more widely*. This is another implication of the proposition that aesthetic character of experience involves its capacity to grow: without art it would be fleeting and truncated.

Consider first the aspect of control. If a consummated aesthetic experience is not a given, reliable fact but a glimmering possibility, that means it often fades as soon as it occurs. Often—indeed, most of the time—experience is arrested. Somebody fumbles, misses a beat, has to take off just at the wrong time. We can work together to keep the story going and the mood alive; Erving Goffman was a master at discerning all the subtle ways we do that in the course of everyday life. But in the flow of social practice, turning our experiences to *a* social experience is mostly serendipitous. It is the glance that reveals the depths of racism in everyday encounters, the meal that discloses all that food and shared meals can be.

Art represents an effort to control those processes by forming experiences in such a way that makes them more likely to occur again, in new places for different people. This need not be restricted to art as paintings hung on museum walls or plays performed in theaters, let alone to any standard form of art, high or popular. As we will see, diagrams such as the Chicago School's maps may constitute Deweyean art objects. Dewey himself often pointed to the art of communication. He highlighted the potential in the trained-up ability to sustain a conversation as it generates momentum toward a revelatory climax. Even more broadly, "the concept of creativity approximates to that of the self-created meaningfulness of what one does. This is something which is not the preserve of geniuses, but is accessible to all actors" (Joas 1986, 140).[9] This is a key feature of aesthetic experience as a variable achievement that can grow toward consummation, or not: it represents the possibility of experience carrying itself through to completion even when it usually stalls. Art for Dewey is an effort to control the course of experience so as to make this possibility a reality. For Dewey works of arts are not superfluous but essential to the continuing growth of experience.

This capacity to channel and control experience allows an experience to widen beyond the local situation and engage a wider audience. This is the point in Dewey's philosophy whereby the art object becomes more central. Art objects have the remarkable quality of not only representing or pointing to an experience but of "containing it" (Eldridge 2010). In art objects, aesthetic experience becomes mobile: the artist produces an object that others may take up elsewhere and later, often at great distances in time and space. By subjecting experience to a formative medium, it becomes public and shareable. Art for Dewey is a dynamo of experience.

To be sure, there is no guarantee that an audience will share the experience of the creator or, for that matter, have *an* experience at all. But for Dewey, it makes little sense to demand that the sadness expressed in a work of art be the same as the artist's sadness, or the audience's. The important question for him is the degree to which a potential recipient can engage with the object in such a way that embodies the rhythmic build-up through tensions and problems toward a completed experience that for Dewey *is* the aesthetic. There is no doubt that in many, if not most, cases the circulation of such objects will run up against the sociological limits of taste groups and, if contact is even made, be met by indifference, disdain, or confusion. Yet once again for Dewey, this is not a neutral fact but a statement of the problem. Art that remains circumscribed within a narrow social circle lives a circumscribed existence and reveals a society marked by narrowness and limited horizons—experience is stunted. The greater the art, the more it contains within itself the possibility to develop further experiences and interactions beyond the intentions and context of its production. As in all pragmatism, successful action creates a platform for further action (Silver 2011).

But this is only a potential, and it is here that critical judgment plays a more important role in Dewey's aesthetic theory. Intelligent criticism carries an experience beyond its initial formulation. Indeed—again in contrast to Martin's approach—if the artist must adopt the audience's point of view to imagine a receiver interacting with the work, the receiver must adopt an artistic orientation by creatively experimenting with the work to permit the experience it might contain to develop. An intelligent critical community probes the object, looking at, listening to, reading, and moving through it in various ways; placing it in different contexts and settings, interpreting it according to various principles. In this way, one discovers the limits of the experiences it is capable of sustaining, often exhausting the object's potential along the way.

Yet critical reception may also permit the work—and the potential experience it contains—to speak to new and different groups, uncovering latent possibilities not originally intended. The result is that if and when criticism aids many others in coming into meaningful contact with an object, its value becomes objective. This is not to say that all agree on a singular meaning of the work; rather, the work attains the status of an object: it stands between us, offering something to and demanding something of us, opening up lines of response and closing down others, pointing toward more than any single individual's intentions or understanding. It becomes not only a representation of experience but an objective vehicle for working through and learning more about experience by exploring the latent potentialities it contains.[10]

III. SOCIOLOGICAL AESTHETICS: THE CHICAGO SCHOOL OF SOCIOLOGY AND THE ROLE OF SOCIOLOGY IN THE GROWTH OF EXPERIENCE

The discussion so far has highlighted basic conceptual issues while pointing toward some implications for and examples from sociological research, including but not exclusive to cultural sociology. I have sought to isolate points of contact and divergence between Dewey's pragmatist aesthetics and Martin's field-theoretical social aesthetics, throughout indicating that the most fundamental issue concerns the very nature of experience. For Dewey experience has a developmental potential that must be closely integrated into any social theory that aims to stay true to his outlook.

This final section moves to a new level of analysis, applying this Deweyan notion to sociology itself. This is important because one might well wonder what role the work of sociologists has in the aesthetic processes Dewey articulates. I argue that sociology can have a critical role: it may enhance the aesthetic experience of social life by creating objects that aid in focusing shared attention on social experience and that may provide objective vehicles for critically developing that experience beyond its initial formulation.[11] In other words, we need to understand sociology as a form of art, in Dewey's sense. It may only do so, however, insofar as it takes seriously its own role in the interaction of the "live creature" with its environment as a participant in the production of objects that are potentially capable of rendering experience enduring, intelligible, and available to searching, critical perception. To illustrate this possibility, I examine the Chicago School's iconic images of the urban process as examples of sociological aesthetics in practice.

Chicago maps as sociological aesthetic objects. In discussing the Chicago School maps as embodying multiple techniques for condensing urban experience into compact objects for critical observation, I follow Owens's (2012) lead. In contrast to other interpreters of the Chicago maps, Owens demonstrates that there was not a single Chicago School mapping tradition but multiple overlapping forms of mapping. Each had a distinct theoretical and historical grounding. The famous concentric circles, for example, grew out of engagement with Von Thünen and related traditions of central place theory; they resonated more with ecological conceptions of urban order as emerging from competition for valuable space. The community area maps aligned more closely with the social survey tradition and embodied more pluralistic ideas about urban areas as symbolic orders with their own enduring local cultures and sentiments that sustain a distinct way of life. Census maps came out of a more atomistic and administrative orientation, in which the city was conceived as a collection of small discrete units that could be analyzed along multiple dimensions according to the researcher's or administrator's interests. Rather than seeking to combine these into a single theoretical orientation, they are evidence of the Chicago School's pragmatic willingness to experiment with multiple representational devices without becoming fixated on one all-purpose tool.

Yet not only do the Chicago School maps have different historical and theoretical backgrounds, they also contain strikingly different aesthetic potentials. Abstracted from the usual wayfinding function of maps, they become vehicles for new meanings. Rendered into circles and lines, they become plastic means for experimenting with the media through which we perceive the city. Building toward a perception of a pervasive quality of urban life, they become objects for collectively probing the scope and limits of different models of urban experience. Articulating these in more detail helps to elaborate how sociological works themselves may play a role in the formulation and growth of experience.

Toward an *experience of the city*. Consider first the iconic zonal maps (figure 5.1). They are in the mode of classical French paintings. All elements are oriented toward a single point; everything flows toward and away from one place. Wherever

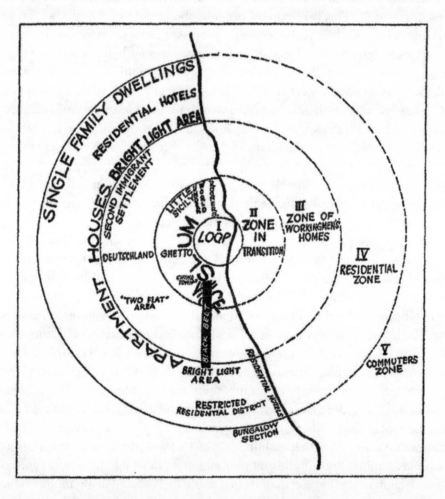

FIGURE 5.1 The Chicago School model of urban growth represented as a set of concentric circles. The diagram embodies a sociological aesthetic where social life is marked by motion and growth flowing outward from a center.

the eye begins, it is drawn in the same direction, as if by an overarching energy that permeates all. This was Diderot's classical ideal, around which so much of the history of French painting flowed: a causally unified order that is internally self-contained, every moment intimately interconnected with any other, growing from one to the other in constant rhythmic motion (Fried 1988).

Engaging with the zonal maps sustains a similar mode of perception. They do not *look* like any actual city, but they do embody and "contain" certain key experiences of contemporary urban life, which come to the fore as one works through their elements. There is the single point at the center. Rings repeat around that point, and this repetition creates a feeling of motion flowing from and toward that center. The rings get wider and wider, and by varying their distance regularly, they produce a perception of rhythmic growth. Motion and growth create a sense of pulsating vitality; social life is *alive*.[12] The use of concentric circles enforces the perception that this growth flows outward, building up and passing through moments or phases, so that what happens *here* is intimately, constitutively involved with what is happening *there*, challenging, pressing up against, pulsing through each other continuously. At the outer regions of the image, we enter into a space of possibility; the rings are surrounded by emptiness, an open environment; growth is ongoing but unpredictable, a center of organization that loses distinct shape as it shades into its environment.

And all of this is there, present for our perception and contemplation, in a single striking yet internally dynamic image. It contains and presents the Chicago-Deweyan ideas of complexity, processuality, tension, and dynamic growth that we (and many Chicagoans, and urbanites writ large) may have vaguely sensed but not perceived as such. To retrieve and map experience, it needs to be rendered articulate. With such an image before us, we can (and Chicago sociologists, of course, did) develop propositions and gather data to test them (e.g., about what we expect to happen in different zones). But it is the image of social life that gives that endeavor an object around which it can focus its efforts. In this way, the aesthetic sociological object builds up certain aspects of normal processes of urban living that we often encounter but rarely directly perceive, condenses them, and carries them to their completion as a meaningful whole. It shows us what the city would be like if those ecological overtones of urban experience became their keynote and came to pervade our habits of inquiry and observation.

In assimilating this experience of Chicago into *an* experience of the ecological potential of urban life, the zonal maps both gave Chicagoans a way to perceive themselves and produced portable techniques for extending that conception globally. The critical work of the sociologist grew the experience and allowed it to circulate more widely. At the same time, the diagrams provided a medium for critique, and generations of commentators have both sought to expose the limits of the zonal diagrams as a universal model for urban life and experimented with multiple alternatives—even as the basic intuition continues to endure as at least providing a partial model for the organization of many cities (Beveridge 2011; Lewinnek 2010).

Perspectivism and pluralism. Less remarked is the fact that, as Owens notes, the Chicago School sociologists themselves did not rely exclusively on the zonal maps; they also developed an alternative mode of representing the city as a plurality of "community areas" (figure 5.2). Not only does this alternative rest on different theoretical bases, but it, too, encourages a distinctive mode of perception. The community area maps are not organized according to the principles of French classicism. Instead, there are multiple regions that one must consider one at a time; there is no single pictorial field but many points of view from which one might begin. One observes one community area, gets a sense for its distinctive character, then moves to the next. Yet even as they undermine any perception of unity, they do not do so in an aggressive mode—but build an alternative perception—of perspectivism and pluralism. In these images there is another experience of the city, as a plurality of worlds and perspectives, with no final or central hierarchical principle governing them. If we often sense this potential but rarely carry it to completion, the iconic

FIGURE 5.2 Community area maps of Chicago. They embody a sociological aesthetic in which social life is marked by perspectivism and pluralism, with no clear center or hierarchical principle.

sociological object makes it available to us as an image of a city pervaded by plural-istic perspectivism.

The influence of the community area maps has proven especially persistent, con-tinuing to this day to shape Chicago policy and perception. Nearly a century later, the names that Burgess and his collaborators gave to the seventy-five community areas they found are still the city of Chicago's official designations, and the bound-aries they assigned continue to inform city policy and research. This example neatly illustrates the feedback loop between experience, sociologist, and iconic image. Bur-gess and his students "saw" community areas around the city as self-created com-munities. Their maps gave those communities names and provided means for representing them. Those representations and names in turn came to define many of the city's official policies and much of its on-the-ground self-understanding as a patchwork of communities with distinct identities (Hunter 1974; Clark, Silver, and Sawyer 2015). This cumulating feedback is a hallmark of the aesthetic process, and the Chicago School maps show how it can operate in the process of social research.

A conversation of perceptions. These two forms of mapping embody crystalliza-tions of two ways of experiencing urban life. Though we may simply leave them side by side, Dewey's notion of art as experience invites us to do more. As we have seen, for Dewey aesthetic objects do not simply represent a form of experience; they are proving grounds for critically discovering and creating experience anew and opening them to alternative possibilities. This occurs when we experiment with the work itself, probe its potentials, and test its limits.

Park, following Simmel, wrote about how in the city nature becomes culture. As urbanites' identities become more fluid and contested, questions of meaning become more pronounced, and the symbolic order becomes an interest in its own right (Park 2019). Literal becomes figural. The zone maps present this very motion, if we consider them in an experimental, critical spirit, as plastic objects to be imag-inatively explored. A striking aspect of the zonal maps is evident in the versions in which the zones are overlayed atop Chicago landmarks. There is a distinctive aes-thetic movement to this mode of presentation. The "residential hotels" line, for example, cuts across the circles, dividing it into a left and a right. The left is messier, with its myriad Chicago references, whereas the right is all clean lines and rhyth-mic regularity. It is as if one could grab the line like a handle and move it side to side, moving from concrete to abstract. This imaginative movement embodies the vital rhythm in the dialectics of literal and figural as we move from left to right; the image moves us from life on the ground in Chicago to the concerted effort to express the meaning and quality of that life in abstract images.

One could even see this movement as an aesthetic expression of one of the Chi-cago School's most challenging topics: the interplay between the ecological and the moral order (Joas 1993). Yet the image does not simply point to this tension; by experimenting with it, we may directly perceive it in the image itself. In this way, we reach the limits of the mode of perception contained in the zonal maps: they ter-minate in a problematic conclusion, in which the symbolic and sentimental order of the city is an emergent phenomenon that is present but not an explicit ordering principle. Yet it is precisely here that the community area maps begin (aesthetically). They in turn elaborate an image of the city pervaded by symbolism and sentiment.

Criticism of the (sociological) art object enables one form of perception to meet its limits and points us beyond itself to another. It does not just gather and retrieve experience (though it does that, too). Without requiring agreement on the substance of the experience, or embodying all its aspects, the Chicago School images provide a medium for honing collective powers of social perception and observation and extending them. The perception of social relations comes into its own in the production of sociological works that are capable of carrying it forward in heightened aesthetic sensitivity to the environment through a more articulate form of intuition.

A scientific or scholarly work may gain currency in a number of ways: truth, explanatory power, novelty, intellectual activism, ideology, and more. The aesthetics of the work play a role as well, often under headings such as "elegance" and "beauty." But what this aesthetic dimension consists in is often relegated to the realm of the vague and ineffable.

In this chapter, I have attempted to approach the aesthetics of sociological work from the point of view of John Dewey's pragmatist theory of art and aesthetics. From this viewpoint, the aesthetically satisfying work permits an experience of social life to run its course to completion. Obstacles and impediments to carrying an experience through to its fulfillment are removed. Such experiences may not be pleasant or happy. Yet without an appropriate medium for their articulation, they remain fleeting and obscure. We do not perceive them in their fullness; they break off before they can come fully to perception. They become durable and intelligible in objects geared toward their expression. Such objects engage the same powers of perception deployed in everyday social experience but organize them in a controlled manner that allows us to probe their limits. Sociology has among its (difficult) tasks the production of such objects.

To articulate this pragmatist notion of sociological aesthetics, I have contrasted Dewey's aesthetics with John Levi Martin's social aesthetics. The two approaches share much in common. Most important, they are united in maintaining the crucial importance of the qualitative character of experience and in the effort to integrate the notion of quality into our theories of social action. They diverge at a very basic level: on the nature of experience itself. For Dewey, experience has a developmental character; it grows. This basic difference leads to a number of other points at which pragmatism and field theory depart: on the centrality of judgment, the nature of sociality, and the relation between art and aesthetics.

Finally, I argued that the pragmatist version of aesthetics issues in a distinctive approach to sociological work—as a work of art. I used the early Chicago School to illuminate this conception of sociology as a form of art, in particular in the intensive use of visual, abstract, nonverbal symbols, most notably maps. These images bring to a head the experience of society as a form of *life*, moving, growing, uncertain, tensive, emotionally fraught, adaptive, competitive, contingent, but also—because it is all of these—potentially meaningful.

These are difficult and complex issues. My primary purpose has been to advance both pragmatist theory and field-theoretic social aesthetics by returning to their fundamental assumptions, searching for points of contact and divergence, and working through their implications.

WORKS CITED

Anderson, Elizabeth. 2014. "Dewey's Moral Philosophy." In *The Stanford Encyclopedia of Philosophy*. Ed. Edward N. Zalta, updated January 14, 2014. https://plato.stanford.edu /archives/spr2014/entries/dewey-moral/.

Apple, Michael W., Stephen J. Ball, and Luís Armando Gandin. 2009. *The Routledge International Handbook of the Sociology of Education*. Routledge.

Beveridge, Andrew A. 2011. "Commonalities and Contrasts in the Development of Major United States Urban Areas: A Spatial and Temporal Analysis from 1910 to 2000." In *Navigating Time and Space in Population Studies*, ed. M. P. Gutmann, G. D. Deane, E. R. Merchant, and K. Sylvester, 185–216. Dordrecht, Springer.

Brett, G., D. Silver, and K. Beelen. 2020. "The Right Tool for the Job: Problems and Solutions in Visualizing Sociological Theory." *Journal for the Theory of Social Behaviour* 50 (2): 223–48.

Brown, R. H. 1978. *A Poetic for Sociology: Toward a Logic of Discovery for the Human Sciences*. Chicago, CUP Archive.

Childress, Clayton. 2017. *Under the Cover: The Creation, Production, and Reception of a Novel*. Princeton University Press

Clark, Terry Nichols, Daniel Silver, and Stephen Sawyer. 2015. "City, School, and Image: The Chicago School of Sociology and the Image of Chicago." In *Institutions and Imaginaries*, ed. Stephanie Smith, 31–46. School of the Art Institute of Chicago.

Dewey, John. 2002. *Human nature and conduct*. Courier Corporation.

Dewey, John. 1925. *Experience and Nature*. Chicago: Open Court Publishing

Efron, A. 1995. "Literature as Experience: Dewey's Aesthetics in an Age of Galloping Theory." *Transactions of the Charles S. Peirce Society* 31 (2): 322–57.

Eldridge, R. 2010. "Dewey's Aesthetics." In *The Cambridge Companion to Dewey*, ed. Molly Cochran. Cambridge University Press.

Fried, Michael. 1988. *Absorption and Theatricality: Painting and Beholder in the Age of Diderot*. University of Chicago Press.

Gusfield, Joseph R. 1976. "The Literary Rhetoric of Science: Comedy and Pathos in Drinking Driver Research." *American Sociological Review* 41 (1): 16–34.

Hunter, Albert D. 1974. *Symbolic Communities: The Persistence and Change of Chicago's Local Communities*. University of Chicago Press.

——. 1990. *The Rhetoric of Social Research: Understood and Believed*. Rutgers University Press.

Joas, Hand. 1993. *Pragmatism and Social Theory*. University of Chicago Press.

———. 2000. *The Genesis of Values*. University of Chicago Press.

Langer, Susanne K. 1953. *Feeling and form*. Vol. 3. London: Routledge and Kegan Paul.

Lewinnek, Elaine. 2010. "Mapping Chicago, Imagining Metropolises: Reconsidering the Zonal Model of Urban Growth." *Journal of Urban History* 36 (2): 197–225.

Nisbet, Robert. 2017. *Sociology as an Art Form*. London: Routledge.

Owens, B. Robert. 2012. "Mapping the City: Innovation and Continuity in the Chicago School of Sociology, 1920–1934." *American Sociologist* 43 (3): 264–93.

Pamental, Matthew. 2011. "Review of the Cambridge Companion to Dewey." *Philosophical Reviews*. http://ndpr.nd.edu/news/the-cambridge-companion-to-dewey.

Park, Robert. 2019. "The City: suggestions for the investigation of human behavior in the urban environment." In *The City*, ed. Robert E. Park and Ernest W. Burgess. Chicago: University of Chicago Press

Roth, Robert J. 1963. "How 'Closed' Is John Dewey's Naturalism?" *International Philosophical Quarterly* 3 (1): 106–20.

Shea, William M., and John Dewey. 1980. "Qualitative Wholes: Aesthetic and Religious Experience in the Work of John Dewey." *Journal of Religion* 60 (1): 32–50.

Silver, Daniel. 2011. "The Moodiness of Action." *Sociological Theory* 29 (3): 199–222.

———. 2020. "Figure It Out!" *Sociological Methods & Research* 49 (4): 868–905.

Tanner, J., ed. 2004. *Sociology of Art: A Reader*. Routledge

Tanner, J., and R. Osborne. 2007. "Introduction: *Art and Agency* and Art History." In *Art's Agency and Art History*, ed. Robin Osborne and Jeremy Tanner, 1–27. Blackwell

Van Maanen, John. 2011. *Tales of the Field: On Writing Ethnography*. University of Chicago Press.

Waks, Leonard J. 1999. "The Means-Ends Continuum and the Reconciliation of Science and Art in the Later Works of John Dewey." *Transactions of the Charles S. Peirce Society* 35 (3): 595–611.

NOTES

1. Though Dewey scholarship suggests treating Dewey's aesthetics as a topic for general sociological theory rather than for the sociology of culture specifically, recent scholarship has drawn some fruitful connections between Dewey and theories of reception in the sociology of culture. In *Bound by Creativity: How Contemporary Art Is Created and Judged* (Chicago: University of Chicago Press, 2021),Wohl, for example, develops her theory of "creative visions" in contemporary art scenes in part by joining Dewey's theory of aesthetic experience as a "movement between formal and conceptual qualities" of a work with other work in the sociology of culture (e.g., Wendy Griswold, "A Methodological Framework for the Study of Culture." *Sociological. Methodology* 17 [1987]: 1–35; Janet Wolff, *Aesthetics and the Sociology of Art* [Boston: Allen and Unwin, 1983]; Jason Kaufman, "Endogenous Explanations in the Study of Culture," *Annual Review of Sociology* 30 [2004]): 335–357). Wohl's work suggests a valuable way to integrate Dewey into ongoing debates in the sociology of culture, but the present chapter does not pursue the matter further, as it seeks to consider Dewey's aesthetics on the more general level staked out in Martin's work.

2. Shusterman has developed a sharp contrast between Bourdieu and Dewey, which focuses more on their divergent approaches to the study of art. Richard Shusterman, "Pierre Bourdieu and Pragmatist Aesthetics: Between Practice and Experience," *New Literary History* 46, no. 3 (2015): 435–457. By contrast, given that Martin's social aesthetics begins not from art but from a theory of judgment and experience, I highlight points of contact and divergence on those issues.

3. To be sure, some thoughtful field theorists do track actors' trajectories over time through a field, as, for example, Leschziner does in her study of chef's careers. Vanina Leschziner, *At the Chef's Table: Culinary Creativity in Elite Restaurants* (Palo Alto, CA: Stanford University Press, 2015). But this approach simply assimilates trajectories as another position in the field, which become part of the typical processes of mutual judgment—"those people" have "these types" of trajectories, while "those others" have "their types" of trajectories. In Dewey's aesthetics, "development" is not so much a longitudinal trajectory as a progressive buildup toward a climactic experience that focuses and reveals the meaning of the entire process.

4. Martin does discuss examples of heightened sensitivity to qualities, specifically with an example of how, after having food poisoning, one may tend to perceive an egg as rotten due to a "temporarily heightened sensitivity to actually existing sulfur compounds in a nonrotten egg" (Martin 2011, 261). Yet this example illustrates the difference from Dewey: for Martin such sensitivity makes the most sense as a temporary condition brought on by external forces, which explains variation across persons and groups; time is assimilated to space. For Dewey aesthetic experience is a temporal process of heightening, which may be controlled and developed.

5. The relationship between Dewey's religion and aesthetics is complex and disputed. For good treatments, see Shea and Dewey (1980) and Roth (1963).

6. "Experience, when it is carried to the full, is a transformation of interaction into participation and communication" (Dewey 2005, 22).

7. "There is that meal in a Paris restaurant of which one says 'that *was* an experience. It stands out as an enduring memorial of what food may be" (Dewey 2005, 37). This kind of ideality is not empty, nor is it a utopian aim laying off in the future; it "seizes on the most precious things found in the climactic moments of experience and projects them" (Joas 2000, 114).

8. "The very presence of an 'artworld,' with its dealers, fadists, intellectual czars, bohemia eccentrics, and even aestheticians should not simply be accepted as empirical data on which to construct a theory, but should occasion critical reflection instead. An 'institutional theory of art' is the predictable outcome of a society that institutionalizes art" (Alexander 1987, 187).

9. For Dewey "art concerns any activity that manipulates things outside the body such that the rearrangement produces an experience not possible with things in their unadulterated state. Such an experience—whether in the artist or in an audience—is aesthetic when the object created brings an enhanced appreciation of its qualities" (Pamental 2011).

10. Susanne Langer has formulated this intuition with remarkable clarity:

> The exhilaration of a direct aesthetic experience indicates the depth of human mentality to which that experience goes. A work of art, or anything that effects us as art does, may truly be said to 'do something to us,' though not in the usual sense which aestheticians rightly deny—giving us emotions and moods. What it does to us is to formulate our conceptions of feeling and our conceptions of visual, factual, and audible reality together. It gives us forms of imagination and forms of feeling, inseparably; that is to say, it clarifies and organizes intuition itself. (Langer 1953, 397)

11. This approach to sociological aesthetics renews themes opened by authors such as Joseph Gusfield and Richard Brown in the 1970s (e.g., Gusfield 1976; Brown 1978) and continued with respect to the rhetoric of social research in, for example, Hunter (1990) and Van Maanen (2011). There is also a tradition of treating sociology as an art form, most notably in Nisbet ([1962] 2017). Whereas these have focused on the literary dimensions of sociological aesthetics, my main interest here is on the visual dimension as well as in pointing the way toward a more general theory of the aesthetic dimension of sociological work. Nevertheless, it would be intriguing to subject nonvisual images of society to a similar Deweyean analysis in dialogue with this literature on the aesthetics and rhetoric of sociological writing, drawing on his treatment of literary works and the scholarly literature on that treatment (e.g., Efron 1995). For more on the visual dimension of sociological theory specifically, see Silver (2020) and Brett, Silver, and Beelen (2020). One might also fruitfully draw on a rich tradition in art history, aesthetics, and anthropology on the role of intentions and agency in the interpretation of images, critically engaging authors such as Michael Baxandall and Alfred Gell in dialogue with Dewey, among others (for useful overviews in this direction, see Tanner 2004; and Tanner and Osborne 2007).

12. On the capacity of these design elements to create a feeling of growing life, see Langer (1953, 67).

6. Disambiguating Dewey; or Why Pragmatist Action Theory Neither Needs Nor Asks Paradigmatic Privilege

JOSH WHITFORD

Do I contradict myself?
Very well, then I contradict myself
(I am large, I contain multitudes)

—Walt Whitman, *Song of Myself* (1892)

That secret of a continuous life which the universe knows by heart and acts on every instant cannot be a contradiction incarnate. If logic says it is one, so much the worse for logic. Logic being the lesser thing, the static incomplete abstraction, must succumb to reality, not reality to logic. Our intelligence cannot wall itself up alive, like a pupa in its chrysalis. It must at any cost keep on speaking terms with the universe that engendered it.

—William James, *A Pluralistic Universe* (1909)

INTRODUCTION

We seem willing enough in this pragmatist revival in sociology to take a page from Whitman, to contradict one another (and perhaps even ourselves) but not worry too much about it. This is perhaps to be expected given that we are borrowing ideas from the classical pragmatists, who had made their name insisting—as Dewey wrote in 1910—that classic philosophies be "squared up with the many social and intellectual tendencies that [had] revealed themselves since those philosophies matured." He described the "pragmatic spirit," in fact, "primarily [as] a revolt against that habit of mind which disposes of anything whatever—even so humble an affair as a new method in Philosophy—by tucking it away . . . in the pigeon holes of a filing cabinet." He was, he wrote, "confirmed in a belief that after all it is better to view pragmatism quite vaguely as part and parcel of a general movement of intellectual reconstruction. For otherwise we seem to have no recourse save to define [it] . . . in terms of the very past systems against which it is a reaction; or, in escaping that alternative, to regard it as a fixed rival system making like claim to completeness and finality."[1]

The pragmatist question is *not* so much whether we contradict *each other* since, as James observed, a contradiction is a property of language and logic, a static incomplete abstraction whereas experience is continuous. We can be wrong about the first, no matter how confident we are of our reasoning. But the second happens whether we like it or not. We need, in short, to ask whether something that presents itself as a contradiction is experienced also *as a problem*. So, for instance, when Dewey's friend and former student, the Cartesian philosopher Albert Balz, wrote in 1949 in a letter to his former teacher of the "perplexities"—that is, the problems— he had experienced as he had read Dewey's *Logic: The Theory of Inquiry*, he got back "a fresh statement of some of the fundamentals of [Dewey's] position." Balz, Dewey suspected, had read the book conventionally, in an "ontological" context, so in reply Dewey tried to "obtain an understanding of what it is that [his] theory of inquiry is trying to do if and when it is taken to be, wholly and exclusively, a theory of knowledge." He did not expect to win a convert but reasoned that, "after all, rejection based upon understanding is better than apparent agreement based upon misunderstanding."[2]

In this chapter, I try as best I can to do what my title promises, which is to disambiguate the implications for sociology of a philosopher whose writings have influenced many of us but that are not always read in the same way. I ask, in effect, what it means in sociology to take Dewey's theory of inquiry as he took it, as "wholly and exclusively" a theory of knowledge in any argument structured as a response to "perplexities" about pragmatism in articles by (a) Gianluca Manzo in the *European Journal of Sociology* (EJS) in 2010; (b) Duncan Watts in the *American Journal of Sociology* (AJS) in 2014; and (c) Monica Prasad in *Socius* in 2021.[3] I select these three in part because they are prominent, and so offer easy comparison, but also because they misconstrue the underlying logic, at least internal to pragmatism, of the so-called pragmatist theory of action. I do not try so much to establish a debate as to clarify, first, the place in Dewey's pragmatism of "realistic social thinking"; second, its implications for our use in sociology of the conventional Weberian distinction between *Verstehen* (understanding) and *Erklären* (explanation); and, finally, why a pragmatist theory of action does not need, and cannot demand, paradigmatic privilege, at least internal to a pragmatist way of thinking.

THREE—AT LEAST—DEWEYS

There are—at least—three Deweys running citationally across contemporary sociology.[4] The first and most prominent is associated especially with arguments that Dewey makes in *Human Nature and Conduct* (*HNC*), which "seriously [set] forth a belief that an understanding of habit . . . is the key to social psychology"; laid out a conceptualization of habits less as rote behavior than as "acquired predisposition[s] to *ways* or modes of response"; and argued that the "function of thought is to guide action in the service of practical problems that arise in the course of life."[5] In contemporary sociology Joas, Whitford, and Gross are often cited for their use of these ideas to deny "paradigmatic privilege" to "portfolio" models of action— including but not limited to rational choice theory—by focusing on the interplay of habit and creativity in "problematic situations" in terms that do not require the analyst somehow to hold actors' goals "strictly separate from the conditions of action."[6] They have recently been credited, for instance, by Prasad (on whom more later) with "major statements, which together have been responsible for much of the revival of attention to pragmatism in sociology."[7]

Then, there is the Dewey associated citationally with the arguments that find their most complete expression in *The Public and Its Problems* (*P&P*), which holds that "the outstanding problem of the Public is discovery and identification of itself," and that "no government by experts in which the masses do not have the chance to inform the experts as to their needs can be anything but an oligarchy managed in the interests of the few."[8] These ideas run in sociological efforts to make sense of— and sometimes to inspire change in—contemporary civil society. The belief that the problem of the public is to discover and identify itself is found, for instance, in Eliasoph and Lichterman's examination of "culture in interaction" to show how "groups put culture to use in everyday life"; Walker's worry that "private efforts to shape public life are on the rise"; Overdevest's identification of "economic and social controversies [as] important sites for the enactment of democratic politics"; Baiocchi et al.'s discussion of the "civic imagination" as they ask how people "individually and collectively envision better political, social, and civic environments and work toward achieving those futures"; and so on.[9]

Finally, there are the ideas that Dewey developed most fully in his more explicitly philosophical writing—*The Quest for Certainty* (*QfC*), *Logic: The Theory of Inquiry* (*TOI*), the *Theory of Valuation* (*TOV*), and the like—where he set his way of thinking in opposition to what he called the "intellectualist fallacy."[10] He defined this fallacy as "the doctrine that calls subjective and phenomenal all objects of experience that cannot be reduced to properties of objects of knowledge"; held instead that "knowing is not the act of an outside spectator but of a participator inside the natural social scene"; and argued that "the true object of knowledge resides in the consequences of directed action."[11] Sociologists tend most often to cite these ideas in discussions like this chapter, where the subject matter is the abstract conduct of social inquiry itself.[12] However, they run in some seemingly "applied" or otherwise focused pragmatist analysis, too. This includes my own past writing on the pragmatist theory of action where I was careful to recognize that I could not claim "to have found 'the' unifying theory of action, the philosopher's stone of social theory," since, if I had, I would "contradict the very pragmatist experimentalism that I advocate, in which a theory is better only insofar as it can usefully solve the problems of the day."[13]

It is impossible in this space to do justice to the substance of these different Deweys as they run through contemporary sociology. I instead exploit the brutal reductionism of modern bibliometrics to compare their citational prevalence, using the Web of Science database to count citations across time only in sociology, and in all academic fields, of *P&P, HNC, ToI, and QfC*. I also count how often citing publications are themselves cited, as a measure of "second-order" influence. Table 6.1 displays summary counts of citing works, the average number of citations per year in the two periods, and the ratio of citing works in sociology to the ratio of citing works in all fields divided into the periods before and after 1998. Figure 6.1 displays cumulative sums from 1998 to 2017 (the Y intercept is the sum of citations prior to 1998), with *P&P* graphed as a square, *HNC* as a circle, *ToI* as an X, and *QfC* as a +. In the figure, citations in all fields are in the top row and citations only in sociology are in the bottom. The leftmost column contains counts of publications citing Dewey directly; the right, second-order citations (i.e., publications citing publications citing Dewey).

TABLE 6.1

Citations of the Different Deweys, Pre- vs Post-1998

		Total Citing			Citations/ Year	Citations/ Year	Citations/ Year
		Publications	Pre-1998	1998–2017	Pre-1998	1998–2017	All years
	All Fields	2,389	601	1,788	8.5	89.4	10.6
P&P	Sociology	286	58	228	0.8	11.4	14.0
	Soc./All	**12%**	**10%**	**13%**			
	All Fields	1,022	290	732	3.8	36.6	9.6
HNC	Sociology	167	52	115	0.7	5.8	8.4
	Soc./All	**16%**	**18%**	**16%**			
	All Fields	1,260	430	830	7.2	41.5	5.8
TOI	Sociology	77	28	49	0.5	2.5	5.3
	Soc./All	**6%**	**7%**	**6%**			
	All Fields	1,190	498	692	7.2	34.6	4.8
QfC	Sociology	101	50	51	0.7	2.6	3.5
	Soc./All	**8%**	**10%**	**7%**			

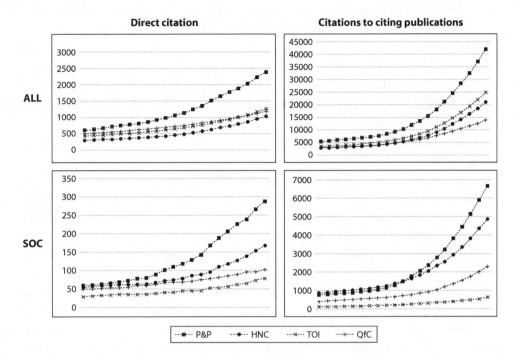

FIGURE 6.1 Citations of the Different Deweys, 1998–2017.

The rate of citation to writing by Dewey and to writing that cites Dewey has been increasing.[14] *P&P*, for instance, was cited by 601 indexed publications (58 in sociology) in its first six decades, which is not a small number; but we still see a tenfold annualized increase across the next two decades. And although the other books are cited less often, there has been rapid acceleration across the last two decades. But, for purposes here, the relevant point is that sociologists have cited *HNC* comparatively more often and *P&P* about as often, but sociologists do not cite Dewey's more philosophical writings (i.e., *TOI* and *QfC*) as often as do scholars in other fields other fields. This is not surprising—*HNC* was Dewey's principal contribution to social psychology—but it is consistent as well with the idea that we should perhaps distinguish more explicitly between, on the one hand, the situational reliance on the so-called (Deweyan) pragmatist theory of action in research in an otherwise "ontological" context and, on the other hand, its use (or not) in the conduct of research grounded instead in Dewey's theory of inquiry understood, "wholly and exclusively, [as] a theory of knowledge."

THREE FOILS

The foils for my argument do not agree with each other about everything or, maybe, about much. Manzo structures his article as a response to critics of analytical sociology (AS)—including pragmatist critics—to clarify a conception of AS as "a set of rules on how hypotheses about mechanisms underlying the regularities of social life can be theoretically designed and empirically tested."[15] Watts argues that sociologists too often "conflate understandability with causality in ways that are not valid by the standards of scientific explanation," writing that if we want in fact to be a "science" we should reframe explanation as prediction "through closer attention to causal inference, experimental methods, and out-of-sample testing."[16]

Prasad engages a "three-sided debate in American sociology between the rationalist tradition, . . . the emancipatory tradition, . . . and the skeptical tradition." Each, she writes, hits a theoretical impasse potentially resolved by an understanding of "pragmatism as problem solving," which, she argues, is her "alternative" to what she characterizes as prevalent conceptions in sociology of "pragmatism as a theory of human action, not a practical method of knowledge generation."[17]

The common thread, again, is that each misunderstands or mischaracterizes the meaning and scope of the pragmatist theory of action associated especially with the writing of Joas, Whitford, and/or Gross. All seem to agree with Watts when he describes it as yet another of "many variants of individualism that have pervaded sociology over the years."[18] We are charged—in Watts's telling—with formalizing and obfuscating ideas marked by their descent from a scare-quoted "ancestor 'theory' [that] is not itself a sociological theory, but rather is a commonsense or folk theory, deployed in practice by ordinary people in everyday circumstances to make sense of behavior they have observed." Watts ("for the sake of argument") argues that our theory therefore amounts to a form of "rationalizable action," to a general reliance on "the claim that actions, whether individual or collective, can be explained in terms of the intentions, beliefs, circumstances, and opportunities of the actors involved." So, he writes, we have been encouraging sociologists to "promise scientific explanations based on generalizable causal mechanisms but in practice produce empathetic explanations that render action understandable."[19]

Watts's contention, summarized, is that pragmatists and others who rely on theories that somehow descend from rationalizable action do not have the theoretical guardrails they need to keep their human capacity to "mentally simulate"—to imagine "what it would be like to be a particular actor in a particular situation"—in check. He identifies this capacity as useful—necessary even—in the *generation* of candidate explanations but worries that it leaks too often into the *evaluation* of those explanations by way of our commitment to *Verstehen*, to our desire for what Hempel and Oppenheim referred to as "empathetic" explanations amounting in fact to "the reduction of something unfamiliar to ideas or experiences familiar to us." We do this, Watts writes, even when looking at "large-scale, spatially distributed, or temporally distant phenomena" for which the necessary scope conditions (i.e., immediacy of feedback) do not hold. His solution, freely offered, is to direct sociologists—pragmatists included—to "place less emphasis on understandability (i.e., sense making)," by reframing explanation as prediction "through closer attention to causal inference, experimental methods, and out-of-sample testing."[20]

Manzo and Prasad, for their parts, add complaints that somehow run opposite to each other, the first accusing pragmatism in sociology of too much ambition, the second worried that there has been too little. Manzo takes specific issue with "Gross's choice of focusing with such insistence on the habitual side of action," on the grounds that Gross's (ostensible) "overall intent" was to identify "a theory of action more *realistic* than standard rational choice theory usable for a general conceptualization of social mechanism." His objection, damning if right, is that "on an empirical level, . . . Gross cites no evidence which demonstrates the *realism* of his model of actor."[21] Prasad believes the genealogy of the pragmatist revival, since it came by way of the theory of action, has been restricted to sociology's "rationalist strand." Joas, Whitford, and Gross, she writes, "see pragmatist understandings of action as more compelling than other understandings of action; adapting Richard Rorty's (2009) terms, they see pragmatism as a better mirror in which to see the true state of the world."[22] But because they "do not attempt to address problems in the world," they are "rationalists" who have not been "very pragmatist themselves."[23]

Plain Misreading

Elements of these characterizations of the so-called pragmatist theory of action are, in my view, plainly wrong on a fair reading of the texts cited, so I will not say much, leaving the reader to decide for herself. Insofar as my 2002 article is one of those cited, it *does not say* that the pragmatist theory of action is, *in general*, "more compelling than other understandings of action." I wrote, (a) "the question of whether anything—including a theory of action—is better or worse is *situational*"; and (b) that "rational choice and other portfolio theories do have their place in the social scientist's theoretical toolbox; but (c) that it is a bad idea to "premise a paradigmatically privileged theory of actions upon fixed ends," since that "limit(s) our ability to speak usefully to the problems of the day." I did at least attempt to address problems in the world in an extended discussion of issues of trust, cooperation, and industrial policy.[24] And though I made no reference to Rorty's metaphor of the "better mirror," I thought and think he is right that the pursuit of that mirror is a philosophical dead end; we should, with Dewey, "give up the notion of science traveling towards an end called 'correspondence with reality' and instead say *merely* that a given vocabulary works better than another for a given purpose."[25]

Watts's assertion that the so-called pragmatist action theory is in some fundamental way a "variant of individualism" is, I think, also just wrong;[26] as is Manzo's belief that pragmatist objections to "structural individualism"—to "the "methodological doctrine according to which all social facts, their structure and change, are in principle explicable in terms of individuals, their properties, actions, and relations to one another"—are grounded in objections to Hedström's "simplistic conception of the problem of the subjective 'sense' of individual actions"[27] Insofar as Gross's use of Dewey's conceptualization of habit as grounding for his pragmatist theory of social mechanisms is cited as the evidence for these assertions, it is worth calling attention, by adding some italics, first to his explicit recognition that pragmatism "is not a form of methodological individualism' and cannot, by its own logic, "*require* that mechanisms operating at the meso or macro-levels be explained exclusively in terms of the actions of the individuals involved, meaning-interpretive or otherwise"; and, second, to the fact that he therefore insists only that the "*potential* contribution of individual action to the operation of mechanisms be taken into account."[28]

These frustrations aside, three prominent scholars, all of whom have produced work I admire, have converged on what I think an errant understanding of the place that Dewey's conception of habits as "ways or modes of response" holds in the broader context of his theory of inquiry. I should recognize, also, that they are hardly alone in their understandings of the associated theory of action and its implications for sociology. So, in what follows, I engage aspects of their arguments that do not amount to what I am calling "misreads" but that seem instead to me—to use Balz's term—to represent genuine "perplexities" in the face of a way of thinking that is in fact atypical in the social sciences. I will try, that is, to clarify three points: (a) Dewey's pragmatist commitment to "realistic social thinking," responding mainly to perplexities in Manzo's 2010 article; (b) Dewey's thinking on *explanation*, responding mainly to perplexities that arise in the Watts 2014 article and in his 2017 exchange with Turco and Zuckerman and (c) to the place of a pragmatist theory of action or, in Dewey's terms, "the idea of organized association" in pragmatist social inquiry writ large responding, in conclusion, also to Prasad.

PRAGMATISM REALISM

There is a revealing passage in Manzo's article where he asks, rhetorically, "What criteria does Gross mobilize to claim that a theory of action which builds on the concept of habit is more 'viable' (p. 359), 'sophisticated' (p. 359), 'solid' (p. 359), 'adequate' (p. 365) or 'promising' (p. 365)" than competitor approaches.[29] He has evidently mined Gross's text for adjectival criteria, does not find "realistic" (it is not there), but seems still honestly to believe that Gross's "overall intent" as a pragmatist must have been to identify a "theory of action more realistic than standard rational choice theory usable for a general conceptualization of social mechanisms." In fact, as a textual matter, Gross provides an explicitly pragmatist standard of evaluation in his conclusion, with pragmatism notably characterized as an orientation toward "problem solving." He writes that sociology should "mark its progress by whether, for any social outcome of interest to us, we are able to identify reasonably well the often hidden social mechanisms responsible for it; gain some insight into how those mechanisms, or related ones, might play out under different circumstances; *and, as a result, intervene effectively to bring society into greater conformity with our values and ideals.*"[30]

Manzo is not exactly wrong, but he is not quite right either. He is, in my terms, perplexed, in the sense that pragmatists *are* realists, so long as that realism requires "neither monism nor dualism."[31] Dewey responded sharply in 1922 to Arthur Rogers's characterization of the "the quarrel between the critical realist and the pragmatist [as] due, primarily, to the fact that they are not dealing with the same problem."[32] As far as Dewey was concerned, they were both "trying to know knowledge" but were quarreling over the "method by which the problem is to be approached and dealt with." The critical realists had fallen prey (in Dewey's view) to the dualisms of the intellectualist fallacy; that is, they thought it somehow possible to know knowledge by holding "the epistemological method as distinct from a method which accepts logical procedure as a fact and then tries to analyze it." Dewey, by contrast, observed that we have learned through painful experience, in most matters at least, that the way to arrive at a sound generalization is by examination and analysis of specific, concrete cases"; saw no reason not to just go ahead and "apply this lesson of scientific procedure to the problem of reaching a conception of knowledge"; and, crucially, argued that this did not entail accepting the "subjective" as our final arbiter of the true. [33]

So, for instance, to characterize Dewey's pragmatism just in "terms of satisfaction of personal desire, as success in activities performed in order to satisfy desires, etc." fails to recognize "the importance in [his] theory of the existence of *indeterminate or problematic situations* as not only the source of, but as the control of, inquiry." Dewey drew in this sense explicitly on Peirce's impatience with the notion that philosophy might reasonably "take its start from one or another state of mind in which no man, least of all a beginner in philosophy actually is," and thus both with the Cartesian direction to *decide* to doubt, "as if doubting were 'as easy as lying'"; and with Hume's legacy, with the direction somehow to distill our "'first impressions of sense,' [thus] forgetting that our very percepts are the results of cognitive elaboration." There is, after all (in pragmatism at least), "but one state of mind from which you can 'set out,' namely, the very state of mind in which you actually find yourself at the time you do 'set out'—a state in which you are laden with an immense mass of cognition already formed, of which you cannot divest yourself if you would; and who knows whether, if you could, you would not have made all knowledge impossible to yourself?"[34]

For Dewey, it was accordingly "a mistake to suppose [as a general matter] that a situation is doubtful only in a 'subjective' sense."[35] He thus uses the same concept in *HNC* to theorize habits as "ways or modes of response," deviated into creative action when there is "something the matter," and it appears more or less unchanged in contemporary pragmatist writing on the theory of action by Joas, Gross, and myself. This continuity of concept is an implication of Dewey's insistence that all knowing, including scientific knowing, is "one kind of interaction which goes on within the world" and is one that is, in my view, a source of some of the confusion around the pragmatist theory of action I am trying to allay in this chapter.[36] For now, though, I need just to explain why Manzo has misidentified the criteria by which pragmatists decide (or don't) to focus on habit sets (or anything else) to theorize social mechanisms (or anything else). Dewey's most succinct explication of those criteria is found, to my read, in the *Theory of Valuation,* in a passage I will return to repeatedly in what follows: "In all inquiry, even the most completely scientific, what is proposed as a conclusion (the end-in-view of that inquiry) is evaluated as to its worth on the ground of its ability to resolve the *problem* presented by the conditions under investigation. There is [therefore] no a priori standard for determining the value of a proposed solution in concrete cases."[37]

Realistic Social Thinking

If we are going to agree to take indeterminate or problematic situations as the source and control of inquiry, we obviously need a clear definition of this concept. Dewey offered perhaps too many, since he used the concept so often, but he provides what I find to be an especially clear and succinct characterization in his exchange with Balz (who, Dewey thought, had like Russell missed their centrality in his theory). *Situation,* he wrote, stood in his theory for "something inclusive of a large number of diverse elements existing across wide areas of space and long periods of time, but which, nevertheless, have their own unity."[38] He clarified then with the example at hand, describing their two letters as "conspicuous features of [a] situation [but as] far from being the only or even the chief ones. In each case there is prolonged prior study: into this study have entered teachers, books, articles, and all the contacts which have shaped the views that now find themselves in disagreement with each other." They were also in a situation they had evidently experienced as problematic in light of the same "complex of fact"—otherwise, why take the time to write the letters?—since *problem* stood in Dewey's writing for "the existence of something questionable, and hence provocative of investigation, examination, discussion—in short, inquiry."[39]

Dewey's definition of what it means to engage in "realistic social thinking" follows. It is, he wrote, "precisely the mode of observation which discriminates adverse and favorable conditions in an existing situation, 'adverse' and 'favorable' being understood in connection with the end proposed." He recognized, though, that his pragmatist willingness to eschew the dualism of fact and value that had set so many of his philosophical contemporaries against him, so he emphasized that this does not imply, in his way of thinking, that we are free to take one observation as more "favorable" than another as a subjective matter, as a bit of *gustibus* about which there is no *disputandum.*[40] We can lie, of course. But, per Peirce, "[d]o you call it *doubting* to write down on a piece of paper that you doubt? If so, doubt has nothing to do with any serious business. [So] do not make believe: if pedantry has not eaten all the reality out of you, recognize, as you must, that there is much that you do not doubt, in the least." Belief, in pragmatist terms, "is a habit of mind essentially enduring for some time," whereas doubt is "of an altogether contrary genus. It is not a habit, but the privation of habit."[41] In short, both are, for pragmatists, *experiential,* not just for those we theorize; *we* are experiencing, too.

By implication, "[a]ny problem that does not grow out of actual (or 'practical') social conditions is factitious; it is arbitrarily set by the inquirer instead of being objectively produced and controlled." It follows, also, that "social conflicts and confusions [must] exist in fact *before* problems for inquiry exist." The former, the social conflicts, are the source of some honest Peircian doubt in the experience of some researcher who, laden with her mass of cognition already formed, intellectualizes her "practical" troubles into inquiry. She can then set to observing more deliberately. But, "[t]that which is observed, no matter how carefully and no matter how accurate the record, is [then] capable of being understood only in terms of projected consequences of activities." In short, we cannot actually do any science if the conditions in these "genuine problems [are] of a piece—[since] otherwise there would be no conflict or confusion involved—and, moreover, they are never so fixed that no change in them can be effected."[42] If we give up our spectator theories, we cannot of course know if something is so fixed that it cannot be changed; but if it cannot, it cannot matter whether we do or do not engage in inquiry, since everything up to and including our reactions is indelibly scripted.

Crucially, we also cannot assume (based on experience) that our understanding of the problem that we start with, or the facts that we first gather, will remain unchanged, since—for Dewey—inquiry is constituted by our "progressive determination of a problem and its possible solution."[43] We cannot apprehend the situation *in toto*, so "the unsettled, indecisive character of the situation with which inquiry is compelled to deal affects all of the subject-matters that enter into all inquiry. It affects, on the one hand, the observed existing facts that are taken to locate and delimit the problem; and, on the other, it affects all of the suggestions, surmises, ideas that are entertained as possible solutions of the problem."[44] It is, Dewey, wrote, "notorious that a hypothesis does not have to be true in order to be highly serviceable in the conduct of inquiry." But if we look also at the "historical progress of any science," we will see that "the same thing holds good of 'facts': of what has been taken in the past as evidential. They were serviceable, not because they were true or false, but because, when they were taken to be provisional working means of advancing investigation, they led to discovery of other facts which proved more relevant and more weighty."[45]

It follows, in pragmatism at least, that "social inquiry, in order to satisfy the conditions of scientific method, must judge certain objective consequences to be the end which is *worth* attaining under the given conditions." That is, it is a fundamentally *evaluative* enterprise, but it can be—and should be—an *aboveboard* evaluation because "this statement does not mean what it is often said to mean: Namely, that ends and values can be assumed outside of scientific inquiry so that the latter is then confined to the determination of the means best calculated to arrive at the realization of such values."[46] It means, instead, "ends in their capacity of values can [then] be validly determined only on the basis of the tensions, obstructions, and positive potentialities that are found, by controlled observation, to exist in the actual situation."[47] It is essential, therefore, that we translate our "influential conceptions into *formulated* propositions," to promote "critical comparison of alternative hypotheses" since "the only logical alternative to open and aboveboard propositional formulation of conceptual alternatives (as many as possible) is formation of controlling ideas on the ground of either custom and tradition or some special interest."[48]

PRAGMATISM, EXPLANATION, AND UNDERSTANDABILITY

Manzo and Watts both fixate on a particular passage in Gross's 2009 article, where he directs pragmatists using his theory to try to "grasp how the relevant individuals understand the situations before them."[49] However, they read it to opposite effect. The first cites it as evidence of pragmatist pursuit of a correspondence realism, the kind that can fit more or less; but the second cites as evidence that, for pragmatists, "presumably causal mechanisms are to be evaluated in terms of their understandability."[50] In fact (again), Gross writes explicitly that pragmatism can, by its own logic, insist only that the "*potential* contribution of individual action to the operation of mechanisms be taken into account."[51] He is more or less just applying what Rorty refers to as the only "general hermeneutical rule" that we can glean from Dewey's pragmatism. That is, "it's always wise to ask what the subject thinks it's up to before formulating our own hypotheses. But this is an effort at saving time, not a search for the 'true meaning' of the behavior." We need not (and should not) buy the confused corollary "that somebody's *own* vocabulary is always the best vocabulary for understanding what he is doing, that his own explanation of what's going on is the one we want."[52]

Still, Watts is not exactly wrong when he reads Gross's gloss on that general hermeneutical rule as evidence that pragmatists evaluate "presumably causal mechanisms" in terms of their understandability. But he is not quite right either. He is assuming, in effect, that Gross is thinking conventionally ("in ontological terms") about the distinction that Weber so famously drew in the context of the *Methodenstreit* between *Verstehen* and *Erklären*, setting himself in opposition to both Menger and Schmoller to stake out space for sociology as "a science concerning itself with the interpretive understanding of social action and thereby with a causal explanation of its course and consequences."[53] This context has since faded, as that very bitter fight turned on other matters, on questions of methodological individualism and holism, shaping divisions between the humanities and the social sciences, and between the economists and the rest of us. Its legacy in sociology, though, remains; we are left with a debate that has gone on for longer than anyone alive can remember, in terms that are so settled that we more or less take them for granted.[54]

So, for instance, Catherine Turco and Ezra Zuckerman responded blisteringly to Watts in 2017, also in *AJS*, but they include the proviso that "*there can be no debating* Watts' premise that the [the causal and the V*erstehen*] modes of inquiry and [their] standards are distinct."[55] They complain about Watts's relative dismissal of ethnographers and others whose stock-in-trade is the "rich interpretive accounts," since he seems to think they constitute "science" only insofar as they restrict themselves to *the generation* of candidate explanations that we are bound then to evaluate across predictions—be they probabilistic, of stylized fact, or of patterns of outcomes. The exchange—Watts replied—is charged, but it seems to me a reprise of our old fight. Watts worries that "interpretability, valued for its own sake, diverts attention from scientific validity."[56] Turco and Zuckerman rise (rightly) in response to defend those who think it enough sometimes to help us just to "see things that we otherwise would not and that the actors themselves cannot," but the authors take the tack of again delivering Weber's "sobering news that verstehen-based sociology will always look less 'scientific' than might be wished by those who use the natural sciences as their standard."[57]

Pragmatists can take a different tack because they can debate the premise itself, to ask why *Verstehen* and *Erklären* and—more important—their standards of evaluation are so necessarily distinct. Balz observed in his letter to Dewey that pragmatists love distinctions that are made *"prospectively,* as factors conditioning the accomplishment of inquiry," but fear their petrification into dualisms, where "the philosophical enterprise fails before it is begun."[58] Our old fight is logically interminable if fought across a dualism between those who unify "science" as Watts does, drawing either on the logical empiricists (and/or their intellectual heirs) or divide it as Weber does in his "methodological" essays, and as so many sociologists have done since. We have two sides joined—as Philip Gorski explains—by the shared assumption that there is some "intransitive realm of fact . . . clearly bounded from the influence of value," with values that we should think of as separable, subjective and relative.[59] We are left, that, is, with that familiar insistence that value commitments can and should influence the research process, with discipline and method (with fights, then, as to which) serving its function if it can protect our findings from those values.

I do not mean here that pragmatists should just ignore that our findings may be hijacked by our values to our scientific detriment, or that Watts is not giving good advice when he worries that we sometimes stop too easily at intuitively satisfying "causal stories," thus ignoring, to our scientific detriment, that "the details of the explanations we construct could in principle have been identified as relevant ex ante, hence predictive."[60] Dewey's insistence that we translate our "influential conceptions" into formulated propositions is aimed precisely toward his worry that inquiry is otherwise "kept in the domain of opinion and action in the realm of conflict," with the effect that we get the "dichotomization of [this or that] social field into conservatives and progressives, 'reactionaries' and 'radicals,' etc."[61] But, for pragmatists, Weber's further distinction between *Wertbezüge* (value relations) and *Wertfreiheit* (value neutrality) just compounds the problem, because it is not itself up for evaluation in the context of inquiry. And Watts, though closer because his direction to think in terms of consequences as our standard of evaluation, commits a parallel sin, in the sense that he would put methodological guardrails on intelligence itself lest we get overly tempted by those oh-so-satisfying "stories."

The point, rather, returns to the *Theory of Valuation*: "in all inquiry, even the most completely scientific, what is proposed as a conclusion . . . is evaluated as to its worth on the ground of its ability to resolve the *problem* presented by the conditions under investigation. There is no a priori standard for determining the value of a proposed solution in concrete cases."[62] It is only "sobering" to think that "verstehen-based sociology will always be less 'scientific' than might be wished by those who use the natural sciences as their standard" if we concede what Turco and Zuckerman concede and are unwilling to fight for what counts as science *in general*. The pragmatist standard, whether in *Verstehen* or *Erklären* or some combination of the two, is always the same. So, to borrow some of Rorty's better writing, we misdescribe the issue between "between those who hanker after 'objective,' 'value-free,' 'truly scientific,' social sciences and those who think this should be replaced with something more hermeneutical as a quarrel about 'method.'" We can certainly talk about the "competing goals of 'explanation' and 'understanding'" but, again, that is less an issue to be resolved than a difference to be lived with.

> The idea that explanation and understanding are opposed ways of social science is [in Dewey's pragmatism] as misguided as the notion that microscopic and macroscopic descriptions of organisms are opposed ways of doing biology. . . . "Explanation" is merely the sort of understanding one looks for when one wants to predict and control. It does not contrast with something else called "understanding." . . . To say that something is better "understood" in one vocabulary than another is always an ellipsis for the claim that a description in the preferred vocabulary is most useful for a certain purpose. If the purpose is prediction, then one will want one sort of vocabulary. If it is evaluation, one may or may not want a different sort of vocabulary. . . . If, with Dewey, one sees vocabularies as instruments for coping with things rather than representations of their intrinsic natures, then one will not think that there is an intrinsic connection, or an intrinsic lack of connection, between "explanation" and "understanding." . . . One will not think that there are two "methods"—one for explaining somebody's behavior and another for understanding his nature.[63]

Pragmatism and Prediction as Production

The distinction—but not the dualism—remains. Dewey defined causal propositions conventionally, as propositions "[dealing] explicitly with subject matters that are connected with one another as means to consequences."[64] His writings are consistent throughout with Watts's assertions: that "prediction is a necessary (but not sufficient) feature of causal explanation" and that prediction in social science should be "defined suitably . . . in the broad sense of out-of-sample testing, allowing both for probabilistic predictions and for predictions about stylized facts or patterns of outcomes."[65] However, he set himself in opposition both to the skeptical semanticism of Russell, for whom "the word 'cause' is so inextricably bound up with misleading associations as to make its complete extrusion from the philosophical vocabulary desirable";[66] and to the logical empiricists, analytical sociologists, Watts (if implicitly), and others, who insist on the *ontic* to explain the stability of belief.[67] Dewey, contra the first, confirmed "the value of the causal category as a leading principle of existential inquiry" but, contra the second, held that we can and should take the "category [as] logical not ontological."[68]

It is straightforward to think of causation as ordered sequence in logical terms, given that we are talking about "an abstract conception of the indefinitely numerous sequences that are established in scientific inquiry:—established by means of the use of generalized propositions as laws."[69] The standard (*ontic*) objection to a strictly logical postulation of the category is that we are then left to adjudicate the arbitrary, since "no event comes to us labelled 'cause' or 'effect' "; we take them as the one or the other out of the welter of experience. The pragmatist response is, as always, that we take our events only in the context of inquiry.[70] Our stock of generalized propositions ("laws") are thus "as much an *antecedent* of observation and assemblage of facts as . . . a consequence of observing and assembling them."[71] The determination of a causal linkage between events is part and parcel of inquiry, but it is neither final nor logically complete. It is, rather, "a means of instituting, in connection with determination of other similar linkages, a single unique *continuous* history"; it either "performs the function of resolution of a problem for the sake of which it is adopted and tried or it does not."[72]

This idea, that causal inquiry never stands alone from *Verstehen*, whether in the generation or the evaluation of our hypotheses, should recall Duneier's crack— in response to Wacquant—that "sociology is constantly criticized for documenting the 'obvious' when, in fact, there is more than one obvious."[73] But it gets there differently and to different effect than Watts's own riff on this same problem, which he expresses as the claim that explanations we think are obvious "once we know the answer" have some tendency to beguile us into "thinking that we know more than we do."[74] Pragmatism, in its self-conception at least, is more worried even than Watts about what Dewey called the "cultural waste, confusion and distortion" that results from our failure to put what we think we know to practical test, by relegating "scientific (that is, competent) methods of inquiry to a specialized technical field."[75] But Dewey's recognition that inquiry, in experience, is the progressive determination of a problem and its possible solutions led him to take seriously that "the first propositions we make as means of resolving a problem of any marked degree of difficulty are indeed likely to be too *vague* and coarse to be effective, just as in the story of invention of other instrumentalities, the first forms are relatively clumsy, uneconomical, and ineffective."[76]

We can and should of course turn to data "as tests of any idea or hypothesis that suggests itself." But, as every honest researcher knows, it is no simple thing to confirm or disconfirm, and, as often as not, our first real discoveries are often just that we had not actually managed to "delimit the problem sufficiently to indicate what kind of solution is relevant."[77] We see in Watts—and in Turco and Zuckerman, too—some respect for the ideal-typical, if stylized, story of the scientific division of labor we all learn in elementary school, the one with Newton, an apple, and the principle of gravitation on the side of *Verstehen*, and some equations and predictions that we can test with experiments giving us our *Erklären*. For pragmatists, by contrast, this stylized story is misleading in even the most scientific of fields. We do not need to (nor should we) eschew our search for systematic social regularities, but we cannot forget that *all* inquiry amounts in practice to the "*progressive* determination of a problem and its possible solutions.".[78] We are not condemned to wrestle with "more than one obvious" so much because—or, at least, *just* because—the dominance in sociology of what Prasad calls the "rationalists," with their endless efforts to map this or that aspect of reality, have given us a few too many mirrors in "the crowded and incoherent funhouse of rationalist sociology."[79]

Our problem, at least in part, is that we really must wrestle with the vague, with determining "*which* propositions in particular *are* instances of [*which*] kind in question."[80] Our theories, after all, neither use nor suggest themselves. We use them, as means, in indeterminate or problematic situations in what Dewey describes as a "continued to-and-fro movement between the set of existential propositions about data and the set of non-existential proposition about related conceptions."[81] We are missing something that matters if we reduce the functional importance of our theories, laws, and the like merely to "means of prediction." We are ignoring that they can be "means of *prediction* only as far as they are means of *production* of a given situation."[82] They are what Lancelot Hogben calls a "a recipe for correct conduct"; that is, they specify "what steps to take if we wish to observe a regularity of nature. . . . Predicting where a planet will be at a certain date is equivalent to prescribing where to put a telescope at a particular time if we wish to see it."[83] We are saying, in effect, "if certain operations are performed then certain phenomena having determinate properties will be observed."[84] But we do so as an intermediate step in inquiry, one we must evaluate—as always—"as to its worth on the ground of its ability to resolve the *problem* presented by the conditions under investigation."[85]

It does not much matter if the best "techniques of observation employed in the advanced sciences [have been] conformed to, including the use of the best statistical methods to calculate probable errors [if] the material ascertained [is] scientifically 'dead,' i.e. irrelevant to a genuine issue, so that concern with it is hardly more than a form of intellectual busy work."[86] The operations we perform may range from, say, a theoretically motivated question in an interview with the intention (prediction) of eliciting an answer that is, in Watts's terms, "understandable," to touching keys as electronic circuitry, silicon, and such display symbols that we interpret as the results of a regression (with controls!) of one variable on another, and so on. And while I recognize, of course, that it is not often useful to take our models quite so literally, we do not evaluate models per se; we evaluate the situations that occur when operations that constitute the model are performed. This mostly entails asking whether we see what we predicted that we would see. But we are always also asking, if implicitly, whether our operations and observations answer to—or, in light of revealed vagueness, militate for reconsideration of—some "plan and policy for existential resolution of the conflicting social situation."[87]

PREDICTION AND ANALYTIC SCOPE

Watts concludes his exchange with Turco and Zuckerman a little cheekily, with the prediction that: (a) an increasingly "data-rich" sociology, aided by "the methods of causal inference and out-of-sample testing" (b) will reveal that "many

interpretatively satisfying explanations are really just stories" and (c) that the sur-
vivors will tend often to be those we find a bit less intuitively "satisfying," leaving us (d) increasingly "to choose between story telling and science."[88] It is leading
to describe sociology as increasingly data rich—the *quantity* of sociological data
is and has always been infinite, if taken in sufficient granularity—but I get that
Watts is referring to machine-mediated and machine-readable data, to the tracking
of fingers across screens and keyboards, and of GPS chips we have "agreed" to haul
from place to place, and so on. Remember that data neither clean nor speak for
themselves; but pragmatists can and should similarly expect that the advent of new
means to translate "influential conceptions into formulated propositions" will generate new ends-in-view (i.e., hypothetical solutions) and—we can auger—will upset
at least some of our once-settled "controlling ideas on the ground."[89]

   That said, I am skeptical that we will see the same "thinning" of theories that
Watts predicts, not because we will opt for storytelling but because I think Watts misunderstands the functional nature of theory and generalization in social inquiry. We
see this in, for instance, his discussion of Jennie Brand's and Yu Xie's 2010 use of distinct longitudinal panels—one from Wisconsin (WLS) and one national (NLSY)—
to show that "individuals who benefit the most from college are those least likely to
attend."[90] Watts cites the study as evidence for his claim that "the more rigorously a
hypothesis is tested and the more data it is tested against, the weaker it must be in
order to survive scrutiny." He argues that the authors' willingness to test their hypotheses using different data sets does "arguably increase confidence in the main finding," but he observes then that seemingly strong effects lose (statistical) significance
or even reverse sign in different panels. We are left, he writes, to wonder whether
"the effect is stronger either for men (national panel) or for women (Wisconsin)"and
to recognize that "evidence for positive selection is scarce—a weaker finding than
could have been concluded if only one data set had been considered."[91]

   I do not mean that Watts is somehow wrong in his reading; I mean that he cannot, as a matter of logic, describe the study as a test of the same hypotheses across
two different data sets (i.e., as an "out-of-sample" test) without some *Verstehen* on
the back end. We cannot assess whether some model (generalization) or other holds
for some population by testing it across a pair of samples from that population without simultaneously testing, at least implicitly, our decision to take them as such for
purposes of analysis. Brand and Xie do everything they should to show that their
"two data sources are . . . complementary in their strengths and weaknesses."[92] But
even in sociology that is (in conventional terms) relatively "scientific," *Verstehen* is
unavoidable, not just in the generation of candidate explanations but in their evaluation as well. I agree, actually, that this variation is a weakening of their main finding,
but it does require excluding by assumption that there is just something different
between the populations. If their second data set were from Germany (or Malawi or
Mars), we would assume from the selection of the data sets that the problem itself
was different, that we were asking about "real" variation across places (populations).

   This is not a profound observation, and I do not intend it as such. I doubt that most
sociologists need telling by Watts or by me that they rely on untested assumptions

grounded in a-*Verstehen*-of-plausibility that, though falsifiable in principle, need not be tested unless to prove—at some stage of inquiry—a source of indeterminacy. Brand and Xie have a national data set and a deeper dive into a geographically and administratively defined subpopulation. It is uncontroversial to think that they are examining similar social processes and straightforward to read variation between the data sets as weakening any general claim about positive selection into college, which we can then transform into additional hypotheses if we are interested in variation across gender and/or place.[93] The fight here is over whether we can trust the application of intelligence not just in the *to* but also in the *fro* of inquiry. That is, it is about how we should react when our findings neither confirm nor disconfirm in ways that tell us that something somewhere is still a bit vague, where Watts worries that our transformation of those findings into the "satisfactory" answer to a different problem amounts too often to storytelling when, of course, he is also telling himself the story that the populations are equivalent for purposes of analysis.

CONCLUSION

"Pragmatism"—as a word—appears only twice in Dewey's *Logic*, and then only to explain its absence. Dewey wrote in the preface that "so much misunderstanding and relatively futile controversy [had] gathered about the word that it seemed advisable to avoid its use." He described the book as a development of ideas that he had first published forty years before, modified in inquiry to more expressly identify "reflective thought with objective inquiry" and, he hoped, in "a mode of statement less open to misapprehension than were the previous ones." Its text, though, remained in his view "thoroughly pragmatic" as he had tried always to use word, to denote "the function of consequences as necessary tests of the validity of propositions, provided these consequences are operationally instituted and are such as to resolve the specific problem evoking the operations."[94] So, I have tried in this chapter to take this lesson that there is little of substance to be won in fights over terminology; I am happy enough to take my pragmatism a bit vaguely, as part and parcel of a general movement of intellectual reconstruction. But I worry that we run some risk of the same futile controversy that forced Dewey from an otherwise useful term. It is, after all, a fool's errand to lay out all your assumptions and priors every time you want to convince someone of something, so I am hoping we are not all forced similarly to avoid its use.

I have tried in response to disambiguate the Deweys that run citationally across contemporary sociology, to argue that we might understand one another better if we understand Dewey's pragmatism—as opposed to the propositions that follow from his pragmatism—as he intended it, as "wholly and exclusively, a theory of knowledge." But I should clarify in closing that it is often unnecessary to state explicitly that one is writing "as a pragmatist." The way of thinking that informs research practice needs to find its way into research exposition only when it can help the reader to grasp the argument. It seems likely to help when one is trying to theorize theorizing, as is my task here. It seems advisable when using "downstream" Deweyan pragmatist concepts and theories pertaining to the interplay of creativity and habit in action;[95] to the examination of the "apprenticeship" and "laboratory" approaches to the instruction of teachers;[96] to a working definition of a public as "those indirectly and seriously affected for good or for evil [who] form a group distinctive enough to require recognition and a name" while still contending that "the problem of the relationship of individuals to associations—sometimes posed as the relation of *the* individual to society—is a meaningless one";[97] and so on.

Put differently, it is advisable to disambiguate when one fears one's writing will be misunderstood if read in the "*ontological* context" that led Balz astray. I have tried to show that Dewey's way of thinking in *QfC*, *TOI*, and *TOV* are a source of the kinds of propositions that pragmatists looking to the Dewey of *HNC* and the Dewey of *P&P* are likely to derive. We can, in this sense, read Dewey's setting forth in *HNC* of "a belief that an understanding of habit and of different types of habit [is] the key to social psychology" as his translation of an "influential conception" into a "formulated proposition." Obviously, "any hypothesis as to a social end must include as part of itself the idea of organized association among those who are to execute the operations it formulates and directs"; so, for those hypotheses we need *some* theory of organized association.[98] But it is contradictory to Dewey's more fundamental theory of inquiry to give "paradigmatic privilege" to *any* theory of action (or even to assume that we need a social psychology for the problem at hand), whether that is the pragmatist theory sometimes associated with my past writing, a portfolio theory, or something else entirely, something we have yet to invent.

That said, I think that a pragmatist theory of creative action that takes habits as ways or modes of response is, on its record, a good candidate theory of organized association. I have used and will continue to use it when it helps in empirical work.[99] But it is not good in *general*; it is good insofar as it "performs the function of resolution of a problem for the sake of which it is adopted."[100] I am not complaining that over the years others have sometimes hived my descriptive claims about habits, situations, means, ends-in-view, ends-in-themselves, and so on away from the pragmatist context in which I tried to place them. When others find ways to generate their own propositions and evaluate them by some alternative standard, perhaps believing that a focus on "habit sets" more accurately (somehow defined) describes the real than does some alternative, I have no objection whatsoever. I am responding to Manzo, Watts, and Prasad, much as they responded to me, because it seems that we have all found "something questionable, and hence provocative of investigation, examination, discussion" that we have intellectualized into inquiry in connection with something I once wrote.[101] I recognize, though, that we are not really asking anyone to evaluate the pragmatist action theory itself, at least in general terms.

We each reference it to delimit some more specific problem to indicate what kind of solution might be relevant and, if Dewey is right, the evaluation that matters is one that takes our formulations of the problem *and* our proposed solutions together. Manzo, Watts, and Prasad make claims I think are demonstrably wrong on a fair reading of the texts they cite but, if they were to concede my version, the contrast would remain. So, for instance, a fair comparison of Manzo's larger argument with my own entails asking (a) whether Dewey's pragmatism, understood "wholly and exclusively" as a theory of knowledge; or (b) analytical sociology, defined as "a set of rules on how hypotheses about mechanisms underlying the regularities of social life can be theoretically designed and empirically tested"; (c) would, if operationally instituted, serve as better means to the goal that Manzo lays out in his conclusion; (d) which is to help move "sociology toward what sociology would be if it were a science like any other"; (e) since this goal is consistent with Dewey's commitment to the "principle of the continuum of inquiry," albeit with all science construed in pragmatism less as rule than as "free intelligence operating in the best manner available at a given time."[102]

To compare Watts's and Prasad's larger arguments with my own, it is worth bringing his assertions elsewhere, in *Nature Human Behaviour* in 2017, into the situation. He writes that the social sciences have an "incoherency problem," by which he means we have "many theories for the very same thing [that]—although often interesting and plausible when considered individually—are fundamentally incoherent when viewed collectively";[103] and that we should therefore "adopt a more solution-oriented approach, starting first with a practical problem and then asking what theories (and methods) must be brought to bear to solve it." The first assertion divides me from Watts in ways that we cannot really commensurate in experience, since we differ as to whether the pursuit of a "better mirror" is a philosophical dead end. If I am right that we do better if we take problematic situations as the source and control of inquiry, we do not want our generalizations to come as "all-or-none contradictory 'truths,'" as "sweeping universals [that] do not delimit the field so as to determine problems that may be attacked one by one, but are of such a nature that, from the standpoint of theory, one theory must be accepted and the other rejected *in toto*."[104]

The second joins but perhaps also divides me from Prasad, who cites it as evidence that scholarship in sociology's "rationalist" tradition has, when pressed, often done more or less what Dewey says it should.[105] I disagree that my past writing on pragmatism is rationalist in its orientation, but Watts certainly belongs there. He is openly committed to the notion that science done well is "traveling towards an end called 'correspondence with reality,'" and he expects the requirement that "solutions work in the real world" to force us to confront our incoherency problem, which, if he is right, it will. It is worth noting, though—as Prasad does—that by telling us to begin with practical problems rather than trying directly to ascertain the validity of some framework or other (let alone grand theory), he is also somehow acknowledging that reframing explanation as prediction does not by itself give us a shared standard that we can use, in general, to convince each other that one theory "corresponds" with the real more closely than does another. He is conceding, in effect, the pragmatist idea that operational truth is a bit more local, grounded in our ability at least to convince each other internal to some definite community of inquiry that one of our theories works — or, at least, worked — better than another for a definite and situated purpose.

I can as a committed Deweyan pragmatist thus happily endorse what Prasad calls "pragmatism as problem-solving"; I believe Dewey was right, that "the supreme business of scientific inquiry [is] to ask about and find out about *what is*" precisely by recognizing that "[k]nowing marks the conversion of undirected changes into changes directed toward an intended conclusion."[106] We need (and can) ask only if we have "a *solution* which answers the requirements of a *problem*." So when "this *unscientific* limitation is removed 'larger social issues' (and moral values as involved in these issues) are necessarily and inevitably an integral part of the subject matter of inquiry."[107] We can and we should translate our influential conceptions into formulated propositions, since this allows us to predict and then asses the consequences that arise if and when they are operationally instituted. But as Clarence Ayres wrote of his own field, let's not forget that economists are not trying principally to predict prices any more than astronomers are really just predicting the next eclipse. Or, as Rorty put it, a vocabulary for the social sciences should allow for "descriptions which permit prediction and control"; but it is a poor vocabulary if it does not also allow for descriptions to help us decide what to do.[108]

The division, if there is one, is over whether there is any useful connection between Watts's assertions. Certainly, we should be doing our sociology with an eye toward "genuine problems." Still, I don't think our problem in sociology is — or at least exactly is — that we have different theories "for the same thing" and that those theories cannot simultaneously be "true." I do not mean there are no logical contradictions between abstractions, and I am not advocating further proliferation of theories and concepts in sociology, at least for its own sake. But we don't have different theories for the same thing; we have different theories for the same *kind* of thing; the contradictions or incoherence, if it occurs, lies in our failure to identify patterns in the kinds of problems that one rather than the other seems more often to have "worth on the ground of its ability to resolve the *problem* presented by the conditions under investigation." A generalization (i.e., a theory) is not by itself true or false, whether we call it 'problem solving or no'; it can be 'fit or unfit, proper or improper, right or wrong,' only on ground of [its] serviceability in the direction of behavior dealing with states of affairs found to be objectionable because of some lack or conflict in them."[109]

NOTES

1. John Dewey, *The Influence of Darwin on Philosophy and Other Essays in Contemporary Thought* (New York: Henry Holt, 1910), iv.
2. Albert Balz and John Dewey, "A Letter to Mr. Dewey Concerning John Dewey's Doctrine of Possibility, Published Together with His Reply," *Journal of Philosophy* 46, no. 11 (1949): 332.

3. Gianluca Manzo, "Analytical Sociology and Its Critics," *Archives Européennes de Sociologie/European Journal of Sociology/Europäisches Archiv Für Soziologie* 51, no 1 (2010): 129–70; Duncan J. Watts, "Common Sense and Sociological Explanations," *American Journal of Sociology* 120, no. 2 (2014): 313–51; and Monica Prasad, "Pragmatism as Problem Solving," *Socius* 7 (2021): 1–13.

4. A fourth strand has been spun from ideas developed most famously in Dewey's *Democracy and Education (D&E)*. I have left this strand out of my analysis because that is the Dewey I know least well, for reasons that reflect in part the discipline of sociology that operates (to its detriment) in silos. The Dewey of *D&E* did not need exactly to be "revived" because he has been consistently influential in social science writing on education, but there is not all that much cross-citation with "mainstream" (whatever that means) sociology. See John Dewey, *Democracy and Education: An Introduction to the Philosophy of Education* (New York: Macmillan, 1923).

5. John Dewey, *Human Nature and Conduct* (New York: Henry Holt, 1922a), i, 42; Neil Gross, "A Pragmatist Theory of Social Mechanisms," *American Sociological Review* 74, no. 3 (2009): 366.

6. Gross, "Pragmatism, Social Mechanisms"; Hans Joas, *The Creativity of Action* (Chicago: University of Chicago Press, 1996); Josh Whitford, "Pragmatism and the Untenable Dualism of Means and Ends: Why Rational Choice Theory Does Not Deserve Paradigmatic Privilege," *Theory and Society* 31, no. 3 (2002): 326.

7. Prasad, "Pragmatism as Problem Solving," 8.

8. John Dewey, *The Public and Its Problems* (New York: Henry Holt, 1927), 185.

9. Nina Eliasoph and Paul Lichterman, "Culture in Interaction," *American Journal of Sociology* 108, no. 4 (2003): 735, 783; Edward Walker, "Privatizing Participation: Civic Change and the Organizational Dynamics of Grassroots Lobbying Firms," *American Sociological Review* 74, no. 1 (2009): 99; Christine Overdevest, "Towards a More Pragmatic Sociology of Markets," *Theory and Society* 40, no. 5 (2011): 536; and Gianpaolo Baiocchi et al., *Civic Imagination: Making a Difference in American Political Life* (New York: Routledge, 2015): 15.

10. John Dewey, *The Quest for Certainty* (New York: Minton, Balch, 1929), 291; Dewey, *Logic: The Theory of Inquiry* (New York: Henry Holt, 1938); and Dewey, *Theory of Valuation* (Chicago: University of Chicago Press, 1939).

11. Dewey, *The Quest for Certainty*, 291, 196.

12. See, for instance, Bente Elkjaer and Barbara Simpson, "Pragmatism: A Lived and Living Philosophy. What Can It Offer to Contemporary Organization Theory?," in *Philosophy and Organization Theory*, ed. Haridimos Tsoukas and Robert C. H. Chia (Bingley, UK: Emerald, 2011); Mustafa Emirbayer and Douglas W. Maynard, "Pragmatism and Ethnomethodology," *Qualitative Sociology* 34, no. 1 (2011): 221–61.

13. Whitford, "Untenable Dualism, Means & Ends," 326.

14. A more careful analyst would try to find some way to control for the increasing risk of citation to all work, in the sense that the population in the database is growing at an increasing rate and the number of citations per article has increased as well. I am mostly interested in comparing the results between sociology and other fields, which mostly

obviates the concern. However, I have done comparisons to "competitor" work from the time and am not worried that these findings are an artifact. I looked, for instance, at Arthur Lovejoy, *The Great Chain of Being* (Cambridge, MA: Harvard University Press, 1963); and at Bertrand Russell, *The Problems of Philosophy* (New York: Henry Holt, 1912).

15. Manzo, "Analytical Sociology and Its Critics," 162.

16. Watts, "Common Sense," 313, 342–43.

17. Prasad, "Pragmatism as Problem Solving," 1, 8.

18. This is not to say that they are equally worried about theoretical individualism per se; Manzo mostly endorses it, if that endorsement is grounded in the principles of analytical sociology.

19. Watts, "Common Sense," 314.

20. Watts, "Common Sense," 314, 318, 331, 342.

21. Manzo, "Analytical Sociology and Its Critics," 158–59; emphasis added.

22. Prasad, "Pragmatism as Problem Solving" 8.

23. Prasad, "Pragmatism as Problem Solving," 8, 2.

24. Whitford, "Untenable Dualism, Means & Ends," 326, 355. See also Josh Whitford, "Waltzing, Relational Work, and the Construction (or Not) of Collaboration in Manufacturing Industries," *Politics & Society* 40, no. 2 (2012): 249–72.

25. Richard Rorty, *Philosophy and the Mirror of Nature* (Princeton, NJ: Princeton University Press, 1979); Rorty, "Method, Social Science, and Social Hope," *Canadian Journal of Philosophy* 11, no. 4 (1981): 571.

26. Watts, "Common Sense," 314.

27. Manzo, "Analytical Sociology and Its Critics," 158. The definition of structural individualism is quoted from Peter Hedström and Peter Bearman, "What Is Analytical Sociology All About? An Introductory Essay," in *The Oxford Handbook of Analytical Sociology*, ed. Peter Hedström and Peter Bearman (Oxford: Oxford University Press, 2009), 9.

28. Gross, "Pragmatism, Social Mechanisms," 369.

29. Manzo, "Analytical Sociology and Its Critics," 159.

30. Gross, "Pragmatism, Social Mechanisms," 376; emphasis added.

31. John Dewey, "Realism Without Monism or Dualism—I: Knowledge Involving the Past," *Journal of Philosophy* 19, no. 12 (1922b): 309–17; Dewey, "Realism Without Monism or Dualism—II," *Journal of Philosophy* 19, no. 13 (1922c): 351–61.

32. Arthur Rogers, "The Problem of Error," in *Essays in Critical Realism: A Co-Operative Study of the Problem of Knowledge*, ed. Durant Drake (New York: Macmillan, 1920), 160.

33. Dewey, "Realism Without—II," 360–61.

34. John Dewey, "Propositions, Warranted Assertibility, and Truth," *Journal of Philosophy* 38, no. 7 (1941): 182; Charles Sanders Peirce, *Collected Papers of Charles Sanders Peirce* (Cambridge, MA: Harvard University Press, 1974; hereafter cited as *CP*), 278. Hilary Putnam has pithily summed up this long and somewhat convoluted—but brilliantly cutting—passage in Peirce in an easy to remember aphorism: "Doubting Is Not as Easy as Lying," in *Pragmatism: An Open Question* (Oxford: Wiley-Blackwell, 1995). Dewey,

in introduction to the *Theory of Inquiry* explicitly identifies his specific debt to Peirce on these matters, writing that "attention [in the book] is called particularly to the principle of the continuum of inquiry, a principle whose importance, as far as I am aware, only Peirce had previously noted"; Dewey, *Theory of Inquiry*, iii.

35. Dewey, Theory of Inquiry, 106.
36. Dewey, *The Quest for Certainty*, 204.
37. Dewey, *Theory of Valuation*, 47.
38. Balz and Dewey, "Letter and Reply," 331.
39. Balz and Dewey, "Letter and Reply," 331.
40. Dewey, *Theory of Inquiry*, 500.
41. Peirce, *CP*, 278.
42. Dewey, *Theory of Inquiry*, 500.
43. Dewey, *Theory of Inquiry*, 110.
44. Balz and Dewey, "Letter and Reply," 331.
45. Dewey, *Theory of Inquiry*, 110.
46. Dewey, *Theory of Inquiry*, 503.
47. Dewey, *Theory of Inquiry*, 503.
48. Dewey, *Theory of Inquiry*, 508.
49. Gross, "Pragmatism, Social Mechanisms," 369.
50. Watts, "Common Sense," 323.
51. Gross, "Pragmatism, Social Mechanisms," 369; emphasis added.
52. Rorty, "Method, Social Science," 579.
53. Max Weber, *Economy and Society*, ed. Guenther Roth and Claus Wittich (Berkeley: University of California Press, 1978), 4.
54. Mats Ekström, "Causal Explanation of Social Action: The Contribution of Max Weber and of Critical Realism to a Generative View of Causal Explanation in Social Science," *Acta Sociologica* 35, no. 2 (1992): 107–22; Uljana Feest, ed., *Historical Perspectives on Erklären and Verstehen* (Dordrecht: Springer, 2010).
55. Catherine Turco and Ezra Zuckerman, "Verstehen for Sociology: Comment on Watts," *American Journal of Sociology* 122, no. 4 (2017): 1275; emphasis added.
56. Duncan Watts, "Response to Turco and Zuckerman's 'Verstehen for Sociology,'" *American Journal of Sociology* 122, no. 4 (2017a): 1293.
57. Turco and Zuckerman, "Comment on Watts," 1781, 1724.
58. Balz and Dewey, "Letter and Reply," 314.
59. Philip Gorski, "Beyond the Fact/Value Distinction: Ethical Naturalism and the Social Sciences," *Society* 50, no. 6 (2013): 546. Gorski's own way out is to take on an "ethical naturalism."
60. Watts, "Common Sense," 343.
61. Dewey, *Theory of Inquiry*, 508.
62. Dewey, *Theory of Valuation*, 46–47.
63. The passage I am quoting at length here runs from pages 574 to 576 in Rorty, "Method, Social Science." I do not endorse Rorty's reading of Dewey in all its elements, but his 1981 essay has substantially shaped my understanding of Dewey's writing on these matters.

64. Dewey, *Theory of Inquiry*, 460.

65. Watts, "Common Sense," 340.

66. Bertrand Russell, *Mysticism and Logic and Other Essays* (London: Allen & Unwin, 1917): 180.

67. Alan Richardson, "Engineering Philosophy of Science: American Pragmatism and Logical Empiricism in the 1930s," *Philosophy of Science* 69, no. 53 (2002): S36–S47; Manzo, "Analytical Sociology and Its Critics."

68. Dewey, *Theory of Inquiry*, 462, 459.

69. Dewey, *Theory of Inquiry*, 458.

70. Dewey, *Theory of Inquiry*, 459.

71. Dewey, *Theory of Inquiry*, 498.

72. Dewey, *Theory of Inquiry*, 445; Dewey, *Theory of Valuation*, 47.

73. Mitchell Duneier, "What Kind of Combat Sport Is Sociology?," *American Journal of Sociology* 107, no. 6 (2002): 1568.

74. Duncan Watts, *Everything Is Obvious:* Once You Know the Answer* (New York: Crown Business, 2011), 29.

75. Dewey, *Theory of Inquiry*, 535.

76. Dewey, "Propositions, Warranted Assertibility," 177; emphasis added.

77. Dewey, "Propositions, Warranted Assertibility," 177.

78. Dewey, *Theory of Inquiry*, 110; emphasis added.

79. Prasad, "Pragmatism as Problem Solving," 8.

80. Dewey, "Propositions, Warranted Assertibility," 178.

81. Dewey, *Theory of Inquiry*, 427.

82. Dewey, *Theory of Inquiry*, 456.

83. Lancelot Hogben, *The Retreat from Reason* (London: Watts & Co., 1936), 49. Cited and discussed by Dewey, *Theory of Inquiry*, 456.

84. Dewey, *Theory of Inquiry*, 456.

85. Dewey, *Theory of Valuation*, 47.

86. Dewey, *Theory of Inquiry*, 499.

87. Dewey, *Theory of Inquiry*, 499.

88. Watts, "Response to T&Z," 1298.

89. Dewey, *Theory of Inquiry*, 508.

90. Jennie Brand and Yu Xie, "Who Benefits Most from College? Evidence for Negative Selection in Heterogeneous Economic Returns to Higher Education," *American Sociological Review* 75, no. 2 (2010): 273–302.

91. Watts, "Common Sense," 343–44.

92. Brand and Xie, "Who Benefits," 282.

93. Dewey, *Theory of Valuation*, 47.

94. Dewey, *Theory of Inquiry*, iii-iv.

95. See, for example, Gross, "Pragmatism, Social Mechanisms"; Whitford, "Untenable Dualism, Means & Ends."; Josh Whitford and Francesco Zirpoli, "Pragmatism, Practice, and the Boundaries of Organization," *Organization Science* 25, no. 6 (2014): 1823–39; and Mark Granovetter, *Society and Economy* (Cambridge, MA: Harvard University Press, 2017).

96. John Dewey, "The Relation of Theory to Practice in Education," in *The Third Yearbook of the National Society for the Scientific Study of Education. Part I*, ed. C. A. McMurry (Chicago: University of Chicago Press, 1904), 9–30; Lee S. Shulman, "Theory, Practice, and the Education of Professionals," *Elementary School Journal* 98, no. 5 (1998): 511–26.

97. David Stark, Balazs Vedres, and Laszlo Bruszt, "Rooted Transnational Publics: Integrating Foreign Ties and Civic Activism," *Theory and Society* 35, no. 3 (2006): 323–49; Dewey, "The Public and Its Problems," 35, 69.

98. Dewey, *Theory of Inquiry*, 503.

99. Whitford and Zirpoli, "Pragmatism, Practice" ; Whitford, "Waltzing, Relational Work."

100. Dewey, *Theory of Valuation*, 47.

101. Balz and Dewey, "Letter and Reply," 331.

102. Manzo, "Analytical Sociology and Its Critics," 163; Dewey, *Theory of Inquiry*, 506.

103. Duncan Watts, "Should Social Science Be More Solution-Oriented?," *Nature Human Behaviour* 1, no. 1 (2017b): 1.

104. Dewey, *Theory of Inquiry*, 506.

105. Prasad, "Pragmatism as Problem Solving," 6.

106. John Dewey, "Liberating the Social Scientist," *Commentary* 4 (1947): 379; Dewey, *The Quest for Certainty*, 205.

107. Dewey, "Liberating the Social Scientist," 379; Dewey, "Propositions, Warranted Assertibility," 178.

108. Rorty, "Method, Social Science," 575.

109. Dewey, *Theory of Valuation*, 47.

PART II. Agency

7. Problem-Solving in Action

A PEIRCEIAN ACCOUNT

IDDO TAVORY AND STEFAN TIMMERMANS

This chapter provides a pragmatist framework for tracing an important cluster of problem-solving situations in action and interaction, and the very definition of such problems. Drawing on Peirce's semiotic theory, we argue that attending to the structure of signification—the kind of sign, how it is related to its object, and how it relates to its presumed effect—provides researchers with a clearer understanding of the unfolding of meaning and how problem-solving takes place. Specifically, we argue that many definitions of and solutions to emerging problems can be understood through "upshifting" and "downshifting" the generalizability of signification. To exemplify the mechanics of the approach and its use-value, we use interactional data about stigma management.

Attracted to its robust theory of action, creativity, and habit, sociology is in the midst of a pragmatist revival. One of the most compelling and oft-cited aspects of this resurgence is the image of people as problem solvers. But although it is deeply resonant both with some sociologists' emphasis on cultural repertoires and with an emphasis on the materiality of action,[1] *problem-solving* has become a floating signifier in the pragmatist theory of action. The term reminds sociologists to embed people's actions in the proximate setting of the situation rather than in the shifting sands of ultimate ends, but it is unclear how problem-solving actually operates as a set of meaningful practices.[2] Besides a ritualistic reiteration of actors as problem solvers and a nod toward the importance of habits, it often does not seem that sociologists gain much analytic leverage from pragmatism as they work through this fundamental tenet of social action.

In order to make good on the promise of problem-solving, some of the most important proponents of the pragmatist revival within sociology, such as Emirbayer and Gross, have instead turned to Bourdieu's theory of habitus.[3] As both pragmatists and Bourdieu stress, ingrained habits provide actors with repertoires of thought and action that become apparent both in a "sense of the game" as well as in creative solutions to novel problems. There is thus a theoretical affinity between Bourdieu's phenomenologically indebted theory of habitus and the pragmatist notion of habit.[4] Moreover, since the theory of habitus has been more extensively developed, and especially as it homed in on inequalities and the patterned distribution of such habits more than pragmatist philosophy ever has, such a move is promising.

Alternatively, in an attempt to develop sociological insights in decision-making, Daipha has synthesized the literature on materiality, organizations, and the cognitive psychology of "fast" and "slow" cognition to specify the contours of problem-solving.[5] Following science and technology scholars, Daipha regards problems as located in materially objictified ways, which shape actors' ability to use specific solutions to a problem, as well as in specific institutional and organizational cultures.[6] When actors encounter problems, they approach them through habits. These habits, however, are refracted by institutional and organizational cultures and the material affordances that these problems might entail.[7] Similarly, Jansen's account of political innovation and problem-solving focuses on the relation between habits and the organizational and institutional affordances that shape those modes of action, showing how political actors innovate new forms of politics.[8]

Although these are useful ways to unpack what problem-solving may entail, this chapter shows what can be gained by remaining closer to early pragmatist thought. We propose a semiotic account of problem-solving that relies on the writings of Charles S. Peirce, the initial architect of pragmatism.[9] After outlining his view of semiotics as a process in motion, we show how such semiotics help us gain traction on questions of "specifying" and "generalizing" social encounters. We do not think that this approach solves the issue of "problem-solving" once and for all, but it provides researchers with an analytic tool set that is sensitive to the ways in which people both construct and solve a set of inherently sociological problems—those of the typification and detypification of social life.

A HANDFUL OF TRIPARTITE DIVISIONS

The fundamental purpose of Peirceian semiotics is to understand how signification is achieved in an ongoing stream of activity. As opposed to the later structuralist division of the sign into signifier and signified, Peirce devised a threefold semiotic partition: "I define a sign as anything which is so determined by something else, called its object, and so determines an effect upon a person, which effect I call its interpretant, that the latter is thereby mediately determined by the former" (CP

8.343).[10] Meaning-making thus consists of three interlinked parts. The first of these elements is the *sign*—whether an arbitrary convention or a vehicle that is more intimately tied to the object. The sign, in turn, does not exist on its own but is always in relationship to an object: a sign signifies or provides meaning about an object. A sign reveals something, and due to the limits of human perception, this revelation is inevitably partial: the sign focuses on only some aspects of the object. The second element, then, is the *object*, any entity about which a sign signifies—including both actual things out there in the world or ideas in our head. It is important to note that objects are not simply docile receptacles of meaning; they can also resist their signification. Objects, in other words, are never completely captured by their grounding in the sign.

Peirce's most original insight in this tripartite division, however, was that meaning-making is a practical achievement. To capture this point, Peirce argued that every act of meaning-making includes an *interpretant*—the effect of the sign-object through which any act of meaning-making is completed. We cannot talk of meaning-*making* unless it has some kind of effect on actors—an emerging understanding, emotion, or action. Temporal movement is thus inherent to a pragmatist semiotic analysis.

Implicit in this image is also the understanding that an interpreter necessarily brings her own habits of thought and action into the situation. Seeing a homeless person, for instance, is possible only because we immediately attend to certain clues about people's dress or where and how they sit. We do not puzzle our world from scratch every time but build on ever-developing habits of thought and action to make sense of the situations we face. This, we think, is crucial—semiotics and habits are inseparable. Peirce thus raises what is perhaps the most well-known aspect of a pragmatist theory of action: its melding of both creativity and habit.[11] We always work through our habits of thought and action as we encounter novel problem situations, but the encounter itself gives rise to the creativity of action—to forms of action and symbolization that could not have been initially guessed at (although they may often seem obvious in retrospect).[12]

This version of meaning-making in motion was partly taken over by later pragmatists and especially by interactionists, albeit without the technical jargon of *interpretant*. However, Peirce's subsequent work on the ways in which signification operates within this basic triad has not been mined by sociologists. Thus, within each aspect of the triad, Peirce developed a further threefold partition. The logic of these new triads relates to the degree of potentiality, actuality, and generalization within each aspect of meaning-making. Thus, the sign itself can be a "tone," a "token" or a "type"—a potentiality, a specific marker (such as a name), or a more general type that refers to a kind of thing ("a sociologist"). The relationship between the sign and the object can be similarly divided into "icon," "index," and "symbol" based on how the sign signifies the object. Finally, the way that the sign-object relationship is taken up by the interpretant can also be similarly divided—through the somewhat ill-named terminology of rheme, dicent, and argument.

We argue that the language that Peirce developed to parse out the ways in which meaning-making operates can be used productively to think about problem solving—and problem-defining—in interaction. We begin with an extended example that demonstrates the merit of Peirce's distinctions and then show (through an example culled from the work of sociologist John O'Brien) how this approach allows us to talk about the processes of making actions, objects, and actors more or less "general" in interaction.[13] That is, we show how actors typify and attempt to detypify their social world—a core "problem" that sociologists study.

EXPLICATING PEIRCE'S SEMIOTIC CATEGORIES

Consider the following heuristic example. Marvin takes a shower, walks into the bedroom, drops the towel, and gets dressed. Ellie, his partner, enters the room and, in a distinctly chilly tone, asks, "Is that your towel?" With a sense of foreboding Marvin quickly picks up the towel, jokingly responding, "How did *this* get here?" Ellie explodes at Marvin. He always leaves the towel on the floor, he never washes the dishes, and he refuses to spend Thanksgiving with her relatives. He seems to take the entire relationship for granted, just like he takes for granted that the towel somehow magically returns to the towel bar after he drops it. Exasperated, Marvin replies, "Are you serious? Relax, it's just a towel . . ."

The basic structure of meaning-making underlying this seemingly trivial towel incident is prevalent. One party constructs a social problem by making a specific incident stand for a wider pattern, and the other party resists this form of signification and the definition of the situation as a "problem situation." It is, at essence, a generalization (or typification) and an attempt at resisting and delegitimizing such generalization—a key semiotic process that is at work in many kinds of claims-making in the realm of interpersonal relationships, social movements, and other institutional processes. In semiotic terms, the towel incident involves a contestation over different modes of signification. A semiotic relationship that, for Marvin, is indexical and highly specific is turned by Ellie into an increasingly symbolic and general form of signification—a transformation that Marvin actively resists when he asks his partner to relax (using, as we show later, another generalizing trope).

So, at this elementary level, what is the sign-object-interpretant in the towel example? Because we are interested in the interactional sequencing of problem-solving and construction, we will divide the event into five scenes:[14]

1. Marvin dropping the towel on the floor after the shower.
2. Ellie asking, "Is that your towel?"
3. Marvin responding, "Oh, how did *this* get here?" while picking it up.
4. Ellie moving from the towel to relationship flaws.
5. Marvin grunting, "Are you serious? Relax, it's just a towel."

These scenes involve an intricate contestation of signs. In Peirce's conception, the sign allows and limits the production of various interpretants based on the object. A sign may *stand for, denote, or represent* an object and *mean or signify* an interpretant. But, as the towel example suggests, it can do so in multiple ways. Following his threefold partition of sign, object, and interpretant, Peirce distinguished three ways in which signification can work on each of these aspects.

First, in terms of the sign itself, Peirce differentiated between what he called "tone," "token," and "type."[15] Thus, a sign can denote the vague potential of something, an actual and specific thing in the world, or a general set of phenomena. The differentiation between token and type is immediately useful. After all, the question of the towel is about what kind of sign it is—whether it signifies a specific and actual occurrence (the towel on the floor as a token for the actual act of dropping it) or a class of things (the many times a towel was left on the floor, and different moments in which similar acts of carelessness have been evidenced).

Second, Peirce distinguished three categories of signs based on how the sign related to an object: icons, indexes, and symbols. An *icon* refers to its object based on resemblance (e.g., a father says "meow" to teach a baby what noises cats make; the color green for grass). An *index* characterizes its object based on a contiguous relationship or, as Peirce put it, "a correspondence in fact" (a footprint in the snow to whoever went past; a wind vane on top of a house to the wind's direction). In our example, once Ellie makes Marvin aware of the towel, his reading of the situation becomes indexical. Like the relationship of a paw print to a passing animal, the dropped towel is an index of the action of "dropping" that located it there. Finally, a *symbol* stands for an object on conventional grounds regardless of the likeness and actual relationship to the object (e.g., the word *horse*; Arabic numerals). Since it is based on convention, any symbol, in Peirce's account, relies on a habitual way of feeling, acting, or thinking.[16]

Third, Peirce differentiated three modalities through which the interpretant could be related to the sign. These distinctions are critical for meaning-making because they highlight the active and creative role that an interpreter plays in signification. Much as signs are related to their objects and objects constrain possible signs, the same sign-objects can be taken up by their interpretants in different ways. In this view, the interpretant could take an iconic sign as iconic (a modality Peirce called a *rheme*), as in the way that a selfie picture is usually taken up in action as saying something about the person who took the self-portrait. An indexical sign, however, could be enacted as an index (a *dicent*) but also as a rheme. Thus, for example, a wind vane indicating the direction of the wind (an index) can be understood in an indexical modality, but it can also be taken as a rheme of its owner's bad taste in matters of aesthetics if we focus on its gaudiness. In the latter case something that is structured as a specific, contiguous relationship is taken up iconically. Similarly, a symbol could be understood as a rheme or a dicent, as well as being understood as a symbol (an *argument*). An American flag flying at half-staff will likely stand for mourning, shared loss, and patriotism, but it can also be interpreted as indexing the wind direction or as a piece of beaten cloth. Thus, the interpretant is part of the "play" of signification—it can align with the sign-object in a straight-forward fashion (an icon as rheme, an index as dicent, a symbol as argument) but can also creatively make it more or less general.[17] Across all three trichotomies, the different categories of signification range from potentiality, to specificity, to high generality and conventionality. As table 7.1 shows, this ordinal nature of semiotic modalities allows for "upshifting" or "downshifting" between sign categories over the course of an interaction—making them more or less general.[18]

Thus, as we describe in more detail, when a towel moves from being a marker of a specific act and becomes the sign for flawed personhood and relationship, it simultaneously moves from token to type, from index increasingly to symbol, and may produce a rheme rather than a dicent interpretant—a general upshifting of the sign category.[19] Conversely, actors can also take a symbol or type and downshift it by making signification more specific—for example, an employee arguing that he arrived late not because he is always tardy but because of the traffic on that particular day, or a student handing in yet another late assignment and explaining that the dog did, in this instance, actually eat his homework.

These semiotic distinctions are highly technical. Still, they allow us to see the towel incident in new ways. In the first scene, the dropping of the towel is not yet a sign.[20] There is nothing necessarily signifying about dropping a towel as we described it. It is in the next scene, when Ellie asks, "Is this your towel?" that the towel becomes a sign. And, at first, it seems to be a token-indexical-dicent modal-ity of semiosis—that is, it signifies only the specific dropping of the towel (thus, a token), the towel is an indexical sign for the dropping (as it is the contiguous trace of this past), and the question seems to be treating it precisely as an indexical token.

TABLE 7.1

Peirce's Semiotic Categories

	Category	Sign Classed by Own Phenomenological Category	The Sign's Relationship to Object	The Sign-Object's Relationship to Interpretant
Upshifting ↑	(X)			Argument
	(IX)		Symbol	Dicent
	(VIII)			Rheme
	(VII)	Type	Index	Dicent
	(VI)			Rheme
	(V)		Icon	Rheme
	(IV)		Index	Dicent
	(III)	Token		Rheme
	(II)		Icon	Rheme
	(I)	Tone	Icon	Rheme	Downshifting ↓

Yet, at the same time, the way this question was asked—icily—foreshadows where signification may go: the construction of an interactional and relational problem.

Indeed, Marvin's reaction in the third scene suggests that he senses the danger ahead and aims to keep the towel signification indexical. By making a joke of it, he signifies that he both treats Ellie's question as a token-indexical-dicent but also shows that he realizes that it can turn into something different.[21] He then counters the accusatory tone of the exchange in the exchange. Here, it is useful to think counterfactually and consider the many other ways in which Marvin could have reacted (claiming he didn't drop it, ignoring his partner, shouting at his partner to leave him alone, etc.). Despite openly leading to an understanding of the situation as a simple index, Marvin already assumes the shift that is potentially on the horizon, and precisely by hinting at the possible transformation, he is subtly trying to diffuse it.

In scene 4, then, the relationship of signification is explicitly altered and the problem situation takes shape. The object of the sign is rapidly changed—from the actual dropping of the towel to a chain of associations building upon one another. This, as we noted earlier, is obviously a shift from token to type. But it is also much more, because the issue at stake is not just a repeated pattern of dropped towels. Rather, what is even more revealing about this transformation is a semiotic double oscillation: both moving from index to symbol *and* simultaneously moving from dicent to rheme.

For (and here we leave the Peircean trodden path) the movement from index to symbol is continuous rather than discrete. For Ellie, the towel never quite ceases to be indexical, but the object of signification shifts from the towel to Marvin's relationship flaws. The towel stands for a type of behavior that signifies increasingly diverse problems in the relationship. This movement toward symbolization occurs through linking the towel to a list of other activities: not washing dishes and refusing to attend Thanksgiving with Ellie's relatives. Each statement is an interpretant becoming a sign in the next iteration, and with each iteration, Ellie moves up on the continuum toward a conventionalized understanding of "a flawed relationship," between indexicality and symbolism. Thus, while she still points to concrete evidence that is contiguously related to the object, this relationship becomes increasingly more abstract, so that the cumulative effect of signification accomplishes symbolization.

However, the semiotic prize that Ellie is after is not a conventional agreement that her partner is careless but an assessment of the kind of person he is. Marvin, she asserts, is someone who takes a relationship for granted. Thus, the effect of her statement shifts a dicent into iconic essentialism—into a rheme. *In an important sense, he is the dropped towel.* From a semiotic perspective, the compounded effect of turning the token into a type, the index in the direction of the symbol, and the dicent into a rheme is an upshifting of the original form of signification—making it more abstract and lawlike than it was. It is, in a sense, the kind of operation that sociologists have long thought about: turning a unique occurrence into a social type; the construction of a *social* problem.

In the last scene, however, the possibility of the interpretant to enact sign-objects in ways that are different from their modality as icons, indexes, or symbols proves critical. Marvin resists the upshifting by keeping the towel a token-indexical-dicent when he replies to Ellie's outburst with "Are you serious? It's just a towel." Whereas Ellie has upshifted the confrontation, Marvin's reaction keeps the indexicality of the sign of the fallen towel intact, producing a dicent interpretation of what was intended as a symbolic argument. With "Are you serious?" Marvin implies an understanding of the towel as increasingly symbolic—in the sense that the sign conventionally refers to the object rather than having an existential connection to it. And he rejects it as a symbol, instead emphasizing the "one off-ness" of a dropped towel as a token-indexical-dicent. The conventionality of the symbolic is reread as arbitrary assignment of value. This maintenance of indexicality under threat of upshifting is as much an accomplishment as the transformation of indexicality into a symbol.

At the same time, and perhaps in the most complicated move in this example, Marvin's reply accomplishes the downshifting back to indexicality in a particular way. In our hypothetical example, he doesn't simply say, "no, it's just this towel." By beginning his downshifting attempt with "Are you serious?" he treats the very act of signification performed by his partner as itself a sign—a token-indexical-rheme signifying the unreasonable, nagging partner who sees patterns in every little act.

This interpretive jump depends on the ready availability of a complex cultural repertoire of gendered expectations and scripts. Indeed, not only does upshifting or downshifting rest on the change of semiotic modality over time or the creativity of interpretants, but the act of signification is also always set in an interdiscursive space, and its movement in this space helps to define it.[22] After all, incidents such as the towel episode are recognizable as gendered relationship conflicts. At least in popular imagination, towel-droppers tend to be men, and the partners who turn the towel into a series of personal and relational flaws are women. Thus, the entire episode is made to fit a patriarchal script about women who "always see stuff that isn't there." And, recursively, the frame also provides Marvin with the possibility of saying, "Relax, it's just a towel." The work of masculinity, in this instance, resides in both constantly guarding the indexical and turning the upshifting itself into an index—that of the feminine figure who always reads too much into the situation as against the unfortunate, simple, token-indexical figure of masculinity.

Teasing out this hypothetical example provides insight into an important class of social problem constructions and attempted solutions. A Peircean semiotics suggests that one useful way to capture this tension is not only the question about *what* the object of signification is but also tying this question to the semiotic struggle between upshifting and downshifting signification, between generalizing and resisting generalizations—asking *how* the object is signified.[23]

DOWNSHIFTING AS A MODE OF PROBLEM-SOLVING

The foregoing example begins to give a sense of the complex semiotic work that goes into even the most mundane exchanges. But this entire episode is also an exercise in the attempted construction and solution of problems. Faced with a problem situation, each party recasts the world in a different way in order to make sense of it and to advantageously position themselves in it while constantly anticipating how their positioning will be understood by the other interactant.

Semiotic registers, then, are the ways through which problems are made and solved. This is so because the situation will unfold differently depending on which meaning structure takes hold. If employees are late, they need to work at downshifting this lateness. If their lateness is upshifted to become symbolic of their attitude toward the work more generally, or if it is presented as the type of thing they do, they will probably be fired. What this example shows is the kind of work that goes into both generalizing and specifying the social world. We have long been accustomed to thinking about generalization as the work of "making things social," as in the important stream of work that examines typification.[24] Making things social is plucking them out of their specificity and making them stand for some larger class of entities. Making things social is the work of upshifting. And yet, what the earlier example shows us is that an equally important, and equally social, process operating on an interactional level is the opposite move: that of "making things specific." Moreover, the example shows that such downshifting can, in some situations, be a way of exercising power in interaction.

Rather than continue with the question of downshifting as an exercise of power, we next present an example from the work of fellow ethnographer John O'Brien.[25] It follows the lead of some sociologists who have noted that modes of particularizing and downshifting may often serve as a weapon of the weak—a way to disarm and challenge stereotyping.[26] As we show, however, such downshifting from a position of weakness requires actors to develop complex, and often quite fragile, semiotic strategies.

As our theoretical benchmark, we build on Goffman's arguments regarding the normative dilemmas that stigmatized people face when encountering "normals."[27] The challenge is that the stigmatized are not expected to explicitly confront the bigotries held by others, while they also cannot expect to be truly accepted as people with stigma. The best they can hope for is feigned acceptance of feigned normality. This catch becomes particularly acute when the stigmatized want to confront and undo prejudice. Professionals and sympathetic outsiders may offer "tricks of the trade" for stigma management, but people facing stigma mostly learn from their peers. Yet, even among peers, the stigmatized are trapped by the double bind of needing to acknowledge that they collectively share a "spoiled" identity in order to negate the grounds for stigmatization. Such backstage interactions of stigma management among peers thus need to simultaneously play on different registers: rehearsing appropriate stigma management strategies is directed at navigating the hostile outside world while also providing morale-boosting, face-saving behavior to an inside audience of peers who partake in such preparatory interactions.

As an example of such collective stigma management, we can reanalyze a short incident noted by O'Brien.[28] He studied high school Muslims coming of age in post 9/11 United States. Some of the prejudice against Muslims following the attacks filtered down to the high school level (several local schools, for example, organized an "Islamo Fascism Week"), rendering the youth vulnerable to stigmatization. Consequently, the mosque that O'Brien studied engaged in what he called "stigma management rehearsals" whereby leaders discussed appropriate responses to provocations—a concerted set of problem-solving sessions. In one instance, a staff member leads a workshop in which small groups of participants act out social problems in a skit and the entire group discusses potential solutions. O'Brien describes what happens:

> Another kid, Waseem, goes up. He tells the group: "Why would you fools call me a terrorist? You (to Ali) you look like Chewbacca! And you, you look like a piece of bleep!" People laugh a lot, and Kim [the staff member] laughs too. Then she says, "Is that a good way to solve it?" Everyone says, "NO!" Next Adam volunteers to step in: "You don't know anything about Islam. You don't know who their families are or where they are from! How do you know they're terrorists?" People nod approvingly.[29]

Taking a semiotic approach to the sequential buildup of the situation, Waseem's first act is to attribute a type-iconic-rheme to his invisible interlocutors—you are a kind of person (a type) who is a terrorist by dint of sharing a quality with "other terrorists" (an icon), and the signification is supposed to define Waseem's essence (a rheme). Starting his turn by defying signification ("you fools"), he then constructs a surprisingly similar semiotic structure to the people sitting in front of him. His utterance "You look like Chewbacca" works on multiple semiotic levels: it is an example of a possible retort to being called a terrorist—a countermove that is dependent on disarming a situation with humor. Since Waseem specifically targets Ali with the comparison to the hairy *Star Wars* character, the skit is also a cover to put in a humorous dig at his friend (a practice well honed in high school interactions).[30] Similarly, when he states that another peer "looks like a piece of bleep," the response registers as a possible type-iconic-rheme retort all the while signaling that he knows that in the mosque context, one cannot curse freely.

Waseem's attempt, then, does not directly downshift the external threat; instead, it plays to the local audience and exposes the ridiculous nature of the stigma by responding in kind—both to his imaginary aggressors and to his friends. He solves Goffman's double bind through the use of humor, which allows him to both denounce stigma but also make it seem that nothing much is going on—thus hedging his bets even as he attempts to respond to the stigmatizing taunt.

With the question "is this a good way to solve it?" the staff member undercuts the semiotic multiplicity, effectively (and rhetorically) asking whether countering one type-iconic-rheme with another constitutes an appropriate response to stigmatization and whether profane humor is the best way to approach the challenge. The unanimous audience rejoinder confirms that the youth agree—at least to the staff member's face—that such a response is wanting. Falling back in line, Adam offers a way out. His statement, "You don't know anything about Islam," explicitly calls into question the basis for signification in the original terrorism association, turning the insult into an essential personal, intellectual flaw with a token-iconic-rheme. The elaboration about specific families uses a type-index-dicent line of signification to question the entire act of symbolization, arguing that to the degree that Muslims are signs at all, they are radically specific. The audience's interpretant, nodding, suggests that they accept this as a downshifting strategy.

In the skit, the youth and the staff provisionally resolve Goffman's double bind of having to see themselves as others see them—as tainted by stigma—in order to condemn the stigma. Downshifting occurs collectively: Waseem, Adam, Kim, Waseem's "targets," and the audience collaborate to disarm a potentially threatening charge that, if it were to stick, could lead to cascading negative consequences. In the safety of a friendly environment, they collectively try out different semiotic solutions. And yet, these stigma management rehearsals produce fragile semiotic techniques—techniques that work better as performances of solidarity than as backstage rehearsals.

Thus, in Waseem's attempt, the humorous register is the key problem-solving moment, even as joking, here, already concedes that downshifting is precarious. But the second strategy, following the staff member's invitation, is actually weaker. Heeding her call, Adam produces a pedagogic moment, effectively stopping the interaction to reflect on the problematic grounds of signification. The move rests on the staff member's ability to disrupt the interaction and change its semiotic register. And although "correct"—as the youth all acknowledge—it is also likely ineffective as an actual interactional downshifting strategy outside the mosque, since it quite abruptly changes frame.[31] Its destigmatizing success depends on the imaginary high school foes responding with the "right" interpretant drawing from the appropriate cultural and interdiscursive framing of the situation. In the imaginary world constructed by the instructor, racist bullies would be persuaded that ignorance of Islam should resignify the situation. But sharing such a perspective as common interactional ground is unlikely. Thus, in essence, the semiotic power of the stigma rehearsal is mostly concentrated at the Goffmanian backstage. Its enactment is more important as a way to perform and construct solidarity than as an actual rehearsal.

This episode constitutes a semiotic game. Actors are imaginatively tackling social problems that they will encounter in the future, as well as puzzling out their current situation. A Peirce-inspired analytic strategy provides a fine-grained way with which we can trace how they attempt to solve problems. By being attentive to the modes of signification, we can begin to gain appreciation for both the creativity manifested in these moments and the semiotic precarity that even their best efforts seem to provide them with.

DIRECTIONS AND POSSIBILITIES

This chapter explores some of the ways in which actors construct and solve problems through a pragmatist lens. Rather than assume that we need to go elsewhere if we want to understand the actual processes of problem-solving, we argued that classical pragmatist thought has rich notions of meaning-making. Pragmatist semiotics, however, is not a magic bullet. The kinds of problems we focused on—those of generalization and specification of signs—constitute but one cluster of problems, albeit a socially critical one that can be found at the basis of any kind of stereotyping and attempts to counter such typecasting. Peirce was no social scientist, and questions of group formation, the distribution of habits, social power, and moments of solidarity were beyond the scope of his thought.

We want to highlight, however, that, at a minimum, social scientists should link accounts of meaning-making with theorizations of problem-solving. Problems are inherently *meaningful.* How we semiotically approach the situation—whether explicitly, semiconsciously, or anywhere in between—is important. As actors attempt to puzzle out their world, they do so by casting and recasting it in slightly different ways and to different effects. In thinking about modes of signification in action, Peirce thus provides us with useful analytic tools for the analysis of interaction and meaning-making. In other words, and in a more pragmatist vein, we argue that semiotics *makes a difference* in how we see the world and in the questions that we ask.

We exemplified one contribution of Peirce's semiotics to a sociological-interactional analysis. Using the stereotypical example of a domestic dispute (and of sexism), we outlined how Peirce's semiotic account highlights the interactional work involved in processes of upshifting and downshifting and why this can be a useful way to think about things we care deeply about as sociologists. These semiotic registers are some of the most pernicious ways in which ethnicity and gender are "done."[32]

This, however, is only one among many possible applications of pragmatist semiotics. As we alluded in both the towel example and O'Brien's work, for instance, another fruitful line of thought is to make semiotic sense of frame shifts in interaction.[33] What humor, for example, means in an interaction (at least in the examples we use) is that while speakers use one semiotic register explicitly, they may also anticipate another semiotic register implicitly. The bifurcation of meaning, which is the hallmark of the humorous mode, becomes apparent as a bifurcation of semiotic modes—something that is hard to capture structurally without a semiotic toolbox.[34] It would be generative to push this line of work further and see whether and how different experiential frames are marked by specific semiotic forms, and where changes in semiotic form can be used as a way to trace frame shifts in interaction.

In short, we argue that the question of problem construction and problem-solving, some of the most important tenets of pragmatist thought, need be tackled more directly. And as more and more sociologists position problem-solving at the center of their work, they should draw on the resources that pragmatist thought has already been developing to link meaning-making to the ongoing semiosis of social life.

NOTES

1. Both these metaphors and research projects, of course, are themselves deeply indebted to pragmatist thought, if often implicitly.

2. John Dewey, *The Middle Works of John Dewey, Volume 14, 1899–1924: Human Nature and Conduct* (1922; Carbondale: Southern Illinois University Press, 1988); Josh Whitford, "Pragmatism and the Untenable Dualism of Means and Ends: Why Rational Choice Theory Does Not Deserve Paradigmatic Privilege," *Theory and Society* 31, no. 3 (2002): 325–63.

3. Mustafa Emirbayer, and Matthew Desmond, *The Racial Order* (Chicago: University of Chicago Press, 2015); Neil Gross, "A Pragmatist Theory of Social Mechanisms," *American Sociological Review* 74, no. 3 (2009): 358–79; Pierre Bourdieu, *Outline of a Theory of Practice*, Cambridge Studies in Social and Cultural Anthropology 16 (Cambridge: Cambridge University Press, 1977); and Bourdieu, *Pascalian Meditations* (Stanford: Stanford University Press, 2000).

4. Pierre Bourdieu, and Loïc J. D. Wacquant, *An Invitation to Reflexive Sociology* (Chicago: University of Chicago Press, 1992).

5. Phaedra Daipha, *Masters of Uncertainty: Weather Forecasters and the Quest for Ground Truth* (Chicago: University of Chicago Press, 2015).

6. See also Ann Swidler, *Talk of Love: How Culture Matters* (Chicago: University of Chicago Press, 2001).

7. Although we do not engage French neopragmatism here, we note that this stream of research relies on a somewhat similar reading of the relation between problem-solving, a repertoire of "solutions" (if organized in "regimes of worth"), and the affordances of the situation. See Luc Boltanski and Laurent Thévenot, *On Justification: Economies of Worth*, Princeton Studies in Cultural Sociology 27 (Princeton, NJ: Princeton University Press, 2006).

8. Robert S. Jansen, "Situated Political Innovation: Explaining the Historical Emergence of New Modes of Political Practice," *Theory and Society* 45, no. 4 (2016): 319–60.

9. Specifically, we focus on the ways in which Peirce's theory of meaning is developed in his "intermediate" semiotic account.

10. Ferdinand de Saussure, *Course in General Linguistics* (New York: Open Court, 1986). CP refers to: Charles Sanders Peirce, *Collected Papers of Charles Sanders Peirce, Volume VIII; Reviews, Correspondence, and Bibliography*, ed. Arthur W. Burks (Cambridge, MA: Harvard University Press, 1958).

11. Hans Joas, *The Creativity of Action* (Chicago: University of Chicago Press, 1996).

12. William H. Sewell, "A Theory of Structure: Duality, Agency, and Transformation," *American Journal of Sociology* 98, no. 1 (1992): 1–29.

13. John O'Brien, "Spoiled Group Identities and Backstage Work: A Theory of Stigma Management Rehearsals," *Social Psychology Quarterly* 74, no. 3 (2011): 291–309.

14. This is not the only way in which a researcher could analyze this interaction. A linguistic anthropologist, for example, may look at each word or phrase, subdividing the incident into a dozen semiotic elements, or focus on one specific kind of question or response. The number of semiotic units depends on the researcher's purpose.

15. Peirce also referred to tone, token, and type as "qualisign," "sinsign," and "legisign." For our purposes, we ignore the general architecture of potentiality, actuality, and generality that underlies the tripartite division within each type of signs. Despite a rich literature in linguistic anthropology (see, e.g., Asif Agha, *Language and Social Relations. Studies in the Social and Cultural Foundations of Language* 24 [Cambridge: Cambridge University Press, 2007]; Lily Hope Chumley, "Evaluation Regimes and the Qualia of Quality," *Anthropological Theory* 13, nos. 1–2 [2013]: 169–83; and Michael Silverstein, "Axes of Evals," *Journal of Linguistic Anthropology* 15, no. 1 [2005]: 6–22), we find this language inadequate to provide a good account of this case. For useful expositions of Peirce's thought on this matter, see, for example, James J. Liszka, *A General Introduction to the Semiotic of Charles Sanders Peirce* (Bloomington: Indiana University Press, 1996); Richard J. Parmentier, *Signs in Society: Studies in Semiotic Anthropology* (Bloomington: Indiana University Press, 1994); Parmentier, "Troubles with Trichotomies: Reflections on the Utility of Peirce's Sign Trichotomies for Social Analysis," *Semiotica* no. 177 (2009): 139–55; and Thomas Lloyd Short, *Peirce's Theory of Signs* (New York: Cambridge University Press, 2007).

16. Winfried Nöth, "The Criterion of Habit in Peirce's Definitions of the Symbol," *Transactions of the Charles S. Peirce Society* 46, no. 1 (2010): 82–93.

17. We note that the sign-object does constrain the forms of signification that are possible. Rather than 27 possible permutations (3 x 3 x 3), Peirce allowed for ten classes of signs. For the purposes of this chapter, however, we do not focus on Peirce's rules of permutation . See Parmentier, "Troubles with Trichotomies," for an exceptionally clear exposition of the logic undergirding these possibilities. We also note that changes in the modality of signification (such as the wind vane becoming a rheme) often also encapsulate a shift in the object of signification.

18. Parmentier, *Signs in Society*; Parmentier, "Troubles with Trichotomies."

19. Technically, a move "up" from the fourth to the eighth category.

20. We take this position because we intend this to be an interpretant-centric semiotics. For a different semiotic take, see Eduardo Kohn, *How Forests Think: Toward an Anthropology Beyond the Human* (Berkeley: University of California Press, 2013).

21. In other words, he is reacting to the paralinguistic message encapsulated in Ellie's tone of voice. John J. Gumperz, *Discourse Strategies. Studies in Interactional Sociolinguistics* 1 (Cambridge: Cambridge University Press, 1982).

22. Silverstein, "Axes of Evals."

23. Eitan Wilf, "Semiotic Dimensions of Creativity," *Annual Review of Anthropology* 43, no. 1 (2014): 397–412.

24. Peter L. Berger and Thomas Luckmann, *The Social Construction of Reality: A Treatise in the Sociology of Knowledge* (New York: Anchor, 1966); Alfred Schutz and Thomas Luckmann, *The Structures of the Life-World, Vol. 1*, Studies in Phenomenology and Existential Philosophy, trans. Richard M. Zaner and H. Tristram Engelhardt, Jr. (Evanston, IL: Northwestern University Press, 1973).

25. Stefan Timmermans and Iddo Tavory, "Racist Encounters: A Pragmatist Semiotic Analysis of Interaction," *Sociological Theory* 38, no. 4 (2020): 295–317; O'Brien, "Spoiled Group Identities," 291–309.

26. Fred Davis, "Deviance Disavowal: The Management of Strained Interaction by the Visibly Handicapped," *Social Problems* 9, no. 2 (1961): 120–32; Michèle Lamont and Crystal Fleming, "Competence and Religion in the Cultural Repertoire of the African American Elite," *Du Bois Review* 2, no. 1 (2005): 29–43.

27. Erving Goffman, *Stigma: Notes on the Management of Spoiled Identity* (New York: Touchstone, 1963).

28. O'Brien, "Spoiled Group Identities," 291–309.

29. O'Brien, "Spoiled Group Identities," 302.

30. Jooyoung Lee, *Blowin' Up: Rap Dreams in South Central* (Chicago: University of Chicago Press, 2016).

31. Erving Goffman, *Frame Analysis: An Essay on the Organization of Experience* (Cambridge, MA: Harvard University Press, 1974).

32. Candace West and Don H. Zimmerman, "Doing Gender," *Gender & Society* 1, no. 2 (1987): 125–51.

33. Goffman, *Frame Analysis*.

34. Arthur Koestler, *The Act of Creation* (London: Hutchinson, 1964); Iddo Tavory, "The Situations of Culture: Humor and the Limits of Measurability," *Theory and Society* 43, nos. 3–4 (2014): 275–89.

8. Projective and Responsive Creativity Among On-Demand Workers

MAZEN ELFAKHANI

INTRODUCTION

This chapter develops a pragmatist framework for conceptualizing human creative action and applies it to understanding the creativity exhibited by Uber drivers. Specifically, it asks, in what ways do workers reorganize their lives around the work they perform as Uber drivers, given the structural properties of on-demand work?

The theoretical motivation is to advance discourse on creative action. Creativity is often implicitly understood in negative terms as "not habit" or, alternatively, a generic descriptor for how actors behave when habits fail. Such conceptualizations leave little room for understanding creative action in its own terms and in situations of "normal functioning"—when habits are *not failing*—and, relatedly, for understanding what creative action means for social change and social reproduction. As Joas demonstrated in *The Creativity of Action* (1996), theorizing creativity in its own terms is a critical step toward a "non-functionalist macrosociology based on social action" (198). In line with pragmatist instrumentalism,[1] using "creative action" as an analytic category is especially useful when the empirical problem involves social change and novelty, the kind associated with the emergent on-demand economy.

This theoretical focus dovetails with an empirical interest in the lives of on-demand workers, a topic with normative dimensions. The emergence of on-demand work during the Great Recession—at a time when economic insecurity (Hacker 2006; Western et al. 2012) and employment instability (Farber 2009; Hollister 2011) were especially severe—heightened normative sensibilities to questions about the growth of "nonstandard" work.[2] Are nonstandard workers being left out of the promises of neoliberal economic prosperity, or are they otherwise structurally disconnected or disembedded (Beck 1992, 2000; Giddens 1990) from the mainstream, living life on the fringe, where they experience the kinds of vicissitudes that constrain human freedoms and potential? Do new forms of labor income and the choices and contingencies around them represent new freedoms or new forms of coercion (Joas 2004)? Such narratives and paradoxes fit the experiences of some workers, but it is important to take a more inductive approach to on-demand work, given its distinctive structural properties.

A key question of both theoretical and empirical interest revolves around work structures and notions of human freedom and values. Should new forms of work created by Uber and the on-demand economy be viewed as freeing or shackling? To this end, this chapter uses the concept of "core" or "ultimate" values,[3] which "define the ideal, most abstract conception of the desirable and even what makes life worth living" (Patterson and Fosse 2015, 13). The more that work structure enables workers to realize their values, the more freeing it is. Insofar as positive freedom is viewed as intrinsically good, investigating some of the ways in which Uber's work structure enables or constrains opportunities for creative action is worthwhile from a pragmatist viewpoint.

THE CASE OF UBER AND ITS WORKERS

This section introduces Uber to highlight the company's significance as an empirical case and establish a fact base around its work structure.

Uber as Purveyor of the On-Demand Economy

Uber is a digital platform-marketplace that relies on a distributed network of drivers ("suppliers") to provide passengers ("consumers") with nearly immediate access to private or shared transportation. On the supply side, drivers use their personal (noncommercial) vehicles to service passengers, with whom they connect via a mobile application (Uber Partner). On the demand side, riders access a separate mobile application (Uber) to connect with drivers. As a corporation, in addition to marketing to both sides of the market, Uber processes the payments, tracks trips for customer safety and data collection, optimizes routes, adjusts prices given in-moment supply and demand, and maintains a mutual rating system, among other intermediary services. Workers retain fares minus a fee adjustment, which has variably been either a transaction fee—usually between 20 and 30 percent of the fare—or a fixed fee per mile traveled, with quantities varying by city-market.

By any measure, Uber is the clearest case of on-demand work in the United States. Prior to its initial public offering in May 2019, it was valued between $60 and $120 billion, touted as the highest-valued private company in the country. A few

months after its public offering, by end of 2019, it was valued (by market capitaliza-
tion) at $69 billion (Isaac, de la Merced, and Sorkin 2019). With respect to work-
ers, in November 2015, Uber reported having 400,000 active monthly drivers in the
United States (Uber Newsroom 2015a); with its rapid growth globally, in 2020, it was
estimated to have 3.9 million drivers globally (Uber Newsroom 2020), with 40 to
50 percent volume concentrated in America. In terms of industry effect, since the
2012 launch of its low-price "mass" product, UberX, Uber has effectively disrupted
the taxicab industry (Romburgh 2015;[4] Gray 2016; Megaw 2016) and triggered what
has been called the "Uber for X" phenomenon (or "uberization")—that is, the
adoption of on-demand models by startups in myriad service areas.

Uber's emergence has been publicly contentious, particularly with respect to
whether its drivers should be classified as independent contractors or employees.
These and other questions have engaged a wide range of stakeholders, including
city officials, taxicab owners, lobbyists and leasers/renters, Uber drivers, and activist citizens. More broadly, Uber has triggered normative debates about the institutionalization of nonstandard work and the conditions of on-demand workers. Thus,
although there are many ride-sourcing, platform-marketplaces today, Uber is usefully viewed as a key purveyor of on-demand work and its social organization.

The Structure of Work for Uber Drivers

Two aspects of driving for Uber are particularly important to highlight for understanding creative action: Uber provides stable, predictable full-time work income—
that is, predictable work hours—and relative autonomy—that is, considerable
control over hours worked, the feeling that one has no employer, supervisor, or boss.

First, with respect to the predictability of full-time work, although Uber's fees and
prices fluctuate, in major cities the availability of work is stable. In this sense, Uber
differs from "precarious" or "contingent"[5] forms of nonstandard work—most typically temporary work (i.e., agencies, direct-hire), contract company work, on-call
work, and day labor—for which the availability of work hours is typically erratic.
In Boston, drivers' mean earning rate of $20.29 per hour (Hall and Krueger 2016)
is at least as high as earnings from taxicab and limousine driving.[6] Marginal wages
from an additional hour of work are similar irrespective of how many hours a driver
has worked; that is, the difference in income between driving ten or eleven hours in
a week versus forty or forty-one hours is similar (Hall and Krueger 2016).

Second, on-demand work provides workers with a considerable degree of *autonomy*, which, for Uber drivers, has two implications: control over work hours and the
feeling of "being one's own boss" or subject to only indirect supervision in the form
of passenger ratings. While Uber has influence over its drivers and many of the "suggestions" it gives its driver-contractors are subtly coercive, Uber drivers are not subject to many of the constraints experienced in more traditional jobs (e.g., controlled
hours). Benenson Strategy Group stated that 87 percent of drivers cite "being [their]
own boss" as a major reason for working with Uber (BSG 2015). Importantly, Uber's

hourly earning structure is what makes this autonomy *flexible*.[7] This eases decisions around working fewer rather than more hours and fluctuating one's work hours week to week, if the need or preference arises. Many drivers vary their hours across weeks, and 62 percent of Uber drivers said they had a second job (BSG 2015). Drivers commonly use Uber to pursue other activities, including working other jobs simultaneously, exploring other opportunities,[8] and enjoying recreation activities.

How do these work structure characteristics help with understanding creativity? Insofar as creativity is partly related to the range of choices available to an actor, it follows that the case of how Uber drivers organize their lives is fertile ground for understanding different kinds of creative action as well as the normative dimensions of Uber's work structure. The suggestion is not that Uber's work structure enables high degrees of creativity but, rather, that its work structure may provide a unique lens for gaining insight into different modes of creative action.

THREE MODES OF CREATIVE ACTION: SLACK, RESPONSIVE, PROJECTIVE

This section synthesizes research on creative action in contexts involving a wide range of problem situations and resources. It constructs three conceptions of creativity: (a) *slack* creativity, which reflects a view most associated with behavioral economics (Mullainathan and Shafir 2013); (b) *responsive* creativity, which reflects a prevailing conceptualization of creativity within contemporary sociology; and (c) *projective* creativity, which reflects particularly important but neglected behavioral dynamics.

Slack Creativity

A general framework for understanding creativity can be derived[9] from Mullainathan's and Shafir's (2013) research into the cognitive effects of scarcity. They argue that when actors "feel [they] have too little" (12), their cognitive capacity and executive control functions become constrained (39–68); the corollary is that creativity tends to be observed when actors have sufficient "slack" or "room" for creativity.

Their argument's generality stems from the fact that scarcity in *any* resource (e.g., money, time, food) generates a similar mindset, which is characterized by "focus[ing] single-mindedly on managing the scarcity at hand" (29), or what they describe as "tunneling." While tunneling predisposes people to efficient management of their present needs, its flip side is a narrowing of planning and other modes of action that involve creativity, or what they call a "bandwidth tax."

However, the usefulness of the concept of slack creativity may be limited to only the most extreme empirical cases. The strongest evidence in favor of the argument that scarcity generates similar cognitive and behavioral effects is based on experimental studies in which the experience of scarcity can be induced. In such situations, scarcity is sharply experienced and negates the effects of other behavioral determinants; for example, extreme hunger likely induces similar effects across most individuals. However, when less extreme scarcity is experienced, there is much more scope for cultural processes to influence the behavior.

For instance, among Mullainathan's and Shafir's most central examples is poverty. Yet, as Patterson has argued (Patterson and Fosse 2015, 4), "the simple truth of the matter is that there is no such thing as *the* culture of poverty. Poor people all over America and the world adapt to their socioeconomic, physical, and political environments in a wide variety of ways." For example, in the United States there is ample evidence over decades that Black and white Americans use different kinds of consumer credit to cope with financial distress, with African Americans disproportionately using payday loans and other kinds of "fringe credit" (Kolb 1999; Logan and Weller 2009; Elliehausen 2009; Wheatley 2010), a fact partly explained by the concentration of payday lenders in Black neighborhoods (Li et al. 2009).

Responsive Creativity

Creative action is most commonly understood in the sociological literature as a response to a new or enduring problem situation. Hall and Lamont (2013) capture this notion as "social resilience," that is, the "capacity of groups . . . to sustain and advance their well-being in the face of challenges to it" (2). Researchers have illustrated this responsive creativity in a wide range of contexts, including neoliberal economic restructuring (Han 2012; Brown-Glaude 2011), negative social categorizations and social exclusion (Lamont and Mizrachi 2012; Fleming, Lamont, and Welburn 2012; Lamont and Molnar 2001), race and consumption (Charles, Hurst, and Roussanov 2009), and political disenfranchisement (Chambers 2006; Mullins 1999; Lee 2002; Chin 2001). For example, Edin's[10] and Shaefer's (2016) $2.00 a Day vividly profiles the ways in which the poorest American families discover new sources of income and ways of saving, including donating blood, using public libraries for internet, and sharing resources.

The construct of responsive creativity helps to explain how actors use available resources and habits to maintain their interests in the face of problems, as well as which resources, including network members, are used or called on in which situations (Dominguez and Watkins 2003; Small and Sukhu 2016). It demonstrates the robustness of human creative problem-solving even in situations of extreme deprivation (e.g., Edin and Shaefer 2016), which helps to limit the generality of Mullainathan's and Shafir's (2013) perspective.

However, the construct of responsive creativity has important limitations. The framing of creative action as *responsive* is evocative of "behavioral stimulus" propositions (Homans 1974), which, in the context of understanding creativity, implicitly views actors as only *beset* by problems rather than having influence over the situations to which they flow in and out.[11] Yet, social experience fundamentally entails continuous transactions between actors and problem situations (e.g., between "mind and world" and "belief and fact"; see Peirce 1877, 1878; Dewey 1922c), a notion that points to a conception of creativity as projective.

Projective Creativity

Creative capacities are often oriented toward *actualizing* or realizing one's values (Goldstein 1934). Rather than being a direct response to a constraining or disruptive problem situation, projective creativity is observed in "normal," harmonious situations. Further, rather than involving actors beset by situational dictates, projective creativity results in actors' forging new flows of action, which shape the kinds of problem situations they encounter. Central to Joas's (1996) thesis was this notion that creativity is an everyday phenomenon displayed in everyday problem-solving and wide-ranging metaphors of expression, intelligence, and reconstruction rather than a representation of sporadic innovation or artistic genius.

Empirical illustrations can be seen in the literature on childbearing (Edin and Kefalas 2005), immigrant mobility (Dominguez 2011), and aesthetic production (Patterson and Fosse 2015; Marshall 2015). For example, Edin and Kefalas show how, somewhat independent of their material circumstances, young women in Baltimore viewed having children as "an absolutely essential part of a young woman's life, the chief source of identity and meaning." Dominguez (2011) describes Latin American immigrant women's "self-propelling agency" based on a deep-seated desire to live up to the expectations of their parents and cultural beliefs about the limited opportunities for upward mobility in their countries of origin.[12] In both examples, the subjects' beliefs and values projectively shape their actions.

The construct of projective creativity sensitizes researchers to how actors can project their cultural knowledge onto their practices and experiences in ways that shape the kinds of situations into which they select. Projective creative action is as heterogeneous as are configurations of habits; different actors have different aspirations and projects (e.g., entrepreneurial, consumption-related, familial); and, indeed, it is the interaction of habits with ecological structures that is most critical. In this way, different kinds of work structures will vary in both the extent and ways in which they elicit projective creativity. It would be expected that Uber's work structure—particularly the relative autonomy it affords workers and the predictability of its wage structure—would create dynamics that are well captured by the concept of projective creativity.

DATA AND METHODS

To understand how Uber drivers reorganize their lives around their work, sixty-two semistructured interviews were conducted with drivers in the Greater Boston Area between September 2015 and June 2017.

TABLE 8.1

Characteristics of Interviewee Sample Versus Sample from Uber's Twenty Largest Markets

Characteristics	Interviewee Sample	Uber-Provided Sample from Largest Markets
Age		
18–29	17%	19%
30–39	26%	30%
40–49	41%	26%
50–64	14%	22%
65+	2%	3%
Education		
No college	18%	12%
Some college	34%	40%
College/post-college	48%	48%
Hours/Week		
1–15	36%	51%
16–34	35%	30%
35–49	18%	12%
50+	11%	7%
Women	10%	14%
Immigrant	78%	N/A

Driver characteristics in twenty largest markets are from Jonathan V. Hall and Alan B. Krueger, *An Analysis of the Labor Market for Uber's Driver-Partners in the United States* (working paper 22843, National Bureau of Economic Research, November 2016, https://www.nber.org/papers/w22843).

The most representative data on Uber drivers comes from Hall and Krueger's (2016) work, which drew on Uber-provided administrative data on drivers in Uber's twenty largest markets.[13] Table 8.1 provides descriptive statistics comparing the characteristics of the interview pool with Hall and Krueger's data. The interview pool had fewer drivers over age fifty, was slightly more formally educated, and had a smaller proportion who drove between one and fifteen hours per week; other characteristics were quite similar.

Regarding format, I accessed Uber drivers by calling an UberX, which is the most basic private car service offered. I asked drivers if I could conduct a short interview with them while they were driving me to an arbitrary destination, after which we would typically continue the conversation in the parked car, at a nearby venue, or by phone later in the day. Of the drivers, 78 percent agreed to be interviewed, resulting in sixty-two interviews ranging from one to four hours.

Interviews were divided into two parts. The first involved structured questions covering educational history, labor market history, financial history, family, friends, and the like. The second part involved open-ended questions focused on understanding the driver's experience with Uber; special attention was given to changes in the driver's life in relation to their Uber experience.

This interview-based data collection approach has limitations, including risks of "errors of inference" (Becker and Geer 1957, 13), "attitudinal fallacy" (Jerolmack and Khan 2014), and social desirability bias (Cook and Campbell 1979); however, interviews were useful for addressing the research question for at least two reasons. First, interviews allowed for constructing a "temporal and narrative structure of events that already have occurred," as argued by Jerolmack and Khan (2014, 180) and to which cultural knowledge can be linked. Second, as Pugh (2013) has argued, interviews can capture emotional dimensions of behavior that are central especially to grasping evaluative cultural knowledge (Patterson 2014) and how it shapes action.

FINDINGS

Findings are organized into three recurrent themes: financial projects, familial aspirations, and behavioral regulation. The first section centers on how Uber's work structure facilitated the development of financial self-efficacy among a subset of drivers; the second on how the Uber experience was often used to realize familial aspirations; and the third on how Uber triggered specific behavioral shifts.

Financial Projects

Many drivers described their Uber experience as being the first time in their lives that they felt they were gaining control over their finances and were accumulating wealth. This newfound financial self-efficacy reduced uncertainty regarding the attainability of various personal financial aspirations, resulting in drivers' taking concrete steps toward realizing these aspirations. These themes are illustrated through the cases of Abe and Lucas.

Abe—who was in his mid-fifties and married with two children and had immigrated to the United States around 1995—had been working with Uber for two and a half years, driving fifty hours a week, and reportedly earning $55,000 in pretax income through the Uber platform.

He had worked as a taxicab driver prior to Uber but described it as "paying less and [involving] more aggravation with the owners and riders." He described the attractiveness of Uber in the first few months as based primarily on pay, but over time, he increasingly came to value the autonomy that Uber provided, specifically the sense of financial self-efficacy (control) that it gave him: "The way I see my job now is . . . now I control my finances better. I can control my spending so I can calculate my future, . . . what I have in mind to do tomorrow." By this, Abe was expressing the relationship between being able to predict his earnings and the *motivation* to want to control his spending and budget, which he described in detail: "I spend $800 per month on my home . . . for food it's about $250 per month . . . car insurance is about $380 per month. Gas is 15 percent less with Uber because of discounts, so about $40 per week."

Abe had bought his current car through one of Uber's auto-financing programs, describing it as his first "investment": "This is a reliable car . . . not like my two cars before, which would always break down. This is reliable. It's $24,000. . . . It's a great investment. I paid for it because I wanted a car in good condition so people like it and so it doesn't break down. It's clean, and I don't have to just lease a car, which is wasted money, like I did when I was a taxi [driver]."

He went on to describe his savings in relation to the car purchase: "Now I have $700 saved with no debt. I've made $13,000 payment on this car. . . . I have $11,000 more and I can do it in a year, and then I'll be saving more money. I'm making about $4,500 [i.e., before expenses] a month now [pretax] and can make more by driving more if I want." These savings were a critical part of his plan: "Then once I'm done with this one [i.e., making payments on current car], I want to start a transportation business. I can buy other cars like this and lease them to drivers." Abe wanted to buy a fleet of Uber cars and generate income by leasing the cars to other Uber drivers and teaching them how to use Uber most effectively.

Like Abe, Lucas also described Uber as giving him a greater feeling of control over his finances and his plans, particularly over his debt. Lucas, in his late twenties had started driving with Uber part-time in early 2015 (six months prior to interview) to supplement his income so that he could pay off his credit card debt (he had five cards) faster. He currently had $8,000 left in these loans, ranging from 9 to 22 percent interest rates, and despite these high rates, he said he was confident that he would be able to pay off this debt in the coming years: "The great thing is that with Uber I know I can pay off my credit cards by driving more. . . . My other job [he worked at a dry cleaner during the day] is for during the day, it's fixed . . . but here I can drive as many hours as I want to make more." He went on to illustrate his strategy: "I make extra money here when I want to [i.e., through Uber] and I pay the highest interest rate card first, then the others . . . you know the snowball method. That's what I do."

Lucas insisted that not only did Uber make him confident that he would pay off his loan in the coming years, but that it made him more meticulous in tracking his income and expenditures more generally: "When I got this Uber app and was seeing the weekly earnings, I wanted to track more of my expenses, so I got other apps that would let me see my progress . . . so I have this one [he showed me Debt Tracker iPhone application] and this [Mywallet application], and I do calculations on credit cards here [pointing to his phone]."

Yet, though Lucas had become more meticulous in tracking his finances, his broader project was entirely recreational; Abe, in contrast, used the financial confidence that Uber afforded him to plan steps to realize his vision for buying more cars to start a transportation business through Uber. In Lucas's case, his newfound financial confidence and motivation to track his finances allowed him recently to save enough money to purchase a boat that he had been planning to buy for years:

"Ever since I was a kid I wanted to buy a boat like this. I just love it so much. So I saved for it and realized I could do it by working more and bought it a few months ago." He went on to describe its significance for him: "It just feels so free and great to have it. . . . I love the water and being out there and I've just always wanted it." He had paid $1,200 for the boat, and when asked why he did not put that money toward his substantial credit card debt given the interest rates, he said, "you see, I'm really not worried about the debt. I can just drive more hours when I need to. So it's fine."

Both drivers did, however, allude to the fact that even with extremely long work hours, they can earn only a good working-class wage, never the kind of middle-class income that would be needed to turn their lives around entirely. Abe said, "at the end of the day, I can work when I want and make more, and that's good, but I won't ever make six figures doing this, and only from that would I have the savings to do more creative things."

Overall, Uber gave drivers a feeling of financial self-efficacy, which made long-term personal projects feel more realizable. This impelled them to meticulously monitor their finances and take concrete steps toward their aspirations. More generally, many drivers expressed a feeling of personal achievement at making regular payments toward ownership of relatively expensive vehicles (often above $20,000 in market value). This feeling of building wealth, and the feeling of self-efficacy that it created, tended to be strongest among drivers who rented their homes (rather than owning a mortgage) and those who were formerly vehicle-leasing taxicab drivers (e.g., Abe). Such drivers described their cars as smart investments in their futures, moving them toward asset accumulation, financial security, and possibly future investment income. However, drivers did feel that the absolute wages themselves put a cap on their creative prospects even while inducing creativity within a certain band of earnings.

Family Aspirations

Drivers with families commonly used Uber, in ways that were otherwise cumbersome for them prior to joining the Uber platform, to realize familial aspirations tied to (a) strengthening relationships with children (e.g., gift purchases, quality time), (b) more effective spousal coordination (e.g., division of parenting responsibilities) and expressions of love; and (c) planning to start a family. To these ends, drivers reorganized their lives around Uber on the basis of the relative predictability of Uber's wages and the autonomy it affords drivers.

First, with regard to predictable wages, drivers described a "financial routine" through which they strengthened their relationships with their children (especially children living with ex-wives) and their wives. It centered on exercising their ability to earn roughly predictable extra income through additional hours worked for the purpose of making targeted gift purchases for their children and partners.

Christopher was in his late thirties, immigrated to the United States around 2005, and had been driving full-time with Uber for just under a year. He had married twice and had two children with his first wife. In order to stay close to them (they lived with their mother), and on the basis of knowing that he could predictably earn extra income by driving more hours, Christopher described the pattern of using extra income for buying gifts: "When I want to buy them a thing they like, I determine to drive an extra hour or two and then buy it for them. . . . I just go home a bit later then."

He went on to contrast Uber with his prior two jobs: "When I worked at the car dealership and at [major retailer], getting extra hours was not so easy as it is with Uber." Christopher described gift-buying as a way of staying close to his children: "I buy them things for their phone and other kinds of stuff. . . . They really like those things from me."

Abe presented a very similar pattern; he also had two biological children who were living with his ex-wife and with whom he sought to show his affection: "I buy my kids things they need like clothes and school supplies, but sometimes I know they like other things like electronics, so for those things that I need extra money for I just drive more hours some night and buy them. . . . It's good for when I don't get to see them. They always ask for stuff, you know."

Gift purchasing allowed Christopher and Abe to both stay involved with their children's lives—that is, because the children's mothers tended to be more accommodating when the fathers brought gifts—and also to show their affection to their children. Critically, it was the *knowledge* that they could generate extra income with little hassle, by simply, for example, starting work a bit early or returning home a bit later, that motivated them to structure their relationships with their children in this way. It was also common for drivers to use the same routine to curry favor with their wives. For example, regarding his girlfriend, with whom he had been in a relationship for almost ten years and who he was planning to marry soon, Abe said laughingly, "I also do the same thing with my girlfriend. . . . I drive a few more hours and buy her gifts for the kitchen . . . and you know, lingerie and things like that."

Second, the relative autonomy that Uber afforded drivers made much more realizable a variety of familial aspirations, including improving the quality of child care, coordinating vacation times with the spouse, and spending more time with the children.

Lucas described how he joined Uber—part-time in addition to his full-time job at a dry cleaner—not only to supplement his income but also because he and his wife preferred that she take care of their children rather than hiring a babysitter: "I think it's much better this way because she can focus better on them, she doesn't have to worry about work. . . . Also the babysitter is expensive and, you know, my wife is better for that."

For other drivers, a substantial benefit of controlling their hours was that they could more effectively carve out recreational time to pursue their hobbies and/or spend more dedicated time with their wives. For example, Sisi, whose wife worked for a state agency, described, how prior to Uber, it was always difficult to coordinate some time with his wife so they could go on short trips together, but that now he is able to do so: "A year ago before I started, it was so hard to go on vacation with my wife because of our schedules. But now I work whenever I want to, so whenever she has free time we can go." Additionally, nearly all drivers with kids described how now it was much easier to find time to spend with their kids. This was usually realized in the form of parenting obligations, such as driving their kids to school rather than stopping work early specifically to go home and spend time with them.

Finally, both predictability of wages and relative autonomy were critical to more life-changing plans such as having a baby. Pedro—who was in his mid-thirties and married but with no children—described how he always wanted to have children but was worried about ensuring that he and his wife (who worked) had the financial stability and time to manage it. He noted that Uber ensured both: "It's also much easier for me and my wife to have kids now. Because she works. So I can stay with the kids when she works. And I can work more if we will need more money. . . . We're gonna have a baby soon."

He went on to describe how he felt that the stress associated with his prior jobs in the restaurant and construction industries had made the prospect of starting a family difficult: "Roofing work is stressful. You deal with a lot of craziness. It pays good, but I actually like what I'm doing now so I'm much happier. So it makes me feel I can move forward with plans [referring to building a family] since my job is good." Thus, the relative wage predictability and work autonomy (i.e., taking care of the kids when his wife is at work), and the personal satisfaction he experienced when driving with Uber tied to wages and autonomy, made it much easier for Pedro to realize his plan of many years.

Overall, for all these drivers, the Uber experience—due to relatively stable (predictable) wages and autonomy (control over work hours)—facilitated personal aspirations involving family, specifically the strengthening of their relationships with children (e.g., gift purchases, quality time), better coordinating schedules with their spouses (e.g., vacations, dividing household work efficiently), and starting a family.

Behavioral Regulation

Uber's work structure was also used by a subset of drivers to regulate personal behaviors. The most common patterns observed were reducing cigarette and alcohol consumption, spending fewer "recreational" weekend nights (usually drinking), and intending to service riders with professionalism and excellence.

Several drivers described Uber as having helped them wean off excessive use of cigarettes or alcohol, largely given rules against cigarette -smoking in the car and federal laws against drinking alcohol while driving. Adil, who was in his early fifties and had been driving full-time with Uber for two years, described how these rules reduced his alcohol consumption: "I just can't drink as much because I'm driving, so I buy less beer than before Uber." Although Adil noted that this change has resulted in more disposable income, saving him roughly $100–$150 per month, he did not seem especially pleased with this behavioral change, viewing it simply as a given aspect of driving with Uber.

This can be contrasted with Jamal—who was in his late twenties and had been driving full-time with Uber for nine months—for whom the rule against cigarette smoke in the vehicle seemed to have a more substantial behavioral and cognitive effect, as he was a heavy smoker. "I smoke a couple packs every day, but I can't do it when driving because of the passengers. Because I want to drive more hours to make money, I just don't smoke as much as I used to before." When asked how this affected his life, beyond mentioning health effects in passing, he emphasized substantial savings: "[Before Uber] I was spending . . . maybe $1,000 [a month] on smoking. Now I spend less, . . . maybe half that." This amounted to roughly $500 per month in cost savings, which was roughly 40 percent of his monthly rent. When asked what he was doing with these extra savings, he said, "I pay off credit debt. I have about $15,000 of it, so it's helping me focus on paying that."

Relatedly, Jamal also noted an aspect of driving with Uber most often observed among younger drivers: given that peak demand for rides tends to be on Friday and Saturday nights in Boston (which translates to higher wage rates at those times), most Uber drivers tended to spend weekend nights working—often earning $250–$350 per night—rather than allocating those nights for personal recreation. Jamal said, "I don't really spend nights at the bars anymore. Before this I would go out drinking with my friends usually on weekend nights, but that is the best time to drive because everyone else is out drinking with their friends."

Another general finding was the personal satisfaction that drivers felt when they had high ratings and how it impelled them to, at the very least, state that they intended to continue to serve riders with excellence. Dwayne, who was in his early thirties and had been driving full-time with Uber for almost a year, noted how pleased he was with his high Uber rating: "I like it when the people I pick up appreciate the service I provide them. My great rating makes me know I'm doing a good job and treating them right, and they appreciate that."

This sentiment was especially common among former taxicab drivers. Sayeed, who had been driving full-time with Uber for the last year and a half and previously worked as a taxicab driver in New York City, said, "in the taxicab industry, you know, these guys [passengers] just come in and out, and you know, you're taking them where they want to go when they need to go there. So you're doing them a service, and yes they pay you, but it is good to know that they are happy with the service, so I try harder as well." He went on to describe the pride he took in maintaining a clean car so that passengers would feel comfortable on their trips.

Generally, in the aforementioned cases, it was the work structure of driving with Uber—specifically, rules against smoking and alcohol consumption, fares proportionate to demand and peak demand on weekend nights, rating systems—that triggered behavioral and emotional changes among drivers. Adil reduced his alcohol consumption; Jamal smoked less (saving money by doing so) and now only rarely went out drinking with his friends on weekend nights; and Dwayne and Sayeed expressed a deeper pride in their work (due to ratings), with Sayeed deliberately stating that with Uber he paid greater attention to rider "customer service" than he did when he was a taxicab driver. These situational triggers were mostly directed (arguably, coercively) at specific behaviors; the slight exception is Uber's rating system which tended to influence a broader set of behaviors that were tied to interactions with riders (e.g., conversational politeness, keeping the car clean).

DISCUSSION

This chapter has argued that projective and responsive creativity capture distinct social processes. Responsive creativity was defined as action oriented toward maintaining (or reconciling) one's interests or goals in relation to a problem situation; it tends to be observed when a problem situation disrupts normal functioning by imposing a constraint on the actor. In contrast, projective creativity was defined as action oriented toward realizing one's core values in relation to a problem situation; it tends to be observed when the problem situation is harmonious with the actor's sense of normality and avails the actor to opportunities to realize personal projects or develop capacities.

Thus, these two kinds of creativity differ in their social-situational antecedents and consequences. Responsive creativity is triggered by the imposition of disruptive constraints and results in the actor's maintaining their lower-order wants, whereas projective creativity is enabled by harmonious actor-ecological experiences and felicitous opportunities, which orient actors to self-actualizing or attaining higher-order wants (e.g., realizing core values). These distinctions are critical at least partly because they bear directly on questions of social change and stability; whereas responsive creativity tends to *reinforce* (or maintain) social relations and experiences, projective creativity tends to *transform* (or alter) the status quo.

These findings are discussed in three sections; the first two sections make inferences about the social processes underlying projective and responsive creativity (respectively), and the third section offers final remarks on how the findings can improve our understanding of human agency, Peirce's semiotics, emotional achievement, and unanticipated novelty.

Specified Attainability and Projective Creativity

In the first two sets of findings, several illustrations of Uber drivers engaged in creative action were characterized as projective.

First, many drivers experienced a feeling of financial self-efficacy regarding their current financial situation and futures, a feeling that they attributed directly to Uber, often describing their Uber experience as the first time that they felt they were gaining control over their finances and accumulating wealth. For example, for Lucas, Uber meant that he could generate additional part-time income whenever he needed it (e.g., consumption smoothing, accelerating debt payments); for Abe, the main difference between working in his former job as a taxicab driver and working as an Uber driver was the financial security he felt with the latter. For both drivers, the financial self-efficacy they experienced through Uber was unanticipated; that is, they had joined Uber for different reasons.

Second, among drivers with families, a pattern was observed of using Uber to realize familial aspirations involving strengthening relationships with children, improving spousal coordination and communication, and starting a family. Drivers related that these aspirations, and the core values that underpinned them, had always been important to them, but prior jobs made sustained commitment to those goals cumbersome.

Each of these cases illustrates projective—rather than responsive—creative action, a distinction best captured by expounding on antecedents and consequences.

With respect to antecedents, these drivers were not triggered into taking particular steps to ensure personal survival, as, for example, did the extremely poor (e.g., donating blood plasma for cash) described by Edin and Shaefer (2016). They were not beset by anticipated or unanticipated situational constraints to which they needed to respond in order to protect their material and/or emotional interests. Rather, given Uber's work structure, these drivers were enabled to realize their personal aspirations in ways that reflected the projection of their values onto their experiences.

Importantly, while in many cases these drivers were enduring severe material constraints, they were nonetheless able to manage and plan paths toward their aspirations; this contrasts with the view that creativity tends to be stifled by scarcity (Mullainathan and Shafir 2013). This is not to suggest that creativity cannot be constrained by material or other kinds of deprivation; rather, consistent with the literature illustrating projective creativity (Dominguez 2011; Patterson and Fosse 2015; Fosse 2015; Edin and Kefalas 2005), creative action can be quite robust to material circumstances; "slack creativity" is mostly, to use Beck and Beck-Gernsheim's (2001) phrase, a "zombie category," relevant only to the most extreme circumstances.

With respect to consequences, in the face of imposed situational constraints, these drivers' actions were not oriented toward maintaining their (narrowly conceived) interests or goals (i.e., lower-order wants); rather, they were oriented toward realizing core values in ways that altered social relations. The upshot was that their actions altered their practices; to the extent that those alterations reverberated more broadly (e.g., entrepreneurship among on-demand workers), then such projective creativity can also have a transformative effect on social relations more broadly. This is notwithstanding the real material limits on their creative prospects in the form of working-class wages.

Common to both of these sets of findings regarding projective creative action is a behavioral mechanism involving Uber's work structure and the certainty it inspires in drivers with respect to *how to attain desired outcomes*. Winship (2015) has described the antithesis of this behavioral circumstance as "unspecified attainability," a circumstance in which the constraints (e.g., uncertainty about costs or risks of a particular action) are unknown (or weakly known). I argue that the practice of driving with Uber tends to imbue particular types of drivers—those who experience on-demand work as "situationally normal"—with reduced uncertainty regarding the attainability of particular expectations of actions (i.e., beliefs about the likelihood that actions will result in particular outcomes).

From these findings, I infer the following social mechanism (i.e., sequence of events or processes; see Gross 2009[14]) as implicated in projective creativity:

Uber's work structure (i.e., nondiminishing wage returns with incremental hours worked + autonomy or control over driver's work hours) (causes) drivers who experience on-demand work as situationally normal (due to habits of thought and action) to have reduced uncertainty regarding the attainability of their personal aspirations or projects (e.g., entrepreneurship, major consumption, having a child) as well as reduced stress regarding their social situation (causes) drivers to orient their actions (e.g., financial tracking, "hyper-saving," gift-purchasing, family planning) to achieving these purposes *irrespective* (within bounds) of material constraints (e.g., credit card debt, many child dependents) (causes) alters social practices (causes) social selection into new kinds of problem situations.

Situational Constraints, Responsive Creativity, and Complications

The third set of findings regarding behavioral regulation can be usefully understood as responsive creativity, with some important qualifications that complicate this conceptualization.

Overall, it was observed that various aspects of Uber's work structure—specifically, rules against smoking in the vehicle, federal laws against drinking under the influence of alcohol, fares that are proportionate (nonlinearly) to demand and the incidence of peak demand on weekend nights, and driver rating systems—triggered behavioral changes among some drivers. Adil reduced alcohol consumption; Jamal reduced cigarette smoking (saving around $500 per month) and spent fewer weekend nights drinking with friends; and Sayeed (and, to a lesser extent, Dwayne) became more committed to excellent customer service.

Synthesis of these findings indicates that these cases illustrate responsive, rather than projective, creative action; this can be recognized when reflecting on the situational antecedents and consequences.

With respect to antecedents, these behavioral shifts were caused by situational triggers that imposed constraints on the actions of the drivers: if they wanted to continue driving with Uber, abiding by these rules was necessary. This is also true of driver ratings: in some city markets, Uber had suggested[15] to drivers that their accounts would be deactivated if their rating fell below a certain threshold. Although Adil and Jamal recognized that reduced cigarette and alcohol use was generally favorable, these behavioral changes were not personal aspirations that the drivers held prior to joining Uber; rather, they were imposed on them.

With respect to consequences, both Adil and Jamal generally adjusted to these constraints by trying to maintain their lifestyle; they merely reduced their alcohol and cigarette use and expressed little personal satisfaction as to the changes that had occurred. For Dwayne and Sayeed, the consequences are less clear; both declared that ratings made them more committed to performing their work with excellence. Further, neither mentioned trying to stay above a minimum threshold rating so they would not be deactivated from UberPartner; rather, they simply wanted as high a rating as possible.

Thus, although minimum rating requirements could be interpreted as a situational constraint that helped drivers realize deeply held aspirations to perform their work *par excellence,* a more precise interpretation is that the continuous rating scale induced some emotional satisfaction at the thought of performing better rather than worse.

From these findings, I infer the following social mechanism (Gross 2009) as implicated in responsive creativity:

Uber's work structure constraints, including behavioral rules, wage rate peaks on weekend nights, and rating systems, (cause) drivers to adjust their behaviors (e.g., smoke less, clean car more often) while nonetheless maintaining their lifestyle.

Conceptual Frontiers for Future Research

I conclude with some final remarks on how the construct of projective creativity can add clarity to conceptions of human agency and also add causal power to Peirce's semiotics.

Human Agency

First, the social process through which values are projected onto experiences and actions adds clarity to the otherwise often muddled concept of human agency by capturing how actors select into problem situations. The classic theoretical challenge is to grasp how human action can have an altering effect on social relations while simultaneously recognizing that, in the strictest sense, all human action is constrained by structural circumstance. The construct of projective creativity offers theoretical leverage in this regard by recognizing that human projects are culturally grounded, yet born of "human powers."

To elaborate on this point, all creativity is grounded in habits that become embodied through knowledge acquisition channels tied to group-level processes[16] (Patterson 2014). For example, in order to understand why entrepreneurship (e.g., owning a transportation business) was meaningful to Abe whereas certain kinds of consumption (e.g., owning a boat) were meaningful to Lucas, we would need to investigate social constructions of habits. In economic terms, Lucas's work-leisure trade-off had crossed the inflection point on a backward-bending labor supply curve; given that Uber (and his other job) satisfied his income concerns and values, he preferred substituting leisure for additional paid work. For Abe, the inflection point was much higher due to his habits. The key point is that the difference between the two is grounded in socially constructed habits. Similarly, to under-stand why starting a family was a meaningful project for Pedro, we would need to better understand his values and their formation (e.g., immigrant or religious influences). Thus, any conception of action as momentarily extricated from ecological processes is just that, a pragmatic "conception" or analytic category.

Nonetheless, it is clear that the cognitive capacity to synthesize information and plan, *project*, and calculate action that accords with one's habits is robust to even often extreme material constraints (as discussed earlier); this is precisely what the concept of projective creativity captures. It describes how actors can project meaning that is central to their identity onto their experiences and ecologies, to the effect of altering or transforming practices and social relations in ways that comport with commonsense understandings of human agency. In contrast, responsive creativity, inasmuch as it is born of disruptive (sometimes coercive) situational triggers and is oriented toward the maintenance (rather than actualizing or transforming) of wants, is arguably incongruent with intuitive understandings of agency.

Yet, even if responsive creativity is understood as a qualitatively distinct kind of agency (broadly defined), its "effects" are different from those of projective creative actions. Responsive creativity tends to imbue actors in their ordinary situational practices and the kinds of problem situations that they tend to select into and that tend to beset them, whereas projective creativity tends to create "horizon changes" for actors, altering the kinds of problem situations they select into and that tend to beset them. In this way, by theorizing projective creativity, we can move toward understanding the processes through which actors socially select into problem situations.

Peirce's Semiotics

Second, the distinction between projective and responsive creativity—particularly their different antecedents and consequences—provides the basis for adding a causal structure to semiotic frameworks that explicitly creates a link between everyday meaning-making and practical action. Peirce's triadic framework (sign, object, interpretant) offers the clearest link; its central thrust is the notion of an *interpretant*, which is the reaction that a person has when making sense of any *sign* (e.g., words, images; anything representing something else) that represents/denotes any *object* (i.e., anything conceivable). An interpretant is the "effect upon a person" (Peirce 1992, 2: 478) of the sign-object relationship and itself can be a sign for another act of meaning-making in a semiotic chain. Tavory and Timmermans (2013) have argued that Peirce's semiotics provides a "useful foundation for a mechanism-based approach to causality" (682) for ethnographers; yet, on its own, "Peirce's semiotics does not tell us why, in a specific case, meaning making operates as it does, only to think of meaning making's constituent parts."

Building on this notion, a specific question emerges: how can we move toward explaining and predicting interpretants or, at the very least, defining their scope (e.g., range of interpretants) for a given interpreter who is enmeshed in a given complex of sign-objects? How do we make semiotics explanatory and predictive?

Explaining and predicting interpretants is an ambitious and critical enterprise, and the constructs of creativity put forth in this chapter offer a step in this direction by specifying some relevant antecedents for which to look: namely, the extent to which the complex of sign-objects (e.g., those embedded in Uber's work structure) disrupts or constrains the interpreter's everyday habits (triggering responsive creativity) or, alternatively, harmonizes with habits (enabling projective creativity). Determining this extent requires inquiry into social structures (e.g., Uber's work structure) and habits of thought and action (e.g., core values).

This chapter focused on the commanding properties of work structures (more so than habits), and from this, the following two patterns emerged. First, in some circumstances, sign-objects have a commanding power over the interpretant; in these situations, interpretants can be viewed as malleable to the power of the sign-objects with which they are interacting. This strongly evokes the concept of responsive creativity, because actors' creative scope is severely limited to the imposing power of social structures. For example, Uber's explicit cigarette restrictions are sign-objects that, practically, can result in only a limited range of interpretants, to the effect of generating homogenous responses from drivers. Second, in other circumstances, it is the actor (interpreter) who possesses the commanding power over the sign-objects that they interpret; that is, they are able to interpret their situation liberally and can seize it to realize core values in the form of personal projects or deeply held aspirations. This evokes the concept of projective creativity, because actors' creative scope is expansive with enough leeway to emanate from one's core values rather than be constrained by narrow situational dictates. For example, the complex of sign-objects associated with Uber's wage and work schedule rules—including the company's explicit advertisements associating driving with calls for freedom—generate interpretants that are relatively free-ranging, to the effect that the *proactive* actions of drivers (i.e., projective creativity) are as heterogenous as are drivers' core or ultimate values (Weber 1949b).

Thus, synthesizing these constructs of creativity with semiotics has the potential to, on the one hand, render meaning-making, a *pragmatic* process rather than, in Patterson's words, a "compulsive, cognitively exhausting" (2014, 8) enterprise, and on the other, an explanandum that is amenable to causal thinking.

REFERENCES

Beck, Ulrich. 1992. *Risk Society: Towards a New Modernity*. London: SAGE.

Beck, Ulrich. 2000. *The Brave New World of Work*. London: SAGE.

Beck, Ulrich, and E. Beck-Gernsheim. 2002. *Individualization: Institutionalized Individualism and its Social and Political Consequences*. London: Sage.

Becker, Howard, and Blanche Geer. 1957. "Participant Observation and Interviewing: A Comparison." *Human Organization*. 16(3):28–32.

Beckert, Jens. 2013. "Imagined Futures: Fictional Expectations in the Economy." *Theory and Society*. 42(3): 219–240.

Benenson Strategy Group (BSG). 2015. "The Driver Roadmap: Where Uber Driver-Partners Have Been, And Where They're Going." Benenson Strategy Group. https://newsroom.uber.com/wp-content/uploads/2015/01/BSG_Uber_Report.pdf.

Brown-Glaude, Winnifred. 2011. *Higglers in Kingston: Women's Informal Work in Jamaica*. Nashville, TN: Vanderbilt University Press.

Bureau of Labor Statistics. 2016. *Occupational Employment and Wage Statistics, May 2016 Metropolitan and Nonmetropolitan Area table. https://www.bls.gov/oes/tables.htm.*

Chambers, Jason. 2006. "Equal in Every Way: African Americans, Consumption and Materialism from Reconstruction to the Civil Rights Movement." *Advertising & Society Review*.

Chang, Gordon. 2010. "Eternally Foreign: Asian Americans, History, and Race." Pp. 216–233 in *Doing Race: 21 Essays for the 21st Century*, edited by H. R. Markus and P. M. L. Moya. New York: Norton.

Charles, Kerwin, Erik Hurst, and Nikolai Roussanov. 2009. "Conspicuous Consumption and Race." *The Quarterly Journal of Economics*. 124(2): 425–467.

Chin, Elizabeth. 2001. *Purchasing Power: Black Kids and American Consumer Culture*. Minneapolis: University of Minnesota Press.

Cook, T. D., & Campbell, D. T. (1979). Quasi-experimentation: Design and analysis issues. Boston, MA: Houghton Mifflin Company.

Dewey. John. 1910. "A Short Catechism Concerning Truth", Chapter 6 in The Influence of Darwin on Philosophy and Other Essays. New York: Henry Holt and Company. 154–168.

Dewey, John. 1922. "Realism without Monism or Dualism—II." *The Journal of Philosophy*. 19(13):351–361.

Dominguez, Silvia, and Celeste Watkins. 2003. "Creating Networks for Survival and Mobility: Examining Social Capital Amongst Low-Income African-American and Latin-American Mothers." *Social Problems*. 50(1): 111–135.

Dominguez, Silvia. 2011. *Getting Ahead: Social Mobility, Public Housing and Immigrant Networks*. New York: New York University Press.

Edin, Kathryn, and Laura Lein. 1997. *Making Ends Meet: How Single Mothers Survive Welfare and Low-Wage Work*. New York, NY: Russell Sage Foundation.

Edin, Kathryn and Luke Shaefer. 2016. *$2 a Day: The Art of Living on Virtually Nothing in America*. Boston: Houghton-Mifflin Harcourt.

Edin, Kathryn, and Maria Kefalas. 2005. *Promises I Can Keep: Why Poor Women Put Motherhood Before Marriage*. California: University of California Press.

Elliehausen, Gregory. 2009. "An Analysis of Consumers' Use of Payday Loans." Accessed on December 20, 2010: http://www.business.gwu.edu/research/centers/fsrp/pdf/m41.pdf.

Farber, Henry. 2009. "Job Loss and the Decline of Job Security in the United States." Working Paper #520.

Fleming, Crystal, Michele Lamont, and Jessica Welburn. "Responding to Stigmatization and Gaining Recognition: Evidence from Middle Class and Working Class African-Americans." *Ethnic and Racial Studies*. 35: 400–417.

Fosse, Ethan. 2015. "The Values and Beliefs of Disconnected Black Youth." in Orlando Patterson's *The Cultural Matrix: Understanding Black Youth*. (2015). Cambridge, Mass: Harvard University Press.

Fromm, Erich. 1941. *Escape from Freedom*. New York: Farrar & Rinehart.

Gavazza, Alessandro, Alessandro Lizzeri, and Nikita Roketskiy. 2014. "A Quantitative Analysis of the Used-Car Market." American Economic Review. 104(4): 3668–3700.

Giddens, Anthony. 1990. *The Consequences of Modernity*. Stanford University Press.

Gross, Neil. 2009. "A Pragmatist Theory of Social Mechanisms." *American Sociological Review*. 74:358–379.

Goldstein, Kurt. 1934. "The Organism: A holistic Approach to Biology Derived from Pathological Data in Man." New York: Zone Books.

Gray, Alistair. 2016. "Taxi Lender Warns on Capital as Uber Competition Woes Deepen." *Financial Times*. Accessed on August 12, 2016. https://www.ft.com/content/90539000-5f3f-11e6-ae3f-77baadeb1c93#axzz4HDfTvj00.

Hacker, Jacob. 2006. *The Great Risk Shift: The Assault on American Jobs, Families, Health Care and Retirement and How You Can Fight Back*. Oxford University Press, USA; First Edition.

Hall, Jonathan, and Alan Krueger. 2016. "An Analysis of the Labor Market for Uber's Driver-Partners in the United States." Working Paper 587 https://www.nber.org/system/files/working_papers/w22843/w22843.pdf.

Hall, Peter, and Michele Lamont. 2013. *Social Resilience in the Neoliberal Era*. Cambridge University Press.

Han, Clara. 2012. *Life in Debt: Times of Care and Violence in Neoliberal Chile*. University of California Press.

Hollister, Matissa. 2011. "Employment stability in the US Labor Market: Rhetoric versus Reality." *Annual Review of Sociology*. 37:305 – 24.

Homans, George. 1974. *Social Behavior: Its Elementary Forms*. Harcourt Brace, USA.

Isaac, Mike, Michael de la Merced, and Andrew Sorkin. 2019. " How the Promise of a $120 Billion Uber I.P.O. Evaporated." New York Times. Accessed on June 4, 2019. https://www.nytimes.com/2019/05/15/technology/uber-ipo-price.html.

James, William. 1904. "What Pragmatism Means" in A. Blunden (Ed.), A New Name for Some Old Ways of Thinking: from William James, Writings 1902–1920 (2005th ed.). The Library of America.

Jerolmack, Colin, and Shamus Khan. 2014. "Talk is Cheap: Ethnography and the Attitudinal Fallacy." Sociological Methods & Research. 43(2): 178–209.

Joas, Hans. 1996. *The Creativity of Action*. Translated by J. Gaines and P. Keast. Chicago, IL: University of Chicago Press

Joas, Hans. 2004. "Morality in an Age of Contingency." *Acta Sociologica*. 47(4): 392–99.

Kolb, Anthony (1999) *The spatial analysis of bank and check-cashing locations in Charlotte, NC*. Chapel Hill: University of North Carolina, Center for Community Capitalism.

Lamont, Michele, and Nissim Mizrachi. 2012. *Responses to Stigmatization in Comparative Perspective*. United Kingdom: Routledge.

Lamont, Michele, and Virag Molnar. 2001. "How Blacks Use Consumption to Shape their Collective Identity: Evidence from Marketing Specialists." *Journal of Consumer Culture*. 1:31–45.

Lee, Jennifer. 2002. "From Civil Relations to Racial Conflict: Merchant-Customer Interactions in Urban America." *American Sociological Review* 67 (1): 77–98.

Lefkowitz, Joel. 2003. *Ethics and Values in Industrial-Organizational Psychology*. Mahwah, NJ: Lawrence Erlbaum Association.

Levine, Linda, Vincent Prohaska, Stewart Burgess, John Rice, and Tracy Laulhere. 2001. "Remembering Past Emotions: The Role of Current Appraisals." *Cognition and Emotion*. 15(4): 393–417.

Li, Wei, Leslie Parrish, Keith Ernst, and Delvin Davis. 2009. "Predatory Profiling: The Role of Race and Ethnicity in the Location of Payday Lenders in California." *Center for Responsible Lending*.

Logan, Amanda and Christian E. Weller. 2009. "Who Borrows From Payday Lenders?" Washington, D.C.: Center for American Progress.

Marshall, Wayne. 2015. "Hip-Hop's Irrepressible Refashionability: Phases in the Cultural Production of Black Youth." in Orlando Patterson's *The Cultural Matrix: Understanding Black Youth*. (2015). Cambridge, Mass: Harvard University Press.

Megaw, Nicholas. 2016. "Uber Expansion Leaves Taxi Industry in Urgent Need of a Lift." *Financial Times*. Accessed on May 18, 2016. https://www.ft.com/content/c4ded228-1910-11e6 -bb7d-ee563a5a1cc1#axzz48rcbIEaO.

Mullainathan, Sendhil, and Eldar Shafir. 2013. *Scarcity: Why Having Too Little Means So Much*. New York: Henry Holt & Company.

Mullins, Paul. 1999. "Race and Genteel Consumer: Class and African-American Consumption, 1850–1930." *Historical Archaeology*. 33: 22–38.

Patterson, Orlando. 2014. "Making Sense of Culture." *Annual Review of Sociology*. 2014. 40: 1–30.

Patterson, Orlando, ed. 2015. *The Cultural Matrix: Understanding Black Youth*. Cambridge, Mass: Harvard University Press.

Peirce, Charles. 1877. "The Fixation of Belief." *Popular Science Monthly*. 12: 1–15.

Peirce, Charles. 1878. "How to Make Our Ideas Clear." *Popular Science Monthly*. 12, 286–302.

Peirce, Charles. 1992–99. *The Essential Peirce*, 2 vols. Bloomington: Indiana University Press.

Plous, Scott. 1993. *The Psychology of Judgment and Decision Making*. New York: McGraw-Hill.

Pugh, Allison. 2013. "What Good are Interviews for Thinking about Culture? Demystifying Interpretive Analysis." *American Journal of Cultural Sociology*. 1: 42–68.

Rokeach, Milton. 1973. *The Nature of Human Values*. New York: Free Press

Romburgh, Marlize. 2015. "Uber in S.F. is Now Three Times Bigger than City's Entire Taxi Industry." *Bizjournals*. Accessed March 20, 2016. www.bizjournals.com/sanfrancisco /blog/techflash/2015/01/uber-valuation-revenue-sf-taxi-industry-kalanick.html

Schiller, Ferdinand. 1895. "The Metaphysics of the Time-Process". *Mind*. 4:13. Pp. 36–46.

Small, Mario, and Christopher Sukhu. 2016. "Because They Were There Access, Deliberation, and the Mobilization of Networks for Support" *Social Networks*. 47:73–84.

Smith, Vicki. 1997. "New Forms of Work Organization." *Annual Review of Sociology*. 23:315–39.

Tavory, Iddo, and Stefan Timmermans. 2013. "A Pragmatist Approach to Causality in Ethnography." *American Journal of Sociology*. 119(3): 682–714.

Uber Newsroom 2015a. "Uber and the American Worker: Remarks from David Plouffe." *Uber Newsroom*. Accessed November 4, 2015. https://newsroom.uber.com/1776/.

Uber Newsroom 2020. "Company Info." Accessed June 25, 2020. https://www.uber.com /newsroom/company-info/

US Government Accountability Office. 2015. "Contingent Workforce: Size, Characteristics, Earnings, and Benefits." www.gao.gov/assets/670/669899.pdf.

Western, Bruce, Deirdre Bloome, Benjamin Sosnaud, and Laura Tach. 2012 "Economic Insecurity and Social Stratification." *Annual Review of Sociology*. 38: 341–359.

Weber, Max. 1949. "Objectivity" in social science and social policy. In *The Methodology of the Social Sciences*, translated. E. Shils, H Finch, pp. 49–112. Glencoe, IL: Free Press.

Wheatley, Parker. 2010. "Economic and Regional Determinants of the Location of Payday Lenders and Banking Institutions in Mississippi: Reconsidering the Role of Race and Other Factors in Firm Location." Accessed on February 2, 2011: http://documents.apec .umn.edu/ApEcSemSpring2010-Wheatley%20paper.pdf.

Winship, Christopher. 2015. "Inchoate Situations and Extra-Rational Behavior." *Working Paper. Harvard University-University of Chicago Pragmatist Conference.*

NOTES

1. Instrumentalism is defined as the position that theories are tools for problem-solving—which in social-scientific context relates to explaining and predicting phenomena—and, importantly, that theories are true to the degree that they produce favorable, practical consequences (i.e., that they are effective in explanation or prediction). This accords with the epistemologies of classical pragmatists including Schiller (1895), Dewey (1910c), and James (1904).

2. Generally, it refers to types of work that deviate from "traditional," full-time, stable employment, such as part-time work, independent contracting, and temporary work. Whereas the research on on-demand work is scant, the broader literature on nonstandard work is well developed (for reviews, see Smith 1997; and Hollister 2011).

3. Patterson (2015) follows Weber (1949b), Rokeach (1973), and Lefkowitz (2003) in making the distinction between ultimate values and particularized values, the latter of which are directed toward particular objects (e.g., attitudes toward groups).

4. As of early 2015, Uber was estimated to be at least three times the size of the entire taxi industry in San Francisco (Romburgh 2015).

5. This group represents 7.9 percent of employed workers, up from 7.1 percent in 2006 (U.S. Government Accountability Office 2015). The growth has been mainly in on-call workers as well as temporary agency workers (US GAO 2015).

6. The Bureau of Labor Statistics' Occupational Employment Statistics, which tracks wages of taxicab and limousine drivers who are employees (rather than independent contractors), estimated mean wages of employee-drivers in Boston at $13.97 per hour as of May 2016 (BLS 2016); this wage rate is net of drivers' gasoline, insurance, and other expenses.

7. *Autonomy* and *flexibility* are defined differently here. Flexibility is autonomy that emerges under particular circumstances. For example, if Uber drivers earned $10 per hour for each of their first ten hours of driving in a week but $20/hour for the next ten hours and $30/hour for any hour beyond the first twenty hours, then in a particular sense, the work is highly autonomous, but *in effect* it will not be used very flexibly. That is, the distribution of work hours per worker per week will be concentrated above twenty hours.

8. This flexibility is likely especially attractive to those at opposite ends of the age distribution; that is, younger drivers use Uber as a bridge for other opportunities, whereas older drivers use it to supplement income or for recreation. As for longevity with Uber, Hall and Krueger (2015) report that after six months into driving, there is a 30 percent drop-off rate, and after twelve months, there is a 50 percent drop-off.

9. Mullainathan and Shafir (2013) do not primarily focus on creative action, but their work has obvious and strong implications for it.

10. This work on extreme poverty is a continuation of a substantial literature on coping with financial distress, much of which can be traced to Edin and Lein's (1997) *Making Ends Meet: How Single Mothers Survive Welfare and Low-Wage Work*.

11. At a pragmatist conference at the University of Chicago in 2015, the lack of work in contemporary pragmatism on how actors select into problem situations was specifically lamented.

12. Dominguez (2011) also advances the notion of "efficient populations" as those in which the concentration of SPAs is high enough to establish social support systems among the population.

13. The twenty markets were Atlanta, Austin, Baltimore, Boston, Chicago, Dallas, Denver, Houston, Los Angeles, Miami, Minneapolis, New Jersey, New York City, Orange County, Philadelphia, Phoenix, San Diego, San Francisco, Seattle, and Washington, D.C.

14. Gross (2009, 364) defines a social mechanism as "a more or less general sequence or set of social events or processes analyzed at a lower order of complexity or aggregation by which — in certain circumstances — some cause X tends to bring about some effect Y in the realm of human social relations. This sequence or set may or may not be analytically reducible to the actions of individuals who enact it, may underwrite formal or substantive causal processes, and may be observed, unobserved, or in principle unobservable."

15. Several years ago, Uber indicated to Boston drivers that they should maintain a rating of at least 4.5 out of 5. Yet, this has never been explicit, given the legal dimensions of "controlling" drivers in this way. I have encountered many Uber drivers whose ratings were below 4.5, although the majority have higher ratings.

16. Joas (1996) made a similar point in grounding creativity in situations, corporeality, and sociality.

9. Words Versus Actions in the Network Behavior of Low-Income African Americans

MARIO L. SMALL, CAYCE C. HUGHES, VONTRESE D. PAMPHILE, AND JEFFREY N. PARKER

INTRODUCTION

One of the primary contributions of pragmatist social theory has been to focus our attention on practice, on what people are actually doing in the course of their everyday lives (Dewey 1922a; Joas 1996). In few contexts is such an orientation as important as when we seek to understand how people manage poverty. The poverty experienced by African Americans in the United States is unique in its high levels of concentration; those who are poor and Black are especially likely to live near other poor people (Wilson 1987, 1996; Massey and Denton 1993; Sharkey 2013). This concentration has been associated with a number of social problems, including limited organizational resources, underperforming schools, and violence (Small and Newman 2002; Sampson, Morenoff, and Gannon-Rowley 2003; Goering and Feins 2003; Sampson 2012). How do people manage, in practice, the deprivations associated with poverty?

Sociologists have offered two different pictures, both consistent with common sense and evident in ethnographic studies. Some have argued, and offered evidence, that concentrated poverty among African Americans has created distrust, isolation, and a sense of independence from others. This outcome, they say, results from a number of factors, including neighborhood violence, lack of resources, and high instability (see, e.g., Wilson 1987; Anderson 2000; Smith 2007; Chan Tack and Small 2017; Mazelis 2017). But others have argued, and offered evidence, that poverty among African Americans has created especially high levels of trust, socialization, and dependence on others. The reason, these sociologists say, is the high level of need created by limited resources and the fact that people realize that interdependence created by the sharing of resources across a network benefits all (see, e.g., Stack 1974; Dominguez and Watkins 2003; Small 2009; Desmond 2012). Over the last several decades, many ethnographers and on-the-ground observers have reported either one or the other version of this story (but see Nelson 2000; Miller-Cribbs and Farber 2008; Murphy 2016; Raudenbush 2016).

This contradiction is the topic of this chapter. Over several years, we conducted research among low-income African American mothers in three high-poverty neighborhoods: one each in New York City (Harlem), Chicago (Woodlawn), and Houston (Sunnyside). Besides the high poverty level, all three neighborhoods were high-unemployment, predominantly African American neighborhoods, but they differed dramatically in population density, organizational capacity, infrastructure, access to public transportation, and local political environment. We conducted participant observation and interviewed scores of mothers about their practices, paying special attention to their social networks. We uncovered notable differences across the three cities, but also substantial similarities. These similarities are important, as they belie the possibility that different ethnographers have reported contrary findings because they have studied different cities (Small, Manduca, and Johnston 2018). On the contrary, on the particular contradiction that motivates the work reported here, we found the same pattern in Harlem, Woodlawn, and Sunnyside. These similarities form the heart of our chapter.

First, we show that across the three cities, people repeatedly expressed distrust, isolation, and independence — but ended up trusting, socializing with, and depending on others anyway. That is, their words and actions appear inconsistent (Raudenbush 2016).

Second, we show that the literature is contradictory in part because researchers reporting high levels of distrust have at times underemphasized trusting behavior among their own respondents, and researchers reporting reliance on networks have often underemphasized expressions of distrust among their respondents. Thus, the totality of the evidence produced by those researchers gives credence to both patterns.

This conflict between what people do and what they say they do, which is a conflict between practice and narrative, presents an interesting problem for the pragmatist sociologist. One could ignore the narrative, and some ethnographers propose that what people say should be taken with a grain of salt, or even dismissed altogether (Becker and Geer, 1957; Jerolmack and Khan 2014; but see Small and Cook 2021). But narrative is itself a form of practice, a verbal articulation of one's understanding of oneself, and it is implausible that such consistent narratives across such different contexts are not indicative of some important social fact. In fact, the narratives reveal important "habits of thought and feeling" (Dewey 1922) that are borne of common experiences. Probing both narrative and practice in greater depth makes clear that the sociologist cannot hope to understand one without the other.

Third, we show that people express distrust while still trusting others because the former is generalized and the latter is specific (Raudenbush 2016): people distrust their neighbors in general but tend to trust particular neighbors, those with whom they have an *institutionally mediated relation*—such as parishioners at church, parents or teachers at school, and kin members down the street.

These mediating institutions play a major role in which neighbors are actually trusted. Such relationships carry expectations that transcend the two parties, increasing their overall trustworthiness, even among people who do not know each other well. A neighbor who happens to be a co-parishioner or family member is, in the mothers' understanding, either more than just a neighbor or not what she conceives of as "people in the neighborhood." Only a close examination of their practices reveals this differentiation.

THREE NEIGHBORHOODS

Background

Our study is based on three neighborhoods that were selected for their core demographic similarities. Harlem in New York City, Woodlawn in Chicago, and Sunnyside in Houston are all historically African American neighborhoods and remain predominantly African American (65 percent in Harlem, 86 percent in Woodlawn, and 84 percent in Sunnyside). During the study period, all three neighborhoods had a poverty rate exceeding 30 percent (U.S. Census Bureau 2015), and nearly a third of households across neighborhoods were headed by a single mother. The unemployment rate among adults was 15 percent in central Harlem, 22 percent in Woodlawn, and 23 percent in Sunnyside, compared with the national unemployment rate of 9 percent in 2014.

Despite these similarities, the neighborhoods diverge on other important characteristics, including population and organizational density, both of which appear to differ markedly across poor neighborhoods nationally (Small and McDermott 2006; Small 2007; Hyra 2008; Small, Manduca, and Johnston 2018). Harlem is quite dense, with approximately 94,285 residents per square mile. Woodlawn is much less dense, with 26,446 people per square mile, and in Sunnyside the density is even lower, with 3,479 people per square mile (American Community Survey 2011–15).

A similar pattern holds for organizational density, with Harlem having far more organizations per square mile than either Woodlawn or Sunnyside. For example, in central Harlem, residents can choose among roughly thirty grocery stores per square mile, whereas in Woodlawn there is an average of one grocery store per square mile and less than one per square mile in Sunnyside.

For most types of neighborhood establishments, this pattern holds whether we measure density by area (number of organizations per square mile) or per capita (number of organizations relative to the population). One important exception is churches. Although there are more churches per square mile in Harlem than there are in Woodlawn or Sunnyside (219 in Harlem, 13 in Woodlawn, and 13 in Sunnyside), a different pattern emerges when we consider organizational density in terms of population. Through this lens, we see that Sunnyside has about 34.9 churches per 10,000 people, compared with 25.4 in Harlem and 14.8 in Woodlawn.

Another salient difference between our focal neighborhoods is related to variation in spatial organization and public transportation infrastructure across cities. Houston is a sprawling, driving-centric city, with over 80 percent of employees commuting to work by car (Davis and Baxandall 2013). In contrast, New York City is geographically compact and ranks first among metro areas in public transportation use, with residents taking on average 230 public transportation trips each year per capita. Chicago ranks ninth, compared with Houston in ninety-first place.

There are important differences at the neighborhood level as well. Sunnyside has been characterized as "rurban," with a mix of typically rural and urban features. There are wide open swaths of pasture adjacent to public housing complexes, and horses can be found grazing in overgrown vacant lots. Many residential streets lack sidewalks and are instead bordered by open ditches. And although Sunnyside is less than a fifteen-minute drive from downtown, it is not easily accessible by public transport, and no train lines service the area.

In contrast, central Harlem is an urban hub, with bustling sidewalks, constant foot traffic, and few vacant properties or storefronts. Public transportation options abound, with ten Manhattan subway lines running through greater Harlem and twelve bus routes traversing the central Harlem area.

Woodlawn is an intermediate case. Formerly a thriving South Side commercial area, the neighborhood has rapidly depopulated, and the main corridor now features not only closed businesses but entire empty blocks, the result of a combination of disinvestment and arson. Woodlawn is, however, accessible via multiple bus lines and an elevated city train route.

What these differences mean in practice is that on a typical day, a mother in Harlem could, without concerted effort, encounter multiple opportunities for interaction with other people in multiple settings as part of her daily round. Within blocks of her home, she would find corner stores, cafes, nail salons, produce markets, and perhaps a movie theater. The same mother in Woodlawn or Sunnyside could just as easily walk several blocks without seeing any commercial establishments or other pedestrians, thus missing those opportunities for chance meetings or conversations. These differences across the neighborhoods are especially notable given the striking similarities we report in how people relate to others.

Data Collection and Analysis

We conducted preliminary observations in each neighborhood over a four-month period in 2013. During this time, we familiarized ourselves with local institutions, established contacts with community members, and conducted a census of all organizations in each neighborhood. To do so, we canvassed each neighborhood by foot or car, recording the address and organization name and type. We then coded according to organization type based on the North American Industry Classification System (e.g., full-service restaurant [72251], beauty salon [812112]) and calculated the density of each establishment type per capita and per square mile.

We conducted interviews with forty mothers in Harlem, sixty-two in Woodlawn, and thirty-one in Sunnyside. Most interviews were conducted in 2013 and 2014; however, we conducted six interviews with Sunnyside mothers in 2016. As a way of finding people in similar circumstances across the neighborhoods, our initial selection strategy called for mothers whose children were enrolled in Head Start (see Small 2009a). However, we also recruited from non–Head Start childcare centers, neighborhood parks, schools, and community centers. Though there was some heterogeneity in mothers' social identities, we focused our analysis on the majority of mothers who were African American to better understand the experience of concentrated poverty among African Americans. Mothers were invited to participate in an interview about how they managed the daily challenges of raising children and about their social networks. Interviews were open-ended and conversational, ranging in length from ten minutes to over three hours. We interviewed mothers in a public location of their choice, such as a donut shop or local restaurant. Topics included mothers' major concerns, daily routines, perceptions of the neighborhood, the composition of their social networks, and the extent to which they participated in organizations. With consent, interviews were audio-recorded and later transcribed verbatim. Participants were given a $20 gift card to local supermarkets or retail stores to thank them for their time.

Our approach to data analysis was inductive (Glaser and Straus 1967; Becker 2009; Small 2009b). First, we open-coded the transcripts to identify broad themes related to mothers' perceptions and practices in terms of social support. We used memos to synthesize our findings and develop working propositions about what the data described. Over the course of this period, the topic of analysis shifted several times until the potential disjuncture between respondents' narratives and actions regarding their interactions with others became central. We then returned to the data with these two themes in mind and identified all passages referring to one or another form of trust or social engagement and all those referring to some form of distrust or isolation. We refined the theoretical categories based on what we uncovered, confirmed their presence across the three neighborhoods, and drafted the argument reported here.

NARRATIVE

The mothers we interviewed repeatedly expressed a general distrust of others, self-characterizing as people who kept to themselves, avoided others, and generally did not trust people unless they were very close. This general distrust could be seen in four different but related kinds of narratives about others.

Trusting no one. One narrative was the statement, offered by mothers across the three neighborhoods, that they trusted almost no one. Christina, an African American grandmother in her sixties in Sunnyside, expressed general mistrust in others. When asked who she would turn to if she wanted to talk about something important to her, she said, "I'd go to my sister, I don't have anybody else to go to. And I can't trust outsiders. Don't you tell, you talk to them about something, next thing you know it's everywhere. So I talk to my sister. . . . I'm the type [of] person, I can't be around anybody. I have to be around people where I feel love."

Similarly, when we asked Nancy, an African American mother of two in her twenties living in Woodlawn, if her six-year-old daughter had friends in the neighborhood, she said, "We have friends that—she has a friend next door, but I'm not trustworthy like a lot of people. I mean I don't let my daughter go to other people's houses and things like that. That's just my trust level. This is just how I am. I never liked it, not unless I'm with her."

Elizabeth, a forty-year-old African American mother in Harlem, also described herself as having a "trust issue." She explained: "So, I don't, I don't trust everybody and I don't get close to everybody. You know, I'll talk to you. But I don't get close." Elizabeth added that her primary focus was her children, and she preferred to care for them independently.

Keeping to myself. The second way mothers generally expressed distrust was to describe themselves as someone who "keeps to myself" or who has "associates" rather than friends (Murphy 2016; Raudenbush 2016). Consider Jocelyn, who lived in Sunnyside with her sister Christina (mentioned earlier) while she looked for permanent housing. When asked who she would go to if she needed to talk about something important to her, Jocelyn said she sometimes talked to her sister but generally avoided people because she found them to sometimes be "mean, evil, and cruel." "They laugh, talk about you, make fun of you. . . . And they got ignorant people in the world that don't care, that do stuff to hurt people's feelings," she said. "So, I try to distance myself. And that way, I stay out of trouble."

We found something similar in Woodlawn. Rachel, an African American mother of two, spoke negatively about people in her neighborhood, claiming they "either drink or have some kind of setbacks." She also avoided people on Facebook, explaining, "I don't know those people. I mean there's a lot of people I don't know. I'm just very cautious and a lot of people try to befriend you and want to meet you and I'm just not into it." She continued, "when you call someone a friend, a friend is not a word that you use loosely. A friend takes work, just like a marriage does and that's how I look at it." When asked how many friends she had, Rachel said "none," only "associates."

Depend on no one. A third way mothers expressed general distrust was to describe a reluctance to rely on others for help. Mary, a Sunnyside African American mother in her twenties, described herself as "staying to myself . . . I don't conversate with people." Mary lived across the street from her sister, but when asked if Mary would turn to her sister if she needed something, she said, "No, I just, I'm like more independent like not gonna ask anybody for anything, I'm gonna find a way to get it myself, that type of situation." When asked who she would go to if she *really* needed something, she insisted she would turn to "nobody."

Patricia, an African American mother in her twenties living in Harlem, was also reluctant to depend on others. She described herself as "a loner," explaining that she had no friends and did not want any. When asked if she had ever needed help with her three-year-old daughter, Patricia replied, "Never, there is no one. You know the emergency contacts? I have none. It's really just me and her" (paraphrased, interview not recorded). Patricia's daughter suffered from an illness and on occasion had to be rushed to the hospital. Patricia said that if it was necessary, she would prefer to drop out of college to care for her daughter rather than rely on anyone else for help.

Stay off the streets. A final way that mothers expressed distrust was to communicate an unambiguous reluctance to spend time in their neighborhood outside the home or to let their children do so. Karen, a Sunnyside African American mother of three in her mid-twenties, said she did her best to keep her children inside, because she was worried about gun violence: "I just go to work, come get them, come in the house." Karen also said that she stayed away from other adults in the complex to keep herself out of trouble: "I'm not friendly. I don't talk to nobody. . . . I'm cool with the girl across the way but somebody don't like her so they gonna start a whole lot of mess. That's how these females is down here. I don't talk to no one. I go to work, I come home, I go to bed."

Jane, a nineteen-year-old African American mother in Woodlawn, said she feared simply being outside, explaining, "Because there's nothing else there [but violence]. I usually—I used to go outside. I just graduated from high school, so I was outside every day 'cause I had to leave to go to school and then come back. But now that I graduated, I don't spend time outside, and then I got a baby, so. There's nothing else outside but violence. You never know who gonna die, so I don't want to get caught in no crossfires." She continued, "Garfield's an open wide street, and not that much cars come so it's easy access for somebody to shoot and keep going, so I don't hang over there no more." Jane reported that she and her daughter "barely go outside anyway, so we'll stay in the house to avoid all of that."

The fear of violence was less prevalent among mothers in Harlem than it was for mothers in Sunnyside and Woodlawn. Nevertheless, Harlem mothers expressed reluctance to spend time in areas that they perceived to have high violence. Describing the Harlem block where she used to live, Donna, a grandmother, said, "Lotta shootin', fightin'. You go out, you take your children outside, you gon' have to run back inside." She eventually moved away from the area because of the violence. One mother transferred her child to a different school after seeing gang activity nearby, and others described taking alternate walking routes to avoid people hanging out on the block. Though mothers did mention spending time at neighborhood parks with their children, they often described going to the park only and then directly home. As Emily described, "I'm just not, like—I'm not too fond of the streets, like, if I'm in the streets, I'm in the streets for a reason. I'm not hanging on the corner with my kids or—I take 'em to the park by me for, like, an hour or two."

In sum, the evidence was strong and consistent with prior accounts. In several ways—expressing distrust explicitly, keeping to themselves, avoiding reliance on anyone, and keeping themselves and their children off the neighborhood streets— mothers expressed the general distrust, reluctance to rely on others, independence, and isolation reported in many ethnographic accounts.

PRACTICE

Yet, in spite of their high distrust and expressed reluctance to rely on others in their neighborhoods, mothers did depend on others, often in multiple ways. That is, the accounts of high interdependence, reliance on others, and supportive social networks found in other studies were also evident in our interviews—including by the same mothers who had reported the opposite. We observed this trend in both socialization with others and helping behavior.

Frequent socializing. In spite of describing themselves as "keeping to myself," mothers described many everyday circumstances that may easily be read as evidence of routine socialization. Judy, a young African American woman in her early twenties, was pregnant with her first child at the time of our interview. She had moved to Houston recently after having lived in Austin for most of her life.

Like others, Judy did not prioritize friends. "I moved here without any friends at all, and I still don't have any to this day. I mean, I have a few associates, but I would rather not. That's how I've been my whole life. I've grown up without having as many friends. . . . I like to be alone, so I'm not worried about friends."

Nevertheless, Judy's description of everyday life communicated a different picture. When asked how often she saw her boyfriend, Judy replied, "all the time." She continued, "He lives with five roommates, okay, so it's a house full of guys. When I go there, I can go whenever I want and leave whenever I want. It's like I live there. Sometimes I'll go there a few times of the week, few days of the week, stay the night, or when he goes to school, I'll stay there and sleep and leave when I want. Or I'll just stay and hang out with the roommates. They're like brothers to me, and I'll be there when he gets out of school, and it's not hard, really. Just come over and stay the night. I'm always there. It's like when I live there. He comes home. He leaves, I'm still there."

Elizabeth, a mother from Harlem discussed earlier, also socialized with others despite saying she kept only a few associates and no friends. "I don't really have friends like that anyway so it doesn't matter. My, my life that I live is for my kids." She had learned from her grandmother "not to use that word friends so frequently because you know, everybody's not your friend." Later in the interview, Elizabeth explained, "some people can take advantage of, you know, your kindness. And it has happened. So now it's like I have this wall, this shell that I won't allow it to happen no more with nobody."

While Elizabeth said she had no friends, she spoke with her neighbors and socialized with one neighbor in particular almost daily. "Yeah, I, um, I speak to them. Like her, I speak to, um, like every day . . . like we talked, and, um, you know, I'm just, you know, starting to get close to her. Like, you know, we talk every day." Elizabeth explained how she speaks to this neighbor when she feels stressed or needs to vent about her children's father, adding that she found it easier to speak to her neighbor than call a family member "because she's right there." This pattern is reminiscent of that reported by researchers in national populations, where people often turn to weak ties because they are available (Small and Sukhu 2016; Small 2017). Moreover, Elizabeth and this neighbor often ran errands together. "Like when she's gonna, you know, she might walk with me to 125th Street today because I have to go there, you know, or she'll . . . you know, and she'll go with me shopping or whatever, you know, she'll buy something, whatever. And we just talk about, you know, we just talk."

Everyday help-seeking behavior. We also observed much of the everyday help-seeking behavior that has been documented by researchers studying low-income African Americans (Stack 1974; Uehara 1990; Mazelis 2017). Consider Susan, a mother in her thirties, who said she kept her distance from others in Harlem. "I mean, I talk to people, but . . . you know now you can't consider people your friends now . . . they like could talk about you and, so, I'm like, . . . you stay your business, I'll stay mine, we have nothing to say." Yet, when Susan was looking for employment, she turned to neighbors in her building for help. She asked another mother who worked in a hair salon, "Please help me out I'm trying to look for something else to do." She also reached out to several other neighbors about finding employment: "There's people in my building, you know cause they got some nice decent jobs, I said 'listen is your job hiring?' They like 'I don't know, can find out.' I say 'alright well you find that out, and you find out if there's any more other jobs around where you at.'"

Some mothers described receiving help that they did not explicitly seek out, which bears evidence of the network of support in which many were embedded. Mary, the Sunnyside woman described earlier, reported that she would not ask anyone for help, even her siblings. However, she also noted that she talked to one of her sisters at least once every day, and that the sister living across the street babysat Mary's children. She also enrolled her kids in a school that was recommended by family members and got her home health care job through a cousin. These examples demonstrate routine receipt of support from network members.

In sum, although mothers expressed generalized distrust, they also depended on neighbors for socialization and advice and both asked for and received help to overcome day-to-day problems. We believe both expressions of high distrust or isolation and a high prevalence of social interaction are common. They are also common in the existing literature.

RELUCTANCE VERSUS RELIANCE

The pattern we have observed, of both reluctance and reliance, can be found in other works—provided one looks carefully at the full scope of their data. Consider two notable cases.

Smith's *Lone Pursuit* (2007) reported high levels of distrust, independence, and what she called "defensive individualism" among low-income African American job-seekers. She examined the long-standing finding that finding work is a network process and that job seekers rely on job holders for information (Granovetter 1974). Among her respondents, Smith found many expressions of distrust consistent with our reports, which made network-based job-seeking more difficult. For example, one respondent offered information about her job and encouraged job-seeking relatives to apply; however, she would not recommend anyone out of concern "that she might vouch for job-seekers who would later reveal themselves to be 'bad workers,' workers 'that might have some effect on, you know, me as a person'" (Smith 2007, 57). Smith proposed that the fundamental lack of trust among her respondents made them unable to use their networks as a source of help in finding jobs.

Nevertheless, a close examination of her work reveals that low-income African Americans may not be that different in this respect from others. Consider the reported rate of network use in Smith's study, in which 50 percent of respondents indicated that they had gotten their most recent job through a personal contact (2007, 99). That percentage indicates a high, not low, level of network-based job-finding. In fact, it is the rate of helping behavior typically found in studies arguing that people do use their networks in job-seeking. In Granovetter (1974) study of men in professional jobs, he reported that 55.7 percent of respondents had found their most recent job through a personal contact (18)—a figure highly consistent with Smith's.[1]

Unlike Smith's work, Stack's *All Our Kin* (1974) reported high levels of support, interdependence, and trust. She argued that the low-income African Americans in her study dealt with poverty by relying not only on those in their nuclear family but also on "kin-like" others in their broader network. Stack found that previous definitions of family were inadequate for explaining the support systems she saw, and she ended up defining "family" as "the smallest, organized, durable network of kin and non-kin who interact daily, providing domestic needs of children and assuring their survival" (1974, 31). Her book repeatedly describes forms of helping behavior consistent with our reports. For example, mothers swap goods and provide childcare among their networks in a system of mutual obligation.

However, Stack's work also demonstrates high levels of distrust. For example, she documented a prevailing distrust of men by women, noting that "many young women . . . feel strongly that they cannot let a man make a fool out of them, and they react quickly and boldly to rumor, gossip, and talk that hurts them" (1974, 111–12). She also reported expressions of conflict and unwillingness to help others. Julia expressed frustration with her cousin Mae in regard to lack of reciprocity with swapping goods, saying, "If someone who takes things from me ain't giving me anything in return, she can't get nothing else" (34). Similarly, Magnolia considered swapping an integral part of friendship and cut off those who did not reciprocate. "Sometimes when you help a person they end up making a fool of you," she said. "If a friend ain't giving me anything in return for what I'm giving her, shit, she can't get nothing else" (57).

Stack acknowledges the distrust that exists in the community but suggests that it is "offset by improvisation: an adaptive style of behavior acquired by persons using each situation to control, manipulate, and exploit others" (1974, 39). Nevertheless, the overall thrust of her argument is unmistakably that "all our kin" constitute a community of help and trust. We suggest that, instead, both helping behavior and strong and frequent expressions of distrust coexist.

UNDERSTANDING THE INCONSISTENCY BETWEEN NARRATIVE AND PRACTICE

Why do people express distrust and isolation but behave in ways that communicate high levels of trust, socialization, and interdependence? We do not believe that respondents are lying. Our argument is in many ways consistent with Raudenbush's (2016); she reported a similar apparent contradiction and referred to it as a kind of selective solidarity. However, we propose that an important part of the issue is what people mean by their narratives and how they perceive their networks. In a nutshell, their narratives of distrust are general and their network behavior is particular—that is, they trust, socialize, and engage with a specific and consistent subset of their network members, those with whom they have institutionally mediated relations (see Raudenbush 2016).

Small (2017) has argued that network ties may differ in the extent to which they are institutionally mediated: "Institutional mediation is the extent to which the norms or rules of an organization, profession, or other formal arrangement governs the expectations underlying the relationship. Examples are the ties between two coworkers, two church members, employee and boss, or parishioner and priest, all of which differ from purely personal ones in that, no matter how close, they are subject to formal expectations of behavior either commonly understood or codified in rule books or the law" (2017, 66).

Institutional mediation takes many forms. One important mediating institution is the family. Fischer (1982) argued, and many have shown, that family relations differ from others in their trust, expectations, and obligations. Regardless of how close or distal they are, family members have expectations toward one another that people who are not family members do not. "Though kin-related expectations may vary across cultures and class backgrounds, they remain perennial aspects of interpersonal relations, the source of phenomena as varied as the family feud, the dowry, the arranged marriage, and the filial obligation" (Small 2017, 71). Another major source of institutional mediation is organizational embeddedness, the extent to which the two parties are members of the same school, church, social club, or other local organization (Small 2009a). "Routine organizations are not merely places, sites where clusters of nodes and ties happen to exist. Instead, they constitute sets of institutional rules, norms, and practices that to lesser or greater extent affect how their members or participants interact, form personal connections, think of one another, build trust, develop obligations, and share information and other resources" (2009a, v). We argue that such contexts provide a measure of legitimacy that increase both the level of trust and the probability of socialization among neighbors.

Our interviews suggest that much of the contrast between narrative and practice rested in the distinction between a neighbor as an abstract category and neighbor as a person who, in practice, was an institutionally mediated relation toward which a pragmatist approach of engagement and interdependence made more sense. Though respondents thought of neighbors as people they might stay away from, many of their neighbors, in practice, were siblings, co-parishioners, school members, teachers, or other institutionally mediated relations toward whom an engaged posture was a practical approach to everyday survival.

Family Members

Logan and Spitze (1994, 1996) have shown that many of the neighbors of people in low-income areas are, in fact, family members. Though only a minority of neighbors are family members, "family neighbors" play a larger role in local social networks and condition the effect of typical neighboring variables (Logan and Spitze 1994). The strong expectations that undergird kin relations affect social behavior among family neighbors. For example, people may complain about an untrustworthy sibling or cousin but feel compelled to help them anyway. In fact, much of Stack's (1974) evidence of a social support network was based on sets of family members, "all our kin," who lived within a few blocks of one another. Understanding the importance of family brings to light what may seem like a contradiction between the sense of lack of support and the presence of a supportive network in practice.

Tamara, an African American mother in her early twenties, did not have a stable permanent residence in Sunnyside. She struggled with basic needs, did not own a car, and explained that she was unemployed because she lacked childcare. Tamara continued, "Because right now I don't have nobody to depend on, I have to get out there and go get it how I get it." However, when Tamara recounted a recent job interview, she explained that she asked her child's father to watch their son. When he was working, she called on other family members, describing a network of potential babysitters much like Stack's depictions of dense kin networks.

Rachel had a similar experience in Woodlawn. Though she described herself as not trusting other people in her neighborhood, she often left her children with neighbors, most of whom happened to be family members. Rachel was briefly incarcerated, and during this time her children stayed with their father or with other nearby relatives. Rachel explained, "I have family. I don't trust all them, but I mean, they're trustworthy people but my kids are okay. They're okay."

Church Members

Other neighbors were members of the same church, an organization that typically places strong expectations of engagement, socialization, and helping behavior on its members (McRoberts 2003). Paula is a Sunnyside grandmother in her late fifties who had custody of her two grandchildren. She described herself as largely anti-social, keeping interactions with neighbors to a minimum. "I basically stay in the house." She was also strict with her grandchildren, who were not allowed outside during the week and could not walk alone to school because of neighborhood violence. Her narrative was consistent with that of many who have explained the negative consequences of violence for trust and interpersonal relations (Chan Track and Small 2017).

Nevertheless, when the conversation turned to her church, Paula revealed an entire set of neighbors with whom she socialized actively. "Sometimes, like I said, I'll sit down with my neighbors. We'll sit out at nighttime sometimes once the kids done went to bed for school the next day. We stand out by the cars and we might talk 15, 20, 25, 30 minutes or so. We go to church together too, the ones I be talking to. So we might sit out there, and sometimes we sit out there 12:30, 1:00 in the morning." Paula referred to one of these neighbors as her sister: "I call her sister. She's like a sister to me, so yeah, she know everything that's going on with me, everything. She know everything that's going on with me. She the only one knew everything that's going on with me other than my sister that lives down the walkway and my niece that live around the corner." These designations, as church member or kin/kinlike, seem to allow Paula to open up when she otherwise might not.

School Members

In some cases, parents, teachers, and staff members in schools or childcare centers were the source of socialization or social support (Small 2009a). Nancy, the Woodlawn mother of two described earlier, expressed a general distrust of other people, specifically with respect to her children. Nevertheless, she came to associate heavily with a group of parents who met daily at her children's school. She considered it a supportive, helping community. "We do projects with our children. They get us off the street. I don't be on the streets, but it's to get like other people off the streets to partake in like helping their child's classroom, like taking me to a project or something or—like staple papers for the class or whatever—put up a billboard for the class, or, you know, stuff like that. So we partake in like helping with the school—the parents, so that's what the parents' class is about." Some relationships have extended beyond the parents' class.

Similarly, Sunnyside sisters Jocelyn and Christina volunteered at the elementary school that their grandchildren attended for eight years and have both asked for and received help from staff members there. Sometimes, the help had been highly consequential, as Jocylen recounted: "For instance, I may go to a teacher that I can trust and say, 'you know, we don't have any food' and then they'll take me and they'll make groceries and you never hear over the school. I may say my children need clothes or something. They'll help me and I don't hear that. Don't do something for me and then put it out and broadcast. And like I say, they, there's times I done come here, walked here with no bus fare and these people done gave me bus fare or took me home. And they look out for us for life. . . . Christmas, Thanksgiving, they make sure we get Thanksgiving baskets, Christmas baskets. And make sure all the kids get Christmas, good stuff. I have to say it, that's why I been here so long." The teacher, whom Jocelyn trusted, did not gossip or share with others that she or her sister needed assistance.

Molly, an African American mother of three in Woodlawn, explained that she mostly stayed in her house and minded her own business. "I be in the house," she said. "If I'm not in the house then I'm trying to get to work." Nevertheless, she was active at her children's school, particularly at parent meetings. "I try to show [the teacher] that I'm all with it, you know, you know because you have to participate because your child attending school, you know, you have to come and sit and talk to the teachers sometime and, you know, get in the program with the parents, you know, other parents, you know." In spite of her self-description as antisocial, Molly explained the importance of "socializing, you know, with the community, with the school and with other parents." For example, Molly lobbied other parents about the need for an afterschool program for their children.

Betty, an African American grandmother in Harlem in her mid-fifties, also said she generally kept to herself at her housing project but had relationships with mothers at her granddaughter's childcare center. Betty preferred church and Bible school to going outside, describing herself as "a mama's girl. I loved to stay in the house." She tried "not to get too involved" with neighbors, adding, "so, I tries to deal with it. I try to stay more to myself." Despite a reluctance to engage others at the housing project, Betty was one of the most active parents at the childcare center. Betty's granddaughter had attended the center for only two months, but Betty had gotten to know other parents, becoming fast friends with one of the younger mothers, Sandra. Sandra and Betty had taken their children to the local children's museum over the weekend and planned to host each other for Thanksgiving and New Year's Eve. Betty planned to help Sandra with the upcoming center potluck, saying, "She don't cook, so I'm tryin' to teach her how to cook now." Betty and Sandra interacted almost daily at the center, and Sandra became part of Betty's daily neighborhood routine. "I come out about 2:25 to catch up with Sandra. Then we're sitting here and see if [the childcare center worker] need help with anything, just sittin' here and chat until it's time to get the girls. Then we'll stay here and chat some more. Then we go outside to her park." Betty had called on Sandra once to pick up her granddaughter from the center when she was running late, and she had introduced Sandra to her family members.

Miscellaneous Contexts

An important aspect of some institutionally mediated relations is that it is less about the institutional norms of the relation than the social and physical context of inter-action. When a mother is sitting at a PTA meeting at school, the fact that the per-son sitting next to her is also a parent at the school makes informal conversation and interaction easier. But the fact that they are sitting in a public space, with chips and drinks in a welcoming environment, probably plays a role as well (Small 2009a). Mothers often encountered other mothers in local organizations, salons, childcare centers, laundromats, and elsewhere, and those places created a space for social-ization, a space where a neighbor shifts from "a stranger out there on the street" to "another person waiting for her clothes to finish drying." In this sense, understand-ing the mothers' survival strategies as being enacted, in practice, in concrete spaces with people who are understood in relation to those spaces, rather than as "neigh-bors" or "the network" or similar abstraction, helps to explain the inconsistency between narrative and practice.

Consider again Rachel, the Woodlawn mother who said she did not and could not trust other people in the neighborhood. We saw that Rachel sought advice and information when it came to raising her children. She was having trouble with her son, who was being bullied at school. His grades and behavior had suffered, and she worried about how it would affect his chances of getting into a high school. When asked how she sought advice and information, she pointed, interestingly, to her neighborhood laundromat. "You know, something, I don't know. I don't know but when I go to the laundromat and stuff like that I'm always talking to other par-ents trying to get some kind of feedback. I'm always networking in some kind of way." She explained what she got from her laundromat neighbors: "One lady which I really respect in her conversation, her opinions, and she said maybe, I've told her everything that I'm telling you and she said, 'Well, maybe your son's not really into school. He just wants to work and he wants to be a man.' Okay, what do I do with that, because education is important? If that fails, if anything fails, whatever he's doing right now, what is he going to have to fall back on? I listen to people but it just don't sound right to me. Like I said, I network to try to find out different peoples' opinions and like I said, I go online."

Elizabeth, described earlier, also networked to find information in the neighbor-hood. She disliked Harlem and planned to relocate down South. She had heard good things about the South from people in the neighborhood with whom she networked. "I network with a lot of people because that is, you know, I try to find out different information, so I network." When asked what she meant by network-ing, Elizabeth explained, "Like I just talk to different people. People, when I go out and I meet different people I just, you know, I just strike up a conversation about . . . anything." She gave an example: "Like let's say if I go get my nails done and I just I start talking. You know what I'm saying? I'll strike up a conversation with maybe, you know, with another person getting their nails done or I have to take a training and there's other, you know, other ladies in there. So, you know, I'm talking about, we talk about different things and then that's how the conversation start. You, you talk about one thing and then you just keep talking. And then that's just how, you know, things come up. That's how you find out, oh, a person, you know, has this business or, you know, a person lived here or information that they can give you that's helpful."

Jennifer, a mother in her forties from Harlem, said she was someone who kept to herself in the housing project where she lived. "I don't wanna get to know no one." One day, Jennifer saw another mother, Michelle, from the housing project at the supermarket. Though the two had not spoken before, "we was in the line, waiting to pay him, we just started a conversation." Their supermarket conversation turned into a friendship. After the supermarket interaction, the two had socialized. "Once or twice we did, just us two we went for breakfast, you know, we went and got our, feet and my nail, our nails done." Jennifer had recently lost her job and turned to Michelle for assistance. "She just called me a few minutes ago. She works in a hospital but . . . she is a dietician. But I don't think they're hiring. She been, you know she been looking for me as well." Moreover, Jennifer had relied on Michelle for help watching her two children. "I guess we had . . . by that time, you know, we had talked so much or whatever, and I think one day I was actually gonna take them to my mom's, . . . so she asked me, 'you know where you going?' I say 'oh I got to take them to my mom's and I have to go back to work at six.' She was like 'no,' she said 'I'll watch them for you, don't worry.' And they love her. So I was like, 'okay, let's try it.' And it was fine." Jennifer explained that she had relied on Michelle for babysitting "around ten times."

DISCUSSION

The apparent inconsistency between narrative and practice can be better understood by probing recent work on neighborhood narratives and on mechanisms from a pragmatist perspective. Small (2002, 2004) referred to "neighborhood narrative frames" as the cognitive understandings people have about their neighborhoods that take the form of narratives or stories about a place. Importantly, such narratives can be about not merely the neighborhood but also the resident's place in it, about the self in relation to the space. The stories of mothers not trusting people on the corner or keeping their children off the streets are narratives about both the neighborhood and the self.

In this respect, they are versions of what Gross (2009), in a pragmatist theory of mechanisms, recently called "cognitive affective habits" (2009, 370); they are "habitual ways individual actors have of [both] understanding and responding emotionally" (370) to their predicaments. Cognitive affective habits are one of three types of habits[2] in Gross's model, the type most closely related to what Dewey, in an extensive discussion of habits, referred to as "habits of thought and feeling" (1922, 108).[3] Dewey emphasized that such habits are "not so easily modified" (108). Often resulting from what Gross called people's "psychosocial experience," they become fundamental to how people think and feel (2009, 370). In the current context, life experience in high-poverty neighborhoods where—especially in Woodlawn and Sunnyside—violence is high and the need for some measure of self-protection is real, necessarily informs these habits of thought.

Gross's use of the term "habits" is not intended to ignore their cultural character. On the contrary, "Insofar as the tendency to employ one cognitive schema for interpreting the world rather than another also falls under this analytic rubric, cognitive-affective habits are major sites of cultural-interpretive activity" (2009, 370). The fact that they are sites of cultural-interpretive activity matter in an important way. Though cognitive habits are dispositional and often not stated, they can certainly be elicited by interviewers when asking respondents to represent their attitude toward their neighbors and neighborhood. That is to say, these particular habits can be articulated, and we refer to these articulated understandings as *narratives* (see also Small, Harding, and Lamont 2010).

Nevertheless, Gross's (and Dewey's) term "habit" is useful, because it speaks to the generality of these understandings. A cognitive habit is built over time through one's daily, repeated neighborhood experiences. Once formed, it becomes a general understanding of the self and the neighborhood; once articulated, either to oneself or an interviewer, it becomes a narrative. The narratives are general because they are the culmination of a multitude of daily experiences; they are not about any person or particular place or often even location (Raudenbush 2016, 1035 ff.). They are general habits of thought about a place and its people that become articulated as attitudes about the self.[4]

This is not to say that narratives are inevitable. After all, not every mother expressed the same general narrative about the neighborhood, and even among those who described what can generally be described as distrust, some focused on how they raised their children while others focused on how they kept distance from others. There was certainly heterogeneity. The key is that narratives are general because they reflect the end result of accumulated experiences, a cognitive generalization that happens individually but will often be shared to the extent that those experiences—neighborhood violence, fear for safety, lack of resources, high poverty—are shared.

For these reasons, describing the narratives as false is inadequate. The mothers are not lying. They are merely representing something other than what researchers have sometimes interpreted respondents to have expressed. They are describing their cognitive understanding of themselves in relation to their neighborhood, a general approach born of experience, not a specific orientation toward any individual. In these narratives, the "people" being described may be technically neighbors but are not necessarily "neighbors," because they are also are specific individuals with whom they have a relation, often institutionally mediated and, as individuals, are immaterial to any general understanding. The mothers can express their dispositions so easily because they are cognitively distinguishing church, school, or family neighbors, whom they describe (particularly) as "the parent in the daycare" or the "lady at the church" or "my sister down the block" from noninstitutionally affiliated neighbors, whom they describe as "people" in the streets.

CONCLUSION

We have argued that low-income African Americans across high-poverty neighborhoods express distrust and isolation but nevertheless also socialize and engage in helping behavior; that they do so because the former is general and the latter targeted; and that the targeting is shaped by whether the neighbor ties are institutionally mediated. Our argument relied on a full and frank examination of our qualitative data, an a priori disinterested view of what the data would uncover, and a heightened sensitivity to what actors did in practice. Ethnographic data, when explored comprehensively, paint fuller pictures than the summary statements about urban poverty we have become accustomed to hearing. We could have taken half of our data and painted a story—a real story—of isolation, distrust, keeping to oneself, and independence. Indeed, we must stress that the loneliness and deep distrust that the mothers experienced are themselves a form of isolation common in high-poverty neighborhoods that we do not wish to underemphasize (e.g., Small 2007). But we could have taken the other half of our data and painted an equally real story of social support, interdependence, community, and reliance on others (see Raudenbush 2016). A full and fair accounting, however, requires us to eschew either story on its own.

We argue not merely that there is truth to both stories; we argue that they point to different phenomena, to people's true narratives of their lives and to the decisions they make over the course of their everyday lives when they need help figuring out how to raise their children, or getting food for the holidays, or avoiding the loneliness that comes from isolation. Furthermore, we argue that the narratives are generalist, describing a self-understanding born of the steady accumulation of daily neighborhood experiences. Their practice, however, is pragmatically specific; the mothers turn to others when institutional expectations from family or organizations make trust, socialization, and interdependence easier, expected, or at least feasible. And in a context in which help from or merely engaging with others is helpful, a modicum of institutional nudging is often sufficient.

Pragmatists often interpret thoughts, words, and reasoning in light of actual practice. The pragmatist's orientation toward practice becomes particularly intriguing when practice and narrative appear in conflict, when what people do and what they say about what they do collide. Sometimes such collisions are easy to explain, such as when people lie about their behavior out of embarrassment. But there are times when the matter is more complicated, wherein honest actors perceive their practice in ways that may seem to the researcher inconsistent with the practice itself. The experiences of low-income mothers in these three neighborhoods presents one such opportunity, wherein the joint study of both narrative and practice improves our understanding of what people do in their everyday lives.

BIBLIOGRAPHY

Anderson, Elijah. 1999. *Code of the Street: Decency, Violence, and the Moral Life of the Inner City*. New York: W.W. Norton & Company".

Becker, Howard S. 2009. "How to Find Out How to Do Qualitative Research." *International Journal of Communication* 3:545–53.

Bourdieu, Pierre. 1990. *The Logic of Practice*. Trans. by R. Nice. Stanford, CA: Stanford University Press.

Chan Tack, Anjanette M. and Mario L. Small. 2017. "Making Friends in Violent Neighborhoods: Strategies among Elementary School Children. *Sociological Science*. 4:224–248.

Davis, Benjamin and Phineas Baxandall. 2013. *Transportation in Transition: A Look at Changing Travel Patterns in America's Biggest Cities*. Boston: U.S. PIRG Education Fund.

Desmond, Matthew. 2012. "Disposable Ties and the Urban Poor." *American Journal of Sociology* 117(5):1295–1335.

Dewey, John. 1922. *Human Nature and Conduct: An Introduction to Social Psychology*. New York: Henry Holt and company.

Domínguez, Silvia and Celeste Watkins. 2003. "Creating Networks for Survival and Mobility: Social Capital among African-American and Latin-American Low-Income Mothers." *Social Problems* 50(1): 111–135.

Fernandez, Roberto M. and Isabel Fernandez-Mateo. 2006. "Networks, Race, and Hiring." *American Sociological Review* 71(1):42–71.

Fischer, Claude S. 1982. *To Dwell Among Friends: Personal Networks in Town and City*. Chicago: University of Chicago Press.

Glaser, Barney G. and Anselm L. Strauss. 1967. *The Discovery of Grounded Theory: Strategies for Qualitative Research*. Chicago: Aldine.

Goering, John, and Judith D. Feins. 2003. *Choosing a Better Life?* Washington D.C.: Urban Institute Press.

Granovetter, Mark. 1974. *Getting a Job: A Study of Contracts and Careers*. Chicago: University of Chicago Press.

Gross, Neil. 2009. "A Pragmatist Theory of Social Mechanisms." *American Sociological Review* 74(3):358–79.

Hyra, Derek. 2008. *The New Urban Renewal: The Economic Transformation of Harlem and Bronzeville*. Chicago: University of Chicago Press.

Jerolmack, Colin and Shamus Khan. 2014. "Talk is Cheap: Ethnography and the Attitudinal Fallacy." *Sociological Methods & Research* 43(2):178–209.

Joas, Hans. 1996. *The Creativity of Action*. Trans. J. Gaines and P. Keast. Chicago: University of Chicago Press.

Kramer, Roderick M. and Karen S. Cook, eds. 2004. *Trust and Distrust in Organizations: Dilemmas and Approaches*. New York: Russell Sage Foundation.

Logan, John R. and Glenna D. Spitze. 1994. "Family Neighbors." *American Journal of Sociology* 100(2):453–76.

Logan, John R., and Glenna D. Spitze. 1996. *Family Ties: Enduring Relations between Parents and Their Grown Children.* Philadelphia: Temple University Press.

Mazelis, Joan Maya. 2017. *Surviving Poverty: Creating Sustainable Ties among the Poor.* New York: NYU Press.

Massey, Douglas and Nancy Denton. 1993. *American Apartheid.* Cambridge, MA: Harvard University Press.

McRoberts, Omar. 2003. *Streets of Glory: Church and Community in a Black Urban Neighborhood.* Chicago: University of Chicago Press.

Miller-Cribbs, Julie E. and Naomi B. Farber. 2008. "Kin Networks and Poverty among African Americans: Past and Present." *Social Work* 53(1):43–51.

Murphy, Alexandra. Unpublished manuscript. *When the Sidewalks End: Poverty in an American Suburb.*

Nelson, Margaret K. 2000. "Single Mothers and Social Support: The Commitment to, and Retreat from, Reciprocity." *Qualitative Sociology* 23(3):291–317.

Powell, Walter and Paul J. DiMaggio. 1991. *The New Institutionalism in Organizational Analysis.* Chicago: University of Chicago Press.

Raudenbush, Danielle. 2016. " 'I Stay By Myself': Social Support, Distrust, and Selective Solidarity among the Poor." *Sociological Forum* 31(4):1018–39.

Sampson, Robert. 2012. *Great American City: Chicago and the Enduring Neighborhood Effect.* Chicago: University of Chicago Press.

Sampson, Robert, Jeffrey D. Morenoff, and T. Gannon-Rowley. 2002. "Assessing 'Neighborhood Effects': Social Processes and New Directions in Research. *Annual Review of Sociology* 28:443–478.

Scott, W. Richard. 1995. *Institutions and Organizations: Ideas, Interests, and Identities.* Thousand Oaks, CA: Sage Publications.

Sharkey, Patrick. 2013. *Stuck in Place: Urban Neighborhoods and the End of Progress toward Racial Equality.* Chicago: University of Chicago Press.

Small, Mario L. 2002. "Culture, Cohorts, and Social Organization Theory: Understanding Local Participation in a Latino Housing Project." *American Journal of Sociology.* 108(1):1–54.

Small, Mario L. 2004. *Villa Victoria: The Transformation of Social Capital in a Boston Barrio.* Chicago: University of Chicago Press.

Small, Mario L. 2007. "Racial Differences in Networks: Do Neighborhood Conditions Matter?" *Social Science Quarterly.* 88(2):320–43.

Small, Mario L. 2009a. *Unanticipated Gains.* New York: Oxford University Press.

Small, Mario L. 2009b. " 'How Many Cases Do I Need?': On Science and the Logic of Case Selection in Field-based Research." *Ethnography* 10(1):5–38.

Small, Mario L. 2017. *Someone To Talk To.* New York: Oxford University Press.

Small, Mario L. and Jenna Cook. 2021. "Using Interviews to Answer Why: Challenges and Strategies in the Study of Motivated Action." *Sociological Methods & Research.*

Small, Mario L., David J. Harding, and Michele Lamont. 2010. "Reconsidering Culture and Poverty." *The ANNALS of the American Academy of Political and Social Science* 629(1):6–27.

Small, Mario L., Robert Manduca, and William Johnston. 2018. "Ethnography, Neighborhood Effects, and the Rising Heterogeneity of Poor Neighborhoods across Cities." *City & Community* 17(3):565–89.

Small, Mario L. and Monica McDermott. 2006. "The Presence of Organizational Resources in Poor Urban Neighborhoods: An Analysis of Average and Contextual Effects." *Social Forces* 84(3):1697–1724.

Small, Mario L. and Christopher Suhku. 2016. "Because They Were There: Access, Deliberation, and the Mobilization of Networks for Support." *Social Networks* 47:73–84.

Small, Mario L. and Katherine Newman. 2001. "Urban Poverty after *The Truly Disadvantaged*: The Rediscovery of the Family, the Neighborhood, and Culture." *Annual Review of Sociology* 27:23–45.

Smith, Sandra. 2007. *Lone Pursuit: Distrust and Defensive Individualism Among the Black Poor.* New York: Russell Sage Foundation.

Stack, Carol. 1974. *All Our Kin.* New York: Basic Books.

Stinchcombe, Arthur L. 2001. *When Formality Works: Authority and Abstraction in Law and Organizations.* Chicago: University of Chicago Press.

Uehara, Edwina. 1990. "Dual Exchange Theory, Social Networks, and Informal Social Support." *American Journal of Sociology* 96(3):521–57.

U.S. Census Bureau, *American Community Survey* 2011–15.

Wilson, William J. 1987. *The Truly Disadvantaged: The Inner City, the Underclass, and Public Policy.* Chicago: University of Chicago Press.

Wilson, William J. 1996. *When Work Disappears: The World of the New Urban Poor.* New York: Vintage.

NOTES

For their generous support, we thank the University of Chicago, Harvard University, and the Harvard Project on Race, Class, and Cumulative Adversity at the Hutchins Center. We thank the editors for valuable and insightful comments.

1. Fernandez and Fernandez-Mateo (2006) found something even stronger: "In contrast with the expectations of certain theories, which suggest that minorities might be reluctant to engage in networking activities, we found that African Americans, Asians, and Hispanics are significantly more likely to produce referral applications than are whites" (66).

2. The other two are habits of behavior and collective habits.

3. Cognitive affective habits also bear some relation to Bourdieu's (1990) "habitus."

4. Raudenbush (2016,1036) describes them as frames: "We should understand statements like 'I stay by myself,' then, as statements that reflect a frame that people develop to navigate a social world in which broader forces make them wary of those around them and cause them to perceive interactions with others as potentially harmful."

10. Scientific Innovation as Environed Social Learning

NATALIE B. AVILES

INTRODUCTION

In recent decades, sociologists have explored the topic of innovation with renewed vigor. Interest in scientific and technological innovation in particular has revived an institutionalist sociology of science largely dormant since the 1970s and has opened new ground to be colonized by field theory. This contemporary sociology of science, informed by the theoretical work of Robert K. Merton and Pierre Bourdieu, revisits the enterprise of explaining the social conditions that make scientific innovation possible or likely. While such recent empirical contributions enrich the discipline, they also lay bare the theoretical limitations of approaches that are insufficiently attentive to the practices of scientists that involve them in transformations with heterogeneous material and social environments.

In this chapter, I bring disciplinary sociological efforts into conversation with theoretical insights on material scientific practice from science and technology studies (STS) to expand the theoretical scope of contemporary sociology of scientific innovation. At the same time, I critique STS approaches that flatten the material world, arguing that issues of scale are central to scientific decision-making and should be studied naturalistically to understand how scientists engage in their environments to effect and encode innovative transformations.

Pragmatism provides an approach for conceptualizing the effects of environmental heterogeneity and scale on scientific innovation, thus addressing some of the shortcomings of sociology of science and STS. Elaborating on a long-running sociological focus on "social worlds" in STS, I discuss how doubling down on the pragmatist origins of social worlds analysis can help sociologists develop a comprehensive approach to temporally extended episodes of scientific problem-solving as a form of what I call "environed social learning." To demonstrate how a pragmatist orientation allows for greater explanatory scope and power in comparison with theoretical alternatives, I offer a case study of human papillomavirus (HPV) vaccine innovation in the U.S. National Cancer Institute (NCI). I argue that revisiting key insights from classical American pragmatism allows us to focus on collective and environed activities, such as social learning, that may be generalizable across a broad range of scientific innovation efforts.

INNOVATION IN SOCIOLOGY AND STS: PROBLEMS OF HETEROGENEITY AND SCALE

Despite the presumed importance of scientific innovation in remaking the modern world, sociology has tended to recreate in its explanations a demarcation between objects of study that are properly "social" and those that are primarily "scientific." The first institutionalist sociologists of science, following Merton, formally abdicated sociology's role in examining the content of scientific knowledge claims and were thus largely reticent on the process of innovation itself. Merton's functionalist take on scientific innovation held that sociologists could study the norms that guided scientific progress quite apart from the substance of scientists' work. Taking for granted that scientific conduct was governed by an "ethos" that sanctioned behavior in ways conducive to continued discovery and rapid diffusion of innovation,[1] Merton and his fellow sociologists of science built an industry of citation analyses exploring the consequences of these norms on the distribution of scientific credit.

The work of many prominent contemporary sociologists of science hews closely to Merton's hallmark concepts and methods.[2] However, these scholars modify many of Merton's functionalist assumptions with insights from new institutionalism and social network analysis. Evans and colleagues substitute Merton's simplistic model of reward-based decision-making with an "academic habitus" inspired by Bourdieu, wherein innovation is a strategic gamble for recognition.[3] Bourdieu's own forays into science studies involved applying his field theoretic to explain science as a field of struggle over scientific authority. Yet his sparing remarks about what scientists are really up to is revealing of his faith in "an idealized picture of the inner workings of scientific fields" that is nothing short of Mertonian.[4]

Bourdieu's approach to innovation in science is similar to his approach to innovation in literature or philosophy: the innovator is someone with sufficient scientific capital and mastery of the rules of the game to ascend to a position of dominance in the field through struggles wherein she transforms the forces structuring the field. Scientific practice is bound up with field position by habitus, which involves the development of a "practical logic" through experimentation.[5] Scientists acquire certain dispositions that structure their research programs around a sense of where they are in their discipline and where they would like to be. Competition among scientists is tempered by "intersubjective agreement" among scientists that certain rules and norms, which neatly coincide with Merton's ethos, will "[provide] guarantees of the quality of the products" scientists come to accept as valid.[6]

As the work of contemporary sociologists demonstrates, the neo-Mertonian and Bourdivin approaches to sociology of science are ultimately compatible with a few simple theoretical trade-offs. The fusion of the two theories also reveals what is centrally up for debate in the Mertonian and Bourdivin approaches: the assumption, aptly stated by Foster, Rzhetsky, and Evans, that "published claims in contemporary biomedicine [can be used] to make inferences about underlying choices and dispositions" of scientists.[7] The goals of a sociology of science informed by Mertonian institutionalism and Bourdivin field theory is to discern the strategies that scientists use to navigate a social world in which science is primarily an ideational pursuit with concrete career consequences. Consider the following passage from the same study:

> Our analysis follows six distinct steps and connects to the vignette of our practicing scientist, described earlier. In brief, our broad goals are as follows: map the space of chemical knowledge (Steps 1 and 2); identify the prevalence and stability of the various strategies (Step 3); construct a simple behavioral model of scientific attention that relates strategy prevalence with opportunity (Step 4); measure risks and rewards associated with various strategies using citations (Step 5); and explore two potential motivational mechanisms for scientists' choices—maximizing citations and seeking outsized recognition (Step 6).[8]

Remarkably, at no point in her work-a-day world does this "practicing scientist" do anything that resembles science. In place of the practicing scientist, the authors model a "strategizing scientist."

Astute readers of Mertonian and Bourdivin sociology of science may also notice their general dearth of citations to works produced after the early 1980s in the now large interdisciplinary field of science and technology studies. In fact, STS enjoys an additional methodological advantage over the ideational and strategic models of Mertonian and Bourdivin explanations in that its focus on material scientific practices highlights the difficulty that scientists confront in making or reproducing successful experimentation, and the preponderance of failure in routine attempts at innovation.[9] If the bales of print generated by STS scholars since the 1980s to support the idea that most innovation comes from attempts to solve practical problems in the laboratory through bootstrapping and bulldogging against failure are any indication, then sociologists are in no position to neglect the role of scientific practice as a causal precipitant of innovation outcomes. To understand science as comprising transformative engagements with the material world is to appreciate that the processes whereby patterns are recognized, become salient, and are named and then refined involve tightly interwoven interactions between social *and* natural elements in scientists' environments.

In its dominant theoretical attitude, STS strives to demonstrate the causal importance of engagement with heterogeneous dimensions of material and discursive environments to the generation of innovations and to their durability through acceptance and adoption. Most prominent among contemporary STS theories of innovation has been posthumanism, particularly in the semiotic interpretation of actor-network theory (ANT) associated with Bruno Latour and Michel Callon,[10] and the "new materialism" developed by scholars like Karen Barad[11] and Jane Bennett.[12] The foundational insight of posthumanist STS is that the nonhuman world participates fully in humans' attempts to represent and transform it. The notion that nonhuman things have the capacity to push back against human intervention has been interpreted by posthumanists to indicate a measure of agency on the part of nonhuman and inorganic matter, such that analysts should treat humans and all other facets of the material world as "actants" with epistemological (in ANT) or ontological (in new materialism) parity with one another. To accomplish this, they flatten the world into a series of relationships, either semiotic[13] or material.[14] In this way, innovation can be studied as the outcome of strategic efforts to enlist networked actants into supporting particular claims about the world (in ANT), or as the product of intra-active processes involving "entanglements" of humans and matter that mirror shifts and recombinations at the quantum level (in new materialism).

Posthumanism's flattened world offers a lens for social scientists to explore scientific innovation involving heterogeneous material and conceptual elements that are analyzable on the same plane of explanation. Both ANT and new materialism propose a synecdochic ontology of the world, such that entities obtaining at small scales (e.g., atoms or microbes) are homologous with those occurring at larger and larger scales (e.g., human actors or nation-states). In this manner, every salient force affecting innovation, from scientists to molecules to nation-states, can be made intelligible in their connections to one another. Such a move enables posthumanist STS to cast a wider net over the world than can ideational Mertonian or Bourdivin sociologists, and it thus accounts for the causal efficacy of heterogeneous features of the environment—such as technological infrastructures and physical or organic matter—over innovation outcomes. Yet in opening inquiry to elements of a heterogeneous environment for scientific action, ANT and new materialism sacrifice important variations in scale that structure scientific practices in ways that affect innovation outcomes. A discussion of the limitations of these theories in relation to scale should precede an analysis that takes many of the basic insights of such STS theorizing seriously.

As Derek Woods has argued, posthumanism's "scale-invariant" approach to scientific innovation is limited in capturing how scientists act in a world in which causation—and, ultimately, ontology—varies according to spatial and temporal scale.[15] Typically, scientists refer to these variations in terms of different "scale domains," which they study along metrics (nanoscopic, microscopic, macroscopic, etc.) relative to human optics. Regardless of where we draw the lines between these scales analytically, Woods argues, there are material constraints on certain ways of being at different scales that analysts must take seriously in understanding the environing factors behind successful scientific innovation. From the perspective of scale variance, we cannot assume that the transition from things that exist at very small or very large scales compared with the human organism will be continual or lossless. Rather, there are distinct ontological rifts between scales that are characterized by "relatively sharp transitions from dominance by one set of factors to dominance by other sets."[16]

Rifts between domains of different size are necessitated by physical features of the world (such as the rate at which oxygen molecules are displaced, which prevents mammals with respiratory systems from shrinking below a certain size) or interdependencies among entities (e.g., regional industries, geophysical systems, and natural ecologies in the phenomenon of climate change). Such physical and interactive constraints limit the possibilities for phenomena manifesting in the different and overlapping "scalar worlds" that characterize scientists' environments. Although such features are easily bracketed in traditional sociological analysis as "nonsocial," they crucially shape the possibilities for developing successful scientific innovations. As Woods argues, is not *merely* a matter of conceptualization, measurement, or persuasion that led nano engineers to design vehicles based on insect bodies. In engaging the nanoscopic world, engineers found that the structural principles of macroscopic design "break down" at the quantum level to the extent that it is impractical or impossible to replicate the architectures of industrial machinery or organismic complexity that characterize human societies and vertebrate bodies.[17] Engineers settled on insect bodies as the closest functional analog on which they could design moving vehicles at the nano scale. Here human creativity could be exercised only in light of the constraints imposed by inorganic matter existing by rules that characterize the smallest level of phenomena on which we are able to intervene, given the technologies available. An explanation of why the insect design succeeded as an innovation that excludes these elements is necessarily incomplete.

The corollary of ontological pluralism along issues of scale as well as type is an epistemological stance that captures, rather than collapses, the dominant sets of factors that obtain and are observable in different scalar worlds. Things-in-the-world, many of which can exist only at comparatively small scales (e.g., molecules) or comparatively large scales (e.g., global economies) vis-à-vis human scientists, are necessary but not sufficient contributors to scientific innovation. To be sure, it is overly ambitious to prescribe for sociology an account of these plural scales of existence. Instead, the challenge is to develop frameworks that bring scientists' transactions with their environments so constituted into analytical focus so that we can better understand the success of scientific innovations as encounters with salient features of their environments *that scientists experience as real and consequential to their ability to act further.* The key is to understand how scientists make sense of and transform these experientially real, heterogeneous, and multiscalar environments (both materially and meaningfully) to create conditions suited toward their situated goals. As sociologist Mark Peter Jones[18] has argued, pragmatism already offers STS the theoretical tools to analyze innovation as a process wherein human actors engage transactionally with heterogeneous and scale-variant worlds. Embracing the humanist impulse of pragmatism allows sociologists to take the activities of scientists from a historicist and empiricist perspective, centering the mutual articulation of moral, ideational, and experimental systems in the practices whereby humans constitute their work environments.

PRAGMATIST APPROACHES TO SCIENTIFIC INNOVATION

The theoretical challenge to which pragmatism is well suited is thus to capture the heterogeneity and scale variance of scientists' environments, alongside the ongoing temporal processes whereby scientific conduct reshapes the environment for subsequent research. The full theoretical potential of a pragmatist theory of scientific innovation is lost if it fails to capture the iterative process of mutual shaping between scientists and their environments. This is because the fact of its sociality makes scientific inference accountable to a *world*, defined by the transactional interplay between the capacities of material environments and the ongoing temporal practices of distinctively human environments ordered by cultural practices. The world thus defined is fully capable of resisting our best attempts to intervene in it, a reality that constantly threatens failure and error as the end result of human conduct.

Scientific practice presents itself as a uniquely generative topic for sociological theory in the central importance of accountability to socio*material* environments. At the same time, a pragmatist interpretation accepts the limitations imposed on explanation by the fact that humans integrate their environments into experience through an active, social, and perspectival process. Pragmatism acknowledges the objectivity and resistance of nonhuman participants in a transaction without granting them ontological parity with humans.[19] Similarly, a pragmatist approach to sociomaterial transaction allows STS scholars to study how the physical environment is integrated into human cognition in mutually transformative processes, without presuming access to the perspectives of nonhuman actants that are independent of humans' situated reconstructions.

The foundational insight of analyzing the activities of scientists from a historicist and empiricist perspective has encouraged naturalistic philosophers of science to remain attentive to the embodied conditions of perception and knowledge, an enterprise for which pragmatism has remained an enduringly useful tool.[20] Drawing in particular on the philosophies of Charles Peirce and John Dewey, naturalist epistemologists have taken an approach to science as a system of knowledge production that develops over time as humans "learn how to learn" by acting toward problems as they present themselves, thereby building on past experiences while producing truly novel insights.[21] Complementary to Peirce's axiom that "abductive inference shades into perceptual judgment without any sharp line of demarcation between them"[22] is Dewey's model of inquiry that presupposes that the value of a certain end is weighed against how well it allows action to proceed given the environment toward which the actor must act.[23] In accounting for the development of specific lines of inquiry, pragmatism encourages sociologists of science to examine the local and historical circumstances whereby a certain course of action proceeds and to appreciate innovation as a product of human desires and interests made meaningful through engagement with the affordances that inhere in the full social, intellectual, and material richness of scientists' lived environments.

The newest generation of pragmatist-influenced philosophers of science has developed a conceptual focus on how the situation of experimentation leads to the emergence of new knowledge and techniques and their subsequent integration into the environment for future scientific conduct. This process has been called "generative entrenchment," and it involves the processes whereby "phenomena investigated by empirical scientists result from the active use of materials, tools, instruments, machines, people, and money. As commitments to their use develop, these elements become part of the constitutive conditions for the occurrence of that particular phenomenon."[24] A similar sentiment about the ecological impulses undergirding such a concept of generative entrenchment has been developed by Joseph Rouse, who draws on neopragmatist Robert Brandom to conceptualize the joint articulation of conceptual, technical, and organizational commitments in science over time as a process of niche construction. Scientific lineages are formed by the ongoing reconstruction of social and material apparatus in experimental performances that are accountable to norms defining what is "at issue" in a given experiment and what is "at stake" in assessing the implications of these experiments beyond their specific contextual performance.[25] Scientific practice is thus intersubjectively evaluated based on its collective reconstruction as a materially accountable and socially meaningful activity relative to the multiple overlapping environments in which scientific performances are embedded.

In their insistence on embedding scientific practice in the organized conditions of its production and continuation, these pragmatist-inspired philosophers advance perspectives on science as an ecological process. Whereas their philosophical projects have addressed the overemphasis on knowledge claims by theorizing how experimental systems become established in laboratories, the more explicitly pragmatist theorizing of sociologists who are committed to social worlds analysis demonstrates how these systems scale up beyond the immediate laboratory context. Leading sociological figures in the STS interpretation of social worlds, including Susan Leigh Star, Adele Clarke, and Joan Fujimura, are professional descendants of early social worlds thinkers like Tamotsu Shibutani and Anselm Strauss.[26] Rooted in the symbolic interactionist tradition of the Chicago School, social worlds are canonically defined as the "organized outlook, built up by people in their interaction with one another," that forms the basis of a "universe of regularized mutual response."[27] STS scholars build on this definition to argue that "reference groups generate shared perspectives which form the basis for collective action organized through the construction of social worlds."[28] Drawing on symbolic interactionist interpretations of Dewey and Mead,[29] these STS scholars analyze the complex and multiscalar material, technological, and discursive environments that characterize different social worlds involved in scientific innovation.

Social worlds analysis in STS entails taking an ecological perspective wherein "the unit of analysis is the whole enterprise" operating in a particular intersection of people and organizations rather than the perspectives of discrete individuals or actants within a network.[30] STS's social worlds scholars are attentive to how scientific practice involves flows within social worlds (e.g., scientific disciplines) and across different arenas for action (e.g., political alliances).[31] These scholars have thus focused on the social and material technologies that allow certain theories, methods, and classificatory systems to be accepted as the "right tool for the job" in laboratory science,[32] medicine,[33] and technology.[34] These studies offer a firm grounding for a more thorough integration of pragmatist insights on creativity and scientific inquiry than is encompassed in symbolic interactionism, both by putting greater emphasis on material environing factors in addition to practical and discursive ones and by paying closer attention to temporal processes whereby phenomena at varying scales develop and change in concert with these environments.

Proponents advocate for social worlds analysis as a humanistic alternative to ANT that better accounts for the distinct properties of supervenient social phenomena, with a particular emphasis on the genesis and exercise of power across social worlds.[35] Attention to networks in social worlds analysis is primarily oriented toward imagining the maintenance of boundaries in the scientific labor process and following the traffic of knowledge and technological objects through organizational spaces. A particularly compelling interpretation of social worlds in STS has emerged from considerations of how large-scale shifts in biomedical practice have been effected through the iterative circulation of technologies, materials, and human laborers. Here sociologists direct their attention to networked collectivities that enact closely coupled cultural conceptions and material practices through the process of experimentation.

Social worlds analysis has thus been explicitly developed by sociologists in STS to address meso- and macro-level organizational and institutional forces that are consequential to the way scientific research is conducted without sacrificing insights gained from analyzing the embodied and material nature of scientific work. Innovation in scientific research often results when conflicting or competing claims within or across social worlds are consolidated into coherent and portable techniques that materialize particular definitions of problems and approaches to their solution. Over time, these techniques can transform the broader arenas for scientific action around particular problems by redefining the stakes of different scientific disciplines or programs and concretizing these stakes in durable changes to the financial, cultural, intellectual, and physical constitution of scientific practice.

These advantages also harken to the social worlds approach's indebtedness to the pragmatism of George Herbert Mead, who had developed an understanding of scientific change as a process of problem-solving wherein scientists continuously reconstructed the objects of their inquiries through their practical experiences of theory construction and experimentation.[36] Mead's understanding of scientific innovation built directly on the more well-known apparatus of his social psychology. In the objectivity of perspectives, Mead suggests a solution to theorizing how scientists act in environments that are characterized by various forces that restrain the direction and consequence of their actions. The manifest and salient aspects of our environments present themselves to experience as dimensions of sociality that are bound up (though not interchangeable) with human sociality. Mead argues that in becoming available to our perception as objective things, all entities emerge from and are characterized by their transactions relative to other aspects of the environment. The projective aspect of human experience and action involves us in the world such that we articulate and respond to nonhuman aspects of the environment in a process similar to that from which we iteratively develop a sense of self. On this Mead was explicit: "Anything—any object or set of objects, whether animate or inanimate, human or animal, or merely physical—toward which he acts, or to which he responds, socially, is an element in what for him is the generalized other."[37] Yet these perspectives are objective because they involve a reckoning with the manifest conditions for human action in particular situations—that "mutual determination of the form and its environment."[38] In regard to human practices, including science, our ability to take the place of nonhuman others is limited by the embodied experience of living as an organism embedded in scalar social relationships with human and heterogeneous others.

Pragmatism is thus a promising solution to the omissions of nonheterogeneous and scale-invariant theoretical frameworks that predominate in sociological and STS accounts of scientific innovation. It enables us to approach science as a situated human enterprise that involves reconstructions of the environment that are at the same time conceptual and material and that are oriented toward fixing heterogeneous worlds in particular spatial and temporal parameters that are nonetheless open to revision. Moreover, this process of revising scalar orders is not predictably located at the flat scale of "actor/actant" or the homogenous arena of "positions in a field." The environment for scientific innovation comprises phenomena that are distinguished along varying qualitative axes as persons, collectives, technological artifacts, and nonhuman matter, where each of these categorizations should be treated as "provisional genre[s] that [include] diverse particles and forces"[39] impinging on research outcomes. Scientific projects are scaled differently by different collectives, and these scaling events can be iterated through action so that they come to characterize part of the environment as material, technological, or political realities.

The resources available to make such claims open to learning and retention are provided not only in the machinations of actors but in the ability of salient features of the environment to accommodate or resist actors' interventions. Here the insights of field theory and actor-network theory are productive for thinking through what the relative stakes may be in a given realm where innovation unfolds, as well as the ways in which actors attempt to mobilize aspects of their environment to strengthen their claims for particular innovations. What pragmatism reminds us is that successful innovation is not a mere *trompe l'oeil*; the environment, scaled to demonstrate in material traces what a new intervention is useful *for*, comprises necessary ingredients for scientific innovations to succeed.

Yet to truly capitalize on the potential of a pragmatist approach to scientific innovation, I argue we should focus more deliberately on transitions across social worlds—not only spatially, as extant social worlds analyses aptly do, but temporally as well. I thus propose to supplement the social worlds approach with an explicit focus on "transitionalism," which pragmatist scholar Colin Koopman defines as the "thoroughgoing historicity and temporality of epistemic, ethical, and political practice"[40] uniting the most productive insights of both classical pragmatists and neo-pragmatists like Brandom and Richard Rorty. Though agnostic about the form that transition may take across social practices, transitionalism emphasizes the importance of reconstruction to the transition process as it unfolds across varying situations. One basic insight offered by transitionalist pragmatism is that reconstruction is often aimed specifically at melioration—at wielding the resources available in a present situation to reconstitute an immediately proximate situation as improved over that present.[41] Reading the germ of a transitionalist pragmatism into the social worlds projects of STS scholars, I argue that we can capture the ways in which sociomaterial environments are recursively reconstructed over historical time as a process of social learning. A pragmatist foundation informs us how we might better observe social learning operating through transformations to the social and material dimensions of scientific environments in which scientists are situated as (borrowing a turn of phrase favored by Dewey) *environed* social learning.

An emphasis on environed social learning as a temporal process of transition moves us from analysis of problem-solving in the short term to innovation along a larger scale and longer time horizon, thus tracking the iterative process of generative entrenchment across successively transformed social worlds. Pragmatism encourages us to understand novelty as arising from situations that are characterized by diverse environing conditions. These conditions range in the scale at which they become factors that are salient for motivating action. Broadly, they can be summarized in terms of the following.

1. *Material systems.* These include, but are not limited to, the behaviors of nonhuman or inorganic matter as it obtains at varying scales (e.g., quantum uncertainty in subatomic particles, molecular transcription of DNA, biochemical mechanisms of metabolism in mammals). The operation of material systems sets parameters in which transformations may be enacted by other processes (e.g., points 2–4).

2. *Physical technologies.* These encompass techniques for generating, representing, and/or intervening on any of the systems listed here. Traditionally, physical technologies embody particular routines in apparatus that humans leverage toward practical use (e.g., automated machinery for manufacture, infrastructure for communications, tele- and microscopics for enhanced visualization).

3. *Human interactions.* Typically encompassed by the micro level of sociological analyses, these involve processes of communication and meaning-making that are often centered in an exchange of symbolic gestures among discrete persons situated in a particular time and place.

4. *Social technologies.* Roughly encompassing the meso and macro levels of sociological analysis, these entail supraindividual processes that structure collective life across space and time (e.g., divisions of labor in organizational fields, rules and rituals in institutions, systems of order and meaning in languages and cultures).

Each of these environing factors is recombined as scientists construct, manipulate, and interpret scientific experiments in light of sensory feedback, collective experimental goals, and scientific standards of proof.

Consideration of these environing conditions also highlights the importance of understanding innovation as a process that unfolds iteratively over a significant time horizon. An additional advantage of a pragmatist approach to innovation lies in its direct applicability to analyzing temporal sequences of problem-solving,[42] each of which may involve redefinitions of the situation that necessitate transformations to other aspects of the environment. Thus the context for innovation does not remain static; rather, it is transformed by scientists to better enable successful innovation in the immediate future. Innovation, as a form of "practical success . . . depends not only on our sentences and our beliefs but also on our bodies, our skills, our tools, and a whole host of other accumulated practical material as well on the realities with which all this material interacts."[43] The continuity of the "interexperiential leadings that draw on all these forms of experience and all their corollary kinds of tools" that contribute to this extended learning process may be lost to the snapshot form of social worlds analysis without careful focus on how environments are reconstructed in the "enormously dense temporal connections that tie past and future experiences together."[44] Careful attention must thus be paid to the way in which environed social learning, as oriented toward meliorism of the environment through problem-solving, unfolds through a "triadic relation of transitionality (from *ab* to *bc* by way of *b*)."[45] We should therefore double down on the pragmatist impulse in social worlds analysis to approach environed social learning in science as an attempt to move from "some present situation to some improved future situation," such that "transitioning from present to future depends on the possibilities of the present as constituted by its historical trajectory."[46]

HPV VACCINE INNOVATION AS ENVIRONED
SOCIAL LEARNING

Elsewhere,[47] I chart the development of vaccines against human papillomavirus (HPV) by federal employees working in a laboratory at the U.S. National Cancer Institute (NCI). I discuss how routines of experimentation, planning, evaluation, and budgeting in the NCI enabled and constrained scientists' ability to develop the first efficacious HPV vaccine alongside an ethics of cervical cancer prevention that reflected their situated labor in this organization. In what follows, I revisit central episodes in HPV vaccine innovation that illustrate the importance of accounting for heterogeneity and scale in the success of this innovation.[48] Using a pragmatist approach that highlights the environing conditions to which scientists creatively responded in developing vaccines, I argue for an approach to innovation that integrates causally precipitating engagements with viruses and technological systems, as well as social technologies of organization and collective creativity. This approach not only demonstrates the analytic gain in tracking transformations to the environment for learning over time but also offers improvements over the dominant alternatives in sociology and STS previously discussed.

The first generation of efficacious vaccines against strains of HPV commonly associated with cervical cancer were approved by the U.S. Food and Drug Administration and the European Medicines Agency in 2006. These vaccines, marketed as Gardasil by Merck and Cervarix by GlaxoSmithKline, originate from publicly funded science, particularly an innovation developed by Douglas Lowy, MD, and John Schiller, PhD, of the NCI Laboratory of Cellular Oncology and patented by the U.S. government. The invention of first-generation HPV vaccines illustrates the importance of creatively interpreting problems generated by the behavior of molecular processes in light of established laboratory routines to the success of this innovation.

Lowy and Schiller are unusual as successful innovators in part because neither had any previous experience in vaccinology or immunology.[49] Furthermore, their research did not focus on human papillomavirus vaccines, because other scientists' attempts to innovate using traditional vaccine techniques proved to be "miserable failures."[50] Instead, they focused on bench science and animal studies on the cellular mechanisms of tumor development, particularly using an assay they developed to detect the growth of bovine papillomavirus (BPV) tumors in cows.

In 1991, a series of studies were published that demonstrated the possibility of isolating harmless structural proteins on the viral envelope of human papillomaviruses (i.e., the L1 and L2 proteins) and showed that L1 proteins were capable of self-folding when expressed through recombinant DNA systems. However, none of the laboratories behind these studies (Queensland University in Australia, the University of Rochester in New York, and Georgetown University in Washington, D.C.) had successfully developed a working vaccine using self-folding L1 HPV proteins.[51] This failure presented a puzzling challenge to scientists at the NCI Laboratory of Cellular Oncology, as they were able to quickly develop vaccines and demonstrate their efficacy using a similar technique for papillomaviruses that infect rabbits and cows.

Lowy, Schiller, and their team interpreted the failure of L1 HPV vaccines based on the routines they had developed over years of in vivo experimentation on BPV and in vitro study of the function of the HPV E6 and E7 proteins, which cause cancer by inactivating the "tumor suppressor" gene $p53$. In these in vitro HPV experiments, the team demonstrated cellular transformation of tissue cultures with "wild-type" (i.e., naturally occurring) $p53$ but not mutated strains of $p53$.[52] Through analogical thinking, the team hypothesized that past attempts at inventing HPV vaccines had failed because they were developed using a mutant strand of HPV. As Lowy recalls,

> we were disappointed to find that whereas the bovine papillomavirus [L1] self-assembled very efficiently, the HPV-16 reference strain that we and virtually everyone else in the world had, that strain was not self-assembling as efficiently. And we did two things: the first was that we considered that, well maybe BPV is different, and what was important was that HPV-16 just doesn't work that way. But the alternative was that HPV-16 might be a mutant in L1. And it turned out that there actually was a publication showing that this reference strain, there was a mutation in another gene that was published. And so it increased the likelihood that maybe there was a mutation.[53]

The laboratory thus designed an experiment testing their theory using a papillomavirus that they were experienced in studying, which they knew to be closely related to HPV:

> HPV-16 [is] very closely related by sequence phylogenetically to a monkey papillomavirus. So the rhesus papillomavirus, we essentially cloned the L1 from that, and Reinhard [Kirnbauer, a postdoctoral researcher in the Laboratory of Cellular Oncology] found that it self-assembled just as well as BPV. So he, you know we, we all inferred that probably the HPV-16 L1 was a mutant [since] it was isolated from a cancer, and so asked colleagues to send us HPV-16 isolates that were from non-cancerous material from cervical dysplasia rather than from that. And when we, when Reinhard expressed HPV-16 L1 from those, they self-assembled just fine. Sequence analysis was done to compare them, and it turned out that indeed there was a point mutation in the reference strain with L1, which dramatically decreased the efficiency of self-assembly.[54]

The NCI team was able to produce the first working vaccine in large part because they discovered that the reference strain of HPV-16 being used in experiments worldwide had a point mutation that prevented its DNA from accurately encoding proteins that were capable of self-folding.[55] Because the epitopes produced by the immune systems of humans, monkeys, cows, and rabbits are conformation-dependent to papillomaviruses, L1 proteins must be properly folded for any vaccine to elicit a stable and sufficient immune response. The mutated reference strain used by other laboratories thus imposed molecular-level material constraints on the possibility of developing a successful vaccine against HPV, even as the technological capacity to do so existed.

Generating a successful vaccine not only necessitated a change in the material resources scientists engaged during experimentation, it also required a disengagement from the institutional networks that are traditionally used to distribute reference strains to laboratories worldwide. Rather than relying on these networks and their suspected mutant strain, the team mobilized colleagues within the NCI to send the laboratory samples of wild-type HPV-16 on which to base their attempts at developing a vaccine. Lowy has reported the ease of such intraorganizational collaborations in the NCI as an instrumental factor in the team's success.[56] Using this new strain, the team generated a system for expressing self-folded HPV L1 and an assay to test its immunogenicity. The laboratory was thus able to produce the first successful HPV vaccine and demonstrate its efficacy.[57]

As Schiller noted, the rapid movement from ideation to experimentation and innovation from 1991 to 1993 "in retrospect was really easy."[58] This is an unexpected revelation, given that the laboratory team lacked expertise in vaccine design, as evidenced by Schiller's recollection of their first attempt at testing the vaccine and assay in rabbits:

> When we first put it in animals, all we did is we took a bunch of cells and ground them up. We didn't even extract these virus-like particles and purify them or anything; we put it in rabbits, then we took out the serum, then we asked: how much can we dilute the serum and still prevent infection in tissue culture cells? And of course we said, we told the postdoc [Kirnbauer] who did this, who was incidentally a dermatologist who had no background in this sort of stuff, and we had no background in this sort of stuff either because . . . we weren't vaccinologists or immunologists, we were studying how the virus caused cancer and decided to do this.[59]

The NCI team did not proceed from identification of a candidate for a vaccine to traditional vaccinology techniques, which might be considered a more direct ideational move. Rather, the knowledge and skills on which the team drew reflected their prior experience in assaying whole-animal tumors. As Schiller recalls, he and Lowy instructed Kirnbauer to

> dilute [the serum] 100 fold, because it can't be more than, you know, you won't have to dilute it more than 100 fold to reach an endpoint where it doesn't work anymore. They did it, and even at 100 fold, you didn't get any infection. So then we said, well, why don't you dilute it 10,000 fold—surely you don't have to dilute it more than 10,000 fold. And he diluted it at 10,000, and even at 10,000, there was no infection. It wasn't until he diluted it in the third experiment—each of the experiments takes about three months—he diluted it out to a million fold, and finally reached an endpoint of 100,000. So in other words, the serum in that

rabbit was ten thousand times . . . more concentrated than was needed to prevent infection of these tissue culture cells. So this is a first example where we just said, man, this is way better than we could've even imagined. And we spent a lot of time after that, actually, just trying to understand why these particles work so well.[60]

Despite the lack of expertise in vaccinology among the laboratory's personnel, their accumulated skills in animal experimentation proved decisive in their success in developing the first working HPV vaccine, as it enabled them to reproduce the laboratory conditions needed to inoculate animals and assay these results into an analogous experimental system for HPV.

The difference that NCI as an organization makes in constituting an environing condition for experimentation becomes clear in comparing the subsequent approaches to clinical trials conducted by the NCI with those in industry. By 1996, animal trials on the NCI-developed L1 VLP vaccine had been well under way,[61] and their findings suggested that the vaccine would be safe enough to test on a larger human population than that included in the current phase I trial being conducted for them by a specialist team at Johns Hopkins. Much in the manner whereby Lowy and Schiller's team depended on clinicians in other divisions of the NCI, they now initiated a series of collaborations with Mark Schiffman, an intramural NCI epidemiologist at the newly restructured Division for Cancer Epidemiology and Genetics. Schiffman was a principal investigator on a study launched in 1993 that aimed to track the natural history of HPV infection in women in Guanacaste, Costa Rica, over seven years. Schiller and Lowy convinced Schiffman to collaborate on modified arms of the Guanacaste trial that would test an enzyme-linked immunosorbent assay (ELISA) for detecting HPV antibodies that they had developed and, beginning in 1997, would serve as Phase II and III trials for their L1 VLP vaccine.[62]

The collaboration with Schiffman would unfold over the course of a few years. As Schiller recalls, these relationships "developed very naturally" in the NCI.[63] Though neither Schiller nor Lowy had worked with epidemiologists prior to their HPV vaccine efforts, they were familiar with Schiffman from joint meetings with their division in the NCI's extension at Shady Grove, Maryland. Encouraged by their collaboration across divisions, institute leaders would invoke joint projects between these bench scientists and epidemiologists as examples of successful collaboration that was encouraged by the NCI's organizational culture.[64] For the NCI leadership, this involved inviting members of the team to discuss their trials during meetings with external advisory bodies appointed by federal statute to oversee the NCI's intramural scientific activities. Among these advisory bodies was the President's Cancer Panel, an independent committee formed in 1971 to supervise the nation's cancer research efforts across government, industry, and academia in order to advise the White House on national health strategy.

In both the Phase I trial at Johns Hopkins and the Phase II/III trials in Guanacaste, Schiller and Lowy's team was able to achieve a goal that many of the NCI's outside advisors found particularly laudable: diversity in clinical trial recruitment.

In particular, Harold P. Freeman, chair of the President's Cancer Panel, had long advocated for attention to health disparities among racial and ethnic minorities in the United States. Cervical cancer disparities were particularly striking among African Americans in the rural south, Hispanic/Latina women in border regions, and low-income whites in the Appalachian region. For years, collaborative efforts for HPV vaccine development in the NCI had been receiving praise for their attention to exactly these underserved populations. As Schiller noted in a 1998 advisory meeting, the Phase I trial at Johns Hopkins included "strong representation" of African American women, and the Phase II/III Guanacaste trial enrolled not only a predominantly Latina population but women whose circumstances more closely resembled those of the majority poor women who would suffer and die from HPV-related cervical cancer.[65]

As I have noted elsewhere,[66] the NCI team's appreciation that the low-income women who bore the brunt of cervical cancer morbidity and mortality—and who were, in the United States and abroad, overwhelmingly women of color—motivated them to pursue alternative dosing regimens as a meliorating public health approach to cervical cancer disparities. The meaningful and material resources that informed this reconstruction of the goals of experimentation were already an ingredient in the situation at hand. Here the organization as a configuration of relational spaces occupied by scientists and their external political advisers is transformative of the science itself. Pragmatism helps us understand how this transformation can be effected through more than mere discourse, as the materiality of experimentation itself becomes involved in redefining the political stakes of the vaccine initiative. Women of color had long constituted the experiments that the NCI team conducted on their vaccine candidate but were not present in the formal discourse whereby these scientists defined the stakes of their research. In the routine administrative task of presenting their work to the advisory boards that formally approved intramural projects at the NCI, the team confronted actors like Freeman, whose political commitments to the inclusion of historically underserved racial and ethnic populations made these women's material presence as research subjects salient to the projects that were under way. The effect was not a mere shift in the rhetoric of vaccine development; it involved the reconstitution of the environment wherein the HPV vaccine could be most usefully deployed. Once the materiality of these women's bodies and circumstances was brought to the fore, the NCI team shifted their experimental protocols to include data collection that could inform them of the efficacy of reducing the number of shots such women might reasonably receive given their vulnerable positions in systems of global inequality.

In the case of the HPV vaccine, answering the central question of why the vaccine was developed by NCI scientists and not more experienced scientists situated elsewhere, we can consider how pragmatism's attention to the distinctive environing factors presented by these scientists' situatedness in the NCI as an organization offers a superior analytic lens compared with both institutionalist sociology and posthumanist STS. Institutionalist and field-theoretic accounts of HPV innovation that exclude the technological and material transformations that the NCI team effected would struggle to account for what enabled their success where other innovation efforts had failed. The difference between success in the NCI and failure in the three other laboratories closest to developing a similar vaccine came down not to superior strategizing or scientific capital. Each of these laboratories came to similar *theoretical* conclusions about how to design a vaccine, and of the four major players, Schiller and Lowy were the least experienced in the requisite fields of vaccinology and immunology. Instead, the HPV vaccine was a practical achievement, based on restructuring material elements in the environment in accordance with previously acquired practical and conceptual skills, that allowed experimentation to succeed.

Neither did the NCI team structure their experiments to improve their position in the field. They had the least to profit from such a discovery, as the National Institutes of Health stringently enforces royalty caps on inventors' patents, as well as retaining ownership and licensing rights in the name of the U.S. government.[67] Indeed, Lowy and Schiller received little in the way of recognition from the scientific community for their role in developing the vaccine until they were awarded the prestigious Lasker-DeBakey Clinical Medical Research Award in 2017, a full twenty-five years after developing the innovation and eleven years after vaccines developed from their patent hit the market. In that time, their laboratory remained roughly the size it had been when they made their discovery.[68] Rather than the reproduction of systems of scientific capital, this example emphasizes the significance of scientists' technological and material interactions with their environment in allowing for the kind of creativity involved in transposing routines of engagement with a specific laboratory environment to innovate in a new scientific area.

Though actor-network theory and new materialism capture a greater range of the environmental factors that are involved in scientific innovation than do institutionalist or field-theoretic explanations, posthumanism in turn reduces the interaction of environmental elements to a single plane of discursive semiotics or nondiscursive materialism. As this case study illustrates, phenomena at both of these levels and more—from individual and institutional practices of meaning-making and structures for resource allocation, to molecular processes of encoding proteins or organismic processes of immunogenesis, and on to the political-economic systems that generate the material vulnerabilities confronted by poor women of color around the globe—are causally necessary, but alone insufficient, for explaining the HPV vaccine as an innovation. Contra ANT and new materialism, a pragmatist approach to innovation can assume that viruses are independently capable of producing certain phenomena at the molecular level, *and* that humans' meaningful practices can either obscure or enable creative transformations of these and other features of their plural environments without having to reduce one to the other.

DISCUSSION

When we consider a definition of innovation as a process involving successful adoption of novel practices at the collective level, it becomes clear that innovation should entail the transformation of scientists' environments over significant timelines and across distributed and varying dimensions of scale. Further empirical study will be necessary to inform our understanding of the conditions that encourage innovation from the first spark of creativity to the establishment of novel social practices. Though this inductive case study is necessarily limited in its generalization, when put into conversation with other recent studies that integrate considerations of environmental heterogeneity and scale, it suggests that pragmatism may continue to inform the analysis of social learning processes beyond the NCI. A pragmatist theory of scientific innovation shifts attention from concrete outcomes to processes of environed social learning that unfold across series of events. Dewey's concept of habit has elsewhere been used to analyze how the process of inquiry and the integration of new information becomes anchored in organizational routines through long-term learning.[69] Such theorizing creates opportunities for sociologists of organization to refine the undertheorized concept of "organizational learning"[70] as it was developed by scholars who were informed by pragmatist philosophy.[71]

Historically, organizational learning has described a process whereby organizations evaluate their past performance or assess the performance of other organizations in their fields to guide goal-setting and decision-making in the present. A central but unsettled debate in the literature on organizational learning concerns which level of analysis organizational learning actually takes place—that is, whether organizational learning is merely the sum of individual knowledge processes or something that is more appropriately attributed to the organization as an agentic force. By focusing on social learning as a sequence of events situated around collective problem-solving, pragmatism cuts through the ambiguity of discussing organizations as agentic learners by showing how social learning processes emerge from the conduct of collective actors operating in heterogeneous and multiscalar environments. At the same time, focusing on iterative cycles of collective evaluation, interpretation, and problem-solving keeps discussions of organizational learning appropriately focused on processes that cannot be reduced to the scale of individual decision-making without losing the phenomenon of interest (i.e., the emergence over time of particular organizational orders related to temporal sequences of problem-solving).

Given a long enough temporal span, we can follow organizations through successive iterations of learning to better grasp the complex and nonlinear processes that remake the boundaries of organizations in the context of routine practices.[72] Maintaining a focus on formal organizations rather than diffuse networks or fields allows us to better analyze how situated actors can iteratively or recursively leverage local structures, rules, and politics to redefine the immediate environment in which technoscientific policy and practice unfold. Social learning has thus gained some traction in STS around issues of science and its publics. It has been especially illuminating in the emerging emphasis of infrastructure studies, where it provides a connecting point between collective learning episodes and policy outcomes. For instance, Jack Stilgoe[73] has shown how technology governance directed toward managing self-driving cars evolves new conceptions of economic, infrastructural, and social needs as collectives informally reconstruct unexpected events, like the 2016 fatal crash involving a Tesla S on autopilot. Other STS works that can be interpreted as cases of iterative social learning involve examples as divergent as the emergence of novel financial instruments in French global banks[74] and the improvisational processes driving meteorological predictions in the U.S. National Weather Service.[75]

Though organizational learning is perhaps more visible in the science and technology sectors due to the concrete manifestations of innovations qua deliverables, sociological analysis of diverse groups indicates that organizational learning processes undergird many collective behaviors that are distinctive to formal organizations. As Daniel Cefaï reminds us, the earliest investigations conducted under the original social worlds framework of the Chicago School revealed how subcultures emerged around locally specialized forms of communication and (often deviant) behavior.[76] Urban ethnographies continue to inform sociological analysis of organized behavior, with an increasingly holistic emphasis on reconstructing the environment for situated action. For example, Rios, Prieto, and Ibarra demonstrate how police draw on diverse cues from the material and symbolic context to guide their interactional strategies during stop-and-frisk encounters with presumed gang-affiliated community members.[77] Police relied on environmental cues in the urban setting or on the bodies of community members to guide situated and temporally unfolding encounters in ways that reflect learned behaviors acquired from imperatives to balance the organizational needs of their policing unit with the tenuous legality of stop-and-frisk as a racial profiling practice.

Attention to collective knowledge practices in different organizational settings promises to enhance the analytical scope of social learning frameworks. Business schools have developed their own, nearly identical, concept of social worlds in the idea of "communities of practice."[78] This influential approach builds on the emphasis on network-based cycles of organizational learning as drivers of innovation in dispersed and knowledge-driven organizations (such as the "heterarchies" described by Stark[79]). One of the most important contributions that communities of practice has made to the discussion of organizational learning lies in its emphasis on failure. Though formal organizations often foreground performance issues in their evaluations of employee progress, research conducted on communities of practice emphasizes that teams often increase their capacity to respond effectively and creatively to problems by learning through failure. The accretive process of organizational learning has been used to explain why some managerial configurations, such as those that are dependent on short-term contracting relationships, seem to lead to a decline in innovation over time. This is exemplified by the U.S. military's turn toward contracting in the 1990s, which stalled innovation in many knowledge-intensive sectors due to poor integration across projects.[80] Without opportunities to learn from failure, even once successful organizations cannot help but fall behind their peers.

CONCLUSION

In critiquing work on scientific innovation in sociology and science and technology studies, I position pragmatism as a useful theoretical remediation. However, I am optimistic about the combinatorial potential of insights gained through these other modes of theorizing that have emphasized particular phenomena to the neglect of environmental heterogeneity and scale. What makes pragmatist explanations of scientific innovation preferable goes beyond avoidance of partiality and omission, for innovation as an outcome necessarily involves alterations to the material, conceptual, and habitual scaffolding on which scientific practices proceed. A successful innovation changes the environing conditions under which subsequent innovations will be made. Appreciating this circumstance allows us to revisit in a new light how certain individuals, techniques, organizations, locations, nations, and so on achieve consistency in innovation, not only as they reap rewards in the form of scientific authority but as they construct environments that encode conceptualizations and evaluations into their collective orientations to action.

Reframing scientific innovation along the lines suggested here may also help remedy one of the persistent theoretical omissions in STS: a lack of substantive theorizing on formal organizations.[81] In demonstrating the "irreducible and emergent effects of organizations"[82] on the production of technoscientific artifacts, we can also develop a way forward in explaining how meso-level social orders emerge from the actions of heterogeneous elements in situations that are structured by organizational routines. By encouraging focused attention on organizations, pragmatism also allows us to localize efforts at scientific innovation in specific environments and activities, hewing to recent developments in organizational theory that "distinguish between 'creativity' as the ideas or products generated by individuals, and 'innovation' as the successful execution of a new product or service by an entire organization."[83] To the extent that innovation involves the transformation of organizational routines as well as other aspects of the environment for action, we should anticipate an ongoing, recursive relationship between scientific action and organizational situation. Indeed, a promising theoretical synthesis of sociology, posthumanism, and pragmatism is already under way in the interdisciplinary field of organization studies, where a number of "practice theorists of organization"[84] and "process theorists of organization"[85] are drawing lessons from these theories to break new ground in analyzing how time, memory, and emergent phenomena shape both stability and change in organizational life. These exciting developments suggest that the study of formal organizations can benefit from ensuring that our inquiries into scientific innovation are sensitive to the complexities that situated action introduce into science and technology, and vice versa.

NOTES

1. Robert K. Merton, *The Sociology of Science: Theoretical and Empirical Investigations* (Chicago: University of Chicago Press, 1973).

2. Alberto Cambrosio et al., "Mapping the Emergence and Development of Translational Cancer Research," *European Journal of Cancer* 42, no. 18 (December 2006): 3140–48; James A. Evans, "Industry Collaboration, Scientific Sharing, and the Dissemination of Knowledge," *Social Studies of Science* 40, no. 5 (October 1, 2010): 757–91; Jacob G. Foster, Andrey Rzhetsky, and James A. Evans, "Tradition and Innovation in Scientists' Research Strategies," *American Sociological Review* 80, no. 5 (October 1, 2015): 875–908; and John N. Parker and Ugo Corte, "Placing Collaborative Circles in Strategic Action Fields: Explaining Differences Between Highly Creative Groups," *Sociological Theory* 35, no. 4 (December 1, 2017): 261–87.

3. Foster et al., "Tradition and Innovation in Scientists' Research Strategies," 878.

4. Charles Camic, "*Science of Science and Reflexivity* by Pierre Bourdieu," *American Journal of Sociology* 111, no. 5 (March 1, 2006): 1569–71.

5. Pierre Bourdieu, *Science of Science and Reflexivity* (Cambridge, UK: Polity, 2004), 39.

6. Bourdieu, *Science of Science and Reflexivity*, 83.

7. Foster et al., "Tradition and Innovation in Scientists' Research Strategies," 876.

8. Foster et al., "Tradition and Innovation in Scientists' Research Strategies," 882.

9. See, for example, Harry Collins, *Gravity's Shadow: The Search for Gravitational Waves* (Chicago: University of Chicago Press, 2010); Joan Fujimura, *Crafting Science: A Sociohistory of the Quest for the Genetics of Cancer* (Cambridge, MA: Harvard University Press, 1996); Peter Galison, *How Experiments End* (Chicago: University of Chicago Press, 1987); Karin Knorr Cetina, *Epistemic Cultures: How the Sciences Make Knowledge* (Cambridge, MA: Harvard University Press, 2009); Andrew Pickering, *The Mangle of Practice: Time, Agency, and Science* (Chicago: University of Chicago Press, 1995); and Sharon Traweek, *Beamtimes and Lifetimes* (Cambridge, MA: Harvard University Press, 2009).

10. Bruno Latour, *Reassembling the Social: An Introduction to Actor-Network Theory* (Oxford: Oxford University Press, 2005b); Latour, *Science in Action: How to Follow Scientists and Engineers Through Society* (Cambridge, MA: Harvard University Press, 1987); Michel Callon, "Some Elements of a Sociology of Translation: Domestication of the Scallops and the Fishermen of St Brieuc Bay," *Sociological Review* 32, no. S1 (May 1, 1984): 196–233; and Michel Callon and Bruno Latour, "Unscrewing the Big Leviathan," in *Advances in Social Theory and Methodology*, ed. Karin Knorr Cetina and Aaron Cicourel, 277–302 (London: Routledge and Kegan Paul, 1981).

11. Karen Barad, *Meeting the Universe Halfway: Quantum Physics and the Entanglement of Matter and Meaning* (Durham, NC: Duke University Press, 2007).

12. Jane Bennett, *Vibrant Matter: A Political Ecology of Things* (Durham, NC: Duke University Press, 2010).

13. Latour, *Science in Action*; Bruno Latour, *The Pasteurization of France* (Cambridge, MA: Harvard University Press, 1993).

14. Barad, *Meeting the Universe Halfway.*

15. Derek Woods, "Scale Variance and the Concept of Matter," in *The New Politics of Materialism: History, Philosophy, Science,* ed. Sarah Ellenzweig and John H. Zammito (London: Taylor & Francis, 2017), 200–224.

16. J. A. Wiens, "Spatial Scaling in Ecology," *Functional Ecology* 3, no. 4 (1989): 385–97: 393, cited in Woods, "Scale Variance and the Concept of Matter," 206.

17. Woods, "Scale Variance and the Concept of Matter," 203.

18. Mark Peter Jones, "Posthuman Agency: Between Theoretical Traditions," *Sociological Theory* 14, no. 3 (1996): 290–309.

19. See Jones, "Posthuman Agency."

20. See, for example, Nancy Cartwright, *The Dappled World: A Study of the Boundaries of Science* (Cambridge: Cambridge University Press, 1999); Hubert L. Dreyfus, *Skillful Coping: Essays on the Phenomenology of Everyday Perception and Action* (Oxford: Oxford University Press, 2014); Helen E. Longino, *Science as Social Knowledge: Values and Objectivity in Scientific Inquiry* (Princeton, NJ: Princeton University Press, 1990); and Pickering, *The Mangle of Practice.*

21. John H. Zammito, *A Nice Derangement of Epistemes: Post-Positivism in the Study of Science from Quine to Latour* (Chicago: University of Chicago Press, 2004), 114.

22. Charles Sanders Peirce, *The Essential Peirce: Selected Philosophical Writings* (Bloomington: Indiana University Press, 1992), 227.

23. John Dewey, *Theory of Valuation* (Chicago: University of Chicago Press, 1939).

24. James R. Griesemer," The Role of Instruments in the Generative Analysis of Science," in *The Right Tools for the Job: At Work in Twentieth-Century Life Sciences,* ed. Adele E. Clarke and Joan Fujimura, 47–76 (Princeton, NJ: Princeton University Press, 2014), 53.

25. Joseph Rouse, *Articulating the World: Conceptual Understanding and the Scientific Image* (Chicago: University of Chicago Press, 2015).

26. Howard S. Becker, *Art Worlds: 25th Anniversary Edition, Updated and Expanded* (Berkeley: University of California Press, 2008); Tamotsu Shibutani, "Reference Groups as Perspectives," *American Journal of Sociology* 60, no. 6 (May 1, 1955): 562–69, https://doi.org/10.1086/221630; and Anselm Strauss, "Social Worlds and Their Segmentation Processes," *Studies in Symbolic Interaction* 5, no. 1 (1984): 123–39.

27. Shibutani, "Reference Groups as Perspectives," 566.

28. Adele Clarke, "A Social Worlds Research Adventure: The Case of Reproductive Science," in *Theories of Science in Society,* ed. Susan Cozzens and Thomas Gieryn, 15–42 (Bloomington: Indiana University Press, 1990), 18.

29. Adele Clarke and Susan Leigh Star, "The Social Worlds Framework: A Theory/Methods Package," in *The Handbook of Science and Technology Studies,* 3rd ed, ed. Edward J. Hackett et al. (Cambridge, MA: MIT Press, 2008), 113–37.

30. Susan Leigh Star and James R. Griesemer, "Institutional Ecology, 'Translations' and Boundary Objects: Amateurs and Professionals in Berkeley's Museum of Vertebrate Zoology, 1907–39," *Social Studies of Science* 19, no. 3 (August 1, 1989): 387–420.

31. For a recent statement on how social worlds analysis informs theoretical and methodological approaches in STS, see Adele E. Clarke, Carrie Friese, and Rachel Washburn, *Situational Analysis in Practice: Mapping Research with Grounded Theory* (Walnut Creek, CA: Left Coast, 2015).

32. Adele Clarke and Joan H. Fujimura, *The Right Tools for the Job: At Work in Twentieth-Century Life Sciences* (Princeton, NJ: Princeton University Press, 2014); Fujimura, *Crafting Science*.

33. Monica J. Casper and Adele E. Clarke, "Making the Pap Smear Into the 'Right Tool' for the Job: Cervical Cancer Screening in the USA, Circa 1940–95," *Social Studies of Science* 28, no. 2 (April 1, 1998): 255–90.

34. Geoffrey C. Bowker and Susan Leigh Star, *Sorting Things Out: Classification and Its Consequences* (Cambridge, MA: MIT Press, 2000); Martha Lampland and Susan Leigh Star, *Standards and Their Stories: How Quantifying, Classifying, and Formalizing Practices Shape Everyday Life* (Ithaca, NY: Cornell University Press, 2009).

35. For an explicit formulation, see Casper and Clarke, "Making the Pap Smear Into the 'Right Tool' for the Job."

36. Daniel R. Huebner, "On Mead's Long Lost History of Science," in *The Timeliness of George Herbert Mead*, ed. Hans Joas and Daniel R. Huebner (Chicago: University of Chicago Press, 2016), 40–61.

37. George Herbert Mead, *Mind, Self, and Society* (University of Chicago Press, 1934), 154n2, quoted in Bradley Brewster and Antony Puddephatt.,"George Herbert Mead as a Socio-Environmental Thinker," in *The Timeliness of George Herbert Mead*, ed. Hans Joas and Daniel R. Huebner (Chicago: University of Chicago Press, 2016), 147.

38. George H. Mead. *The Philosophy of the Present* (London: Open Court, 1932), 34.

39. Woods, "Scale Variance and the Concept of Matter," 200.

40. Colin Koopman. *Pragmatism as Transition: Historicity and Hope in James, Dewey, and Rorty* (New York: Columbia University Press, 2009), 16.

41. Koopman, *Pragmatism as Transition*, 166–67.

42. Neil Gross, "A Pragmatist Theory of Social Mechanisms," *American Sociological Review* 74, no. 3 (June 1, 2009): 358–79.

43. Koopman, *Pragmatism as Transition*, 128–29.

44. Koopman, *Pragmatism as Transition*, 129.

45. Koopman, *Pragmatism as Transition*, 170.

46. Koopman, *Pragmatism as Transition*, 195.

47. Natalie B. Aviles, "Situated Practice and the Emergence of Ethical Research: HPV Vaccine Development and Organizational Cultures of Translation at the National Cancer Institute," *Science, Technology, & Human Values* 43, no. 5 (January 29, 2018): 810–33.

48. Methodological note: I present evidence from oral history interviews with key figures in the NCI Laboratory of Viral Oncology to support claims about laboratory practices around the vaccine innovation developed from 1991 to 1993. In the interest of limiting

biases in actors' accounts caused by post hoc reconstruction, I exclude specific recollections that cannot be corroborated with documents produced contemporaneously with the reported scientific activities ($n = 2$). All laboratory activities reported here have been cross-referenced for accuracy with data from peer-reviewed publications and laboratory project summaries that are included in NCI annual reports issued from 1991 to 1993.

49. Oral history interview with John Schiller, April 22, 2015

50. Interview with Schiller, 2015.

51. For a summary of these projects and their outcomes, see Caroline McNeil, "Who Invented the VLP Cervical Cancer Vaccines?" *Journal of the National Cancer Institute* 98, no. 7 (2006): 433.

52. National Cancer Institute, "Project Report of the Laboratory of Cellular Oncology: Analysis of Papillomaviruses," in *Division of Cancer Biology, Diagnosis and Centers Annual Report* Bethesda, MD: National Cancer Institute, 1991), 208–10.

53. Oral history interview with Doug Lowy, February 23, 2017.

54. Interview with Lowy, February 2017.

55. Interview with Lowy, February 2017.

56. "2017 Lasker Award Ceremony—Douglas Lowy Acceptance Remarks" (video), September 15, 2017, https://laskerfoundation.org/winners/hpv-vaccines-for-cancer-prevention/.

57. National Cancer Institute, "Project Report of the Laboratory of Cellular Oncology: Analysis of Papillomaviruses," *in Division of Cancer Biology, Diagnosis and Centers Annual Report* (Bethesda, MD: National Cancer Institute1993), 213–15.

58. Interview with Schiller, 2015.

59. Interview with Schiller, 2015.

60. Interview with Schiller, 2015.

61. National Cancer Institute, *Division of Basic Sciences Annual Research Directory 1996*, 195.

62. Director, National Cancer Institute, *The Nation's Investment in Cancer Research: A Budget Proposal for Fiscal Year 1999*. (Washington, DC: Government Printing Office, 1997), 9.

63. Interview with Schiller, 2015.

64. Department of Health and Human Services, Public Health Service, National Cancer Institute, "124th National Cancer Advisory Board, Summary of Meeting, December 4–5, 2002" (Bethesda, MD: National Cancer Institute, 2002), 33-34, https://deainfo.nci.nih .gov/advisory/ncab/archive/124_1202/04dec02mins.pdf.

65. National Cancer Institute, Division of Extramural Activities, National Cancer Advisory Board, "Minutes of the 108th Regular Meeting, December 8-9, 1998"(Bethesda, MA: National Cancer Institute, 1998), 17, https://deainfo.nci.nih.gov/advisory/ncab/archive /108_1298/ncab1298.pdf.

66. Aviles, "Situated Practice and the Emergence of Ethical Research."

67. September 1, 1994, memo from NIH Legal Advisor to Robert H. Purcell, NIAID, "The $100,000 Cap on Royalties to Inventors in the Federal Technology Transfer Act," Harold Varmus papers, box 7, folder 1 (Bethesda, MD: National Library of Medicine,1994).

68. Oral history interview with Doug Lowy, April 21, 2017.

69. Neil Gross, "Pragmatism and the Study of Large-Scale Social Phenomena," *Theory and Society* 47 (February 26, 2018): 87–111, https://link.springer.com/article/10.1007/s11186-018-9307-9; David Stark, *The Sense of Dissonance: Accounts of Worth in Economic Life* (Princeton, NJ: Princeton University Press, 2009); and Josh Whitford and Francesco Zirpoli, "Pragmatism, Practice, and the Boundaries of Organization," *Organization Science* 25, no. 6 (June 24, 2014): 1823–39.

70. Mark Easterby-Smith, Mary Crossan, and Davide Nicolini, "Organizational Learning: Debates Past, Present And Future," *Journal of Management Studies* 37, no. 6 (September 1, 2000): 783–96.

71. Chris Argyris and Donald A. Schön, *Organizational Learning: A Theory of Action Perspective* (Reading, MA: Addison-Wesley, 1978); Barbara Levitt and James G. March, "Organizational Learning," *Annual Review of Sociology* 14 (1988): 319–40.

72. Whitford and Zirpoli, "Pragmatism, Practice, and the Boundaries of Organization."

73. Jack Stilgoe, "Machine Learning, Social Learning and the Governance of Self-Driving Cars," *Social Studies of Science* 48, no. 1 (February 1, 2018): 25–56.

74. Vincent Lépinay, *Codes of Finance: Engineering Derivatives in a Global Bank* (Princeton, NJ: Princeton University Press, 2011).

75. Phaedra Daipha, *Masters of Uncertainty: Weather Forecasters and the Quest for Ground Truth* (Chicago: University of Chicago Press, 2015).

76. Daniel Cefaï, "Social Worlds: The Legacy of Mead's Social Ecology in Chicago Sociology," in *The Timeliness of George Herbert Mead*, ed. Hans Joas and Daniel R. Huebner, 165–84 (Chicago: University of Chicago Press, 2016).

77. Victor M. Rios, Greg Prieto, and Jonathan M. Ibarra, "Mano Suave–Mano Dura: Legitimacy Policing and Latino Stop-and-Frisk," *American Sociological Review* 85, no. 1 (February 1, 2020): 58–75.

78. Etienne Wenger, Richard Arnold McDermott, and William Snyder, *Cultivating Communities of Practice: A Guide to Managing Knowledge* (Cambridge, MA: Harvard Business Press, 2002).

79. Stark, *The Sense of Dissonance.*

80. Kendall Hoyt, *Long Shot: Vaccines for National Defense* (Cambridge, MA: Harvard University Press, 2012).

81. Diane Vaughan, "The Rôle of the Organization in the Production of Techno-Scientific Knowledge," *Social Studies of Science* 29, no. 6 (December 1, 1999): 913–43. For an important recent exception, see Janet Vertesi, *Shaping Science: Organizations, Decisions, and Culture on NASA's Teams* (Chicago: University of Chicago Press, 2020).

82. Vaughan, "The Rôle of the Organization," 931.

83. R. Keith Sawyer, *Explaining Creativity: The Science of Human Innovation* (Oxford: Oxford University Press, 2011), 8.

84. Barbara Simpson, "Pragmatism, Mead and the Practice Turn," *Organization Studies* 30, no. 12 (December 1, 2009): 1329–47.

85. Barbara Czarniawska, "STS Meets MOS Commentary," *Organization* 16, no. 1 (2009): 155–10; Tor Hernes, *A Process Theory of Organization* (Oxford: Oxford University Press, 2014).

11. Why Do Biologists and Chemists Do Safety Differently?

THE REPRODUCTION OF CULTURAL VARIATION THROUGH PRAGMATIC REGULATION

SUSAN S. SILBEY

Explanations for the variation in compliance with legal regulations range from accounts of inconsistent and lax enforcement to misaligned incentives (Hawkins and Thomas 1984b; Wilson 1980; Deutch and Lester 2004), with much recent scholarship and policy advocates recommending innovative nudges to push behavior to reduce anticipated risks (Thaler and Sunstein 2008). Rather than traditional policy levers such as restrictions, penalties, and education, nudge promoters recommend designing choice contexts to push decisions in desired directions. Nudge enters the panoply of regulatory approaches by addressing individual cognition as the means of aligning decisions with legal mandates and goals. Yet, the empirical studies that test nudges for shaping regulatory compliance and pro-social behavior challenges meaningful synthesis or clear predictions (Huising and Silbey 2018). Moreover, "what is typically missing is any evidence about the underlying mechanisms through which these policies affect behavior" (Grüne-Yanoff 2016, 464) or how individual action aggregates to produce compliance at the organizational level.

If the organization is the salient actor, observers also identify a range of responses to regulatory requirements and pressures (Gunningham, Kagan, and Thornton 2004). Managerial attention to and interpretation of the legal environment, competitive forces, strategic issues, and operational factors are said to generate variation in organizations' responses to regulation. This body of work identifies organization-level variables that predict formal responses to regulations but overlooks the internal organizational processes and mechanisms through which the everyday priorities and work routines, decision-making networks, and ways of interacting and talking coordinate with regulatory requirements.

For decades, studies of regulatory implementation and compliance have proposed one or another dimension of social action—institutional, legal, economic, or cognitive—with which to explain variation in responses to regulatory requirements. Whatever is proposed ultimately fails to fully account for or affect the variations at the organizational or individual level; empirical observations consistently document a gap between the explanatory model and practices on the ground.

Because the ostensible goal of regulation is to shape what constitutes routine action, attention to the internal and habitual processes offers an alternative path to understanding how compliance (or noncompliance) is actually produced. Eschewing at the outset a formal, abstracted model or explanation allows us to see what may be more often overlooked as the detritus of organizational performance: the local variations that are overlooked or discarded as we search for a central tendency in the data.

This chapter describes the distinctive ways in which biologists and chemists respond to the legal regulation of their laboratories, to increased surveillance and inspection, prescribed training programs, and retraining. Although academic scientists enjoy unusual degrees of autonomy in setting their professional agendas, we describe how scientists forgo more common resistance to organizational nudges and instead defer to a range of institutional pressures and incentives to transform laboratory routines. Why do they comply when resistance is more common? We suggest that deference to the varied cultures of biology and chemistry encouraged compliance: each science can do safety in ways that are consistent with the history and sociology of its science. Deference to local epistemic cultures worked to improve regulatory compliance.

Importantly, those charged with implementing the legal mandate to create consistent conformity with environmental, health, and safety laws adopted a pragmatic approach. Instead of succumbing to legal pressures to enforce standardized, one-size-fits-all procedures, they varied details of implementation to the local cultures of different disciplines and departments, thus seducing scientists to accept a surveillance system they more likely may have resisted. This was not, however, planned as such. It developed step by step as professionals with expertise in various technical fields (e.g., radiation, toxins, chemical waste, biological hazards, air quality) confronted competing mandates and interests: to create consistent conformity in compliance with environmental and safety regulations and to support the cutting-edge scientific research that was the source of institutional reputation and resources.

In this institutional encounter between law and science, law seems to triumph but, importantly, does so because it adjusts to the local circumstances to become part of scientific practice. Both biologists and chemists defer to the law's authority to set limits to laboratory practices. Crucially, however, what might look like institutional conformity (Drori et al. 2003) on closer observation turns out to be an instance of scientific variation[1]: biologists and chemists vary in *the ways in which*

they defer. The deference to law, the acceptance and participation in the environmental health and safety (EHS) management system, is based not on a simple vic-
tory of law against science but on multiple interpretations (Rosental 2003) of the
responsibility of scientists and the procedures of compliance. I provide evidence of
three forms of disciplinary variation that together explain biologists' and chemists'
interpretations and positioning before the law.

First, the authority and expertise of biology and chemistry have been built with
different meanings and relevance of contamination and hazard. As such, the introduction of the law into the processes of doing science takes on very different interpretations—*as part of science for the chemists; as part of the context but not the
content for the biologists.* For centuries, chemists have been constructing labs with
protections against contamination, fumes, and fire. Since the mid-nineteenth century, close relations among academic and industrial labs reinforced the legitimacy
of safety protocols, including periodic lobbying and support for uniform government
regulations. In contrast, molecular biology is a young science with a recently developed industry that emerged during an era of hostility to government regulation.

Second, the social and spatial organizations of the labs vary. Academic biology
labs normally have a permanent staff of managers, technicians, and longer-term
postdoctoral fellows as well as graduate students. Chemistry labs rarely employ any
permanent staff and rely entirely on an ever-changing population of postdocs and
students. At Eastern University, every biology lab was constructed from a common
template with substantial space shared among colleagues; each chemistry lab was
individually designed to the specifications of the principal scientist with very limited common spaces.

Third, biologists and chemists produce their results differently. Biologists seek
statistically significant variation in a population, whereas organic and inorganic
chemists are trying to create a particular chemical reaction, to increase the yield
in a system in which they can already detect a useful difference. Notably, not every
chemist was on board, "doing safety" perfectly well by himself, and not every biologist was less than welcoming. Nonetheless, there were marked differences in the
responses of the departments in the name of their faculty: the chemists considered
the environmental and safety regulations as part of the practice of chemistry, and
the biologists defined the new system as yet another, inescapable institutional constraint on science, something they could delegate to others.

Regulatory compliance was embedded within familiar activities through adaptation of the system's requirements to the local contexts. While the particularities varied from one department to another, a general script prescribing obligations and
expectations was differentially implemented. The abstract demand for consistent
conformity was achieved through pragmatic adjustment of historic custom to new
purposes.

This chapter proceeds by first establishing the legal context for the regulation of scientific laboratories. In the mid-1990s, the U.S. Environmental Protection Agency (EPA) decided to turn its attention to heretofore ignored sources of

pollution: municipalities, the military, and educational institutions. I begin with an EPA inspection of a university that became the impetus for mandated changes for containing environmental, health, and safety hazards in research laboratories. The following section, "Trouble in the House of Science," points to the habitus of academic scientists that was disturbed by the EPA inspection and the subsequent consent decree promising organizational changes. I continue with an account of the ethnographic methods used to track the creation, introduction, and responses to this legal intervention, describing what turned out to be a natural experiment comparing different organizational responses to the mandated change. The biologists' and chemists' responses are presented topically and chronologically. The departmental variations are explained in terms of the different sciences' histories and relations with industry, organization of laboratory spaces and research groups, and, finally, experimental processes. In sum, I show how legal challenges to organizational autonomy are mediated through professional expertise and local habitus. In a process of pragmatic regulatory implementation, cultural variation among the sciences is reproduced, a new form of variation — legal subjectivity — is observed among scientists, and deference to legal regulations is achieved specifically by accommodating these different interpretations of the legal responsibilities of the scientific researcher.

A MANAGEMENT SYSTEM FOR LABORATORY HAZARDS

The Provocation

In late June 2001, the federal court[2] recorded a consent decree between the EPA and Eastern University in which the EPA alleged that the university violated certain provisions of the Resource Conservation and Recovery Act (RCRA), the Clean Air Act (CAA), and the Clean Water Act (CWA).[3] Without admitting any violation of law or any liability, the university agreed in the decree to settle the matter without a trial on any matters of fact or law. From the district court's perspective, this was a minor case that took little time or attention. From the perspective of the EPA and the university, however, this was a major occasion, the culmination of three years of lengthy, detailed negotiations that both parties hoped would ultimately produce the means for sustainable, environmentally sound research practices for the nation. All parties viewed this agreement as an opportunity to create a model of safe and "green"[4] laboratories.

Three years prior to the filing of the consent decree, the EPA gave notice to Eastern, along with dozens of other universities, that it would be conducting campus inspections. Immediately, negotiations began to determine which of the more than four hundred laboratories would be inspected and when. Given the wide range of activities and types of possible contaminants, it was important to see different kinds of laboratories and functional areas; yet, it would be impossible to visit every location where there might be emissions, spills, or hazardous waste. Eastern had established a very good record for compliance with Occupational Safety and Health Administration (OSHA) regulations. It had also invested heavily in a diverse array of expert managers with over a dozen different offices and committees distributing responsibility for keeping toxic and radioactive materials secure and the animals, students, staff, and faculty safe. Although there were accidents every once in a while—a fire in a laboratory, an eye damaged by a laser because the warning light was not observed by an intruder—Eastern's record displayed a relatively low rate of accidents. Most important, there had been no toxic emissions, spills, radioactive leaks, and improper disposal of hazardous materials.

Nonetheless, when the EPA completed its five-day inspection, it recorded more than three thousand violations of RCRA, CAA, CWA and their implementing regulations. Despite the large number of discrete violations, both the EPA and the university regarded all but one as minor infractions. Eastern's major failure, according to the EPA, was its lack of uniform practices across the laboratories. One laboratory was a model of good practice, whereas another produced no accidents, spills, or emissions but was littered with uncapped chemical bottles, unlabeled waste, and students working without protective clothing or safety glasses. The university could not identify which policies enabled such extraordinary variation and yet prevented serious accidents. There was no clear, hierarchical organizational infrastructure for compliance with environmental laws, no systems approach to environmental management, no clear delineation of roles and responsibilities, and, most important, no obvious modes of accountability for either compliance or violations. The line of command from the laboratory through the safety office to the leadership of the university was opaque to the inspectors, and thus it was impossible to say who was responsible for what. The academic freedom celebrated and protected by the faculty and Eastern administration looked like mismanagement and anarchy to the EPA.

The consistent, uniform conformity required by the EPA is abhorred by the university (Paradeise and Thoenig 2013; Thoenig and Paradeise 2014). Yet, herein lies the gravamen of the EPA's complaint and the heart of the organizational problem. In response to having the university's culture of autonomy and invention exposed as chaotic and irresponsible, the consent decree required what had never before existed: consistent uniform practices across all departments and labs, clear lines of command, and transparent legibility for all environmental and safety procedures.

The consent decree stipulated a five-year deadline for compliance. Normally, EPA consent decrees demand compliance within a year. The five-year window signaled a new kind of regulation "that seeks directly to promote the management of private firms in ways that meet public goals" (Coglianese and Lazar 2003). Although most regulation attempts to manage some activities of private firms, this strategy supplants more conventional policies that mandate either the use of specific technologies or specific levels of performance. This management-based strategy locates the design, standard-setting, and implementation of regulation squarely within the regulated organization itself, creating a form of private management in the public interest, a form of corporatism, or what scholars of governmentality call "regulation at a distance" (Foucault and Lemke 1999). A private organization not only reforms its own practices but assumes responsibility to invent and publicly disseminate new models of environmental, health, and safety management.

From the point of view of both the Eastern administration and the EPA, the consent decree turned liabilities into investments, creating the possibility of a win-win situation. From the government's perspective, private educational institutions are notoriously difficult to regulate. Not only do they enjoy privileged autonomy, moral responsibility, and epistemological authority, but the vast range of activities, dispersed and opaque practices typical of institutions of higher education create seemingly intransigent obstacles to regulation, especially environmental and workplace safety standards that were designed primarily for mass-production industries with more tightly disciplined and coordinated workforces. By extending the time frame for compliance, and contracting with Eastern to invent a new management system for research universities across the nation, the consent decree offered the EPA an opportunity to solve some of its most intractable problems.

From the Eastern administration's point of view, the agreement was an opportunity to repair what it saw as its now tarnished reputation for excellence and innovation. The alleged violations threatened the university's reputation while also creating the prospect of heavy fines and costs. Litigation to challenge the allegations would expose Eastern to unfavorable publicity and expense, with no assurance of an ultimately favorable outcome. Although it took three years to negotiate, the EPA considered Eastern a compliant and cooperative organization, *"gracefully acknowledging its failures"* and *"immediately asking what it could do to make repairs."*[5] In addition, from the perspective of the university's attorney, this was the first hurdle in what would become a make-or-break case for career advancement. And from the perspective of the university's environmental and safety staff, it was also an opportunity to rebuild their credibility and professional status.

A Management System

The consent order between Eastern University and the EPA promised the adoption of a comprehensive EHS management system, which was designed and put in place between 2001 and 2007. The management practices in the consent order call for control systems specifically designed to ensure accountability through constant surveillance, data collection, and informational feedback loops. Designed to make organizational functions and ground-level performance immediately transparent to university administration as well as internal and external auditors, such systems are promoted as the preferred means for containing risks (e.g., financial, environmental, safety) as well as assuring regulatory compliance (itself a form of risk management). Often referred to and marketed as *enterprise resource planning systems* (ERP; ERM, or enterprise resource management; or CBS, computer business systems), these omnipresent software packages use relatively simple linked digital applications to electronically represent the organization and its workflow.

From the perspective of the scientists at Eastern University, the management system is a tool for surveillance, routinely observing and recording performance and outcomes. From the administration's point of view—especially the EHS staff dedicated to supporting laboratory science (for example, by managing licenses to work with radioactive isotopes, proscribed toxins, and chemical and biological materials to prevent their introduction into water systems or uncontrolled waste)—the system is a tool for collecting, analyzing, and responding to information about laboratory hazards. All groups seemed to understand that if the management system functioned as expected, it would become an apparatus for controlling scientific work: information collected through inspections of laboratories would become information for new policies, training, and, ultimately, changed practices. All hazardous activities within the labs would be made visible, if not entirely legible, to observers outside the labs.

In general, management systems work by mechanizing these functions—storing and analyzing data—through the digital technologies. At one end of a continuum of constraint, the system can be used to channel and control work as completely as possible. Here, the management system functions like the Taylorist assembly line, where the production process is divided into sequential units, each of which is designed to require the minimal human action (or decisions) necessary to add a particular supplement to a progressive assembly of the work process or final product. The system recommended for the Eastern laboratories, as well as labs at other universities, operates at the other end of a spectrum of standardization and control. The Eastern EHS system would be designed to coordinate and make visible the labor of actors whose work processes are more varied, often complex, with many interconnected procedures, each requiring expert decision-making, and whose work product cannot be standardized or completely digitized. Although any individual may do the same task many times, variation in the workflow is much greater than in the assembly-line model. These university and research management systems are designed for workers who are themselves decision makers who must interpret rules and protocols within the immediate, diverse, and variable conditions of production. Often this work is invisible to others not immediately involved, and even sometimes to those involved as well.

In practical and immediate effect, the creation of the system involved the reallocation of responsibility within the labs, within the administrative staff, and between the two that constitute the loosely coupled organization of the university (Perrow 2011; Weick 1976). This chapter describes and analyzes the responses of biologists and chemists to these legally mandated changes.

TROUBLE IN THE HOUSE OF SCIENCE

Under any circumstances, planned organizational change is famously difficult (Barnett and Carroll 1995; Armenakis and Bedeian 1999). Decoupling of organizational practices from institutional norms is common, and change projects rarely enact prescribed designs completely (Turco 2012; Huising 2015). Imposed from outside or above, legally mandated change simply exacerbates the normal difficulties. Professional agendas frequently shape organizational compliance because regulations are not self-enforcing, not until they become, with time and repetition, commonplace, habituated features of organizational everyday life. Although implementation can be built into product designs or instantiated in urban planning through traffic signals and lane markers, within complex organizations, experts and professionals often become the active enforcement agents. Professions can enhance their status by taking on new regulatory responsibilities or retain greater control by self-regulating in line with legal mandates. However, professional agendas and organizational interests may also undermine regulatory mandates (Gallagher, Jung, and Dobbin 2015). Policy goals may be contested even after legislative enactment (Stone 2002); compliance may be primarily symbolic (Edelman 1992); and well-intentioned implementation may produce intractable struggles among managers and experts or among different, if not competing, professional communities (Waring and Currie 2009; Kellogg 2009, 2011; Brivot 2011; Barrett et al. 2012; Huising 2014; Galperin 2015).

Although all social fields rely on interchange with other social fields, scientists may be distinguished by an unusual degree of autonomy in setting professional agendas and in the degree to which they successfully guard their authority and conditions of work (Bourdieu 1975, 1991). Scientists aggressively police the boundaries of what constitutes science and nonscience, denying legitimate or merely comparable authority and status to pseudoscientists, "protecting the autonomy of scientific research from political interference" (Gieryn 1983, 781). Of course, this autonomy is not absolute, and as "pressure to patent and commercialize scientific research increases, the scientific field becomes less autonomous and more subject to external forces impinging from without" (Foster, Rzhetsky, and Evans 2015, 902; see also Berman 2008, 2012; Camic 2011, 2013; Powell and Owen-Smith 1998). Despite the law's direct authorization for so much of the recently generated wealth for scientists and innovation for the nation (through patenting and licensing of scientific discoveries), transactions between law and science are often characterized by incomprehensibility and opposition, producing what one scholar calls the "use and misuse of science in law" (Faigman 1999).

Thus, it is not unusual to observe scientists actively resisting legal efforts to constrain the ways in which science is done, including requirements adopted in the name of health and safety. For example, nanotechnologists and materials scientists have been shown to display "extremely hostile reactions" to studies of the risks of their research for human health, claiming instead that "such research was itself a major risk to the health (i.e. funding and public acceptance)" of science itself (Kelty 2009, 80). And although most scientists may—usually after multiply repeated requests—complete mandatory safety training, respond to legal requirements to label hazardous waste, or remove equipment blocking corridors and exits, they often interpret these mandates as impediments to their work (Gray and Silbey 2014) and frequently do not sustain compliance with required changes beyond particular inspection or audit (Bruns 2009).

Safety regulations aim to prevent adverse effects of lethal substances on the scientists themselves as well as the public, but the scientists are primarily concerned about the adverse effects on their experiments (Evans and Silbey 2021). Scientists may rely on administrative nonscientist staff for financial and material support, response to accidents, and actually improved laboratory management at the same time that they resent requirements to wear lab coats and safety glasses (Huising and Silbey 2011), material handling and storage, security measures, the disposal of contaminated and hazardous materials, institutional review boards (Stark 2011), and required documentation (Stephens, Atkinson, and Glasner 2011). Scientists interpret such prescriptive rules as more than intrusions. To the extent that legal regulations engender activities "separate from those actions that suffice to meet the scientists' professional concerns" (Bruns 2009, 1399), legal mandates are experienced and described as hindrances to the smooth operation of the laboratory, obstacles to the autonomy of science, and impediments to scientific progress (Evans 2012, 2014). Outsiders' demands for new or different ways of working "are trivialized by insiders because outsiders make those claims without understanding what will be displaced" (Heimer 2008, 30). To scientists, legal regulators, like most nonscientists, lack understanding of the real processes of science and organization of laboratories (Gray and Silbey 2014).

To the degree that the consent decree between the EPA and Eastern University sought to achieve uniform, consistent and legible practices across the university's laboratories, it threatened the scientists' expertise instantiated in their research processes but also in their relatively autonomous control of their laboratories and supervision of their graduate students' education and training. There is reason to believe that the proposed EHS system signaled a direct challenge to the authority and expertise of the university scientists, which would have discernible consequences for the shape, capacities, and penetration of the system into laboratory routines.

RESEARCH METHODS

A Case Study

The negotiated settlement between the EPA and Eastern University to design and implement an environmental health and safety system for academic laboratories represented trouble for science, locally for the scientists at Eastern but also for American academic scientists in general, because Eastern agreed to make its system available for the nation's research universities. In their now canonical 1941 account of how to study the "law-stuff of a culture," the anthropologist E. Adamson Hoebel and fabled jurisprudential scholar Karl Llewellyn[6] urged scholars with interests in understanding how law really worked—especially in settings where formal professions and institutions were not immediately observable—to look at "instances of hitch, dispute, grievance, trouble," inquiring what the trouble was and what was done about it. "It is rare in a . . . group or society," they wrote, "that the 'norms' which are felt or known as proper ones to control behavior are not made in the image of at least some of the actually prevalent behavior; and it is rare, on the other hand, that [the norms] do not to some extent become active in their turn and aid in patterning behavior further." Norms build up over time with amazing emotional and material power, often attaching moral meanings to what may be simply accident, habit, or convenience. Thus, instances of hitch, trouble, or dispute lay bare the community's norms as both moments of deviation and repair. What may be latent is made manifest and what appeared consensual becomes the subject of open, explicit contest. By following the events set in motion by this consent order between Eastern and the EPA, by observing the ways in which it is trouble for the university, I began a journey into the taken-for-granted, habitual, reputably consensual norms of contemporary laboratories to discover whether—and if so, in what ways—the law is part of the constitution of modern science.

This chapter is based on six years of ethnographic fieldwork at Eastern University to document and analyze the creation of the new EHS system for research laboratories. As such, it is a single case with both common and atypical features. Eastern University, included among the sixty Association of American Universities in the United States and Canada, shares with others the common organizational structure of a professional bureaucracy (Mintzberg 1979; Freidson 2001). Disciplinary departments are managed by chairpersons who report to deans managing collections of departments within schools. Deans report to the provost, who is responsible to the president, with whom s/he continually confers. The highest-level academic meetings for budget, appointment, and policy decisions include participation by the president, provost, school deans, and chair of the faculty, plus high-level administrators such as the vice president for finance, vice president for research, general counsel, heads of facilities and libraries, as well as the administrators for undergraduate and graduate student affairs. The president reports monthly to an executive committee of the board of trustees and thrice annually to the full board.

On paper it looks like a standard bureaucracy, although, as mentioned earlier, authority on the administrative side flows from the top down, whereas on the academic side, faculty ostensibly located at the ground of the hierarchy populate the highest academic offices (president, provost, deans, chair of the faculty) enjoying enormous autonomy as the ostensible source of the university's educational and research value.

The university is a loosely coupled but complex organization in which multiple goals can be pursued through nonlinear yet simultaneous, often unpredictable interactions (Perrow 2011). Unexpected or negative events can occur because of unplanned, unforeseen interactions and will occur regardless of the intentions or planning processes (Merton 1936). Sources of error or malfunction—whether financial, educational, or environmental—are not easily identifiable in complex systems. This is the case for laboratory hazards, especially during the confusion that accompanies an accident.

The university is a loosely coupled system also characterized by decentralized operations, multiple interests, amorphous and ambiguous performance standards, and, as already mentioned, flexible social control mechanisms. Processes do not flow in rigid Sequences. Locally practical solutions are often instituted, providing alternative paths to any particular goal with substitute processes and equipment. Variation is readily accommodated. This was, of course, exactly the situation that the EPA found to be chaotic in its inspection of Eastern. Just as importantly, loosely coupled complex organizations are not designed for efficiency or for unidirectional action. Thus, the creation of an EHS management system represented a major challenge to the university's organization, processes, and culture.

Although Eastern's organizational profile is not unusual, I make no claim that this is a typical large organization or an average university. Eastern is an elite institution and as such commands greater-than-average private endowment, national attention, public and private research support. The terms of the EPA consent decree were explicitly negotiated because of Eastern's resources—human, economic, and cultural—to serve as a national prototype for more effective management of laboratory hazards across the nation's hundreds of universities. If Eastern could manage to secure faculty compliance and a more reliable safety culture, its model could, it was hoped, replace previous compliance efforts that had turned out to be unsuccessful in mobilizing faculty support for safer laboratory practices. As an atypical institution, this is an outlier case pursued as an opportunity to identify new empirical facts and conditions of variation, build rather than test theory, uncover mechanisms, and trace processes (Small 2009a). The persuasiveness of the evidence will depend less on the representativeness of the events (although I do think they are not uncommon) than on the "logically sensible" linkages (Small 2009a) identified between scientific expertise and legal subjectivity, between actors' and groups' professional authority alongside efforts at organizational change.

Data Collection

The fieldwork activities included interviews, observation, and document collection. These were supplemented by systematic data collection with standardized instruments for observation and surveys. Because my focus is the intersection of three social phenomena—government agencies and regulations, university organization, and scientific laboratories—my sites included the university administration, changes in those offices in response to the regulatory mandate, scientific laboratories and changes in response to regulation, as well as interviews with government officials and observations of their interactions with university personnel. Given the breadth of the sites and length of time, I worked with a team of research assistants, some very accomplished, others in training.

We began observations with the announcement of the consent decree to faculty just preceding the court hearing and followed through the next six years when the EPA came to inspect and assess compliance. The formal meetings we observed included those of a committee for facilities, a committee for research laboratories, and a committee of administrators and faculty overseeing the work of these two working committees. One or two of us attended each meeting, sitting silently at the side of the room, taking notes on the proceedings. I interviewed members of the committees individually; we received copies of all documents and were included in all mailing lists. We also conducted individual interviews with senior administrators, key faculty, and members of the committees overseeing health, safety, and environmental policies. This includes safety and chemical hygiene officers within labs and on the EHS staff. We observed most meetings where the university attorneys and EHS representatives met with EPA attorneys. We followed the intermediate audits of the system conducted by consulting firms contracted for this purpose and the final audit and inspection conducted by the EPA before the consent decree was lifted.

Laboratory observations are key to this project. These observations took place in laboratories across a spectrum in which past practice and need for improvement varied, as did the authority structure and degree of environmental and health risk in the lab. We conducted participant observation in more than twenty laboratories in five sciences, plus medical and engineering departments, for at least three months each. We expected the observations to provide us with evidence of the variations in managerial style of the principal investigators (PIs): how involved each was in the logistical and material organization of the lab.

I approached faculty members for permission to "hang around" their laboratories, and for my research assistants to do so as well. Although it is important to follow the discussions out of which the EHS system design emerged, it is even more critical to trace the ways in which the law, the EPA, and the regulatory regime were being interpreted and responded to by actors at the ground level of the organization. The entire EHS organization is created and mobilized to serve ongoing research in the laboratories. The culture of autonomy and freedom that characterizes the university has its *raison d'être* at this ground and center of the university's organization. If there is to be compliance, or violation of federal law, it will be in the laboratories. If trust and autonomy are threatened or enhanced by this systemic surveillance, it will be visible at this ground level. If there will be routine changes in scientific practices spurred by this legal intervention, they will be apparent in the labs.

All field notes were typed up using Microsoft Word and kept in files arranged by organizational locus and topic. We recorded descriptions of what was going on in front of us as well as our queries about what was happening that we did not understand. These notes were typed at the end of every day or, at most, at the end of two days. All notes and queries were shared among the team members and discussed in weekly group meetings (Evans, Huising, and Silbey 2016). All recorded interviews were transcribed by a person hired for this purpose. The transcriptions and notes were entered into and coded using Atlas.ti.

Data Analysis

A natural experiment. This work, at its base, analyzes how the authority of one form of knowledge interacts with the authority of other forms of knowledge and expertise (Espeland 2003;1998; Heimer and Staffen 1998; Guetzkow, Lamont, and Mallard 2004; Lamont 2009). Here, a legally mandated organizational change, a management system with scripted protocols and laboratory routines, as well as standard operating procedures, was imposed uniformly across hundreds of laboratories. The introduction of the management system constituted, in effect, a natural experiment in which to observe organizational responses to legally mandated changes, a treatment applied across the varied subjects. How would scientists respond to this legally mandated intrusion into their professional domain? We had every reason to believe that they would resist if they did not find ways to make the requirements minimally intrusive. The job of the administration was to make the burden as light as possible. As the university attorney told me, "It is my job to make this work. We are not going to stop their research, so it has to work in one way or another." Eventually, managers hoped, it would become just another lab routine, part of the expert knowledge and habits of experimental science.

Of course, we did not believe that responses would be uniform. At the outset, we hypothesized that the responses to the new regulations might vary with aspects of laboratory organization and levels of risk. For example, some labs are tightly managed with weekly group meetings that include reports of all "problems," "accidents," and other housekeeping matters as well as detailed discussion of the research. As one PI told me, "I don't want them to tell me every time there is a jar without a cap, or a torn label, but they sure enough better tell me at the end of the week how many there have been this week. Otherwise how I am going to correct the problem?" "How do you correct the problem?" I asked. "It depends. This is an educational institution after all. You always get a chance to improve. But if there is a character who is creating repeated problems, and dangerous conditions for everyone, I don't want him in my lab." Other PIs don't want to be bothered daily, weekly, or monthly. They want this delegated to a dedicated person.

Laboratories also vary in the degree to which they pose health, safety, or environmental risk. Some laboratories are using toxic chemicals and biological and radioactive materials. Others are using lasers on biological and/or toxic substances. Yet others use no biological or radioactive materials but very heavy equipment with high voltage. Finally, some laboratories have no specifically designated biological substances, radioactive materials, or large equipment but may have relatively harmless solvents and cleaners that nonetheless require special handling. Solvents and cleaners constitute environmental hazards, exactly because of the lack of local sensitivity to their risks. Using the legislated standards of risk for controlled substances, the laboratories we observed range from those in which there are only solvents and cleansers (low risk)—for example, used in stage productions or for care of musical instruments—to those using radioactive materials on biological phenomenon (high perceived risk). In between, we have laboratories that use lasers and other potentially risky equipment on various materials. Finally, the laboratories vary by the degree to which they have been considered good or bad actors in the past, model citizens, or needing improvement.

Thus, we expected some variation by standard organizational features: past practices, organizational hierarchy or collegiality, and material conditions of greater or less risk. We did not expect variation by discipline. Nor would we have expected variation between biology and chemistry, disciplines that shared more features than those distinguishing them. All labs in both departments have an abundance of chemical solvents and radioactive materials. Many chemistry labs have biomatter. Together they produce 70 percent of all hazardous waste on campus and occupy adjoining buildings. In terms of hazards and risk, they looked more like each other and different from many other departments, for example physics. We expected resistance to legal intrusion; we did not expect deference, and we did not expect disciplinary variation.

How could we explain these unanticipated findings? We analyzed the field notes and interviews in search of an explanation for the different reactions of the biologists and chemists to the EHS system. For this chapter, we collected all text that referenced or was coded for biology and chemistry, authority, expertise, history, industry, laboratory fixtures and spaces, dispute or conflict, as well as specific codes for components of the management system.

In the next section, I lay out the responses of biologists and chemists to the proposed regulatory regime. The implementation of EPA guidelines is observable not just through differences in outcome measures—whether one set of actors complies more or less than another—but also in the ways in which the legal norms of environmental regulation are part of the culture of the organizational units (table 11.1).

TABLE 11.1
Differential Responses to Legal Regulation of Laboratories

	Biology	Chemistry
Introduction of EHS system	No time for this; need to do research.	Do it already and do it better; part of being a chemist and good scientist.
Staff positions for EHS	EHS coordinator cannot be a member of the department; needs authority of university administration to reign in difficult or resistant faculty.	EHS coordinator must be a member of the department; no one other than chemistry member could navigate the varied lab materials and hazards. Prized autonomy and did not want central administration looking closely inside the department.

(continued)

TABLE 11.1 *(continued)*
Differential Responses to Legal Regulation of Laboratories

	Biology	Chemistry
Compromise: EHS staff and department partners	Partnership welcomed with expectation that the central EHS partner would be the leader. First appointment immediately embedded and comfortable handling crises as well as routines within department.	Partnership accepted with expectation that the department partner would be the leader. Several personnel changes before settling on coordinator accepted by department.
Inspections and auditing	Inspection by central EHS staff contact and department coordinator.	Inspection by a department committee of the EHS coordinator, rotating faculty member, and rotating graduate students.
Inspection tools	Prefer standard form used in all lab inspections across all university labs.	Use inspection form designed by chemistry, not limited to university-wide form or digital record.
Standard operating procedures	Requested list of most important safety procedures to post above sink in every lab.	Objected to posting of a standard list, as there are no standard hazards or processes across all labs.
Other variations	Requested training by central EHS staff for students. EHS to keep records of training and inspections; since they insist on these procedures, they should have the responsibility.	Provide own training and will continue to do so. Keep their own records; these are learning and research processes, not policing.

DIFFERENTIAL RESPONSES TO LEGAL REGULATION

How have faculty responded to this generalized apparatus for identifying, preventing, and responding uniformly to environmental, health, and safety risks? Very early in the process of planning the new system, it became unambiguously clear that the responses were patterned along disciplinary and departmental lines rather than any of our hypothesized organizational features, degrees of risk, or possibly idiosyncratic inspection histories. In full department meetings, when the system was being introduced to faculty across the university, as well as in the smaller committee meetings, in which the system was being designed, biologists and chemists interpreted and responded to the new system differently. Laboratory observations and interviews confirmed these variations.

Introduction of New EHS System

At the outset, the biologists were skeptical, if not outright hostile, to this project. They were reluctant to be burdened, the biologists said, by additional demands on their time and resources that were not part of their research. They were like many others for whom the law usually looks like a hindrance, an impediment to productivity. Those who view the regulations this way offer accounts of how constrained they are by all the rules and how afraid they are by what might happen with a "new improved" system, which is surely going to mean yet more rules.

One biologist explained to me that outside monitoring of laboratory materials and processes is a waste; no one cares more than the PI[7] to secure his laboratory and the students and postdocs within it, and for sure to protect the research animals. "Look," he said, "it's a big pain because we want the mice healthy. People are going to want them healthy because they can't do their experiments [otherwise]." The scientists care more because they have a direct interest in securing the health and safety of their experimental animals, he claimed. There are years of investment in these animals; the loss of any one could mean years of work down the drain. The spot inspections and detective work that the government agencies require were described as a big waste of time and energy.

The most consistently voiced complaint had less to do with the animals than with that most precious commodity: human labor time. A typical response was repeated at almost every stage of the design and implementation of the management system: "My students don't have the time for this; they have to do their research." When the organizational scheme, training, inventory, and auditing processes were presented at a meeting of the biologists, the first faculty member to speak asked, "Why don't we just tell them that we don't want to do this?" This called forth a great deal of laughter. The notion that the university could "just say no" had not occurred to the rest of the group as a possible or reasonable tactic. When the laughter died down, the speaker went on to explain that the hazards in her lab were considerably less than what gets poured down the drain in every kitchen and laundry every day. "Why doesn't the EPA go bother the real problems?" Thus, the earliest and loudest message was that the safety regime—the law—was external to the research. It created unnecessary and costly obstacles to doing great science. "We are doing important work, and we are not the nation's problem."

In contrast to this reaction, a chemist remarked one day in conversation with one of the biology faculty, "The environmental practices we're trying to get everyone to adopt are not additions to what we do. We have to see these things as part of what we do. We can't be scientists one way and environmental citizens in another." This carefully parsed statement does not fully capture the energy and emotion that was expressed both orally and bodily, as the chemist almost leapt across the table to restrain the biologist who kept insisting that he and his students had no time for all "this bureaucratic stuff."

The chemists did not necessarily have greater respect for the safety inspectors. Indeed, it turns out they had much less. But their immediate response was that they already do it better. "We didn't think all that much of the guys who did come by, or the guys who make the rules," a chemist told me, "because they weren't as smart in chemistry as we are, and they came and were saying 'you're not using this or that properly.' But they didn't know what the structure and properties of the chemicals were. They would lose credibility in front of the students. It was a really bad situation." As a consequence, the chemists did not object to a renewed commitment by the university to address laboratory hazards, but they insisted that they would do it themselves.

I don't want to misrepresent this. Not every chemist was on board, already "doing safety" perfectly well by themselves, and not every biologist was less than welcoming. Nonetheless, there were differences in the responses of the departments in the name of their faculty and the faculty in university committees in the name of their departments. Importantly, although chemists were not at all deferential to what they called "the environmental police," they considered the environmental and safety regulations as part of the practice of chemistry; the biologists defined the new system as yet another institutional constraint on science.

Staff Positions for EHS

These initial differential and resistant responses to the prospect of a university-wide environmental, health, and safety management system were resolved when the Eastern administration agreed to hire personnel in new positions to handle the new rules and procedures. The resistance that had characterized the initial discussions dissipated entirely when the administration said that it would allocate five positions to the science and engineering departments proportionately according to need. Need was defined by the degree and amount of regulation to which the labs in each department were subject. Degree of regulation (from most to least regulated) was scaled quantitatively and qualitatively; that,is, by the amount of hazardous waste and number of different hazards. The EHS staff generally recognizes five classes of hazard: chemicals; biological materials; radiation, including lasers; air quality; and safety, including heavy equipment, magnets, hoists, and major electrical power. Biology and chemistry were the most heavily regulated departments. From the very beginning, before this conception of regulatory oversight was actually operationalized in the design of the new system, the disproportionate attention was developed intuitively. When a metric was needed with which to justify the allocation of new resources, the impressionistic assessment of need was confirmed with what was described as hard data. As such, the allocation of resources received no critique or pushback. Together, chemists and biologists represented approximately

70 percent of all the hazardous waste on campus. Together, they were assigned four of five of the new coordinators for the EHS system. Other departments would reallocate existing staff.

Once the commitment was made to hire additional staff to manage the new EHS regime in the labs, another difference emerged between the two sciences. The biologists did not want the EHS coordinator, whom they called an "agent," to be a member of the department. They voiced concern that a member of the department would be unable to assert sufficient authority to ensure success of the EHS system. How could a member of the department staff tell a senior faculty member that his or her lab was dirty or dangerous? What if the faculty member resisted complying with rules or recommendations for good practice? Faculty status and pressure would compromise the new EHS role. Apparently, the previous record of the department, known to the EHS staff and revealed in the EPA inspection, was notably checkered. Some labs were models of safety; others were among those that had some of the most flagrant and numerous violations recorded by the EPA. In their comments, members of the department suggested a history of individualistic favoritism rather than consistent management by department heads. Thus, the biologists thought it entirely appropriate that the university should provide the manpower to handle these new demands. The system would work best, they argued, if the new EHS staff were indeed agents of the central administration who could act with authority, rather than department personnel who might become embedded in local politics within the department. Consistent with their view that these EHS regulations were demands from outside of science, the staff entrusted with their enforcement belonged with the source of those regulations, outside of science.

In contrast, the chemists would not have an EHS coordinator involved in training or auditing chemistry labs and personnel. One account focused on practicality. Only members of the department—students, faculty, staff—could function effectively. Only members of the department could understand sufficiently the range of hazards, varieties of practice, and legitimacy of particular routines. Only department members could understand the actual chemistry of matter and the culture of the chemists, including the various subcultures among organic, inorganic, bio, and physical chemists. And only members of the department "command the respect and authority to influence what goes on in a department." Here the chemists seemed to agree with the biologists that the ability to influence what happens in the department would affect the ability to secure a safe environment: the biologists sought to create a countervailing authority to the faculty within the department, and the chemists sought to secure and guard that which already existed within. To an important extent, this difference may have derived from the fact that the chemists did not want, and seemed not to need, change, while the biologists recognized that their distribution of influence and authority had not heretofore secured uniformly good practices and that they needed organizational change.

The second ground for resisting an EHS agent within the chemistry department was simply scientific autonomy. As one member of the department said, " I look at this from my point of view in chemistry. Do I want someone from central administration overseeing my department?" They did not want safety to become a matter of policing.

Since 1990, when OSHA enacted what is known as the Lab Standard, the chemists had demonstrated their expertise in self-regulation by putting in place training and inspection processes, a system that had won national recognition and become a model for others. They saw no need to change what they had already institutionalized. They could easily expand their existing system to include environmental hazards but would not trust someone from outside to take over the job. Experience had demonstrated the effectiveness of their practices, at the same time as other departments were revealed in the EPA inspection to have deficient practices.

The 1990 Lab Standard had been created because the OSHA rules in place at the time had been designed and implemented primarily for industrial sites and seemed not to work well for research laboratories. Industrial sites do the same things over and over again.[8] Because of this standardized repetition, the forms and processes of industrial safety can, like the work, also be routinized. By contrast, most scientific laboratories perform a wide array of activities, some of them infrequently. They also typically perform these actions on a smaller scale, using smaller quantities of potentially hazardous materials. Because of the variation in processes and materials, it is difficult to anticipate the kinds of dangers that might be involved. "There are lots of things," Professor Laslett, the Chemistry Department safety and chemical hygiene officer, said, "for which hazards are not known. They're new substances we've created as part of our research. And so research lab people said [to the federal government about the OSHA regulations] that the laws that are being applied to us really are not relevant." In other words, the dangers that attach to research laboratories are to a significant degree unspecifiable in advance. As a consequence, according to Laslett, the chemists have taken on the role of regulating themselves. Laslett described the department's process.

> We tried to change the culture of safety. . . . I would say the prior situation was an adversarial relationship between the safety police and researchers and faculty. Occasionally some sort of proclamation would come through—like you can't wear shorts if you work in the lab—that people would treat derisively and ignore totally. . . . It was a really bad situation.
>
> We had, in a sense, to reinvent our whole safety regime. So it was an opportunity to do this differently. It's as if you're saying we're throwing out our entire legal code and rewriting it.
>
> The OSHA lab standard is an interesting performance-based law, which means that it doesn't lay out in detail [that] under the following conditions you must wear safety glasses, under the following different conditions you don't. Instead, what it comes down to is [that] it says you must appoint a person called the chemical hygiene officer and you must write something called the chemical hygiene plan. And it doesn't specify what you put in there. What it does say is that this has to be effective in protecting all researchers from hazards. We're not telling you what a safe laboratory is. You are going to make up rules that make a safe

laboratory. That's what the law, the federal law says. . . . They did not lay out in excruciating detail one-size-fits all safety rules. It says "we will allow you to . . . design your own safety plan." We may inspect and determine if it is effectively protecting people . . . but we are not going to micromanage things.

When the law went into effect, the first thing [we] had to do was to decide how are we going to comply with it. Are we going to have a single safety chemical hygiene officer who would be safety czar over the entire [university], or are we going to make every PI, every professor, a chemical hygiene officer . . .

So, the most important decision we made was that safety should begin at the grass roots. . . . If we didn't enlist the people affected by these rules in the creation of new rules [it wouldn't work]. . . . The idea was that we would create a structure. The creation of the new safety rules would be done cooperatively by faculty, students, and administrators within each department. And the enforcement of compliance—monitoring the compliance and enforcing would similarly involve not only faculty administrators and authority figures but those researchers, the people who are affected by the rules. [This was] to overcome the adversarial relationship that otherwise inevitably develops if you have people outside of the community creating rules and monitoring compliance and enforcing them.

After a lot of debate we came up with a plan, which would be more or less equivalent [across the university]. Every department would have its own chemical hygiene officer and plan. We felt that it was unrealistic for each individual laboratory professor to have one.

But, he continued, it was also not good policy to have one policy for the entire university. In the past, that hadn't produced an effective safety system because of the hostility between the researchers affected and the professional safety people.

The researchers felt that they had no stake in the creation of the laws. And the laws, any rules, tend to interfere in some way with research if only in terms of making it less convenient to do certain things. And the fact is that some of the benefits are not immediately apparent, like am I going to get cancer thirty years from now. It is not necessarily easy for people to see the long-term benefits of these short-term inconveniences. The inconveniences are being applied from on high, naturally people are less cooperative.

My agenda was that if we involved everybody at the beginning making rules, they were more likely to appreciate why these are important and necessary; they are more likely to cooperate.

Of course, their cooperation must be verified, Lasslett explained.

It is very important not just to have an initial training lecture and to give people copies of these documents, it's also important that we check that they're working in compliance with it. So what we have, in our department, is a system of inspections. Every research lab—that means every group—is inspected, unannounced, unannounced inspection twice a year . . . by a team consisting of one faculty member and one graduate student from the chemical hygiene and safety committee.

The chemistry department's success at self-regulation, under the requirements of the OSHA lab standard, encouraged resistance to newly centralized regulation under the EPA consent order. Although all departments had created chemical hygiene plans and appointed chemical hygiene officers in response to the 1990 OSHA lab standard, uniformity had ended there. The chemical hygiene officers met once a year for one to two hours to go over any new regulations. Most plans inscribed in thick binders sat on shelves gathering dust, rarely changed from year to year. It was unclear whether departments other than chemistry were doing as well; some others, including biology, had training protocols in place, although it seemed that few had instituted the systematic and rigorous inspection system that was the central feature of the chemists' program.

If the OSHA lab standard had initiated a process of self-regulation, adopted very unevenly across the university, the consent order, unlike the OSHA rules, demanded consistent conformity across the university, just that conformity that the EPA inspection exposed as absent under the OSHA lab standard. Thus, whereas the biologists wanted someone who operated with the authority of the university administration behind them, not an employee subordinate to the department faculty, the chemists would have no one working in the department who was not a member, one of themselves, familiar with the local, existing, rigorous safety culture of chemistry.

Compromise: Partners in Regulation

These different approaches stymied the committees that were designing an organizational structure for the new EHS system. The consent decree required direct, transparent lines of authority. Individual faculty PIs and the department chairs had to be included within the lines of reporting as well as responsibility. The biologists wanted these lines to include an EHS person who would be dedicated to the department but reporting to the university administration, and the chemists wanted someone within the department who would report to the department chair.

In the end, a compromise was developed whereby each department would have an internal EHS person and a partner in the EHS central office. In this way, teams composed of both internal and central administrative personnel would serve every department. For the biologists, it was imagined during discussions, the central EHS partner might be the dominant actor. Reporting to the EHS office hierarchy up to a vice president, such a staff member could draw on central administrative authority to persuade or discipline uncooperative faculty, if it were necessary. For the chemists, it was imagined, the department EHS coordinator would be the dominant team member, and the central EHS office partner would be an additional resource only if needed, which was not expected.

The biologists hired a department EHS coordinator (to partner with the central staff EHS contact person), who very quickly and quietly immersed herself in the local organization, becoming immediately both acquainted with and comfortable in the department. Indeed, her incorporation was so facile and uneventful that by her second month on the job, she was handling crises and reorganizing hazardous practices with minimal resistance. The chemistry department EHS coordinator (also to partner with a central EHS contact person) was hired at the same time but left within three weeks, unhappy at her lack of authority and autonomy. It took several personnel changes until a satisfactory person was in place in chemistry.

Inspection and Auditing

Inspection and auditing are central features of the new EHS system, features that are stipulated in the consent order in greater detail than any of the other elements, such as requirements for universal training and inventory control. The consent order required five levels of monitoring: weekly self-examination of each investigator's laboratory and group; regular department-level inspections at intervals to be determined but not less than once a year; inspections by the central EHS office, at intervals to be determined but not less than once a year; auditing by the university auditors every few years; and outside auditing every three to five years.

In the standard accounts of audit culture (Power 1997; Strathern 2000), inspection and auditing are distinct activities. Inspections are thought to be universal oversight and surveillance of all relevant aspects of work and the spaces of work. Inspection involves the collection of empirical evidence of compliance with protocols and possibly standardized metrics operationalizing the prescriptive rules. For example, each lab is expected to have weekly checks of the short-term (less than thirty-day) hazardous waste collection areas to ensure that all containers are properly capped and labeled, ready for pickup and transfer to the long-term (up to ninety-day) central university storage areas. Those conducting the weekly inspection will verify that the procedures are being followed by observing consistency between the rules and practices while noting and correcting any inconsistencies. Similarly, the weekly, monthly, or semiannual departmental and EHS inspections will also survey every laboratory space and all materials to ensure full compliance with all relevant rules; for example, availability and good working condition of all personal protective equipment such as lab coats and safety glasses, as well as exhaust hoods, emergency eye washes, and safety showers.

Audits, however, do not actually involve observing the subject phenomena; audits do not collect empirical evidence, as inspections do, that the laboratory looks and functions as the regulations prescribe. Audits are procedures that are adopted to see that the inspection system itself, rather than the lab, is working properly. Audits sample the data collected by the inspections and the responses generated by the organization but do not normally match the samples to the field evidence. They operate at a remove from the hazards themselves to monitor the system for producing safety (inspections, training, etc.) rather than the system's product (safe labs).

As discussions for implementing the inspection system progressed, it became clear that the commitment to five levels of inspection and audit could create a significant burden on laboratory time, especially if each inspection was independent of every other as originally anticipated. Since the department and central EHS staff were to be partnered, some on the planning committees suggested that the central inspection might be conducted alongside, simultaneously with the department inspection. This compromise was communicated to and approved by the EPA attorneys.

With regard to the forms to be used at each inspection level (auditing was left to future discussions), the EHS office had hoped to computerize the entire process so that lab inspections might be quickly entered into a data bank for central collation and analysis while identifying not only systematic overall compliance but perhaps also problem patterns across the university, as well as individual so-called bad apples. In the second year of the design and implementation process, financial resources were significantly constricted, and plans for computerized inspection via handheld devices with checklists that would automatically send the data to a central storehouse, as well as automation of the future inventory system, were put on hold. Planning would focus on a temporary data collection system for inspections, leaving computerization and automation for future discussions and richer budgets. This paper-based system remained in place for at least fifteen years.

Two heated discussions within the faculty planning group revealed yet another source of variation among the scientists. The biologists were now basically satisfied with the design of the roles and staffing and had become supporters of the university-wide management system. Their approach in year two had become more than conciliatory. They sought out the EHS planning group and staff to help them do a better job. Could the EHS staff provide them with some standard rules or operating procedures for the most common waste materials that could be printed and posted above the hazardous waste collection areas? Could the EHS staff help them standardize the processes in order to create greater efficiency? Specifically, with regard to the inspections, they were perfectly happy to have the central EHS accompany the departmental EHS coordinator on inspections. They had hoped that the central staff would do these inspections all along, and the partnering solution, they thought, had formalized this. If the EHS central staff wanted to use a standard set of questions for all university lab inspections, it was fine with them. If the EHS staff wanted to use multiple forms, some tailored for the department and some for general use, that was also fine.

The chemists did not agree. Not only would they not use a standard university-wide form for their inspections, they did not want the department committees who conducted the semiannual inspections to be burdened with the need to coordinate with any central staff EHS personnel. The rationales for this resistance varied from one meeting to another. At one of the first general meetings on the subject, the chemistry representative voiced his lack of confidence in the EHS staff. He said that the department did not trust the central staff, whom they believed were deficient in the basic science and thus ignorant of the degrees of hazard in the great variety of materials in chemistry labs. Here, the public discussion reiterated what I had been told in one-on-one interviews when I began the project: nonchemists just did not have sufficient chemical knowledge to recognize unusual hazards or, conversely, what was not actually a hazard. The intrusion of nonexperts in the labs had been the source of resistance to regulation over a decade earlier and had been over-come, the chemists argued, by instituting their own system of self-regulation. This would be going backwards.

At a smaller subsequent meeting, the dismissive tone of a highly expert academic speaking to the rabble was moderated considerably. Now, the objection was practical and voiced as a concern that the university's entire system would falter by trying to spread limited resources too thinly. It was just not possible, the chemists claimed, for the central EHS staff to inspect every university lab twice a year. This was minimally a two-hour activity for more than forty department labs, no less the more than four hundred laboratories university-wide, each inspection requiring the presence of at least three persons (a member of the department faculty or staff, a graduate student, and now a member of the central staff). Just coordinating the persons to schedule these inspections — which were to be unannounced, surprise visits — would be an impossible job. The effectiveness of the surprise — for ensuring daily compliance — would be impeded if they tried to systematize the visits, and without systematizing, it would be impossible to schedule without hiring many more people, which was just not possible. The EHS staff would never have enough people, the chemistry representative claimed, to go on all the inspections. The central EHS participation in inspections would just have to be less frequent so as not to complicate the department's well-oiled surveillance machine. At the end of this meeting, it appeared to this observer that the collaboration with the central staff had come to an end, at least in the chemistry department.

In a series of committee and then one-on-one meetings between representatives of the department and the Eastern attorneys participating in the design of the EHS system, the chemists continually objected to being included in any general set of university-wide processes, although they wanted such a system for everyone else. One of the attorneys managing the project explained to me as I followed along after one of these meetings that he was not all that worried. Indeed, the chemists were not really a *safety* problem, because they had produced an effective system of self-regulation. They were an *organizational* and *regulatory* problem, however, if they would not participate in the general university-wide system because the EPA required consistency across the university. The attorney recognized the posturing and was not surprised, he said, that the roles had become reversed between the difficult (first biology and now chemistry) and cooperative (first chemistry and now biology) departments. Over time, he expected the roles might shift again. He explained the situation: "In essence, they were saying, 'don't mess with what we have here. We do it well, and will continue to. Stay out.' I can understand that. We will work it out."

For perhaps six months, the chemists continued to refuse to use a standard form for their departmental inspections, although the form adopted by the planning committees was developed by tweaking the chemists' existing protocols. Over time, they moderated the disrespectful language about the competence of the EHS staff and compromised their reservations about the logistical problems of having EHS personnel observe or accompany them on inspections. There would be twice-a-year, unannounced, surprise inspections. One semiannual inspection would be done by the departmental committee alone, and one inspection would include the EHS staff partner along with the department committee members.

Other Variations

The biology department said it would like the central staff to provide training for students and postdocs and a simple poster to be tacked above every lab sink with the ten most important rules. Furthermore, the department had no problem with EHS staff keeping training and inspection records centrally so long as they were kept and the department would not "have to reproduce something in the future for which they were unprepared because the EHS took responsibility and did not fulfill it." In contrast, the chemists did not want the central staff involved in training. Also, it was not possible to have a single poster with rules for every lab; not only did the particular chemicals create different risks, but if you posted only ten rules, the nonposted safety practices would be ignored. Chemistry had a system in place, and it worked fine. Moreover, they did not want any central recordkeeping. This was a learning and research activity, not a police surveillance activity.

Before moving to possible explanations, I reiterate that this variation was not what we expected at the outset of the research. We originally thought that variation in responses might derive from the degree of risk from the number and degree of hazards in the different laboratories, or the organization of the labs as more or less hierarchical or as one big family, and, finally, whether the lab's previous experience indicated that it was problematic (that is, dirty, or a site of violations in the inspection) or a reliably compliant lab. We never imagined that the differences would fall out along department and disciplinary lines. Today, departments and disciplines may be considered somewhat arbitrary because, for example, biological research and nano-scale (molecular/chemical) investigations are everywhere in the university. Radiation and chemical waste are also ubiquitous. Moreover, some members of the chemistry department are biochemists doing basic chemical reactions on biological molecules, and all biologists use chemical reagents. But it turns out that these two departments are excellent sites from which to learn about responses to regulation and surveillance because they do constitute 70 percent of all the chemical waste on campus. Even if there were some biologists who resembled chemists and some chemists who sounded more like biologists, there were very few such outliers, and those responses were silenced by the conversations in department meetings and policies established at the departmental level.

Although we may see an increasing movement to interdisciplinarity across universities, departments are the organizational location and normative community in which academic scientists live and work: gathering material resources, being allocated space, teaching courses, and admitting, selecting, training, and mentoring graduate students who perform the laboratory research. Departments constitute the organizational node through which faculty are linked hierarchically to the

TABLE 11.2

Accounting for Differences

	Biology	Chemistry
History of the field and relationship to industrial practice	Contemporary molecular biology begins in 1970s with invention of recombinant DNA, causing public panic and research moratorium.	Over two hundred years old.
	Biologists collaborate at Asilomar in 1975 to develop criteria for safe handling of bio-matter, protection against spread. Typology of levels of hazard adopted by Centers for Disease Control and NIH. Protections built into lab architecture and standardized equipment and clothing protections.	Long-standing recognition that chemists working with very with hazardous materials.
	Biology industry grows exponentially during 1980s, period of antigovernment regulation. Development of bio-safety industry with dedicated professionals.	Since 1700s, laboratories built with chimneys to exhaust fumes, separating materials to prevent fires. Hoods invented in 1800s.
		First requested U.S. government regulation for safe handling of chemicals in 1880s.
		Two-hundred-year-old industry adopting relatively uniform safety procedures and equipment for exhausts, separation of materials, protective clothing.
Social organization of the lab	Permanent staff of lab managers and technicians supervising work within each lab, with often large number of postdoctoral fellows and much smaller number of graduate and undergraduate students. Multiple layers of hierarchy before reaching principal investigator.	No lab managers or technicians. Many graduate students and fewer postdoctoral fellows and undergraduates. Relatively flat hierarchy within the lab: the PI and her students.
	All labs built from a standard model.	Each lab individually designed.
	Approximately one-third of biology building space shared, e.g., autoclaves, refrigerators, culture rooms.	No shared spaces of facilities, other than those shared across all university departments, e.g., magnet lab, atomic force microscopy.

(*continued*)

TABLE 11.2 (*continued*)
Accounting for Differences

	Biology	Chemistry
Experimental practices	Often work with standard kits for repetitive steps of an experiment of many steps.	Organic and inorganic chemists create a particular reaction or molecule; variation and contamination must be excluded.
	Chemical reactions are technical resources.	Chemical reactions are the epistemic object to be explored, controlled.
	Seeking small but significant statistical or probabilistic variation in a large population of samples.	Seeking to increase the yield in a system where they have already detected a useful product in some amount, to become standard process for kits that biologists and others use.
	Integrated dynamic, complex systems where much still unknown.	Foundational knowledge relatively secure and well accepted.

larger university and where the local matters of curriculum, teaching, research, and employment are coordinated and contested with other departments. How can we account for these differences in the responses of the chemists and biologists? Table 11.2 outlines the differences in the disciplines' histories and relations with industry, social and physical organization of the labs, and epistemological foundations of their experimental processes that together account for the different responses of the chemists and biologists to the new legal regulations governing their labs.

INHERITED EXPERTISE, DIFFERENTIALLY ORGANIZED, AND EXPERIMENTALLY ENACTED

Important scholarship in the sociology of science lends support to the notion that part of the cultural authority of science derives from its ability to guard its boundaries (Gieryn 1983) to make persuasive claims for science as against pseudoscience, ideology, faith, and administrative demands as much as it does from its claim to objective methods and powerful technologies of observation. Neither the chemists nor the biologists willingly ceded authority to define the boundaries of their fields. Although both biological and chemical research is spread across many university departments—for example chemical engineering, geology, civil engineering, and neuroscience—neither the chemists nor the biologists deferred to others outside their departments the authority to define "good biology" or "good chemistry." Nonetheless, despite this common practice of boundary control, one science erected repeated hurdles to the intrusion of institutional safety systems and personnel while the other staked its claim to scientific autonomy by defining the safety regime as not science, inviting the safety personnel to inhabit, not merely visit, the biology labs.

How can we account for these differences in the responses of the chemists and biologists to the prospect of new and intrusive legal regulation? I suggest that this variation in response to the emergent EHS system is consonant with the different ways in which science is done in biology and chemistry. What do I mean? If we look at the different aspects of doing science and being a scientist, we can find variations in the way the work is organized, the relationship between academic and industrial or corporate science, as well as the embodied and cognitive tasks of being a biologist or chemist—what science studies describe in ethnographies of laboratory practices and the epistemologies of the different sciences (Knorr Cetina 1995; Doing 2008; Shapin 2004). Pragmatist philosophy (Haack 2006) and practice sociology (Bourdieu 1977, 1990) urge us to take note of how strongly individuals are committed to and invested in their hard-won knowledge and how much of what seem like minor interactions or small adjustments seem to threaten long-established habits, knowledge, and consequent authority. In effect, this literature argues that knowledge, including scientific knowledge, is localized, embedded, and invested in practices (MacIntyre 2007). Planned systems of change and innovation must take account of these local practices in order to create boundary-spanning objects or practices. If the law seeks to regulate these dense practices, it, too, needs to be a system of not only abstract logical principles but also practical tools, "thought on its way to action" in Holmes's words (Novick 1995, 3:502). In other words, for law to succeed, it may also need to be practical as well as principled (Ewick and Silbey 1998).

History of the Fields and Relationship to Industrial Practice

Modern chemistry is simply older than biology—older in the sense that its foundational knowledge was in place more than a century before modern molecular and genetic biology started. Indeed, alongside evolutionary theory, much of contemporary biology derives from advances in chemistry. Almost every chemist with whom I inquired about the newly planned EHS system mentioned the age of the field and the fact that chemists have understood for several centuries that they are working with hazardous materials. "Doing chemistry—especially doing chemical experiments—was a smelly, dangerous business, best kept below stairs, well away from polite society," which may help to explain why "eighteenth century chemists—whether they were doing experiments or producing commercial products—worked in laboratories, while most natural philosophers (physicists) did not" (Jackson 2016, 299).

Even the earliest proto-chemical laboratories, spaces for alchemists, assayers, and pharmacists, displayed a recognition of contamination and hazard by placing the multiple furnaces of different configurations at a distance from the work with vessels of flammable materials. The archetypal safety device, the fume hood, evolved from the chimneys that drew furnace smoke upward while coincidentally drawing off the noxious odors with the smoke. As far back as the seventeenth century (Morris 2015, 98), there are examples of early exhaust devices. Placing the hood above the work table, as we know it today, rather than the furnace began in the mid-eighteenth century with labs in Germany, London, and Pennsylvania. The standard histories describe the development of modern chemistry throughout the nineteenth century as a progression of increasing control over laboratory hazards with elaborate ventilation systems for frequent air changes, specialized cabinets for hydrogen sulphide, bomb ovens (also called *ballistic cabinets*) for explosive mixtures, rooms for gas analysis, clean rooms for balances, and workspaces at windows and in adjoining outdoor areas for dissipating fumes.

Technologically elaborated features of these nineteenth-century labs are the ubiquitous features of contemporary labs. Some fixtures address storage issues; others provide for new apparatus, especially glass lines for controlling syntheses and characterization of substances within relatively closed systems; "but many others [are] concerned with maintaining a safe working environment, particularly for inexperienced chemists in training" (Jackson 2016, 299). "The novel risks inherent in teaching and doing organic synthesis were significant in driving and shaping the construction of late-nineteenth century institutional chemical laboratories, and . . . these laboratories were essential to the disciplinary development of chemistry" (Jackson 2011, 55). "The management of risks [was] so severe [that] they could no longer be left in the hands of the individual" and thus became an institutional, professional obligation built into chemistry pedagogy (Jackson 2011, 61). Purpose-built laboratories became essential. "Chemists understood the significance of the purpose-built laboratories in advertising the status of their discipline, but their laboratories were also manifestations in bricks and mortar of the integrated system of training and research by which chemical knowledge was produced" (Jackson 2011, 61).

As important as the chemists' familiarity with laboratory hazards has been, the existence of an established chemical industry, also more than two hundred years old, is part of the disciplinary legacy. Industrial labs were the site, for example, where specialized laboratory clothing first became commonplace[9] (Morris 2015, 257). The movement back and forth between industry and academia created an intimacy with legal regulation and safety regimes in chemistry that has emerged only in the last few decades in biology. Thus, part of the local culture among chemists—which has distinguished them from biologists until recently—is their shared understanding of the dangers attached to the materials with which they work and the techniques, instruments, and habits that mitigate these hazards, which have become an engineered part of the chemical industry. As one chemist told me, "we don't want to be embarrassed when we send out students to DuPont. They have one of the best safety regimes anywhere. We don't want them telling us that we don't train our students well."

For biologists, industrial development is new; and the history of contemporary biology may have worked against a concern with safety. Several centuries after chemistry labs included safety precautions, and while the profession regularly requested regulations for containment through prescribed modes for shipping and handling chemicals, a National Research Council report on the design, construction, and equipment of laboratories for teaching and industry was published with no specific mention of biology or the particular needs of biology labs (Coleman and Wank 1951). Although containment cabinets were fashioned in the mid-1940s for use in the biological warfare laboratories at Fort Dietrich, Maryland, and, by the mid-1950s, the biological warfare experts began distributing their expertise more widely, it was not until the mid-1960s that nonclassified researchers were included in these biosafety discussions.

When recombinant DNA techniques—the foundation of contemporary microbiology—were first announced, a public panic developed, associating basic research with the fears of biological warfare and unconstrained contamination. Immediately, a moratorium on academic biological research was instituted in Cambridge, Massachusetts, where recombinant DNA was developed, while negotiations ensued between local officials and academic researchers. Commissions were set up, public hearings were held; scientists were required by government and the public to account for themselves and to assuage fears that they, the researchers, were not creating genetic agents in their laboratories that would leak into the local air and water systems, infiltrating the urban infrastructure and contaminating the human genetic pool. About one hundred forty biologists across the nation responded to the Cambridge moratorium, organizing themselves at a meeting held at Asilomar in Monterey, California, during which they formulated processes for working safely with genetic material. The researchers had been taken unawares; they were unprepared for the public furor, surprised by what they regarded as unfounded hysteria. Nonetheless, they took the lead in controlling the consequences, ultimately succeeding in muting the discourse surrounding the implications of genetic engineering and limiting attention to the technical problems of containing unfamiliar hazards. Silencing the discussion of purposive genetic engineering allowed the biologists to control the discourse when it entered Congress and to counter emerging regulatory legislation. They also succeeded in defanging new guidelines by the National Institutes of Health (NIH) to create what the biologists saw as real obstacles to the pursuit of particular lines of research and development (Wright 1994, 256).

Discussions at the 1975 Asilomar conference produced the current standard definitions of risk and protocols for managing four levels of biohazard risk based on the particular agents or organism on which the research is being conducted. The Centers for Disease Control and NIH adopted the Asilomar protocols as the model for mandated federal regulations for containing unknown as well as known hazards in biology laboratories. Each level builds on the previous one, adding constraints and barriers. Beginning with agents that pose a minimal potential threat to laboratory workers and the environment and do not consistently cause disease in healthy adults, the regulations call for dedicated training in standard microbiological techniques, personal protective equipment (lab coats, glasses, shoes rather than open sandals), prescribed handling of sharps (needles), decontamination of work surfaces and hands, and a prohibition on eating or drinking within labs. At each of the levels of greater hazard, the regulations prescribed enhancements in physical containment, waste handling, and body protection. The laboratories are built with prescribed airflow direction, limited or no air recirculation, and surfaces that resist contamination and ease of decontamination. At the highest level of hazard (BSL 4), the laboratories are physically isolated in buildings located at a distance from populations and other labs, workers wear full body-suits, and air is not only exhausted but filtered.[10]

For our effort to understand the different responses of biologists and chemists to the university safety system and thus the varied contexts within which successful regulation would need to adapt, two features seem important. First, there may be remnants of resistance to government regulation and overreaching, as we heard in the biologists' early responses, "Why don't we just tell them that we don't want to do this?" Second, biosafety has become a major industry with a worldwide professional field of specialists (Huising 2019). Scholars of regulation and public policy have begun to refer to the network of private actors who offer assistance to secure not only biosafety but regulatory compliance generally as "regulatory intermediaries" (Abbott, Levi-Faur, and Snidal 2017). The public fears concerning research processes, the demonizing of the researchers, and the drift from biosafety to biosecurity may have encouraged what now seems like the biologists' more comfortable remove from the management of local hazards.

Social Organization of the Laboratory

Scientists live and work within university-wide hierarchies of power and authority. Both chemists and biologists occupy privileged positions with respect to university staff, for example, radiation experts overseeing licensing and handling of all radioactive isotopes as well as lasers, and industrial hygienists working to design hoods, airflow, surfaces, and bodily protections. Scientists also enjoy almost total power within in the organization of their individual research groups: postdocs, technicians, graduate students, and undergraduates, all of whom are aware of their place in the hierarchy and the absolute and ultimate authority of the principal investigator.[11] Yet, again, there are significant differences between the biologists and the chemists in the ways in which their laboratories are organized. I suspect, moreover, that this difference may be even more salient than their histories and relations to industry, which may be slowly converging. There are many more technicians, permanent assistants, and lab managers in biology laboratories than in chemistry, where there are almost no permanent technical staff or managers—only the regular flow, cycling in and out, of students and postdoctoral fellows. Moreover, biology labs often have many more postdocs than graduate students. The relationship between the chemistry professor and her students is much more direct and unmediated by the layers of lab workers.

There are also systematic differences in the architecture of the biology and chemistry laboratories. Two items illustrate this spatial variation. Both the biology and chemistry departments at Eastern experienced large-scale renovations in recent years with construction of entirely new buildings. In the biology buildings, approximately half of the new construction comprises standard-issue labs: that is, there is a single model that was repeated in over half the allocated space. In the chemistry building, every lab was individually designed. The necessities are all there—hoods, benches, student desks, refrigerators, freezers, stock closets—but in each chemist's allocated space, the spatial organization of equipment and work surfaces is individually designed. When an entirely new biology building was constructed ten years earlier, not one laboratory was individually designed. I asked the dean, "how come the chemists got to design each of their labs individually and the biologists used a standard arrangement?" He replied that the then chair of biology did not want cost overruns and would not allow any variations. But that explanation really avoids the issue. The dean does not claim that cost overruns are permitted in chemistry but not in biology. When I asked the vice presidents for finance and research, I was told that it is "just the way the chemists are." But that is the question; I am trying to figure out "the way chemists are" that is different from the way biologists are.

Further inquiry at the biology department provided more information. Touring all the spaces and analyzing the architect's plans, I noticed that the main biology building (where all the labs had a single design) allocated approximately one-quarter to one-third of all floor space to shared facilities: autoclaves, refrigerators and freezers, steam baths, centrifuges, and so on. Further inquiry revealed that there were three kinds of shared spaces among the biologists. Very large facilities, such as the mouse-breeding facility that served many faculty, were staffed by a permanent team of specially trained technicians and "governed" (a term used by faculty who described this to me) by a director and faculty committee. There were also partnered facilities when two—or, less often, three—faculty members applied for funding for a particular piece of equipment. Finally, there were spaces and machines that were provided by the department for everyone's use but that required no special governance, for example, autoclaves (for destroying all biological matter before disposal: a consequence of those RDNA regulations). In contrast, the chemistry department had few shared spaces or facilities (a few large computers and access to general university facilities, such as the spectroscopy or magnet labs, which were also used by biologists and physicists as well as engineers.) They were not solely chemistry department space or facilities, although the director might be a chemist or a physicist.

Experimental Practices

Although both chemists and biologists are "generator(s) of surprises" (Hoagland 1990, xvii), there are notable differences between the biologists and chemists in their experimental practices, specifically different bench routines and explanatory logics. Indeed, the repetitive routine in biological experiments may be one of the major differences. Microbiologists produce their results through statistical analysis of variation in their samples. One biochemist explained to me that "biologists are still looking for basic determinants; they work with more integrated, dynamic systems where mechanisms may not be as easily isolated. Because there is still much unknown in the fundamentals, it is what I call an open system where biologists seek small differences in their data that can be built upon as a heretofore unannounced if minor mechanism. Because so much is still unknown, the probability of purification—the chemist's task—is not analytically possible." The explanations are within quite large error bars, as compared with the synthetic chemists. "In molecular biology and cloning studies, the desired species may be a very minor component (e.g., chemical), yet the methodologies may not be sensitive enough to detect the minor components that are being sought. Biologists thus often select for some activity (e.g., infectivity by a nucleic acid or replicative expansion), shown by the minor component, allowing enrichment based, for example, one function rather than abundance." Organic and inorganic chemists are not attempting to create or document systematic variation in a population. They are trying to understand and create a particular, unique chemical reaction, or to increase the yield in a system where they can already detect a product in some amount. They vary conditions and experimental parameters, optimizing what they can produce. They are able to do this because their foundational knowledge has become validated and entered the core of scientific truths. In comparison with the microbiologists, chemistry is a relatively closed system with the foundational knowledge—the elements and most but, of course, not all molecular structures—well known.

Here are some indicators of the different experimental practices. Ironically, despite the openness of biology relative to chemistry, biologists purchase many standard packages or kits for the various steps in their experimental protocols that are in effect closed. Scholars of science studies call ready-made processes "black boxes" (Clarke and Fujimura 2014; Fujimura 1992), a stabilized tool that "is no longer questioned, examined or viewed as problematic, but is taken for granted. A black boxed tool has become part of the tacit skills or material equipment of the laboratory, a circumstance or element of the situation, often rather invisible."[12] The chemists, however, use relatively fewer, if any, ready-made packages and expend a great deal of effort "unboxing" chemical reactions that take place within what may have become standard tools. In addition, it appears that the biologists use a wider array of materials and techniques than do the chemists, more numerous as well as more fixed recipes. As one chemist explained, "We try to invent a new process, a new reaction, that then can be used by the others—chemists and biologists—to produce something they need. But what we do is figure out a generic or universal reaction." Obviously, this is just one kind of chemistry.

Here is a further indicator about equipment. The glass lines in chemistry laboratories with which the syntheses are produced were early recognized by chemists as an independent source of hazard, with exploding glass a not-infrequent occurrence. The absolute amount of glass as against plastic may be another source of variation. Nonetheless, the number of steps, number of machines, and use of standard recipes and packages seem to vary between the fields.

These differences in experimental systems have been described in terms of variations in the particular *epistemic and technical objects*, as well as local cultures (Knorr Cetina 2009). The epistemic objects "are material entities or processes— physical structures, chemical reactions, biological functions—that constitute the object of inquiry . . . present[ing] themselves in a characteristic irreducible vagueness . . . embody[ing] what one does not yet know" (Rheinberger 1997, 27). The object is not yet defined, so much so that its description is merely a list of components into which the addition of any new component changes the object (Latour 1987). The technical things/objects compose the experimental process through which the definition of the epistemic object emerges. Whereas the epistemic object is in progress and unstable, with experiments composed of technical things used to define the epistemic object, technical objects have become stabilized. Importantly, "it is through these technical conditions that the institutional context passes down to the bench work in terms of local measuring facilities, supplies of materials, laboratory animals, research traditions, and accumulated skills. . . . In contrast to epistemic objects, these experimental conditions tend to be characteristically *determined within the given standards of purity and precision*" of the particular science (Rheinberger 1997, 29; emphasis added). Although with time, epistemic objects can become stabilized to become themselves technical things, part of the technical repertoire, "both types of elements are engaged in a non-trivial interplay" (29).

This analysis of the differences between chemists' and biologists' responses to safety regulations shows how that transformation can work in the opposite direction: the biologists' technical objects can serve as the chemists' epistemic object. If chemists work to make the reaction that biologists use to decode DNA, one scientist's epistemic thing can be another's technical object with associated standards of purity and precision.

DISCUSSION

Although professional agendas frequently shape regulatory compliance, scientists may be extraordinary in the degree to which they successfully guard their professional authority to control their laboratories and conditions of work, as well as status and expertise. Using data from a study of the creation of a system to manage environmental, health, and safety hazards in laboratories, this chapter shows that rather than resist legal intrusions, biologists and chemists ultimately deferred to legal demands to transform laboratory routines. This willingness to bow before the law was not a product of generalized respect or deference; rather, the biologists and chemists mobilized their disciplinary authority, relying on their historical relations with government regulation, conventional lab organizations and practices, and ways of doing science to insist that if they comply with the new regulatory regime, they do so in ways that did not disturb their disciplinary habitus. By accommodating what appeared to be idiosyncrasies of these departments, the in-house regulators (EHS staff of Eastern University) were able to install the new management system, pass an EPA audit, and thereby comply with the federal court order. The system worked because it was locally responsive, instantiating a basic pragmatic insight. Semiannual inspections conducted within the EHS system processes show that both departments have indistinguishable numbers of findings—that is, noncompliance. Can we claim that variation in legal subjectivity—the ways in which the biologists and chemists interpret law and regulation—is a generalizable observation beyond Eastern University? Perhaps there is something extraordinary about this particular university.

Because "every experimental scientist knows just how little a single experiment can prove or convince" (Fleck 1979, 96), we attempted to assess the generalizability of our findings about the deference of these scientists to the legally mandated regulation of their labs. We distributed a survey to EHS managers at several hundred American universities (receiving 177 responses) to determine ways in which our observations at Eastern were or were not comparable with other universities. The survey was designed to assess whether the extent and structure of a university's EHS system—its design and formal properties—led to differential rates of penetration into the labs. We hypothesized that the scientific status of the university (measured by department rankings, research funding, and AAU membership) and legal environment (EPA inspection status, presence of in-house counsel and risk management officer, and membership in an EPA partnership, section alliance or university consortium) would influence the shape and extent of the EHS management at the university.

The data showed that the presence of an EHS system did not affect the attention to at least ten or more EHS-related issues on campus: 58 percent of universities without EHS and 66 percent with management systems addressed ten or more issues. We did not find strong support for the argument that penetration is a function of the broader university environment. Only professional networks have a marginally significant effect on penetration, such that universities that are members of an environmental, health, and safety consortium tend to have a penetration score that is approximately 8.6 percent higher than universities not involved in these networks. Also, penetration into the labs does not vary with the degree of legal regulation to which the university was subject (having had an EPA inspection or legal counsel on campus) or its professional status relative to other universities. However, we did find that discipline influenced penetration of environmental, health, and safety procedures into the laboratories. Specifically, we explored whether pene-tration was more pronounced when biology or chemistry departments were heavily involved in EHS. We found that penetration, measured by responses to questions about routine laboratory safety practices, is significantly stronger when chemistry is heavily involved in EHS policies, irrespective of the biology department's involve-ment. Penetration is greater when chemistry is a key player, and this effect holds both when biology is also heavily involved and when biology is not heavily involved. I reiterate that this variation is not what we expected at the outset of the fieldwork, and thus we developed the survey to see whether the observations at Eastern were reproduced at other universities. They were.

The introduction of an environmental, health, and safety management system into scientific laboratories brings the audit culture (Power 1997; Strathern 2000) — in this case, legally mandated — directly into the habitat of the scientist. This approach to regulation is a response to experience and learning, itself a form of pragmatic, experimental public policy (Dewey [1927] 1954). It is the consequence of a shift in the EPA's and other agencies' agendas to focus on classes of organizations whose activities have proved much harder to regulate: the military, municipal and state offices, and the subject of this paper, educational and research institutions. But, more fundamentally than the site of regulation, this form of performance-based reg-ulation signals a direct response to criticisms about the limitations of regulation as command and control (Deutch and Lester 2004) and increasing demands for reg-ulations adapted to local organizational cultures (National Research Council 2014; Huising and Silbey 2018). Although most legal regulation attempts to manage some activities of organizations, this strategy supplants more conventional policies that mandate either the use of specific technologies or specific levels of performance by locating the design, standard-setting, and implementation of regulation within the regulated organization itself, in the hopes of co-opting the local governance processes that operate within these institutions to meet public, rather than private, goals (Coglianese 1997, 2001; Huising and Silbey 2011).

From a larger perspective, however, this risk management strategy is not just about accommodating and thus mobilizing existing organizational capacities; it is also symptomatic of a long historical shift in social relations, which Giddens (1990, 17) refers to as "reflexive modernization": the systematic, "reflexive order-ing and reordering of social relations in the light of continual inputs of knowl-edge." A series of transformations in the loci and objects of trust, differentiating modern from traditional societies, mark this historical shift. Trust is "a form of faith in which confidence vested in probable outcomes expresses a commitment to something rather than just a cognitive understanding"(1990, 27). In contempo-rary societies, trust no longer attaches as critically and pervasively to kin, commu-nities, or religious cosmologies as it does to personally chosen networks alongside the very opposite: abstract systems, especially expert systems. Those expert systems are technical accomplishments that organize large areas of the material and social environments in which we live and work today. Knorr Cetina (2009) describes the knowledge-based organizations that suffuse our daily life as epistemic cultures, practiced and practicing knowledge; scientific research laboratories are the ideal type of a knowledge-based organization, an expert system that has evolved over the last four centuries. By assigning responsibility to the university for designing, implementing, and, most important, auditing its own protocols for environmental safety, the consent order required that the scientists' expert knowledge be extracted, collected from its local authorities in the labs and safety personnel, generalized, and embedded in protocols distributed and audited through the management system (Huising 2014).

Further, we can see this regulatory apparatus as just another in the long stream of administrative ordering of society, what Scott (1998) describes as projects of high modernist faith (i.e., trust) in the ability to rationally plan and, most importantly, make legible and transparent what is usually unspoken and tacit. For sure, the EHS management system did just that; it revealed the deeply sedimented routines and taken-for-granted practices that differentiated biology from chemistry, so much so that consistent conformity with safety demands required locally crafted protocols. While Scott (1998, 5) describes modernist nation-building projects as features of authoritarian states' capacities to "run roughshod" over a prostrate civil society, the scientist subjects of the EHS systems successfully marshalled forms of legitimation denied to ordinary citizens even in flourishing democracies. If legibility creates the capacity for social engineering, it remains an open question how much scientists will be able to retain their privileges in the face of concerted efforts at social control.

The biologists and chemists at Eastern University went along with this appropriation of their authority and expertise only to the extent that the processes were consistent with their varied local habitus. I suspect that the willingness to bow down to the legal demand to produce safe laboratories and reorganize local cultures to do so is only in part a deference to law. More likely, I think, there is an aspect here of that recursive reflexivity Giddens describes, because this particular legal authority is constructed in part by science in its identification and specification of what constitutes a safety hazard. The identification of hazards is an ongoing process, constantly in the making. Thus, as science contributes to the institutionalization of safety as a part of our regimes of knowledge and risk, it subordinates itself, like the canonical liberal legal subject, to the principles and knowledge it helps to establish.

Nonetheless, by subjecting science to the same processes and techniques of accountability as just about everyone else—including industry, finance, and the police—this risk management of laboratories challenges the independence and autonomy that have characterized, if not fueled, the productivity of science. By demanding attention to the safety of laboratory habits, the regulatory regime appropriates attention, always a scarce resource. Regulatory activity is ultimately "focused on devising methods for ensuring that organizations and their staff pay attention to the "right" things. . . . Allocation of attention is not just about using a scarce resource efficiently, but is also about the right to decide for oneself what is important" (Heimer 2008, 30). Here is where the challenge to scientific authority may be most significant.

"In responding to the demand for [accountability], scientists are reshaping the relationships between existing disciplines . . . [and] the very matter they are creating" (McCarthy and Kelty, 2008, 3; 2010), engineering safety concerns into the very molecules they are synthesizing, making them "safe by design" (Kelty 2009).

If legally mandated organizational change is notoriously difficult, there is also evidence that organizational practices do change, often in response to institutional pressures and regulatory enforcement (Coslovsky 2011; Pires 2011; Huising and Silbey 2011), to which this chapter contributes another example. Perhaps repeated proclamations of regulatory failure and organizational sluggishness are simply a consequence of concentrated focus on the tails rather than the hump of the distribution of implementation and compliance practices (Silbey 2013; Land 2014; Basbug and Silbey 2021). Most legal regulation succeeds. That is, most people follow the rules most of the time (Ewick and Silbey 1998). This applies to the widest range of activities concerning, for example, economic markets and production, financial transactions, the education of children, the provision of medical care, and the organization of city streets and traffic lanes. Active law enforcement is normally directed to the few transactions, often less than 5 to 10 percent, that fall outside prescribed pathways. Success goes unnoticed because it "has become thoroughly institutionalized" (Heimer 2013; Heimer and Kuo 2021; Short 2013), part and parcel of the habituated and taken-for-granted conditions of everyday life, for example, through safety standards for building materials, logistical organization of public spaces, or the security of drinking water. Thus, while we might have appropriately expected faculty to be among the ten percent who frequently resist new regulatory mandates, especially those that interfere with investigator autonomy and laboratory habits, it is also possible that the mandated environmental management system might eventually become as routine—even if resented—as equal employment personnel policies, conflict-of-interest protocols, and institutional review boards (Stark 2011).

It is certainly too early to say whether these observations and hypotheses will prove prescient, or how the several variables (history, organization, practice) will plait to describe other laboratory cultures. If asked to predict, I would imagine that both the biologists and the chemists will sustain well-functioning EHS processes within their departments. I would expect that the next EPA inspection would not show much variation in compliance or violations between the two departments. What remains unclear, however, is how they connect to the university in general and what this experience bodes for other forms of legal regulation and control. After all, it was the particular cultures of biology and chemistry that mediated—by moderating—the demands for change. To the biologists, the EHS system appears to be just another piece of equipment, like another technician or a facility made available by the department—a set of externally imposed or available constraints, like the rules they so much opposed at the outset. Conversely, for the chemists, their work, labs, and students are personalized, and the safety regime is as well. For the chemists, the safety regime will be an internalized part of their laboratory practice and identity—while for the biologists, it will be another material resource.

The chymists are a strange class of mortals, impelled by an almost insane impulse to seek their pleasures amid smoke and vapor, soot and flame, poisons and poverty. Yet among all these evils I seem to live so sweetly that may I die if I were to change places with the Persian King.

—Johann Joachim Becher, *Physica Subterranea*, 1667

REFERENCES

Abbott, Andrew. 1988. *The System of Professions*. Chicago: University of Chicago Press.

Abbott, Kenneth W., David Levi-Faur, and Duncan Snidal. 2017. "Theorizing Regulatory Intermediaries: The RIT Model." *Annals of the American Academy of Political and Social Science* 670 (1): 14–35.

Aptean, http://www.aptean.com/additional-crm-and-erp-related-links-pages/erp-resources -folder/erp-system-definition, 1–26.2015.

Armenakis, Achilles A., and Arthur G. Bedeian. 1999. "Organizational Change: A Review of Theory and Research in the 1990s." *Journal of Management* 25 (3): 293–315.

Barley, Stephen R. 1986. "Technology as an Occasion for Structuring: Evidence from Observations of CT Scanners and the Social Order of Radiology Departments." *Administrative Science Quarterly* 31 (1): 78–108.

Barnett, William P., and Glenn R. Carroll. 1995. "Modeling Internal Organizational Change." *Annual Review of Sociology* 21 (1): 217–36.

Barrett, Michael, Eivor Oborn, Wanda J. Orlikowski, and JoAnne Yates. 2012. "Reconfiguring Boundary Relations: Robotic Innovations in Pharmacy Work." *Organization Science* 23 (5): 1448–66.

Barthe, Yannick. 2014. "Scientific Expertise in Situations of Controversy: A Sociological Testimony." *European Journal of Risk Regulation* 5: 14–24.

Basbug, G. and Susan S. Silbey. 2021. "Rank Has Its Privileges: Explaining Why Laboratory Safety Is a Persistent Challenge." (On file with author.)

Berman, Elizabeth Popp. 2008. "Why Did Universities Start Patenting? Institution-Building and the Road to the Bayh-Dole Act." *Social Studies of Science* 38 (6): 835–71.

——. 2012. "Explaining the Move Toward the Market in US Academic Science: How Institutional Logics Can Change Without Institutional Entrepreneurs." *Theory and Society* 41 (3): 261–99.

Bourdieu, Pierre. 1975. "The Specificity of the Scientific Field and the Social Conditions of the Progress of Reason." *Social Science Information* 14 (6): 19–47.

——. (1972) 1977. *Outline of a Theory of Practice*. Trans. Richard Nice. Cambridge Studies in Social and Cultural Anthropology 16. Cambridge: Cambridge University Press.

——. 1990. *Logic of Practice*. Trans. Richard Nice. Palo Alto, CA: Stanford University Press.

——. 1991. "The Peculiar History of Scientific Reason." *Sociological Forum* 6 (1): 3–26. ——. 2000. *Pascalian Meditations*. Palo Alto, CA: Stanford University Press.

Brivot, Marion. 2011. "Controls of Knowledge Production, Sharing and Use in Bureaucratized Professional Service Firms." *Organization Studies* 32 (4): 489–508.

Bruns, Hille C. 2009. "Leveraging Functionality in Safety Routines: Examining the Divergence of Rules and Performance." *Human Relations* 62 (9): 1399–1426.

Bumiller, Kristin. 2008. *In an Abusive State: How Neoliberalism Appropriated the Feminist Movement Against Sexual Violence*. Durham, NC: Duke University Press.

Camic, Charles. ——. 2011. "Bourdieu's Cleft Sociology of Science." *Minerva* 49 (3): 275–93.

——. 2013. "Bourdieu's Two Sociologies of Knowledge." In *Bourdieu and Historical Analysis*, ed. P. S. Gorski, 183–214. Durham, NC: Duke University Press.

Clarke, Adele E., and Joan H. Fujimura. 2014. *The Right Tools for the Job: At Work in Twentieth-Century Life Sciences*. Princeton Legacy Library 149. Princeton University Press.

Coglianese, Cary. 1997. "Assessing Consensus: The Promise and Performance of Negotiated Rulemaking." *Duke Law Review* 46:1255.

——. 2001. "Is Consensus an Appropriate Basis for Regulatory Policy?" Cambridge: Research Programs, John F. Kennedy School of Government, Harvard University.

Coglianese Cary and David Lazar. 2003. "Management-Based Regulation: Prescribing Private Management to Achieve Public Goals." *Law & Society Review* 37 (4) 691–730.

Cohen, Bernard P. 1989. *Developing Sociological Knowledge: Theory and Method*. 2nd ed. Monterey, CA: Wadsworth.

Cole, Simon. 1999. "What Counts for Identity? The Historical Origins of the Methodology of Latent Fingerprint Identification." *Science in Context* 12 (1): 139–72.

Coleman, Harry S., and Roland Wank, eds. 1951. *Laboratory Design: National Research Council Report on Design, Construction and Equipment of Laboratories*. New York: Reinhold.

Collins, Harry M., and Robert Evans. 2002. "The Third Wave of Science Studies: Studies of Expertise and Experience." *Social Studies of Science* 32 (2): 235–96.

Collins, Harry M., Robert Evans, and Mike Gorman. 2007. "Trading Zones and Interactional Expertise." *Studies in History and Philosophy of Science Part A* 38 (4): 657–66.

Collins, Harry M., and Trevor Pinch. 1998. *The Golem: What You Should Know About Science*. Cambridge University Press.

Collins, Randall. 2009. *The Sociology of Philosophies*. Cambridge, MA: Harvard University Press.

Cook, Karen S., Margaret Levi, and Russell Hardin. 2009. *Whom Can We Trust?: How Groups, Networks, and Institutions Make Trust Possible*. New York: Russell Sage Foundation.

Coslovsky, Salo V. 2011. "Relational Regulation in the Brazilian Ministério Publico: The Organizational Basis of Regulatory Responsiveness." *Regulation & Governance* 5 (1): 70–89.

Daston, Lorraine, and H. Otto Sibum. 2003. "Introduction: Scientific Personae and Their Histories." *Science in Context* 16 (1–2): 1.

Deutch, John M., and Richard K. Lester. 2004. *Making Technology Work: Applications in Energy and the Environment*. Cambridge University Press.

Dewey John. 1954 [1927]. *The Public and Its Problems*. New York: Henry Holt.

Dobbin, Frank. 2009. *Inventing Equal Opportunity*. Princeton, NJ: Princeton University Press.

Doing, Park. 2008. "Give Me a Laboratory and I Will Raise a Discipline: The Past, Present, and Future Politics of Laboratory Studies in STS." In *The Handbook of Science and Technology Studies*, 3rd ed., ed. Edward J. Hackett et al., 279–95. Cambridge, MA: MIT Press.

Drori, Gili S., John W. Meyer, Francisco O. Ramirez, and Evan Schofer. 2003. *Science in the Modern World Polity: Institutionalization and Globalization*. Palo Alto, CA: Stanford University Press.

Edelman, Lauren B. 1992. "Legal Ambiguity and Symbolic Structures: Organizational Mediation of Civil Rights Law." *American Journal of Sociology* 97 (6): 1531–76.

Ehrlich, Eugene. (1913) 1962. *Fundamental Principles of the Sociology of Law*. Livingston, NJ: Transaction.

Espeland, Wendy Nelson. 1998. *The Struggle for Water: Politics, Rationality, and Identity in the American Southwest*. Chicago: University of Chicago Press.

——. 2003. "Understanding Law in Relation to Other Forms of Authority." In *AMICI, Newsletter of the Sociology of Law Section, American Sociological Association* (Fall 2003).

Evans, Joelle. 2012. "Moral Frictions: Ethics, Creativity and Social Responsibility in Stem Cell Science." PhD thesis, Massachusetts Institute of Technology.

——. 2014. "Resisting or Governing Risk? Professional Struggles and the Regulation of Safe Science." In *Academy of Management Proceedings*. https://doi.org/10.5465/ambpp.2014.18.

Evans, Joelle, Ruthanne Huising, and Susan S. Silbey. 2016. "Accounting for Accounts: Crafting Ethnographic Validity through Team Ethnography." In *Handbook of Qualitative Organizational Research: Innovative Pathways and Methods*, ed. Kimberly D. Elsbach and Roderick M. Kramer, 143–55. New York: Routledge.

Evans, Joelle, and Susan S. Silbey. 2021. "Co-opting Regulation: Professional Control Through Discretionary Mobilization of Legal Prescriptions and Expert Knowledge." *Organization Science*.

Evans, Robert, and Harry Collins. 2008. "Expertise: From Attribute to Attribution and Back Again?" In *The Handbook of Science and Technology Studies*, 3rd ed., ed. Edward J. Hackett, Olga Amsterdamska, Michael Lynch, and Judy Wajcman, 609–30. MIT Press.

Ewick, Patricia, and Susan S. Silbey. 1998. *The Common Place of Law: Stories from Everyday Life*. University of Chicago Press.

Ezrahi, Yaron. 1990. *The Descent of Icarus: Science and the Transformation of Contemporary Democracy*. Cambridge, MA: Harvard University Press.

Faigman, David L. 1999. *Legal Alchemy: The Use and Misuse of Science in the Law*. New York: W. H. Freeman.

Fleck, Ludwik. 1979. *Genesis and Development of a Scientific Fact*. Chicago: University of Chicago Press (First published in German, 1935).

Fligstein, Neil, and Doug McAdam. 2012. *A Theory of Fields*. Oxford University Press.

Foster, Jacob G., Andrey Rzhetsky, and James A. Evans. 2015. "Tradition and Innovation in Scientists' Research Strategies." *American Sociological Review* 80 (5): 875–908.

Foucault, G, and T. Lemke. 1999. "Governmentality and the Risk Society." *Economy and Society* 28 (1): 138–48.

Freidson, Eliot. 2001. *Professionalism, the Third Logic: On the Practice of Knowledge*. Cambridge: Polity.

Fujimura, Joan H. 1987. "Constructing 'Do-Able' Problems in Cancer Research: Articulating Alignment." *Social Studies of Science* 17 (2): 257–93.

——. 1992. "Crafting Science: Standardized Packages, Boundary Objects, and 'Translation.'" In *Science as Culture and Practice*, ed. Andrew Pickering, 168–211. University of Chicago Press.

Galison, Peter. 1997. *Image and Logic: A Material Culture of Microphysics*. University of Chicago Press.

Galison, Peter and Emily Thompson (editors). 1999. *The Architecture of Science*. Cambridge, MA: MIT Press.

Gallagher, K. P., Jung, J., Dobbin, F. 2015. "The Chief Risk Officer as Trojan Horse: How Sarbanes-Oxley Promoted the Abuse of Risky Derivatives." Paper presented at 2015 annual meeting of the American Sociological Association. Paper on file with author.

Galperin, R. 2015. "Organizational Powers: New Entry and Change in Professionalized Fields." SSRN, http://papers.ssrn.com/sol3/papers.cfm?abstract_id=1873545, downloaded 5.11.2016.

Giddens, Anthony. 1991. *The Consequences of Modernity*. Palo Alto, CA: Stanford University Press.

Gieryn, Thomas F. 1983. "Boundary-Work and the Demarcation of Science from Non-Science: Strains and Interests in Professional Ideologies of Scientists." *American Sociological Review* 48 (6): 781–95.

——. 1998. "Biotechnology's Private Parts (and Some Public Ones)." In *Making Space for Science: Territorial Themes in Shaping of Knowledge*, ed. Crosbie Smith and Jon Agar, 281–312. New York: St. Martin's.

——. 1999a. *Cultural Boundaries of Science: Credibility on the Line*. Chicago: University of Chicago Press.

——. 1999b. 'Two Faces on Science: Building Identities for Molecular Biology and Biotechnology." In Peter Galison & Emily Thompson (eds), *The Architecture of Science*, ed. Peter Galison and Emily Thompson, 423–55. Cambridge, MA: MIT Press.

——. 2002. "Three Truth-Spots." *Journal of the History of the Behavioral Sciences* 38 (2): 113–32.

Gray, Garry C., and Susan S. Silbey. 2014. "Governing Inside the Organization: Interpreting Regulation and Compliance." *American Journal of Sociology* 120 (1): 96–145.

Grüne-Yanoff, Till. 2016. "Why Behavioural Policy Needs Mechanistic Evidence." *Economics & Philosophy* 33 (3): 463–83.

Guetzkow, Joshua, Michèle Lamont, and Grégoire Mallard. 2004. "What Is Originality in the Humanities and the Social Sciences?" *American Sociological Review* 69 (2): 190–212.

Gunningham, Neil, Robert A. Kagan, and Dorothy Thornton. 2004. "Social License and Environmental Protection: Why Businesses Go Beyond Compliance." *Law & Social Inquiry* 29 (2): 307–41.

Gusterson, H. 2000. "How Not to Construct a Radioactive Waste Incinerator." Science, Technology, and Human Values 25 (3):332–51.

Guston, David H. 1999. "Stabilizing the Boundary Between US Politics and Science: The Role of the Office of Technology Transfer as a Boundary Organization." *Social Studies of Science* 29 (1): 87–111.

——. 2000. *Between Politics and Science: Assuring the Integrity and Productivity of research*. New York: Cambridge University Press.

——. 2001. "Boundary Organizations in Environmental Policy and Science: An Introduction." *Science, Technology & Human Values* 26 (4): 399–409.

Haack, Susan. 2006. *Pragmatism, Old and New: Selected Writings*. New York: Prometheus.

Hackett, Edward J. 1994. "A Social Control Perspective on Scientific Misconduct." *Journal of Higher Education* 65 (3): 242–60.

——. 2005. "Essential Tensions: Identity, Control, and Risk in Research." *Social Studies of Science* 35 (5): 787–826.

Hardin, R. 2002. *Trust and Trustworthiness*. New York: Russell Sage Foundation.

Hawkins, Keith, and John M. Thomas. 1984a. "The Enforcement Process in Regulatory Bureaucracies." *Enforcing Regulation* 3: 13–15.

——. eds. 1984b. *Enforcing Regulation*. Kluwer-Nijhoff.

Heimer, Carol A. 1999. "Competing Institutions: Law, Medicine, and Family in Neonatal Intensive Care." *Law and Society Review* 33 (1): 17–66.

——. 2008. "Thinking About How to Avoid Thought: Deep Norms, Shallow Rules, and the Structure of Attention." *Regulation & Governance* 2 (1): 30–47.

——. 2013. "Resilience in the Middle: Contributions of Regulated Organizations to Regulatory Success." *Annals of the American Academy of Political and Social Science* 649 (1): 139–56.

Heimer Carol A., and Kuo E. 2021. "Subterranean Successes: Durable regulation aand regulatory endowments" *Regulation & Governance* July.

Heimer, Carol A., and Lisa R. Staffen. 1998. *For the Sake of the Children: The Social Organization of Responsibility in the Hospital and the Home.* Chicago: University of Chicago Press.

Hoagland, M. 1990. *Toward The Habit of Truth: A Life in Science.* New York: Norton.

Hoebel E.A. and Llewellyn, K. 1941. *The Cheyenne Way.* Norman: University of Oklahoma Press.

Huising, Ruthanne. 2014. "The Erosion of Expert Control Through Censure Episodes." *Organization Science* 25 (6): 1633–61.

——. 2015. "To Hive or to Hold? Producing Professional Authority Through Scut Work." *Administrative Science Quarterly* 60 (2): 263–99.

——. 2019. "Pragmatic Regulatory Design: The Case of Human Pathogens and Toxins Regulations in Canada." *Entreprises et histoire* 4: 58–69.

Huising, Ruthanne, and Susan S. Silbey. 2011. "Governing the Gap: Forging Safe Science Through Relational Regulation." *Regulation & Governance* 5 (1): 14–42.

——. 2018. "From Nudge to Culture and Back Again: Coalface Governance in the Regulated Organization." *Annual Review of Law and Social Science* 14: 91–114.

Jackson, Catherine M. 2011. "Chemistry as the Defining Science: Discipline and Training in Nineteenth-Century Chemical Laboratories." *Endeavour* 35 (2–3): 55–62.

——. 2016. "The Laboratory." In *A Companion to the History of Science,* ed. Bernard Lightman. Wiley.

Jasanoff, Sheila. 1987. "Biology and the Bill of Rights: Can Science Reframe the Constitution." *American Journal of Law and Medicine* 13: 249–89.

——. 2003. "(No?) Accounting for Expertise." *Science and Public Policy* 30 (3): 157–62.

——. 2009. *The Fifth Branch: Science Advisers as Policymakers.* Cambridge, MA: Harvard University Press.

Jones C.A. 1994. *Expert Witnesses.* Oxford: Clarendon Press.

Kaiser, David. 2005. *Pedagogy and the Practice of Science: Historical and Contemporary Perspectives.* MIT Press.

Kaiser, David, Kenji Ito, and Karl Hall. 2004. "Spreading the Tools of Theory: Feynman Diagrams in the USA, Japan, and the Soviet Union." *Social Studies of Science* 34 (6): 879–922.

Kellogg, Katherine C. 2009. "Operating Room: Relational Spaces and Microinstitutional Change in Surgery." *American Journal of Sociology* 115 (3): 657–711.

——. 2011. *Challenging Operations: Medical Reform and Resistance in Surgery.* University of Chicago Press.

Kellogg, Katherine C., Wanda J. Orlikowski, and JoAnne Yates. 2006. "Life in the Trading Zone: Structuring Coordination Across Boundaries in Postbureaucratic Organizations." *Organization Science* 17 (1): 22–44.

Kelty, Christopher M. 2009. "Beyond Implications and Applications: The Story of 'Safety by Design.'" *NanoEthics* 3 (2): 79–96.

Knorr Cetina, Karin D. 1995. "Laboratory Studies: The Cultural Approach to the Study of Science." In *Handbook of Science and Technology Studies*, ed. S. Jasanoff. Thousand Oaks, CA: Sage.

——. 2004. "Capturing Markets? A Review Essay on Harrison White on Producer Markets." *Socio-Economic Review* 2 (1): 137–47.

——. 2009. *Epistemic Cultures: How the Sciences Make Knowledge*. Cambridge, MA: Harvard University Press.

Knorr Cetina, Karin, and Urs Bruegger. 2002. "Global Microstructures: The Virtual Societies of Financial Markets." *American Journal of Sociology* 107 (4): 905–50.

Knorr Cetina, Karin, and A. Preda. 2004. *The Sociology of Financial Markets*. New York: Oxford University Press.

Lamont, Michèle. 2009. *How Professors Think: Inside the Curious World of Academic Judgment*. Harvard University Press.

Lamont, Michèle, and Virág Molnár. 2002. "The Study of Boundaries in the Social Sciences." *Annual Review of Sociology* 28 (1): 167–95.

Land, Kenneth C. 2014. "Delinquency Referrals; Predictive and Protective Factors for Serious, Violent, and Chronic Offenders; and Juvenile Justice Interventions." *Criminology & Public Policy* 13: 79–82.

Latour, Bruno. 1987. *Science in Action: How to Follow Scientists and Engineers through Society*. Cambridge, MA: Harvard University Press.

Latour, Bruno, and Steve Woolgar. 1986 [1979]. *Laboratory Life: The Construction of Scientific Facts. Princeton*: Princeton, NJ: Princeton University Press.

Lazega, Emmanuel. 2001. *The Collegial Phenomenon: The Social Mechanisms of Cooperation in a Corporate Law Firm*. Oxford: Oxford University Press.

Lépinay, Vincent Antonin. 2011. *Codes of Finance: Engineering Derivatives in a Global Bank*. Princeton University Press.

Lynch, Michael E. 1985. *Art and Artifact in Laboratory Science*. London: Routledge and Kegan Paul.

——. 1991. "Laboratory Space and the Technological Complex: An Investigation of Topical Contextures." *Science in Context* 4 (1): 51–78.

Lynch, Michael E., Simon A. Cole, Ruth McNally, and Kathleen Jordan. 2010. *Truth Machine: The Contentious History of DNA Fingerprinting*. Chicago: University of Chicago Press.

MacIntyre, Alasdair. 2007. *After Virtue*. South Bend, IN: University of Notre Dame Press.

McCarthy, Elise, and Christopher Kelty. 2008. "Responsibility and Nanotechnology." Department of Anthropology, Rice University.

——. 2010. "Responsibility and Nanotechnology." *Social Studies of Science* 40 (3): 405–32.

Merton, Robert K. 1936. "The Unanticipated Consequences of Purposive Social Action." *American Sociological Review* 1 (6): 894–904.

——. 1973. *The Sociology of Science: Theoretical and Empirical Investigations*. Chicago: University of Chicago Press.

Miller, Clark. 2001. "Hybrid Management: Boundary Organizations, Science Policy, and Environmental Governance in the Climate Regime." *Science, Technology, & Human Values* 26 (4): 478–500.

Mintzberg, Henry. 1979. *The Structuring of Organizations*. Upper Saddle River, NJ: Prentice Hall.

Moore, Kelly. 1996. "Organizing Integrity: American Science and the Creation of Public Interest Organizations, 1955–1975." *American Journal of Sociology* 101 (6):1592–627.

Morris, Peter J. T. 2015. *The Matter Factory: A History of the Chemistry Laboratory*. London: Reaktion.

Myers, Natasha. 2008. "Molecular Embodiments and the Body-Work of Modeling in Protein Crystallography." *Social Studies of Science* 38 (2): 163–99.

——. 2012. "Dance Your PhD: Embodied Animations, Body Experiments, and the Affective Entanglements of Life Science Research." *Body & Society* 18 (1): 151–89.

National Research Council. 2010. "Surrounded by Science: Learning Science in Informal Environments. Washington, DC: The National Academies Press, doi:10.17226/12614

National Research Council (US) Committee on Prudent Practices in the Laboratory. (2011). Prudent Practices in the Laboratory: Handling and Management of Chemical Hazards: Updated Version.

National Research Council. 2014. *Safe Science: Promoting a Culture of Safety in Academic Chemical Research*. Washington, DC: The National Academies Press. https://doi.org/10.17226/18706.

Novick, Sheldon M, ed. 1995. *The Collected Works of Justice Holmes: Complete Public Writings and Selected Judicial Opinions of Oliver Wendell Holmes*, Vol 3. Chicago: University of Chicago Press, 1995.

Owen-Smith, Jason, and Walter W. Powell. 2001. "To Patent or Not: Faculty Decisions and Institutional Success at Technology Transfer." *Journal of Technology Transfer* 26 (1): 99–114.

Owens, Larry. 1990. "MIT and the Federal 'Angel': Academic R & D and the Federal-Private Corporation before World War II." *Isis* 81 (2):188–213.

Paradeise, Catherine, and Jean-Claude Thoenig. 2013. "Academic Institutions in Search of Quality: Local Orders and Global Standards." *Organization Studies* 34 (2): 189–218.

Perrow, Charles. 2011. *Normal Accidents: Living with High-Risk Technologies*. Princeton, NJ: Princeton University Press.

Peterson, David. 2015. "All That Is Solid: Bench-Building at the Frontiers of Two Experimental Sciences." *American Sociological Review* 80 (6): 1201–25.

Pires, Roberto R. C. 2011. "Beyond the Fear of Discretion: Flexibility, Performance, and Accountability in the Management of Regulatory Bureaucracies." *Regulation & Governance* 5 (1): 43–69.

Porter, Theodore M. 2020. *Trust in Numbers: The Pursuit of Objectivity in Science and Public Life*. Princeton, NJ: Princeton University Press.

Powell, Walter W., and Jason Owen-Smith. 1998. "Universities and the Market for Intellectual Property in the Life Sciences." *Journal of Policy Analysis and* 17 (2): 253–77.

Powell, Walter W., Douglas R. White, Kenneth W. Koput, and Jason Owen-Smith. 2005. "Network Dynamics and Field Evolution: The Growth of Interorganizational Collaboration in the Life Sciences." *American Journal of Sociology* 110 (4): 1132–1205.

Power Michael. 1997. *The Audit Society: Rituals of Verification*. Oxford: Oxford University Press.

Rheinberger, Hans-Jorg. 1997. *Toward a History of Epistemic Things: Synthesizing Proteins in the Test Tube*. Palo Alto, CA: Stanford University Press.

Roqueplo, P. 1997. *Entre savoir et decision, L'expertise scientifique*. Paris: INRA.

Rosental, Claude. 2003. "Certifying Knowledge: The Sociology of a Logical Theorem" *American Sociological Review* 68: 623–644.

Scott James C. 1998. *Seeing Like a State: How Certain Schemes to Improve the Human Condition Have Failed*. New Haven, CT: Yale University Press.

Seron, Carroll, and Susan S. Silbey. 2009. "The Dialectic Between Expert Knowledge and Professional Discretion: Accreditation, Social Control and the Limits of Instrumental Logic." *Engineering Studies* 1 (2): 101–27.

Shapin, Steven. 1994. *A Social History of Truth: Civility and Science in 17th Century England*. University of Chicago Press.

——. 1988. "The House of Experiment in Seventeenth-Century England." *Isis* 79 (3): 373–404.

——. 1998. "The Philosopher and the Chicken: On the Dietetics of Disembodied Knowledge." In *Science Incarnate: Historical Embodiments of Natural Knowledge*, ed. Christopher Lawrence and Steven Shapin, 21–50. University of Chicago Press.

——. 2004. "Who Is the Industrial Scientist? Commentary from Academic Sociology and from the Shop-Floor in the United States, ca. 1900–ca. 1970." In *The Science–Industry Nexus: History, Policy, Implications*, ed. Karl Grandin, Nina Wormbs, and Sven Widmalm, 337–63. Science History Publications.

Shibayama, Sotaro, John P. Walsh, and Yasunori Baba. 2012. "Academic Entrepreneurship and Exchange of Scientific Resources: Material Transfer in Life and Materials Sciences in Japanese Universities." *American Sociological Review* 77 (5): 804–30.

Short, Jodi L. 2013. "Self-Regulation in the Regulatory Void: 'Blue Moon' or 'Bad Moon?'" *Annals of the American Academy of Political and Social Science* 649 (1): 22–34.

Silbey, Susan S. "Organizational Challenges to Regulatory Enforcement and Compliance: A New Common Sense About Regulation," Editor's Introduction." *Annals of the American Academy of Political and Social Science*, September 2013.

Silbey, Susan S. and Patricia Ewick. 2003. "The Architecture of Authority: The Place of Law in the Space of Science." In *The Place of Law*, ed. Austin Sarat, Lawrence Douglas, and Martha Umphrey, 77–108. University of Michigan Press.

Small, Mario Luis. (2009). "'How many cases do I need?' On Science and the Logic of Case Selection in Field-Based Research." *Ethnography* 10 (1), 5–38.

Stark, Laura. 2011. *Behind Closed Doors: IRBs and the Making of Ethical Research*. Chicago: University of Chicago Press.

Star, Susan Leigh, and James R. Griesemer. 1989. "Institutional Ecology, 'Translations' and Boundary Objects: Amateurs and Professionals in Berkeley's Museum of Vertebrate Zoology, 1907–1939." *Social Studies of Science* 19 (3): 387–420.

Stephens, N., Atkinson, P., & Glasner, P. 2011. "Documenting the doable and doing the documented: bridging strategies at the UK Stem Cell Bank." Social Studies of Science, Vol 41 (6) pp. 791–813.

Stone, Deborah. 2002. *Policy Paradox: The Art of Political Decision Making*. New York: Norton.

Strathern, Marilyn. 2000. *Audit Cultures: Anthropological Studies in Accountability, Ethics, and the Academy*. Psychology Press.

Thaler, Richard H., and Cass R. Sunstein. 2008. *Nudge: Improving Decisions about Health, Wealth, and Happiness*. New York: Penguin.

Thoenig, Jean-Claude, and Catherine Paradeise. 2014. "Organizational Governance and the Production of Academic Quality: Lessons from Two Top US Research Universities." *Minerva* 52 (4): 381–417.

Turco, Catherine. 2012. "Difficult Decoupling: Employee Resistance to the Commercialization of Personal Settings." *American Journal of Sociology* 118 (2): 380–419.

Waring, Justin, and Graeme Currie. 2009. "Managing Expert Knowledge: Organizational Challenges and Managerial Futures for the UK Medical Profession." *Organization Studies* 30 (7): 755–78.

Weber, Max. [1946] "Science as a Vocation." In *From Max Weber: Essays in Sociology*, trans. H. H. Gerth and C. Wright Mills. Oxford: Oxford University Press

Weick, Karl E. 1976. "Educational Organizations as Loosely Coupled Systems." *Administrative Science Quarterly* 20(1): 1–19.

Wilson, James Q. 1980. *The Politics of Regulation*. New York: Basic Books.

Wright, Susan. 1994. *Molecular Politics: Developing American and British Regulatory Policy for Genetic Engineering, 1972–1982*. Chicago: University of Chicago Press.

NOTES

1. The sociology of science has documented the ways in which science varies: by the degrees of social embeddedness and material exchange (Kaiser, Ito, and Hall 2004; Shibayama, Walsh, and Baba 2012); networks of collaboration (Powell et al. 2005; Collins, Evans, and Gorman 2007); organization of space (Lynch 1991; Gieryn 1999b, 2002; Silbey and Ewick 2003) and of bodies (Myers 2008, 2012; Peterson 2015); degree to which scientists invest in tradition or innovation (Foster, Rzhetsky and Evans 2015); production of intellectual property (Owen-Smith and Powell 2001); relationships among theory, experiments, and available technology (Galison 1997); experimental systems (Rheinberger 1997); meanings of data (Latour and Woolgar 1986; Lynch 1985; Collins and Pinch 1998); and the differential constructions of truth, or what Knorr Cetina (2009) calls the "epistemic cultures"—the ways in which different fields of science constitute knowledge.

2. I do not specify the exact date or federal circuit because we do not name the institution or the persons, using pseudonyms only.

3. Resource Conservation and Recovery Act 1976 (RCRA), 40 C.F.R. part 260–280; Clean Air Act 1990 (CAA) Title 42, chap. 85; Clean Water Act (CWA) P.O. 92–500, 86 Stat. 816 (1972), 33 U.S.C. 1251 et seq.

4. I use the term *green* as a colloquial label to designate a wide spectrum of conditions and practices designed to secure clean air and water and conservation of natural resources. It is not meant to suggest or ally with any political party or lobby.

5. Interview with EPA attorneys on file with author.

6. For Hoebel and Llewellyn (1941), one route to the law stuff of a culture was ideological and traced the extant rules of social control for proper channeling and controlling behavior. In this first path, the scholar would attempt to map the official, formal norms of a society, those rules of right behavior for which individuals do not retain authority to define. The second mode of legal inquiry should explore, they urged, the patterns

according to which behavior actually, rather than ideally, occurs. This became the standard model of empirical and sociological research for several generations. The third path, outlined here, involves the search for trouble cases by which to explicate what Ehrlich ([1913] 1962) called the living law, which regulates social life, often commanding much more authority and conformity than may be the rules of decision for particular cases. By excavating cases of trouble, Llewellyn and Hoebel attempted to integrate the three methods and show the relationship between the living and the jurisprudential law.

7. *PI* is the colloquial term used by the federal government as well as universities to refer to researchers with authority to secure funding to conduct research without supervision.

8. OSHA Lab Standard 29 CFR 1910.1450. *Federal Register* 55, no.21 (Wednesday, January 31, 1990), Rules and Regulations. The OSHA Lab Standard required the appointment of a department chemical hygiene officers, production of a safety handbook, rules for regular meetings, and yearly review and revision of the handbook.

9. Although many academic chemists worked in ordinary street clothes until the mid-1930s, when lab coats became more common, there are many pictures of chemists wearing protective aprons from the mid-nineteenth century on.

10. CDC partners with the U.S. National Institutes of Health to publish biosafety guidelines for protecting workers and preventing exposures in biological laboratories (https://www .cdc.gov/safelabs/resources-tools/biosafety-resources-and-tools.html). CDC also serves as the World Health Organization's Collaborating Centre for Applied Biosafety Programmes and Training. CDC partners with renowned organizations to sponsor the biennial International Symposium on Biosafety, produces online training, and offers other downloadable materials that may be useful to laboratorians nationally or around the world.

11. This authority is, however, increasingly confined by an escalating number of regulations; for example, concerning limits on uses associated with funding from public and private sources as well as regulations concerning harassment and appropriate interactions with subordinates, including students and staff.

12. Clarke and Fujimura (1992, 30) note that historians use the term "black box" differently, to mean questions that are set aside and not pursued for the moment. This is similar to use of the term by philosophers and engineers, where the functioning mechanism is unquestioned, and focus is concentrated on the inputs and outputs of the box.

PART III. Democracy

12. Accidental Discovery and the Pragmatist Theory of Action

THE EMERGENCE OF A BOSTON POLICE AND BLACK MINISTERS PARTNERSHIP

CHRISTOPHER WINSHIP

INTRODUCTION

It is a Tuesday afternoon in July 2019. A crowd of more than fifty individuals is gathered in front of the East Boston Police Precinct Station for the weekly Tuesday night Neighborhood Walk for Peace. The walks, which started with the good weather in June, will last until the cold weather arrives in October. They are organized by the Reverend Mark Scott, associate pastor at the Azusa Christian Church in North Dorchester, in conjunction with the Boston Police Department (BPD).

Several ministers and priests from local churches are present. Today, as is often the case, Boston Police Commissioner William Evans is here, along with half a dozen members of his command staff and officers from the precinct. Several times over the summer, Mayor Walsh will join the group, resulting in the march being covered by local TV stations.

The most commanding presence, however, are the local residents. Several dozen are here, holding signs that read "Peace," "Peace Now," or "No More Guns." They range in age from young children to the elderly. There is much excited banter. They talk among themselves, and with the police and clergy. The walk tonight will proceed like a parade.

After a prayer, a procession winds through the East Boston neighborhood. Members of the group, particularly BPD officers and the clergy, stop and talk with residents standing in their yards in front of their houses. A little more than an hour later, the group stops in a small square for a concluding prayer. Local junior high school students present a dance performance from different Latin American countries. Thirty minutes later, the crowd disperses and the police commissioner is off to another engagement.

I have been and will go on many of these walks over multiple summers. There is a ritual quality to their performance. They occur weekly in East Boston and in three other neighborhoods where gang violence is common. The predominantly Latinx East Boston has less violence than the other three neighborhoods (which are majority Black), but it is also home to Boston's most violent gang, MS-13. In other neighborhoods, fewer residents attend. In Mattapan, a neighborhood with few nonprofit organizations (Levine 2016), a Peace Walk may involve only police and clergy.

The weekly Peace Walks in Boston's neighborhoods are one manifestation of an informal partnership that has existed between Boston's communities of color and the Boston Police Department since the mid-1990s. Besides the Peace Walks, there are meetings every Wednesday morning at the Ella J. Baker House, home of the Azusa Christian Church, involving clergy, various police officers—precinct captains, the gang unit, mass transit police, the school police, and community residents—along with staff from the government and nonprofit social service organizations. These meetings have been going on since 1998; similar meetings occur regularly in other neighborhoods. As part of the several decades-old Home-Front program (https://bpdnews.com/operation-homefront), clergy and police officers spend Thursday nights visiting the homes of youth whom schools have identified as being in trouble and at risk of becoming gang involved. On a less regular basis, there are basketball games with police and youth, neighborhood barbecues, and "flashlight walks," which occur later at night.

From late 1996 through the mid-2000s, the BPD and the Ten Point Coalition, which is comprised of inner-city Black ministers, have worked together to address youth violence across Boston (Braga and Winship 2006). Today, the Ten Point Coalition exists mostly in name only, its initial founders engaged fully in other agendas (Braga, Hureau, and Winship 2008). Numerous other churches and nonprofits have taken up the coalition's original aim, working with the BPD to reduce violence in their neighborhoods.

Although the idea of a partnership between inner-city ministers and the police may seem unusual, it is particularly surprising given Boston's long history of racial turmoil. During the 1970s and early 1980s in particular, Boston's school busing crisis rendered the city a national symbol of northern racism. The partnership is equally unexpected given the prior animosity between the Ten Point ministers and the Boston police. As I detail below, during this earlier period, the BPD was under constant and vehement criticism by both the local press and community activists. Among the most vehement critics of the Boston police was Reverend Eugene Rivers, one of the founders of Boston's Ten Point Coalition.

How did two groups who were figuratively at each other's throats at the beginning of the 1990s form a partnership just a few years later—a partnership that has been recognized internationally for effectively addressing youth violence? No leadership from above demanded that the two parties negotiate a more constructive relationship for the public good. The two groups never met to develop any sort of master plan. And there was no attempt to follow the example of other cities or other groups. In short, there was no formal deliberative process that produced this collaboration. Putting it figuratively, in this story there was no table around which ministers and police discussed how to form a parternship. Yet, after a few short years, these groups had institutionalized a relationship that relied on a complex set of mutual understandings.

The goal of this chapter is to explain this surprising Boston story. My purpose in doing so is twofold. First, I show that pragmatist ideas can at least partly explain the curious emergence of this police-ministerial partnership. Second, I use this case to argue that the pragmatist concept of periods of interdeterminancy and problem-solving based on creative intelligence needs to be expanded to include what I call *wandering* and the possibility of unintended or accidental discovery. This expansion would more accurately recognize instances of effective problem solving that do not originate from individual agents actively experiementing with alternatives.

Consider a mundane example. I have left my wallet at home and have no money for lunch. I find it too embarrassing to ask my colleagues for a loan. As I am walking (wandering) with no idea how to solve my problem, I look down and see (discover) a ten-dollar bill, which I pick up. My problem is solved. There is discovery, but no specific intentionality or creativity.

The problem to be solved with respect to lunch is minor. The Boston story shows that an analogous process may take place in the context of problems that are far more serious and even existential. A central pragmist argument is that changes in the environment can create problems (Dewey 1910). Conversely, I suggest that solutions may simply appear, though they are solutions only if they are recognized as such.

In my analysis I rely on two key components of pragmatist theory. First and foremost is the theory's focus on habits, problems, problem-solving, and creativity as found principally in Dewey (1910) and discussed at length by Joas (1996, 126–27). I use these elements of the theory to explain how change became necessary and how it came about. Second, I use Mead's analysis of the central importance of intersubjectivity for establishing meaning and for the coordination of human behavior. As I argue here, it is the breakdown of the police and ministers' separate intersubjectivities and the establishment of a new, shared one that forms the core of the Boston story.

Although Karl Weick was not explicitly recognized as a pragmatist, his work touches on many pragmatist themes.[1] Weick's concept of retrospective sensemaking is an essential part of my explanation of the emergence of the police-minister partnership. Most important, as I describe in this chapter, I use his notion of sensemaking as a way to delineate the different stages of the Boston story.

As will be clear in the telling, events of different types are critical elements in moving the story forward. Although events are components in Mead's (1932) theory, his discussion of events is abstract and complicated (Joas 1997). A more relevant and contemporary discussion of events is that by Sewell (2005), who points out the importance of events as creating demands for cultural change. Within a pragmatist framework, events potentially create problems that need to be solved, but, as I will argue, they also can provide solutions. In the Boston story, it is events of various types that propel the story forward and, as such, are the critical factor in causing the BPD and the Ten Point ministers to change their understanding of themselves, each other, and inner-city violence.

This chapter contributes to the sociological literature in two ways. First, I show that a pragmatist theory of action can explain change at the meso level. A number of authors of both classic pragmatism and neopragmatism have primarily provided theories of change at an individual or micro level (Dewey 1930, 1938; Putnam 1989; Anderson 2006; Gross 2009, 2018). Second, in explaining the partnering of police and ministers in Boston, a precursor to the Ten Point Coalition's full institutionalization, I contribute to the nascent sociological literature on institutional emergence (Stark 1996; Sawyer 2005, Padgett and Powell 2012).

In the following section, I briefly summarize the pragmatist theories of action, creativity, and intersubjectivity. In the subsequent sections, I describe the Boston story at length, pausing at critical points to introduce pragmatist interpretations of the events that I describe. In the discussion section, I more thoroughly develop the pragmatist themes that emerge from this story. In the appendix, I discuss my methodology. I conclude by articulating the importance of the Boston story for pragmatist-based sociological theory.

PRAGMATISM'S THEORETICAL MODEL

The pragmatist theory of action is perhaps pragmatist's theory of action most important contribution to sociology. Numerous authors—including the classic pragmatists Peirce, James, Dewey, and Mead—all described key components of this theory (Peirce 1931–58; Dewey 1922, 1925; James 1890, 1909; Mead 1932, 1938) as have contemporary scholars, such as Joas (1996), Kilpinen (2008), Whitford (2002), Gross (2009), Anderson (2010), and Wehrwein and Winship (2018). The effort here is to move beyond a purely instrumental understanding of action (Joas 1990, 1996; Gross 2009; Whitford 2002). To quote Joas,

> My claim is not, therefore, that sociology must be opened up to these currents of thought. Rather, I am saying the conception of action which is so crucial to how sociology understands itself needs to be reconstructed in such a way that this conception is no longer confined to the alternative of a model of rational action versus normatively oriented action, but is able to incorporate the creative dimension of human action into its conceptual structure and thus also take adequate account of the intellectual currents which hinge on this dimension. (Joas 1996, 72)

Creativity is central, as it allows pragmatists to move beyond more traditional socio-logical theories of action. Pragmatists believe that action can be instrumental, but generally only in a highly localized way (Whitford 2002). This assumption is captured by Dewey's famous phrase that individuals have "ends-in-view" in contrast to long-range goals (Dewey 1922, 223–37).

The key sequence in the pragmatist theory of action is as follows: current habits, problems that undermine habits, creative/intelligent problem-solving, new habits. To quote Joas again,

> According to this model, all perception of the world and all action in the world is anchored in an unreflected belief in self-evident given facts and successful habits. However, this belief, and the routines of action based upon it, are repeatedly shattered; what has previously been habitual, apparently automatic procedure of action is interrupted. The world reveals itself to have shattered our unreflected expectations. . . . And the only way out of this phase is a reconstruction of the interpreted context. . . . This reconstruction is a creative achievement on the part of the actor. (Joas 1996, 128–29)

"Habits" here are to be understood broadly as "regular behavior" and may be conscious or unconscious (Kilpinen 2009). Joas's "shattering" is change that results from the inapplicability of our current habits and the necessity of finding new ones. As we formulate these new habits, problem-solving in the form of creative intelligence comes into play. Thus, the central sequence in the pragmatist theory of action is: current habits, problem creativity/problem-solving, new habits.

My analysis will point to a tension between the facts of the Boston story and the creativity/problem-solving stage within this pragmatist sequence. According to Joas (1990, 1770), creative solutions are found through "experimenting intelligence." The emphasis here on "intelligence" possibly, though not necessarily, suggests that the individual is the critical agent in problem-solving. The notion of "experimenting" suggests the active trial of different possible solutions to the current problem.

Neither individual intelligence nor the active, conscious pursuit of alternatives fits the Boston story. Rather, much of the story is closer to directionless wandering, or Lindblom's (1959) "muddling through," a concept that Joas explicitly rejects as representing a type of intelligence (Joas 1996, 127).[2] As such, muddling is not, in Kilpinen's (2008) terms, a "mind-first" theory that creativity would seem to imply. The Boston story thus calls into question the claim that problem-solving is *always* a function of creativity. By putting so much emphasis on creativity, the pragmatist theory of action implies a limited type of instrumentality. As I argue in this chapter, it is possible for action to be both noninstrumental and nonhabitual (also see Winship 2017).

One of the most important contributions of Mead to pragmatist thought is his focus on intersubjectivity.[3] As Joas states, Mead is concerned implicitly with "practical intersubjectivity" (Joas 1990, 1996, 1997). For Mead, social order is established not in normative agreement but, rather, in the ability of a group to coordinate its action in order to solve problems and achieve common goals (Joas

1990, 172, 185).[4] A key implication is that creativity is found in the transformation of a past set of intersubjective understandings to a new set. As Joas notes in critiquing Schopenhauer and Nietzsche, their theories of creativity fail in that they see creativity as isolated from "the intersubjective and objective context of human action" (Joas 1996, 124).

Over several decades, Weick has analyzed the problem of intersubjectivity, theorizing about how individuals, groups, and organizations engage in sensemaking in order to coordinate their behavior. For Weick, a central "question for scholars of organizations" is, "How do people produce and acquire a sense of order that allows them to coordinate their actions in ways that have mutual relevance?" (Weick 2001, 26). Weick's answer is that this occurs through the creation of intersubjectivity.

Weick's work is theoretically rich but complicated. Rather than attempt to address his theory as a whole, my analysis of the Boston story relies on specific theoretical insights that he has developed over the years. In particular, I draw on his claim that sensemaking is often retrospective (Weick, 2001), an idea that is fully consistent with Mead:[5]

> It is idle, at least for the purposes of experience, to have recourse to a 'real' past within which we are making constant discoveries; for that past must be set over against a present within which the emergent appears, and the past, which must then be looked at from the standpoint of the emergent, becomes a different past. The emergent when it appears is always found to follow from the past, but before it appears it does not, by definition, follow from the past (Mead 1932, 2).

As already noted, I use Weick's notion of sensemaking to describe the Boston story as one of "changing senses." I posit this in terms of understandings—that is, types of senses—that constitute the three stages to the Boston story. First, in the late 1980s and early 1990s (and almost certainly earlier), groups had *established senses* of who they were and their relationships with one another. For police officers and ministers—and the Black and white communities more generally—these established senses of self stood in opposition to one another. Second came a period characterized by ambiguity and confusion, or, in Dewey's (1938) terms, a period of interdeterminancy. In this period, roughly 1992–96, the problem was that there was a *lack of sense*. Police officers and ministers had limited (if any) understanding of themselves, their goals, and one another. They did, however, find themselves interacting unintentionally, bumping into one another on the streets at night or dealing with the same specific events. On several occasions, they discovered a need to depend on one another. Finally, we see a period of *shared sense*, whereby police officers and ministers—at least at some minimal level—have a common understanding of the problem of youth violence and the mutual goal of "keeping the next kid from being killed." In this period, cooperation and coordination become possible, and a formal, institutionalized relationship develops.

Besides positing a set of stages, my analysis needs to explain why and how these groups move from one stage to the next. With regard to the transition from a

TABLE 12.1

Changing Senses

Stage	Period	Description
Established senses	< 1992	Fixed but disconnected or conflicted understandings, identities
Collapse of sense	1992–93	Collapse of previous understandings and identity
Lack of sense	1991–1995	Liminality, ambiguity, confusion
Sensemaking	1995	Coordinated sensemaking, retrospect interpretation
Shared sense	> 1995	Coordination activities, cooperation, formal partnership

situation of established senses to lack of sense, I argue that a series of exogenous events that police and ministers cannot understand within their extant frameworks come to undermine their senses of who they are. In Weick's (2001) terms, there is a collapse of sensemaking. Subsequently, a shared sense emerges through a process of joint sensemaking based on retrospective interpretation (Weick 2001). In pragmatist terms, interaction leads to intersubjectivity. Table 12.1 provides an outline of the hypothesized process.

At various points in this narrative, I pause to underscore pragmatist insights. In the discussion section, I examine how the Boston story does and does not fit the multistage pragmatist theory of action.

In presenting this story, I have decided to separate its telling from the analysis. Specifically, I describe a portion of the story and then analyze it. I do this for two reasons. First, much of the narrative can be found in earlier papers, many coauthored with Jenny Berrien (Berrien and Winship 1999, 2002, 2003), and is, in part, based on the interviews that she conducted for her senior thesis (Berrien 1998).[6] As such, I think it is appropriate to keep this descriptive work separate from the novel theoretical analysis done in this chapter. Second, I aim to provide readers with every opportunity to interpret the data as they see fit. Separating the narrative from the analysis seemed like the best way to accomplish this. The appendix provides a detailed description of the methodology behind this work.

THE BOSTON STORY

Established Senses

Boston Police Department. During the 1980s, the BPD resembled most other departments across the country in taking a reactive approach to law enforcement. Police activity typically consisted of patrolling streets in squad cars and responding to 911 calls. Police saw their charge as solving crimes, not preventing them from occurring (Goldstein 1990). Crime was going to be reduced by locking people up.

Crack cocaine hit Boston between 1987 and 1988, later than in many other cities. As the crack market developed in Boston, so did turf-based youth gangs. Gangs that previously engaged primarily in low-level criminal activity, such as stealing down jackets, became more active and violent; they engaged in fist and occasionally knife fighting as they realized that there was significant money to be made through the sale of crack. Gang colors and geographically based gang names such as "Corbett Street Posse" indicated strong, almost familial, levels of loyalty toward and respect for one's gang affiliation (see Irons 2011).

Since Boston law enforcement agencies had little experience with turf-based gang activity, their initial response was limited. Until 1990, a department-based policy directed police officers and the administration to publicly deny the existence of a "gang problem." Throughout this period of public denial, the department's focus on the traditional *reactive* policing was evident. In terms of enforcing gang violence, the BPD responded to youth homicides on a case-by-case basis, focusing on who killed each individual. Police focused aggressively on individuals and specific incidents rather than pursuing crime management through preventive strategies.

In 1988, the City Wide Anti-Crime Unit (CWACU), traditionally responsible for providing intense, targeted support across district boundaries of the city, was permanently assigned to the most violent neighborhoods of Boston's inner city. In 1989, the BPD issued a policy statement indicating that any individual involved in a gang would be prosecuted to the full extent of the law. In this way, the Boston police acknowledged the existence of a gang problem. However, it still had no targeted plan for tackling the specific challenges of turf-based gang violence. According to one police captain, in order to make the "big hit," the CWACU was expected to "go in, kick butts, and crack heads." The BPD adopted the mentality that "they could do anything to these kids" in order to put an end to their violent activity, which resulted in highly aggressive and reportedly discriminatory policing tactics.

Black ministerial community. Historically, Boston's Black churches have served the Black middle and working classes. As McRoberts (2005) has described, churches saw themselves as "safe houses" where "decent" people could meet, away from the violence of the inner city. More important, as McRoberts (2004) has documented, the congregants of many inner-city churches do not live in the neighborhoods where their churches are located. Rather, churches are often located where they are because ample size is available at very low rent. As a result, few of Boston's Black churches had programs focused on youth violence. Instead, mainstream Black clergy responded to the increased violence in Boston's neighborhoods by offering a sanctuary from the "war." They avoided taking on any activist role that would bring attention to and combat the so-called inner-city problem. They worked to build their congregations from the inside out and hoped to strengthen the broader community as a positive side-effect. Churches viewed outreach to youth in their neighborhoods as not only dangerous but also incredibly difficult. Youth who were connected to drugs, gangs, and violence maintained a different set of values, which hindered traditional ministry. As the following quote suggests, there was a strong sentiment among Black clergy that youth were not equipped with an understanding of basic faith-based traditions and convictions:

> Many ministers agree that there is a great distance today between the teenagers in the streets and the pastors in neighborhood churches. 'It is so far removed,' said Reverend Wall, who works with many street youths, 'that they don't even understand the sanctity of the church and the role of the preacher' (Jordan 1992).

This perceived gap in values, traditions, and basic beliefs posed a significant hurdle for traditional Black ministers to confront if they were to reach out to youthful offenders in their communities. There was no accessible or familiar method to approach or influence these youth; they could not count on an ingrained sensibility about church and faith. Ministers did not know how to reach them and were reluctant to try.

Reverend Eugene Rivers' ministry was a notable exception at that time. Rivers was born in Chicago. As a youth, he had been a gang member and had fathered a child out of wedlock. In his late twenties, he decided to go to college, crashing courses at Yale and receiving a perfect A average. Yale was not willing to admit him as a regular student, but Harvard was. In the early 1980s, he founded the Seymour Society, a Black Christian student group. In his junior year, he dropped out, and then a few years later, he and his wife—a Jamaican native who had graduated *summa cum laude* from Harvard—together with their two young children, moved to the Four Corners neighborhood of North Dorchester, at that time one of the most violent neighborhoods in Boston. It was there that he established his first ministry.

Throughout his early career, Rivers was very vocal in criticizing other Black ministers and prominent Black figures in Boston for their lack of response to the violence and drug crises in their communities:

> It was another audacious volley in Gene Rivers' holy war. Since establishing an outpost in the gritty Four Corners neighborhood of Dorchester in 1988, he has conducted an unconventional ministry, challenging the criminal element among his own people and criticizing the Black establishment (Wilkie 1993).

Rivers's "holy war" left him essentially partnerless. Boston's Black clergy was not only struggling to respond to violence on the street but also grappling with its own internal conflicts.

Throughout the late 1980s and early 90s, members of Boston's Black religious community were among the most vocal and public critics of the BPD's policing tactics. Reverend Rivers levied particularly harsh criticism of Boston's law enforcement agencies. There was little potential for cooperative work because their relationships to the so-called culprits of inner-city youth violence were entirely in conflict. On the clergy side, many Black ministers were highly aware of the intense level of police attention directed toward the youth of their community, especially young Black males.

Rivers's close contact with youth and especially youthful offenders provided him with unique insight into how police officers treated these individuals. He heard stories of the officers who had notorious reputations for their hard-hitting, "no joke" treatment of young Black males. According to Rivers, police abuse was not rampant, but cases of abuse were substantial. These stories and incidents placed Rivers on the attack and led to him to fiercely protect the youth of his neighborhood. In addition to supporting youth during court hearings, much of Rivers's advocacy centered on direct criticism of and confrontation with the BPD. According to one police lieutenant, Rivers intentionally criticized police in order to make waves within the city and bring attention to the needs of his community. As a result, Rivers received the reputation of being a "cop basher."

ANALYSIS

In this initial period, both police officers and ministers have established set habits. The police are committed to reactive policing, a common model at the time (Goldstein 1990). They respond to 911 calls and attempt to solve crimes after they have been committed.

The inner-city ministers' strategy for dealing with inner-city violence was similarly reactive. They saw their job as keeping street matters out of the churches and providing safe houses for "decent folk" (McRoberts 2005). Reverend Rivers, who worked with youth in inner-city neighborhoods, was the exception.

Police and ministers have well-established senses of their situation and how they see themselves and others. There is intersubjectivity within each group and what might be called complementary intersubjective understandings. As in war, each side has a firm understanding of the other and a different perception of who are the "good" and who are the "bad" guys. In addition, each side understands how the other side understands them. In general, the ministers saw the police, who were disproportionately white and predominantly Irish, as racist. Police saw inner-city residents as immoral and prone to crime.

The Collapse of Sense

In important respects, the situations of both the police and the ministers were unstable. Violent crime was soaring in Boston's inner-city neighborhoods, and neither group had a strategy to deal with it. A series of exogenous events independently undermined the situation of both groups, shifting them into a situation that I have labeled *lack of sense*.

Boston Police Department. Two events in 1989, the Carol Stuart murder investigation and the "stop and frisk" scandal, brought fierce, widespread attention to and evaluation of the BPD's initial approach to the violence crisis. Carol Stuart, a pregnant white woman, was murdered in the primarily Black neighborhood of Mission Hill. Her husband Charles was with her at the time of her death and reported that a Black male had committed the crime. Relying on Charles Stuart's account, the

Boston Police Department scoured Mission Hill for suspects. There were widespread reports of police abuse as well as a coerced statement that implicated a Black male suspect, William Bennett. Charles Stuart himself was later identified as the alleged murderer, though he committed suicide before an investigation could be completed. The mishandling of the Stuart murder investigation and Charles Stuart's dishonesty created an atmosphere within the Black community of extreme distrust of and disillusionment with the Boston Police Department. As Rivers has since described, the Black community came to feel that it was "open season on Black males."

Later in 1989, the stop-and-frisk scandal intensified the tension. A precinct commander initiated this scandal by describing the Department's approach to preventing gun-related violence as a policy of stop and frisk en masse. This outraged the Black community and solidified the Boston public's suspicion of the police. There is some dissension within the BPD about the extent to which its policy truly was to indiscriminately stop and frisk all Black males within high-crime areas, an approach that police describe as "tipping kids upside down." Several officers related that they targeted individuals who were either previously spotted performing some illegal activity or known gang members. However, officers also acknowledged that this approach was critically flawed because it was often difficult to "distinguish the good guys from the bad guys." Officers also agree that there were "bad seed" cops who acted far too aggressively and indiscriminately. In any case, the community did not view such activity as fair or justified. Accusations of stop-and-frisk tactics led to a court case in the fall of 1989 in which a judge threw out evidence acquired in what he viewed as an unconstitutional search and seizure (Globe Staff 1992).

These two scandals, combined with smaller-scale, less visible incidents, eventually led the Boston press to question BPD's capacity to effectively handle even basic policing activities. In 1991, the *Boston Globe* published a harshly critical four-part series, "Bungling the Basics," which detailed a succession of police foul-ups during the previous few years (Locy 1991a–d). The misguided investigations and questionable policing exposed by the press eventually led to the appointment of the St. Clair Commission, which was assigned the task of thoroughly reviewing the BPD and its policies.

The CWACU took the rap for much of the questionable policing tactics during this time and was consequently disbanded in 1990. "Bad-seed" cops were weeded out. A new unit—the Anti-Gang Violence Unit (AGVU)—which espoused a "softer approach" to violence prevention, was established. The aggressive and indiscriminate street tactics of the past were sharply curtailed. Possibly as a result, the decrease in homicides from 1991 to 1992 was followed by a sharp increase in 1993.

The release of the St. Clair Commission's report in 1992 spurred further administrative changes at the highest level (St. Clair Commission 1992). The report cited extensive corruption within the department and recommended major changes. In 1993, Mayor Flynn resigned, and the New York Transit Police's Bill Bratton replaced Police Commissioner Mickey Roache. Bratton brought a new philosophy—community policing—to the BPD (Bratton and Knobler, 2009).

Ministers. It was not until the violence on the streets literally entered the confines of a Mattapan church that Black clergy as an entity began to address the violence oppressing much of their community. In May 1992, the Morning Star Baptist Church held a service for a youth murdered in a drive-by gang shooting. During the service, a shootout and stabbing occurred among several of the gang members. A melee ensued within the sanctuary, shots were fired, and nearly four hundred people stampeded out of the church. Fortunately, no one died.

The Morning Star Church tragedy was a clear challenge to the sanctity of the church and its status within the Black community. The message was clear: if the church was not going to deal with the problems of the streets, those problems would enter the church. For approximately six months, established and more marginal ministers came together in a series of meetings. Eventually, these meetings met an impasse; the ministers were divided on whether or not to work directly with youth. It was out of this division that the Ten Point Coalition was founded. "After the Morning Star Baptist Church incident, dozens of ministers met to determine a course of action, Rivers invited those who wanted to make a direct intervention to meet at his home the next Friday night." As the Reverend Jeffrey L. Brown, another prominent Ten Point Coalition leader, told the *Boston Globe*: "We started going out every Friday night, walking in the streets, talking to whoever would talk to us" (Wilkie 1993).

ANALYSIS

Neither the police nor the ministers had an effective way of dealing with increasing levels of youth violence in Boston. More important, the violence itself resulted in specific events that destablized their existing modes of operation—that is, their habits. In the language of the philosopher Rahel Jaeggi (2018), the police's and minister's "forms of life" in pragmatist terms no longer "worked" for them. Their problems were not a matter of fixing past mistakes but, rather, in Jaeggi's terms, were of a second order; they needed to find a new way of doing things. In true pragmatist fashion, events shattered the routine activities of both the police and ministers.

Lack of Sense

During the first half of the 1990s, neither the police nor the ministers had a clear definition of their goals or purposes. This was true both of their own activities and their relationship to each other. Speaking about the police, one captain stated: "The police department had no plan of how to deal with the drug problems that the districts and neighborhoods were having. Their idea was a city wide, centralized unit that was really locked into the big hit, the big score with drugs." What was killing the neighborhoods was the kids on the corner, the drug houses, etc. Both groups, however, were committed to dealing with the problem of youth violence, even though they had no idea how they were going to do it. This commitment was parallel, not shared, as there was no agreement to collaborate.

The fact that they had the same concern—youth violence in general, and gangs in particular—did have an important implication: they often found themselves in the same social space. They literally bumped into each other at night in the streets. There was thus a great deal of unstructured social interaction between the two groups. To understand the underlying dynamics of this period, I discuss it in terms of three concepts: purposeless engagement, ambiguous relationship, and accidental dependence.

Purposeless engagement. After the founding of the Ten Point Coalition, the ministers would meet every Friday night in collar to walk the streets of Boston's inner-city neighborhoods as Reverend Brown put it, "talking to whoever would talk to us." In these walks the ministers would often run into gang members. After the first few months, gang members would chat with them. Sometimes these conversations would get very serious. As Berrien's interviews with the ministers revealed, they did not know what they were trying to accomplish with their walks. All they knew was that they were called by God to be present (Berrien 1999).

In 1993, Commissioner Roache was replaced by Superintendent William Bratton, who had been brought from the New York City Transit Authority the previous year to help professionalize the BPD. Bratton spoke of a particular interest in community policing, the new buzzword in policing circles across the country. Bratton held a single meeting with the ministers in 1993 to discuss working together. At that meeting there was discussion of the "one in ten rule"—that out of every ten gang members and wannabes, perhaps one was sufficiently dangerous that they needed to be incarcerated; the other nine needed help and services. This is the first evidence of a possible emerging intersubjectivity based on a shared understanding of gangs.

What Bratton meant by community policing is unclear. Within less than a year, he left Boston to head up New York City's Police Department. There, he, along with Mayor Rudolph Guliani, pursued a repressive style of policing that both distressed New York's communities of color and stood in sharp contrast to the policies that Boston would later become famous for (Patterson and Winship 1999).

Throughout 1994 and 1995, gang violence in Boston continued unabated. The Boston police were joined by two Harvard researchers, David Kennedy and Anthony Braga, with the goal of designing initiatives to reduce violence under a program called the Boston Gun Project. They worked full-time with the police for the entirety of 1995. The question of what they might do was unclear. As Kennedy and Braga described it, "we had essentially moved in with the Working Group, spending day after day at Warren Street, riding with YVSF [Youth Violence Strike Force] and probation officers, and holding one-on-one conversations with Working Group members to probe more deeply into what they did and could do, what they thought was going on, and what might be done about it. It was an intense and a deeply disturbing time, with no clear way forward" (Kennedy, Braga, and Piehl 2001, 26).

The police appeared to have been successful in at least one geographic area. The Wendover Street area and its associated gang was inactive for a period of more than nine months during 1995. Less clear was why the policing in this area had been successful, and the BPD's own theory—that they had been "honest with them"—was just as vague. The Harvard team eventually revealed what had happened. In many respects, Wendover Street had experienced a classic crackdown.

> YVSF officers enforced every law they could against gang members, shutting down street drug sales and making arrests for trespassing, public drinking, overt drug use, and disorder offenses," but what was different was that gang members were told "why the crackdown was occurring and what it would take to make it stop (Kennedy et al. 2001, 27).

To the Harvard researchers, this seemed like an innovative approach to dealing with gang violence. Thus, the seed of Operation Ceasefire was planted.

Ambiguous relations. Throughout the first half of the 1990s, the relationship between the police and the Ten Point ministers was complicated and ambiguous. At the most general level, the police simply did not understand what the ministers were doing. The ministers' understanding of the police was also complicated. In 1992, Reverend Rivers initiated what he called the People's Police Tribunal. The Tribunal provided a forum for community members (particularly young Black males) who thought that they had been mistreated by the police to present their cases. Although the tribunal had no legal authority, there was the possibility that it was likely to receive considerable press, something Rivers was generally quite good at attracting, although the initiative did not get much attention.

After the tribunal was established, Reverends Brown and Ray Hammond, the other two core members besides Rivers of the Ten Point leadership, began to worry that it might send the police the wrong message—that cops were generally bad and should be presumed to be racist. To counter this, they developed a program that they named the Community Youth Service Awards: awards to police deemed to have been exemplary in the work they had done in the community and with youth in particular.

Accidental dependence. By being in the same space at the same time, the police and ministers could potentially find that they needed to depend on each other. This was particularly true given how dangerous the space was. For ministers, there was the possibility that they would have to deal with violence directly. For the police, there was the danger that their actions might lead to charges of racism and discrimination. I describe two illustrative events.

One night in 1991, a group of drug dealers shot at Reverend Rivers's home; a bullet passed within inches of his six-year-old son's head.[7] Rivers had a choice. He could move his family out of the neighborhood into safer quarters, be seen as a coward, and have to give up on his efforts in the neighborhood. Alternatively, he could work with police. He chose the latter. The two officers with whom he had the most tense relationships volunteered to investigate. This was an opportunity for them to discover what Reverend Rivers was truly about. Was he for real or a drug dealer, as they thought? Six months later, a local drug dealer was arrested for the shooting. It turned out that he had not even been aiming at Rivers's house but the house next door. He was simply a bad shot.

Just as the ministers—and in particular Rivers—found that they had to rely on the police, so, too, did the police find that they needed the ministers. Two incidents occurred in 1994 in which police misconduct had the potential to be highly racially explosive. I discuss one here.[8]

On March 24, 1994, police carried out a full-force SWAT-style drug bust, complete with battering rams, M-16s, tear gas, and much yelling and confusion. Unfortunately, the information that a "snitch" had passed on to them was wrong. The police had not broken into a drug dealer's apartment but, rather, into the apartment of Accelynne Williams, a retired Black minister. In the melee that followed, the Reverend Williams was thrown to the ground and handcuffed, suffered a heart attack, and died.

Given Boston's tense racial past, Police Commissioner Paul Evans realized that there was enormous potential for racial unrest, even riots. Not knowing what to do, he consulted Reverend Rivers and asked for advice. Rivers told him that he needed to hold a press conference immediately, acknowledge that that the BPD had made a terrible mistake, apologize, and indicate that there would be a full investigation of Williams's death and that those responsible would be held accountable. The commissioner took Rivers's advice. In subsequent weeks, BPD leadership met with various community groups. At their side were several Ten Point ministers, providing the implicit message that although what had occurred was horrendous, the BPD was responding in a responsible way.

ANALYSIS

I have described the first half of the 1990s as a period of lack of sense, with neither the police nor the ministers possessing an overall sense of themselves and their relationship. More specifically, (a) each party had little to no understanding of what they wanted to accomplish, and (b) each party was unclear about the other's disposition and goals. This second point is particularly apparent from the incongruous efforts of the People's Tribunal and the Youth Service Awards. In the sense of Mead, there was no intersubjectivity across the two groups.

Both groups, however, had limited, immediate goals in the sense of Dewey's concept of "ends-in-view" (1922, 223–37). The Wendover Street intervention, with its immediate purpose of disrupting the gang's current violence, illustrates this point for the police. The ministers' street walks provide a parallel example. There was not, however, a longer-term or global strategy. Weick speaks directly to this point:

> In turbulent periods, orderliness is limited to short-lived transactions, intelligence is reduced to local expertise, and determinacy covers only those events close together in time and space. While no one questions that it would be desirable to have grand and stable designs in times of turbulence, the organization is not sufficiently homogenous to support concerted action, nor is the environment sufficiently determinant to encourage accurate, long-term prediction. Instead, the way out of turbulence may lie in continuous improvisation in response to continuous change in local details (Weick 2001, 88).

This "lack of sense" phase is similar to Dewey's notion of a period interdeterminacy (1938). It does not, however, fit neatly the pragmatist theory of how such a period is responded to. This should be a time of "creative intelligence," where both groups are imagining new options for future habits. Although each group has particular ends-in-view in the context of specific situations, I never saw any evidence of either group considering different options involving an overall plan.

As I have described, the lack of sense period is a time of purposeless engagement, ambiguous relations, and accidental dependence. At a general level, one might describe this stage of the Boston story as "undirected wandering" or "muddling through." As noted earlier, Joas (1996, 127) explicitly rejected this latter phrase as an example of creative intelligence.

Even though this period of lack of sense seems to be one of undirected wandering, it is not a period of "blind" wandering. Both the ministers and the police are open to new experiences and trying new initiatives, even when the goals of those initiatives are no more than ends-in-view. As such, a common history of events is being constructed over time, even if both parties—at least at the moment—fail to recognize this.

Sensemaking

On September 25, 1995, Paul McLaughlin, a local assistant district attorney, took the subway home to West Roxbury. For the past several years, McLaughlin had been prosecuting various gang-related drug cases. As he started his car, which was parked at the commuter train stop, a Black male approached, put a gun to McLaughlin's head, and pulled the trigger. Boston's gangs were letting everyone know who was in control of the city (McGrory and Dowdy 1995).

The BPD, the Ten Point ministers, and the *Boston Globe* immediately recognized the potential for McLaughlin to become another Carol Stuart. The *Globe* is said to have assigned twenty reporters to follow the cops who were investigating the case. Realizing the potential enormity of the situation, the police and the ministers held a joint press conference. The message from the ministers was clear: this was an outrageous crime and needed to be investigated aggressively, but there would be no "open season" on young Black males (Anand 1995). The *Globe* withdrew the vast majority of their reporters. It took two years to arrest a suspect; one year later, he was convicted (Kahn 1999).

The media, particularly the news media, contributed to sensemaking in important ways during this period. In May 1996, Operation Ceasefire began its gang forums, with the Ten Point ministers joining six months later. Almost immediately, the youth homicide rate dropped. This positive outcome became of enormous interest to the press. Of particular interest was the fact that cops and Black inner-city ministers were working together. This unusual mixture appeared to have produced magic, what the press called the "Boston Miracle": a sharp 80 percent drop in homicides along with substantially improved police-community relations, indicated by a 60 percent drop in complaints against police. The provocative and colorful Reverend Rivers captured special media attention, culminating in *Newsweek*'s June 1, 1998, cover story on the role of religion in fighting crime. The magazine's cover featured a photo of Reverend Rivers with the caption, "God vs. Gangs."

Whether the ministers had in fact contributed to the Boston Miracle has been hotly contested (Kleiman 2002; Kennedy 2002b). Skeptics argue that because the ministers joined Operation Ceasefire after crime rates had fallen, their involvement could not have had a causal effect. I, however, contend that the police's partnership with the ministers created a political environment in which it was possible for the police to innovate. In addition, it appears that the BPD's anticipation of the ministers' criticism caused them to drop various policy options in designing Operation Ceasefire (Braga and Winship 2006).

ANALYSIS

The fact that the police and ministers decided to hold a joint press conference is critical. Their intent was to send a single unified message, one that their understandably cynical audience might perceive as internally inconsistent: McLaughlin's murder was going to be investigated vigorously, but the rights of young Black males were going to be respected. Arguably, this message is believable only if it comes simultaneously from both parties. There had been some coordination in the past with one party helping the other. In response to the McLaughlin murder, however, coordination was oriented toward supporting both parties' needs. Key players used the past (Carol Stuart) to understand the present (McLaughlin) and to shape current actions. Past joint events provide evidence that coordination could be successful.

If there is any creative intelligence in the Boston story, it comes at this stage. What is critical about the McLaughlin case is that both sides were intelligent enough to recognize that they needed each other in order to convince the public that the murder investigation would be both aggressive and fair. This is distinct from previous incidents in which one party needed the other.

As I discuss in more detail later, the previous two stages of the Boston story, lack of sense and sensemaking, suggest that the pragmatist concept of creativity should be expanded. During the lack-of-sense component of the story, the openness of both the police and ministers to different events and experiences is essential to their common, though yet unrecognized, history. In the sensemaking component, the creative intelligence is for the parties to recognize their joint need to work together.

Shared Sense

After the McLaughlin murder, the BPD and the Ten Point Coalition began to formalize their joint ventures and develop a shared language; in short, they institutionalized their relationship. Precisely how this occurred is beyond the scope of this chapter, though various descriptions exist (Winship 2004b; Braga et al. 2008). Instead, I discuss this period and its legacy from three angles: joint activities, shared language, and collaborative problem-solving.

Joint activities. In December 1996, three months after Assistant District Attorney Paul McLaughlin's murder, the Ten Point ministers joined Operation Ceasefire as formal participants. In subsequent years, the BPD and ministers, along with others, started various other programs—including school visits and prisoner reentry—with a parallel structure. Beginning in 1998, as part of Operation Homefront, the police and ministers conducted home visits on Thursday nights. During these visits, two officers and one minister would arrive (uninvited and unannounced) at the home of a young person whom the schools had identified as high risk. There, they would talk to the youth and their family about specific challenges that they were facing and how minister and police might be of support.

How tenuous was the BPD-minister relationship was crystallized for me during a meeting with Reverend Rivers in the spring of 2000. Over breakfast that day—four years into the coalition's active partnership with the BPD—Rivers reported with great excitement that he had worked out a formal agreement with the police: he could criticize them in the press as long as he gave them a "heads-up" first.

Through the late 1990s and beyond, the police officers and ministers negotiated about a variety of matters. Prior to each gang forum, the BPD and the Ten Point Coalition would discuss what exactly should be required of gang members in order to avoid a police crackdown. There were also frequent negotiations about the appropriate outcome for individuals who had been arrested.

Shared language. Throughout his work, Mead emphasizes the importance of language—in the form of gestures and actual speech—as a basis of intersubjectivity (Joas 1997). For individuals to work together, they must have not only a common vision of their mutual goals but a language with which to relate to each other (Hirsch 1986). Except in the trivial sense that they both speak English, cops and ministers do not generally share a common language: one group's language can often be highly militaristic; the other's obviously has strong religious themes.

By 1997, it became clear that the police officers and ministers had developed a common language, at least to a minimal degree, which supported a shared sense of their cooperation in tackling youth violence. After the 1991 shooting at his home, Rivers began to talk about how "some kids were so out of control that they needed to be put in jail, both for their own good and for the good of the community." By the mid- and late 1990s, this phrase was being frequently repeated by the core ministers. It also became the basis for a message they jointly used in gang, school, and prison reentry forums. By the late 1990s, both police officers and ministers were talking about how some kids needed a "prison ministry." I also began to hear more frequently about the "one in ten" deal. At the most general level, police officers and ministers started describing their shared goal as "keeping the next kid from getting killed."

Although the language that the officers and ministers shared is simple, behind it lay a complex set of latent understandings. From what I can determine, these

agreements have never been made explicit. Rather, they are a set of implicit principles that guide the actions of both groups. I have identified and confirmed through
interviews three shared principles: (1) although poverty, singleparent households,
poor schools, and other conditions may be factors in youth violence, any short-term
effort to reduce violence needs to treat it as a criminal problem; (2) only a small
number of youths are responsible for most of the violence;[9] and (3) the ministers
would have an informal role in determining the justice system outcomes for specific individuals.

Collaborative problem-solving. On January 1, 2003, two police officers were shot
and wounded after responding to a call involving a man named Jermaine Berry
(Dade and Daley 2003). It was said that the police and the media planned to present
this case as an example of the moral decay and danger of the inner city. This theme
seemed particularly relevant given the sharp rise in crime and homicide rates over
the prior year.

Reverend Rivers intervened immediately. Jermaine Berry had a long history of
mental illness; his parents had immigrated from Haiti and were illiterate. Rivers
helped them write a note of apology to the police officers' families. He then worked
to reframe the incident, efforts that resulted in newspaper stories describing the failure of state social services and the inadequate treatment that Berry had received for
his illness (Barry and Stockman 2003).

On the morning of February 13, 2002 Willie Murray, a Black thirty-seven-year-
old, while sitting in the driver's seat of his car, was shot and killed by a Black BPD
officer, Shawn West. This was the sixth police killing of a civilian in Boston in fifteen months—an anomaly in a city which on average sees about one police killing
each year. As in the case of many police shootings, the circumstances of the Murray
killing were unclear. The only witness to the shooting was an individual who was in
the backseat of Murray's car. West claimed that his life was threatened by Murray's
actions and thus that the shooting was justified.[10]

The *Boston Globe* immediately posed a question that was almost certainly on
the minds of many community members: did the Murray killing indicate excessive
use of force by the BPD more broadly?[11] The day after the shooting, BPD Commissioner Evans responded to these charges by attending a joint meeting of the Ten
Point Coalition and the Black Ministerial Alliance, Boston's more traditional organization of Black churches. At this meeting, he explained what he knew about the
circumstances of the shooting, indicated that the shooting was being thoroughly
examined by internal investigators, suggested that there well might be problems
with the shooting (i.e., that it was not justified), and recognized the clergy's, as well
as the broader city's, concern about the number of recent killings by police. He also
promised to consider the appropriateness of current police policy on the use of firearms. The approximately thirty-five Black clergy in attendance had no questions for
the commissioner.[12]

Shortly thereafter, the BPD had the local District Attorney's Office send the
case to a grant jury, essentially admitting that they believe that the shooting was

not justified. The police commissioner also followed through with his promise to review departmental policy. A disproportionate share of problematic shootings by police occurred when police used firearms and a suspect was in a car. Particularly egregious was the fatal shooting of Eveline Barros-Cepeda, an unarmed passenger. The commissioner issued a new policy prohibiting the use of a firearms by police to protect themselves from suspects in cars. The rationale was that a firearm was of little use in these circumstances and the risk of a problematic shooting was much too high. The police union went into an immediate uproar. It demanded that the commissioner resign. The sole group to publicly support the commissioner and his new policy was the Ten Point ministers. The commissioner stayed, and the policy remains in place today.

ANALYSIS

After the McLaughlin murder, the police and the Ten Point ministers jointly developed a new set of habits—gang forums, strategy meetings, Homefront visits, Peace Walks—which, in one form or another, continue to this day. A new intersubjectivity allowed for this coordination and development of shared activities. Most important, their partnership allowed them to deal with potential crises, whether the shooting of two police officers or the fatal shooting of a citizen by the police.

As Mead has argued at length, intersubjectivity is based in great part on shared language. At least as important to the Boston story have been shared activities, both in the present and in the past. To quote Weick, "People commit to and coordinate instrumental acts (means) before they worry about shared goals. . . . But shared goals do emerge as people search for reasons that justify the earlier interdependent means to which they have become bound" (2001, 17).

DISCUSSION

The Boston story is consistent with some aspects of the pragmatist theory of action but requires other aspects to be expanded. Certainly, the period of established senses exemplifies the pragmatist concept of habitual action. The events involved in the collapse of sense also seem consistent with pragmatist theory. In Joas's language, this collapse involves a series of events that shatter existing intersubjectivity and habits. The lack-of-sense stage, however, seems hard to reconcile with pragmatist theory, which focuses narrowly on this as a period of creative intelligence. This time more closely resembles aimless or undirected wandering. What creates the opportunity for change is not the deliberate consideration of different options but, rather, a continual flow of events that forces people to change how they act and how they interact. That said, the police and ministers do act in a way that is consistent with Dewey's notion of ends-in-view. Rivers calls the cops when his house is shot up. The police ask the ministers for advice when a retired Black minister dies in a botched drug raid.

In Winship (2017), I discuss situations in which rational action in the narrow sense of economists is not possible: people don't understand their situation, don't know their options, or are unaware of particular constraints on their actions. In the terminology of Kilpinen (2009), these are situations in which "mind-first" behavior often is not possible. I label these *inchoate situations*. In such situations, even localized instrumental action (i.e., ends-in-view) may not be feasible. I describe a wide variety of *extrarational behaviors*, ways in which individuals may act in inchoate situations and which may lead to accidental discoveries. Wandering is one type of extrarational behavior.

The Boston story suggests that we need to expand pragmatist problem-solving to include the concepts of wandering and accidential discovery, in addition to that of creativity. Certainly, there are cases in which individuals and groups consciously go about creatively considering options for solving some problem. But there are also situations in which a solution may simply present itself. Thus, events and general environmental change may not only create problems for actors but also provide solutions.

What discovery does require is recognition. I need to notice the ten-dollar bill and recognize that it is a solution to my lunch problem. This brings us to the next moment in the Boston story" sensemaking. After the McLaughlin murder, the police and ministers independently and then together recognized the potential for a repeat of the past—the disastrous Carol Stuart investigation. They further recognized that it was necessary for them to hold a joint press conference. Arguably, these moments of recognition are creative in some sense. If one is going to discover solutions to a problem, one certainly needs to be able to recognize a solution when it presents itself.

What is important here is not just that the police and ministers independently developed a understanding of their situation, but that their their understanding was shared. In this way, the Boston story shows that a history of shared events and history, as well as common actions, provide the "grist" needed to establish intersubjectivity. What the Boston story shows is that such a shared understanding may result from common discovery.

The final stage in the Boston story, shared senses, certainly fits the pragmatist theory of action. We are back to the world of habits in the broadest sense of unreflective action. The police and ministers initated myriad joint activities, most of which continue to this day.

My foregoing analysis suggests that the pragmatist theory of action needs to go further in recognizing the importance of noninstrumental action—action that is not "mind first"—in the context of problem-solving, one of its key intellectual agendas. In particular, as the Boston story exemplifies, action can take place in the absence of understanding, even if that action then becomes the basis for future understandings (for a related argument, see Bearman, Faris, and Moody 1999). To underscore this point, we might contrast the idea of action in a lack-of-sense period with how symbolic interactionism (SI), the subfield of sociology most influenced by pragmatism, understands action. To quote Blumer from his program-defining book, *Symbolic Interactionism*, "In order to act the individual has to identify what he wants, establish an objective or goal, map out a prospective line of behavior, note and interpret the actions of others, size up his situation" (Blumer, 1986, 64). This is clearly a mind-first theory of action. This mind-first approach is also apparent in the importance that SI places on the process of negotiation. A key maxim of SI most closely associated with Strauss (1978) but repeated by many (e.g., Farberman 1979; Fine 1984) is that "there is no order without negotiation." Unless we interpret negotiation *very* broadly as social interaction, then negotiation requires a choate situation with defined preferences and choices.

It is nearly impossible to see formal negotiation in the Boston story. Yet, it is a story about the emergence of order. The notion that negotiation is not possible necessarily precedes order is problematic in that it assumes that negotiation is possible without individual goals and a shared understanding of what is to be negotiated—that is, without intersubjectivity. Negotiation is simply not possible in a chaotic situation that "lacks sense." Although the specifics of a social order may be negotiated, this is only possible if there are already understood terms of negotiation, a type of order. In the Boston story, once there was a degree of intersubjectivity between police and ministers, it was possible to negotiate how they would work together and when things would be done (e.g., whether an individual would have their probation revoked). Prior to this, coordination of activities was possible only in the most limited, ends-in-view sort of way.

At the heart of my point about the limitations of the concepts of creativity and negotiation is that people may not always be aware of the options available to solve a problem. They may not even be able to imagine them (Winship 2017). Even in these situations, problem-solving does not stop. One can wander aimlessly and still hope to stumble on discover a solution—whether by discovering a ten-dollar bill or a way to productively coordinate with a former adversary. Of course, one needs the intelligence to recognize that solution for what it is.

CONCLUSION

In this chapter, I have argued for a broader conception of the role of action in problem-solving than what is found in standard instrumental models or in pragmatist models of creative experimentation. Although both of these models may describe a large subset of human behavior (Weick 2001; Whitford 2002; Winship 2017), they assume a mind-first model of action (Kilpinen 2009). Here I argue for the importance of aimless wandering and discovery as types of action that fall outside of mind-first models. To support this position, I examine how the Ten Point Coalition—a group of Black ministers in Boston—developed a partnership with the Boston Police Department in order to reduce youth violence. There is no table in this story; that is, the ministers and the police never met formally to figure out (negotiate) how to work together. Rather, they discovered their partnership when an assistant district attorney was murdered by a drug dealer. Key to the story is a period of lack of sense, several years in which neither the police nor the ministers were sure of their goals. There were multiple instances of joint action, but goals were limited, as in Dewey's famous phrase, to "ends-in-view." There is a deep-seated pragmatist assumption that external change disrupts habits, creating a situation that requires deliberate problem-solving. The Boston story demonstrates that external change can also provide solutions to existing problems, though actors need the intelligence to recognize when a solution arrives.

REFERENCES

Anderson, Elizabeth. 2006. "The Epistemology of Democracy." *Episteme: A Journal of Social Epistemology* 3 (1): 8–22

——. 2010. *The Imperative of Integration*. Princeton, NJ: Princeton University Press.

Barry, Ellen and Farah Stockman. 2003. "Shooting Suspect Left Menthal Health System." *The Boston Globe*, January 3, p. A1, B4.

Bearman, Peter, Robert Faris, and James Moody. 1999. "Blocking the future: New solutions for old problems in historical social science." *Social Science History* 23 (4): 501–533.

Berrien, Jenny. 1998. "The Boston Miracle: The Emergence of New Institutional Structure in the Absence of Rational Planning." Senior Thesis. Department of Sociology. Harvard University.

Berrien, Jenny, and Christopher Winship. 1999. "Lessons Learned from Boston's Police-Community Collaboration," *Federal Probation* 63 (2): 24–32.

——. 2002. "An Umbrella of Legitimacy: Boston's Police Department-Ten Point Coalition Collaboration" With Jenny Berrien in *Securing Our Children's Future: New Approaches to Juvenile Justice and Youth Violence*, Gary Katzman (ed.). Brookings Institution Press.

——. 2003. "Should We Have Faith in the Churches? The Ten-Point Coalition's Effect on Boston's Youth Violence." With Jenny Berrien in *Guns, Crime, and Punishment in America*. New York: New York University Press.

Berrien, Jenny, Christopher Winship, Omar McRoberts. 2000. "Religion and the Boston Miracle: The effect of Black ministry on youth violence." In Mary Jo Bane, Brent Coffin and Ronald Thiemann, *Who Will Provide? The Changing Role of Religion in American Social Welfare*. Boulder, CO: Westview Press.

Blumer, Herbert. 1969. *Symbolic Interactionism: Perspective and Method*. Berkeley: University of California Press.

Braga, A., D. Kennedy, E. Waring, and A. Piehl. 2001. "Problem-Oriented Policing, Deterrence, and Youth Violence: An Evaluation of Boston's Operation Ceasefire." *Journal of Research in Crime and Delinquency* 38: 195–225.

Braga, Anothony, and Christopher Winship. 2006. "Partnership, Accountability, and Innovation: Clarifying Boston's Experience with Pulling Levers." In *Police Innovation: Contrasting Perspectives*, ed. David Wiesburd, and Anthony A. Braga. Cambridge: Cambridge University Press.

Bratton, William, and Peter Knobler. *The Turnaround: How America's Top Cop Reversed the Crime Epidemic*. New York: Random House, 2009.

Braga, Anthony A., David Hureau, and Christopher Winship. 2008. "Losing Faith—Police, Black Churches, and the Resurgence of Youth Violence in Boston." *Ohio State Journal of Crimnal Law* 6: 141.

Brown, Jeffrey L., Ray Hammond, Eugene Rivers, and Samuel Wood. 1995. "Facing Our Common Enemy: Violence." *Boston Globe*, October 1: A39.

Chacon, R. 1995. "Boston Police Investigators Seek Cause of Undercover Officer's Injuries." *Boston Globe*, February 4: 22.

Dade, Corey, and Beth Daley. 2003. "Shooting Wounds Two Hub Officers: Suspect Also Hit in New Year's Confrontation." *Boston Globe*, January 2: 1, 6.

Dewey, John. 1910. *How We Think*. New York: Heath.

——. 1922. *Human Nature and Conduct: An Introduction to Social Psychology*. New York: Modern Library.

——. (1925). *Experience and Nature*. La Salle, IN: Open Court.

——. 1930. "The Quest for Certainty: A Study of the Relation of Knowledge and Action." *Journal of Philosophy* 27 (1): 14–25.

——. 1938. *Logic, The Theory of Inquiry*. New York: Henry Holt.

Farberman, Harvey A. 1979. "A Review Symposium: Anselm L. Strauss—Negotiations: Varieties, Contexts, Processes, and Social Order." *Symbolic Interaction* 2 (2): 153–68.

Fine, Gary Alan. 1984. "Negotiated Orders and Organizational Cultures." *Annual Review of Sociology* 10 (1): 239–62.

Gillespie, Alex, and Flora Cornish. 2010. "Intersubjectivity: Towards a Dialogical Analysis." *Journal for the Theory of Social Behaviour* 40 (1): 19–46.

Globe Staff. 1992. "Events Leadings to the St. Clair Report." *Boston Globe*, January 15: 23.

——. 2002a. "Police Questions." *Boston Globe*, February 14: A18.

——. 2002b. "Suspect Shootings." February. *Boston Globe*, February 21: A16.

Goffman, Erving. 1959. *The Presentation of Self in Everyday Life.* Garden City, NY: Doubleday Anchor.

Goldstein, Herman. *Problem-Oriented Policing*. New York: McGraw-Hill, 1990.

Gross, Neil. 2009. "A pragmatist theory of social mechanisms." *American Sociological Review* 74.3: 358–379.

Gross, Neil. 2018. "Pragmatism and the Study of Large-Scale Social Phenomena." *Theory and Society* 47 (1): 87–111.

Grunwald, M. and G. Anand. 1995. "Authorities Are Praised; Some Blacks Wary." *Boston Globe*, September 30: 80.

James, William ([1890], 1950). *The Principles of Psychology, I-II*. New York: Dover.

——. ([1909], 1977). "A Pluralistic Universe." In *The Works of William James*. Cambridge, MA: Harvard University Press.

Jerolmack, Colin, and Shamus Khan. 2014. "Talk Is Cheap: Ethnography and the Attitudinal Fallacy." *Sociological Methods & Research* 43 (2): 178–209.

Joas, Hans. 1990. "The Creativity of Action and the Intersubjectivity of Reason: Mead's Pragmatism and Social Theory." *Transactions of the Charles S. Pierce Society* 26 (2): 165–194.

——. 1996. *The Creativity of Action*. Chicago: University of Chicago Press.

——. 1997. *G. H. Mead: A Contemporary Re-examination of His Thought*. Cambridge, MA: MIT Press.

Jordan, Robert A. 1992. "Clergy's Anger Can Bring Hope." *Boston Globe*, May 16: 13.

Hirsch, Paul M. 1986. "From Ambushes to Golden Parachutes: Corporate Takeovers as an Instance of Cultural Framing and Institutional Integration." *American Journal of Sociology* 91 (4): 800–837.

Hutchins, Edwin. 1995. *Cognition in the Wild*. Cambridge, MA: MIT Press.

Irons, Meghan E. 2011. "Community Recalls Devastation of Crack." *Boston Globe*, April 10.

Jaeggi, Rahel. 2018. *Critique of Forms of Life*. Cambridge, MA: Harvard University Press.

Jerolmack, C., & Khan, S. (2014). Talk Is Cheap: Ethnography and the Attitudinal Fallacy. *Sociological Methods & Research*, 43(2), 178–209.

Kahn, Ric. 1999. "Cocksure Bly Cross the Line." *Boston Globe*, May 30: 5.

Katzmann, G. (ed.), *Securing Our Children's Future: New Approaches to Juvenile Justice and Youth Violence*. Washington, DC: Brookings Institution Press.

Kennedy, David M. 1997. "Pulling Levers: Chronic Offenders, High-Crime Settings, and a Theory of Prevention" *Valparaiso University Law Review* 31:449–84.

Kennedy, David A. 2002a. "A Tale of One City: Reflections on the Boston Gun Project." In *Securing Our Children's Future: New Approaches to Juvenile Justice and Youth Violence*, ed. G. Katzmann, 229–61. Washington, DC: Brookings Institution Press.

——. 2002b. "We Can Make Boston Safe Again." *The Boston Globe*, July 15: A11.

Kennedy, David M., Anthony A. Braga, and Anne M. Piehl. 2001. "Developing and Implementing Operation Ceasefire." In *Reducing Gun Violence: The Boston Gun Project's Operation Ceasefire*, 5–54. Washington, DC: National Institute of Justice, U.S. Department of Justice.

Kennedy, David M., Anne M. Piehl, and Anthony A. Braga. 1996. "Youth Violence in Boston: Gun Markets, Serious Youth Offenders, and a Use-Reduction Strategy." *Law and Contemporary Problems* 59 (1): 147–96.

Kilpinen, E., 2008, June. Pragmatism as a Philosophy of Action. In *First Nordic Pragmatism Conference, Helsinki, Finland*.

Kilpinen, Erkki. 2009. "The Habitual Conception of Action and Social Theory." *Semiotica*, 173 (1): 99–128.

Kleiman, Mark. 2002. "Policing Boston's Violence." *Boston Globe*, April 16: A21.

Latour, Francie. 2002. "Grand Jury to Get Police Shooting." *Boston Globe*, February 15: A1, A5.

Lehr, Dick, and Lianne Attersley. 2009. *The Fence: A Police Cover-Up Along Boston's Racial Divide*. New York: Harper.

Leifer, Eric Matheson. 1991. *Actors and Observers: A Theory of Skill in Social Relationships*. New York: Garland.

Levine, Jeremy. 2016. "Slow Train Coming: Power, Politics, and Redevelopment Planning in an American City," PhD Dissertation, Harvard University.

Lindblom, Charles E. 1959. "The Science of 'Muddling Through.'" *Public Adminstration Review* 19 (2): 79–88.

Locy, Toni. 1991a. "Bungling the Basics: Poor Police Work Hampers Investigations." *Boston Globe*, April 7: 24–25.

——. 1991b. "Bungling the Basics: Many Arrests Are Based on Problem-Prone Procedure." *Boston Globe*, April 8: 1, 8.

——. 1991c. "Bungling the Basics: A Question of Preparation Inadequate Group-Work by DA's Office Dooms Some Cases." *Boston Globe*, April 9: 10.

——. 1991d. "Bungling the Basics: Supervision, Facilities Found Lacking." *Boston Globe*, April 10: 1, 16.

——. 1992. "Suffolk DA May Find Post Tough to Keep." *Boston Globe*, July 30: 1, 21.

MacIntyre, Alasdair. *After Virtue*. A&C Black, 2013.

McGinn, Kathleen L., and Alexis Gendron. 2002. *Reverend Jeffrey Brown: Cops, Kids and Ministers*. Harvard Business School Case Study 9-801-284. Harvard University.

McGrory, Brian, and Zachary R. Dowdy. 1995. "Prosecutor of Gangs Is Shot Dead." *Boston Globe*, September 26: 1, 26.

McRoberts, Omar M. 2004. *Streets of Glory: Church and Community in a Black Urban Neighborhood*. University of Chicago Press.

——. 2005. "H. Richard Niebuhr Meets 'The Street.'" In *Taking Faith Seriously: Valuing and Evaluating Religion in American Liberal Democracy*, ed. Mary Jo Bane and Brent Coffin, 94–112. Harvard University Press.

Mead, George Herbert. 1932. *The Philosophy of the Present*. LaSalle, IN: Open Court.

——. *Mind, Self and Society*. Vol. 111. University of Chicago Press.: Chicago, 1934.

——. 1938. *The Philosophy of the Act*, ed. C. W. Morris et al. Chicago: University of Chicago Press.

Merton, Robert K., and Elinor Barber. 2011. *The Travels and Adventures of Serendipity: A Study in Sociological Semantics and the Sociology of Science*. Princeton, NJ: Princeton University Press.

Padgett, John F. and Walter W. Powell. 2012. *The Emergence of Organizations and Markets*. Princeton, NJ: Princeton University Press.

Patterson, Orlando, and Christopher Winship. 1999. "Boston's Police Solution." *New York Times*, March, 2.

Peirce, C. S. 1931–58. *Collected Papers of Charles Sanders Peirce*. 8 vols., vols. 1–6 ed. C. Hartshorne & P. Weiss; vols. 7–8 ed. A. W. Burks. Cambridge, MA: Harvard University Press

Putnam, Hilary. 1989. "A Reconsideration of Deweyan Democracy." *Southern California Law Review* 63: 1671.

Sawyer, R. Keith. *Social Emergence: Societies as Complex Systems*. Cambridge: Cambridge University Press, 2005.

Sewell Jr, William H. 2005. *Logics of History: Social Theory and Social Transformation*. Chicago: University of Chicago Press, 2005.

St. Clair Commission Report. 1992. "Report of the Boston Police Department Management Review Committee." Submitted to Mayor Raymond L. Flynn, January 14. http://vault. blackstonian.org/wp-content/uploads/2016/10/St.-Clair-Commission-Report.pdf.

Stark, David, 1996. "Recombinant Property in East European Capitalism." *American Journal of Sociology* 101 (4): 993–1027.

——. 2011. *The Sense of Dissonance: Accounts of Worth in Economic Life*. Princeton, NJ: Princeton University Press.

Strauss, Anselm L. 1978. *Negotiations: Varieties, Contexts, Processes, and Social Order*. San Francisco: Jossey-Bass.

Sunstein, Cass R. (1995). "Incompletely Theorized Agreements," *Harvard Law Review*, 108 (7): 1733–1772.

Tench, M. 2002. "Group Offers Support for Evans, Points to Progress in Curbing Violence." *Boston Globe*, September 21: 34.

Wehrwein, Zach and Christopher Winship. 2018. "Facts or Tools: Strong Realist versus Pragmatist Understandings of Morality." Unpublished. Harvard University.

Weick, Karl E. 1993. "The Collapse of Sensemaking in Organizations: The Mann Gulch Disaster." *Administrative Science Quarterly* 38 (4): 628–652.

——. 2001. *Making Sense of the Organization.* Oxford: Blackwell.

——. 2009. *Making Sense of the Organization: The Impermanent Organization. Vol II.* New York: Wiley.

Whitford, Josh. 2002. "Pragmatism and the Untenable Dualism of Means and Ends: Why Rational Choice Theory Does Not Deserve Paradigmatic Privilege." *Theory and Society* 31 (3): 325–63.

Wilkie, Curtis. 1993. "The Holy War of Rev. Rivers." *Boston Globe,* July 18: 1, 26.

Winship, Christopher. 2004a. "End of a Miracle? Crime, Faith, and Partnership in Boston in the 1990s." In *Long March Ahead: African American Churches and Public Policy in Post-Civil Rights America,* ed. R. Drew Smith, 171–92. Durham, NC: Duke University Press.

——. 2004b. "Veneers and Underlayments: Critical Moments and Situational Redefinition." *Negotiation Journal* 20 (2): 297–309.

——. 2006. "Policy Analysis as Puzzle Solving." In *The Oxford Handbook of Public Policy,* vol. 10, ed. Robert E. Goodin. Oxford: Oxford University Press.

——. 2017. "Inchoate Situations and Extra-Rational Behavior." In *Rationality in the Social Sciences,* ed. Helmut Staubmann and Victor Lidz, 223–43. New York: Springer.

Winship, Christopher, and Jenny Berrien. 1999. "Boston Cops and Black Churches." *Public Interest* 136: 52–68.

Wong, Doris S. 1989. "Police Vow to Continue Searches." *Boston Globe,* August 31: 31, 35.

APPENDIX

Methodology

Most research on the emergence of new social forms—whether partnerships, organizations or institutions—is carried out ex post. The researcher chooses a particular structure to analyze and then uses interviews and archival materials to reconstruct its history. There are at least two major limitations to this approach. First, it is difficult to reconstruct evidence of what actually happened, particularly at the level of interactions between individuals. Second, interviewees may share post hoc rationalizations for what has occurred, rather than an accurate description of the causal process that took place, though the post hoc rationalizations can be interesting in themselves (Jerolmack and Kahn 2014). Individuals are quite likely to present activities of the past in a far more coherent and rational fashion than likely occurred, with inconsistent events dropped and supportive material invented.

Fortunately, but also problematically, the analysis reported here is the result of my unknowingly finding myself in a research project. In the summer of 1994, I worked regularly with the Ten Point ministers in an evaluation of a program they were running called "Boston Freedom Summer." During the summers of 1994, 1995, and 1996, I visited the Four Corners neighborhood of North Dorchester, the principal site for the camp, between one and three times a week. During these visits I almost always spent time with the key Ten Point ministers and their staff. In this regard, I was a participant observer. The only problem was that, at tha time, neither the ministers nor I had any idea that they were in the process of creating a partnership with the BPD. In the many days I spent with individuals in Ten Point, I never once heard the ministers or their staff discuss the Boston police. In late 1996, the Ten Point ministers first accepted the BPD's invitation to participate in gang forums. Just as the ministers did not realize that they were forming a partnership with the police, I did not realize that I was a participant observer in what would become a research study. This serendipitous research project allowed me to watch a partnership materialize in real time. Unfortunately, as I was not aware that I was doing research, I was not collecting field notes.

In order to bolster my informal observations, my undergraduate advisee, Jenny Berrien, carried out a series of interviews as part of her senior thesis research (Berrien 1998). All interviews took place during 1997 and 1998. They represent key players' recollections of events that occurred between approximately 1990 and the end of 1996. There is certainly some degree of bias in these recollections. How serious this is not clear, particularly given the theoretical interest here is in understanding how a set of individuals came to understand a common situation. In this regard, retrospective reports most importantly provide evidence of the shared understanding of what emerged.

An additional source of evidence is newspaper articles. From the late 1980s to the present, there has been intense local interest in youth violence, first because of its sharp increase and then later because of the nation-leading drop of 80 percent in the homicide rates during the 1990s, the so-called Boston Miracle. Both locally and nationally, Boston was seen as a city that had succeeded in simultaneously reducing crime rates and improving police/community relations.[13] Hundreds, perhaps thousands, of stories on this topic have been published in the local, national, and international press.

Although newspaper stories may or may not accurately report all of the facts, they do represent a form of public discourse. As such, they can be analyzed for the content of the messages they contain. Various actors, most importantly the ministers, have been quoted frequently in these stories and have written numerous Op-Eds in the Boston Globe and other local newspapers. These Op-Eds contain strong statements about how to think about and tackle the issues of youth violence and race. Thus, articles and Op-Eds are a texts worthy of direct analysis.

All three data sources have their limitations: my direct observations were informal rather than systematically documented; interviews are not always accurate; and newspapers present a very select set of voices. Thus, for this analysis I regularly triangulate on sources. In addition, because I have and have had ready access to key players in the story, I have been able to quickly check any questionable facts. Furthermore, I have solicited factual corrections from the individuals involved after they have read earlier related papers, this paper, and attended talks that I have given on the Boston story.

NOTES

1. Weick acknowledges this. "Most obvious is the affinity with several ideas in pragmatism. To depict impermanent organizing is to presume that people have agency, that there is

an ongoing dialectic between continuity and discontinuity from which events emerge, that humans shape their circumstances, and that minds and selves emerge from action (Maines 1991, 1532). Frequent citations to the work of William James and John Dewey will attest to the pragmatic grounding of this line of argument" (Weick 2009, 5–6).

2. Merton and Barber's (2011) concept of serendipity is related to my concept of wandering. In both cases, there is a chance finding. The difference is that in the case of serendipity, one is not consciously looking for a solution; in fact, there may be no immediate, recognized problem. As I describe later, wandering involves consciously looking for a solution, though with no idea of where to look.

3. Scholars have posed many definitions of intersubjectivity (Gillespie and Cornish 2010). For my purposes, intersubjectivity is a basic shared understanding of a situation. A shared understanding may not mean that the parties involved agree on how something is understood, merely that they know what each other's understanding is. See Winship (2004a) for a discussion of Goffman's (1959) concept of a surface agreement, one possible definition of intersubjectivity.

4. An extreme example of intersubjectivity in Mead's sense is Hutchins's (1995) detailed discussion of how a battleship is brought to dock. Here, no one actor has a full picture of what needs to be done. Rather, myriad actors know what they need to do and how to coordinate their actions with those of immediate relevance to them. Hutchins suggests that failure in this coordination would result in a battleship's stopping many miles inland.

5. Also see MacIntyre (2013) for the importance of history—particularly tradition—as a basis for formulating a new future.

6. Previous accounts of the Boston story that primarily focus on its policy implications for policing can be found in Berrien and Winship (1999, 2000); Winship and Berrien (2000); Winship, Berrien, and McRoberts (2000); and Winship and Berrien (1999).

7. In 1994, Rivers's house was shot up for a second time.

8. A incident that had a parallel structure and outcome was the 1994 beating of a Black undercover police officer by four uniformed officers, both white and Black, who thought he was the suspect they were pursuing. See Lehr and Attersley (2009) for a detailed discussion of this event.

9. David Kennedy suggests that this is the case, at least in Boston, with approximately 1 percent of the youth constituting the real problem (Kennedy 1997; Kennedy, Piehl, and Braga 1996).

10. Informant interview; also see *Globe* Staff (2002a).

11. Globe Staff (2002b, 2002d).

12. See Globe Staff (2002c).

13. Since 2003, homicide rates have varied from year to year, but have remained at approximately half or less of what they were at the worst point in the 1990s.

13. Pragmatist Comparative-Historical Sociology

ISAAC ARIAIL REED AND PAUL LICHTERMAN

In this chapter, we propose a pragmatist approach to theory and method in comparative-historical sociology. We discuss the meaning and purpose of sociological comparisons between cases, the understanding of causality that should inform such comparisons, how to think reflexively about using historical comparisons to make explanatory claims, and the way in which the interpretation of conduct articulates with counterfactual thinking. We also consider the potential of *normative counterfactuals* in comparative-historical research, a fraught topic that we believe needs much more attention.

A pragmatist historical sociology departs significantly from prevalent epistemologies of historical comparison by crafting interpretive explanations of conduct. The term *conduct*, taken from John Dewey and Charles S. Peirce, indicates both our philosophy of human action and our understanding of inquiry in historical sociology. We see both as forms of "controlled conduct," always involving meaningful communication, with varying amounts of reflexivity.[1] Since historical sociology is about *human* history and history contains *action* in the form of conduct, our perspective introduces a particular set of challenges for the historical sociologist— which overlap with the problems that attend the work of historians and scholars of comparative literature.[2]

Specifically, the historical sociologist must interpret meaning, and account for how human creativity and idiosyncrasy introduce contingencies into the making and unmaking of social forms and patterns. To illustrate this distinctive approach and grasp its implications, we compare a historical sociology centered on conduct and its multiple interpretations with a well-known approach to causal comparison in historical sociology that is centered on set theory and necessary and sufficient causality. This comparison reveals certain surprising but useful features of pragmatist accounts of action for historical sociologists.

Our discussion draws on several classic studies in historical sociology to make our argument—most prominently, Leon Trotsky's *History of the Russian Revolution* and W. E. B. Du Bois's *Black Reconstruction in America*. We also avail ourselves of Reed's work for a "backstage" look at how to develop the kind of comparison we are advocating. Finally, read in tandem with an earlier article by the same authors, our argument highlights several concerns common to historical sociology and ethnography.[3]

CHAINS OF MEANINGFUL ACTIONS AND THEIR INTERPRETATION

To start, consider the social world as chains of meaningful actions. Action emerges in relation to problems inside or between unfolding chains of further action that crisscross and crystallize into larger webs of relationships in time and space. Viewed in this way, the social world is made up of an extended network of actions and reactions that flow in relation to each other, cocreating the world.[4] From the pragmatist perspective, action traverses an arc between reflexively planned conduct and habit. In this view, then, the investigator must be willing to comprehend the world of social causes through the interpretation of the meanings embedded in action and left as traces of meaningful action in archives.

There is a stark divide between this approach to action and approaches in social science that resist the interpretation of meanings and focus primarily on observable behavior. Those approaches are driven by a strong and strict epistemology in which all claims boil down to claims about efficient causality. As we will see, this tension, while abstract to the point of being metatheoretical, becomes palpable at key moments in conducting historical-sociological research and constructing sociohistorical explanations. At these moments, a pragmatist concern with theorizing *action* meets a long-standing concern, in the "historical-hermeneutic sciences" with *interpretation*.[5] Let us clarify what we mean by both terms.

We understand action as experimental: actors try out different comprehensions of others' actions and different understandings of the coherence of their own future actions with the present.[6] Actors perform that ongoing, interpretive work in relationship to ends-in-view.[7] Custom, habit, creativity and deliberation link together as actors devise and revise their ends, crafting trajectories of action and forming the sinews of the world. Although this pragmatist theory of human action is well known, it has a variety of useful, if sometimes startling, consequences for historical sociology. Perhaps first and foremost, it means that historical sociological knowledge claims are instances of interpretive explanation.[8]

An *interpretive* explanation is a knowledge claim that merges meaning with causality, just as they cohabit unfolding action in history. An investigator attempts to comprehend the actions of another by carefully translating the other's meaningful horizons of action using the researcher's own horizons of meaning reflexively. When the persons under study acted, they left behind various traces of the meanings embodied in their actions; these provide clues for comprehending why, as well as when and how, they did what they did and what it meant to them when they did so.[9] The investigator who spends enough time with these traces can begin to reconstruct the meaningful background for action. But this is not merely a matter of collecting traces of meaningful action, but rather a matter of *colligation*.[10] Colligation requires the use of concepts from the investigator's own community of inquiry, which is to say, the use and refinement of abstract terms that might or might not be in and of the world of action under study.[11]

The result is an account of what drove the action, what "explains" it. But what do we mean by this term *explain*? In interpretive explanations, explanation means that (a) the actions are contextualized adequately enough that they "make sense" within causal stories that include the actors' meanings reconstructed by the researcher, *even if the interpretive component of the explanation goes beyond those meanings in part*; and (b) the researcher's account answers a "why" question about the causal etiology of the actions under study, concerning why action went in one direction *rather than* another. Now, from whence comes the "rather than" in this second question? "Thinking comparatively," in some sense of the term, is one way in which historical sociologists—and, in different ways, sociologists writ large, as well as historians—refine their why-questions.[12]

As Reed explains in detail, an interpretive explanation need not be "cultural" in the specific sense of preferring solidarity, norms, or "ideation" as the motivating drivers of action. Interpretive explanations can point to powers and interests, domination and exploitation, trade and moneymaking, and various forms of social hierarchy in their construction of a causal story.[13] But interpretive explanations do such pointing in a way that is conditioned by the landscapes of meaning on which (for example) exploitation occurs.

Historical sociology offers vivid examples of locating sociological explanations within landscapes of meaning. Richard Biernacki argued that the exploitation of labor in early capitalism had to be examined against the background of how German and English workers conceptualized and signified labor and labor time differently.[14] Philip Gorski argued that the construction of state hierarchies and the manifestation of state power in Prussia and the early modern Netherlands occurred against the background of confessional similarities that obtained between rulers and their agents in, for example, the tax ministry.[15] As these examples indicate, in interpretive explanation, there is a great deal to be gained from comparative thinking. However, comparison has not, in sociological thought, generally been imagined as a manifestation of historical hermeneutics, in the sense that "depth" interpretation is often thought of as the approach that is appropriate for the highly detailed and contextualized study of a *single* case. We will take a different tack, suggesting that a pragmatist understanding of action provides the necessary background for pursuing comparison across small numbers of cases, in the pursuit of interpretive explanations for each case. First we discuss a comparative imagination that has become prominent in historical sociology among those who do not aim for interpretive explanation, in order to clarify what is distinct about our own proposal.

COMPARISON IN HISTORICAL SOCIOLOGY AND THE MOVE TOWARD CAUSAL COMBINATORICS

As historical sociology emerged as a recognizable cluster of work with a set of shared problems, the boundary between sociology and history became a location for intense reflection on concept and method.[16] The comparison of cases in the form of national trajectories, and the powerful causal claims that such comparison enabled, set up a clear contrast between sociology and history with regard to both how investigation was justified and how it was practiced; this contrast mirrored an older distinction between nomothetic and ideographic argumentation in the human sciences.[17] A typified, even stereotypical, image emerged: the sociologist, relying on secondary sources, produced a set of claims about an object or an outcome that spanned many more specific histories or cases, whereas the historian, in touch with specific archival materials, engaged in the discovery of new evidence and the writing of noncausal narratives. While this image is surely far from an accurate description of the messy process of knowledge construction about history and society,[18] it has often played a soft regulatory role in the evaluation of knowledge and provided a thumbnail sketch of how different communities of inquiry could expect to relate to each other.

If we look past this image and a little more closely at the formation of a collective identity for "comparative-historical sociologists," we quickly realize that, as Thomas Kuhn might have predicted, the interpretation and reinterpretation of exemplary studies by practitioners helped to make the subfield into a self-conscious community of inquiry. Barrington Moore's *Social Origins of Dictatorship and Democracy* and Theda Skocpol's *States and Social Revolutions*, in particular, asked and answered a series of questions about the emergence of the modern world; and though full of historical narrative and interpretive judgment, they also finished their studies in a positivistic veneer. Suggested (in Moore's case) or stated (in Skocpol's), the Millian method of similarity and difference became the basis for strong causal claims in the field. And so, comparative-historical sociology emerged via a fraught relationship with empiricism as a philosophical orientation.[19] On the one hand, comparative-historical sociology was full of resolutely theoretical, even deductive, argumentation played out on history as empirical territory, whether in the form of Moore's Marx/Weber synthesis or in the form of rational choice hypothesis generation from .axiomatic principles.[20] On the other hand, as comparative-historical sociology developed a variety of methods for sifting through evidence, it retained an understanding of the relationship between knower and known that most would recognize as having a familial resemblance to logical empiricism in its understanding of scientific inquiry.[21]

The methodological arguments that ensued from this and other initial tensions in the field have been well documented.[22] The vibrancy of these debates led to the development of alternative epistemological frames for understanding inquiry, including pragmatist and interpretive ones.[23] But among these, surely one of the most important and influential strands of methodological reflection was the careful formalization and regrounding of comparative logic in set theory, which we take as a foil to our own efforts.

In response to the philosophical difficulties invoked by the Millian method, Charles Ragin, James Mahoney, and Gary Goertz, among many others, made a radical and creative departure, which nonetheless embodied in a clear way the intellectual torque of the classics of the field. Keeping the spirit of Moore and Skocpol alive, they replaced the reliance on Mill with a turn to J. L. Mackie and INUS causality,[24] focusing on the combinations of necessary and sufficient causes.[25] This was an act of creative reinterpretation. These scholars' formalization took several shapes and produced along the way its own language—qualitative comparative analysis (QCA), fuzzy set qualitative comparative analysis (fsQCA), "smoking gun" and "hoop" tests, and "INUS causality" (which takes its name from "insufficient but necessary elements of unnecessary but sufficient causes"). We choose the moniker *causal combinatorics* to refer to the larger arc of compare-and-contrast approaches to historical sociology that runs from the exemplars of the second wave to these later formalizations of the comparative method.[26]

The causal combinatorics approach thinks of cases as the complex interactions between aspects or variables, linked together via the operators "and" and "or," which then produce an analytically defined outcome with varying probability (e.g., "fascist state" or "liberal welfare regime"). Formally, both causes and effects, both process and outcome, are understood to be empirical instances that are inside or outside various sets—for example, those countries or nation-states with a "democratic regime," "autonomous state elite," and so on. This has led to important work on sets as analytically defined representatives of social kinds,[27] but what matters here is the pragmatics of investigation that we get from grounding comparison in set theory.

The reliance on INUS causality thematizes a core intuition in the field. For outcomes that historical sociologists care deeply about (e.g., a country developing a fascist government, whether or not there is a revolution, whether or not a revolution succeeds, etc.), there are routes to those outcomes that go through opposing values on a "variable" or "property of a case." Thus, there might be a causal combination that leads to fascism that involves strong unions and another route to fascism that involves weak unions. To account for these sorts of possibilities, which are frequent in the classics of the field (consider, for example, the massive combinatorics of power contained in Michael Mann's four-volume *Sources of Social Power*), Ragin and others realized that a causal philosophy focused on the drawing together, by the "and" and "or" operators, of various (in)sufficient and (un)necessary causes would be particularly appropriate. The advocates of causal combinatorics are fond of contrasting their approach to a more mainstream sociological understanding of causality in terms of average effects. In so doing, they share the basic view of their more informal predecessors Moore and Skocpol. That is, they are interested in *combinations of qualities*, not average effects of linearly defined correlations interpreted as causes. In particular, there is a way in which the formalizations pursued by Ragin, Mahoney, and Goertz do seem to capture the "different histories can lead to similar outcomes" *feel* of several, if not all, of the paradigm-setting tomes of comparative-historical sociology.

In short, causal combinatorics has worked as a congenial field-builder for comparative-historical sociology. First, it formalizes the idea, widely respected among historical sociologists, that momentous historical events (e.g., the French Revolution) and world-changing macro-trajectories (e.g., the triumph and spread of British-style capitalism) can be understood as the result of historical conjunctures or "overdetermination."[28] Second, it maintains a bright line between the sociologist and the historian and thereby articulates historical sociology with comparative thinking in social science more broadly construed—for example, with contemporary comparisons between labor struggles in different countries. Causal combinatorics justifies how contemporary historical sociologists tend to approach history and teach a historical-sociological imagination to their students. Put even more practically, one great advantage of causal combinatorics is that it gives a clear and distinct way forward for a student who wants to study X in different settings (countries, colonies, movements) and thereby to write a dissertation.

A final, well-fleshed-out intellectual advantage to causal combinatorics is that it domesticates in a satisfying way the philosophically troubling aspects of counterfactuals in causal analysis. Confronted with the infinite regress that results from combining the question "Why A?" with a counterfactual understanding of causality,[29] causal combinatorics *reduces the set of counterfactuals of concern* to those combinations of the chosen causes that do not (yet?) have actual cases to represent them. This means that, in effect, the only counterfactuals on offer are those for which there is a predesigned variable lodged in the study, a variable that can take on different values (or, in the case of crisp sets, one of the two values of A or ~A). This leads to the essential distinction between an *easy* and a *difficult* counterfactual, defined by the proportion of the causes considered that differ, in the counterfactual, from known cases.[30]

Causal combinatorics has found fans in both so-called qualitative and quantitative approaches to methods in social science.[31] It represents a promising departure from the general linear reality model that, whatever its relationship to statistical method, certainly dominates sociological imagery regarding causality.[32] Nonetheless, voices have arisen to criticize the approach. One set of critiques has emerged from statistical analysis, where the concern is whether QCA, "interpreted as an attempt to formalize qualitative research" and as a method that "combines qual-itative and quantitative methods," turns out to offer "a particularly inauspicious combination of the two."[33] This line of critique generated a rather fierce debate,[34] including contention over whether or not the method can be properly described as "case-oriented."[35]

A second critical conversation concerns the role of temporality in what is, after all, supposed to be a *historical* method. This conversation is centered on certain interventions in historical method made by William Sewell, Jr. In contrast to exper-imental time—which belongs to the causal combinatorics approach—and teleo-logical time—which belongs to world-systems theory and Hegelian Marxism (not considered here)—Sewell advocates eventful time, which "recognizes the power of events in history."[36] This third type bids historical sociologists to a more textured image of temporality. For in this view, social life "may be conceptualized as being composed of countless happenings or encounters wherein persons and groups of persons engage in social action." Most of these "occurrences" do not rise to the level of events, because they tend to reproduce the structures that constrain them. In contrast to occurrences, however, "*events* may be defined as that relatively rare subclass of happenings that significantly transforms structures."[37] Such transfor-mations are transformations of the *structure of causality itself* in the social world, and thus, for Sewell, "social causality is temporally heterogeneous."[38] This focus on eventfulness, if interpreted in a strong sense, scuttles causal combinatorics inso-far as the latter's grounding in set theory presumes a stability of qualities across eras and/or regions. Causal combinatorics has responded to these concerns, in turn— incorporating notions of path-dependence, critical events, and even formalizing temporality in the schemas of INUS causality.[39]

Our departure from causal combinatorics shares in some of the skepticisms that have been articulated in the field. But we also start from a different place—spe-cifically, from a pragmatist interest in the gap between justificatory discourse and actual practice in the profession. On the one hand, the formalization of INUS causality represented by causal combinatorics points clearly to the imperative of "medium-N" historical sociology—that is, the use of twenty, forty, or one hundred cases, as is common in, say, comparative politics when many countries are com-pared using the "polity scale" measuring amount of democracy from −10 to 10.[40] *And yet, on the other hand, comparative-historical dissertations in sociology continue to involve the careful study of between two and five cases.* Detailed knowledge of the cases, sequences of actions within the cases, and historiographical debates about the cases are used to illuminate each case in terms of the others and against the background of a widely shared set of theoretical concerns in "the literature." Fur-thermore, researchers often say that one case is "made to speak to" another. When we say this, what do we mean? Put directly, if our implicit logic of inquiry is that of set theory and INUS causality, why do we continue to craft small-N case studies in search of historical explanations? Could it be that the implicit logic of our inquiry is not causal combinatorics but something else?

Perhaps the practice of constructing small-N comparisons is outmoded, un-useful research conduct, and thus we should all shift to the medium-N model, grounded in comparative politics. But we propose a different possibility. We attempt to make explicit what regulative ideal of truth-seeking is implicit in this widely held and widely taught practice of small-N comparison between cases. Our gambit is that if comparativists pursue interpretive explanation built on a pragmatist theory of action, we will quickly see the need for, and intellectual advantages of, small-N comparison. To do this, we need to reconceptualize what a case is. We need to shift from the idea of a case as the member of an intersection of sets (including an outcome set) to the idea of a case as a theoretically interpreted chain of meaningful action. We will also need to redesign the conceptual operations that the investigator performs on cases to make them illuminate each other. We propose to use *action-sensitive concepts*, which highlight that social patterns result from *conduct*, not behavior, even when the patterns are large-scale entities like states or voting blocs.

PRAGMATIST ALTERNATIVE: ACTION, COMPARISON AND THE COMMUNITY OF INQUIRY

Imagine a typical three-case-study dissertation in historical sociology. Treat each case as a world unto itself (as perhaps an ethnographer would[41]), *and* also as components of a scholarly puzzle demanding interpretive explanation. Each of these interpretive explanations builds up through comparison with the other two. The researcher produces the comparison by way of one conceptual framework, illuminating the case-specific meanings that help to explain each case while solving the puzzle. Let us clarify how this "illumination" differs from that produced in much comparative-historical research.

For the investigator, each case is simultaneously an *end-in-view* (that is, an object for explanation, which, when explained, constitutes the "completion" of a project) and the *means* for the successful interpretive explanation of the other cases. This language of case-based interpretive explanation contrasts with the language researchers typically use to justify case studies. The typical language is a generalized formula for including values on an analytically defined outcome of interest (or perhaps as a "crucial experiment," testing such a formula on a "key case"). In this combinatorics mode of comparison, the investigator sees a case as a particular, independent collection of factors or variables. The investigator supposes these different collections of variables have led to variation on the outcome variable. Instead, we are proposing that cases form a kind of mini-world of comparative explanation, each case helping the investigator to complete a context-bound explanation of the others. In this mini-world, the cases relate to each other because the investigator interprets and explains them through the same, small set of action-sensitive concepts. These concepts illuminate different chains of conduct—meaningful action—that the concepts have made comparable. The investigator defines cases in terms of different action sequences and different meanings rather than as different outcomes to the same class of event produced by different configurations of variables. Cases, in other words, are co-informing because the investigator carves them out from the world of myriad intersecting action chains via the process of theoretical interpretation.

In what follows, we trace the research process that leads to co-informing cases. That process involves three phases: theoretical casing, comparison via theoretical translation, and critical-reflexive judgments by a community of inquiry that reads and interprets the interpretation offered by the investigator. With these three moves, we address an essential problem confronting historical sociology: its concepts must open to meaningful action (as, indeed, Max Weber repeatedly argued), and yet, at the same time, its explanations often treat patterns of human social life that are massive in scope and scale, requiring such concepts as "the state." By way of careful small-N comparisons, the researcher may admit meanings into explanations of conduct over time, across space. This form of inquiry allows historical sociology to address macrosociological questions with claims that are, in a philosophical sense, about action rather than behavior.

The Work of Casing Constructs Meaningful Chains of Action

If the world is made up of overlapping chains of meaningful action, which must be somehow parsed and brought into view for analysis, then the first step is to *construct* the object of interpretive explanation. Researchers who pursue historical ethnography have transferred this long-standing issue of casing in ethnography to the project of historical sociology.[42] In this vein, the first point of struggle for the investigator is the complex relationship between the investigator's meanings and those of the actors the researcher is studying.[43] What is at stake in rendering historical sociological investigation hermeneutic in this way?

Consider the study of the French Revolution.[44] In her causal story about the revolution, Skocpol dismissed the relevance of revolutionary consciousness to the event's causal trajectory. Interpretive sociologists of the French Revolution, like Sewell, objected.[45] They insisted that better explanations would be achieved by interpreting, for example, the importance of Enlightenment thought to the Parisian elite. This part of the intellectual history of historical sociology is well known. What has been subject to less reflection are the intellectual problems that this interpretive route to explanation encounters.[46]

One potential problem is the historical equivalent of the ethnographer who is duped by informants. François Furet argued that the Marxist historians of the French Revolution had been *taken in by*, and *uncritically adopted*, the self-understanding of the revolutionaries themselves, which they then elaborated into an "objective" history of the revolution from the perch of their twentieth-century academic offices.[47] This is a specifically hermeneutic difficulty. The way out of (or perhaps through) the difficulty is to imagine a relationship between theoretical conceptualizations of the French Revolution, or whichever "case" or sequence is at hand, and the meanings of the actors involved in the chains of action that make up the revolution, without collapsing one into the other or obliterating the latter.[48] This, then, is the first point of conceptual struggle for the pragmatist sociological historian, who must render her cases in a variety of ways. She must decide a question of duration—where to snip the chains of action, how to consider the contested interpretations that actors make of their actions as they unfold, and how to grasp and summarize these contested interpretations as part, but not the entirety, of the flow of action that makes up the "revolution itself."

This is one point at which our approach departs from causal combinatorics. The latter would seek to define revolution in terms of outcome, thus rendering, in one fell swoop, actions taken under different meanings, in different times and places, as *prima facie* comparable insofar as they involved a radical shift in state-society relations, regardless of their meaning. (But how do we measure what makes a shift radical?) We are insisting, in contrast, that the historical sociologist should develop an interpretation of the cases under study *that readily admits of meaningful action* and that also opens, for each case, onto wide-ranging debates that have interpreted and reinterpreted those actions in different terms. For the researcher, this means bringing action-sensitive concepts even to the interpretation and explanation of structures such as states or conjunctures of manifold events such as revolutions. Our upcoming discussion of Reed's research illustrates this move to conceptualize historical cases in an action-sensitive way.

We recognize that there is no getting around an engagement with the historiography of the French Revolution, if that is our object of interpretive explanation. Yet, our approach suggests that the investigator should use historiographic work to inform casing with concepts different from those that often have anchored historical inquiry. before there can be a sociological why-question about the French Revolution, a series of intellectual decisions have to be made about how to think about the revolution "as" a case of something (contentious politics, societal collapse, transformation of power, a violent contest between different political theologies, the advent of bureaucracy and the audit society). Still, we argue that underneath these choices is the substrate of meaningful chains of action that become the focus of comparison. In this way, the theoretical operation of casing the French Revolution proceeds from our pragmatist view of conduct: persons in action situations solving problems and acting on projections of what the future could or should be. Even Jacobins were actors with shifting ends-in-view.

This tension between the meanings of the historical actors and the concepts of the various investigators who have studied those actions is a classic location for pondering historical interpretation. However, insofar as one pursues an interpretive explanation, this hermeneutic tension must be brought into conversation with the problems of historical causality and counterfactuals. Specifically, one could ask of the (myriad, historical) interpretation of chains of action in the French Revolution the same questions that John Levi Martin addressed to the *infinite* chains of causality that sit behind any given event: "No protozoa, no French Revolution." How to contain or reduce this impossible infinity? Even if one manages to snip the chains of action in a theoretically guided way and render the revolution as a particular kind of action situation, one is then confronted with the problem of "instead of what?" Even if we identify and interpret in a way that includes actors' meanings in a chain of action, we still need a clear contrast or foil for that chain to become an object of interpretive explanation.[49]

Theoretical Translation Makes Chains of Action Comparable

Interestingly, comparison and theoretical translation show up in some works by revolutionary actors themselves. Leon Trotsky's *History of the Russian Revolution* repeatedly veers into accounts of conduct and meaningful action that are grounded in comparison. For example, in a key moment early in his text, Trotsky draws a threefold comparison between the royal houses of England in 1688, France in 1789, and Russia in 1917, with specific attention to the mood and character of royal *action*. This is so he can show the degree to which, in each case, nobility (both high and rank and file) can become discontented with a "blind" monarchy and, in their discontent, open space for other action. In evocative language, he writes in comparing France and Russia: "Although separated from each other by five quarter centuries, the tsar and the king were at certain moments like two actors playing the same role. . . . They both make the impression of people who are overburdened by their job, but at the same time unwilling to give up even a part of those rights of which they are unable to make any use. . . . They both go toward the abyss 'with the crown pushed down over their eyes.'"[50]

This similarity is drawn out, in Trotsky's narrative, as itself in contrast to a series of differences between the capacities for action of the Russian proletariat and its European counterparts (in both the early twentieth century and during the age of revolutions). Trotsky plays the role, in his text, of both actor and investigator. *History of the Russian Revolution* is full of arguments not only comparing Russia 1917 with France 1789, and not only comparing Russia 1917 with Russia 1905, but also with notes on how the Russian Revolution *could have or should have gone*. His tracking of the why and wherefore of the Bolshevik project takes comparisons from all sorts of places — including ones that exist only in the (his?) revolutionary imagination. For interpretive explainers who are not revolutionary actors, we would point out another aspect of Trotsky's comparisons: they are descriptions of action situations that were navigated in a certain way given the habits of persons in monarchical positions.

For Trotsky, the hermeneutic circle between actor and investigator could, in part, be closed by his own revolutionary consciousness. In contrast, for many investigators, the starting point for conducting historical sociology is a rather radical *alienation from* the consciousness of those being interpreted. This perhaps accounts for why, while Trotsky was sure he had a case of revolutionary action and its sources, most of the time in intellectual life, such casing is a difficult interpretive issue.

Trotsky took for granted precisely those theoretical renderings of phenomena that preoccupy dissertation writers in sociological history and ethnography: what is this a case of?

To compare chains of action and build interpretive explanation, we first must make those chains comparable through a process of *theoretical translation*. We translate them into a common set of conceptual terms that can illuminate situated action.[51] It is important to note that this theoretical translation embeds cases in a particular *abstract* language, without making assumptions about how generally applicable that language may be.[52] To try to get a handle on how this works, we turn to a much more mundane example, in which coauthor Reed pursued theoretical translation, in the hopes of grasping two (seemingly) very different cases in a way that would productively pair them. Reed compares action and communication in the Whiskey Rebellion (1794) and the Salem Witch Trials (1692).[53] What is being compared? A rebellion is not a witch hunt, even presuming that we could agree on generalizable definitions of those terms. Instead, Reed compared the use of elaborate, coherent metaphysical worldviews—for example, the seventeenth-century "Puritan mind" or late-eighteenth-century millenarian Christianity—by actors in response to their experience of social and political uncertainty and chaotic unpredictability.[54]

Reed's interpretation of the Salem Witch Trials articulated the process whereby a highly public witch trial became the opportunity for certain actors to grasp at power via the rendering of a coherent ideology, which brought some sort of (imagined) order to an otherwise uncertain moment for Massachusetts Bay Colony. Reed found in Salem ample evidence of a situation in which the usual guardrails of action and reaction had been removed. Amid the uncertainty bequeathed by a relative lack of political authority, a group of ministers were able to use the rhetorical power of coherence to render their interpretation of the crisis convincing.[55]

Having originally chosen the Whiskey Rebellion case to represent the "modern" 1790s in contrast with the "metaphysical" 1690s, Reed stumbled upon a different question: why did the Whiskey Rebellion, at least on the surface, not involve the use of a coherent worldview to "fill in" for the lack of political authority during a crisis? The whiskey rebels certainly had access to a coherent millenarian worldview, complete with an apocalyptic narrative structure—one of their leaders was the millenarian preacher and all-around charismatic itinerant Herman Husband. Why did his world-ordering views fail to become dominant, given their ability to cognitively tame the uncertainty of the situation? Thus, via theoretical translation of a concern with "crisis action," Reed constructed a counterfactual for 1794 taken from Salem in 1692, even though the two events and their outcomes typically would not belong in the same "class" of event or involve the same "outcome"—as they would need to in order to participate in the same causal-combinatoric explanation. Rather, there was useful comparison to be drawn between specific strands of *conduct*—both conceptualized as action taken in a mood of uncertainty.

Translating the Salem episode into the language of action helped to constitute the Whiskey Rebellion as a case and explanatory problem. In contrast to the rhetorical evidence found in the Salem case, the whiskey rebels' speeches and communications among one another often evinced incoherence, humor, and nervousness, a stark difference from the epic seriousness and apocalyptic narratives of Cotton Mather and other Salem ministers. Following this lead, Reed discerned in the Whiskey Rebellion a series of *varyingly coherent* interpretations of the ongoing event, rather than a preponderance of explicit and coherent worldviews circulating among a wide circle of relevant actors. One of these interpretations of the rebellion—that emanating from the federal government in Philadelphia—attempted to exert power via its rhetorical coherence; others did not. But this difference in actors' self-conscious quest for coherence in each case demanded an explanation, given that only some reached for the power of coherence. The reasons for these differences (in particular, the way the whiskey rebels vacillated between various understandings of their project and who they represented) enabled Reed to propose a new interpretation of the course of events in each case and, furthermore, articulate *variation* in the interpretation of uncertainty that helps to constitute "crisis."

Simultaneously, the case of the Whiskey Rebellion, theorized this way, became a contrast for understanding Salem. On further investigation, the actors' contest of public interpretations during the Whiskey Rebellion revealed a shared focus on sovereignty and law, a thematization of extant political conflicts and grievances widely experienced among the American electorate at the time. In contrast, the focus on the threat of witches in the ministerial interpretation of unsettled times in Massachusetts Bay Colony redirected public attention away from the concerns evinced by others in the uncertain milieu, opening a gap between the institutions that were crumbling and the representation of threat. In sum, the contrast between the Whiskey Rebellion and the Salem Witch Trials enabled Reed to distinguish between a *thematic* series of interpretations of crisis as guides for action (Whiskey Rebellion in 1794) and a *fetishized* series of interpretations of crisis as guides for action (Salem Witch Trials in 1692). These were two different formats of rhetorical struggle, each emerging when the parameters of social and political life were ill-defined *and* that condition *was understood as a crisis*. The study joined its findings to a scholarly inquiry into crisis, though conspicuously not the inquiries into violent responses to increases in taxation or witchcraft—the literatures that might seem most obvious for the topics at hand. The point here, for comparative-historical sociology, is that the same events may be cased and theoretically translated in different ways for different scholarly contributions.

Theoretical translation, then, involves interpreting historical episodes in terms of action-sensitive theoretical concepts, such that comparing those episodes contributes to developing an interpretive explanation of each case. The action-sensitive theoretical concepts here were interpretations of crisis, use of coherent ideological formations, and claims-making over shared problems.

It is an interesting and difficult question whether such action-sensitive concepts can do this work for all of the pressing questions of comparative-historical sociology. One might also ask whether a causal combinatorics could be constructed around the set "responses to crisis." Should we try to render well-honed concepts and operationalizations from comparative social science (e.g., the democracy scale, the distinction between social and political revolutions, the emergence of welfare-state policy) in this way? And should the *rhetoric of crisis* become, in itself, a kind of reified point of study for fuzzy-set analysis? In lieu of final answers to these questions, we would point out that Weber repeatedly wrestled with these difficulties of interpretation and generalization—often with a certain amount of irony and humility concerning the capacities of social science—when conceptualizing historical sociology. For example, consider the following passage:

> The causal analysis of personal actions proceeds logically in exactly the same way as the causal analysis of the "historical significance" of the Battle of Marathon, i.e. by isolation, generalization, and the construction of judgments of possibility. . . . Let us assume a temperamental young mother who is tired of certain misdeeds of her little child, and as a good German . . . gives it a solid cuff. . . . Let us assume that the howls of the child release in the paterfamilias, who, as a German, is convinced of his superior understanding of everything, including the rearing of children, the need to remonstrate with "her" on "teleological" grounds. . . . We proceed logically in the same way in the analysis of a decision of Napoleon or Bismarck as we did in the example of our German mother.[56]

Interpreters of Weber have discussed at length the implication of passages like these, usually in the context of asking about "individualist" versus "collectivist" tendencies in different classical theorists. We bring it in here for a different reason. Read from a pragmatist point of view, the implication of Weber's work on action is that the basis for comparison in sociology is the way in which meaningful action is the substrate out of which grows substantive variation in social formations. Thus, a classic interest in historical sociology—for instance, state-formation—must, even when working at higher levels of aggregation or abstraction, provide some kind of account of action, understood not in a methodologically individualist way but in a pragmatist way. This would mean (a) a grounding in the creativity of action and action-reaction chains[57] and (b) a tracing of social process and relationality at multiple levels.[58]

A Community of Inquiry Judges Comparisons and Counterfactuals

If investigation is itself a form of conduct, then this conduct happens through communication and, in particular, through links with a series of overlapping publics, whose "matters of concern" inform the intellectual process of constructing, publicizing, and justifying an interpretive explanation. Following the classical pragmatists—and especially Peirce and Dewey—we propose that knowledge claims are worth believing when evidence for them emerges from experimental encounters with reality *and* those claims with evidence survive cross-examination in relevant communities of inquiry. Communities of inquiry justify the scientific believability, or "integrity," as Peirce put it, of those claims—until future tests give a community reason to doubt them.

Peirce, the scholar probably most identified with the notion of a community of inquiry, imagined scientists continually disputing one another's knowledge claims and vetting the evidence behind those claims.[59] Participants in such a community would commit to heeding and even encouraging their own and their colleagues' doubts regarding some belief about the world. They would work to resolve doubt through inquiry presented to a community of inquirers for assessment and public criticism, rather than trying to bar doubt by fiat, tenacious attachment to what one wants to believe, or appeal to preexisting popular conceptions.

Since any community of historical inquiry will have access to an impossibly wide variety of cases, selection requires balancing two features that pull the community in different, even opposed, directions. One is the community's aspirations, its commitment to the ongoing reality testing and cross-examination that Peirce and Dewey both championed. In Dewey's view, those aspirations bid the scholar choose cases that will facilitate "inference" that is fruitful for future empirical inquiry. For us, that could be further inquiry into a process we are trying out as part of the explanation, or simply further inquiry that meets the end-in-view for one case.[60] Communities of inquiry are also empowered—yet constrained, too—by a second feature: commonsense assumptions. These include relevance criteria— the conventions through which the community deems certain kinds of cases relevant for a question that is itself widely viewed as relevant, but also less articulate, commonsense understandings.[61] As Dewey was at pains to show his colleagues in both the philosophy of science and political philosophy, the commonsense constraints set by communities of inquiry can limit a researcher's possibilities of experimental thinking. The community of inquiry results as an ambivalent medium for communication. The community can be an obstacle to innovative research; yet it also empowers the inquiry, because it takes the community's collective knowledge to channel an investigator's finite energies usefully toward solving research problems.

Problems are important not because any individual deems them so but because a community of cooperating, competing scholars deems them to be so. Put directly, scholarly common sense is indispensable yet always risks diminishing the future inferential value of a comparative explanation in ways Dewey warned against.[62] The historical sociologist needs to cultivate experimental savvy that balances these two research-shaping capacities of the community.

Experimental savvy in addressing some research problems will require the investigator to engage the community of inquiry in *metacommunicative dialogue*, or what is sometimes called *theoretical critique*. In this kind of dialogue, investigators reflect on the foundational assumptions behind the concepts we use, the entire line of inquiry we are propounding, and the criteria we use to situate ourselves in one conversation ("a literature") rather than another. Sometimes inquirers reconstruct literatures to highlight passing observations as facts that are significant for the community's longer lines of inquiry. They also engage in these reconstructions to challenge the meaning of concepts, sometimes providing alternative genealogies and different futures for a well-worn concept. As argued elsewhere,[63] this kind of dialogue is not a supplement to empirical or causal claims that emerge first. Rather, it is integral to what gives those sociological beliefs their scientific warrant or integrity. From the Peircian or Deweyan point of view, empirical claims-making is a social process, not simply an unmediated report on so-called reality tests from the empirical world. On the arc from reflective to habitual action in communities of inquiry, metacommunicative dialogue represents the strongly reflective end.[64] The *language* and, in particular, the *abstract concepts with varying denotations and connotations* through which this dialogue takes place is what we call *theory* in the human sciences.

This concern with language—and indeed, with common sense—in metacommunicative dialogue is perhaps evidenced by the way in which Reed uses *metaphor* to engage with theories of crisis in the aforementioned paper. The essential tension in social science talk about "crisis" is one between an objective account of crisis focused on institutions and long arcs of social and political development that come together in a conjuncture, and a subjective account of the feeling and naming of crisis. In seeking to move through this opposition in a productive way, Reed replaced geological metaphors of "rupture" and "building tension" and their opposite, the idea of a crisis as "vacuum" of power, with the metaphor of crisis as a prism. This metaphor attempts to shift the background common sense of what a crisis is slightly, suggesting that instead of an explosion of forces that destroys structures and creates a vacuum, a crisis *projects* previous power formations into a new shape or space, like a prism transforming or differentiating an image as it projects it onto a wall.

Debating Relevance Criteria Bolsters Small-N Interpretive Explanation

Interpretive explanation invites comparison in the wild—off the grid of previously defined outcomes and combinations of variables, though very much within the space of metacommunication within one or more communities of inquiry. In this approach, the language of investigation re-renders meaningful action that has left traces of itself in archives and has been subject to interpretation and reinterpretation in varied, overlapping communities of inquiry over successive generations of historians. We have been concerned with how theory in the human sciences can render meaningful action,[65] and in the case of historical sociology, our programmatic argument has been that this means introducing action-sensitive theoretical concepts. Comparison, then, contributes to interpretive explanation while retaining the end-in-view of a context-sensitive explanation of each particular case we compare. Comparison via theoretical translation provides an image of different ways conduct could have gone.

This way of thinking about what historical sociology is and does as a knowledge project prescribes close readings of only a few cases. This is, in part, because this approach asks the investigator to engage in a study of the interpretations of interpretations (of interpretations . . .) that make up the historiography of an event, process, or time period. It then asks her to move beyond these into an interpretive explanation of conduct. This is the moment of abstraction, when the relationship between history and sociology is (re)forged—a historical sociological version of maximal interpretation.[66] This is, necessarily, an abstraction away from the inference of historical details from indexical signs.

The introduction of action-sensitive concepts, and the investment in interpretation, means that, in pragmatist historical sociology, the line between sociology and history becomes a knife's edge. On the one hand, there is an inescapably theoretical aspect of these interpretive explanations and the invocation of certain theoretical traditions, concerns, and conflicts between schools of thought that would make many historians uneasy, for they lead quickly away from the specificity of a given historical interpretation. On the other hand, the historical sociologist is tasked with appreciating contingency in a way that is familiar from debates about historical knowledge that sit well outside standard sociological methods.[67]

For a pragmatist comparative-historical sociology, this recovery of contingency comes at a price: the difficulty of rendering myriad counterfactuals manageable for thought requires a solution different from that on offer in causal combinatorics. This process, of *choosing contrasts to a given reconstructed variation*, is essential to explanation, as we have tried to show for ethnography as well.[68] We derive insight and language from the philosopher of explanation Alan Garfinkel, whose one major work—*Forms of Explanation: Rethinking the Questions in Social Theory*, from 1981—insisted on giving the *pragmatics* of explanation pride of place (as opposed to its semantics or syntax).

Garfinkel remarks that "explanations have presuppositions which, among other things, limit drastically the alternatives to the thing being explained."[69] He called the process of coming up with such contrasts "limited negation," insisting on the need to have "a determinate sense of a consequent's 'not' happening. Lacking such a determinate sense of alternatives, one has difficulty seeing how we could give explanations at all; they would have to be so all encompassing as to be impossible."[70] In historical sociology, a community of inquiry's assessments depend heavily on relevance criteria that help scholars decide which contrast cases make sense and are relevant for a given chain of action. Metacommunicative dialogue takes effort, and overturning communal common sense *should* require multiple efforts at limited negation. For if explanations are a species of sensemaking, then they, too, rely on background meanings granted to the investigator by the community of inquiry.

NORMATIVE THEORY AND COUNTERFACTUAL CONTRAST IN THE HUMAN SCIENCES

Thus far, we have explored how theoretical translation via action-sensitive concepts turns other concrete chains of action under study—other cases—into contrast cases. The navigation of crisis in the Salem Witch Trials (fetishization) throws into relief the navigation of crisis in the Whiskey Rebellion (thematization), and vice versa. However, sometimes our research conduct positions historical actors' conduct in relation to normative interpretation about how future action *should* have gone. In those instances, a different source of counterfactuals appears on the scene for interpretive explanation in historical sociology.

There is a large body of literature on pragmatism and social science highlighting the pragmatist break with the fact/value distinction. It argues that democracy as a way of life inflected not only Dewey's public politics but also his logic of inquiry, and it lauds the pragmatist route out of stark oppositions between objectivism and subjectivism.[71] What there have been less of—for sociology, at least—are explicit and specific accounts of how engagement with "ought" can, does, or should inflect engagement with the "is" in a way that manifests the insights of pragmatist philosophy.

How should normativity affect the choice of cases, the analysis of evidence, the writing up of results, or the evaluation of research? Indeed, the salutations bestowed upon pragmatist philosophy for its transcendence of fact and value quickly become discomfort when we face the possibility that the normative project of the investigator would somehow help to determine their findings. In our view, this is in part because we have not done enough work to parse out *how* such a partial determination could happen, thus making it very difficult to gauge the "somehow" in the previous sentence. In this section, we explore a very specific way in which normativity can structure an interpretive explanation in historical sociology: by providing one of the *determined alternatives* to what happened and therefore make an explanatory question valid as well as meaningful to a scientific community of inquiry. Normative interpretation of actually existing history can help to set up a more complex and revealing contrast space to what actually happened and thus inflect the development of interpretive explanations. We begin with a classic example of this research move, at once normative and analytic, in historical sociology and, then briefly sketch how contemporary communities of inquiry could negotiate such a move.

In *Black Reconstruction in America* Du Bois narrates his argument about historical labor struggles in the United States after the Civil War in consistent contrast to two alternatives.[72] Du Bois arrives at one comparison via the theoretical translation of labor and politics in industrialized Europe, as articulated in Marxist concepts and social theories of modernity centered on Europe. But another comparison also comes in: the promise of an American republic that would host a more democratic social life for the entire population of an industrial(izing) society. The first comparison is well known as a critique of classical sociology, which, Du Bois shows, missed the racialized aspects of transitions to modernity. For example, Du Bois's narration of the trajectory of the white worker and the Black worker in America is consistently accompanied by a comparison with the plight of the European working class under industrial capitalism. This contrast of the American case, in which the labor question could not be disentangled from the race question, would in turn inspire renderings of European cases as themselves explainable, in part, by dynamics of racial power. The second contrast has received less attention, but we propose that it is just as important to the meaning of the text. For example, when Du Bois discusses U.S. political history, he often contrasts actual political history with a normatively articulated possibility, as in the following passage:

> In the North, a new and tremendous dictatorship of capital was arising. There was only one way to curb and direct [this dictatorship] to implement public opinion by the weapon of universal suffrage [so] that it would function in the interest of the mass of working men.
>
> To accomplish this end there *should have been* in the country and represented in congress a union between the champions of universal suffrage and the rights of the freedmen, together with the leaders of labor, the small landholders of the West, and logically, the poor whites of the South . . .
>
> This union of democratic forces never took place. On the contrary, they were torn apart by artificial lines of division. The old anti-Negro labor rivalry between white and black workers kept the labor elements after the war from ever really uniting.[73]

In comparison to this unactualized possibility, then, Du Bois advances his interpretive explanation of how "masters of industry" in the north submitted to "the reassertion of the old land-slave feudalism with increased political power."[74]

In passages such as these, a *historically grounded normative counterfactual* is entering the contrast space of determinate alternatives. In so doing, it is giving meaning and structure to the question to which Du Bois's interpretive explanation in *Black Reconstruction* is the answer. Du Bois develops a specific, historical contrast between a process that did take place and one that both could have and should have taken place. He knows it could have taken place because of his analysis of incipient efforts to unite white and Black workers, actual instances of Black suffrage before the end of Reconstruction, and the actual post–Civil War political ambitions of what had been the abolitionist movement.[75] Then, Du Bois's explanation details the causal sequences of action that differentiate this counterfactual "could and should" from the actual historical trajectory.

We find that this practice of making normative counterfactuals part of the contrast space for interpretive explanation, in implicit and sometimes explicit form, has helped to produce many sociohistorical explanations. Sometimes, it comes in a widely shared, explicit explanatory question (e.g., "why no socialism in the United States?"). From pragmatist perspectives, that normative counterfactuals would make their way into social-scientific arguments should not be such a surprise. Dewey held that a community of inquirers is not fundamentally different in its habits, potentials, social blind spots, and projectivity from other modern communities, even though it uses a specialized, more reflexively refreshed vocabulary and maintains what Dewey called a "self-developing and self-correcting" character.[76] Communities of scholarly inquiry wonder about the possibilities for a better society just as do nonscholarly communities; sometimes citizens' frustrations become professors' research problems.

Whether normative concerns emerge inside a community of inquiry or migrate in from outside, metacommunicative dialogue affords the space for scrutinizing potentially normative visions embodied in the research. Furthermore, if we are correct that normative concerns propel some significant part of research in historical sociology, then efforts to rule out explicit discussion of those normative concerns would risk making cases, questions, and contrasts less available to the community's scrutiny. This would make the community of inquiry less generative for future research and more inclined to the fixation of normative projects via authority, rather than by the experimental controlled conduct that constitutes research, according to Peirce and Dewey.

Still, it is important to recognize the risks involved in opening inquiry explicitly to normative counterfactuals, particularly because it is hard to imagine many studies that would reach the magisterial heights of *Black Reconstruction* or *The Eighteenth Brumaire*. Entertaining normative concerns in this way raises the specter of a researcher who will use commonsense dogma to pose research questions, or even to supply interpretations of actors when the record is ambiguous.

Peirce and Dewey were alive to this issue. Dewey considered the social sciences "backward" in relation to the physical sciences because social inquiry relied too much on beliefs that lack empirical findings, or even more subtle and subconscious "intellectual habitudes" shut away from freely circulating, critical communication.[77] We could suppose that unexamined normative predispositions figured large among the beliefs and habitudes on which Dewey wanted to shine fresh, critical light. It is only within "self-developing and self-correcting" communities of inquiry that researchers could try out normative counterfactuals fruitfully. This is not an easy matter. Yet, this mode of inquiry is already under way—for example, in comparisons that serve double duty: David Thacher has set out the category of the "normative case study," and sociologists will be familiar with uses of the Swedish welfare state or anarchist collectives in the Spanish Civil War as cases that carry the aspirations of "ought" as well as the facticity of "is."[78] Such uses have been, in turn, criticized.[79]

If historical researchers articulate questions and develop contrasts in concert with normative concerns, those concerns should be subject to metacommunicative dialogue within the community of inquiry. That dialogue can sustain and even enhance a community of sociohistorical inquiry in three ways. First, when a study at hand *explicitly* notes a normative interest, the community may subject the role of normative influence on the study's contrasts to reflexive scrutiny. Rather than assume that normative concerns should play no part, the community may ask whether and how different normative arguments would reframe the questions that elicit an investigator's interpretive explanation.

Second, when the research community's dialogue allows in normative counterfactuals, the community may embrace and expand research that connects historical sociology to political philosophy. Some signal historical studies already probe the conditions of possibility for political philosophers' ideals.[80] Besides expanding researchers' horizons for what may count as a suitable comparison case, these studies can produce new empirical inferences and new research questions for the community's participants, *even if a given participant is in normative disagreement with a given inquirer.*

Third, by recognizing the role of normative concerns, communities of inquiry may strengthen the metacommunicative dialogue that some studies already sustain when they challenge commonsense normative understandings of social change. For example, some historical scholars have mobilized empirical cases to challenge declensionism—regarding civic participation, political commitment, or personal autonomy and integrity.[81] Others have shown that cultural phenomena such as advertising or self-expressive intimate relationships have more ambivalent, less thoroughly pernicious consequences than scholars often have assumed.[82] In each of these ways, metacommunicative dialogue about normatively inspired counterfactual cases or research questions may expand researchers' intellectual fecundity. Correspondingly, that dialogue diminishes dogmatic reliance on scientism or various forms of scholastic common sense. Clearly, there are more risks and complications to considering normative questions and cases in pragmatist sociological history, but we propose that these are sufficient grounds to have the conversation.

CONCLUSION

We have invited comparative-historical sociology to several distinct challenges. Can the field recognize that history unfolds in chains of meaningful action, forged by creativity as well as habit, linked in temporally heterogeneous patterns of social causation? Can it treat both the inquiry and the objects of inquiry as conduct?

Our argument is that causal combinatorics cannot meet the challenges and opportunities created by viewing historical sociology as a (fully?) human science, but a pragmatist approach can. Instead of comparing sets of factors taken together as the cause of an outcome of interest, we propose to compare chains of meaningful action with concepts that grasp their contours. And rather than take cases as largely self-enclosed entities, we view them as co-informing constructions brought onto paper by the explanatory project that needs them.

Without the relatively routinized procedures of set theory, or Mill's method of similarity and difference, the role of the community of inquiry in actively casing, discerning, and disputing becomes especially salient in pragmatist historical sociology. The community's metacommunication develops an individual scholar's habits of mind, cultivating seasoned judgment about what works as a good comparison or a good counterfactual. For the pragmatist historical sociologist, good comparisons depend on an experimental savvy that can balance the inquiring community's dedication to critical-reflexive scrutiny of evidence and tentative explanations, on the one hand, and commonsense but necessarily parameter-setting assumptions that undergird the community, on the other. Because those commonsense assumptions include relevance criteria as well as less obviously useful, more limiting presuppositions about actors, society, or research questions themselves, we say experimental savvy "balances" the different tendencies of the community rather than exorcising any of them. By way of theoretical translation, the researcher's study joins one or more ongoing lines of scholarly conversation. There is no starting from zero; only a careful reinterpretation of historiographical interpretation can ground historical sociology in the pursuit of truth.

In creating comparison through theoretical translation, with interpretive explanation as the end-in-view, historical researchers may reach for comparisons that would transgress strict definitions of categories of event or outcome. Is a rebellion really enough like a witch hunt that each instance could teach us anything about the other? As Dewey put it, "everything in the world is like everything else in some respects."[83] The savvy researcher may find usefully comparable chains of meaningful action even when conventional notions of subject matter would suggest otherwise. The comparability, however, cannot work via the identification of necessity and sufficiency. Instead, researchers must seek theoretically informed casing that synthesizes concepts from a preexisting scholarly conversation with meanings that animate the chains of action we hope to explain. We have proposed that historical researchers use action-sensitive concepts to guide our comparison of those chains, even if we intend to rejoin inquiries conceived in less action-sensitive ways. States are continually constituted by different forms of doing, including acts of meaning-making; revolutions are constituted by myriad acts that happen in specific sites, real or virtual.

Finally, a close look at case comparisons and counterfactuals in actual research projects suggests to us that in historical sociology, implicit and occasionally explicit normative concerns motivate explanatory projects. Causal combinatorics, with its ultimate focus on comparing outcomes, makes the admission of normative cases or normative questions look like an unscientific imposition of an "ought" onto a "was." In contrast, we suggest several grounds for thinking that pragmatist insights may assist sociological historians in folding normative cases and even normative questions into the ongoing, generative work of communities that seek truth through investigation.

NOTES

1. This argument is developed extensively in Richard Bernstein, *Praxis and Action: Contemporary Philosophies of Human Activity* (Philadelphia: University of Pennsylvania Press, 1999), 177–87, wherein Bernstein develops an interpretation of the theories of action in Dewey and Peirce.

2. See, e.g., Philippa Levine, "Is Comparative History Possible?" *History and Theory* 53: 331–34; Michiel Baud and Willem Van Schendel, "Toward a Comparative History of Borderlands," *Journal of World History* 8, no. 2 (1997): 211–42; and Rita Felski and Susan

Stanford Friedman, *Theories, Approaches, Uses* (Baltimore, MA: Johns Hopkins University Press, 2013).

3. Paul Lichterman and Isaac Ariail Reed, "Theory and Contrastive Explanation in Ethnography," *Sociological Methods and Research* 44, no. 4 (2015): 585–635. For a different, though not entirely incompatible, rendering of this nexus, consider Josh Pacewicz, "What Can You Do with a Single Case? How to Think About Ethnographic Case Selection Like a Historical Sociologist," *Sociological Methods & Research* (2020), https://doi.org/10.1177/0049124119901213.

4. Andreas Glaeser, *Political Epistemics: The Secret Police, the Opposition, and the End of East German Socialism* (Chicago: University of Chicago Press, 2011); Glaeser, "Hermeneutic Institutionalism: Towards a New Synthesis," *Qualitative Sociology* 37, no. 2 (2014): 207–41.

5. Isaac Ariail Reed, "What Is Interpretive Explanation in Sociohistorical Analysis?" in *Inheriting Gadamer: New Directions in Philosophical Hermeneutics*, ed. Georgia Warnke (Edinburgh: Edinburgh University Press, 2016); Hans Joas, *The Creativity of Action* (Chicago: University of Chicago Press, 1996); Wilhelm Dilthey, *Selected Writings*, trans. and ed. H. P. Rickman (New York: Cambridge University Press, 1976); Jürgen Habermas, *The Theory of Communicative Action*, vol. 1, trans. Thomas McCarthy (Boston: Beacon Press, 1984, 1987); and Isaac Ariail Reed, *Interpretation and Social Knowledge: On the Use of Theory in the Human Sciences* (Chicago: University of Chicago Press, 2011).

6. John Dewey "The Need for a Recovery of Philosophy," in *Creative Intelligence: Essays in the Pragmatic Attitude* (New York: Henry Holt, 1917); Bernstein, *Praxis and Action*, 207.

7. Mustafa Emirbayer and Ann Mische, "What Is Agency?" *American Journal of Sociology* 103, no. 4 (1998): 962–1023; Neil Gross, "A Pragmatist Theory of Social Mechanisms," *American Sociological Review* 74, no. 3 (2009): 358–79; and Joas, *The Creativity of Action*.

8. Reed, *Interpretation and Social Knowledge*.

9. Carlo Ginzburg, "Clues: Roots of a Scientific Paradigm," *Theory and Society* 7, no. 3 (1979): 273–88.

10. William Dray, " 'Explaining What' in History," *Theories of History: Readings from Classical and Contemporary Sources*, ed. Patrick Gardiner (New York: Free Press, 1959).

11. Lyn Spillman, "Causal Reasoning, Historical Logic, and Sociological Explanation," in *Self, Social Structure, and Beliefs: Explorations in Sociology*, ed. Jeffrey C. Alexander, Gary T. Marx, and Christine L. Williams (Berkeley: University of California Press, 2004) 216–33. Ethnographers perform a parallel interpretive move. They make sparing use of abstract terms to render the meaningful world of the researched more accessible to researchers who never visited that world but would be able to communicate more accurately in the idioms of the researched after reading the ethnographer's interpretation. See Paul Lichterman, "Thick Description as Cosmopolitan Citizenship," *in Interpreting Clifford Geertz: Cultural Investigations in the Social Sciences*, ed. Jeffrey C. Alexander, Philip Smith and Matthew Norton (New York: Palgrave, 2011) 77–91.

12. Lichterman and Reed, "Theory and Contrastive Explanation in Ethnography."

13. Reed, *Interpretation and Social Knowledge*.

14. Richard Biernacki, *The Fabrication of Labor: Germany and Britain, 1640–1914* (Berkeley, CA: University of California Press, 1995).

15. Philip Gorski, "The Protestant Ethic and the Spirit of Bureaucracy," *American Sociological Review* 60, no. 5 (1995): 783–86; Gorski, *The Disciplinary Revolution: Calvinism and the Rise of the State in Early Modern Europe* (Chicago: University of Chicago Press, 2003).

16. James Mahoney, "Comparative-Historical Methodology," *Annual Review of Sociology* 30 (2004): 81–101.

17. Maurice Mandelbaum, "Historical Explanation: The Problem of Covering Laws," *History and Theory* 1, no. 3 (1961): 229–42.

18. Damon Maryl and Nicholas Hoover Wilson, "What Do Historical Sociologists Do All Day? Analytic Architectures in Historical Sociology," *American Journal of Sociology* 125, no. 5 (2020): 1345–94.

19. Philip Gorski, "The Poverty of Deductivism: A Constructive Realist Model of Sociological Explanation," *Sociological Methodology* 34, no. 1 (2004): 1–33.

20. Edgar Kiser and Michael Hechter, "The Role of General Theory in Comparative-Historical Sociology," *American Journal of Sociology* 97, no.1 (1991): 1–30; Kiser and Hechter, "The Debate on Historical Sociology: Rational Choice Theory and Its Critics," *American Journal of Sociology* 104, no. 3 (1998): 785–816.

21. John H. Goldthorpe, "The Uses of History in Sociology: Reflections on Some Recent Tendencies," *British Journal of Sociology* 42, no. 2 (1991): 211–30.

22. Theda Skocpol, ed., *Vision and Method in Historical Sociology* (New York: Cambridge University Press, 1984); James Mahoney and Dietrich Rueschemeyer, eds., *Comparative Historical Analysis in the Social Sciences* (New York: Cambridge University Press, 2003); and James Mahoney and Kathleen Thelen, eds., *Explaining Institutional Change: Ambiguity, Agency, and Power* (New York: Cambridge University Press, 2009).

23. Margaret Somers, "'We're No Angels': Realism, Rational Choice, and Relationality in Social Science," Symposium on Historical Sociology and Rational Choice Theory,. *American Journal of Sociology* 104, no.3 (1998): 722–84.

24. J. L. Mackie, *The Cement of the Universe: A Study of Causation* (London: Clarendon, 2002).

25. Gary Goertz and James Mahoney, *A Tale of Two Cultures: Qualitative and Quantitative Research in the Social Sciences* (Princeton, NJ: Princeton University Press, 2012); Charles Ragin, *Redesigning Social Inquiry: Fuzzy Sets and Beyond* (Chicago: University of Chicago Press, 2009); Ragin, *Fuzzy-Set Social Science* (Chicago: University of Chicago Press, 2000); Carsten Q. Schneider and Ingo Rohlfing, "Case Studies Nested in Fuzzy-Set QCA on Sufficiency: Formalizing Case Selection and Causal Inference," *Sociological Methods and Research* 45, no. 3 (2016): 526–68; James Mahoney, "The Logic of Process Tracing Tests in the Social Sciences," *Sociological Methods and Research* 41, no. 4 (2012): 570–97; and Mahoney, "Toward a Unified Theory of Causality," *Comparative Political Studies* 41, nos. 4–5 (2008): 412–36.

26. As one version of this arc, consider the passage from Theda Skocpol, *States and Social Revolutions: A Comparative Analysis of France, Russia, and China* (New York: Cambridge University Press, 1979), 33–39; to Charles Ragin, *The Comparative Method: Moving Beyond Qualitative and Quantitative Methods* (Berkeley: University of California Press, 1987); to Goertz and Mahoney, *A Tale of Two Cultures*; to the new introduction (2014) to Ragin, *The Comparative Method*, xix–xxix.

27. James Mahoney, *The Logic of Social Science* (Princeton, NJ: Princeton University Press, 2021).

28. There is also a realist approach to overdetermination that we do not discuss here. See George Steinmetz, "Critical Realism and Historical Sociology. A Review Article," *Comparative Studies in Society and History* 40, no. 1 (1998): 170–86; and Gorski, "The Poverty of Deductivism." The classic debates in Marxism form a background for the realist argument, in particular the passages on overdetermination in Louis Althusser, *Reading Capital: The Complete Edition* (London: Verso, 2016).

29. John Levi Martin, *The Explanation of Social Action* (New York: Oxford University Press, 2011).

30. Ragin, *Redesigning Social Inquiry*, 160–75; Goertz and Mahoney, *A Tale of Two Cultures*, 115–24.

31. On the one hand, see Kristin Luker, *Salsa Dancing Into the Social Sciences: Research in an Age of Info-Glut* (Cambridge, MA: Harvard University Press, 2010). On the other hand, see Bernard Grofman and Carsten Q. Schneider, "An Introduction to Crisp Set QCA, with a Comparison to Binary Logistic Regression," *Political Research Quarterly* 62, no. 4 (2009): 662–72.

32. Andrew Abbott, *Time Matters* (Chicago: University of Chicago Press, 2001).

33. Samuel R. Lucas and Alisa Szatrowski, "Qualitative Comparative Analysis in Critical Perspective," *Sociological Methodology* 44, no. 1 (2014): 1–79; 67.

34. See the articles collected in *Sociological* Methodology 44, no. 1 (2014).

35. Charles C. Ragin, "Comment: Lucas and Szatrowski in Critical Perspective." *Sociological Methodology* 44, no. 1 (2014): 80–94.].

36. William Sewell, Jr., *Logics of History: Social Theory and Social Transformation* (Chicago: University of Chicago Press, 2005), 100.

37. Sewell, *Logics of History*, 101.

38. Sewell, *Logics of History*, 101; emphasis added.

39. Neil Caren and Aaron Panofsky respond to the absence of a concept of time in causal combinatorics. Notably, however, in their articulation of TQCA, Caren and Panofsky explain precisely why this notion of sequence is *not* a notion of path dependence. They explain: if path dependence is represented by the contrasting sequences: A—B—C—D and A—b—X—Y, then the following expression captures "the path not taken": A—b—D—C (x, y). They then note that this creates a pragmatic problem of creating far too many configurations of variables. This is, in essence, the problem of the infinity of counterfactuals, in the sense that the "alternate path" is so different from the identified variables in each case that it requires a new set of attributes to describe it. This would seem to describe something very similar to what Sewell means when he

describes transformative events as "changing the game." Neal Caren and Aaron Panofsky, "TQCA: A Technique for Adding Temporality to Qualitative Comparative Analysis," *Sociological Methods & Research* 34, no. 2 (2005): 147–72; Mahoney and Thelen, *Explaining Institutional Change*; and James Mahoney "Path Dependence in Historical Sociology," *Theory and Society* 29, no. 4 (2000): 507–48.

40. Goertz and Mahoney recognize explicitly that "good qualitative theories must be able to explain substantively important cases," as does Ragin. We share this metatheoretical commitment. However, when it comes to research design, the tendency in fsQCA and related work has been to pursue limitations on the scope of models that end up with, for example, N = 130 or I = 124 On the lower end of the "medium-N" scale, the essential chapter eight of Ragin's *Fuzzy-Set Social Science* includes a table of twenty cases and their degree of membership in the outcome "social revolution" and the necessary condition "state breakdown." Goertz and Mahoney, *A Tale of Two Cultures*, 185, 212–13; Ragin, *Fuzzy-Set Social Science*, 216.

41. Pacewicz proposes the inverse for ethnographers, in "What Can You Do with a Single Case?"

42. Glaeser, *Political Epistemics*.

43. Lichterman and Reed, "Theory and Contrastive Explanation in Ethnography."

44. For considerations of how the study of the revolution has itself become something of an iconic case or model system for the development of social theory, see Michael Guggenheim and Monika Krause, "How Facts Travel: The Model Systems of Sociology," *Poetics* 40, no. 2 (2012): 101–17; Reed, "What Is Interpretive Explanation in Sociohistorical Analysis?"; Isaac Ariail Reed, "Power and the French Revolution: Toward a Sociology of Sovereignty," *Historická Sociologie* 10, no. 1 (2018): 47–70.

45. William H. Sewell, Jr., "Ideologies and Social Revolutions: Reflections on the French Case," *Journal of Modern History* 57, no. 1 (1985): 57–85.

46. But see Reed, *Interpretation and Social Knowledge*, 117–21.

47. François Furet, *Interpreting the French Revolution* (New York: Cambridge University Press, 1981).

48. Isaac Ariail Reed, "Epistemology Contextualized: Social-Scientific Knowledge in a Postpositivist Era," *Sociological Theory* 28, no. 1 (2010): 20–39.

49. On this point, see the extended discussion of *contrastive* explanation, and especially the question of "foils" and "contrast classes," in Lichterman and Reed, "Theory and Contrastive Explanation in Ethnography."

50. Leon Trotsky, *History of the Russian Revolution*, trans. Max Eastman (New York: Penguin, 2017), 68–69.

51. This can be Goffman's situation or Geertz's situation. We do not adhere to a strictly interactionist definition of situations as co-presences. Erving Goffman, "The Neglected Situation," *American Anthropologist* 66, no. 6 (1964): 133–36; Clifford Geertz, *Local Knowledge: Further Essays in Interpretive Anthropology* (New York: Basic Books, 2008).

52. In philosophical conversations, a common location for discussing the opposition between general and particular is the argument about "ceteris paribus laws." In contrast, the difference between abstract and concrete is subject to a different set of arguments;

for example, in the attempt to define "abstract objects." For the former, see James Wood-ward, "Explanation and Invariance in the Special Sciences," *British Journal for the Philosophy of Science* 51 (2000): 197–254. For the latter, see Bob Hale, *Abstract Objects* (Oxford: Basil Blackwell, 1987).

53. Isaac Ariail Reed, "Between Structural Breakdown and Crisis Action: Interpretation in the Whiskey Rebellion and the Salem Witch Trials." *Critical Historical Studies* 3, no. 1 (2016): 27–64.

54. One commonly cited source in sociology is Ann Swidler, "Culture in Action: Symbols and Strategies," *American Sociological Review* 51, no. 2 (1986): 273–86. However, the concern is broader, occupying different thinkers in different human sciences; for example, Gordon S. Wood, "Rhetoric and Reality in the American Revolution," *William and Mary Quarterly: A Magazine of Early American History* 23, no. 1 (1966): 3–32.

55. Isaac Ariail Reed, "Deep Culture in Action: Resignification, Synecdoche, and Meta-narrative in the Moral Panic of the Salem Witch Trials," *Theory and Society* 44: 65–94, 2015.

56. Max Weber, *The Methodology of the Social Sciences*, trans. and ed. Edward Shils and Henry A. Finch (New York: Free Press, 1949), 177–79.

57. Joas, *The Creativity of Action*; Glaeser, *Political Epistemics*.

58. Andrew Abbott, *Processual Sociology* (Chicago: University of Chicago Press, 2016); Mustafa Emirbayer, "Manifesto for a Relational Sociology," *American Journal of Sociology* 103, no. 2 (1997): 281–317.

59. Charles S. Peirce, "Some Consequences of Four Incapacities," in *The Essential Peirce: Selected Philosophical Writings, Volume 1: Selected Philosophical Writings (1867–1893)* ed. Nathan Houser et al. (1868; Bloomington: Indiana University Press, 1992b), 28–55; Peirce, "The Fixation of Belief," *The Essential Peirce: Selected Philosophical Writings, Volume 1: Selected Philosophical Writings (1867–1893)*, ed. Nathan Houser et al. (1877; Bloomington: Indiana University Press, 1992a) 109–23; David Hildebrand, "Genuine Doubt and the Community in Peirce's Theory of Inquiry," *Southwest Philosophy Review* 12, no. 1 (1996): 33–43; and Helen E. Longino, *The Fate of Knowledge* (Princeton, NJ: Princeton University Press, 2002), 4–5.

60. See Dewey's discussion of judgment in designating material as a case. Using the rather different terminology of "kinds," and "traits" that the researcher would use to designate a "kind," he is referring to the same process of deciding what will make for a useful case. John Dewey, *Logic: The Theory of Inquiry* (New York: Henry Holt, 1938), 268–69.

61. Lichterman and Reed, "Theory and Contrastive Explanation in Ethnography."

62. John Dewey, *The Public and Its Problems* (New York: Henry Holt, 1927); Dewey, *Logic*.

63. Lichterman and Reed, "Theory and Contrastive Explanation in Ethnography."

64. Helen E. Longino, *Science as Social Knowledge: Values and Objectivity in Scientific Inquiry* (Princeton, NJ: Princeton University Press, 1990), 5; Longino, *The Fate of Knowledge*, 126.

65. Reed, *Interpretation and Social Knowledge*; Lichterman and Reed, "Theory and Contrastive Explanation in Ethnography."

66. Reed, *Interpretation and Social Knowledge*.

67. Geoffrey Hawthorne, *Plausible Worlds: Possibility and Understanding in History and the Social Sciences* (New York: Cambridge University Press, 1993).

68. Lichterman and Reed, "Theory and Contrastive Explanation in Ethnography."

69. Alan Garfinkel, *Forms of Explanation: Rethinking the Questions in Social Theory* (New Haven, CT: Yale University Press, 1981), 48.

70. Garfinkel, *Forms of Explanation*, 30.

71. Richard J. Bernstein, *Beyond Objectivism and Relativism: Science, Hermeneutics, and Praxis* (Philadelphia: University of Pennsylvania Press, 2011).

72. W. E. B. Du Bois, *Black Reconstruction in America: An Essay Toward a History of the Part Which Black Folk Played in the Attempt to Reconstruct Democracy in America, 1860–1880* (1935; New York: Oxford University Press, 2014).

73. Du Bois, *Black Reconstructon in America*, 197; emphasis added.

74. Du Bois, *Black Reconstruction in America*, 197.

75. Du Bois, *Black Reconstruction in America*, 165, 171.

76. See Dewey, *Logic*, 490. For further development of this point, see Paul Lichterman, "A More Dialogical Community of Inquiry, or, Dredging the Collective Collegial Subconscious," paper presented at Pragmatism and Sociology Conference, University of Chicago, August 2015.

77. Dewey, *Logic*, 487; Dewey, *The Public and Its Problems*, 169–71.

78. David Thacher, "The Normative Case Study," *American Journal of Sociology* 111, no. 6 (2006): 1631–76.

79. Ann Shola Orloff, "Feminist Theories, Sociologies of Gender and Historical Social Sciences," paper presented at the Annual Meeting of the American Sociological Association, August, Montreal, Canada, 2017.

80. Joan B. Landes, *Women and the Public Sphere in the Age of the French Revolution* (Ithaca, NY: Cornell University Press, 1988); David Zaret, *Origins of Democratic Culture: Printing, Petitions, and the Public Sphere* (Princeton, NJ: Princeton University Press, 2000); Michael Warner, *The Letters of the Republic: Publication and the Public Sphere in Eighteenth-Century America* (Cambridge, MA: Harvard University Press, 2009); Sonali Chakravarti, *Sing the Rage: Listening to Anger After Mass Violence* (Chicago: University of Chicago Press, 2014).

81. Michael Schudson, *The Good Citizen* (New York: Kessler, 1998); Francesca Polletta, *Freedom Is an Endless Meeting* (Chicago: University of Chicago Press, 2002); T. J. Jackson Lears, *No Place of Grace: Antimodernism and the Transformation of American Culture, 1880–1920* (Chicago: University of Chicago Press, 1981).

82. Michael Schudson, *Advertising, the Uneasy Persuasion: Its Dubious Impact on American Society* (New York: Basic Books, 1984); Francesca Cancian, *Love in America: Gender and Self-Development* (Cambridge: Cambridge University Press, 1990).

83. Dewey, *Logic*, 268.

14. American Pragmatism and the Dilemma of the Negro

KARIDA L. BROWN AND LUNA VINCENT

Born in the aftermath of the American Civil War, and in the flux of the rapid industrialization, bureaucratization, and professionalization of the country's first industrial revolution, pragmatism was cocreated by a generation of thinkers as a specifically American philosophical apparatus. It is in this era that the imperative of the American intellectual became divorced from European ruminations that were too often concerned solely with the metaphysical aspects of the human condition. Pragmatism instead demanded a turning toward a more reflexive examination of the meaning of Americanness—the "who are we" of it all. In his 1989 book *The American Evasion of Philosophy: A Genealogy of Pragmatism*, Cornel West aptly captures its essence, defining pragmatism as "a specific historical and cultural product of American civilization, a particular set of social practices that articulate certain American desires, values, and responses and that are elaborated in institutional apparatuses principally controlled by a significant slice of the American middle class."[1]

From this articulation we gather that pragmatism is not a static philosophy based on a fixed set of presuppositions; it is instead a mode of inquiry, an intellectual disposition, or, as Hans Joas puts it, "a medium of discourse."[2] It is also steeped in American ideals of liberalism—individuality, meliorism, human will, meritocracy, freedom, and democracy. For this reason, pragmatism remains in a state of striving toward as-yet possibilities.

So what of the subaltern subject? Specifically, what are the possibilities and limits of the pragmatist philosophical tradition for thinking through the "who we are" in America as it relates to the tens of millions of unintended or uncounted peoples—the Native and Black folks whose land, labor, and negation of person-hood the nation-state was founded on?[3] It is here, within this inherent contradic-tion of the American project of democracy, that the continuities and fault lines exist between pragmatism—the great American philosophy—and the political theories derived from the standpoint of the subaltern subject.

Such an analysis is central to a reflection on the utility of pragmatism in the twenty-first century. Today we still live in two Americas; the one for whom these United States were originally fashioned, and the other America, where Black and brown people's very existence is *always already* deemed a problem by the state, in public opinion, and in the soul of the nation.[4] If you agree with these presupposi-tions, the question remains: what is the utility of pragmatism for the subaltern sub-ject? Specifically, how, if at all, can it be useful for thinking from the margins of society?

This chapter explores these questions through a close reading of W. E. B. Du Bois's lifelong engagement with pragmatism and his encounters with its lim-its. A student of William James and the first Black person to earn a PhD from Har-vard University, Du Bois was one of the most influential American thinkers of the twentieth century.[5] He spent his seven-decade career of scholarship, organizing, and activism striving toward achieving the ideals of freedom and equality for the millions of racialized Others around the world: those whose lives were made to exist on the other side of the global color line. His sociology was emancipatory in that it sought earnest incorporation into national life for those "impossible subjects" not granted the entitlements of democracy. In true pragmatist fashion, Du Bois's thinking and approach changed dramatically with the tides of time. However, he remained deeply influenced by pragmatism for most of his life.

It is important to keep in mind that Du Bois came to sociology not as a student of the discipline but as one of its architects. When he began his scholarly career in the mid-1890s, sociology had not yet been recognized as a discipline in the United States. In fact, Du Bois himself could not have earned a PhD in sociology from his alma mater, Harvard University; at the time he attended, the institution did not even offer sociology courses. Instead, like most of his contemporaries, he found his way to the social sciences by way of bricolage. Reflecting on his journey to sociol-ogy during his Harvard days, Du Bois wrote, "Thus in my quest for basic knowledge with which to help guide the American Negro, I came to the study of sociology, by way of philosophy and history rather than by physics and biology, which was the current approach; moreover at that day, Harvard recognized no 'science' of sociol-ogy and for my doctorate, after hesitating between history and economics, I chose history."[6]

Du Bois completed his studies in 1894 with a doctorate in history from Harvard and two years of extended study in sociology and economics at the University of Berlin. On his return from Germany, he immediately turned to the task of estab-lishing his sociological program.

From the outset, he committed his attention to the study of the "Negro Problem," which he described as the mismatch between America's national ideals and its treatment of ten million members of its citizenry.[7] He was unsatisfied with purely philosophical modes of inquiry that pondered the human condition based on universal abstractions. Du Bois instead designed an intellectual program that was empirically based and aimed at realizing radically humanistic ideals. He found what he was looking for at Harvard:

> With the addition of a course in chemistry in a Harvard laboratory under Hill, some geology under Shaler and history under Hart, I was in possession of the average educated man's concept of this world and its meaning. But now I wanted to go further: to know what man could know and how to collect and interpret facts face to face. And what "facts" were. Here I reveled in the keen analysis of William James, Josiah Royce and young George Santayana. But it was James with his pragmatism and Albert Bushnell Hart with his research method, that turned me back from the lovely but sterile land of philosophic speculation, to the social sciences as the field for gathering and interpreting that body of facts which would apply to my program for the Negro.[8]

It was here, during his undergraduate and graduate studies at Harvard, that Du Bois encountered the building blocks that would lay the foundation for the distinct sociological program he would build. Du Bois did not bind his thinking within any one school of thought or political disposition. In fact, he deeply engaged pragmatism, Marxism, communism, social psychology, and socialism throughout his life. However, Jamesian pragmatism was one intellectual framework that he continued to think with.

Du Bois was first and foremost a scholar of *racialized modernity*,[9] meaning that he understood modernity as a product of racial colonial capitalism.[10] His concerns lay with the global color line and the capitalist system that conditioned, structured, and reproduced it. While his work attended to the global consequences of the color line for people of color, Du Bois's central focus in his early work was on the "Negro Problem" in the United States. As a Black person in America, Du Bois could not escape the force of the color line in his own life, personally or professionally, nor could he allow himself to think outside of it. The realities of structural racism, perpetual racial injustice, and spectacular racial violence denied Du Bois the luxury of living in a world of abstraction.

BETWEEN LAW AND CHANCE: DU BOIS'S PHILOSOPHY OF SCIENCE

Whereas the abstract metaphysical leanings of philosophy and theology maintained a stronghold on the social sciences at the beginning of the twentieth century, pragmatism established itself in direct opposition to this approach to understanding the social world. This is because the early thinkers who propagated this new American philosophy, such as Charles Sanders Peirce and William James, were directly shaped by and utterly preoccupied with their shock and dismay brought on by the Civil War and the subsequent proliferation of industrialization, mass professionalization, corporatism, and bureaucracy that emerged in its aftermath. Pragmatism presented an intellectual framework through which to understand, critique, and act against those rapid social transformations that some early thinkers believed were posing a threat to American democratic ideals.[11] It is this inherent dualism that makes pragmatism distinct in character—the commitment to *understand* and to *act*—that makes it antithetical to the metaphysical abstraction that is the hallmark of European philosophy.

Du Bois followed in this tradition. Not only did he rail against the metaphysical leanings that he feared were diluting the potentiality of sociology, he also dedicated his life and career to solving a social problem that, in his view, plagued the world over in the twentieth century: the color line.

Du Bois most clearly articulates his vision for sociology—or at least what it had the potential to be—in his short essay, "Sociology Hesitant." He wrote the essay in 1905 in response to the previous year's Congress of Arts and Sciences, which took place during the Universal Exposition in St. Louis.[12] In it we find not an empirical study but Du Bois's own philosophy of science for the budding discipline that he was helping to shape.

Drawing from pragmatist thinkers of the day, Du Bois was adamant that a true sociological study must be empirically based and systematically conducted and that it must have practical aims. This vision was a departure from many of his European predecessors, whom Du Bois accused of falsely invoking sociology as the abstract investigation into abstract things. He airs this frustration with this invocation of sociological writing that "there is scarce a sociologist the world over that would acknowledge such a plan. Rather, turning from so startling a task, they have assured the world that their object is to study a certain metaphysical entity called society— and when they have been asked earnestly and rather insistently just what society is, they have replied in language at once curious, mystical and at times contradictory."[13] Du Bois was bothered not by the theorization of the concept of society but, rather, by the lack of any empirical basis for the arguments put forth. He found the work of English philosopher-turned-sociologist Herbert Spencer especially harmful in this way and took him to task for purporting what he called "metaphysical wanderings":

> Spencer and his imitators have done good inspiring but limited work. Limited because their data were imperfect—woefully imperfect: depending on hearsay, rumor and tradition, vague speculations, traveler's tales, legends and imperfect documents, the memory of memories and historic error. All our knowledge of the past lay to be sure, before them. But what is our knowledge of the past as a basis for scientific induction? . . . Yet here, they lovingly lingered changing and arranging, expressing old thoughts anew, inventing strange terms and yet withal adding but little to our previous knowledge."[14]

Du Bois believed that sociology was a hands-on sport and that the scientific study of human action and social problems was achievable through rigorous empirical research. To Du Bois, sociology was the scientific quest to find the limits of natural law in human action: "Has not the time come however when we should face our problems? In reality we seek to know how much of natural law there is in human conduct. Sociology is the science that seeks to measure the limits of chance in human action, or if you will excuse the paradox, it is the science of free will."[15] What was remarkable about this statement is that Du Bois believed that the limits and possibilities of human action were knowable through social-scientific research. He applied this belief to his empirical studies throughout his early career, including studies such as *The Philadelphia Negro*.[16]

In his early days, Du Bois believed that racism could be dismantled with facts and truth. He believed that white audiences could be convinced with scientific evidence that racial inequality was determined by social conditions and not by biological inferiority. However, from the outset of his career, Du Bois was deeply concerned that the findings in extant sociological studies were adulterated by the biases of race prejudice. For Du Bois, unsystematic data collection left social science results particularly vulnerable to manipulation that would "humor the whims of the day."[17] He was strict in his belief that sociological results and interpretations should be based solely on facts, not wishes, myths, or prejudices, even if those results did not work to the researcher's advantage.

Du Bois voiced this concern as early as 1898 in his speech and essay, "The Study of Negro Problems," in which he asserted that "students must be careful to insist that science as such—be it physics, chemistry, psychology, or sociology—has but one simple aim: the discovery of truth. Its results lie open for the use of all men— merchants, physicians, men of letters, and philanthropists, but the aim of science itself is simple truth. An attempt to give it a double aim, to make social reform the immediate instead of the mediate object of a search for truth, will inevitably tend to defeat both objects."[18] Du Bois's concern was that sociology was already losing its way, as much of the research being produced seemed either too abstract or without an empirical base. For example, in "Sociology Hesitant," Du Bois expresses this concern through a reflection on what he views as Comte's subtle hesitation to name sociology as the science of an abstract "society" instead of human action:

> And on this dictum has been built a science—not of Human Action but of "Society", a Sociology. Did Comte thus mean to fix scientific thought on the study of an abstraction? Probably not—rather he meant to call attention to the fact that amid the bewildering complexities of human life ran great highways of common likenesses and agreements in human thoughts and action, which world-long observation had already noted and pondered upon. Here we must start the new science, said the Pioneer, this is the beginning. Once having emphasized this point, however, and Comte was strangely hesitant as to the real elements of Society which must some time be studied—were they men or cells or atoms or something subtler than any of these? Apparently he did not answer but wandered on quickly to a study of "Society." And yet "Society"

was but an abstraction. It was as though Newton noticing falling as characteristic of matter and explaining this phenomenon as gravitation had straightaway sought to study some weird entity known as Falling instead of soberly investigating Things which fall. So Comte and his followers noted the grouping of men, the changing of government, the agreement in thought, and then, instead of a minute study of men grouping, changing, and thinking proposed to study the Group, the Change, and the Thought, and call this new created Thing, Society.[19]

Du Bois believed that sociology is the science of the actions of men within the limits and constraints of social structures, or what he calls the "great highways of common likenesses and agreements in human thoughts and action."[20]

Du Bois asserted that although structure and power constrained and in many ways determined human action, human will and agency always presented the possibility for social change. Du Bois called these bookends of human action "Law" and "Chance": "What then is the future path open before Sociology? It must seek a working hypothesis which will include Sociology and physics. To do this it must be provisionally assumed that this is a world of Law and Chance. That in time and space, Law covers the major part of the universe but that in significance the area left in that world to Chance is of tremendous import."[21]

Du Bois defined chance as the "actions undetermined by and independent of actions gone before."[22] For him, human action was always in the making, situated within time and place, and full of unprecedented possibilities. It was within this arena that sociology offered its most fecund possibilities: "Chance being the scientific side of inexplicable Will. Sociology then, is the Science that seeks the limits of Chance in human conduct."[23] Deeply concerned with liberal ideals of free will, individualism, meliorism, creativity, and hope, the early Du Boisian sociology is steeped in pragmatist philosophy.

To Du Bois, the concept of "Society" was unmoored from the lived experience of people. Contra to this conception, he believed that sociology should be the study of the actions of men. He saw lawlike regularities in the social world exemplified in rates of birth and death but also in customs, public policies, and even trade and ethics. But he believed that these lawlike regularities could be punctured by human action.

In "Sociology Hesitant" Du Bois asked why sociologists don't openly "state the Hypothesis of Law and the Assumption of Chance, and seek to determine by study and measurement the limits of each?" Nearly forty years later, in his book *Dusk of Dawn*, he rephrased this vision, saying that the goal of science is "to explore and measure the scope of chance and unreason in human action, which does not yield to argument but changes slowly and with difficulty after long study and careful development."[24] Here he proposed an idea of society as constituted by its structures and laws but also made and remade through human action. This is very important for Du Bois's analysis of race, racism, and racialized processes of dehumanization: although there is nothing natural about them, they have been constructed historically and perpetuated through systems and institutions.

THE STUDY OF NEGRO PROBLEMS:
DU BOIS'S EMPIRICAL PROGRAM

Du Bois first articulated this empirical program in his essay, "The Study of Negro Problems," published in 1898 in the *Annals of the American Academy of Political and Social Sciences*, which was first presented as a speech at the November 1897 meeting of the academy.[25] In this article, written soon after he completed the data collection for *The Philadelphia Negro*, Du Bois presented his program for research on the "Negro Problem" in the United States, focusing on the material social conditions that defined African Americans' built environment, the intangible social forces of racism and prejudice, and the inner workings of the Black social world in the United States. He intended to implement this program longitudinally at Atlanta University, where he had been recently appointed as a professor of economics and sociology. Years later he would assert that at this point in his life, he aimed to "put science into sociology through a study of the condition and problems of my own group."

Du Bois was committed to what he referred to as "the social study," which he described as a study that "definitely and, within limits, exhaustively [examines] the conditions of life and action in certain localities." Du Bois thought it irresponsible to make broad generalizations about groups of people based on singular observations of a few folks who shared group membership. In *The Study of Negro Problems* he writes, "We must admit, for instance, that the field of study is large and varying, and that what is true of the Negro in Massachusetts is not necessarily true of the Negro in Louisiana; that what was true of the Negro in 1850 was not necessarily true in 1750; and that there are many distinct social problems affecting the Negro." He convinced that a useful sociological study not only account for intragroup heterogeneity but also for time. Not only were people different, but they evolved over time: "Now to bring about this result it is certain that we cannot at once compass all human action in time and eternity—the field is too vast and much valuable time has already been wasted in trying to do the impossible under the brilliant but questionable leadership of Herbert Spencer. We must more and more school ourselves to the minute study of limited fields of human action, where observation and accurate measurement are possible and where real illuminating knowledge can be had."[26] Du Bois understood that it was a vast undertaking to approach the study of an entire population with such exacting precision, but he believed it imperative for dismantling the destructive forces of prejudice and racism.

Du Bois also insisted that the study of Black life in America has to include two parts: "the study of the Negro falls naturally into two categories, which though difficult to separate in practice, must for the sake of logical clearness, be kept distinct. They are (a) the study of the Negro as a social group, (b) the study of his peculiar social environment."[27] The two are necessary in order to assess the experience of Black communities. Without the study of the context in which Black communities developed, the context in which people believed that "people of Negro blood should not be admitted into the group life of the nation no matter what their condition might be," it would be impossible to understand the lives and lived experiences of Black people in America.

The empirical program for the study of social problems that Du Bois put forward in that article—his vision of a scientific sociology—included four components: historical study, statistical investigation, anthropological measurement, and sociological interpretation. The last component was to include the most rigorous analysis of the preceding three and was not to rely solely on the casual observation of the social ills of a people. According to Du Bois,

> it should include the arrangement and interpretation of historical and statistical matter in the light of the experience of other nations and other ages; it should aim to study those finer manifestations of social life which history can but mention and which statistics can not count, such as the expression of Negro life as found in their hundred newspapers, their considerable literature, their music and folklore and their germ of esthetic life—in fine, in all the movements and customs among them that manifest the existence of a distinct social mind.[28]

RACIALIZED MODERNITY AND THE GLOBAL COLOR LINE

As noted earlier, Du Bois was a sociologist not of race but of racialized modernity.[29] For him, race and modernity are inextricably linked, and he thought through these two global master categories to formulate an intellectual framework through which to understand the times in which he lived (and we live). To this end, Du Bois proposed a distinct sociological methodology to understand the modern world: a world order based on the endless accumulation of capital along the racial, gender, religious, and regional hierarchies that would determine its flows and the unique set of problems that resulted from this recent world order. He developed this system of thought from the standpoint of subalterneity, from the global majority who live at the margins of power.

Racialized modernity was the social problem that preoccupied Du Bois's thinking and writing, and he examined it from various levels of analysis. What was race, and how was it constructed? To what end? From early on in his scholarly journey, he built a body of work that attempted to demonstrate that race was an invention of modernity constructed to serve the economic imperative of uneven and endless capital accumulation. From the 1492 encounter onward, the color line emerged as a "structuring structure" that would determine the accumulation of capital and power globally. It set a new stage. It dehumanized in a new way. It established what Charles Mills calls a "racial contract" along the real, yet intangible, global color line.[30]

Biological conceptions of race were the prevailing scientific paradigm during Du Bois's life. Leading scholars in the life sciences and the emerging social sciences held a long-standing position that race was a biological fact, to the extent that entire schools and institutes were built on this notion.[31] Du Bois points out in several texts that he does not believe that "race" is an ontological characteristic of human beings but, instead, is the way that humans have learned to cognate difference in the era of modernity. In his 1917 book of essays, *Darkwater*, Du Bois opens by stating, "I believe in God, who made of one blood all nations that on earth do dwell. I believe that all men, black and brown and white, are brothers, varying through time and opportunity, in form and gift and feature, but differing in no essential particular, and alike in soul and possibility on infinite development."[32] He holds onto this constructionist perspective of race throughout his career. For example, nearly twenty years later, he opens *Black Folk Then and Now: An Essay in the History and Sociology of the Negro* with the same conviction: "It is generally recognized today that no scientific definition of race is possible. Differences, and striking differences, there are between men and groups of men, but in so far as these differences are physical and measurable they fade into each other so insensibly that we can only indicate the main divisions in broad outline. . . . Race would seem to be a dynamic and not a static conception, and the typical races are continually changing and developing, amalgamating and differentiating."[33]

Du Bois began his analyses of racialized modernity from his own lived experience as a Black man living in the United States during the Jim Crow era. He did so by first turning his attention of the workings of race and racialization in New England and, later, in the South. These early writings, such as *The Philadelphia Negro*, *Souls of Black Folk*, and *Darkwater*, were published between 1899 and 1920, when he was experiencing the United States within the Black-white binary. In these works and others, Du Bois examined the material manifestations of the color line from multiple perspectives, including phenomenological (or from the standpoint of lived experience), the social organization of rural and urban places, and various political formations.

However, the scope of Du Bois's analytical frame was never limited to the United States or to just the Black experience.[34] He was well aware of the particular and universal manifestations of the global color line from his time studying and working abroad in Germany and the rest of Europe during his post-undergraduate studies in the 1890s. During this time, Du Bois became a sociologist without borders. He developed a global critique of racial colonial capitalism that examined the relations between the core and the peripheral geographic regions and the way in which these axes of power were constituted around whiteness.

In this way, Du Bois's early sociological program took up questions of freedom, citizenship, and humanity while consistently centering racialized groups who were systematically denied the opportunity to fully experience these ideals within their own lives. He designed a specific empirical approach to examine these phenomena, which he applied through much of the first quarter of his seventy-year career. His initial aim was to prove that race prejudice was unscientific and in fact harmful to national progress. However, as time went on, he came to realize that racism was not rooted in logic and therefore could not be wholly combated with facts and science alone.[35]

AMERICAN DEMOCRACY AND THE DILEMMA
OF THE NEGRO

Over the course of Du Bois's long career, he occupied many roles in the public sphere—as an academic, public intellectual, editor, novelist, and activist. He served two long-term appointments in the Department of Sociology at Atlanta University, bookending his career. Over the course of his seventy-year career, Du Bois's scientific program evolved in response to the world around him. Between 1898, at the time of his first major publication, and 1955, at the time of his last, Du Bois had witnessed the aftermath of Reconstruction, two world wars, the aggressive expansion of the American empire, and the continued oppression and dehumanization of people of color around the world.

Du Bois started off in the 1890s believing that facts, truth, and scientific evidence were all that the world needed to alleviate itself from the ills of race prejudice. To that end, he approached his studies aiming at objectivity and with exacting precision. Reflecting on his evolving thought over the course of his career, he revealed that "this plan was directed toward the majority of white Americans, and rested on the assumption that once they realized the scientifically attested truth concerning Negroes and race relations, they would take action to correct all wrong."[36] However, the persistence and acceleration of racial colonial capitalism and its globally oppressive forces on people of color left Du Bois disillusioned. He realized that white supremacy was not upheld by reason and could not, therefore, be destroyed by reason. Between the 1910s and 1930s, he dabbled in Marxism, decolonial theory, and other emancipatory frames. However, like a prodigal son, he ultimately returned to his pragmatist roots. In 1944 he wrote,

> In accord with what unchangeable scientific law of action was the world of interracial discord about me working? I fell back upon my Royce and James and deserted Schmoller and Weber. I saw the action of physical law in the actions of men; but I saw more than that: I saw rhythms and tendencies; coincidences and probabilities; and I saw that, which for want of any other word, I must in accord with the strict tenets of Science, call Chance. I went forward to build a sociology, which I conceived of as the attempt to measure the element of Chance in human conduct. This was the Jamesian pragmatism, applied not simply to ethics, but to all human action, beyond what seemed to me, increasingly, the distinct limits of physical law.[37]

He returned to pragmatism in the last phase of his career, in the 1930s, but carried with him cynicism that he would never shed. Instead of setting his aims outward to the white majority, Du Bois set his aims toward "scientific investigation and organized action among Negroes, in close cooperation, to secure the survival of the Negro race, until the cultural development of America and the world is willing to recognize Negro freedom."[38] He reasoned that this plan— temporary, he hoped—was a holdout to maintain hope in the American ideal. "This plan realizes that the majority of men do not usually act in accord with reason, but follow social pressures, inherited customs and long-established, often sub-conscious, patterns of action. Consequently, race prejudice in America will linger long and may even increase. It is the duty of the black race to maintain its cultural advance, not for itself alone, but for the emancipation of mankind, the realization of democracy and the progress of civilization." In this sense, Du Bois's vision for truth and scientific knowledge changed according to the extent to which he imagined it would affect the lives of American Negros.

However, in the end, Du Bois, like Comte, hesitated. For he came to the conclusion that what belies the highest ideals of American democracy—life, liberty, and the pursuit of happiness—are this nation's ugly historical foundation: settler colonialism, genocide, racial slavery, and white supremacy. In that way, the ideal of American democracy would always collapse on the question of the Negro. In a farewell note to a friend, sent before his expatriation to Ghana, Du Bois wrote, "I just cannot take any more of this country's treatment. We leave for Ghana October 5th and I set no date for return. Chin up, and fight on, but realize that the American Negroes can't win."[39]

CONCLUSION

What is the import of pragmatism for theorizing from the subaltern standpoint? Du Bois's long-standing engagement with Jamesian pragmatism is illuminating in this regard. Though there is no doubt that his empirical and theoretical program, especially his early work, was deeply influenced by pragmatism, he was by no means bound to it as an intellectual project. Further, he was just as influenced by his own lived experience as he was as a racialized subject. Pragmatism, Marxism, literature, Pan-Africanism, socialism, and his own experience riding the Jim Crow car all influenced Du Bois's sociology. And in true pragmatist form, Du Bois's thoughts and actions adapted with the times.

His commitments were always to attaining the outcome of freedom, liberty, and humanity for Black people and people of color around the world. He was unwavering in his desired end. The previous section revealed that Du Bois eventually gave up on that project for Black freedom and equality in the United States of America; however, that does not mean that he gave up on the ideals themselves. However, in his own life he ran up against the barriers of law and realized that his only chance was to emancipate himself. He left the nation that he had devoted his life to perfecting, and in one of his last acts of agency, he chose to make his final resting place in the land of his forepersons—in Africa.

In our contemporary moment, racial colonial capitalism has further accelerated, and forms of racism have grafted themselves onto religious groups, anti-immigrant sentiment, the global refugee population, sexual minorities, and the poor. The aims of pragmatism are historically rooted in ideas of human freedom and a quest to ponder social action from the standpoint of the human condition. For this reason, there certainly is a place for this philosophical tradition within the larger project of human abolition and liberty. However, it can play only a supporting role in service of the long tradition of subaltern knowledge production. What we mean by this is that pragmatism does not go far for theorizing the subaltern condition without employing other analytical frameworks that have been used to understand modernity from the margins, such as Black feminism, the Black radical tradition, racial capitalism, Du Boisian sociology, and decolonial theory, to name a few. In the words of James Baldwin, "I can't be a pessimist because I'm alive. To be a pessimist means that you have agreed that human life is an academic matter." However, it is at the same time prudent to take heed of Du Bois's cautionary tale:

No one is coming to save us.

NOTES

1. Cornel West, *The American Evasion of Philosophy: A Genealogy of Pragmatism* (Madison: University of Wisconsin Press, 1989), 4.

2. Hans Joas, *Pragmatism and Social Theory* (Chicago: University of Chicago Press, 1993).

3. Patrick Wolfe, "Land, Labor, and Difference: Elementary Structures of Race," *American Historical Review* 106, no. 3 (2001): 866–905.

4. Aziz Rana, *The Two Faces of American Freedom* (Cambridge, MA: Harvard University Press, 2011).

5. José Itzigsohn, and Karida L. Brown, *The Sociology of WEB Du Bois: Racialized Modernity and the Global Color Line* (New York: New York University Press, 2020); Aldon Morris, *The Scholar Denied* (Berkeley: University of California Press, 2015); Earl Wright II, *The First American School of Sociology: WEB Du Bois and the Atlanta Sociological Laboratory* (London: Routledge, 2016).

6. W. E. B. Du Bois, "My Evolving Program for Negro Freedom," *Clinical Sociology Review* 8, no. 1 (1990): 5.

7. W. E. B. Du Bois, "The Study of the Negro Problems," *Annals of the American Academy of Political and Social Science* 11 (1898): 1–23.

8. Du Bois, "My Evolving Program for Negro Freedom," 34.

9. *Modernity* refers to our contemporary historical period. It is defined by reference to various social processes, including urbanization and industrialization, the rise of bureaucracy, the application of science and technology to production, the deepening of the division of labor, and the spread of secularization and democracy. It is usually seen as the image of a successful present or a desirable future. But modernity was always entangled with colonialism and racism. For Du Bois, the defining characteristic of modernity was the *color line*: the invention of whiteness and the multiple forms of exclusion, oppression, exploitation, and inequality constructed along colonial and racial lines. For Du Bois *modernity* is *racialized modernity* from its inception (Itzigsohn and Brown, *Sociology of WEB Du Bois* 220).

10. Itzigsohn and Brown, *Sociology of WEB Du Bois*.

11. Louis Menand, *The Metaphysical Club: A Story of Ideas in America* (New York: Farrar, Straus and Giroux, 2001); West, *American Evasion of Philosophy*.

12. W. E. B. Du Bois, *The Problem of the Color Line at the Turn of the Twentieth Century: The Essential Early Essays*, ed. Nahum Dimitri Chandler (Oxford: Oxford University Press, 2014); W. E. B. Du Bois, *Sociology Hesitant: Thinking with WEB Du Bois*, trans. R. A. Judy (Durham, NC: Duke University Press, 2000); and Dan S. Green and Robert A. Wortham, "Sociology Hesitant: The Continuing Neglect of WEB Du Bois," *Sociological Spectrum* 35, no. 6 (2015): 518–33.

13. DuBois, W. E. Burghardt, "The Atlanta Conferences." *Voice of the Negro* 1, no. 3 (March 1904): 85–90, 85.

14. Du Bois, *Sociology Hesitant*, 39.

15. Du Bois, *Sociology Hesitant*, 44.

16. W. E. B. Du Bois, *The Philadelphia Negro: A Social Study*, Political Economy and Public Law Series 14 (Philadelphia: University of Pennsylvania Press, 1899); Marcus Anthony Hunter, "A Bridge Over Troubled Urban Waters: W. E. B. Du Bois's The Philadelphia Negro and the Ecological Conundrum," *Du Bois Review: Social Science Research on Race* 10, no. 1 (2013b): 7–27; and Hunter, *Black Citymakers: How the Philadelphia Negro Changed Urban America* (New York: Oxford University Press, 2013a).

17. W. E. B. Du Bois, *Dusk of Dawn: An Essay Toward an Autobiography of a Race Concept* (Oxford: Oxford University Press, 1940).

18. Du Bois, "The Study of the Negro Problems," 1–23, 16.

19. Du Bois, *Sociology Hesitant*, 38.

20. Du Bois, *Sociology Hesitant*, 38.

21. Du Bois, *Sociology Hesitant*, 43.

22. Du Bois, *Sociology Hesitant*.

23. Du Bois, *Sociology Hesitant*, 44.

24. Du Bois, *Dusk of Dawn*, 7.

25. Du Bois, "The Study of the Negro Problems."

26. Dan S. Green and Edwin D. Driver, *W. E. B. Du Bois on Sociology and the Black Community* (Chicago: University of Chicago Press, 1980), 54.

27. Du Bois, "The Study of the Negro Problems," 17–18.

28. Du Bois, "The Study of the Negro Problems," 20.

29. Itzigsohn and Brown, *Sociology of WEB Du Bois*.

30. Charles W. Mills, *The Racial Contract* (Ithaca, NY: Cornell University Press, 1997).

31. Menand, *The Metaphysical Club*.

32. W. E. B. Du Bois, *Darkwater: Voices from Within the Veil* (New York: Dover, 1999), 3.

33. W. E. B. Du Bois, *Black Folk Then and Now: An Essay in the History and Sociology of the Negro Race*. Oxford W. E. B. Du Bois, (Oxford: Oxford University Press, 2007), 1.

34. Katrina Quisumbing King, "Recentering U.S. Empire: A Structural Perspective on the Color Line," *Sociology of Race and Ethnicity* 5, no. 1 (2019): 11–25.

35. Du Bois, *Dusk of Dawn*; Du Bois, "My Evolving Program for Negro Freedom."

36. Du Bois, "My Evolving Program for Negro Freedom," 57.

37. Du Bois, "My Evolving Program for Negro Freedom," 47.

38. Du Bois, "My Evolving Program for Negro Freedom," 57.

39. West, *American Evasion of Philosophy*, 159.

15. The Public Arena

A PRAGMATIST CONCEPT OF THE PUBLIC SPHERE

DANIEL CEFAÏ

The concept of the public was put back on the agenda by Habermas (1962) with his book *The Structural Transformation of the Public Sphere*, followed by numerous studies on the public sphere and public opinion. The translation of his work into English, and the many commentaries that ensued, launched the career of the concept of the *public sphere*, accompanied by renewed reflection on civil society, and gave rise to the concept of "marginal" or "subaltern" counter-publics. It is only recently, however, that the question of the public raised by John Dewey (1927)[1] seems to have gained a second wind in the United States and that the influence of the intellectual movement known as *pragmatism* has been felt in the social and political sciences. In France, interest in pragmatism—and, more specifically, in Dewey's concept of "the public"—dates from the beginning of the 1990s to a small group of researchers who were concerned with the sociology of public problems. The concept of the public arena, which will be discussed in this chapter, thus began to be developed at the end of the 1990s.[2]

A first concern was to demonstrate the importance of the study of social problems for an inquiry into democracy, turning them into public problems and making of them more than a topic for undergraduate programs. A second concern was to reconnect this genealogy of publics and public problems with pragmatist philosophy and the Chicago tradition of sociology, for which there has been a strong interest in France since the 1980s. A third important issue was to pinpoint the limits of and to reframe the study of social movements or civic associations in terms of the resource mobilization, rational choice, and political process models, as well as organizational theory, network analysis, and cultural analysis. And fourth, we were looking for an alternative way to deal with the concept of the public sphere and propose a perspective divergent from those of Hannah Arendt[3] and Jürgen Habermas,[4] as well as from the reduction of the public sphere to a "market" or a "field." Dewey, Robert Ezra Park, and George Herbert Mead were taken as starting points for such a pragmatist conception of the public arena. An ecology of public experience and action was thus developed based on a vision of democracy geared toward defining and resolving public problems. This pragmatist inquiry on a problem-driven democracy[5] may be taken as a counterpoint to recent research in political science on state transformations, evolutionary learning, agenda setting, and policy framing. The public arena hosts the social processes in which these institutional, legal, and political changes are grounded; and it is shaped, in turn, by the laws enacted and policies implemented in the name of the public.

DEWEY, MEAD, AND PARK: FROM PROBLEMATIC SITUATION TO POLITICAL PROCESS

Our starting point will thus be the John Dewey of *The Public and Its Problems*. Dewey's basic idea is that when people, confronted with a problematic situation, perceive and evaluate the consequences of this situation as harmful to humans and the that goods they value and, moreover, to life forms and the Earth itself, they worry, reflect, inquire, experiment, and discuss. They try to define what the problem is, determine the contributing factors, assign causality, and ascribe responsibility. They unite and organize themselves and appoint leaders to make their voices heard, convince others, and mobilize support on a large scale. They speak out, testify, judge, argue, criticize, deliberate, and forcefully appeal to public opinion and public authorities. When the latter do not act, they seek solutions to meet their needs, envisage possibilities, plan alternatives, and try to establish how to control or resolve the problematic situation. This collective dynamic simultaneously gives rise to a problem and its public.

The first important concept is that of the "problematic situation."[6] In the functional psychology attributed to the Chicago School, a situation becomes problematic when an organism's habitual responses to the demands of its surroundings no longer satisfy its needs and desires. The well-integrated whole formed by the *transactions*[7] of the organism and its environment undergoes a crisis. The organism, as a life form, must engage in an inquiry to identify the problem and try to solve it by transforming its living environment and the way they relate to each other.

The same holds when the routine and standard types of response made by people toward their environment are revealed to be maladjusted, inadequate, or insufficient: a *trouble* arises from the *indeterminacy* of the situation, requiring the members of a collective to define, understand, explain, contain, regulate, and control it. The problem is not in our heads; it is in the cooperative process of organisms and environments, which go through a disruption of habitual situations. In Thomas's and Park's language of sociology at Chicago, with its mix of human ecology and social psychology, the multiple processes of collective organization and personal organization, mediatized by social institutions,[8] are no longer attuned. This lack of integration generates problematic situations in milieus of collective life and individual life stories. It creates tension and conflictual relationships that cannot be solved by mere processes of accommodation and assimilation.

People, groups, organizations, and institutions then mobilize themselves, in various places and at various times, and try to grasp, from each one's perspective, the nature of the trouble and, where applicable, establish it as a problem. They examine aspects of the situation to escape the fog of indeterminacy, try to grasp "what is wrong," formulate hypotheses or conjectures, and suggest explanations and interpretations. They do an inquiry. This inquiry necessarily has a normative dimension: it simultaneously involves assigning responsibility, denouncing negligence or transgression, and eventually designating victims and offenders, in each case making moral, legal, or political judgments in order to call for reparations or punish wrongdoing.[9]

This work of defining a problematic situation incorporates an attempt at resolution: the participants are driven not by the pursuit of "knowledge for knowledge's sake" but by the pursuit of knowledge insofar as it empowers them to take action. "*Doing is knowing, knowing is doing.*" They intend to select useful information and resources from their environment the better to control it; they discover causal clusters and chains on which to act; they make allies and designate opponents; and they compete on different stages for different audiences—all this to reestablish an orderly and norm-governed course for the situation, which then ceases to be problematic. They invent, in theory and practice, devices of intervention whose effectiveness depends on convincing other people, in private and public, of the sound basis of their diagnoses. These others must be alerted, interested, concerned, and perhaps mobilized. In short, they project themselves into a logic of *problem-defining* and *problem-solving*.

As soon as this dynamic of problematization and publicization extends beyond the circle of those immediately affected to involve a greater number of people, it assumes the character of a *political process*.[10] Robert E. Park put forward an account of this that strongly resembles that of Dewey. "Politics is concerned with *issues*," he used to say: it breaks with the moral consensus. Politics begins when the tacit regulation of social relations through social accommodation and cultural assimilation is no longer effective: people can no longer get along by adjusting their respective ecological niches or by mixing and mingling their meaning-contexts. It results from open conflict over problems. This conflict is not, however, a head-on collision between brute forces, as in total warfare, but is often guided by questions of law or justice. According to Park, political conflict can lead to outbursts of crowd violence—the dark side of collective behavior—but it can also give rise to a *public* when two camps contest pacifically with each other over a problem while addressing an audience. The conflict becomes organized and stabilized through processes of rational discussion, community-mobilizing, opinion-forming, and sometimes lawmaking and institutional transformation. The crisis situation is thus creative, and this dynamic of publicization, while altering the legal and political order, has knock-on effects on the moral order—that is, on beliefs, customs, and "mores and folkways."

The analytical framework of the problematic situation is found again in Dewey's *Logic: Theory of Inquiry* (1938) and underlies his definition of the public in *The Public and Its Problems* (1927). A collective mobilization emerges when the members of a *collective* (as yet indeterminate but whose contours, size, and composition will be specified in the process), feeling *concerned*, directly or indirectly, by a "trouble" that they confront (initially in a vague way, not easily grasped or named, and not yet available to a public), define it as a problematic situation and undertake (in a manner inseparably collaborative and divisive, given the many forms of cooperation and competition they engage in) to resolve it. These "members" of a "collective" are prompted into action by a "trouble"—from the most intangible (dread of the consequences of the growing hole in the ozone layer) to the most palpable (grief over the poisoning of newborns by contaminated milk in China); from the most local (the perception of green algae proliferating on the Breton coast) to the most global (scientific observations of melting glaciers, symptomatic of global warming)—a trouble whose nature will be clarified at an inquiry stage.

THE FORMATION OF A FIELD OF EXPERIENCE

A public arena is thus formed around a problematic situation. There has been much insistence on the "construction" of social problems, but the return to pragmatism shifts the discussion toward an *ecology of public experience*. "Experience": the trouble often arises from *affective, perceptive, and evaluative tests*, which undermine the evidential basis for matters of everyday life and lead to inquiries being conducted to make clear what the difficulty consists in and to gain experience of it. "Ecology": this experience is not only of the "subjectively lived" kind, as is often claimed; rather, it must be grasped in its "experiential habitat";[11] that is, in the transactions between life forms and their environment.[12]

The trouble is of an affective, perceptive, and evaluative nature. Though not yet articulated in descriptive and conceptual language, it is experienced in the form of worry, unrest or confusion, anxiety or fear. It signifies disruption in the normal order of things—the denaturalization of a taken-for-granted situation or the sudden appearance of an unknown in a usual environment. It goes hand in hand with the interruption of habits governing our relationship to the world, to other people, and to things. It leaves us disoriented. In some cases, it robs us of our faculties, destroys our sense of ontological security, and impedes our ability to take things in hand. The trouble, as Dewey calls it, "stands for the existence of something questionable, and hence provocative of investigation, examination, discussion—in short, inquiry. However, [it] covers such a great variety of occasions for inquiry that it may be helpful to specify a number of them. It covers the features that are designated by such adjectives as confusing, perplexing, disturbed, unsettled, indecisive; and by such nouns as jars, hitches, breaks, blocks—in short, all incidents occasioning an interruption of the smooth, straightforward course of behavior and that deflect it into the kind of behavior constituting inquiry."[13] This trouble is experienced as a threat to our lives or our belongings, an obstacle to our dealings with other people and things, or a disruption to our harmony with the situations we find ourselves in. It has a dimension of passivity. A public problem is not constituted wholly in action but also in *passive experience, both individual and shared.*

Before being driven by strategic aims and constructing explanations and rationales, with full awareness, those involved in clarifying a trouble are affected by the situations that they are helping to define and understand. They proceed by evaluating what is unpleasant, repugnant, unacceptable, or intolerable and what would be, by contrast, desirable. They are exposed to events that overwhelm and disorient them—talk or gossip about the destruction of the neighborhood, series of indispositions not yet linked to the close high-voltage line, electricity prices or water bills that increase without any apparent justification, attitudes of firm managers and foremen that disrupt the moral economy of work relationships.[14] Sometimes, when the so-called precautionary principle is involved, they are not even in the presence of what troubles them—they anticipate what might happen to their bodies if they eat genetically modified organisms, or they imagine a tidal wave of migrants or homeless people invading their familiar surroundings. And, oddly enough, they may have feelings of discomfort, grief, indignation, affliction, frustration, or distress without being directly threatened by any predicament—they care about child labor in the Antipodes or feel concerned by the killing of baby seals.

This element of *shared passive experience,*[15] which is inherent in sensing the trouble, can turn into a context for action, but not necessarily. Without engagement in a process of defining and resolving problematic situations, leading to their recognition, definition, clarification, and understanding, as much affective as cognitive and normative, the trouble remains tacit or latent. It is lived through but has no public formulation. While awaiting its own expression, the trouble is not yet identifiable and recognizable as a problem. For phenomenologists, the quality of "the unquestionably given" (*fraglos gegeben*) or "taken for granted," which is attached to experiences in the natural attitude, is altered, but this disorientation is not yet expressed in a reflective attitude. For pragmatists, ordinary beliefs, in Charles Peirce's sense, or warranted assertions, in Dewey's, which are operative during an action, have been threatened, but without this trouble having been reconceptualized as a problem, and even less as a "public problem."

Here, it is vital that a collective experience be *mediated* in order for the trouble to be *problematized* and *publicized,* and for people to know what they are dealing with. People revise their criteria of understanding and readjust their bounds of sense. They try to convert the trouble into a concern about an issue to grapple with; that is, to problematize it and gain a hold over it, thus generating collective experience. A *field of collective experience* encompasses shared ways of seeing, saying, and doing, articulated through a network of serviceable numbers, categories, types, accounts, narratives, and arguments, which allow a state of affairs to be grasped as an identifiable and recognizable problem. It also encompasses sets of customs, "mores, and folkways," and "shared habits," which function as matrices of a "moral order,"[16] which in practice make it possible to experience all sorts of positive and negative moral attitudes and to feel and express outrage.

Finally, the transformation of collective experience is usually mediated by a system of concrete supports and stepping stones—bodies of knowledge, data banks, statistical means, and rules and techniques for implementation: it is translated into a "space of equivalences"[17] through operations of "commensuration."[18] For example, it is inserted into series of meteorological measures, subsumed under medical nosological classifications, or compared with previous legal cases. And, of course, such operations require organizational mediations, which already exist or are yet to emerge—associations, parties, or unions standing for a cause, media through which accusations and demands might be heard, research laboratories, legal or medical specialties, administrative offices to whom complaints might be addressed, Parliament representatives or government officials to challenge and convince, and the like.

Without such a network of devices that are symbolic, financial, legal, media-related, institutional, and so on, the trouble gains no substance and never reaches the forum of public attention. Defining the problematic situation is not only a creative accomplishment but also an institutional endeavor. A public problem does not arise in a vacuum: it is shaped in advance by precedents. It finds its bearings in a "public culture" in which responses to previous problematizations have sedimented. The most basic condition is that people understand what fighting together for the public interest means—an attitude resulting from long-term empowerment through struggles for democracy. Either it is channeled into available devices of categorization and intervention, and then collective habits are sufficient to deal with it; or it is crystallized through different operations (for example, through judicial inquiry or scientific experimentation). It makes dramatic and rhetorical moves (for example, by imitating the Civil Rights movement's framing activities). It aims at gaining credibility and courts the approval of public authorities, specific publics, and the general public.

The trouble becomes a problem by combining elements from already established institutions, devices, and habits in its formulation of new critiques, blames, and claims.[19] The transformation of collective experience may go through aesthetical mediations, as when the public denunciation of industrial hazards or environmental damages is performed through novels or movies that strike the public spirit. The journalistic or scientific inquiry, based on fact-gathering, may take the form of a fiction (a point of which Dewey, in *Art as Experience*,[20] was aware): Upton

Sinclair's *The Jungle* (1906) or Rachel Carson's *Silent Spring* (1963) are two good examples, which led, respectively, to the creation of the Food and Drug Administration and the prohibition of the use of DDT pesticides. The reception of these books altered the public sensitivity, caused a scandal, induced anxiety and anger, and ignited people's mobilizations, imposing a collective feeling of emergency and obtaining a state response to the problem. Sometimes, however, the public problem fails to gain expression. But in such a case, the impossibility of problematizing and publicizing the trouble—as when farmers suffering cancers plausibly due to contact with chemicals, or manual workers living with musculoskeletal pain, refuse to have them defined as occupational diseases—has effects nonetheless. It paralyzes people, imprisons them within doubt and indecision, robs them of capacities for comprehension and self-direction, nourishes unproductive resentment, gives rise to explosions of violence, or silently destroys lives.[21]

This way of seeing things in terms of a field of experience has implications for how the sociology of social movements could rethink its concepts. Dynamics of collective mobilization configure private and public fields of experience. They articulate what matters as *capital, resource, objective, constraint,* and *opportunity.* No analysis can "objectively" determine the meaning of these key categories: the transformations—in the course of collective action, ends-in-view, and, concurrently, evaluative standards and interpretive schemes—organize the experience of actions and their circumstances. Resource mobilization choices and the perception of opportunity structures have to be understood within this process of meaning-making, just as the categories of *class, gender,* or *race* arise not from preestablished "inequality or domination structures" but from the midst of action in context.[22] In such an inquiry, it is crucial to describe the first steps of a dynamic of problematization and publicization. The emergence of the definition of chemical hypersensitivity syndrome may take advantage of networks of physicians already involved with similar diseases—sick building or electro-hypersensitivity syndromes—or use the same web platforms as for other diseases—myopathy or AIDS—through which patients claim for active monitoring of their illness.[23] But to understand this process, one has to account for how ordinary people transform themselves into clinicians, epidemiologists, or pharmacologists; how they learn to describe their experience, compare it with others', identify common features, create new categories, discover causes, and test therapies. They carry out an inquiry by and on themselves; discuss with relatives, kin, and friends; build up an arena of expression and argumentation; and empower themselves as a collective actor amalgamated by the same interests and concerns.

Moreover, according to the ecological reasoning of pragmatists, the dynamics of collective mobilization concern both the dispositions of those involved—their motivations, beliefs, and habits of thought, action, communication, or judgment—and the *instrumentalities* that mediate what they know, say, and do. These collective dynamics transform environments and reconfigure the contexts of perception and manipulation of physical and social objects.[24] They rearticulate *fields of experience,* with their *horizons of anticipation, memory, sensibility, and imagination* and the ecologies that support them. Sometimes, they develop emotional and imaginary visions that strike hearts and minds and that sketch alternative possibilities; sometimes they invest more in facts and try to give detailed accounts of the problematic situations and infer out of them the most reasonable solutions. The researcher can understand what is going on only by way of these situated perspectives.

Another way to formulate this question would be to appraise the field of experience from the point of view of an *anthropology of evaluation.*[25] What counts for people, and how do they account for and take account of it? What has a hold on them, and what do they hold to? And how do these evaluations play out in other relevant areas? Furthermore, the word *experience* here can be understood in at least three different ways, corresponding to different ways in which we are affected. Experience is an *aesthetic test:*[26] the affective (*pathos*) and aesthetic (*aisthesis*) senses are those that, prior to reasoning and judgment, give us access to the world. They are the hinges of experience; they enable us to get a grip on situations that grip us: we are receptive to ambiance and atmosphere, we are sensitive to the beauty of things and to the harmony of circumstances. Experience is also a *practical experiment:*[27] we recognize what is real by subjecting situations and consequences to tests on which we must rely, strengthening our capacity to act by adapting to a reality that resists us. If we succeed in controlling situations, it is because they are "natural laboratories" within whose bounds action depends on the expected consequences of tests on working hypotheses.

Finally, experience is an *interactional exchange:*[28] we achieve access to the truth, the good, and the right not on our own, in our private world, but through interactions with other people and things, via processes of cooperation and communication. These sometimes take the form of actual deliberations, whereby we expose ourselves to others' points of view and take these into account within a widened perspective. The experience of troubles, the way we sense our private life and engage in public life, has aesthetic, experimental, and interactional dimensions.

INQUIRY, PROBLEMATIZATION, AND PUBLICIZATION

Beneath the rational strategies or structural conditions, taken into account by social scientists, the incipient collective dynamic—emerging from its confrontation with specific actions or events—sometimes seems only to interest people as "private persons." Nobody sees beyond his or her personal property, has sufficient trust in his or her neighbors or in institutions, or believes in the possibility of common solutions. Sometimes, however, the collective dynamic takes on another dimension. It shifts the contours of a new experience, making the individuals' interests, beliefs, and desires transcend their usual perspectives. And it succeeds in involving people far removed from those directly affected, pushing them to *form a collective experience, express shared grievances, and mobilize themselves publicly.* This collective experience is bestowed not only on members of the same family, clan, caste, or nation: the political community that is formed is gathered around, and united by, *common concerns for public issues*. It requires an ability to feel and endure in common, which is realized through collective action. People gather together, unite, discuss, worry, share grievances, begin inquiries, and discuss further. They find allies to support them, representatives and experts to make their voices heard, or other organizations to unite with. They investigate and later experiment, draw lessons, generalize, and make known their observations, censures, and claims. Throughout the process, they pinpoint problems that are of public significance. In doing so, they constitute themselves as a *public*; that is, a certain kind of political community.

What tasks do they accomplish?

Sensing the trouble is the ground for the inquiry into the matter at hand and for the evaluation of situations, actions, and events in terms of their unacceptability, illegitimacy, or intolerability in the eyes of those affected by their consequences. This process is inseparably both cognitive and evaluative. Without such a process of valuation, supported by affect, it is impossible to know what is worth finding out, defending or rejecting, or endorsing or dismissing.[29] A major part of the process for alerting, concerning, and mobilizing people around what will be a public problem lies in demonstrating how a situation can be cruel, unjust, disastrous, worrying, and the like. The task of investigating is based on this initial experience. The inquiry recognizes a certain number of things that it describes and evaluates as harmful. In doing so, it tries to identify causal chains that explain how they came about and allow their probable or plausible consequences to be foreseen and predicted. *It organizes a field of explanation and foresight of the problematic situation.* The inquiry can retrace the latter's historical genesis; create tools for categorizing, classifying, and quantifying; and establish criteria of equivalence with other similar situations. For example, it builds up maps and graphs that show the inequalities in salary between men and women or establish the social factors of underperformance at school. It invents new forms of imagery for the visualization of the ozone hole or sets up laboratories near the poles to monitor climate changes; and it may couple these undertakings with epidemiological surveys of the distribution of skin cancers or mathematical modeling for predicting global warming.

At the same time, the inquiry *attributes varieties and degrees of moral and legal responsibility* and brings forth the figures of offender and victim, advocate and compensator. It does so mostly by normatively informing the public discourses of journalists and politicians through mediation by technical investigations and operations of weighting by experts, or through conversion of police conclusions into administrative, legal, and judicial deliberations and decisions. Who has done what? With what consequences? Who must answer for his or her deeds? Who has suffered damages and can demand justice? Who is authorized to judge? Who is responsible for punishing or compensating?

For example, identifying the cluster of causes leading to the mass death of bees and uncovering a correlative link to the use of certain pesticides is already to outline a practical solution: the elimination of contributing factors, the development of alternative pesticides, or the adoption of organic farming methods. It is also, for the environmentalists, to identify offenders by pointing the finger at large, semi-monopolist manufacturers of agricultural chemicals or major cereal farmers who wantonly continue to reject any environmental awareness. Studying the causes of road accidents is also to select one range of causes rather than another in a "multiplicity of possible realities"[30] and, doing so, to attribute responsibility to car manufacturers, the state of the road network, drivers' lack of training, premises where alcohol is consumed, or drivers who take to the wheel after drinking. And if this moral character, the drunk driver, is the one who is to blame, the solution is to invent mechanisms for detecting and measuring alcohol on the breath or in the blood and to enact legal measures for preventing and clamping down on drunk driving.

The task of describing, explaining, and interpreting, which enables the problematic situation to be defined, can be summarized as follows: who has done what, with whom, to whom, where, when, how, why, with what aim, with what degree of awareness, and with what consequences, direct or indirect? Of course, there is nothing consensual about the endeavor of problematization and publicization. On the contrary, a public arises when there is neither consensus around a dominant reality nor consent to the public authorities. Starting from the first emotions and evaluations, points of view diverge and clash. A *public is a political community organized around contested issues.* The inquiry gives rise to competing inquiries; facts are disputed or presented in a different light; each explanation and interpretation is subject to challenge. Each inquiry—a police or legal investigation, news report, scientific experiment, parliamentary hearing, nongovernmental organization report, and so on—tries to balance accounts that are more or less acceptable to different sections of the public and to establish what is at stake in the conflict. Often, the public problem, which goes through a highly contentious phase at an early stage when it is taking shape, then gives way to a phase of stabilization around shared points of contention or controversy. The public arena becomes institutionalized. Perspectives settle within it. The game of cooperation and competition, of alliance and opposition, becomes more stable.

But problems never come alone: the end of a contest often leads to new bifurcations. New conflicts shape and are shaped by new issues. The inquiry refashions the problematic situation through numerous *reality and value tests* that help to both interpret and reconstitute it. It determines the spatial and temporal scale for intervention: where in space and time does a problematic situation begin and end? How far should the inquiry delve into the causes and responsibilities, and how far should it explore the consequences? The inquiry is an action that induces other actions. It indicates ends and objectives to be achieved, marshals means and resources to realize them, determines the nature of constraints and opportunities, and enters into strategies of alliance and opposition. It assigns agents to deal with the problem, specifies the nature of the damages or wrongs, and gives instructions for compensating them. By identifying causes, interpreting motives, foreseeing consequences, evaluating risks, attributing responsibilities, and contriving solutions, *the inquiry structures a field of intervention.*

Most important, it transforms the trouble into a problem and the problem into a *public problem*; that is, one not addressed by a private entity such as the market, given a technical solution unbeknownst to the people, or hushed up behind closed doors. It is taken over by public institutions—Dewey speaks of "public officials," often officers of the state or trouble-shooters authorized by the state[31]. To publicize is to make visible, to dramatize, thematize, and narrate the problem, and to address, through acts of communication, audiences who need to be persuaded and convinced. It is also to give substance to the characterization and resolution of the problem by making its existence in different ecologies tangible; and it is to cause the problem to be recognized, investigated, and resolved through devices and institutions of public action. Either there are already laws, facilities, and personnel suitable for dealing with it and authorized to do so, or new public functions must arise, leading to new sectors and new actions by public authorities. The public, in Dewey's sense, maintains relationships with experts and leaders who represent it; help to settle battle lines between identities, interests, and opinions; and give form and substance to problems within different material environments and semantic frameworks.

All the while, in the background lurk the twin threats of the usurpation and abuse of power and of the exclusive appropriation of control and administration of the problem—ironically illustrated by Joseph Gusfield with the metaphor of ownership, with its "risks of loss" and "possibilities of transfer."[32] This threat overlaps with another one, the manipulation of the public, easily fooled by those "stereotypes" whose power of suggestion Walter Lippmann[33] had perceived, in an era in which techniques of public relations, propaganda, and advertisement were taking off. It leads to the development of strategies of deliberate falsehood, rumor, engineered silence, and misinformation, as shown by Robert Proctor's[34] inquiry on tobacco companies' conspiracy or David Rosner and Gerald Markowitz's[35] on lead wars. Doubt-mongers and spin doctors create a pseudo-publicity, imitating the rhetoric of scientific inquiry.

THE PUBLIC ARENA: NEITHER MARKET
NOR FIELD NOR AGORA

The concept of the public arena stems from the Chicago School of sociology, relayed through Mead and Dewey. If we felt it necessary to build up this concept and shift of perspective in the 1990s, it was to reframe three other concepts. Reframing them did not mean invalidating them: what we intended was to put them into a different light and then do different things, ask new questions, focus on new topics, and develop another experience of democracy. A public arena is thus different from a market (logic of profit-making through exchange), from a field (logic of domination between social groups), or from an agora (logic of argumentation and deliberation). It encompasses these different logics under an *ecology of public problems.*[36] One could say that the models of the market, the field, and the agora are subspecies of a model of social arena. They grasp only one dimension of the complex generative and interactional processes that make it up.

1. First, there is the concept of the market, in which interests and opinions are "negotiated," sort of a stock exchange on which *public problems end up being settled by the law of supply and demand.* The demand is that of consumers who formulate a problem and are numerous enough to represent a critical mass and constitute an economic interest. The supply is that of owners of the means of production of goods, services, information, and ideas who, seeing an opportunity for profit, acknowledge the existence of a problem (the law of the environmental market— entrepreneurs take action when wind or solar power production becomes profitable) or who, on the contrary, foreseeing costs and losses, ignore or cover up the problem (the denial of public health problems—the asbestos scandal). In the media sector, it is thus *newsworthy* information, that which sells and so is profitable, which is exploited: whether or not public problems are given media coverage depends on their expected value as news items (value that is inextricable from both a market and an audience). And, of course, the presence of a public problem on the market has performative consequences: that is where it wins credibility and legitimacy.

This market-centered view has a well-known corollary: the difficulty that individuals experience in engaging in collective enterprises to obtain "indivisible collective goods."[37] If the individuals involved do not anticipate subjective utility or private benefit as the result of their actions (the low marginal utility and profitability of public commitments), if they do not succeed in according each other minimal trust (the prisoner's dilemma), and if they decide that the most rational thing to do is to wait and do nothing (the self-interest behind the conduct of the *free rider*), there is little chance that they will come together to impose a definition of a public problem. One must then depend on the mechanism of the invisible hand that converts private vices into public virtues and personal troubles into collective issues. In this way, entrepreneurs and consumers can engage in a public arena that is understood as a market, where the investment of their time, money, and energy will receive a worthwhile return by the happy coincidence of individual and public interests.

But this perspective has limitations. Often, the actors do not conceive of themselves as isolated individuals dealing with situations according to an economic rationality: they are members of communities, are under obligations, and have responsibilities that are not taken into account by the market model. For example, they aim at the preservation or the institution of common goods that they share with co-owners—the kind of common property of land or water that was described by Elinor Ostrom and her team[38] and, before them, by E. P. Thompson.[39] Today, they fight for the recognition of public goods, typically welfare, education, or health or, most recently, the development of source code available to the general public.

The open-source software and data movement can be seen as a mobilization that chooses in favor of public goods and against privatization and reverses Olson's expectations. What Ostrom calls "commons" is actually close to a certain species of Dewey's "public goods." And this claim for commons is a critique of the supposed universality of Olson's model: economic rationality is no more than one mode of human action. Social worlds are not commodities.

2. Another concept is that of the "field" (Bourdieu 1979). The existence and nature of social problems depend on the state of power relations and the conflicting interests of classes or class fractions in different social fields or subfields. Political sociology has expanded the language of class that prevailed in the 1970s, but the analytical framework remains the same. Agents are driven by the fact that they have different amounts of capital to reproduce, invest, and make profitable through more or less costly strategies. On the one hand, the "dominated," deprived of capital, struggle to be heard in the subfields of the economy, politics, administration, and information; on the other, the "dominants" control the game, possess the means of inquiring and informing, occupy political decision-making positions, and have the firepower necessary for mobilization. Beyond objective complicity between the elites of different subfields, there may be tensions, but the dominants still define the problems and decide on solutions for everybody. The classic example is the press, organized as a social subfield working as a closed-loop system: newspapers and magazines follow strategies for reproducing available information and distinguishing themselves from their direct competitors—a world in which there is no room for a public in Dewey's sense. The audience is made up of dominated consumers, who seem unable to have any judgment and change their minds through any kind of inquiry. Their convictions and opinions are formed by the media, and it is difficult to imagine them having the capacity to turn themselves into members of a public.

One corollary, according to Bourdieu,[40] is that there is only a slim statistical chance that those most deprived of capital will express dissatisfaction, defend their interests, and claim rights. They possess neither the material means to do so nor the organizational and informational tools, even if they have acquired specific social and cultural capital through activism. In general, they simply do not have the time for it—occupied as they are by survival strategies—and they feel ill-qualified to do it. The only way to achieve mobilization is through the mechanism of the "magic of representation," through which "representatives" perform dominated communities and speak on their behalf, and "those represented" put their future in the hands of political professionals who can formulate demands, have ways to act through unions or parties, and are entrusted to do it.

This framework has, of course, undergone alterations since the beginning of the 1980s—in France, through the development of a sociohistory of politics; but the importation of the resource mobilization perspective and the generalization of a rhetoric of the "general economy of practices" have served only to strengthen this restrictive conception of representation, as controlled by "entrepreneurs" of social movements and political parties. And if the dominated seem to have rediscovered some ability to think and act by themselves, they are far from constituting publics: the logic of reproduction of fields and "habitus" leaves barely any room for such collective dynamics.

We should note that these two paradigms, which emphasize *market value* and *power relationships*, are all the more credible now that social worlds are increasingly colonized by economic logics and engaged in processes of financialization; now that the rule of law retreats and devices of security control multiply, and the welfare state shrinks through the destruction of social policy programs. The meaning and relevance of concepts depend on their contexts of use.

3. The third view conceives of a public arena as a *forum* or an *agora—a place of deliberation*. It departs from a vision of exchange based on the law of profit or on the law of the strongest and adopts a vision of *public reason*. Individuals who strive to be rational and reasonable, and who subscribe to a shared conception of public reason, agree on premises of public justification, endowed with universal value, or discuss the best procedures for formulating good arguments. And once they have debated or deliberated—depending on the details of Jürgen Habermas, John Dryzek, or James Bohman's versions—they make decisions and act in accordance with the rational consensus that they have reached. The public problems that emerge are the result of not only a *systemic rationality*—of the government, legislature, or administration—or of a *strategic rationality* of interest groups—businessmen, the media, parties, etc.—but of a *communicative rationality*. In *Law and Democracy*, Habermas[41] thus analyzes how the discussion of social problems in "autonomous public spaces" can generate new values independently of institutions that organize and regulate the political order and of agents who *manufacture consent* by means of political communication.

This approach has affinities with the pragmatist view, encountered as much in Dewey, Mead, and Park as in many other writers of the 1920s who extolled the virtues of public discussion. The social reform movements—urban, journalistic, pedagogical, and so on—in which Park, Mead, and Dewey in one way or another participated had created, in the prewar years, formidable *hotbeds of public culture* in which the progressivist imagination could have free rein. Other interwar activists, such as Mary Parker Follett, Eduard C. Lindeman, and Alfred D. Sheffield, also bet on "creative intelligence"[42] arising through public discussion. That is, moreover, the lesson drawn by contemporary theorists of deliberative democracy, without necessarily linking it to this moment of social reform. The public arena is jointly produced as a *forum of discussion*: the fact that disputed points must be defended and justified, and opposing positions criticized and invalidated, entails processes of evaluation, deliberation, and judgment. In such a public arena, representatives of opposing sides demand justification for arguments and decisions, take up positions, and respond to criticism. Through dialogue, their arguments become more and more aligned with the *public interest*. Mead describes this bootstrapping onto the plane of moral community and mutual recognition as an adoption of the standpoint of the generalized Other. Human beings have a capacity to transcend their self-interest to work toward the public good. They do all that in their living environments not only through speech communication but also by conducting inquiries and experiments.

THE ECOLOGICAL FOUNDATIONS OF PUBLIC REASON

It is therefore justified to think together pragmatism and deliberative democracy. At this point, human ecology comes into play. Disputes involving collective action take on distinct forms according to the type of environment in which they occur. These disputes are usually expressed as journalistic polemic, judicial process, scientific controversy, political struggle, administrative arbitration, and the like, and they are realized in open meetings, parliamentary hearings, street demonstrations, proposals and rebuttals in journals, news reports, petitions, and editorials, to name a few. Communication is indeed the vehicle of cooperation and competition between participants: any action aiming to transform the public order must employ the form and content of reasoning and argumentation, tailored in each case to specific environments, with their strategic moves, specialized jargons, and publics involved. In this way, an act of communication takes place, which outlines an arena of approved roles, legitimate issues, and appropriate involvements. Having a pragmatist perspective on the public arena means not forgetting that it is made of the complementarity of "production and reception roles" (Goffman 1982) through which participants engage in the public game. And they do that using specific formats of communication, vocabularies, and grammars—not the same as when the speaker is a lawyer proceeding in a trial, a researcher reporting experiments, a politician addressing her electors, or a journalist recounting a public event.

A communicative approach does not, therefore, grant absolute power to speech. A public arena is constituted not just by a conclave of people of good faith who come together to discuss and solve problems. It is formed according to an *ecological logic*, through the adjustment and readjustment to the transformations of *symbolic, instrumental, and organizational environments*. This perspective is traditionally that of Chicago sociology (as well as Dewey and Mead's pragmatism, and Thorstein Veblen and John R. Commons's institutionalism). It was developed by Robert E. Park, Ernest W. Burgess, and Roderick D. McKenzie in the 1920s and would be partly redeveloped, in different ways, by Tamotsu Shibutani,[43] Anselm Strauss,[44] and Howard Becker.[45]

A problem is not only a mental construct; it is rooted in environments. The same goes for its resolution: a kind of *creative intelligence* unfolds through a collective action that reorganizes these environments, modifies the *order of things*, discovers new facts and devises new rules, and creates new tools for comprehending situations and intervening in them, to reshape them in accordance with goods aimed at.

The composition of the public arena as an "organizational field" is not given in advance and depends on the ongoing process of checking the consequences of what has been done, conflicting around their diagnosis and prognosis, and projecting new paths for action. New collective protagonists and antagonists come together over this contested resolution, the possibilities for which depend on the problematic situation's material form. Interest groups and social movements spread out around new battle lines and power relations: they try to interest, convince, and enlist other actors on the basis of the sharing of ideological affinities, the agreement over argumentative lines, the alignment of rational strategies, or the convergence of political analyses. Ann Mische[46] proposed an interesting network analysis of such an organizational dynamic and described how spokespersons emerge, send messages to the media and their audiences, and find compromises around common platforms of action. Doing that, these organizations mobilize resources and allies, spot adversaries and aim at targets, and organize themselves to resolve the situation, often while trying to influence government decisions, legal regulations, and administrative arrangements.

Here, we face a *specific process of emergence and invention* that is not easy to describe, even if we can draw on the perspectives of a few thinkers of democracy[47] and of social movements,[48] as well as of the creativity of action, in a pragmatist perspective.[49] The collective dynamics is not determined by structural conditions in a field, nor is it reducible to effects of aggregation on a market. Our bet is that it should be seen as a process of reorganization of communities, organizations, and institutions that pull through a crisis situation. The members of the social worlds affected or concerned by such a test of personal or social disorganization (which means experienced as such) look for a solution. They can try to change their personal environment through private strategies: they get a new job or leave the place they lived in; they invest new capital or acquire new skills by attending training programs. They can become aware that common solutions may be more relevant and are worth trying and commit themselves, collectively, to reallocate resources or reorganize facilities, help to develop new technologies, or ask for a shifting to new public policies—including new ethical and legal standards. This means that their social worlds are subject to new alignments and configurations of action, at different spatial and temporal scales, which lead to sometimes limited, other times more radical consequences for their living environments and life stories.

This entire process, which constitutes a public arena, is a matter not only of field structure or market strategies, or of public discussion, but of *institutional, legal, and political ecology*. We can give a good example of this, contemporary with the golden age of pragmatism at the beginning of the twentieth century. The concern to educate citizens and create a "public consciousness" or a "public mind"[50] suited to democratic life led to the creation of environments of civic institutions such as schools, universities, theaters, libraries, hospitals, journals, social settlements, and community centers, with their programs of evening lectures and adult training courses. Each of these civic institutions opened up new opportunities for public discussion, but, most importantly, they were designed and implemented through the organization of material means, oriented by a political concern for their potential consequences. The emergence of such settings of civic institutions has been described as a matter of pride for the affluent and cultured metropolitan elites from Chicago, New York, Boston, or Philadelphia, who, in competition with one another, sought pastimes befitting their social status—if not, for other facilities, as the manifestation of a kind of philanthropic paternalism of do-gooders worrying about the poor. Even if that is what they were, they could also be seen as vessels of public experience, at the same time products and producers of publics, discussing, experimenting with, and inquiring into the best ways to make their cities livable, working on welfare, educational, and health projects for all.

Similarly, the social inquiry and experimental method not only signal the growth of the scientific mind-set, the professionalization of academic disciplines, and the technocratization of public administration—some classical criticisms of pragmatism in social sciences. They also indicate a shift in the relationship to society: it is possible to have some reflective control over the transformation of an environment by exploring its potentialities and guiding the changes made to it. This was the point of social surveys, at the time of Mead and Dewey and, after them, of sociological inquiry into social work and the urban policy of the 1920s. In other words, *the work of defining and mastering public problems gave rise to agencies in specific environments, which in turn contributed to reframing these public problems and institutionalizing their management.*

In Chicago, for example, garbage collection, city planning and beautification, the creation of children's playgrounds and public baths, legislation on the employment of women and children, reduction of alcoholism in saloons, and reform of housing conditions were first suggested by progressive activists who confronted problems of this kind and little by little transformed their environment to solve them.[51] These battles took place at the local level of Hull House in Chicago's near West Side, at the level of the state of Illinois for issues of juvenile delinquency, and sometimes beyond, at the federal level, for legal and employment matters. Similar struggles grew up at the nationwide level through federations of social centers, community organizations, women's clubs, workers' unions, and the like, which constituted progressive networks and interest groups and put the pressure on political parties and public authorities.[52] The civic management of public problems led to the vote of public regulations, the creation of public services, and the launch of public policies. This came about even though the complexity of technological and economic development and the diversification of customs, habits, and beliefs signaled the end of "local town meeting practices and ideals" and made it difficult to identify a "scattered, mobile and manifold public."[53]

Approaching the issue of participatory democracy in terms of discussion forums for solving public problems thus has its limits.[54] For residents of Chicago at the beginning of the twentieth century, communication was mediated by multiple interrelationships between political decision makers and citizens involved in universities, civic clubs, survey committees, community centers, and, at the local level, in more or less formal associations, from groups of friends to community organizations.

These networks of academics, activists, and philanthropists, who mingled with the city's elite, shared the same preoccupations, relating equally to urban patriotism, the liberal ideal, and the progressive creed. These networks also spanned social, ethno-linguistic, entrepreneurial, and trade union worlds, between which they mediated, translated, and allowed passage and in which they made possible the emergence of something like a "public reason."[55] Movements and countermovements, interest groups and mass media, civil society and public authorities interact with one another, creating constellations of experience, discourse, and action, which intersect, interpenetrate, and divide and counterbalance, unite, and oppose one another. Anselm Strauss employed the concept of the "social arena,"[56] which he explicitly claimed as an empirical extension of the legacy of Thomas, Park, and Mead—to whom he added Herbert Blumer, and Everett C. Hughes. He developed the idea of a "negotiated order," which emerges, takes shape, and stabilizes through transactions both within and between organizations as well as between organizations and their environments. Strauss merged it with the idea of "social worlds," which sprout, grow and multiply, and fuse and fragment, articulating habitualized and recurring orders of interactions and activities.[57] A public arena is a social arena in which the actors aim at public goods, refer to a public interest, frame problems as public, and feel, act, and speak accordingly using public motives. Like a social arena, a public arena is an organized set of bargains and agreements, protests and concessions, promises and commitments, contracts and conventions, tensions and compromises, more or less symbolized and ritualized and formalized and codified, but in this social arena, a public interest is played out. It is a world of social worlds that establishes territories, understandings, technologies, organizations, and institutions and that is organized for securing a public good or preventing a public evil. A sociological version of Dewey's public.

A public arena is configured temporally without the possibility of assigning it preestablished boundaries. It develops by drawing support from and building bridges between different public stages. It opens up social worlds and institutions to one another. It creates new links between them. It brings them into contact, enriches and propels them, and contributes to processes of transformation, fragmentation and rearranging, segmentation and intersection, and denial and legitimization. It transforms environments in which relations of production, property, and power are established, and by raising new cases, it creates precedents that may become the rule. The public arena sets new bundles of *habitual responses*[58]— that is, repertoires of typical understandings of problematic situations and typical reactions to solve them: configurations of actors, ideas, and values; political institutions; cultural meanings; and technical instruments organize the horizons of experience of the public and its capacity to grasp the problem and give it an answer. But beyond this habitualized dimension of the transactions of people with their environments (and their precipitation and crystallization into "social mechanisms"[59]), *overlapping* and *overspilling* appear to be regular processes in the public arena. The idea of "segmentation" as a form of organizational or institutional innovation, which is found in the work of Rue Bucher[60] and is in a direct line of descent from Everett C. Hughes's sociology of professions, clearly expresses this *force of innovation* at work in public arenas. New problems, methods, devices, and capacities; new repertoires of knowledge and beliefs; new sets of staff and materials; new operations of inquiring, training, categorizing, and measuring emerge through this process of mushrooming or burgeoning. Public problems are thus addressed as they pass between different "jurisdictions,"[61] which contribute to organize what is done with them and the experience of these doings. They percolate into "linked ecologies" whereby they take on new dimensions and, conversely, generate new environments.

The work of Shibutani, Becker, and Strauss, and further research following the latter from the 1980s onward, in a confrontation between the social worlds perspective and science and technology studies, have provided new tools with which to grasp the *generative power* of public problems. Processes of dissemination and amplification are mediated by all kinds of master frames and, more interestingly, by *boundary objects*,[62] which help to rally audiences and facilitate translation into other environments. A public problem gains power as the degree of mobilization of large numbers of individuals and the degree of resonance among numerous audiences increase: different stages begin to resonate with each other, interrogate and respond to each other, and borrow themes, resources, people, and information from each other. Its transformation seems to accelerate and its structure seems to branch out in new processes and undergo numerous twists and turns—in terms of topics, domains (media, industrial, political, consumer, etc.), and complexity (opening of new rhetorical fronts; hybridization, linkage, or subordination with other problems). The public problem then transcends the boundaries of social, organizational, and institutional worlds; it establishes new *stages of publicization*[63] straddling them, and it enters, directly or peripherally, into the agendas of a number of decision makers. It spreads by provoking transformations in the worlds of daily life as well as the ecological niches of the market or the State—a phenomenon that theories of *collective behavior* characterized as "contagion." It rearranges environments or creates new ones (redistribution of material resources, growth of professional careers, financial and organizational investments, emergence of technologies and educational methods, production of norms and standards, etc.).

BEYOND NEGOTIATED CONFLICT: PUBLIC INTELLIGENCE

For Strauss and Becker, negotiated arrangements and strategic interactions appear to be the whole story. The young Hans Joas,[64] still under the influence of Habermas, had already pointed out the limitations of a view that does not distinguish between negotiation and deliberation and does not take a communicative rationality into account. Another omission, unnoticed by Joas, as by Habermas, but detrimental to a sociology of democracy, concerns joint activities of inquiry and experimentation.

A public arena is also organized as an archipelago of *fields of inquiry* and *laboratories of experimentation.*

We have already seen how the emergence of public problems at the beginning of the twentieth century in the United States was rooted in a network of social inquiries and experiments. In addition, the Chicago School sociologists established banks of statistical and cartographical data as tools for acquiring scientific knowledge of the city and for planning its development rationally—an undertaking already in process in progressive circles. The idea, pragmatist *par excellence,* was to formulate and confirm working hypotheses about the city, thus treated like a "social laboratory,"[65] in the open, to discover the laws governing its organization and development. This metaphor of experimentation was widespread from the end of the nineteenth century onward; Mead and Dewey revived it and, above all, scrutinized the logic of building and testing hypotheses, including through abduction. The study of public problems—juvenile delinquency, interracial conflict, difficulties in assimilating immigrants, local government corruption, blue-collar working conditions, the disorganization of urban environment, and so on—with a view to explaining and regulating them is central to the burgeoning disciplines of sociology and political science. On the basis of this knowledge, experts in social science can contribute to establishing agencies for urban planning and public policy: in other words, they "organize" and "incorporate" a form of *collective intelligence* into *public institutions.* Urban policy implements a rational approach whereby cities have only known "natural growth"; regulatory and legislative bodies curb forms of industrial exploitation or manage the coexistence of ethnic groups; educational and rehabilitative institutions try to guide children and adolescents and put their lives back on course.

Collective living is a natural laboratory, in the open, where ways of life, patterns of public action, and commonsense knowledge are tried out, examined, tested, and evaluated. It does not simply reproduce customs and traditions; it is not governed by the law of the market alone; it is driven no more by class struggle than by the image of the City of God. Dewey and Mead have often reiterated that politics must define and resolve public problems by a *method of inquiry and experimentation.* Doubtless, some of the actors involved in the public sphere try to impose sectarian prejudices, arguments based on authority, or transcendent truths and engage in fantastical attempts to reinstate an imaginary tradition at the heart of modernity. Others do not pay much attention to law and science and rely more on force, patronage, cronyism, and corruption, or, alternatively, they resort to pseudoscientific rationales to further their interests. The growing body of literature on agnotology[66] describes how the harmful effects of tobacco or the fact of global warming have been concealed by firms and lobbies, and how the latter succeeded at orienting the laboratories' agendas according to their self-interest—the very opposite of free public life. Last, we know now, better than they did in Mead and Dewey's time, that science can have negative effects and that its prescriptions often conflict with public opinion—actually, there were already critiques of "specialism" and "expertise" in the 1920s, which anticipated some of the pernicious effects of the scientific attitude.[67] But the idea that there is an element of inquiry and experimentation in the constitution of a field of democratic experience is crucial, as much from a normative point of view as from a descriptive or analytical one.

From this perspective, *public problems are taken as social movements*[68] whose members piece together facts, embark on investigations, analyze official data, seek points of comparison, suggest explanations and interpretations, imagine strategies of intervention, test hypotheses, and act accordingly. This brings us to another problem inherent to the rhetoric of adjustment and accommodation between interests. While acknowledging that there can be other modes of interaction, such as persuasion, convention, or education, Strauss and Becker do not match the richness of pragmatist theories of the beginning of the century. The normative dimension of publicity is lost in their work, and the ethical and political significance of the constitution of public problems, which was central for Park, Dewey, and Mead, is no longer conceived of as such. However, the dynamic of social reform was of equal importance for *public ethics*: the common good is inseparable from its being tangibly put to the test, and standards for what is right and just, which politics will try to meet, derive not from abstract principles but from collective experience, understood as inquiry and experimentation.[69] A *creative, rational, and organized intelligence*, tested in specific environments, leads to the invention and selection of new ways of seeing, speaking, and doing that are seen as preferable or desirable for the public good. Whether concerning the transformation of the status of women championed by the suffragettes, the implementation of new forms of urban planning, the demand for new rights for industrial workers, or the educational activism aimed at reforming schools, the constitution of public problems always involves an element of inquiry and experimentation. This allows for better pinpointing of the issues that involve conflict or disputation with the conservative elites, interest groups, and opinion movements promoting the status quo or advocating a laissez-faire attitude.

An important point, which Park, Mead, and Dewey had observed and which has since been reformulated by network analysis, is that of the "decoupling" of members involved in the public from roles and statuses and opinions and convictions that are ordinarily theirs and "switching" to others.[70] Structural analyses that trace a public commitment to a position in a field or to the possession of capital have their limits—empirical inquiry delivers counterexamples, even when the publics have a social basis and are rooted in local, ethnic, professional, religious, gender, class, and other types of communities. The point is not to deny this state of affairs but to recognize that *the public reorganizes the field of experience of its members, their sense of what is possible or not, and their critiques and claims, as well as their evaluation of constraints on and opportunities for action*. These different dimensions of experience and action are not completely determined by field or market structures; they emerge in the collective dynamics. By selecting the relevant data that define a problematic situation according to the dialectic of means and ends that they project forward, ahead of them, members of the public free themselves from the grip of this problematic situation by putting themselves in control, formulating and testing hypotheses so as to better understand what they are dealing with. They discover a *capability* to navigate the world, control their destinies, understand the events affecting them, and on this basis, they achieve *positive liberty*—a freedom to not be passive in the face of what happens to them, to regain autonomy within power relations, and, sometimes, to realize ideals of law or justice. This focus on a capability of acting, for which Dewey offers precious resources, demonstrates the power of the public to act—the *potestas in populo*.[71] Taking into account the dynamics of problematization and publicization provides a new framework for the literature on collective mobilizations and social problems. It shows its political scope. It revives the concern for emancipation of the *progressive reformism* of Jane Addams's,[72] Dewey's, and Mead's time—if not a concept of "radical democracy" such as Mary P. Follett's—sensitive to such a collective capacity for acting together.[73]

CONCLUSION: THE PUBLIC AS AN EMERGENT POLITICAL COMMUNITY

The connection between pragmatism and social sciences returns to the fore these days.[74] We hope in this chapter to contribute to this revival and propose new avenues of inquiry and analysis. In the first place, the constitution of public problems, according to Dewey's model, enriches the collective experience with a new wealth of moral sentiments, practical beliefs, collective habits, social representations, and the like. It also augments it with explanatory models, interpretative schemas, and evaluative arguments. It gives rise to a cognitive and normative environment, with its material and conceptual apparatus. One of the driving forces of this collective dynamic is found in inquiries, experiments, and discussions conducted by members of publics, who strive to overcome problematic situations. When they do not take an active stance, they at least maintain a receptive one: they read the news, become well-informed citizens, and exchange points of view in conversations, in line with Tarde's figure of the "public."[75] They gain awareness, feel concerned by a problem, and sometimes engage in collective mobilizations, commuting from receptive to active modes of engagement. The notion of public experience is not far removed from much research done in the United States under the label of *cultural sociology*. But one may add to the topics usually under study—emotions, memory, symbolism, rituals—the question of inquiry and experiment in the transactions between forms of collective life and their environments.

In a pragmatist perspective, democracy is not considered only as a system of laws, policies, and institutions but also as a way of life. The best way to study such a way of life and the public order it relies on is to start with the observation of situations of disruption of what was taken for granted. Pragmatists start with a *problem-centered conception of democracy*. How do new public issues make their way into public experience? How do tiny troubles turn themselves into nationwide causes to defend, stand for, and fight for? We have learned with Gusfield and others how new public stages, driven by the quest for scientific evidence and legal and political responsibility, attract, capture, and hold the attention of the public, and outline new "public issues/causes," in process and in conflict.

But this dramatist and rhetorical perspective has its limits. The members of the public, both active and receptive, are not in a merely contemplative state: the constitution of a public experience provides new grips on problematic situations, which allow them, directly or indirectly involved, to regain their power to understand and take action. The building up of public arenas crafts new *capabilities for action*.[76] Changing reference viewpoints, diffusing poignant narratives, generating counter-information and counterarguments, reframing habits of feeling and thinking, inviting to some kind of cooperative inquiry and experimentation, public arenas let arise a new public experience, which fashions the fields of personal experience of Selves and may transform their lives: having the right to live out sexual preferences with no risk of being ostracized; taking back control over one's life and gaining freedom of action through access to education; increasing autonomy in fulfilling one's desires and realizing one's work projects; controlling one's own body through contraception and escaping male power, among others. Public arenas give rise to new moral sensibilities; redistribute resources, rights, and capabilities more fairly; recognize a plurality of beliefs, opinions, and identities; and create new opportunities for better individual and collective living. They institute new hierarchies of credibility, turn upside down the distribution of rights and powers, invent new forms of knowledge, and circulate new versions of reality. They do that by developing new environments—with their organizations, technologies, literatures, legislations, public policies—thanks to which collective experience gains consistency and durability (and gets disciplined in the same process).

Such a set of questions, of course, crosses the areas of sociology of social problems and sociology of social movements. The public arenas perspective changes the vantage point. Instead of focusing in the first place on environment resources, field reproduction, mobilization structures, political process, or social networks in order to explain a new mobilization, it takes as a point of departure the relevant perspectives (in Mead's sense) of the different participants in the public arena. This means that it is only through their ways of engaging into a struggle around a public issue that one knows what is at stake in the public arena. It is through their ways of understanding, describing, arguing, interpreting, and explaining, valuating, and judging problematic situations (or refusing to do so and staying on side when other actors are invoking your responsibility) that it becomes possible for the observer-analyst to know about their so-called frames and identities and to discover which are the issues, claims, critiques, denunciations and what makes sense as "structural constraint," "political opportunity," "social capital," "network block," and so on.

Much research is done as if these notions were referring to something objective, but if we follow Dewey or Mead, the ways in which we understand the present, reconstruct the past, and plan for the future, the ways that we make deals with allies

or oppose adversaries, discover assets, and experience constraints in a given environment, the ways in which we aim at ends and organize means depend on the kind of
perspectives we take on a problematic situation. These perspectives are not subjective either but depend on how they were set in the social mind (some kind of culture structures grounded in social structures), and they change over time while the
public arena is unfolding. Perspectives are not only constructed on the agendas of
the mass media, civic organizations, government, Parliament, or the administration:
they depend on strong *ecologies of the social mind* (including institutional and legal,
technological and media environments). The fact is that in public arenas, such perspectives shift: people concerned by a public issue go through an experience of
decoupling and switching from their habitual statuses, beliefs, relationships that is
social worlds and social perspectives. This is how, in the public arena perspective,
new groups are represented, new interests satisfied, new rights recognized, and new
organizations created.

Public arenas are nevertheless not reducible to markets in which rational strategies are aggregated, fields of power relations, or agoras for exchanging arguments—
we have to enlarge this conception of the public reason. They are milieus in the
ecological sense of the word, embodied into fields of collective action and experience, which can be concentrated spatially in territories or dispersed in sprawling constellations. New collectives are formed there and regulated around mutual
expectations, complementary beliefs, and shared habits—though in contention.
These milieus are webs of collective life, which means that they are populated with
life-forms in transaction with one another—the connection point between human
ecology and political ecology. They are equipped with artefacts that the publics'
members deal with in their process of defining and mastering problematic situations. There grow up and are constructed, concomitantly, the instrumentalities of
public experience and public action, through which the public intelligence organizes itself. Of course, these milieus are universes of discourse[77] and, more broadly,
"forests" of symbols, signs, and images, which mediate communication, open horizons of intelligibility, draw the boundaries of what is thinkable and doable, and
sometimes project into imaginary worlds. The public mind is made of practical
tools as well as languages, imageries, and symbolisms that our experiences, feelings,
memories, projects, moralities, and fantasies are made of and through which they
can express themselves. The opening of a public arena generates a specific kind
of public affectivity, public memory, and public discourse; it organizes new sets of
resources, topics, and frames, used in public strategies and struggles.

Last, public arenas are milieus insofar as the public, made up of a thousand eyes,
hands, and brains adjusted to their ecological niches, is *embodied in flesh*.[78] The old
metaphor of the superorganism is nothing more than a metaphor, but it is interesting
to play with for an *ecology of publics*. No public exists without sentient bodies, which
feel and are felt on the public stage of a *theatrum mundi*, affected by situations that
they find unbearable, occupied in keeping up appearances, exchanging ideas and
conveying emotions, and eager to find ways to survive and live together—with the

twin dimension of passivity and activity that Dewey brought to light. There is no public without a common sense revealed through feeling, memory, and imagination—without a public experience that creates new channels for common life.

Joining together, exploring situations, inquiring and experimenting, discussing and protesting: these are many ways of engaging in processes of collective action and political judgment and of building, in plurality and conflict, a common world around public issues. The public is such a political community, however divided and disputed it might be.

NOTES

1. John Dewey, *The Public and Its Problems* (New York: Henry Holt, 1927).

2. Daniel Cefaï, "Qu'est-ce qu'une arène publique? Quelques pistes pour une approche pragmatiste," in *L'Héritage du pragmatisme: Conflits d'urbanité et épreuves de civisme*, ed. D. Cefaï and I. Joseph (La Tour d'Aigues: Éditions de l'Aube, 2002), 51–82.

3. Hannah Arendt, *The Human Condition* (Chicago: University of Chicago Press, 1958).

4. Jürgen Habermas, *The Structural Transformation of the Public Sphere: An Inquiry Into a Category of Bourgeois Society* (1962; Cambridge: Polity, 1989).

5. Christopher Ansell, *Pragmatist Democracy: Evolutionary Learning as Public Philosophy* (Oxford: Oxford University Press, 2011).

6. John Dewey, *Logic: The Theory of Inquiry* (New York: Henry Holt, 1938). The principle of the definition of the situation had been set down in sociology by William Isaac and Dorothy Swaine Thomas's famous mantra, "If men define situations as real, they are real in their consequences," in *The Child in America* (New York: Knopf, 1928), 572.

7. Arthur Bentley and John Dewey, *Knowing and the Known* (Boston: Beacon, 1949), 121–39.

8. Daniel Cefaï, "Ecologies of Institutions: The Chicago Perspective," in *Pragmatic Inquiry*, ed. J. R. Bowen, N. Dodier, J. W. Duyvendak, and A. Hardon (New York: Routledge, 2020), 35–52.

9. Joseph Gusfield, *The Culture of Public Problems: Drinking Driving and the Symbolic Order* (Chicago: University of Chicago Press, 1981).

10. Robert E. Park and Ernest W. Burgess, *Introduction to the Science of Sociology* (Chicago: University of Chicago Press, 1921), 52.

11. George H. Mead, *Mind, Self, Society: The Definitive Edition*, ed. H. Joas and D, Huebner (1934; Chicago: University of Chicago Press, 2015), 90.

12. Daniel Cefaï, "Social Worlds: The Legacy of Mead's Social Ecology in Chicago Sociology," in *The Timeliness of G. H. Mead*, ed. D. Huebner and H. Joas (Chicago: University of Chicago Press, 2016), 165–184.

13. John Dewey, "Letter to Albert G. A. Balz," in *Knowing and the Known. The Later Works 1949–1952*, ed. A. Bentley and J. Dewey (1949; Carbondale: Southern Illinois University Press, 1989), 280–94.

14. Edward P. Thompson, "The Moral Economy of the English Crowd in the Eighteenth Century," *Past & Present* 50 (1971): 76–136.

15. Daniel Cefaï, and Cédric Terzi, "Présentation," in *L'Expérience des problèmes publics. Perspectives pragmatists*, series *Raisons pratiques* no. 22, Paris: Éditions de l'EHESS, 2012), 9–47; Louis Quéré and C. Terzi, "Pour une sociologie pragmatiste de l'expérience publique. Quelques apports mutuels de la philosophie pragmatiste et de l'ethnométhodologie," *Sociologies*, (February 23, 2015), https://doi.org/10.4000/sociologies.4949.

16. Robert E. Park, "The Urban Community as a Spatial Pattern and a Moral Order," in *The Urban Community*, ed. E. W. Burgess (Chicago: University of Chicago Press, 1926), 3–18.

17. Alain Desrosières, *The Politics of Large Numbers: A History of Statistical Reasoning* (1993; Cambridge, MA: Harvard University Press, 1998).

18. Wendy Espeland and M. Stevens, "Commensuration as a Social Process," *Annual Review of Sociology* 24 (1998): 313–43.

19. William L. F. Festiner, Richard L. Abel, and Austin Sarat, "The Emergence and Transformation of Disputes: Naming, Blaming, Claiming," *Law and Society Review* 15, nos. 3–4 (1980–81): 631–54.

20. John Dewey, *Art as Experience* (New York: Minton, Balch, 1934).

21. Joan Stavo-Debauge, "Des 'événements' difficiles à encaisser. Un pragmatisme pessimiste," in *L'Expérience des problèmes publics*, series "Raisons pratiques" no. 22, ed. D. Cefaï and C. Terzi (Paris: Éditions de l'EHESS, 2012), 191–224.

22. Daniel Cefaï, "Comment se mobilise-t-on ? L'apport d'une approche pragmatiste à la sociologie de l'action collective," *Sociologie et sociétés*, 41 (2009), 245–69.

23. Francis Chateauraynaud and Didier Torny, *Les sombres précurseurs. Une sociologie pragmatique de l'alerte et du risque.* (1999; Paris: Éditions de l'EHESS, 2013); Michel Callon and Volovona Rabeharisoa, *Le pouvoir des malades. L'Association française contre les myopathies et la recherche* (Paris: Les Presses de l'École des Mines, 1999).

24. George H. Mead, *The Philosophy of the Act*, ed. C. W. Morris (Chicago: University of Chicago Press, 1938).

25. John Dewey, *Theory of Valuation* (Chicago: University of Chicago Press, 1939).

26. Dewey, *Art as Experience*.

27. George H. Mead, "The Working Hypothesis in Social Reform," *American Journal of Sociology* 5, no. 3 (1899): 367–71.

28. Jane Addams, *Democracy and Social Ethics* (New York: Macmillan, 1902).

29. Dewey, *Theory of Valuation*.

30. Alfred Schutz, "On Multiple Realities," *Philosophy and Phenomenological Research* 5, no 4 (1945): 533–76.

31. Robert M. Emerson and Sheldon L. Messinger, "The Micro-Politics of Trouble," *Social Problems* 25, no. 2 (1977): 121–35.

32. Joseph Gusfield, "Constructing the Ownership of Social Problems: Fun and Profit in the Welfare State," *Social Problems* 36, no 5 (1989): 431–41.

33. Walter Lippmann, *Public Opinion* (New York: Harcourt, Brace, 1922), part 3.

34. Robert N. Proctor, *Golden Holocaust: Origins of the Cigarette Catastrophe and the Case for Abolition* (Berkeley: University of California Press, 2011).

35. Gerald Markowitz and David Rosner, *Lead Wars: The Politics of Science and the Fate of America's Children* (Berkeley: University of California Press, 2014).

36. Daniel Cefaï, "Publics and Publicity: Towards a Pragmatist Inquiry," *Politika. Encyclopédie des sciences historiques et sociales du politique* (Paris: Tepsis, 2016), https://www.politika.io/en/notice/publics-and-publicity-towards-a-pragmatist-enquiry.

37. Mancur Olson, *The Logic of Collective Action: Public Goods and the Theory of Groups* (Cambridge, MA: Harvard University Press, 1965).

38. Elinor Ostrom, *Governing the Commons: The Evolution of Institutions for Collective Action* (Cambridge: Cambridge University Press, 1990).

39. Edward P. Thompson, *Whigs and Hunters: The Origin of the Black Act* (London: Allen Lane, 1975).

40. Pierre Bourdieu, *Distinction: A Social Critique of the Judgment of Taste* (1979; Cambridge, MA: Harvard University Press, 1984), chap. 7.

41. Jürgen Habermas, *Between Facts and Norms: Contributions to a Discourse Theory of Law and Democracy* (1992; Cambridge, MA: MIT Press, 1996).

42. John Dewey, A. W. Moore, H. C. Brown, G. H. Mead, B. H. Bode, H. W. Stuart, J. H. Tufts, and H. M. Kallen, *Creative Intelligence: Essays in the Pragmatic Attitude* (New York: Henry Holt, 1917).

43. Tamotsu Shibutani, *Social Processes* (Berkeley: University of California Press, 1986).

44. Anselm Strauss, *Continual Permutations of Action* (New York: de Gruyter, 1993).

45. Howard Becker, *Art Worlds* (Berkeley: University of California Press, 1982).

46. Ann Mische, *Partisan Publics: Communication and Contention Across Brazilian Youth Activist Networks* (Princeton, NJ: Princeton University Press, 2008).

47. Cornelius Castoriadis, *The Imaginary Institution of Society* (1975; Cambridge, MA: MIT Press, 1987); Claude Lefort, *L'Invention démocratique* (Paris: Fayard, 1981).

48. Alberto Melucci, *Challenging Codes* (Cambridge: Cambridge University Press, 1996).

49. Hans Joas, *The Creativity of Action* (Chicago: University of Chicago Press, 1996).

50. Charles H. Cooley, *Social Organization: A Study of the Larger Mind* (New York: Scribner's, 1909), 124.

51. Kevin Mattson, *Creating a Democratic Public: The Struggle for Urban Participatory Democracy During the Progressive Era* (University Park, PA: Penn State University Press, 1998).

52. Elisabeth S. Clemens, *The People's Lobby: Organizational Innovation and the Rise of Interest Group Politics in the United States 1890–1925* (Chicago: University of Chicago Press, 1997).

53. John Dewey, "Search for the Great Community," in *The Public and Its Problems* (New York: Henry Holt, 1927).

54. James Bohman, "Realizing Deliberative Democracy as a Mode of Inquiry: Pragmatism, Social Facts, and Normative Theory," *Journal of Speculative Philosophy* 18, no 1 (2004): 23–43.

55. Roberto Frega, "What Pragmatism Means by Public Reason," *Etica & Politica/Ethics & Politics* 12, no 1 (2010): 28–51.

56. Anselm Strauss, "The Hospital and Its Negotiated Order," in *The Hospital in Modern Society*, ed. E. Freidson (New York: Free Press, 1963), 147–69; and Anselm Strauss et al., *Psychiatric Ideologies and Institutions* (New York: Free Press, 1964).

57. Adele E. Clarke, "Social Worlds/Arenas Theory as Organizational Theory," in *Social Organization and Social Process: Essays in Honor of Anselm Strauss*, ed. D. Maines (New York: de Gruyter, 1991), 119–58.

58. John Dewey, *Human Nature and Conduct* (New York: Henry Holt, 1922).

59. Neil Gross, "A Pragmatist Theory of Social Mechanisms," *American Sociological Review* 74 (2009): 358–79.

60. Rue Bucher and Anselm Strauss, "Professions in Process," *American Journal of Sociology* 66, no. 4 (1961): 325–34.

61. Andrew Abbott, "Linked Ecologies," *Sociological Theory* 23, no. 3 (2005): 245–74.

62. Susan L. Star and James R. Griesemer, "Institutional Ecology: 'Translations' and Boundary Objects: Amateurs and Professionals in Berkeley's Museum of Vertebrate Zoology 1907–1939," *Social Studies of Science* 19, no. 3 (1989): 387–420.

63. For one possible proposal of topography, see Mustafa Emirbayer and Mimi Sheller, "Publics in History: A Programmatic Statement," *Theory and Society* 28, no 1 (1999): 161.

64. Hans Joas, "George Herbert Mead and the 'Division of Labor': Macrosociological Implications of Mead's Social Psychology," *Symbolic Interaction*, 4, no. 2 (1981): 187.

65. Robert E. Park, "The City as a Social Laboratory," in *Chicago: An Experiment in Social Science Research*, ed. T. V. Smith and L. D. White (Chicago: University of Chicago Press, 1929), 1–19.

66. Naomi Oreskes and E. M. Conway, eds., *Merchants of Doubt: How a Handful of Scientists Obscured the Truth on Issues from Tobacco Smoke to Global Warming* (New York: Bloomsbury, 2000).

67. Mary P. Follett, *Creative Experience* (New York: Longmans, Green, 1924).

68. Armand L. Mauss, *Social Problems as Social Movements* (Philadelphia: Lippincott, 1975).

69. John Dewey and James H. Tufts, *Ethics*, rev. ed. (New York: Henry Holt, 1932).

70. Harrison C. White, *Identity and Control: A Structural Theory of Social Action* (Princeton, NJ: Princeton University Press, 1992); and White, "Network Switchings and Bayesian Forks: Reconstructing the Social and Behavioral Sciences," *Social Research* 62 (1995): 1035–63.

71. On civil rights movements, see Hannah Arendt, *On Violence* (New York: Harcourt, Brace, 1970): 44.

72. Jane Addams, *Twenty Years at Hull House with Autobiographical Notes* (New York: Macmillan, 1910).

73. Mary P. Follett, *The New State: Group Organization, the Solution of Popular Government* (New York: Longmans, Green, 1918).

74. Daniel Cefaï, Alexandra Bidet, Joan Stavo-Debauge, Roberto Frega, Antoine Hennion, and Cédric Terzi, "*Pragmatisme et sciences sociales: explorations, enquêtes, expérimentations*," *SociologieS* (online February 23, 2015), https://doi.org/10.4000/sociologies.4915.

75. Gabriel Tarde, *L'Opinion et la foule* (Paris: Alcan, 1901).

76. Bénédicte Zimmermann, "Pragmatism and the Capability Approach: Challenges in Social Theory and Empirical Research," *European Journal of Social Theory* 9, no. 4 (2006): 467–84.

77. Mead, *Mind Self and Society*, 89–90 and 156–58; Park and Burgess, *Introduction*, 423 and 764.

78. Maurice Merleau-Ponty, *The Visible and the Invisible*, ed. C. Lefort (1964; Evanston, IL: Northwestern University Press, 1968).

16. Finding the Future in Pragmatist Thought

IMAGINATION, TELEOLOGIES, AND PUBLIC DELIBERATION

ANN MISCHE

Pragmatism is generally perceived as adopting a radically presentist theory of thought and action. While people engage in experimental deliberation over the future, as well as reflective consideration of the past, they remain firmly grounded in the habits and problems of the present. This insight has underpinned the recent resurgence of sociological interest in pragmatist philosophy, particularly as applied to institutional creativity and change.[1] At the same time, this insistence on presentism in recent appropriations of John Dewey (as well as sociological theorists influenced by Dewey, such as G. H. Mead and Alfred Schutz) underplays the critical role of the *future imaginary* in pragmatist thought and, by extension, the role of future projections in political and institutional change efforts.

This neglect of the future is partly the fault of Dewey himself; his deep skepticism of teleologies—in both thought and politics—led him to emphasize the situational groundedness of intelligent action. Developing a biting critique of the rationalizing forces of industrial capitalism, together with skepticism about the polarizing politics of "Marxian socialism," he was equally wary of instrumentalist "progress" narratives and of grand utopian solutions. He preferred an approach to both knowledge and action that is rooted in local context and emergent temporal horizons ("ends-in-view"). However, I will argue that this emphasis on presentism in recent neopragmatist scholarship does not tap all that Dewey and other pragmatist-inspired thinkers have to say about the ways in which we actively engage the future—in fact, constructing teleologies—even if those futures are often murky, limited, tentative, fantastical, and context-dependent.

In this chapter, I take a closer look at how Dewey conceives of the experimental relationship to the future in his classic psychological work, *Human Nature and Conduct*. I examine Dewey's critique of utilitarian and utopian perspectives, putting this in dialogue with Paul Ricoeur's work on ideology and utopia. I consider the historical grounding of Dewey's critique, as well as its promise and limitations for understanding contemporary power and politics. I examine the ways in which Dewey's ideas were elaborated by Schutz, who took us deeper into the phenomenology of the projective imagination and the role of "projects" in human choice and action. I argue that Dewey and Schutz, taken together, provide conceptual tools with which to challenge functionalist and optimization-based teleologies and instead understand the multistranded, culturally embedded, situationally evolving, and yet still *orienting* and *steering* character of future projections.

At the same time, however, I argue that the pragmatist distrust of teleologies is problematic for understanding how futures work in messy and contentious public deliberations. This is because Dewey's critique of teleologies is both an epistemological and a moral-political positioning; just because he thought we *should* engage in intelligent action (in which future deliberations are experimentally grounded in present problems) does not mean that we always do so. Moreover, as Ricoeur argues, the cultural resources provided by ideologies and utopias enable people to map and disrupt power relations—critical components of political debate and contestation. I close by putting Dewey's psychological thinking on futures in dialogue with his later work on publics, considering how the notion of "soft teleologies" proposed by pragmatist theories of democracy can help us understand how futures shape public deliberation amid the rough and tumble of power and politics.

1. THE PUZZLE OF THE FUTURE

For those of us who study and engage in social change efforts, the future presents a puzzle and a challenge. The future is puzzling as an object of study; because it hasn't happened yet, it falls outside of the arena of facticity, punted into the epistemologically tenuous realm of the imagination. And yet the future also permeates action in the present in tangible and observable ways—through our expectations and aspirations, institutional scaffoldings, routinized temporal schemas, and heuristics for practical decision-making. A growing literature in sociology has begun to examine the role of future anticipations in social life, focusing on ideational variants on futures thinking[2] as well as on how cultural schemas and aspirations steer action,[3] the coordination challenges these pose,[4] difficulties in anticipating worst cases,[5] the management of predictive uncertainty,[6] and the structuring force of future expectations on economic life.[7] Clearly, the future is present for us, although it does not necessarily behave in the way we anticipate or want.[8]

In addition to this epistemological puzzle, futures pose a challenge for action. While dilemmas about the future provoke us all in mundane, everyday ways, they are particularly acute for collectivities that attempt to address problems of urgent common concern; that is, for what John Dewey called "publics."[9] While we know that action is grounded in the present and channeled by the past, the goal of social change efforts is to escape both of these and alter existing expectations and lines of action. The degree of proposed rupture with past and present varies from the meliorative to the messianic, and from short-term redesign to long-term transformations.

A common approach to examining the future in social change efforts is to tag them to the twinned concepts of ideology and utopia. As Ricoeur tells us, both have their social uses; ideologies provide schematized dramatizations of a society's view of its own structure and trajectory, whereas utopia subverts these schemas by imagining radically transformed alternatives. And yet, as Ricoeur also notes, both of these can be problematic—ideology for its tendency toward teleological rigidity and abstraction from context, and utopianism for its idealized normative ruptures and lack of interest in pragmatic pathways toward not-yet-existing futures.[10]

To both of these problems, pragmatist action theory as developed by Dewey and others would seem to provide a response. In pragmatism's antifoundationalism, skepticism about teleologies, deep attention to situation and context, and multi-perspectival approach to knowledge construction we find explicit challenges to the dichotomies underlying our usual tool kit for understanding the role of futures in social change efforts. Dewey himself dedicates careful thought to the process by which people imagine possible futures and the ways in which future deliberations inform action in the present. At the same time, pragmatist theory is notoriously weak in conceptualizing power and contention as essential components of political change—exactly the issues with which theorists of ideology and utopia are critically concerned.

This focus on the future has been downplayed in recent discussions of Dewey's contribution to sociological theory. The neopragmatist revival has highlighted the work of Dewey, Mead, and others on habit and routine, as well as on public deliberation, collective problem-solving, and institutional creativity.[11] But despite frequent references to Dewey's statements on the "experimental" relationship to the future, this revival has largely neglected the diverse forms and contents of people's engagement with future possibilities.[12] Instead, neopragmatist scholars have emphasized Dewey's challenge to the duality between means and ends and his argument that action is "intentional" but "non-teleological."[13]

This perspective has generated a powerful critique of rational choice approaches as well as functionalist normative theory, both of which posit fixed "portfolios" of goals, values, and/or interests. As Josh Whitford argues, actors do not have fixed goals or interests (or "ultimate ends") that remain stable across contexts.[14] Ends and means, Dewey says, are simply "two names for the same reality," with no ontologically distinct status.[15] Instead, ends-in-view flow in a continuous relationship from the array of perceived means, which are rooted in particular social contexts and problem situations. The implication is that we don't generally construct clearly defined goals or plans but rather are propelled forward by habits (conceived here in an active and dynamic sense) until we hit a stumbling block or barrier to action. At that point, reflective human intelligence is engaged as we reorganize our habits and impulses, considering possible responses to the problematic situation: "The actor is an experimenter who encounters problem situations, but without a preformed set of values to dictate a desired end-state with its (necessary) means and actions. Instead, the actor hypothesizes activities—*means-to-ends*—that might resolve the problem and makes predictions about their results—the formation of the desire—choosing a best course of action but constantly adjusting it upon receiving new information about the actual effects of means chosen."[16]

This interpretation of Dewey is compatible with important research in historical and organizational analysis that stresses the accidental, network-embedded, recombinatory basis of political and institutional creativity.[17] At the same time, it underplays the nuanced and variable way in which Dewey considered the future imagination and the ways in which these ideas were carried forward by phenomenological theorists such as Schutz. My discussion does not contradict the interpretation offered by Whitford, Joas, and others, but it does flesh out the analytic richness of Dewey's conceptualization of projectivity and its implications for theories of action and political change.

I argue that pragmatism offers important resources for thinking about futures that go beyond offering a more flexible, non-teleological understanding of ends-in-view. It gives us a way to understand the *cultural scaffoldings* by which individuals and collectivities "stop and think" and carry out "rehearsals in imagination" about possible future pathways as part of deliberate efforts to intervene in those futures. This allows us to perceive the social power of public representations of possible futures as "already having happened," at the same time as it preserves the contingency, context grounding, and open-endedness of action. And though Dewey underplays power, we do not need to. We can focus our attention on the variable ways in which scenarios for possible futures—albeit ambiguous and multistranded—become nodes, magnets, or hinge-points in political contention and institutional change.

2. THE PROBLEM WITH TELEOLOGIES

To understand the role of the future imaginary in the public change efforts that Dewey championed, we need to wrestle with the social role of teleologies, understood as organized, temporally extended representations of imagined future states and the pathways to get there. Teleologies serve as visualizing and steering devices in fields of action characterized by power and contention. At the same time, we need to take to heart Dewey's skepticism of teleologies and his insistence that both knowledge and action are situationally grounded and temporally open-ended. How can action be open-ended yet steered by imagined future states? This is the puzzle for a pragmatist understanding of futures in action.

We can find clues to this puzzle in a deep reading of Dewey's early work on the nature of human thought and action. Dewey's strong suspicion of teleologies—as well as his insistent presentist grounding—was a response to the tensions and debates of the historical period in which he was writing. His rejection of preset future pathways reflects his frustration with alternatives posed by the grand trans-formative narratives of Progressive Era politics. This frustration was both political and epistemological. In an extended passage in *Human Nature and Conduct* on "The Present and the Future," he associates most of the evils and ills of modern civilization—including the dehumanization, exploitation, and class struggle result-ing from industrial capitalism—with the propensity to split off future ends from present activity. As a result of this split, the enjoyment and satisfaction that comes from the creative use of intelligence in response to present conditions becomes sub-ordinated to technical and instrumental concern with production.

In a passage that radiates pathos and frustration, Dewey is equally critical of advanced industrial society and the Marxian socialist response to it for their "subor-dination of the living present to a remote and precarious future."[18] He slams modern "industrial education" as "a determined effort on the part of one class of the com-munity to secure *its* future at the expense of another class," while declaring that the modern separation of production and consumption under industrial capitalism as the source of the "enslavement" of both workers and capitalists: "Socially, the sep-aration of production and consumption, means and ends, is the root of the most profound division of classes. Those who fix the 'ends' for production are in con-trol, those who engage in isolated productive activity are the subject-class. But if the latter are oppressed the former are not truly free. Their consumptions are acci-dental ostentation and extravagance, not a normal consummation or fulfilment of activity. The remainder of their lives is spent in enslavement to keeping the machin-ery going at an increasingly rapid rate."[19]

In this critique of the class divisions resulting from industrial capitalism, Dewey comes very close to advancing a labor theory of alienation, and in fact he declares that "the Marxian reads aright the character of most current economic activity."[20] But at the same time, he criticizes the Marxian alternative narrative on several fronts: not only for its overemphasis on production (as split off from consumption), or for its "monstrous belief that class-struggle civil war is a means of social progress, instead of a register of the barriers to its attainment," but also for its utopian ideal-ism and its teleological fixation on an imagined future state that is radically discon-nected from present conditions.

In this critique, both the "idealist" and the "practical man" come under critical scrutiny. The idealist, he complains, "sets up as the ideal not fullness of meaning of the present but a remote goal." Utopia is a poor remedy for the lack of meaningful and pleasurable engagement in the present: "since human nature must have pres-ent realization, a sentimental, romantic enjoyment of the ideal becomes a substi-tute for intelligent and rewarding activity. The utopia cannot be realized in fact, but it may be appropriated in fantasy and serve as an anodyne to blunt the sense of a misery which after all endures." On the other hand, the practical man searching for a "good thing" also falls prey to the utopian fallacy: "In his utopian search for a future good he neglects the only place where good can be found. He empties present activity of meaning by making it a mere instrumentality. When the future arrives it is only after all another despised present."[21]

And yet although Dewey decries a focus on either idealized or instrumentalized futures, he does argue that imaginative engagement with the future is a critical dimension of intelligence, as long as we do not subordinate the present to the future. "Thought about future happenings is the only way we can judge the present; it is the only way to appraise its significance. Without such projection, there can be no projects, no plans for administering present energies, overcoming present obstacles."[22] Future projections, in other words, are valuable to the extent that they emanate from and in turn intelligently inform deliberations about present action.

Note that even as he critiques them, Dewey does acknowledge utopian, idealistic, fanciful, and instrumental thinking as observed modalities of thought about the future. This recognition of these forms of future engagement is important in itself for a sociological understanding of projectivity, even if he believes that they contribute to "a regime of accident, waste, and distress."[23] In other words, teleologies inform (or perhaps, in his view, infect) not only our theories of action but also our actions themselves. There is a certain degree of pathos in this discussion, as Dewey wrestles with the difficulties we have in intelligently engaging the future amid the complexities, dualisms, and oppressive forms of social organization of modern society. Nevertheless, he resolutely argues for an alternative conception of future engagement, one that he says corresponds more closely to the human capacity for intelligent action.

3. DELIBERATION AND THE EXPERIMENTAL FUTURE

What does such a revised understanding of future projection consist of? Despite his resolute harnessing of the future to the present, Dewey does in fact offer a rich understanding of the cognitive and emotional processes by which we engage with future possibility. If we link the primarily individual and psychological account offered in *Human Nature and Conduct* to Dewey's later work on public deliberation (i.e., in *The Public and Its Problems*), we can find resources for understanding how the projective imagination—as a (semi-)teleological mapping of future possibilities—can in fact contribute to the reorganization and redirection of social and political action.

First of all, as Whitford has noted, Dewey says we need to rethink the relationship between ends and means.[24] Ends, he tell us, are simply the "last act thought of" in a series of projected future events, whereas means are events earlier in the series.[25] Or in an alternative framing, Dewey argues that the "end" is the term for a series of actions taken collectively—that is, the entire trajectory of action seen as a whole—whereas the "means" is the "same series taken distributively"—that is, the distribution of "next acts" in the overarching series. In both cases, an expanded perspective on ends-in-view requires the cognitive work of stepping back from the immediacy of situation, impulse, and next steps and seeing action rather as trajectory and series. The possibility of an enhanced cognitive perception of action as a series of interrelated acts, reaching backward and forward in time, entails variability in what I have elsewhere called the "dimensions" of projectivity.[26] Future perspectives vary in their temporal extension, clarity, and breadth of alternatives; attention to contingency; sense of volition; and theorization of connections between steps in a causal series.

Dewey does not go so far as to theorize this variation, but he does hint at it in some of his formulations. For example, he discusses the "vices of reflection as well as of impulse." We are at risk of not looking far enough ahead "because we are hurried into action by the stress of impulse." But at the same time, we can be too obsessed with the future; "we may become so curious about remote and abstract matters that we may give only a begrudged, impatient attention to things right about us."[27] Narrow fixation on either the short- or the long-term future can be harmful; or, in other words, variability in the depth and clarity of our future projections makes a difference in our ability to respond intelligently to present situations. Moreover, his normative admonitions imply variation in connectivity and volition; we should not focus on "mere ends" (what he calls "dreams") but, rather, attempt to theorize causality, connection, and sequence. "As soon as we have projected it, we must begin to work backward in thought. We must change *what* is to be done into a *how*, the means whereby. The end thus re-appears as a series of 'what nexts.'"[28]

Dewey does note that in the early stage of mapping out lines of action, we often stumble on solutions without a clear purpose; we "shoot and throw" instinctively in reaction to situations. However, our observations and evaluations (like or dislike) of the results of those actions turn instinctive responses into reflective aims: "The result when it is observed gives new meaning to activity. Henceforth men in throwing and shooting think in terms of its outcomes; they act intelligently and have an end."[29] Learning from the natural consequences of such responses, we then subject those lines of action to more focused attention and deliberation. "Old consequences are enhanced, recombined, modified in imagination. Invention operates. Actual consequences, that is, effects which have happened in the past, become possible future consequences of acts still to be performed."[30]

These imaginative projections of the consequences of action have the power to redirect action in the present, even if the projections themselves are not the source or even the target of those actions: "Ends are foreseen consequences which arise in the course of activity and which are employed to give activity added meaning and to direct its further course. They are in no sense ends of action. In being ends of deliberation they are redirecting pivots in action."[31] He clarifies this point further with the metaphor of the mariner:

A mariner does not sail towards the stars, but by noting the stars he is aided in conducting his present activity of sailing. A port or harbor is his objective, but only in the sense of *reaching* it not of taking possession of it. The harbor stands in his thought as a significant point at which his activity will need redirection. Activity will not cease when the port is attained, but merely the *present direction* of activity. The port is as truly the beginning of another mode of activity as it is the termination of the present one.[32]

We orient ourselves by signposts and intermediate targets, each of which can become an opportunity for reflection and redirection, although more often they guide us from one step to the next in a routine, unreflective fashion. Deliberation kicks in when we encounter obstacles along the way that provoke "shock, confusion, perturbation, uncertainty." This in turn triggers reflective, investigative thought; "a new impulse is stirred which becomes the starting point of an investigation, a looking into things, a trying to see them, to find out what is going on. Habits which were interfered with begin to get a new direction as they cluster around the impulse to look and see." As the problematic pathway itself swings into clearer view, the sorting out of possible future actions receives explicit, self-conscious attention: "The momentum of the activity entered upon persists as a sense of direction, of aim; it is an anticipatory project. In short, he recollects, observes and plans."[33]

This kind of projective deliberation is admittedly difficult to do amid the routines and exigencies of daily life. Dewey notes that we often have to suspend action and step away from our routines in order let the imagination move into scenario-building mode; in fact, we are often *forced* to stop, given the contradictory pressures ("propulsive tendencies") that assail us in situations of crisis. During these moments in which we slow down and "stop and think," we gain a more expansive temporal perspective: "The resulting period of delay, of suspended and postponed overt action, is the period in which activities that are refused direct outlet project imaginative counterparts." In such periods of (often enforced) reflection, we pull back from execution mode, mediate and control our conflicting impulses, and begin to rehearse in our minds contending scenarios of action. "Variety of competing tendencies enlarges the world. It brings a diversity of considerations before the mind, and enables action to take place finally in view of an object generously conceived and delicately refined, composed by a long process of selections and combinations."[34]

Dewey's much-cited description of the imaginative, experimental character of deliberation is worth quoting in full, given that it is usually taken telegraphically and out of context. In the expanded passage, we can see a few themes in Dewey's thinking that are often overlooked, including his focus on the suspension of overt action, as well as the sense of both multipronged foresight and imaginative revocability:

We begin with a summary assertion that deliberation is a dramatic rehearsal (in imagination) of various competing possible lines of action. It starts from the *blocking of efficient overt action,* due to that conflict of prior habit and newly released impulse to which reference has been made. Then each habit, each impulse, involved in the temporary suspense of overt action takes its turn in being tried out. *Deliberation is an experiment in finding out what the various lines of possible action are really like.* It is an experiment in making various combinations of selected elements of habits and impulses, to see what the resultant action would be like if it were entered upon. But the trial is in imagination, not in overt fact. The experiment is carried on by *tentative rehearsals in thought* which do not affect physical facts outside the body. *Thought runs ahead and foresees outcomes*, and thereby avoids having to await, the instruction of actual failure and disaster. An act overtly tried out is irrevocable, its consequences cannot be blotted out. *An act tried out in imagination is not final or fatal.* It is retrievable.[35]

In Dewey's view, imagination "runs ahead" of action in the relative safety of reflective thought, tentatively dramatizing the progression and outcome of multiple possible pathways and experimenting with putting elements of these "lines of action" together in new combinations. How does such imaginative scenario-building result in choice? Dewey conceives of choice not as a rational calculation or maximization of benefits but rather as the recovery of a sense of cognitive and emotional coherence in a situation of conflict and blockage. Problem situations release conflicting habits and impulses, which prompt a search for synthesis: "We are striving to unify our responses, to achieve a consistent environment which will restore unity of conduct. Unity, relations, are prospective; they mark out lines converging to a focus. They are 'ideal.'"[36]

This newly synthesized "solution" may appear and even feel ideal (or, at least, provisionally acceptable or "adequate" given the circumstances), but it is not necessarily "optimal" in any objective sense. More importantly, it reconstitutes a cognitive and emotional focus that allows us to perceive a way forward, recover energy for action, and pull out of the suspended mode that characterizes deliberation. Choice consists of "simply hitting in imagination upon an object which furnishes an adequate stimulus to the recovery of overt action. Choice is made as soon as some habit, or some combination of elements of habits and impulse, finds a way fully open. Then energy is released. The mind is made up, composed, unified."[37]

To sum up, we can take five important points from Dewey in developing a theory of how futures work in public deliberation and action. (1) The movement from routine to deliberative thought is triggered by situations of blockage, conflict, and uncertainty in otherwise habitual paths of action. (2) Such deliberation requires a suspension of overt action, whether chosen or enforced by situational pressures and constraints. (3) This temporary withdrawal from action in turn allows for an expanded temporal perspective that conceives of action as series and system, stretching forward and backward in time. (4) In order to solve problems in the present, we engage in imaginative dramatization and scenario-building about possible future lines of action, which in turn contributes to recombination and synthesis. (5) Optimization is less important for choice than perceived actionability and its capacity to release forward-directed energy and motion.

Dewey provides a compelling framework for understanding how future projections contribute to practical action and problem-solving while avoiding the traps of rational choice or functionalist theorizing. While acknowledging that much of our thought and action is organized by habit and schema, Dewey argues that problem situations force us to slow down and engage in more effortful, investigative, hypothetical, and reflective forms of thinking. Value and interest are linked as we theorize about desired and possible futures based on our current situations and experiences of the past. The imaginative engagement with future scenarios can reorganize habit and impulse, even while drawing on these more routinized processes for input about the feasibility and value of projected lines of action.

Although this perspective helps to move us toward a better understanding of how futures steer action, it has a number of important limitations. First, while Dewey's theory is resolutely nonteleological, nevertheless even he acknowledges that much of our thinking is in fact teleological. People often divorce ends from means and fail to think about such ends as stemming from particular contexts and contributing to action in the present. What role do such teleologies play, whether destructively or constructively, in deliberation and decision-making? Here we head back toward realm of ideology and its powerful hold on human thought and action.

Second, and relatedly, our capacity for imaginative recombination and creative synthesis is often limited by available scripts and genres, which may strongly constrain the ways in which we dramatize and rehearse future possibilities. Such cognitive scaffoldings are in turn implicated in larger institutional and discursive formations, positioned with respect to hegemonic and counterhegemonic power relations. Dewey's theorization of power is famously underdeveloped;[38] how can we keep such power relations and discursive-institutional constraints in view while maintaining a sense of the potential reflectivity and creativity of action?

To build on Dewey's framework while addressing questions of power and cultural constraint, we need a stronger understanding of how existing cultural schemas shape the imaginative engagement of future possibilities. To address this problem, I next examine how Schutz's social phenomenology elaborates on the pragmatist conception of the projective imagination. While Schutz is similarly concerned to move away from a purely instrumentalist view of futures, he provides us with more tools for understanding the cultural and institutional embedding of futures, as well as their teleological force. We then return to the question of how imagined futures are mobilized as part of collective deliberations in power-laden publics.

4. SCHUTZ: PROJECTS OF ACTION IN THE FUTURE PERFECT TENSE

Imagination, Dewey argues, is a key operator in the interplay between habitual and reflective thought. But how do we understand the imaginative process itself? Dewey's imagery is resonant but underdeveloped in this respect. Building explicitly on Dewey's formulations, Schutz takes us deeper into the phenomenology of the projective imagination.[39] He provides additional tools for challenging optimization-based theories by theorizing the multistranded, culturally embedded process of future projections as unfolding in the temporal *durée* of consciousness. Although he does not directly address the problem of power and discursive constraint, he helps us to understand how habitualized, schematic understandings—in the form of "stocks of knowledge" and "systems of relevances"—become the building blocks of future projections and reflective deliberation over contending possibilities of action.

Schutz is generally recognized in sociology for his contributions to theories of social construction, ethnomethodology, and symbolic interaction, which have focused on his discussions of typification and intersubjective meaning-making. Largely left by the wayside is his intense preoccupation with what his calls "projects of action" and his consideration of the conditions for reflective foresight. His theorization of projectivity is critical for our purposes because of the way in which he carefully distinguishes his ideas from the rational action theories that were gaining currency in the social sciences as he was writing. Drawing on his seminal analysis of projects in *The Phenomenology of the Social World*, as well as his later essays on deliberation and choice, I will discuss Schutz's conception of the movement from unreflective to deliberative consciousness, as subjectively experienced by the forward-looking, biographically (and, we might add, historically) situated actor.

For Schutz, the meaningfulness of action is rooted in the construction of projects; that is, in our reflective anticipation of completed intentional acts, elaborated in the "future perfect tense." He distinguishes such projects from the Husserlian notion of "protentions," the immediate future awareness inherent in all spontaneous activity. These are closely linked in experience to "retentions," the awareness of "just-having-been" or the immediately evolving past. Anticipations (or "foreseeing expectations") reflectively "represent" the future, whereas protentions only "present" it.[40] The idea of the "project" takes such anticipations a step further by implying reflective intentionality; that is, action in accord with a preconceived, motivated goal (or set of goals). However, those goals can be perceived with varying degrees of clarity or detail, and our perception of the project itself (and our valuation of the choices it entails) changes as we "grow older" or move forward though time and experience.

Schutz's conception of projects moves us back toward the notion of teleologies, if we understand these as ideas about "already realized" futures pulling us forward. What makes action "conscious," according to Schutz, it that "before we carry it out, we have a picture in our mind of what we are going to do."[41] These pictures, or "projected acts," constitute maps that we consult through retention and reproduction (that is, we remember and represent these pictures to ourselves repeatedly over time). "Our actions are conscious if we have previously mapped them out 'in the future present tense,'" that is, if we have imagined them as completed acts in the future toward which we are intentionally directing our action.[42] This process of imagination occurs before the action itself, which then "enlarges" our experience and shifts the focus of attention as we move from anticipation toward the accomplishment of the projected act. "What was inside the illuminated circle of consciousness during the moment of projection now falls back into the darkness and is replaced by later lived experiences which had been merely expected or protended."[43]

Projects, Schutz argues, give unity to action; "the unity of the act is a function of the span or breadth of the project."[44] And yet this unity is internally complex and not necessarily perceived as such until after the act is completed. For the forward-facing actor, projects are often perceived in terms of tensions between contending possibilities; they are "polythetic" or internally differentiated, as multirayed "shafts of attention" shine successively on multiple possibilities of action.[45] Schutz draws on Henri Bergson's metaphor of the "overripe fruit," in which the mind moves successively between different possibilities of action, growing older as each stream of attention informs the next, until the "free choice" drops off and can be retrospectively perceived as such through post hoc accounting practices.

Although Bergson's metaphor of the overripe fruit is highly resonant, it denies the possibility of foresightful deliberation; we drift into choices and see them clearly only after they have happened. However, Schutz modifies Bergson's formulation by arguing that the fact that we can imagine the project as *already having been completed* (i.e., in the future perfect tense) means that we can reflectively consider alternatives before we embark on action itself. The unity of the act is a synthetic unity composed of both the multirayed, forward-looking, as-yet-undetermined (fantasized or shadow) futures and the process of pursuing and completing the act itself: "In our view, the process of choice between successively pictured projects, plus the action itself right up to its completion, comprises a synthetic intentional Act of a higher order, an Act that is inwardly differentiated into other Acts."[46]

The "unity of the act" thus looks very different when viewed prospectively, from the vantage point of multiple possible completed acts, than when it is viewed retrospectively, when the act is behind us. We are pulled forward, so to speak, by the repeated acts of scanning future possibilities. At the same time, the imagination of those possible futures as "already having happened" composes our projects. In other words, imagined end states have a propulsive force; they shape and undergird action and, when viewed from behind, appear to function teleologically. At the same time, these teleologies are temporally contingent and internally complex. They frame choices between multiple futures, even if those choices seem to disappear once we pass them by.

5. MULTIPLE FUTURES AND THE PROBLEM OF CHOICE

Schutz wrestles with how to maintain the multiplicity and reflectivity of action while also addressing how choice is constrained by experience, history, and culture. The choice between contending possibilities is often highly problematic, an issue he addresses more deeply in his 1951 paper, "Choosing Among Projects of

Action." In this essay, he directly engages with Dewey's theory of deliberation, putting Dewey in dialogue with Husserl, Bergson, and Leibniz. While deepening our understanding of how imagination shapes choice, he also helps us understand how choices are focused, funneled, and evaluated, as well as how they come into conflict with each other. In this way, he gives us tools to consider how futures work in complex and contentious public arenas.

Projects, Schutz tells us, are different from "mere fancying" not only because of their motivated and intentional nature (i.e., we desire and propose to carry them out) but because they are constrained and limited by practicality. We cannot enact our "phantasies" at will, but we need to consider feasibility, risk, and personal control as these affect the realistic probability that we can successfully carry them out. Projects are thus not just "a thinking in the optative mode, but a thinking in the potential one."[47] This leads him into his well-known discussion of the typification of knowledge; the demands of practicality require "that according to my present knowledge the projected action, *at least as to its type*, would have been feasible, its means and ends, *at least as to their types*, would have been available if the action had occurred in the past."[48]

Thus, projections are not free-form imaginative play but involve typified knowledge based in prior experience, through either our own direct experiences or our cultural and historical familiarity with the experiences of others. Echoing Dewey, Schutz argues that these typifications include theorizations of cause and effect, or the relationship between means and ends. These perceptions of possibility are themselves shaped by what he calls our "biographically determined situations"; that is, our "position in space, time and society."[49] Our particular positions and histories affect what we experience as imposed, unchangeable, and taken for granted, as well as what we feel we have some actual or potential control over, thus shaping what we understand to be practical (or not).

Moreover, our biographical situations shape the systems of relevances by which we *select* particular elements for attention, interest, and purposeful action. The actor's history, which consists of "the sedimentation of all his previous subjective experiences,"[50] provides the experience of subjectivity and uniqueness, even if typification leads us to the opposite sensation—that projections are objective and anonymous. Here we might note in passing the strong foreshadowing of Pierre Bourdieu's concept of the habitus: the typified or "objective" knowledge of relations of cause and effect implicit in our position in the field, which is nevertheless experienced as "subjective" due to our own sedimented biographical experiences.

However, at this point, Schutz takes a critical (if often forgotten) step away from the mere reproduction of typified and taken-for-granted knowledge and experience and toward deliberation over multiple possible futures, with the possibility for novelty and reformulation. Although many of our experiences and purposes are typified and taken for granted (shaped by what Dewey calls "habits"), this very routinization creates the conditions for doubt and questioning when expectations are challenged. Such challenges occur because interests and projects do not occur in isolation but, rather, are organized into larger systems; "any end is merely a means for another end; any project is projected within a system of higher order."[51]

Projects for work and leisure are nested into larger life and societal projects, and subordinate levels may be in tension with each other. Due to these interrelationships, "there is always the possibility of overlapping and even conflicting interests and consequently of doubt whether the elements selected from our surrounding world taken for granted beyond question are really relevant to our purpose at hand." Schutz argues that this emergence of doubt out of conflict (or what Dewey calls "problem situations") leads to the "rehearsal in imagination" that Dewey describes. "What has been unquestioned so far has now to be put into question. . . . A true alternative has been created. This situation of doubt, created by the selection of the actor in his biographically determined situation from the world taken for granted, is what alone makes deliberation and choice possible."[52]

To explain where such alternatives come from, Schutz links Dewey's theory of deliberation to Husserl's distinction between open and problematic possibilities. Open possibilities are "empty anticipations"; we take for granted that they will continue as expected even though there is no guarantee that they will. In the absence of explicit counterpossibilities, "this general indeterminacy constitutes a frame of free variability."[53] In contrast, problematic possibilities are situations in which counterposed alternatives face off in the light of a "questioning intention" to decide in favor or one or another. This counterposition, in which alternative futures stand to choice, binds them together within a common field of attention: "in the unity of contest and of being apprehended by disjunctive oscillation, A, B, and C become known as being in opposition and, therefore, united."[54]

Whereas Husserl's discussion refers primarily to our perception of objects in the world, Schutz says that we can extend this distinction to deliberation over conflicting possibilities of action. However, he is careful to distinguish this conception from rational action theories, which he says it admittedly resembles. Rational action theories take for granted that both options are readily available, that they are pregiven in form, and that they exist simultaneously in external time. However, projects are produced by actors themselves and can be modified and recreated in the process of production. Citing Bergson, Schutz describes the iterative processes of sequential revisitings of possible futures within the *durée* of internal time:

> The mind by its phantasizing acts creates in succession in inner time the various projects, dropping one in favor of the other and returning to, or more precisely, re-creating, the first. But by and in the transition from one to the succeeding states of consciousness I have grown older, I have enlarged my experience, I am, returning to the first, no longer the "same" as I was when originally drafting it and consequently the project to which I return is no longer the same as that which I dropped; or, perhaps more exactly; it is the same, but modified.[55]

Thus, each time we revisit an imagined projected act, our perception of that act is modified by intervening visits to other imagined futures in the unified field of alternative, contending possibilities. Sequential position in the *durée* of internal time matters, Schutz argues, and principles of selectivity and relevance also inform our imagination of alternatives. Moreover, not only do we perceive these alternatives, but we also evaluate them. Here he brings in Leibniz's theory of choice between "good" and "evil" options; we assign our projections positive and negative weights, which are combined back and forth with each other as we successively revisit possibilities. In the end, the final volition is a combination and synthesis of all of the previous "intermediate volitions" of evaluation and weighting.

Lest we confuse this with simple optimization, however, Schutz notes that this reasoning process is complicated by the limits to our knowledge, by the difficulty of comparing present pleasures and displeasures with future ones, and by the risk of miscalculations of positive and negative values. Moreover, emotions also affect (and sometimes short-circuit) the reasoning process. Schutz acknowledges that our more confused thoughts often elicit stronger emotions and thus compel action in the absence of more effortful and focused deliberation:

> But this knowledge is not homogeneous; it is either distinct or confused. Only distinct knowledge is the realm of Reason, our senses and our passions furnish merely confused thoughts and we are in their bondage as long as we do not succeed in basing our actions on distinct knowledge. This situation is frequently complicated by the fact that our confused thoughts are felt clearly whereas our distinct thoughts are only potentially clear: they could be clear if we were willing to make the necessary efforts to explicate their implications, for instance by penetrating into the meaning of words or symbols.[56]

Schutz notes limits to the rationality of our future projections, but he does not abandon the possibility of deliberative, future-oriented thought as a potentially transformative form of intervention in the social world. However, he conceives of such projection as channeled by temporal, cognitive, and emotional processes that are both biographically and situationally constrained. Moreover, his discussion of the systemic quality of goals and projects, as well as the communicability of typifications, point toward the broader cultural, institutional, and historical embedding of projection and choice. Such typifications serve as scaffoldings for future projection, allowing us relatively sturdy frameworks on which to build our images of possible completed actions in the future perfect tense. And yet they are not immutable and often seem more flexible and fluid when viewed forward than they do in post hoc accounts.

We can take forward the following insights from Schutz's phenomenological perspective as we consider the role of futures in public deliberation and change efforts: (1) Although we do imaginatively engage the future teleologically (as "already completed," or in the future present tense), we do this in selective, partial, multistranded, and often confused and ambiguous ways. (2) While projects are often typified and taken for granted, their systemic and overlapping nature generates tensions that in turn create contending alternatives and choice. (3) Deliberation over such choices is iterative, sequentially influenced, and affected by where we shine our "rays of attention," which is both biographically and situationally conditioned.

In this sense, projections may be influenced both by deep-seated cultural schemas and by more immediate situational pressures and problems. Routinized schemas—grounded not only in individual biographies but also in institutions and in larger political-discursive formations—are essential in providing input to imaginative processes of anticipation and choice. These schemas constrain attention and choice via typified models of plausibility ("it can happen again"). Schemas are organized into systems of relevance, which in turn reflect locations in larger relations of symbolic and material power (underplayed by Schutz but keenly visible to contemporary analysts). Nevertheless, the imaginative process itself—particularly when we allow ourselves reflective space in which to do it—may lead to reevaluations of both desirability and practicality and thus influence projects (and resulting actions) going forward. This is particularly the case when reflective deliberation addresses live tensions and problems, such as those posed by the complex and interlocking character of institutions and events.

6. SOFT TELEOLOGIES, DEMOCRATIC POLITICS, AND PUBLIC DEBATE

One limitation of Schutz's perspective is that his focus on the internal *dureé* of consciousness can lead to a misperception that this projective deliberation happens solely "inside people's heads," thereby contributing to a radicalized understanding of subjectivity. Certainly, generations of social constructionists of varying stripes can trace their intellectual genealogies back through Schutz. However, Schutz's own concern with the practical grounding of action, as well as with intersubjectivity— how we share typifications, lifeworlds, and deliberative processes with others—leads us toward a more communicative understanding of future projections, as theorists such as Jürgen Habermas have noted.[57] This communicative dimension of reflective thought was also central to Dewey's preoccupation with public deliberation about problems of shared concern.[58]

In taking these theories forward, I focus not simply on individual cognition and consciousness but, rather, on communicative processes in public deliberative settings. In such settings, multiple alternatives for the future (Schutz's "problematic possibilities") are counterposed, often in debate with others. These conversations may be both contentious and collaborative, drawing on available cultural resources ("stock of knowledge") in power-laden discursive and institutional fields. While these discussions may be scripted and routinized, interactions within and across settings can challenge and disrupt those routines. This can generate conflict, doubt, and the kind of problem situations that Dewey and Schutz say are the precursor to deliberation, that is, to the reflective consideration—and possible imaginative reconstruction—of potential lines of future action.

As we have seen, both Dewey and Schutz are concerned to avoid a priori and detemporalized futures, harnessing the imagination to the problems and conditions of the present (for Dewey) and to the *durée* of emerging consciousness (for Schutz). Ideologies and utopias are both suspect, from this perspective, in that they impede intelligent action by taking the future outside of its relationship with the emergent and contingent present. But have these theorists gone too far in their critique? To what extent are the schematic maps of future pathways—which constitute ideologies—and the subversive uprootings of the future—which constitute utopias—critical for political debate and action?

Ricoeur offers a somewhat more sympathetic reading of both phenomena. In *From Text to Action*, he elaborates on Karl Mannheim's classic polarity in order to develop a broader theorization of the social imaginary. Ideology, Ricoeur argues, has both an integrative and a performative function; it enables a society to "give itself an image of itself, to 'play itself,' in the theatrical sense of the word, to put itself at issue and on stage."[59] If it does this through "simplification, schematization, stereotyping and ritualization," nonetheless it represents the symbolic process by which "a group becomes conscious of itself and its practice." That is, ideologies are routinized ways of dramatizing the accepted and valued pathways of action in a given society, providing narrative maps and heuristics for decision-making. In that sense, they demonstrate what Dewey describes as the propulsive character of habits of thought. In the pragmatist spirit, ideologies reject Kantian dualism by linking identity and strategy, interests and values—even as they depart from the pragmatist ethos by becoming decontextualized from particular social and historical situations.

The pathology of ideologies, Ricoeur argues, arises when they are captured by systems of authority as means of legitimation and domination. This is where utopias become useful. Ricoeur argues that as a counterpoint to ideology, utopia serves a critical social role in challenging and subverting systems of authority, and in provoking a rethinking of forms of social organization. Utopias "expose the undeclared surplus value of authority and unmask the pretense common to all systems of ideology."[60] In other words, he says, they challenge and unmask power. However, like ideologies, utopias also have their "pathology"—and here we hear echoes of precisely the problems that worried Dewey. Both Dewey and Ricoeur note the limitations of the utopian focus on an idealized future state without a concomitant focus on the steps needed to reach that future:

> Because utopia arises from a leap elsewhere, nowhere, it develops unsettling features that are easy to spot in the literary expressions of utopia: A tendency to subordinate reality to dreams, a fixation with perfectionist designs, and so on. [Utopias express] a preference for the schematism of space; disdain for intermediary stages and an utter lack of interest in taking a first step in the direction of the ideal; blindness with respect to the contradictions inherent in action—whether they make certain evils inseparable from certain desired ends, or whether they heighten the incompatibility between equally desirable goals.[61]

So, if ideologies undermine intelligent action by schematizing and decontextualizing pathways of action—and utopias undermine it by turning a blind eye to practical pathways of action altogether—then what use are they to politics, and in particular to the progressive political change efforts that were dear to Dewey's heart? Here we need to draw on Ricoeur's more sympathetic reading. As we engage in contentious public debate about possible futures—often in agonistic arenas characterized by disparities in power, resources, and symbolic capital—we need to simplify and schematize in order to spin the hypothetical scenarios that allow us to map alternative pathways of action. And we need to engage in narrative ruptures—even if they are ambiguous, internally contradictory, and detemporalized—in order to destabilize the schematic narratives that have settled into the condition of legitimizing *doxa*. To think otherwise is a naiveté on Dewey's part—and reflects his undertheorization of power and contention—despite the compelling and sympathetic character of his appeal for intelligent action.

In recognizing the positive interventions of ideology and utopia, we are also acknowledging discursive and institutional constraints on the future imaginary, as well as its embedding in persistent relations of exclusion and inequality. How can we keep power relations and discursive-institutional constraints in view while maintaining a sense of the reflectivity and creativity of action? I would propose that by examining how futures are directly and (at times) systematically engaged in social change efforts—and by seeing how these play out within messy and complex political contexts—we can maintain the pragmatist commitment to the practical reflectivity and flexibility of action without losing sight of how power, context, and institutions limit and constrain our deliberations and choices.

Chris Ansell helps us to understand the political implications of this reflective process in his theoretical elaboration of "pragmatist democracy."[62] He notes that large-scale institutional change efforts involve the development of ambiguous, multivocal, highly schematic, and symbolically infused "meta-concepts," of which ideologies are arguably one variant. These are detached from particular settings (and thus have a "cosmopolitan" dimension) but need to be put to work through local experimentation. It is precisely the decontextualized, symbolic nature of these concepts that allows them to serve as "boundary objects" that span multiple networks and provoke debate across diverse publics, including among actors who strongly disagree with each other. Such deliberative processes should not avoid disagreement in the interest of solidarity and consensus building but rather should embrace "fruitful conflict." As Ansell notes, "the purpose of Pragmatist collaboration is not to minimize conflict or produce consensus, but to use the interplay of different perspectives to generate mutual learning."[63]

Though responsive to reflection and learning, such meta-concepts have a "soft teleology." Ansell notes that these soft teleologies are implicit in pragmatist thinking (such as in Dewey's conception of ends-in-view), but they are distinct from Aristotelian (or rational choice) conceptions of final causes. Meta-concepts thus contain at least shades of utopia: "[s]uccessful meta-concepts typically have a teleological element; they set up an attraction toward some ideal end state."[64] Ansell argues that the soft teleology of meta-concepts is a necessary component of the recursive, reflective, and experimental process through which institutions change. Moreover, he says that they are critical for advancing a collaborative model of democratic governance in which public agencies engage deeply with the hopes, fears, frustrations, and preferences of their respective audiences (i.e., their concerned publics and counterpublics).

What, then, keeps these teleologies from turning into the kind of instrumentalizing, paralyzing, and potentially blinding reifications that Dewey feared? And how do we maintain the capacity for deep critique that Ricoeur argues is one of the vital contributions of utopias? One answer can be found in Daniel Cefaï's call in this volume for a "pragmatist concept of the public sphere" as vibrant arenas of contestation and debate in which problems are defined through argument, inquiry, dramatization, and public narration. Cefaï notes the element of future projection in this process; as contending actors debate public problems, they engage in a process of inquiry that "tries to identify causal chains which explain how they came about and allow their probable or plausible consequences to be foreseen and predicted. *It organizes a field of explanation and foresight of the problematic situation.*"[65] This effort at foresight in turn maps out possible pathways of intervention, including via political mobilization.

In the pragmatist spirit, we thus understand public deliberation as a process of imaginative, collective scenario construction that dramatizes and "rehearses in mind" alternative future possibilities in arenas of contestation and debate. People elaborate these scenarios via difficult, sometimes painful conversations that contest assumptions and challenge dominant narratives, even while using imagined futures to connect with others across social divides. These conversations may be highly conflictual, as Jason Springs notes in his recent work bridging pragmatist thought and theories of agonistic democracy.[66] Contending futures—both good and bad—may be framed as alternatives that stand to choice in a unified, if oppositional field of potential action (to use Schutz's imagery). But debates over the ends and means of possible future actions may also facilitate collective learning and shifts in the framing of problems and strategies. Such reflective (if sometime unruly or uncomfortable) learning processes are critical to social movements and grassroots activism of various kinds,[67] as well as to processes of democratic participation and governance.[68]

Ansell and Cefaï help us to see what a pragmatist conception of the experimental engagement with the future might look like in the messy, contentious, and power-laden arenas of democratic politics. This requires a critical analysis of the cultural scaffolding underlying future projections, with attention to the ambiguity, multivocality, schematic character, and symbolic resonance of the soft teleologies that pull us forward. It also requires attention to how these cultural schemas and symbolic meta-concepts can be reconfigured as concerned publics respond to the urgency and uncertainty of problem situations. Hopes and fears about possible futures can pull us toward and push us away from certain imagined end states, becoming ideational nodes in public debates and pivots to collective action. Contentious deliberation about such problems forces us to "stop and think," in Dewey's sense, loosening us from routinized projects and pathways and letting us see alternative lines of action. This in turn can allow "problematic" possibilities, in Schutz's sense, to swirl around, smack up against each other, recombine, and, in some cases, lead to a reorientation of thought and action.

7. FUTURES IN HISTORY: BEYOND ACCIDENTAL RECOMBINATION

Let me close by emphasizing that this is neither a rationalistic nor an idealized perspective on future anticipations. We need to move beyond the opposition between seeing the future as the object of our instrumental calculation and control and taking the dreamier view that if only we imagine that "another world is possible," we will be able to achieve it. This polarized approach has led to an impoverished understanding of projectivity that is detached from a sociological analysis of practical action, as well as to the severing of "choice" from cultural, institutional, and historical context. As we have seen, this polarization was explicitly attacked by Dewey early in the last century, a critique carried forward by Schutz. But as Talcott Parsons divided the social sciences into functional boxes mid-century, he separated cultural norms and values from rational interests and assigned these to separate disciplinary paradigms. As a result, the insights of the pragmatist and phenomenological thinkers were submerged or carried forward in ways that largely abandoned the focus on future-oriented projects of action.

I have argued that in order to challenge the neglect of the future in sociological theory, it is useful to revive the insights of Dewey and Schutz into the imaginative and experimental potential of future-oriented deliberation. However, we need to do this from a critical perspective that recognizes, more centrally than these theorists did, the workings of power and contention, as well as the constraining and exclusionary effects of discourse and institutions. In fact, many important analysts of power, conflict, exclusion, and inequality in contemporary society have deep, sometimes unacknowledged roots in pragmatist and phenomenological thought, including W. E. B. Du Bois, Habermas, Bourdieu, and Charles Tilly, along with philosopher Cornel West and Black feminist scholars bell hooks and Patricia Hill Collins.[69] The challenge, then, is to understand this potential in the light of its tensions and contradictions. Our task is to make visible the potentially redirective and recombinatory character of anticipatory deliberation without assuming that this redirection necessarily indicates the realization—or the moral-political value—of the projects in question.

We might summarize this program as that of analyzing teleologies nonteleologically, yet with attention to their propulsive force. If Dewey was anguished by the failures of intelligence involved in teleological thinking, we can perhaps side-step this anguish by understanding the productive value of such projective scaffold-ings. Our culturally grounded imagination of action in the "future present tense," in Schutz's terms, can lock us onto pathways experienced as regulatory and con-straining, even as they enable us to function as competent and (sometimes) suc-cessful and satisfied producers of certain kinds of processes and outcomes. Such "cultural models"[70] or "schemas of devotion"[71] often lead people to generate pre-dictable careers, buttressed by institutional positions and differential access to cul-tural, social, and economic capital, even if they feel like they are exercising agency and choice. More recently, Jens Beckert and colleagues have drawn on pragma-tist and phenomenological theory to describe the ways in which "fictional expecta-tions" about imagined futures undergird capitalist dynamics, providing "props" for action in the face of uncertainty while also constituting our sense of the future as being open, restless, and responsive to our interventions.[72]

Although future expectations can contribute to the reproduction of existing dis-tributions of power and resources, in times of historical upheaval, they can play the opposite role. The mere anticipation of institutional reorganization can change everyday practices and forms of political engagement, as Michal Federowicz argues in relation to the advent of market reforms in Eastern Europe.[73] Social movement analysts describe how changing perceptions of political opportunities—that is, see-ing futures as more open to challenge than previously thought—can energize the strategies of those mobilizing to disrupt established power relations.[74] And even overly simplified and schematized ideological conceptions of the future—as Kim Voss shows us in her analysis of "fortifying myths" in labor movements—have the capacity to sustain social change efforts in the face of adversity.[75] Moreover, uto-pian narratives about transfigured worlds can invigorate the political imagination, sustain communities amid trauma and suffering, and serve as cultural resources for movements combatting injustice, as Alex Zamalin argues in his work on Black Utopia.[76] In both their "hard" and "soft" variants, teleologies can thus provide long-term orientation and steering for action seeking to reform institutions and chal-lenge social inequalities and exclusions.

Rather than discounting the steering force of the future imaginary, we can use the insights of pragmatist and phenomenological theory to understand how it works. We gain insight into social and historical change by examining the ways in which future revaluations are provoked, even coerced, by moments of failure, incompe-tence, blockage, or frustration. The frequent "unsettlings"—collisions, dilemmas, injustices, inefficiencies, and roadblocks—of our turbulent, exclusionary, and inter-secting worlds generate frequent needs for the self-conscious reevaluation of our projects of action, which can (under some conditions) spur the investigative, recom-binatory spirit of anticipation that underlies social learning. Debates about alterna-tive futures in contentious publics can constitute and redirect action and thus steer history, even if these futures are fragmentary, opaque, ambiguous, or unevenly elab-orated over the multiple time horizons that frame the unfolding present.

The personal and collective learning occasioned by such demands to "stop and think" takes us beyond a conception of historical process as simply accidental recombination, or even as situational problem-solving. Problem situations—from small diversions and roadblocks to broad systemic crises—disrupt our routine practices and anticipations, requiring us to experimentally revisit and reframe future possibilities. New projects and choices arise from our imaginative visits back and forth between multiple possible futures, even as we "grow older"—and take our debates and learnings forward—with each visit. This does not mean that our projects necessarily take us where we want to go; history is shaped by unintended consequences, despite our best efforts at foresight and anticipation.[77] But just because our destinations are often unexpected does not mean that our projects have not steered us there. Understanding how our actions are pulled, pushed, and guided by imagined future states—that is, by soft and hard teleologies and their collective reformulations—is well within the mandate and method of pragmatist inquiry.

NOTES

1. For example, see Josh Whitford, "Pragmatism and the Untenable Dualism of Means and Ends: Why Rational Choice Theory Does Not Deserve Paradigmatic Privilege," *Theory and Society* 31, no. 3 (June 1, 2002): 325–63, https://doi.org/10.1023/A:1016232404279; Gary Herrigel, *Manufacturing Possibilities: Creative Action and Industrial Recomposition in the United States, Germany and Japan* (Oxford: Oxford University Press, 2010); and Christopher K. Ansell, *Pragmatist Democracy: Evolutionary Learning as Public Philosophy* (Oxford: Oxford University Press, 2011).

2. Ann Mische, "Projects and Possibilities: Researching Futures in Action.," *Sociological Forum* 24 (2009): 694–704; Mische, "Measuring Futures in Action: Projective Grammars in the Rio+20 Debates.," *Theory and Society* 43 (2014): 437–64; John R. Hall, *Apocalypse: From Antiquity to the Empire of Modernity* (New York: Polity, 2009); and John R. Hall, "Social Futures of Global Climate Change: A Structural Phenomenology," *American Journal of Cultural Sociology* 4 (2016): 1–45.

3. Mary Blair-Loy, *Competing Devotions: Career and Family Among Women Executives* (Cambridge, MA: Harvard University Press, 2003); Alford Young, *The Minds of Marginalized Black Men* (Princeton, NJ: Princeton University Press, 2004); Stephen Vaisey, "Motivation and Justification: A Dual-Process Model of Culture in Action.," *American Journal of Sociology* 114, no. 6 (2009): 1675–1715; Vaisey, "What People Want: Rethinking Poverty, Culture, and Educational Attainment.," *Annals of the American Academy of Political and Social Science* 629 (2010): 75–101; Margaret Frye, "Bright Futures in Malawi's New Dawn: Educational Aspirations as Assertions of Identity.," *American Journal of Sociology* 117 (2012): 1565–1624; Neil Gross and Ethan Fosse, "Why Are Professors Liberal?," *Theory and Society* 41 (2012): 127–68; and Gianpaolo Baiocchi et al., *The Civic Imagination: Making a Difference in American Political Life* (London: Routledge, 2014).

4. Iddo Tavory and Nina Eliasoph, "Coordinating Futures: Toward a Theory of Anticipation," *American Journal of Sociology* 118, no. 4 (2013): 908–42.

5. Karen A. Cerulo, *Never Saw It Coming: Cultural Challenges to Envisioning the Worst* (Chicago: University of Chicago Press, 2006); Lee Clarke, *Worst Cases: Terror and Catastrophe in Popular Imagination* (Chicago: University of Chicago Press, 2006).

6. Gary Alan Fine, *Authors of the Storm: Meteorologists and the Culture of Prediction* (Chicago: University of Chicago Press, 2010); Phaedra Daipha, *Masters of Uncertainty: Weather Forecasters and the Quest for Ground Truth* (Chicago: University of Chicago Press, 2015); and Andrew Lakoff, *Unprepared: Global Health in a Time of Emergency* (Berkeley: University of California Press, 2017).

7. Luc Boltanski and Ève Chiapello, *The New Spirit of Capitalism*, trans. Gregory Elliot (New York: Verso, 2005); Jens Beckert, *Imagined Futures: Fictional Expectations and Capitalist Dynamics* (Cambridge, MA: Harvard University Press, 2016); Beckert, "Imagined Futures: Fictional Expectations in the Economy," *Theory and Society* 42 (2013): 219–40, https://doi.org/10.1007/s11186-013-9191-2; Jens Beckert and Richard Bronk, eds., *Uncertain Futures: Imaginaries, Narratives, and Calculation in the Economy* (Oxford: Oxford University Press, 2018); and Benjamin H. Snyder, *The Disrupted Workplace: Time and the Moral Order of Flexible Capitalism* (Oxford: Oxford University Press, 2016).

8. See the excellent review of the emergence of sociological work on futures since 1950 in Jens Beckert and Lisa Suckert, "The Future as a Social Fact. The Analysis of Perceptions of the Future in Sociology," *Poetics* 84 (February 2021), https://doi.org/10.1016/j.poetic.2020.101499. Beckert and Suckert note three clusters of sociological work on futures. The first focuses on the causal dynamics of aspirations, the second focuses on images of the future, and the third focuses on contestation over the construction of futures. There is also a growing interdisciplinary field of scholarship focused on futures and anticipation studies, for example: David C. Engerman, "Introduction: Histories of the Future and the Futures of History," *American Historical Review* 117 (2012): 1402–10; Roberto Poli, *Introduction to Anticipation Studies*, Anticipation Science 1 (Cham, Switzerland: Springer, 2017); and Jenny Andersson, *The Future of the World: Futurology, Futurists, and the Struggle for the Post Cold War Imagination* (Oxford: Oxford University Press, 2018).

9. John Dewey, *The Public and Its Problems* (New York: Henry Holt, 1927).

10. Paul Ricoeur, *From Text to Action: Essays in Hermeneutics, II*, trans. Kathleen Blarney and John B. Thompson (Evanston, IL: Northwestern University Press, 1991).

11. For example, see Hans Joas, *Pragmatism and Social Theory* (Chicago: University of Chicago Press, 1993); Joas, *The Creativity of Action*, ed. J. Gaines and P. Keast (Chicago: University of Chicago Press, 1996); Mustafa Emirbayer, "Manifesto for a Relational Sociology," *American Journal of Sociology* 103 (1997): 281–317; Mustafa Emirbayer and Ann Mische, "What Is Agency?," *American Journal of Sociology* 103 (1998): 962–1023; Mustafa Emirbayer and Erik Schneiderhan, "Dewey and Bourdieu on Democracy," in *Bourdieu and Historical Analysis*, ed. Philip S. Gorski (Durham, NC: Duke University Press, 2013), 131–57; Margaret R. Somers, "We're No Angels: Realism, Rational Choice, and Relationality in Social Science," *American Journal of Sociology* 104, no. 3 (1998): 722–84; Whitford, "Pragmatism and the Untenable Dualism of Means and Ends"; Neil

Gross, "Richard Rorty's Pragmatism: A Case Study in the Sociology of Ideas," *Theory and Society* 32 (2003): 93–148; Gross, "Pragmatism, Phenomenology, and Twentieth Century Sociology," in *Sociology in America: A History*, ed. Craig Calhoun (Chicago: University of Chicago Press, 2007), 183–224; Gross, "A Pragmatist Theory of Social Mechanisms," *American Sociological Review* 74 (2009): 358–79; Paul Lichterman, *Elusive Togetherness: How Religious Americans Create Civic Ties* (Princeton, NJ: Princeton University Press, 2005); Ann Mische, *Partisan Publics: Communication and Contention Across Brazilian Youth Activist Networks* (Princeton, NJ: Princeton University Press, 2008); Erik Schneiderhan and Shamus Khan, "Reasons and Inclusion: The Foundation of Deliberation," *Sociological Theory* 26, no. 1 (2008): 1–24; Erik Schneiderhan, "Pragmatism and Empirical Sociology: The Case of Jane Addams and Hull-House, 1889–1895," *Theory and Society* 40 6 (2011): 589–617; Herrigel, *Manufacturing Possibilities*; Ansell, *Pragmatist Democracy*; and John Levi Martin, *The Explanation of Social Action* (Oxford: Oxford University Press, 2011).

12. Some notable exceptions of recent work on futures informed by a blend of pragmatist and phenomenological approaches include Frye, "Bright Futures in Malawi's New Dawn"; Tavory and Eliasoph, "Coordinating Futures"; Daipha, *Masters of Uncertainty*; and Beckert, *Imagined Futures*. See also the extended discussion of future "projectivity" in Emirbayer and Mische, "What Is Agency?"

13. Joas, *The Creativity of Action*; Whitford, "Pragmatism and the Untenable Dualism of Means and Ends."

14. Whitford, "Pragmatism and the Untenable Dualism of Means and Ends."

15. John Dewey, *Human Nature and Conduct: An Introduction to Social Psychology* (New York: Modern Library, 1922), 36.

16. Whitford, "Pragmatism and the Untenable Dualism of Means and Ends," 354.

17. David Stark and László Bruszt, *Postsocialist Pathways: Transforming Politics and Property in East Central Europe* (New York: Cambridge University Press, 1998); Walter W. Powell et al., "Network Dynamics and Field Evolution: The Growth of Interorganizational Collaboration in the Life Sciences," *American Journal of Sociology* 110, no. 4 (2005): 1132–1205; Walter W. Powell and Kurt W. Sandholtz, "Amphibious Entrepreneurs and the Emergence of Organizational Forms," *Strategic Entrepreneurship Journal* 6, no. 2 (2012): 94–115, https://doi.org/10.1002/sej.1129; and John Padgett and Walter Powell, *The Emergence of Organizations and Markets* (Princeton, NJ: Princeton University Press, 2012).

18. Dewey, *Human Nature and Conduct*, 270.

19. Dewey, 272.

20. Dewey, 273.

21. Dewey, 274–75.

22. Dewey, 267.

23. Dewey, 277.

24. Whitford, "Pragmatism and the Untenable Dualism of Means and Ends."

25. Dewey, *Human Nature and Conduct*, 34.

26. Mische, "Projects and Possibilities."

27. Dewey, *Human Nature and Conduct*, 197.

28. Dewey, 36.

29. Dewey, 225–26.

30. Dewey, 225.

31. Dewey, 225.

32. Dewey, 226.

33. Dewey, 181–82.

34. Dewey, 197.

35. Dewey, 190; italics added.

36. Dewey, 183.

37. Dewey, 192.

38. Emirbayer and Schneiderhan, "Dewey and Bourdieu on Democracy."

39. Alfred Schutz, "Choosing Among Projects of Action," *Philosophy and Phenomenological Research* 12, no. 2 (1951): 161–84; Schutz, *The Phenomenology of the Social World.*, trans. George Walsh and Frederick Lehnert (Evanston, IL: Northwestern University Press, 1967).

40. Schutz, *The Phenomenology of the Social World.*, 57–58.

41. Schutz, 62.

42. Schutz, 63.

43. Schutz, 65.

44. Schutz, 62.

45. Schutz, 68–69.

46. Schutz, 68.

47. Schutz, "Choosing Among Projects of Action," 165.

48. Schutz, 165–66.

49. Schutz, 168.

50. Schutz, 169.

51. Schutz, 181.

52. Schutz, 169.

53. Schutz, 172.

54. Schutz, 172.

55. Schutz, 175.

56. Schutz, 179.

57. Jürgen Habermas, *The Theory of Communicative Action*, vol. 1, trans. Thomas McCarthy (Boston: Beacon, 1985).

58. Dewey, *The Public and Its Problems*.

59. Ricoeur, *From Text to Action*, 182. See also Karl Mannheim, *Ideology and Utopia: An Introduction to the Sociology of Knowledge* (New York: Harcourt, Brace, 1936).

60. Ricoeur, 184.

61. Ricoeur, 185.

62. Ansell, *Pragmatist Democracy*.

63. Ansell, *Pragmatist Democracy*, 181.

64. Ansell, 50.

65. Cefaï, this volume, chap. 15, , italics in original.

66. Jason A. Springs, *Healthy Conflict in Contemporary American Society: From Enemy to Adversary* (Cambridge: Cambridge University Press, 2018); Jason Springs et al., "Pragmatism and Democracy: Assessing Jeffrey Stout's Democracy and Tradition," *Journal of the American Academy of Religion* 78, no. 2 (2010): 413–48.

67. Lichterman, *Elusive Togetherness*; Jeffrey Stout, *Blessed Are the Organized: Grassroots Democracy in America*, repr. ed. (Princeton, NJ: Princeton University Press, 2012); Kathleen M. Blee, *Democracy in the Making: How Activist Groups Form* (Oxford: Oxford University Press, 2012); Baiocchi et al., *The Civic Imagination*.

68. For example, Archon Fung and Erik Olin Wright, eds., *Deepening Democracy: Institutional Innovations in Empowered Participatory Governance* (New York: Verso, 2003); Ansell, *Pragmatist Democracy*; Rebecca Neara Abers and Margaret Keck, *Practical Authority: Agency and Institutional Change in Brazilian Water Politics* (Oxford: Oxford University Press, 2013).

69. Paul C. Taylor, "What's the Use of Calling Du Bois a Pragmatist?," *Metaphilosophy* 35, no. 1/2 (2004): 99–114; Robert J. Antonio and Douglas Kellner, "Communication, Modernity, and Democracy in Habermas and Dewey," *Symbolic Interaction* 15, no. 3 (1992): 277–97; Veith Selk and Dirk Jörke, "Back to the Future! Habermas and Dewey on Democracy in Capitalist Times," *Constellations* 27, no. 1 (2020): 36–49; Emirbayer and Schneiderhan, "Dewey and Bourdieu on Democracy"; Neil Gross, "Charles Tilly and American Pragmatism," *American Sociologist* 41 (2010): 337–57; Cornel West, *The American Evasion of Philosophy: A Genealogy of Pragmatism* (Madison, WI: University of Wisconsin Press, 1989); V. Denise James, "Theorizing Black Feminist Pragmatism: Forethoughts on the Practice and Purpose of Philosophy as Envisioned by Black Feminists and John Dewey," *Journal of Speculative Philosophy* 23, no. 2 (2009): 92–99.

70. Andrew Abbott and Alexandra Hrycak, "Measuring Resemblance in Sequence Data: An Optimal Matching Analysis of Musicians' Careers," *American Journal of Sociology* 96 (1990): 144–85.

71. Blair-Loy, *Competing Devotions*.

72. Beckert, *Imagined Futures*; Beckert and Bronk, *Uncertain Futures*.

73. Michal Federowicz, "Anticipated Institutions: The Power of Path-Finding Expectations," in *Democratic and Capitalist Transitions in Eastern Europe: Lessons for the Social Sciences*, ed. M. Dobry (Dordrecht: Springer, 2000).

74. Doug McAdam, Sidney Tarrow, and Charles Tilly, *Dynamics of Contention*, Cambridge Studies in Contentious Politics (Cambridge: Cambridge University Press, 2001); Sidney Tarrow, *Power in Movement: Social Movements and Contentious Politics* (New York: Cambridge University Press, 2011).

75. Kim Voss, "Claim-Making and the Interpretation of Defeats: The Interpretation of Losses by American and British Labor Activists, 1886–1895," in *Challenging Authority: The Historical Study of Contentious Politics*, ed. Michael Hanagan, Leslie Page Moon, and Wayne Te Brake (Minneapolis: University of Minnesota Press, 1998), 136–48.

76. Alex Zamalin, *Black Utopia: The History of an Idea from Black Nationalism to Afrofuturism* (New York: Columbia University Press, 2019).

77. Robert K. Merton, "The Unanticipated Consequences of Purposive Social Action," *American Sociological Review* 1, no. 6 (1936): 894–904, https://doi.org/10.2307/2084615; Frank de Zwart, "Unintended but Not Unanticipated Consequences," *Theory and Society* 44, no. 3 (2015): 283–97; and Adriana Mica, "The Unintended Consequences in New Economic Sociology: Why Still Not Taken Seriously?," *Social Science Information* 56, no. 4 (2017): 544–66, https://doi.org/10.1177/0539018417734322.

INDEX

abductive analysis, 65–66
accidental discovery, 307–13; Boston story, 313–26; changing senses, 313; theoretical pragmatism model, 310–13. *See also* Boston Police Department (BPD); pragmatism; sensemaking
actants, 22, 179, 234, 236, 238–39
actor-network theory (ANT), 22, 234, 240, 247
Addams, Jane, 9, 64, 74–77, 79
aesthetics, 122–23; aesthetic test, 384; art and, 130–32; Chicago School of Sociology and, 133–39; developmental character of, 125–32; growth of experience, 133–39; in sociological perspective, 123–25. *See also* Dewey, John; pragmatism; sociology
affordances, 92, 101, 110, 172, 237
African Americans, 211–12, 214–17, 219, 221, 223. *See also* accidental discovery; Boston Police Department (BPD); Du Bois, W. E. B.; poverty, studying action working in; sensemaking

agency, 15–16; accidental discovery, 307–35; biology, 256–303; chemistry, 256–303; creative action, 186–209; future thinking, 406–32; high-poverty action, 210–30; human agency, 15–16, 199–200, 202–3; Negro dilemma, 364–76; problem-solving in action, 171–85; public sphere, 377–405; satisfying regulations, 256–303; scientific innovation, 231–55; self-propelling agency, 191; theme matrix, 17. *See also* democracy; inquiry; problem-solving
agora, concept, 390–91. *See also* public sphere, pragmatist concept of
Alexander, Thomas, 124
American Journal of Sociology (AJS), 144, 154
analytical sociology (AS), 148, 162
Anderson, Elizabeth, 13–14, 29, 127
Ansell, Chris, 423–24
art, aesthetics and, 130–32. *See also* aesthetics
Asilomar conference (1975), 285–86